ECONOMICS
of the
PUBLIC SECTOR

Second Edition

ECONOMICS of the PUBLIC SECTOR

Second Edition

JOSEPH E. STIGLITZ

Princeton University

W. W. NORTON & COMPANY • New York • London

Printed in the United States of America.

Cover photo: Grant V. Faint/The Image Bank

Library of Congress Cataloging-in-Publication Data

Stiglitz, Joseph E.
Economics of the public sector / Joseph E. Stiglitz.—2nd ed. p. cm.
Bibliography: p.
Includes index.
ISBN 0-393-95683-0
1. Finance, Public—United States. 2. Fiscal policy—United States. I. Title.
HJ257.2, S84 1988
336.73—dc19 88-12611

ISBN 0-393-95683-0

W. W. Norton & Company, Inc., 500 Fifth Avenue, New York, N.Y. 10110

W. W. Norton & Company Ltd., 10 Coptic Street, London WC1A 1PU

3 4 5 6 7 8 9 0

To My First Teachers,
Nat and Charlotte

Contents

Part Three Expenditure Programs

Part Four Taxation: Theory

Preface

In one sense, fortune was not kind to the First Edition of this book: no sooner had it appeared than Congress enacted the Tax Reform Act of 1986. In another sense, fortune was kind: the enthusiastic response accorded the First Edition more than compensated for the long hours of writing and rewriting that went into it. For the response, I am grateful. As for the Tax Reform Act, let's just say that—from my perspective as textbook author—I am thankful that, even though it was hailed by politicians as the most sweeping tax reform since the enactment of the income tax, the act did not really represent a radical departure in tax policy. Thus, the concepts and even much of the institutional detail that I described in the First Edition have remained relevant. Still, the Tax Reform Act was of sufficient import to necessitate an immediate and thorough revision of Part Five of the book, which analyzes the U.S. tax structure.

There is a tendency of textbooks to grow in size with each successive edition. I have been wary of falling into this trap—yet it seemed wrong not to include some discussion of two of the central issues facing the United States public sector in the late 1980s: the causes and consequences of the huge federal deficits, and the design of policies to stimulate the economy's growth and productivity. Chapters 2 and 28 provide an introduction to these questions.

Those familiar with the First Edition will note a few other major changes. The discussion of the (Pareto) efficiency of the market economy (Chapter 3) now precedes the introduction to welfare economics (Chapter 4), which focuses on the trade-offs between efficiency and distribution. I have, moreover, added an appendix to Chapter 3 explaining in more detail the conditions required for the Pareto efficiency, and why competitive economies, in the absence of market failures, are Pareto efficient.

Later, in Part Four, on the theory of taxation, I have divided the discussion of the effects of taxation on economic efficiency into two chapters, one dealing with general principles, and one dealing in particular with the effects on labor supply (Chapter 19). I use that occasion to familiarize students with some of the important empirical work in that area, including the results of income maintenance experiments, econometric studies, and surveys.

As part of the thorough revision of Part Five, I discuss a broad range of issues related to capital taxation (Chapter 22), such as depreciation and capital gains, before I present the specific issues related to the taxation of corporate income (Chapter 23).

Though there have been no changes in expenditure programs quite as dramatic as the Tax Reform Act, the chapters discussing specific expenditure programs have all been updated, not only to reflect the latest data, but also to include issues of current policy concern. Thus, the chapter on health (Chapter 11) includes a discussion of the impact of the new system of reimbursements for Medicare, and the chapter on Welfare Programs (Chapter 14) includes a discussion of recent proposals for reform of the welfare system.

My major aims in writing this book remain the same, however. I wrote it in the belief that an understanding of the issues it addressed was central to any democratic society. Among the most important of these issues are the appropriate balance between the public and private sectors, and how governments can more effectively meet their objectives, whatever those objectives are. Issues in public-sector economics often become highly charged politically, but I tried to present the analysis in an impartial manner, with a clear delineation between the analysis of the consequences of any policy and the value judgments associated with assessing the desirability of the policy. The favorable reception of the First Edition by instructors of a wide variety of political persuasions suggests that I succeeded.

An unexpected bonus was the international enthusiasm for the book. Though I had focused my attention on issues facing the United States, similar issues confront countries around the world, where it has become widely adopted. Most exciting from my perspective is that I seemed to have provided a useful framework within which those in a number of other countries could address the particular policy issues which they faced; adaptations of the book to the economies of Japan, Germany, and Italy are presently under way.

Had this text been written twenty-five years ago, it would have been entitled *Public Finance,* and its focus would have been on sources of revenues. The title *Economics of the Public Sector* and the broader coverage it implies is, however, no accident. In recent years, government spending has reached record levels, and it now accounts for more than a third of gross national product. The accompanying federal budget deficits have alarmed economists of all political and intellectual persuasions. It is no longer enough to know where the money comes from; one must give equal time to how it is spent.

Meanwhile, the economic theory of the public sector has burgeoned. Some of this recent literature is devoted to analyzing government expenditures. From cost-benefit analysis to public choice theory, economists now have much to say about how government spends its funds. Much of the recent literature in public economics reflects the development of new and more sophisticated models, such as the theory of optimal taxation. I have chosen to present the modern view of public-sector economics in a simple and intuitive way, to relate the most important contributions of this fast-growing literature to undergraduates taking a first course in public finance.

Public-sector issues include some of the most exciting in all of economics. Health, defense, education, social security, welfare programs, and tax reform all receive steady attention in the news media. Economic analysis brings special insights to the debates. Should education be publicly provided? What is the long-term outlook for our social security program? How do current proposals for tax reform match our knowledge of incidence, efficiency, and equity? These kinds of questions breathe life into the course, which is why I give them careful attention.

Examining specific tax and expenditure programs offers an additional benefit: it underscores the importance of design features. One of the lessons we have learned in the past decade is that good intentions are not enough. Urban renewal programs, intended to revitalize our cities, had the unintended consequence of reducing the supply of housing to the poor. One of the major objectives of the tax reform of 1986 was to simplify the tax code, but it seems, instead, to have made it even more complex. I use examples like these, of unintended consequences, not only to enliven the course but also to instill in students the important habit of testing theory against the complex environment in which public-sector decisions are enacted and implemented.

The organization of this book is based on the principle of flexibility. The sequence I follow is, first, to introduce in Part One the fundamental questions, institutional details, and a review of the microeconomic theory underlying the role of the public sector. Part Two develops the theory of public expenditures, including public goods, public choice, and bureaucracy, while Part Three applies the theory to the five largest areas of public expenditure in the United States: health, defense, education, social security, and welfare programs. Parts Four and Five repeat this pattern, presenting the theory of taxation and its analysis, respectively. Part Six takes up two further topics: issues concerning state and local taxation and expenditure and fiscal federalism; and issues concerning stabilization and growth, with particular emphasis on the relation between microeconomic analysis and macroeconomic performance.

A perfectly workable alternative to this sequence would be to cover taxation before expenditures. Parts Four and Five have been carefully developed so that the teacher wishing to go straight to taxation after Part One can do so without loss of continuity. Further tips on how courses can be organized, as well as lecture notes, test questions, and coverage of advanced topics that some teachers may wish to include in their lectures, are contained in the *Instructor's Manual*, for which Eleanor Brown of Pomona College has done the lion's share of the work for this edition. Another ancillary, the new *Study Guide and Readings*, by Edward C. Kienzle of Stonehill College, helps students to review the material in this book at the same time that it puts accessible portions of the literature in their hands.

The list of those to whom I am indebted is a long one. I owe a special acknowledgment to Karla Hoff, who was more than just a graduate research assistant. She not only updated the figures, she uncovered unpublished data and checked the accuracy of the entire text. More than that, she served as my harshest critic. In writing any textbook at this level, one often has to make simplifications to make the ideas accessible. The problem is how to make those simplifications, while at the same time doing full justice to the complexity of the subject. Karla insisted that there be no compromises on either account: that each passage be clearly accessible to a student with no background in economics, but at the same time that it not oversimplify the subject.

My teachers at Amherst College, James Nelson and Arnold Collery, not only stimulated my interest in economics, and in the particular subject of this course, but laid the foundations for my later studies. They also showed me, by example, what good teaching meant; I hope that some of what I learned from them is reflected in this book. At M.I.T. Dan Holland (currently editor of the *National Tax Journal*) and E. Cary Brown introduced me to the formal study of public economics. Again, I hope some of the blend of policy, theory, and institutional detail that marked their work is reflected here. The insights of my colleagues and collaborators at the institutions at which I have worked (M.I.T., Yale University, Stanford University, Princeton University, Oxford University, Cambridge University, and the National Bureau of Economic Research) and the government agencies (Treasury, Labor, Interior, Energy, Agency for International Development, State of Louisiana, State of Texas) and international organizations (World Bank, Interamerican Development Bank, Organization of Economic Cooperation and Development) for which I have consulted have also proved invaluable. I should mention Henry Aaron (Brookings Institution), Alan J. Auerbach (University of Pennsylvania), Greg Ballantine (former Assistant Secretary of the Treasury for Tax Policy), William J. Baumol (Princeton University), Charles T. Clotfelter (Duke University), Partha Dasgupta (Cambridge University), Peter A. Diamond (M.I.T.), Avinash Dixit (Princeton University), Martin Feldstein (Harvard University), Harvey Galper (Brookings Institution), Robert E. Hall (Stanford University), John Hamilton (University of Florida), Arnold C. Harberger (University of Chicago and University of California, Los Angeles), Charles E. McClure (Hoover Institution; former Deputy Assistant Secretary of the Treasury), James A. Mirrlees (Oxford University), Alvin Rabushka (Stanford University), Michael Rothschild (University of California, San Diego), Agnar Sandmo (Norges Handelshøgskole, Norway), Eytan Sheshinski (Hebrew University), Nick Stern (London School of Economics), Lawrence Summers (Harvard University), and in particular Anthony B. Atkinson (London School of Economics), Peter Mieskowski (Rice University), Raj Kumar Sah (Yale University), and Steven L. Slutsky (University of Florida).

Comments and suggestions I have received from those who have taught from the book or read various stages of the manuscript have been enormously helpful in shaping this text. Here I particularly want to thank Donald N. Baum (Temple University), Jim Bergin (Queens University, Canada), Michael Boskin (Stanford University), Lawrence Blume (University of Michigan), David Bradford (Princeton University), John Burbidge (McMaster University), Paul N. Courant (University of Michigan), Lieutenant Colonel Floyd Duncan (Virginia Military Institute), J. Eric Fredland (U.S. Naval Academy), Victor R. Fuchs (Stanford University), Don Fullerton (University of Virginia), Roger Gordon (University of Michigan), William F. Hellmuth (Virginia Commonwealth University), Mervyn King (London School of Economics), Laurence J. Kotlikoff (Boston University), Robert J. Lampman (University of Wisconsin), Jerry Miner (Syracuse University), Joseph A. Pechman (Brookings Institution), Jim Poterba (M.I.T.), Anora Robbins (UNC Greensboro), Balbir S. Sahni (Concordia University, Montreal), Catherine Schneider (Boston College) Robert Sherry (Keene State College), John Shoven (Stanford University), Joel Slemrod (University of Michigan), Sun-Tien Wu (Chung Hsing University, Taipei), and Qiang Zeng, (Tsing Hua University, Beijing).

My indebtedness to Jane Hannaway is more than that customarily owed to a spouse, for her insights into the behavior of governments in general, and bureaucratic behavior in particular, have been instrumental in shaping my own views, although I am afraid I have had less influence on her than she has had on me.

As in the First Edition, I am deeply indebted to Drake McFeely, my editor at Norton, for his thoughtful and insightful editorial comments that greatly improved the book and for the care and attention he paid in shepherding the book through the various stages of production. The final thanks are due to his colleague, Sandra Lifland, who also helped shape the Second Edition.

Princeton, N.J. J.E.S.
March 1988

PART ONE

INTRODUCTION

How does the government affect the economy? Why are some economic activities undertaken in the public sector, some in the private? How has the government grown over the past fifty years? These are some of the basic questions addressed in Part I of this book.

The first two chapters describe the scope of the book and of the public sector in the United States. The United States has a mixed economy, with some economic activities undertaken in the public sector, some in the private.

Chapter 3 delineates those circumstances in which private markets may not work well, so that some form of government action may be required.

Alternative government actions often present trade-offs between efficiency and equity. Chapter 4 presents the framework within which economists make judgments concerning the desirability of different government programs and policies.

1

The Public Sector in a Mixed Economy

From birth to death, our lives are affected in countless ways by the activities of government.

• We are born in hospitals that are publicly subsidized, if not publicly owned, and our delivery into this world is supervised by doctors who were trained in medical schools that were, at least partly, publicly supported. Our arrival is then publicly recorded (our birth certificate), entitling us to a set of privileges and obligations as American citizens.

• Most of us (almost 90 percent) attend public schools.

• Though the Thirteenth Amendment of the Constitution abolished slavery, or involuntary servitude, the government has frequently resorted to compulsion, to the military draft, to recruit young men to fight our country's wars.

• About 15 percent of us live in housing that is either directly subsidized by the federal government or whose mortgages are insured by the federal government; about 10 percent of us receive food or food subsidies from the government, and more than 40 percent of our medical expenditures are paid by the government.

• Virtually all of us, at some time in our lives, receive money from the government, either as children—for instance, through the government's student loan program; as adults, when we are unemployed, disabled, or impoverished; or in retirement, through social security and Medicare.

• All of us pay money to the government—in local and state sales taxes, in federal excise taxes on such commodities as gasoline, liquor, telephones, air travel, perfumes, and tires, in property taxes, in income taxes, and in social security (payroll) taxes.

• Almost a sixth of the work force is employed by the government, and for the rest, the government has a significant impact on employment conditions. If we are injured on the job in spite of the safety precautions insisted upon by the government, we are protected by workmen's compensation. Unions, whose rights and responsibilities are defined by the government, negotiate work conditions including the hours and pay of a substantial fraction of the labor force. The government encourages pension plans through tax incentives and insures them against an employer going bankrupt.

• The prices for wheat, corn, and dairy products are controlled or strongly influenced by the actions of the government. In many areas of production—steel or automobiles, shoes or shirts, television sets or computers—profits and employment opportunities are greatly affected by whether the government allows foreign competitors to sell goods in America without a tariff or quota.

• As consumers, we are affected by the government: the prices we pay for cigarettes, alcohol, automobiles, and many other commodities are high because of the taxes, tariffs, quotas, and regulations government imposes; while the prices of other goods (utilities, telephones, water, electricity, and housing) *may be* lower because of government regulation. What we eat and drink is regulated by the government. Where we can live and what kinds of houses we can live in are regulated by various public agencies.

• We are all the beneficiaries of public services: we travel on public roads and publicly subsidized railroads. In most communities our garbage is collected and our sewage is disposed of by a public agency; in some communities the water we drink is provided by public water companies, and the cleanliness of the air is regulated by public agencies.

• Our legal structure provides a framework within which individuals and firms can engage in mutually beneficial interactions. Our laws specify the nature of the contracts that we can sign. When there is a dispute between two individuals, the two may turn to the courts to adjudicate the dispute.

THE MIXED ECONOMY

The United States has what is called a **mixed economy:** while many economic activities are undertaken by private firms, others are undertaken by the government. In addition, the government alters the behavior of the private sector, either intentionally or unintentionally, through a variety of regulations, taxes, and subsidies. By way of contrast, in the USSR and the Soviet bloc countries, most economic activities are undertaken by the government. In many Western European economies, the government is responsible for a much larger share of economic activity than in the United States. For instance, in Britain the government is responsible for the production of coal and steel. What the government is responsible for in the United States has also changed dramatically. One hundred years ago there were some private highways and all railroads were private; today there are no major private roads and most interstate railroad passengers travel by Amtrak, a publicly established and subsidized enterprise. It is because mixed economies are constantly facing the problem of defining the appropriate boundaries between government and private activities that the study of public finance in these countries is both so important and so interesting.

Why does the government do some things and not others? Why has the scope of government activity changed over the past hundred years, and why does it do more in some countries than it does in the United States, while in other countries it does less? Does the government do too much? Does it do what it attempts to do well? Could it do it better? These are the central questions with which public finance is concerned. They have been at the center of political, philosophical, and economic debates for centuries. The debates continue. Even though economists cannot provide definitive answers, they have contributed enormously to our understanding of the issues by making us aware of the strengths and limitations of both the public and private sectors.

AN IMPETUS FOR GOVERNMENT ACTION: MARKET FAILURES

In the period between the Great Depression (1930s) and the early 1960s, economists (and politicians) became aware of a large number of ways in which the free-market economy, even the richest free-market economy in the world, seemed to fail to meet certain basic social needs. The economy had always suffered from periodic episodes of unemployment, some of them massive. In the Great Depression, the unemployment rate reached 25 percent and national output fell by about 30 percent from its peak in 1929. The depression brought to the fore problems that, in less severe form, had been there for a long time. Many individuals lost virtually all of their money when banks failed and the stock market crashed. Many elderly people did not have the resources on which to survive. Many farmers found that the prices they received for their products were so low that they could not make their mortgage payments, and defaults became commonplace.

In response to the depression, the federal government not only took a more active role in attempting to stabilize the level of economic activity, but it also passed legislation aimed at alleviating many of the specific problems: unemployment insurance, social security, federal insurance for depositors, federal programs aimed at supporting agricultural prices, and a host of other programs aimed at a variety of social and economic objectives. Together, these programs are referred to as the "New Deal."

After World War II the economy recovered, and the country experienced an unprecedented level of prosperity. But it became clear that the fruits of that prosperity were not being enjoyed by all. Many individuals seemed, by the condition of their birth, to be condemned to a life of squalor and poverty; they received inadequate education, and their prospects for obtaining good jobs were bleak.

These inequities provided the impetus for many of the government programs that were enacted in the 1960s, when President Lyndon B. Johnson declared his "War on Poverty." While some programs were aimed at providing a "safety net" for the needy—for instance, programs to provide food and medical care to the poor—others, such as job retraining programs, were directed at improving the economic opportunities of the disadvantaged.

Could government actions alleviate these problems? How was success to be gauged? The fact that some program did not live up to the hopes of its most enthusiastic supporters did not, of course, mean that it was a failure. Medicaid, which provides medical assistance to the indigent, was successful in eliminating some of the differences in access to medical care between the poor and the rich, but the difference in life expectancy between these two groups was not eliminated. Medicare, which provides medical care for the elderly, was successful in relieving the elderly and their families of much of the anxiety concerning the financing of their medical expenses, but it left in its place a national problem of rapidly increasing medical expenditures. While the social security program provided the aged with an unprecedented level of economic security, in the late 1970s and early 1980s it ran into financial crises that raised questions about whether future generations would be able to enjoy the same benefits.

Twenty years after the War on Poverty began, it is clear that poverty has not been eradicated from America. But have the expenditures had a significant effect in reducing it? While there is no consensus on the answer to this question, both critics and supporters of the government's programs agree that it is not enough to have good intentions: many of the programs designed to alleviate the perceived inadequacies of the market economy have had effects that differed markedly from those the proponents thought (or hoped) they would have. Urban renewal programs designed to improve the quality of life in inner cities have, in many instances, resulted in the replacement of low-quality housing with high-quality housing that poor people cannot afford, thus forcing them to live in even worse conditions. Though many programs designed to promote integration of public schools have succeeded, some have instead increased residential segregation or led some parents to enroll their children in private schools, which has in turn weakened support for public education. A disproportionate share of the benefits of farm programs has accrued to large farms; government programs have not enabled many of the small farms to survive. There have been allegations that government welfare programs have contributed to the breakup of families and to the development of an attitude of dependency.

Supporters of continued government efforts claim that critics exaggerate the failures of government programs. They argue that the lesson to be learned is not that the government should abandon its efforts to solve the major social and economic problems facing the nation, but that greater care must be taken in the appropriate design of government programs.

GOVERNMENT FAILURES

While market failures led to the major government programs of the 1930s and 1960s, in the 1970s the shortcomings of the programs led economists and political scientists to investigate government failure. Under what conditions would government programs not work well? Were the failures of government programs mere accidents, or were they predictable results, following from the inherent nature of governmental activity? Are there lessons to be learned for the design of programs in the future? There are four major reasons for the systematic failures of the government to achieve its stated objectives: the government's limited information, its limited control over private responses to its actions, its limited control over the bureaucracy, and the limitations imposed by political processes.

1. *Limited information.* The consequences of many actions are complicated and difficult to foresee. When the federal government adopted its urban renewal programs, it did not anticipate that they might lead to a decline in the supply of housing available to the poor. Similarly, the government did not anticipate the precipitous increase in expenditures on medical care by the aged that followed the adoption of the Medicare program.

2. *Limited control over private market responses.* The government has only limited control over the consequences of its actions (particularly within a democracy such as ours). When New York City passed its rent control legislation, many advocates overlooked the fact that apartments were supplied by individuals who would turn elsewhere for investment opportunities if the return to their investment declined. Advocates thus failed to anticipate that the supply of rental housing would decrease and that the quality of services provided by landlords would deteriorate. Though the government attempted to control this deterioration by imposing standards on landlords, these attempts were only partially successful and exacerbated the decline in the supply of rental housing. There was little the New York City government could do to stop this, short of repealing the rent control statutes.

3. *Limited control over bureaucracy.* Congress and state and local legislatures design legislation, but delegate implementation to some government agency. This agency may spend considerable time writing

detailed regulations; how these detailed regulations are drafted is critical in determining the effects of the legislation. The agency may also be responsible for ensuring that the regulations are enforced. For instance, when Congress passed the Environmental Protection Act, its intent was clear—to ensure that firms did not pollute the environment. But the technical details—for instance, determining the admissible level of pollutants for different industries—were left to the Environmental Protection Agency (EPA). During the first two years of the Reagan administration, there were numerous controversies over whether the EPA had been lax in promulgating and enforcing regulations, thus subverting the intentions of Congress.

In many cases, the failures to carry out the intent of Congress are not deliberate attempts to avoid the wishes of Congress, but are a result of the ambiguities in Congress's intentions. And, there is a further problem of ensuring that administrators whose job it is to execute the law will do so fairly and efficiently. Just as a principal subject of inquiry in standard economics is the analysis of the incentives within the private sector, so one of the subjects of study here is the analysis of incentives within the public sector: What causes bureaucrats to take the actions they take?

4. *Limitations imposed by political processes.* Even if government were perfectly informed about the consequences of all possible actions, choosing among those actions through the political process would raise additional difficulties. Government actions affect many persons, but they are decided upon by only a limited group—their elected representatives. The decision makers have to ascertain the preferences of their constituencies and they have to find some way of reconciling or making choices among conflicting preferences. It is often alleged that the government acts in an inconsistent manner. We will show in Chapter 6 that under certain circumstances this is a natural consequence of democratic decision making. Moreover, our political process is one in which those who are elected to serve the public sometimes have incentives to act for the benefit of special-interest groups. Thus, the failure of politicians to carry out what would seem to be in the public interest is not just the consequence of the greed or malevolence of a few wayward politicians, but it may be the inevitable consequence of the workings of political institutions in democratic societies.[1]

Critics of government intervention in the economy believe the four sources of government failure are sufficiently important that the government should be restrained from attempting to remedy alleged deficiencies in markets. But even if one does not agree with this conclusion, recognition of the four limitations on government action is a prerequisite for the design of successful government policies.

[1] This view has been particularly argued by George Stigler. See, for instance, his "Theory of Regulation," *Bell Journal,* Spring 1971, pp. 3–21.

EARLIER VIEWS CONCERNING THE ROLE OF GOVERNMENT

The vacillation in views concerning the role of the government that has occurred during the past fifty years has also occurred frequently in the past.[2] For instance, in the eighteenth century a dominant view, particularly among French economists, was that the government should take an active role in promoting trade and industry. Those who advocated this view were called *mercantilists.*

It was partly in reaction to this view that Adam Smith (who is often viewed as the founder of modern economics) wrote his book *The Wealth of Nations* (1776), in which he advocated a limited role for government. Smith attempted to show how competition and the profit motive would lead individuals—in pursuing their own private interests—to serve the public interest. The profit motive would lead individuals to supply the goods other individuals wanted. Competing against one another, only firms that produced what was wanted and produced it at as low a price as possible would survive. Smith argued that the economy was led, as if by an **invisible hand,** to produce what was desired and in the best possible way.

Adam Smith's ideas had a powerful influence both on governments and on economists. Many of the most important nineteenth-century economists, such as the Englishmen John Stuart Mill and Nassau Senior, promulgated the doctrine known as **laissez faire,** which argued that the government should leave the private sector alone; it should not attempt to regulate or control private enterprise. Unfettered competition would serve the best interests of society.

Not all the nineteenth-century social thinkers were persuaded by Smith's reasoning. They were concerned with grave inequalities in income that they saw around them, with the squalor in which much of the working classes lived, and with the unemployment that workers frequently faced. While nineteenth-century writers like Charles Dickens attempted to portray the plight of the working classes in novels, social theorists, like Karl Marx, Sismondi, and Robert Owen, attempted not only to develop theories explaining what they saw but also to suggest ways in which society might be reorganized. To many, the evils in society could be attributed to the private ownership of capital; what Adam Smith saw as a virtue they saw as a vice. Marx, if not the deepest of the social thinkers, was certainly the most influential among those who advocated a greater role for the state in controlling the means of production. Still others saw the solution neither in the state nor in private enterprise but in smaller groups of individuals getting together and acting cooperatively for their mutual interest.

These continuing controversies have stimulated economists to attempt to ascertain the precise sense in which, and the precise condi-

[2] See A. O. Hirschman, *Shifting Involvements: Private Interest and Public Action* (Princeton, N.J.: Princeton University Press, 1982). Hirschman has put forth an interesting theory attempting to explain the constant changes in views on the appropriate role of the government.

tions under which, the invisible hand guides the economy to efficiency. It is now known that the presumption of the efficiency of the market economy is valid only under fairly restrictive assumptions. The failures we noted above make it apparent that there are many problems with which the market does not deal adequately. Today, among American economists, the dominant view is that *limited* government intervention could alleviate (but not solve) the worst problems: the government should take an active role in maintaining full employment and alleviating the worst aspects of poverty, but private enterprise should play the central role in the economy. There is still considerable controversy about how limited or how active a role the government should take. Some economists, such as Harvard University Professor John Kenneth Galbraith, believe that the government should take a more active role, while others, such as Nobel laureates Milton Friedman of Stanford University's Hoover Institution and George Stigler of the University of Chicago, believe that the government should take a less active role. Views on this subject are affected by how serious one considers the failures of the market to be and by how effective one believes the government can be in remedying them.

WHAT OR WHO IS THE GOVERNMENT?

Throughout this chapter we have referred to "the government." But what precisely is the government? We all have some idea about what institutions are included: Congress and state and local legislatures, the president and state governors and mayors, the courts, and a host of the alphabet-soup agencies, such as FHA, IRS, FAA, FTC, SEC, and NLRB. The United States has a *federal* governmental structure—that is, governmental activities take place at several levels: federal, state, and local. The federal government is responsible for national defense, the post office, the printing of money, and the regulation of interstate and international commerce. On the other hand, the states and localities have traditionally been responsible for education, welfare, police and fire protection, and the provision of other local services, such as libraries, sewage, and garbage collection. Though the Constitution asserts that all rights not explicitly delegated to the federal government reside with the states and the people, the Constitution has proven to be a sufficiently flexible document that the exact boundaries are ambiguous. While education is primarily a local responsibility, the federal government has become increasingly involved in its support. The constitutional provision giving the federal government the right to control interstate business has provided the basis for federal regulation of almost all businesses, since almost all businesses are involved, in one way or another, in interstate commerce.

At the local level, there are frequently several separate governmental structures, each of which has the power to levy taxes and the responsibility for administering certain programs. In addition to townships and counties, there are school districts, sewage districts, and library districts. In 1982, there were 82,000 such governmental entities in the United States, down from 155,000 in 1942.[3]

The boundaries between what are public institutions and what are not are often unclear. When the government sets up a corporation, a public enterprise, is that enterprise part of the "government"? For instance, Amtrak, which was set up by the federal government to run the nation's interstate passenger railway services, receives subsidies from the federal government, but otherwise it is run like a private enterprise. Similarly, in Britain, the government nationalized the steel industry. But the British Steel Company is still run in most respects like companies in the United States. Should the British Steel Company be included in the government? Matters become even more complicated when the government is a major stockholder in a company but not the only stockholder.

What distinguishes those institutions that we have labeled as "government" from private institutions? There are two important differences. First, in a democracy the individuals who are responsible for running public institutions are elected, or are appointed by someone who is elected (or appointed by someone who is appointed by someone who is elected. . .). The "legitimacy" of the person holding the position is derived directly or indirectly from the electoral process. In contrast, those who are responsible for administering General Motors are chosen by the shareholders of General Motors; while those who are responsible for administering private foundations (such as the Rockefeller and Ford foundations) are chosen by a self-perpetuating board of trustees.

Secondly, the government is endowed with certain rights of compulsion that private institutions do not have. The government has the right to force you to pay taxes (and if you fail, it can confiscate your property and/or imprison you). The government has the right to "force" its young males to serve in the armed forces, at wages below those that would induce them to volunteer. The government has the right to seize your property for public use provided it pays you just compensation (this is called the right of eminent domain).

Not only do private institutions and individuals not have these rights, but the government actually restricts the rights of individuals to give to others similar powers of compulsion. For instance, the government does not allow you to sell yourself into slavery.

In contrast, all private exchanges are voluntary. I may want you to work for me, but I cannot force you to do so. I may need your property to construct an office building, but I cannot force you to sell it. I may think that some deal is advantageous to both of us, but I cannot force you to engage in the deal.

This ability to use compulsion means that the government may be able to do some things that private institutions cannot do. And the differences in the processes by which those who administer public and private

[3] *Facts and Figures on Government Finance*, Tax Foundation, Table A–2, 1986.

institutions are chosen may have important implications for the behavior of those institutions. It is important to keep these differences in mind as we discuss, in later chapters of this book, alternative views of the role of the government.

THE PUBLIC SECTOR AND THE FUNDAMENTAL ECONOMIC QUESTIONS

Economics is the study of *scarcity*, of how societies make choices concerning how to use their limited resources. Four questions are asked:

What is to be produced?

How is it to be produced?

For whom is it to be produced?

How are these decisions made?

Like any field of economics, the economics of the public sector is concerned with these fundamental questions of choice. But it focuses on the choices made within the public sector itself, on the role of the government, and on the ways that government affects the decisions made in the private sector.

1. *What is to be produced?* How much of our resources should be devoted to the production of public goods, such as defense and highways, and how much of our resources should we devote to the production of private goods, such as cars, TV sets, and video games? We often depict this choice in terms of the **production possibilities schedule,** which traces the various amounts of two goods that can be produced efficiently with a given technology and resources. In our case, the two goods are public goods and private goods. Figure 1.1 gives the various possible combinations of public goods and private goods that the society can produce.

Society can spend more on public goods, such as national defense, but only by reducing what is available for private consumption. Thus, in moving from *G* to *E* along the production possibilities schedule, public goods are increased, but private goods are decreased. A point such as *I*, which is below the production possibilities schedule, is said to be *inefficient:* society could get more public goods and more private goods. A point such as *N*, which is above the production possibilities schedule, is said to be *infeasible:* it is not possible, given current resources and technology, to have at the same time that quantity of public goods and that quantity of private goods.

2. *How should it be produced?* The second question, how what is produced should be produced, is as important as the first question. When should the government take direct responsibility for production of the goods that are publicly provided, and when should the government procure these goods from private firms? While most of the weapons used by the military are produced by private firms, only a small percentage of public educational expenditures goes to private schools. In many countries, government enterprises produce goods (such as telephone serv-

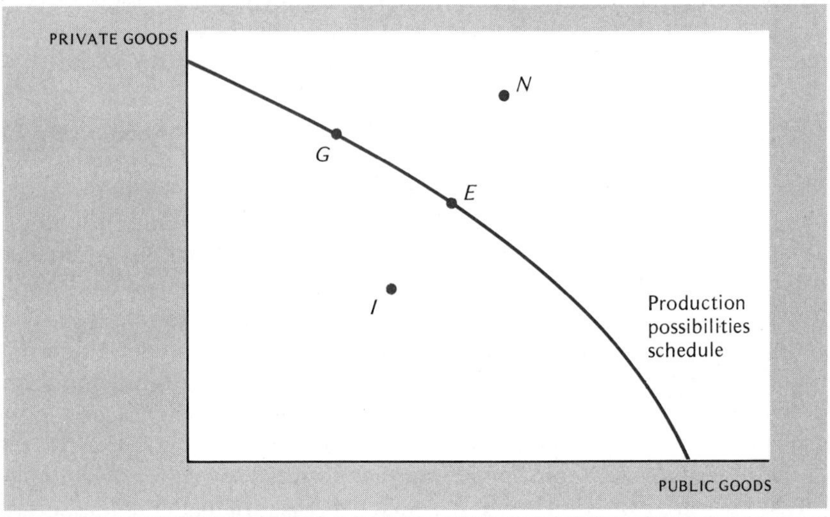

1.1 SOCIETY'S PRODUCTION POSSIBILITIES SCHEDULE This depicts the maximum level of private goods that society can enjoy for each level of public goods. If society wishes to enjoy more public goods, it has to give up some private goods.

ices, steel, and electricity) that are sold to individuals. While some individuals believe that, unless such commodities are directly produced by public enterprises, consumers will be exploited, other individuals believe that state enterprises are inevitably less efficient than private enterprises.

Other issues are subsumed under this second question. Government policy affects how firms produce the goods they produce: environmental protection legislation restricts pollution by firms; payroll taxes that firms must pay on the workers they employ make labor more expensive and thus discourage firms from using production techniques that require much labor; other provisions of the tax code may change the attractiveness of one machine relative to another. Though discussion of these questions seldom comes to the center of political debates, recent debates about the distorting effect of taxation and the desirability of nuclear reactors as energy sources are important exceptions.

3. *For whom? The question of distribution.* Government decisions about taxation or welfare programs affect how much income different individuals have to spend. Similarly, the government must decide what public goods to produce; some groups will benefit from the production of one public good, others from another.

4. *How are collective choices made?* There is one area that is of more concern to public-sector economics than to other branches of economics: the processes by which *collective* choices are made. Collective choices are the choices that we as a society must make together—for instance, concerning our legal structure, the size of our military estab-

lishment, our expenditures on other public goods, etc. Economics texts in fields other than public-sector economics focus on how individuals make their decisions concerning consumption, how firms make their decisions concerning production, and how the price system works to ensure that the goods demanded by consumers are produced by firms. Collective decision making is far more complicated, for individuals often disagree about what is desirable. After all, just as some individuals like chocolate ice cream and some like vanilla ice cream, some individuals get greater enjoyment out of public parks than do others. But while with private goods, the individual who likes chocolate ice cream can simply buy chocolate ice cream, and the individual who likes vanilla ice cream can buy vanilla ice cream, with public goods we must make a decision together. Anyone who has lived in a family knows something about the difficulties of collective decision making (should we go to the movies or go bowling?). Public decison making is far more complex. One of the objectives of public-sector economics is to study how collective choices (or, as they are sometimes called, social choices) are made in democratic societies.

The recognition of this divergence of views is important in itself. It should make us wary of expressions such as "It is in the public interest" or "We are concerned with the good of society." Different policies may be good for different individuals. One should carefully specify who will benefit from and who will be harmed by each policy.

STUDYING THE ECONOMICS OF THE PUBLIC SECTOR

The study of the economics of the public sector can be divided into three categories.

1. *Knowing what activities the public sector engages in and how these are organized.* The complexity of the government's operations is so great that it is difficult to assess what its total expenditures are and what they go for. The budget of the federal government alone is a document that is more than 1,000 pages, and within the budget, activities are not easily compartmentalized. Some activities are undertaken in several different departments or agencies. Research, for instance, is funded through the Department of Defense, the National Science Foundation, the National Institutes of Health, and the National Air and Space Administration, among others. Also, a department such as the Department of Health and Human Services undertakes a myriad of activities some of which are only vaguely related to others.

Further, as we have noted, taxes and expenditures occur at several different levels: in some places, individuals pay not only federal and state taxes but a separate tax to the school district, another tax to the township, another tax to the county, still another tax to the jurisdictions that provide water and sewage, and still another tax to support the library.

2. *Understanding and anticipating, insofar as possible, the full consequences of these governmental activities.* When a tax is imposed on a corporation, who bears the tax? It is unlikely that the tax will do nothing more than reduce corporate profits. More likely, at least part of the tax will be passed onto consumers through higher prices. Or, perhaps, onto employees, as wages fall. When the government passes a rent control law, what will be the long-run consequences? Will renters really be better off in the long run? What are the consequences of the government's changing the age of retirement for social security? Of charging tuition in state universities? Of providing free medical care to the aged?

We have already noted that the consequences of government policies are often too complicated to predict accurately. There is often controversy about what the consequences will be. Indeed, even after a policy has been introduced, there is often controversy about what its effects are. In this book we shall attempt not only to present all sides of some of the major controversies, but also to explain why such disagreements have persisted, and why it is difficult to resolve some of these important questions.

3. *Evaluating alternative policies.* To do this, not only do we need to know the consequences of alternative policies, but we need to develop criteria for evaluation. First we must understand the objectives of government policy, and then we must ascertain the extent to which the particular proposal meets (or is likely to meet) those criteria. But even that is not enough. Many proposals have effects other than the intended effects, and one must know how to predict these other consequences and to bring them into the evaluation.

NORMATIVE VERSUS POSITIVE ECONOMICS

The distinction we have just made, between analyzing the *consequences* of a government policy and making *judgments* concerning the desirability of particular government policies, is an important one. The former kind of analysis is often referred to as **positive economics,** the latter as **normative economics** (or **welfare economics**). Positive economics is concerned not only with analyzing the consequences of particular government policies, but with describing the activities of the public sector and the political and economic forces that brought these particular programs into existence. When economists step beyond the pure analysis of positive economics, they move into the realm of normative economics. Normative economics is concerned with judging how well various policies work and designing new policies that better meet certain objectives.

Normative economics makes statements like, "If the government wishes to restrict the importation of oil in a way that is least costly to the government and consumers, tariffs on the importation of oil are preferable to quotas." Or, "If the objective of the farm program is to assist the poorer farmers, a system of price supports is not as good as a system of appropriately designed income transfers." In other words, in normative economics, economists compare the extent to which various government programs meet desired objectives, and determine which programs better meet these objectives. In contrast, positive economics makes statements like, "The imposition of quotas on oil in the 1950s led to higher domestic prices and the more rapid depletion of our natural resources." Such statements simply describe the effects of a program without evaluating whether intended objectives have been met. No judgments about the desirability or undesirability of the consequences are made.

When economists make such statements, they try not to impose their own criteria, their own values. They often view themselves as providing "technical assistance" to policy makers, helping them to attain their objectives.

At the same time, economists often comment on the objectives that politicians and policy makers put forth; sometimes stated objectives of politicians are not their real objectives. There is a hidden agenda. Economists may use the fact that a program differs from that which would be designed to achieve the stated objective to argue that the "true" objective is different, and they make *inferences* about what the true objectives of a program are by examining its consequences.

Economists also attempt to see, to what extent various objectives may be in conflict with one another and, when they are in conflict, to suggest how these conflicts can be resolved. Economists also try to clarify the full implications of alternative value systems. They attempt to see which values are basic and which values can be derived from other, more fundamental values. Economists' work on these questions often comes close to that of political philosophers.

The two approaches, the positive and the normative, are complementary; to make judgments about what activities the government *should* undertake, one must know the consequences of various government activities. One must be able to describe accurately what will happen if the government imposes one tax or another or attempts to subsidize one industry or another.

Some examples may help clarify the scope of positive and normative economics. Assume Congress is considering increasing a tax on cigarettes or alcohol. Positive economics is concerned with questions such as:

a) How much will the prices of cigarettes or alcohol rise?

b) How will this affect the demand for cigarettes or alcohol?

c) Do lower-income individuals spend a larger proportion of their income on smoking (drinking) than do higher-income individuals?

d) What are the likely consequences of the tax on the profits of the cigarette industry or the liquor industry?

e) What will be the repercussions of a cigarette tax on the prices of tobacco and hence on the income of tobacco farmers? Of an alcohol tax on the price of alcohol and hence on the income of distilleries and breweries?

f) What will be the consequences of reduced smoking for the incidence of lung cancer and heart disease? What fraction of the associated medical expenditures is borne directly or indirectly by the government itself? What will be the consequences of reduced drinking on automobile accidents, and on the associated medical costs? What effect will the increased longevity from reduced smoking have on the social security system?

On the other hand, normative economics is concerned with *evaluating* the various consequences and coming to a judgment concerning the desirability of the tax changes:

a) If our primary concern in the choice of taxes is their impact on the poor, which tax is preferable, the liquor tax or the tobacco tax?

b) If our primary concern in the choice of taxes is how the tax distorts behavior (from what it would be in the absence of the tax), which tax is preferable, the liquor tax or the tobacco tax?

c) If our concern is reducing medical costs, which tax is preferable, the liquor tax or the tobacco tax?

d) Are there better taxes than either of these for attaining any particular objective of the government?

As a second example, assume the government is considering imposing a fine on steel firms generating pollution to discourage them from polluting, or a subsidy on pollution abatement equipment to encourage them to clean up their act. Positive economics is concerned with questions such as:

a) How much of a reduction in pollution will be caused by fines (or subsidies) of different magnitudes?

b) How much of an increase in the price of steel will be caused by the imposition of fines?

c) How much will this price hike reduce the demand for steel produced in the United States?

d) How will these reductions in demand affect employment and profits in the steel industry?

e) How much are those living in the vicinity of steel mills willing to pay for the reduction in the level of pollution? That is, how much is it worth to them?

Again, normative economics is concerned with evaluating the different effects:

a) If our concern is primarily with the poor, which system, a tax or a subsidy, would be preferable? The poor are affected as consumers by the change in prices of all commodities using steel. Since they are more likely to live near steel mills, pollution is more likely to affect them than the rich. But if a fine reduces the demand for steel and employment in the steel industry, the poorer, unskilled workers are the ones who would suffer the most. How do we add up all these effects? And what is the level of tax or subsidy that maximizes the welfare of the poor?

b) If our concern is with maximizing the value of national income, which system, a tax or a subsidy, would be preferable? Or should we have neither? And again, if it is desirable to have one or the other, what is the level of tax or subsidy that maximizes national income?

This example is typical of many such situations that we face in economic policy analysis: there are some gainers (those who can now breathe the cleaner air) and there are some losers (consumers who pay higher prices, producers who have lower profits, workers who lose their jobs). Normative economics is concerned with developing systematic procedures by which we can compare the gains of those who are better off with the losses of those who are worse off, to arrive at some overall judgment concerning the desirability of the proposal.

The distinction between normative statements and positive statements arises not only in discussions of particular policy changes but also in discussions of political processes. For instance, economists are concerned with *describing* the consequences of majority voting. When there are differences in views concerning how much should be spent on national defense, how do the divergent viewpoints get reflected in the outcome of any particular political process? What will be the consequences of requiring a two-thirds majority for increments in public expenditures exceeding a certain amount? What will be the consequences of increasing politicians' pay? Of restricting private contributions to political campaigns? Of public support for political campaigns? But economists are also concerned with *evaluating* alternative political processes. Are some political processes better, in some sense, than others? Are they more likely to produce "consistent" choices? Are some political processes more likely than others to yield equitable or efficient outcomes?

DISAGREEMENTS AMONG ECONOMISTS

In the preceding paragraphs, we have divided the analysis of policy into two steps: analyzing the consequences and evaluating them. Both steps are fraught with controversy.

Unanimity is rare in many of the central questions of policy debate. Some individuals think school busing is desirable, some do not. Some think that the income tax should be more progressive (i.e., that wealthy individuals should pay a higher percentage of their income in taxes, while poor individuals should pay a lower percentage); some believe it should be less progressive. Some believe that the government should provide a tuition tax credit for private schools, some believe that it should not. Some believe that the government's loan program to college students should be cut back, others that it should be expanded. One of the central concerns of policy analysis is to identify the sources of disagreement.

There are three broad areas in which disagreements arise. The first two are disagreements that arise from the positive analysis of the policy;

they arise from the failure of one side or the other to trace the full consequences of the policy, and from differences in views about how the economy behaves. The third has to do with the judgments that are the basis for normative analysis, with disagreement over values.

Failure to Trace the Full Consequences of a Government Policy

Many controversies arise because one side or the other (or both) fails to trace the full consequences of a government policy. We have already noted several examples of this: in rent control, where the proponents failed to take into account the consequences for the supply of rental housing, or in Medicare, where some economists failed to take into account the sharp rise in expenditures on medical care by the aged.

An early example of the failure to think through the full consequences of a government policy was the window tax which was enacted in England in 1696 (under the Act of Making Good the Deficiency of the Clipped Money). At the time, windows were a luxury, and wealthy individuals had houses with more windows than those of poor individuals. It would have been administratively difficult to have an income tax; the government did not have the capacity to ascertain what each individual's income was. Indeed, individuals did not keep the kinds of records that would enable them to ascertain what their income was. Thus, the window tax base may have been a good measure of ability to pay. Those who could afford to have many windows were presumably in a better position to pay taxes; windows may have provided, in other words, an equitable basis of taxation. It was undoubtedly not the intention of those who levied the tax that the windows should be blocked up, but this was one of the major consequences of the tax. To avoid the tax, individuals built houses with few windows. The tax led to dark houses.

In the following chapters we shall frequently point out that the consequences of government policies are markedly different from the intended result. In the *long run,* individuals and firms respond to changes in taxes and other government policies, and these long-run responses need to be taken into account. Moreover, as a result of these adjustments, a tax or subsidy on one good may have consequences for others. Any major tax change is likely to lead to repercussions for the whole economy. Although many of the individual effects may be small, in total, when all the effects are taken into account, these indirect repercussions may indeed be serious. In later chapters, we shall point out some dramatic examples of this—where, for instance, a tax on wages turns out to leave workers unaffected but to lower the price of land.

Differences in Views about How the Economy Behaves

Economists agree that in evaluating a policy one should take into account all consequences; in fact, they view the identification of these consequences as one of their primary roles in policy analysis. They often disagree, however, about how the economy behaves, and hence about what the consequences of a government policy will be. Unlike other scientists, economists are not able to do controlled experiments. The standard way that science has found to test competing theories of how a system behaves is to carry out an experiment. With luck, the results of the experiment will bear out the predictions of only one theory, while discrediting others. But economists ordinarily do not have the possibility of doing controlled experiments. Instead, the experiments that economists can observe are the uncontrolled experiments that are being done for us in different markets and in different time periods, and the historical evidence often does not permit us to resolve disagreements about how the economy behaves.

In analyzing the consequences of various policies, economists make use of what are called **models.** Just as a model airplane attempts to replicate the basic features of an airplane, so too a model of the economy attempts to depict the basic features of the economy. The actual economy is obviously extremely complex; to see what is going on, and to make predictions about what the consequences of some change in policy will be, one needs to separate out the essential from the inessential features. What features one decides to focus on in constructing a model depend on what questions one wishes to address. The fact that models make simplifying assumptions, that they leave out many details, is a virtue, not a vice. An analogy may be useful. In going on a long trip, one often uses several maps. One map, depicting the interstate highway system, provides an overview, enabling one to see how to get from the general area where you are to the general area where you wish to go. You then use detailed maps, to see how to get from your point of origin to the expressway and from the expressway to your final destination. If the interstate highway map had every street and road in the country, the map would have to be so large as to limit its usefulness; the extra detail, though important for some purposes, would simply get in the way.

All analysis involves the use of models, of simple hypotheses concerning how individuals and firms will respond to various changes in government policy, and how these responses interact to determine the total impact on the economy. Everybody—politicians as well as economists—uses models in discussing the effects of alternative policies. The difference is that economists attempt to be *explicit* about their assumptions, and to be sure that their assumptions are consistent with each other and with the available evidence.

1. *The degree of competition.* One broad source of disagreement among economists is the extent to which the economy is competitive. In much of the analysis of this book we shall assume that the economy is very competitive; that there are many firms in each industry competing actively against each other. Each is so small relative to the market that it has no effect on the market price. There are no barriers to entry into the industry, so that if there are profitable opportunities in the industry, they will be quickly seized upon.

Few economists believe that in all sectors of the economy these assumptions are valid, but many economists believe that the economy is sufficiently competitive that the insights that one obtains from analyzing a competitive economy are relevant to an understanding of the effects of government policy in the American economy. Most economists also agree that there are some industries that are not well described by the competitive model, and that the analysis of the effects of taxation in those industries requires an analysis of how monopolies (industries with a single firm) or oligopolies (industries with a few firms) operate.

But there are other economists, such as Harvard's John Kenneth Galbraith, who believe that the economy is basically not very competitive, and that one obtains little insight into the effects of a tax by assuming that it is. These economists believe that most industries are dominated by three or four large firms; that though they may compete vigorously in some directions—for instance, in attempting to develop new products —in other areas, such as pricing policy, there is often tacit collusion. In their view, the traditional competitive model is likely to give misleading results. They contend that an appropriate model needs to take into account the limitations on the extent of competition.

Still others believe that there is a great deal of competition in the long run, but that in the short run competition is more limited. We cannot resolve these disagreements, but what we can do is to show how and when different views lead to different conclusions.

2. *The magnitude of response.* Even when economists agree about the kind of response that a particular policy will elicit, they may disagree about the magnitude of the response. That is, they may agree that income tax cuts will induce individuals to work harder, but some may feel that the effect is very likely to be small, while others may believe that the effect is likely to be large. This was one of the sources of dispute about the consequences of President Reagan's 1981 tax cut. Proponents of the tax cut believed that the lower rates would provide such a spur to the economy that tax revenues would actually increase. Critics agreed that the tax cut might provide some spur to the economy, but they argued that the increase in national income was likely to be so small that tax revenues would decline.[4] This decline would, in their view, lead to large deficits, which would, in turn, have a deleterious effect on the economy. As it turned out, in the short run, the response of the economy was even smaller than some of Reagan's critics had predicted.

Although a central concern of modern economics is ascertaining the magnitude of the response of, say, investment to an investment tax credit, of consumption to a change in the income tax rate, of savings to an increase in the interest rate, etc., it is an unfortunate fact that various studies, using different bodies of data and different statistical techniques, come up with different conclusions. As economists obtain more

[4] See, for example, Don Fullerton, "On the Possibility of an Inverse Relationship between Tax Rates and Government Revenues," *Journal of Public Economics*, October 1982, pp. 1–22.

data and develop better techniques for analyzing the limited available data, some of these disagreements may be resolved.

Disagreement over Values

While the two previous sources of disagreement arise within positive economics, the final source of disagreement lies within normative economics. Even if there is agreement about the full consequences of some policy, there may be a disagreement about whether the policy is desirable. There are frequently *trade-offs:* a policy may increase national output but also increase inequality; a policy may increase employment but also increase inflation; a policy may benefit one group but make another group worse off. There are, in other words, some desirable consequences of the policy and some undesirable consequences. Individuals may weigh these consequences in different ways, some attaching more importance to price stability than to unemployment, others attaching more importance to growth than to inequality.

On questions of values, there is no more unanimity among economists than there is among philosophers. What we shall do in this book is to present the major views and assess some of the criticisms that have been leveled against each.

SUMMARY

1. In mixed economies, such as the United States, economic activity is carried on by both private enterprise and the government.
2. Since the time of Adam Smith, economic theory has emphasized the role of private markets in the efficient supply of goods. Yet economists and others have come to recognize important limitations in the ability of the private sector to meet certain basic social needs. The attempt to correct these failures has led to the growth of government's role in the market economy.
3. The government, however, is not necessarily the solution to private-sector failures. The failure of many public programs can be attributed to four factors: (a) The consequences of any action by the government are complicated and difficult to foresee. (b) The government has only limited control over these consequences. (c) Those who design legislation have only limited control over the actual implementation of the government programs. (d) Politicians may act to further special private interests.
4. The United States has a federal government structure, with certain activities being primarily the responsibility of states and localities (such as education) and other activities being primarily the responsibility of the federal government (such as defense).
5. Economics is the study of scarcity, of how resources are allocated among competing uses. Public-sector economics focuses on choices between the public and private sectors and choices within the public sector. It is concerned with four basic issues: what gets produced; how it gets produced; for whom it gets produced; and the processes by which these decisions are made.

6. In studying the public sector, positive economics looks at the scope of government activity and the consequences of various government policies. Normative economics attempts to evaluate alternative policies that might be pursued.
7. Disagreements about the desirability of policies are based on: failures to trace out the full consequences of government policies; disagreements concerning the nature of the economy; and disagreements concerning values and objectives.

KEY CONCEPTS

Mixed economy	Public sector
Market failure	Production possibilities schedule
Invisible hand	Normative economics
Laissez faire	Positive economics
Private sector	Economic models

QUESTIONS AND PROBLEMS

1. Consider the following discussion of our current program of support for farmers:

   A. The objective of our farm program is to ensure that all farmers have a reasonable standard of living. The way it does this is to ensure that farmers receive fair prices for their commodities. It is no more right that farmers should produce for substandard prices than that workers should work for substandard wages.
   B. Our farm program has been a failure. The benefits of the price subsidies accrue largely to large farmers (because they produce more). Many farmers still have incomes below the poverty line. The high prices have induced increased production, which has meant high costs for the government. Acreage restrictions have had only limited effect, since farmers have kept their best land in production. Direct grants to farmers would be preferable to our price-support program.
   a) Which of the statements in this discussion are normative, which are positive? (The fact that you disagree with a normative statement or that you think a particular "positive" statement is inaccurate does not change the nature of the statement.)
   b) Identify the sources of disagreement: Are they due to differences in values and objectives? Differences in perceptions about the nature of the economy? Or to a failure on one (or the other) side of the debate to take into account the full consequences of the government's action?
2. For each of the following programs, identify one (or more) "unintended" consequences:
   a) Rent control
   b) Minimum wages
   c) Medicare (free hospital care to the aged)
   d) Improved highways making suburbs more accessible to the city
   e) Forced integration of central city schools
   f) Agricultural price supports
   g) Lowering the speed limit to 55 miles an hour to save on gasoline
3. Before the legislative changes enacted in 1983, there was considerable concern that our social security (old-age and survivors' insurance) program was

not adequately financed: with expected birth rates, death rates, etc., the current level of benefits could only be sustained with marked increases in taxes. Some believed that the appropriate response was to reduce the current level of benefits, others believed the appropriate response was to increase taxes in the future. Still others, worried about the effects of even higher tax rates but believing that it would be unfair to lower the benefits of those presently receiving social security, argued that benefits in the future should be cut.

In this discussion, separate out the positive statements from the normative statements. To what extent are the disagreements attributable to differences in views of the economy?

2

The Public Sector in the United States

A central question of debate in the United States, and in other mixed economies, is the appropriate size of the public sector. There are those who believe that the public sector is too large. They are skeptical of government's ability to solve social and economic problems because of the kinds of government failures we discussed in Chapter 1—for example, government's limited control over private market responses. Or they may believe on philosophical grounds in limited government because of a fear that big government undermines economic and political freedom.[1] Still others believe, like Harvard economist John Kenneth Galbraith, that the public sector is too small. In this view, greater government spending could solve the problems of blighted inner cities and inadequate schools. Galbraith argues that public spending for these activities has been inadequate in our society, which is characterized by private affluence.[2]

No matter what view you take, there is no doubt that the government today is larger, far larger, than it was a half century ago. In 1986, tax revenues collected at all levels of government were $1.3 trillion, or 30 per-

[1] A leading proponent of this view, a form of libertarianism, is Robert Nozick. His ideas are summarized in the preface of his *Anarchy, State, and Utopia* (Oxford: 1974, Basil Blackwell). See also Milton Friedman, *Capitalism and Freedom* (Chicago: University of Chicago Press, 1962).

[2] See his best-selling book, *The Affluent Society*, 4th rev. ed. (New York: New American Library, 1985).

cent of total U.S. production. Government expenditures were $1.5 trillion, or 35 percent of total production. By contrast, in 1913, prior to World War I, taxes and government expenditures were less than 10 percent of total production. How do we account for this dramatic change in the size of government? What does the government spend all this money on?

In this chapter, we will give an overview of the scope of the U.S. public sector and how it has broadened over time. We will show the ways in which government actions affect private markets. In the next chapter, we will explain the economic rationale for government intervention in markets: private markets may fail in important instances, and even a perfectly functioning competitive economy may result in a distribution of income that society finds undesirable. These chapters will not resolve the debate over whether the U.S. public sector is too big or too small, but they will provide a basis for formulating a reasonable position on this issue.

THE KINDS OF GOVERNMENT ACTIVITY

A primary role of government is to provide the legal framework within which all economic transactions occur. Beyond that, we can divide the activities of government into three categories: (a) the production of goods and services, and the regulation and subsidization of private producers; (b) the purchase of goods and services, from missiles to the services of street cleaners; and (c) the redistribution of income, that is, payments to particular groups of individuals to enable them to spend more than they otherwise could; such payments are called **transfer payments,** and include welfare payments and social insurance.

These three categories—production, purchase, and redistribution—are simply a convenient way of grouping the vast array of government expenditures and activities. But they do not correspond to the way the federal government organizes its budget or divides responsibilities between its various departments—Commerce, Health and Human Services, Interior, and so on. Moreover, most government activities are undertaken at the state and local levels as well as at the federal level, with the relative importance of state, local, and federal expenditures of various types having changed over time.

A final complication is that the nature of some government expenditures is ambiguous. For example, government subsidies to small farmers could be considered a production subsidy or a redistributive (transfer) payment. Pension payments to military retirees are often counted as transfer payments, but they are more appropriately treated as part of the cost of national defense, just as the pension costs of a private firm are counted among its labor costs.

Thus, the task of constructing a quantitative description of the government's activities is a formidable one.

PROVIDING A LEGAL SYSTEM

An important activity of the government, but one that accounts for very little expenditure, is the establishment of the legal framework within which firms and individuals can engage in economic interactions. Economists and philosophers often try to imagine what life would be like in the complete absence of government. Without laws defining property rights, only the exercise of force would stop one individual from stealing from another. Without the ability to protect property, individuals would have little incentive to accumulate assets. Needless to say, economic activities would be severely restricted.

The U.S. legal system does much more than just protect property rights. It enforces contracts between individuals. It also imposes restrictions on the kinds of contracts that are legally enforceable. Our bankruptcy laws limit the liability of investors. Product-liability laws have an important effect on the quality of goods produced. Antitrust laws attempt to encourage competition among firms: they restrict mergers, acquisitions, and unfair business practices.

The effects of our legal system are pervasive, but expenditures on running the court system and maintaining law and order are relatively small: if police and prisons are included, expenditures are slightly higher than 4 percent of total government expenditures. Less than 2 percent of total government expenditures are for general administration, legislative, and judicial activities.[3]

GOVERNMENT AND PRODUCTION

In addition to providing the basic legal framework within which individuals and firms interact, the government has taken an increasingly active role in production decisions. The government produces only a few goods and services itself, but it has a pervasive effect on production decisions through regulation, taxes, and subsidies that alter the behavior of private firms. Government motives are many. There may be dissatisfaction with particular actions of firms—such as pollution. There may be a concern about the monopoly power of some firms. Special-interest groups may convince Congress that they are particularly deserving of help. The private sector may fail to provide certain goods and services that are felt to be important.

Producing Goods and Services

One of the major differences between the United States and many of the Western European countries is the limited role that the U.S. govern-

[3] In 1985, the last year for which comparable data for federal, state, and local expenditures were available, expenditures were as follows: administrative, legislative, and judicial activities, $23 billion; police and prisons, $39 billion. See *Survey of Current Business,* July 1987, Tables 3.15 and 3.16.

ment takes as a producer of goods and services. The Constitution of the United States gives the federal government responsibility for running the postal service and for printing money. The U.S. Postal Service has a monopoly on the delivery of first-class mail, but more than 50 percent of all parcels and an even higher percentage of express mail are now delivered by private firms.

In the United States, local government has taken a major responsibility for the production of education: approximately 90 percent of elementary and secondary-school students and 80 percent of college students are enrolled in public schools.[4]

Many of the production activities of the government are similar to corresponding activities carried out by private firms. Electricity is produced both by government enterprises (the most famous of which is perhaps the Tennessee Valley Authority) and by private firms. The government sells electricity just as private firms do.

The distinction between government enterprises and private enterprises is sometimes not a clear one. The government may own more than 50 percent of a firm but allow it to operate as if it were totally private. In the United States, the government has established several enterprises. These include Amtrak, which runs the nation's passenger railroad system, and Comstat, which is working on commercial uses of satellites. These firms, too, operate much like private firms.

Comparing the public and private sectors in various countries, we see that some industries frequently fall within the public sector, while other industries seldom do. Agriculture appears to be one of the more difficult industries for public production. On the other hand, in most countries, telephones, railroads, and at least part of the radio and TV broadcasting industry are in the public sector. In some countries, such as Britain, the government produces steel and coal. In many countries, the banking system is owned and operated by the government; in the United States it is closely regulated but privately owned.[5]

The process of converting private enterprises to government enterprises is called **nationalization;** the process of converting government enterprises to private enterprises is called **privatization.** Between 1982 and 1986, the British government undertook a wave of privatizations: it turned over its telephone system and natural gas and petroleum operations to newly created private firms (in which it retains a part of the shares). In 1986 France began what is expected to be the largest sale of government-owned enterprises to private investors ever undertaken, including many enterprises that it had nationalized (when its leading party was socialist) just five years earlier.

For the United States, the colored line in Figure 2.1 traces the levels

[4] *Projections of Education Statistics, 1990–91*, Table 4, p. 32. (Washington, D. C.: Department of Education, National Center for Education Statistics, 1987).

[5] The Federal Reserve Banks, which are responsible for the management of the banking system, are publicly owned. Their profits are turned over to the Treasury. In 1985 these amounted to $17.8 billion.

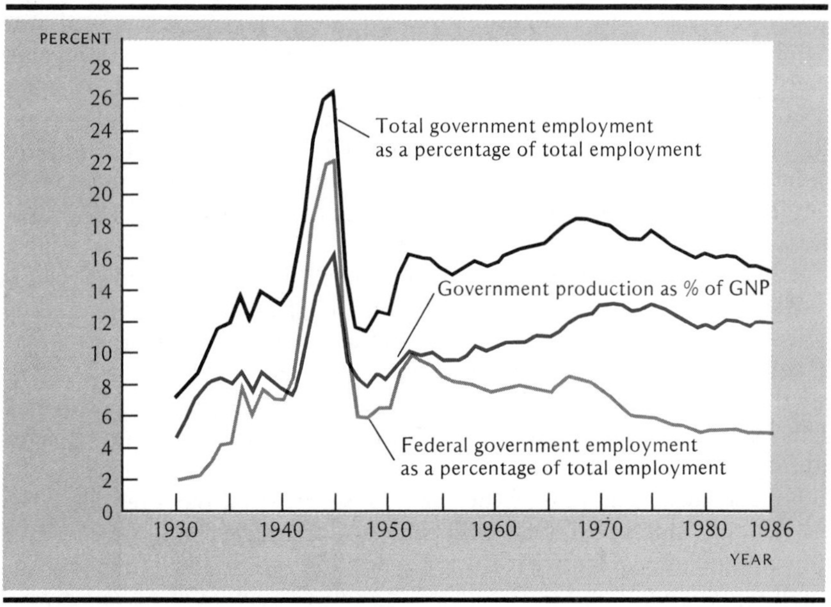

2.1 THE SIZE OF THE PUBLIC SECTOR IN THE UNITED STATES Government production as a percentage of GNP and government employment as a fraction of total employment provide a view of the government's role as producer. SOURCE: U.S. Department of Commerce, *National Income and Product Accounts, 1929–1982,* Tables 6.1, 6.7; *Survey of Current Business,* July 1987, Tables 6.1, 6.7.

of government production since 1930. Public production by federal, state, and local governments currently accounts for 12 percent of national output. This is up considerably from just 8 percent in 1948, but down from the peacetime peak of 13.2 percent it reached in the years 1970–1972.

Government production (like the production of any firm) is measured by the difference between the value of output and the value of materials purchased. This is called the **value added.** But while the value of output in private firms is measured by the price the goods and services are sold for, most publicly produced goods are not sold but are used directly in the public sector or provided freely to the public. Since there is no market price to value such items, they must be valued at the cost of their inputs. Thus, while the value added of a private enterprise is equal to its wages, interest payments, and profits, the value of government production is just equal to wages plus interest. A firm that decided to pay its workers 5 percent more (without eliciting any increased productivity) would find its value added unchanged: wage payments would be up by 5 percent, but profits would be down by a corresponding amount. If the government decided to pay its workers 5 percent more, however, since the value of output is measured by the value of input, the wage increase would appear as a 5 percent increase in production.

Because of these problems, many economists believe that one obtains a better picture of the size of government as a producer by looking at its employment. This is shown by the black line in Figure 2.1. In 1986 there were 17 million public employees (including public education and the armed forces),[6] which represented 15.3 percent of total employment. This was more than double the percentage in 1930 (when it was 7 percent of the labor force) but down slightly from that in 1980. The expansion in the public sector appears to have proceeded at a fairly steady pace until 1970 (apart from World War II). It increased as rapidly during Hoover's administration (1929–1933) as it did during Roosevelt's New Deal (1933–1945). Though there was a slight decrease in the pace of growth during the Eisenhower years, the size of the public sector did not begin to decline until the Nixon and Ford administrations. This decline continued during both the Carter and Reagan administrations.

It is also important to note the variations in the relative roles played by the federal, state, and local governments, as suggested by the bottom line in Figure 2.1. Comparing it to the top line, we see that total government employment and federal government employment do not always move together. While federal employment as a percentage of total employment declined in the early 1970s, this decline was offset by the rise in employment at the state and local level. It is important to bear this in mind: reductions in federal expenditures (or employment) do not, of themselves, necessarily imply a reduction in government expenditures (or employment). More of a burden may simply be placed on states and localities.

Subsidizing Production

In industries in which the government is neither a producer nor a consumer, it may nevertheless have a pervasive effect on the decisions of private producers. This influence is exercised through subsidies and taxes—both direct and indirect—and through regulations.

AGRICULTURAL PROGRAMS

In the United States, the most important set of direct subsidies are for agriculture. These amounted to $26 billion in 1986, up from $7 billion in 1980.[7] Most of these expenditures are for government purchases of agricultural crops to maintain the prices of these crops at a high level. Farm subsidies have been rising precipitously in the 1980s. In 1986, government outlays for corn, wheat, and rice represented 57 percent of the crop value, compared to only 7 percent in 1980.[8]

[6] This figure is the number of "full-time equivalent employees." Two half-time employees are counted as one employee.

[7] *Economic Report of the President, 1987*, p. 155; *Historical Tables: Budget of the United States Government, Fiscal Year 1987*, Table 3.3.

[8] *Economic Report of the President, 1987*, p. 155.

But government expenditures on agriculture represent only a fraction of the total cost of its agricultural programs. Most of the cost is borne in the form of higher prices consumers must pay.

In evaluating these or any other government programs, it is useful to distinguish between two kinds of costs. One is the cost to society resulting from resources not being put to the most efficient use—for instance, workers who remain in agriculture because of the government subsidies, even though their productivity elsewhere may be higher. The other is a **transfer,** a redistribution of income from one group in society to another. Much of the cost of agricultural programs represents a transfer from those outside the agricultural sector to farmers.

Our agricultural programs illustrate another general principle to which we shall return later: governments can subsidize industries and individuals in a variety of ways, and only some of the (costs of these) subsidies show up as government expenditures.

TAX EXPENDITURES

Some of the most important government subsidies are extended through the tax system. If the government gives educational grants to students, these appear as an expenditure; but if the government gives a tax credit for educational expenditures (that is, if the government allows the individual to reduce his tax payments by the amount of the education expenditure), then it does not appear as an expenditure. The government could just as well tax the individual, and then give him a grant; the two are, for all intents and purposes, equivalent. Yet they show up in the statistics in a very different way.

Similarly, if the government gives a grant to a producer to assist him in buying a machine, it appears as an expenditure; if the government allows him to take a tax credit on his expenditures on machines (that is, if he buys a \$100 machine with a 7 percent tax credit, he will get a \$7 tax credit, which reduces the taxes he otherwise would have paid by \$7), it does not appear as a government expenditure. But again, the two are, for all intents and purposes, equivalent.

We call these implicit grants **tax expenditures.** The federal government is required to make estimates of the tax revenue losses associated with each tax expenditure. In recent years, they have become very large. To calculate their value, we first calculate how much each individual or firm would have paid in taxes if there were not special provisions allowing deductions and credits for a variety of categories of expenditures. We then compute the difference between this figure and the actual tax. This difference is the revenue lost because of the tax expenditure. We can think of the government as taxing the individual without these special provisions, and then giving the individual a grant (to buy a machine, to go to school, to buy medical services).

Table 2.1 lists the six budget areas enjoying the bulk of federal tax expenditures in 1986. The tax expenditures for commerce can be

Table 2.1 FEDERAL TAX EXPENDITURES: THE MAJOR RECIPIENTS (1986) *(in billions of dollars)*

Budget Function	*Direct Federal Outlays*	*Revenue Loss Estimates for Tax Expenditures*	*Tax Expenditures as a Percentage of Direct Outlays*
Commerce	2.6	140.4	5,400%
Housing credit	1.9	44.3	2,300
Health	106.1	31.4	30
Income security	318.6	95.3	30
General purpose fiscal assistance to state and local government	6.4	35.5	550
Education, training, employment, and social services	30.6	28.7	94

Source: The United States Budget in Brief, Fiscal Year 1988, Tables 3 and 4; *Special Analyses: Budget of the United States Government, Fiscal Year 1988,* Table G-2.

thought of as production subsidies, encouraging some particular economic activity (investment, research, timber, cattle, etc.). These amounted to \$140 billion in 1986, or fifty-four times direct federal subsidies to firms (other than farmers). The remaining tax expenditures can be thought of as consumption subsidies and redistribution. The housing tax expenditure of \$44 billion (provided largely in the form of a deduction of interest on home mortgages) is a consumption subsidy to owner-occupied housing. The nontaxability of employer contributions to medical care encourages the consumption of health care. The partial tax exemption of social security benefits and employer contributions to pensions is a form of income redistribution. Federal tax expenditures for state and local governments, which were more than five times the level of direct federal outlays for general-purpose assistance to state and local governments, reduce the effective cost of state and local tax payments. The Tax Reform Act of 1986 eliminated the deductibility of state and local sales taxes, but it retained the far larger deduction for state and local income and property taxes. Tax expenditures for education, including the deductibility of contributions to educational organizations and the nontaxability of scholarship income, were nearly equal to the level of direct federal outlays.

HIDDEN SUBSIDIES

Many government subsidies show up in neither the statistics on government expenditures nor those on tax expenditures. For instance, when the government restricts the importation of some foreign good or imposes a tariff on its importation, this raises the prices of those goods in the United States. American producers of competing goods are helped. There is an effective subsidy to American producers paid not by the government but directly by consumers. The government also provides extensive hidden subsidies through low-interest loans and loan guarantees, and it imposes both hidden taxes and subsidies through its regulations. We will turn to these issues below.

Regulating Business

Government regulates business activity in an attempt to protect workers, consumers, and the environment, to prevent anticompetitive practices, and to prevent discrimination.

The Occupational Safety and Health Administration attempts to ensure that workers' places of employment meet certain minimal standards. The National Labor Relations Board attempts to ensure that management and unions deal fairly with each other. The Federal Trade Commission attempts, among other things, to protect consumers from misleading advertising. The Environmental Protection Agency attempts to protect certain vital parts of our environment by regulating, for instance, emissions from automobiles and toxic-waste disposal.

In addition to these broad categories, there are regulations that apply to specific industries. The banking industry is regulated both by the Federal Reserve Board and the Comptroller of the Currency. Trucking and railroads are regulated by the Interstate Commerce Commission. The airlines are regulated by the Federal Aviation Administration. The telephone and telecommunications industry is regulated by the Federal Communications Commission. The securities industry is regulated by the Securities and Exchange Commission.

In recent years, there has been a concerted effort to reduce the extent of federal regulation. The process of reducing or eliminating regulations is referred to as **deregulation.** There has been deregulation in the airline industry (with the elimination of the Civil Aeronautics Board in 1984), in natural gas (gas prices have been allowed to rise gradually to market levels), in trucking, and in banking (the range of services that banks are now allowed to provide has been greatly increased).

Federal outlays for the regulatory agencies represent just under 1 percent of the federal budget.[9] But these expenditures do not give an accurate view of the impact of the federal regulatory agencies. The extent to which they influence virtually every aspect of business practices goes well beyond the simple measure of government expenditures. Many regulations have effects that are similar to those of taxes and subsidies. For example, regulations on utility prices may reduce prices for certain users below the free-market level, while they raise the price to other users.

A very indirect measure of the scope of federal regulations may be had by looking at the costs of reporting, including filling out forms, costs that are borne by firms. During the Carter administration an effort was made

[9] This percentage fell from 1.2 percent in 1975 to 0.9 percent in 1985. See Kenneth Chilton, *The Effects of Gramm-Rudman-Hollings on Federal Regulatory Agencies*, Center for the Study of American Business, 1986.

to reduce paperwork costs, and a Paperwork Commission was established with this as its objective. In its last detailed report, in 1979, the commission estimated that 786 million hours were spent by nongovernmental employees in completing government forms.[10] This corresponds to approximately 400,000 workers working full time for a year. These "indirect employees" equaled 14 percent of direct federal employment in 1979.

Government Activities in Financial Markets

Government activities in one sector—financial markets—are particularly pervasive. Financial markets provide several critical services. They allocate capital. They provide the institutions through which savings of individuals get translated into investments by firms. Stock markets enable entrepreneurs to shift the risks of business to the general public, and insurance firms enable individuals to divest themselves of some of the important risks that they face.

Government affects the financial sector through a variety of regulatory agencies. As we have noted, the banking system is regulated by the Federal Reserve Board and the Comptroller of the Currency, and the securities industry is regulated by the Securities and Exchange Commission. Savings and loan institutions are regulated by the Federal Home Loan Bank Board. Each of the fifty states has an insurance commission to regulate the insurance industry.

In addition to these regulatory activities, the government has both subsidized certain private lending activities and has established governmental bodies to carry on credit and insurance activities.

PROVIDING CREDIT

When it extends credit at below market interest rates, the government in effect subsidizes the credit, assuming that the high market interest rate extended to some groups accurately reflects the market's assessment of the risks of lending to them. The actual subsidy only shows up on the government's books when and if the borrowers default on their loan. (The implicit subsidy on educational loans made in the 1960s and 1970s is only now becoming apparent, as many of these borrowers fail to repay these loans.)

In some cases, the government has not issued credit, but it has provided a loan guarantee, which enables the borrower to obtain credit at a much lower rate than he otherwise could. Since there are not current budgetary costs, loan guarantees are a less painful (at least in the short term) method of subsidizing an industry.

When the Chrysler Corporation was on the verge of bankruptcy in 1979, the government guaranteed its loans. Though it turned out that

[10] *Paperwork and Red Tape: New Perspectives, New Directions*, Office of Management and Budget, 1979.

Chrysler was able to meet its debt obligations, the loan guarantee represented a large subsidy to Chrysler. Because Chrysler met its debt obligations, the government guarantee did not entail any government outlay. Instead, its real cost was only the reduction in the supply of credit to other (possibly more profitable) firms.

Much of the government's lending activity grew in response to a perceived failure of the private markets to provide credit at reasonable terms. Government loan programs (either direct loans or loan guarantees) are available to farmers, homeowners, small businesses, exporters, utilities, shipbuilders, and foreign governments.

To quantify the role of the federal government in affecting the flow of funds between savers and borrowers, it is useful to compare net lending under federal auspices to total net lending in the United States. Annual lending under federal auspices is the difference between the amount of direct and guaranteed federal loans at the beginning and end of the year. This was $129 billion in 1986. The domestic supply of credit is the net increase in the holdings of all U.S. investors. In 1986, this was $889 billion. The ratio of federal and federally assisted lending to total lending, therefore, was 14.5 percent in 1986. This is below the peak of 22.6 percent in 1980.[11]

These ratios should be used with caution because they do not distinguish between a dollar of loans at, or close to, the private market rate of interest, and federal loans that provide a large implicit subsidy. The full extent of federal influence in allocating credit to favored borrowers depends on the degree of subsidy implicit in federal and federally guaranteed loans. The federal government is only beginning to develop an accounting system that would include a good measure of the amount of implicit federal credit subsidies.

PROVIDING INSURANCE

In the period since the Great Depression, the government has taken an increasingly large role in providing insurance. There are two groups of government insurance programs. The first, called **social insurance,** includes social security (old-age retirement and survivors' insurance), Medicare (medical insurance for the aged), unemployment insurance, disability insurance, and workmen's compensation (insurance for injuries on the job). Social insurance has grown to 18 percent of total government expenditures and 28 percent of federal government expenditures. As we shall see later, some of these so-called insurance programs are not just insurance programs that provide each individual with benefits whose actuarial value is equal to his contributions.[12] They also pro-

[11] *Special Analysis: Budget of the United States Government, Fiscal Year 1988,* p. F–30.

[12] The actuarial value reflects the true chance of the insured event occurring. Thus, if an individual insures himself against an accident that would cost him $10,000 if it occurred, and there is a 1 percent chance it will occur, we say the actuarial value of the insurance is $100. If the government insures the risk, charging a premium of $50, there is, in effect, a $50 subsidy.

vide a means by which income gets redistributed to some groups who are felt to be particularly needy. For this reason, they are generally classified as transfer programs, programs that simply transfer income to particular groups in the population. With transfer programs, government is redistributing income, an activity we will discuss later in this chapter.

The second category of government insurance programs is focused on **commercial risks.** Though these insurance programs are intended to be self-sustaining, in recent years several of the agencies that administer them have had losses exceeding their income. While the Federal Deposit Insurance Corporation (which insures deposits in commercial banks) has built up $18 billion of reserves, other programs have used up all of their reserves. This is the case for Pension Benefit Guaranty Corporation, which guarantees the workers of participating private firms against the possibility that their pension funds will be unable to meet their obligations; it is also true of the Federal Savings and Loan Insurance Corporation. (When premiums exceed losses, the difference is added to reserves; when losses exceed premiums, the difference is taken out of reserves.) Many economists believe that the potential losses facing these corporations are enormous. Other federal insurance programs administered by the Federal Emergency Management Agency, provide flood, crime, and riot insurance.

GOVERNMENT PURCHASES OF GOODS AND SERVICES

Every year the government buys billions of dollars' worth of goods and services. It does this to provide for our national defense, to maintain a network of highways, to provide education, police protection, fire protection, and parks. These purchases of goods and services amount to one-fifth of the total production in the United States.

Though there is a close link between "government as purchaser" and "government as producer," the two are conceptually and practically distinct. Much of what the government purchases is produced by it. But the government also makes many purchases from private firms (including most military hardware), while it sells some of what it produces (most notably electricity and passenger rail services) to private firms and consumers.[13]

What we characterize as government purchases are amounts spent for goods and services freely available to the public, such as national defense, public schools, and highways. Government payments to the aged through the Medicare program to finance their hospital expenses or to the poor through the food stamp program, are categorized as transfer payments, not as direct government purchases. Hence, we will discuss them in the separate section below on government redistribution of income.

[13] Figure 7.1 in the text illustrates the relation between government's activities as producer and purchaser.

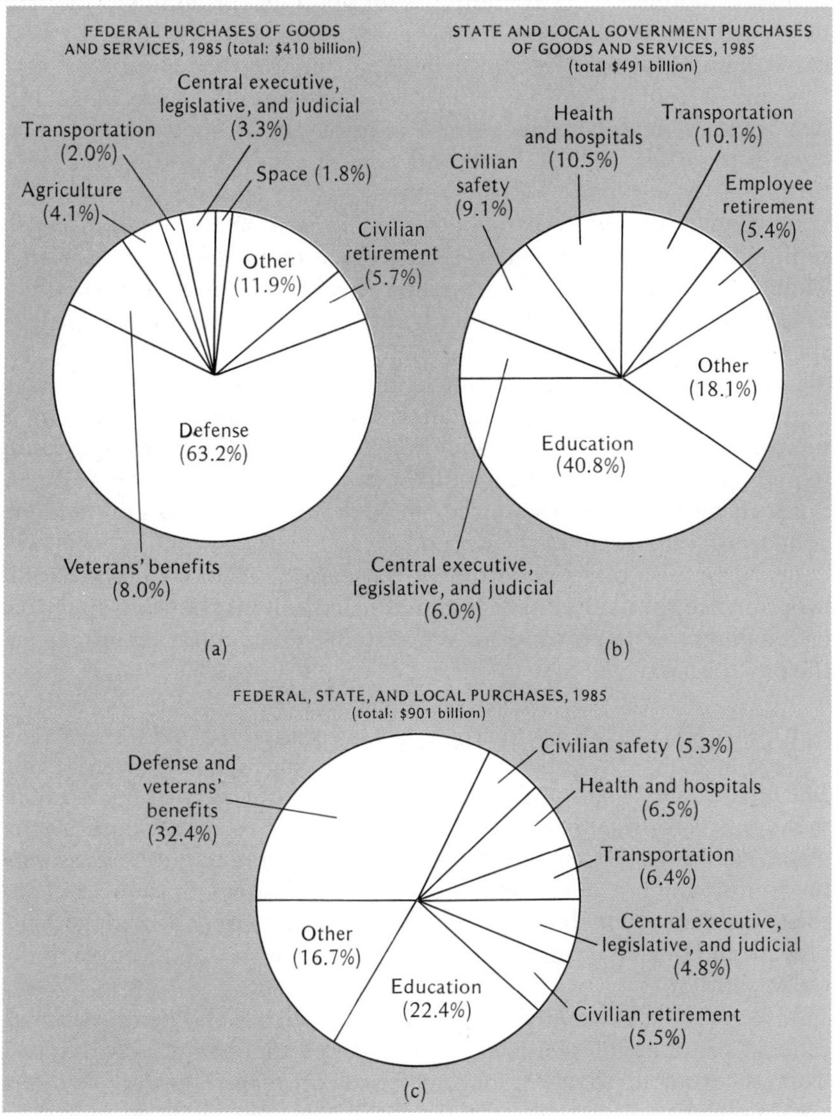

2.2 ALLOCATION OF GOVERNMENT PURCHASES OF GOODS AND SERVICES (EXCLUDING NET INTEREST PAID), 1985 Defense spending dominates federal purchases, while at the state and local levels, education is the major purchase. When federal grants finance state and local purchases, the purchases are attributed to the administering unit. SOURCE: *Survey of Current Business,* July 1987, Tables 3.11, 3.15, and 3.16.

The sum total of government purchases was somewhat less than $1 trillion in 1985. Figure 2.2 shows what the federal, state, and local governments spent this money on. At the federal level, most purchases were for national defense—the army, navy, marines, and development of military hardware. There are two other expenditures that are closely related to defense: (1) expenditures for veterans' programs, which can be thought of as payments for previous services in the armed forces; these amounted to 8 percent of federal purchases of goods and services, and (2) much of the space research and technology program, which was originally motivated by defense considerations. If we add these categories together, then defense and related expenditures amounted to three-fourths of the federal government's purchases.

For state and local governments, the largest item is education, representing close to half of their total purchases of goods and services. Though federal government expenditures have increased markedly in recent years, they still represent only 8 percent of total education spending by government.[14]

Looking at combined spending by all levels of government (shown in Figure 2.2C), the major items after defense (32 percent) and education(22 percent), are health and hospitals (7 percent) and transportation (6 percent). Almost half of all public sector spending on transportation is financed by the federal government, but state and local governments administer 86 percent of the expenditures.[15]

There are also other government purchases in the form of programs for promoting and regulating commerce, for building housing and urban development projects, and for maintaining our natural resources and the environment.

GOVERNMENT REDISTRIBUTION OF INCOME

The government takes an active role in redistributing income, in taking money away from some individuals and giving it to others. There are two major categories of explicit redistribution programs: public assistance programs, which provide benefits to those poor enough to qualify; and social insurance, which provides benefits to the retired, disabled, unemployed, and sick. We will also see some ways in which government hides redistribution.

As we saw above, outlays for explicit redistribution programs are called transfer payments. These expenditures are qualitatively different from government spending on, say, roads or guns. Transfer payments are simply changes in who has the right to consume goods. In contrast, a government outlay for a road or a gun reduces the amount of other goods (e.g., private consumption goods) that society can enjoy. Transfer payments affect the way in which society's total income is divided among its members, but (neglecting here the disruption to incentives

[14] Most of this is in the form either of aid to students or grants to states and localities (and hence is included under state and local expenditures). Of the $16.9 billion expenditure in 1985, $8.5 billion was distributed to state and local governments and $6.8 billion was given directly to individuals.

[15] Of total public sector spending of $58 billion on transportation, $8 billion are federal funds administered by the federal government, $17 billion are federal transportation grants to state and local governments, and $33 billion are state and local funds administered by state and local governments. See *Survey of Current Business*, July 1987, Tables 3.15 and 3.16. Chapter 26 of the text will discuss the interactions between federal and state and local governments.

caused by transfers) transfers do not affect the total amount of private goods that can be enjoyed.

Public Assistance Programs

Public assistance programs (like social insurance programs) take two forms. Some provide cash, while others provide payment only for specific services or commodities. The latter are referred to as **in kind benefits.** Of the *cash* programs, the largest are Aid to Families with Dependent Children (AFDC), and Supplemental Security Income (SSI), which provides cash to the poor who are aged, blind, or disabled. The largest *in-kind* public assistance program is Medicaid, which covers the medical costs of the poor. In 1986, Medicaid accounted for 44 percent of total public assistance, or $45 billion.

Table 2.2 GOVERNMENT PUBLIC ASSISTANCE PROGRAMS *(in billions of dollars)*

Program	*Date Enacted*	*1972 Outlay*	*1986 Outlay*
CASH BENEFITS			
AFDC	1935	$6.9	$16.2
SSI	1972	3.4	12.1
General Assistance	—	0.7	2.5
Earned Income Credit	1978	—	1.4
Other Assistance	—	1.7	3.6
IN-KIND BENEFITS			
Medicaid	1965	8.5	45.2
Food Stamps	1964	2.0	10.6
Lower Income Housing Assistance	1937	1.5	9.0
National School Lunch Program	1946	—	2.1
TOTAL		24.7	102.7

Source: *Survey of Current Business*, July 1987, Table 3.11; General Accounting Office, *Federal Benefits Programs: A Profile, 1985.*

Table 2.2 lists the main public assistance programs with their date of enactment and their benefits. (In-kind benefits are valued at government cost in the table; we will see later that this may be more than their value to the recipients.) The table shows that most (approximately 65 percent) benefits were in-kind, not cash.

Social Insurance Programs

Social insurance differs from public assistance in that an individual's entitlements are partly dependent on his contributions, which can be viewed as insurance premiums. To the extent that what the individual receives is commensurate with his contributions, social insurance can be viewed as a government "production activity" not a redistribution activity. But since what some receive is far in excess of what they contribute

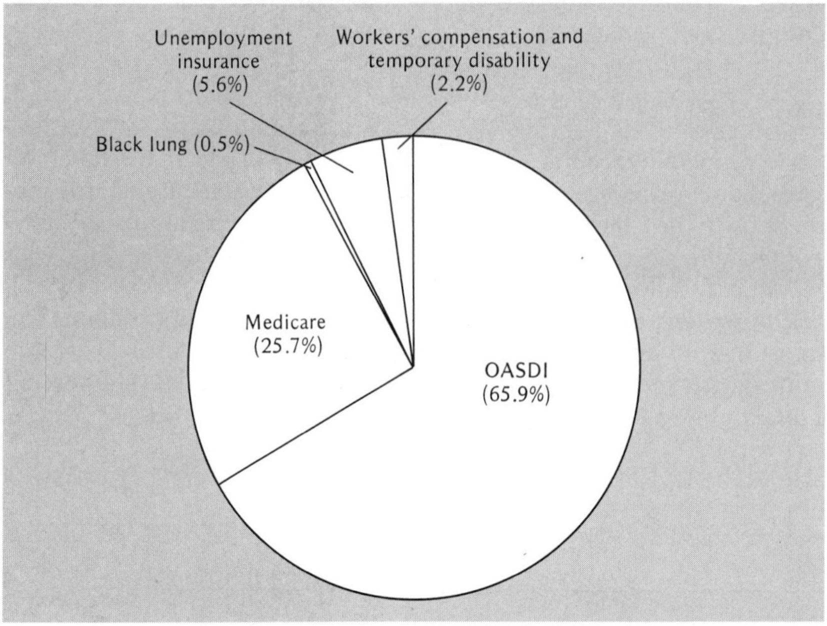

2.3 RELATIVE IMPORTANCE OF SOCIAL INSURANCE PROGRAMS, 1986 (Total expenditure: $294 billion) Social security (OASDI) is by far the largest social insurance expenditure. SOURCE: *Survey of Current Business,* July 1987, Table 3.11.

(on an actuarial basis), there is a large element of redistribution involved in government social insurance programs.

The largest of these programs is the Old-Age, Survivors, and Disability Insurance program (**OASDI**, the proper name for social security). Figure 2.3 gives the relative size of the various social insurance programs. The Medicare program, providing medical services to the aged, has (like Medicaid) grown rapidly since it was first introduced in 1965, and now is the second largest program.

The social security and Medicare programs are sometimes referred to as **middle-class entitlement programs,** because the main beneficiaries are the middle class, and benefits are provided not on the basis of need but because the beneficiaries satisfy certain other eligibility standards (e.g., age). As soon as they satisfy these criteria, they become entitled to receive the benefits.

Hidden Redistribution Programs

The government affects the distribution of income not only through direct transfers but also through the indirect effects of the tax system and other government programs. One could imagine the government taxing everyone at the same rate but then giving grants to those whose income fell below a certain level. This would have the same effect as taxing the lower-income individuals at a lower rate. Thus there is a certain arbitrariness in distinguishing between transfer payments through spending programs and the implicit transfers through the tax system.[16]

The government also redistributes income in the guise of subsidy programs and quotas. Our agricultural programs in effect redistribute income to farmers. The oil import quotas of the 1950s redistributed income to owners of oil reserves. The alleged reason for the quotas was to ensure the energy independence of the United States; nonetheless the redistributive effects were among the primary consequences, and they may indeed provide the true motivation for the legislation.

Spending for goods and services also has its redistributive consequences; subsidies to urban bus transport may help the poor, while subsidies to suburban rail lines may help the middle class. As we shall see in later chapters, assessing the redistributive consequences of any government program—expenditure, tax, or regulation—is an extremely complicated matter.

TOTAL GOVERNMENT EXPENDITURES: A BIRD'S EYE VIEW

We can now give a bird's eye view of total government expenditures through subsidies to government producers, purchases of goods and services, and payments to individuals. Figure 2.4A shows that purchases of goods and services, primarily for defense and education, constituted more than a half of total public sector outlays in 1986. Another one-fourth of outlays went for transfer payments.

Transfer payments are somewhat more important within the federal budget, shown in Figure 2.4B, than within total public sector outlays. Transfer payments in 1986 were 37 percent of federal outlays. The rest of federal spending was divided between defense purchases (32 percent), interest (13 percent), grants-in-aid (8 percent), and everything else (11 percent, or $114 billion). The 1986 federal deficit of $203 billion was larger than this last category. Thus, balancing the budget without reducing transfers, cutting defense, or raising taxes, was impossible.

Federal vs. State and Local Responsibilities

We saw in Chapter 1 that the U.S. government has a federal structure: the federal government takes primary responsibility for the provision of certain goods and services, while state and local governments provide others. Today, the federal government pays for all of national defense, 98 percent of social insurance, three-fourths of public assistance, but less than one-twelfth of public education. The federal budget is some-

[16] Some of the tax expenditures can be viewed explicitly as forms of social insurance. The fact that unemployment insurance and social security are only partially taxed, and disability benefits not taxed at all, means that a dollar of direct expenditures for those purposes goes further than it would if subjected to taxation.

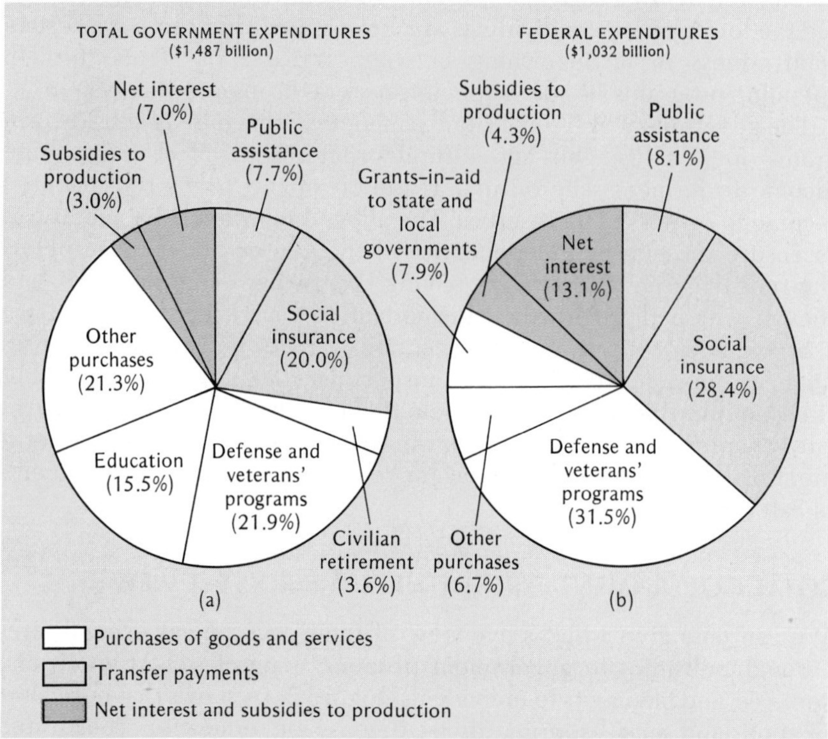

2.4 DISTRIBUTION OF GOVERNMENT EXPENDITURES, 1986 Defense and social insurance are the largest categories of expenditure for government as a whole (panel A) and for the federal government alone (panel B). (Total government expenditures are less than the sum of federal, state, and local expenditures because federal grants-in-aid to state and local governments are included within both federal spending and state and local spending.) SOURCE: *Survey of Current Business,* July 1987, Tables 3.12, 3.14, and 3.16; Estimates from Executive Office of the President, *Up from Dependency,* Vol. I, Table 1.

what less than twice the combined budgets of all state and local governments.

The relations between the federal government and the states and localities are complicated. The federal government gives direct grants (now almost exclusively limited to specific programs), and it uses the states and localities to administer federal programs. Such expenditures thus may be reported as both a "federal" expenditure and a "state and local" expenditure.

In recent years there have been marked changes in the relative importance of these different levels of governments. One way of seeing these changes is to note that the federal share of all nondefense government spending grew from slightly less than a fifth in 1902 to more than a half in 1986.[17]

[17] From R. Inman, "Fiscal Allocations in a Federalist Economy: Understanding the New Federalism, in J. Quigley and D. Rubinfeld, eds., *Urban America and the Reagan Budget* (Berkeley: University of California Press, 1985), and *Survey of Current Business,* July 1987, Tables 3.1 and 3.15.

PERSPECTIVES ON THE SIZE OF THE PUBLIC SECTOR IN THE UNITED STATES

Since the government's impact on the private economy depends on its regulatory and tax policies as well as on its outlays, no single number can provide an accurate indicator of the government's effect on the American economy. Nonetheless, one number that economists have found particularly convenient to use is the size of public expenditures relative to the size of the total economy. A standard measure of the size of the total economy is Gross National Product (GNP), which is a measure of the value of all the goods and services produced in the economy during a given year.

The Growth in Expenditures and Their Changing Composition

During the past fifty years, public expenditures as a share of GNP have grown rapidly. In 1930 they were 11 percent of GNP. Today, they represent 35 percent of GNP, as we see in Figure 2.5.[18]

DEFENSE EXPENDITURES

From 1960 to 1977 defense expenditures declined as a percentage of GNP (from 9 percent to 5 percent) and as a percentage of government expenditures. Though the period since has seen a reversal in this trend, by 1986 defense expenditures as a percentage of GNP were still not up to the level they had attained in 1960. In fact, during the period 1960 to 1977, the actual expenditures increased at a rate slower than the rate of inflation.

In order to avoid the misleading impressions that can be caused by failing to take appropriate account of inflation, economists like to express expenditures in "constant dollars"; thus, if last year the government spent $1 billion on some program, and this year it spends $1.1 billion, but prices have increased by 10 percent, we say that the current expenditures (measured in last year's prices) are $1 billion; in constant dollars, expenditures have not increased at all. Thus, in constant 1982 dollars, defense expenditures *shrank* from an average of $175 billion in 1970–1974 to $156 billion in 1980, but they increased to $227 billion in 1985. Further increases are projected for the future. This 45 percent increase in real defense expenditure within a space of five years has, not surprisingly, engendered enormous controversy.

TRANSFER PAYMENTS AND INTEREST

Growth in expenditures for social security, government retirement programs, Medicare, and interest account for much of the increase in public

[18] Recall from our earlier discussion the arbitrariness of this measure. For instance, if the government switches from providing aid to education through direct grants to providing it through tax expenditures, these statistics would show a fall in the share of public expenditures.

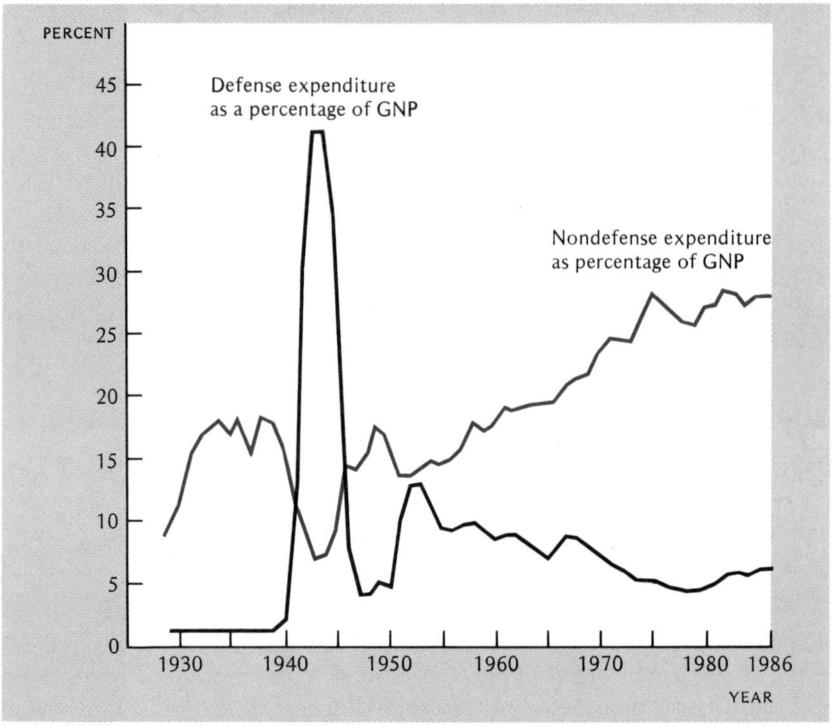

2.5 THE GROWTH OF THE PUBLIC SECTOR IN THE UNITED STATES, 1929–1986 Defense expenditures as a percentage of GNP declined slowly after the Korean War, with a slight increase during the Vietnam War, and they have grown in recent years under President Reagan. By contrast, the percentage of government expenditure on nondefense items has slightly declined in recent years. Defense expenditures shown do not include veterans' benefits and military retirement. SOURCE: U.S. Department of Commerce, *National Income and Product Accounts, 1929–1982,* Tables 1.1, 3.1, 3.15; *Survey of Current Business,* July 1987, Tables 1.1, 3.1, 3.15

expenditures since 1950, as shown in Figure 2.6. Though public assistance is often blamed for the growth in public expenditures, its share in total government expenditures has only increased from 4 percent to 6 percent of total government expenditures.[19]

INTERPRETING THE DATA

There are a number of widespread views concerning how public sector expenditure levels and patterns have changed during the past quarter century, on which the data we have been discussing shed some light.

The data do not show a large increase in expenditures in the late

[19] Only the principal public assistance programs are included in this figure. When we include the smaller programs, too, as in Figure 2.4A, they represent 7.7 percent of total government expenditures in 1986.

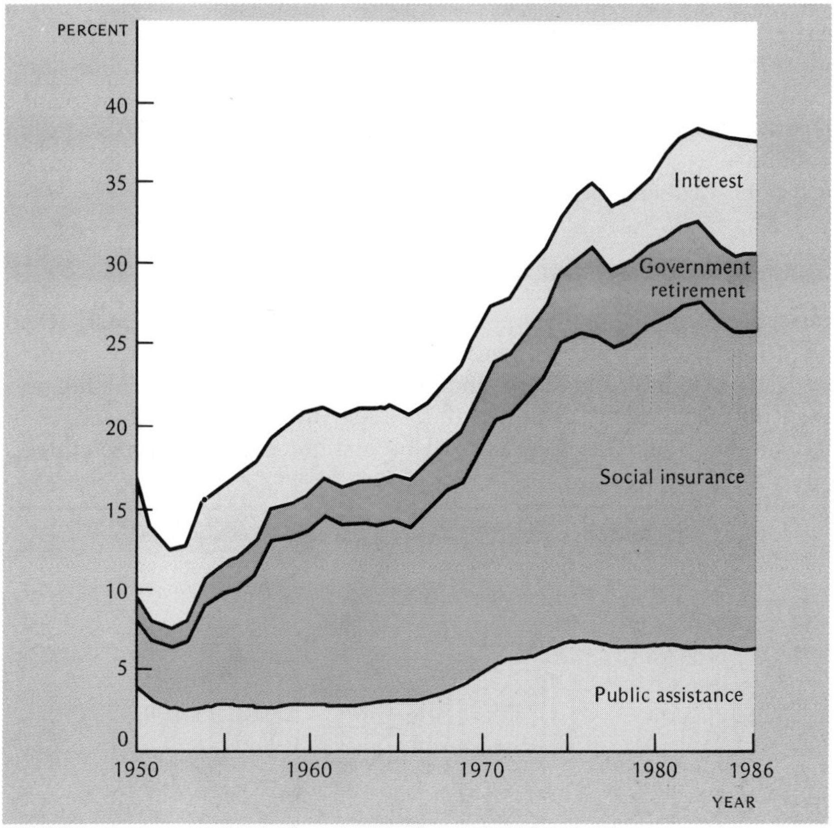

2.6 GOVERNMENT TRANSFERS AND INTEREST PAYMENTS AS A PERCENTAGE OF TOTAL GOVERNMENT EXPENDITURES Since 1950, government transfer programs have grown from less than 10 percent of total government expenditure to more than 30 percent, with the bulk of the increase accounted for by social security (OASDI). This figure includes as transfer programs some expenditures, such as government retirement programs, that might properly be thought of as deferred compensation. It does not include some of the redistributive programs we identified earlier. (Public assistance programs include all items listed in Table 2.2 except housing assistance and the school lunch program.) It does show, however, the major sources of increase in transfer payments. SOURCE: *Survey of Current Business,* July 1987, Tables 1.1, 3.1, 3.15.

1960s, as is commonly thought to have resulted from the War on Poverty. They also do not show a decrease in expenditures in the early 1980s in spite of Reagan's efforts to cut the size of government. The period of rapid increase in nondefense expenditures began before 1960, though it was sustained not only through the Johnson administration (1963–1969), but also through the Nixon administration (1969–1974). It was under Jimmy Carter that the most notable recent decline occurred.

These statistics may, however, be somewhat misleading. Expenditures in one year may be the consequence of programs adopted much earlier. The Medicare and Medicaid programs were adopted in 1965, but the full costs of these programs were not realized until much later. The current high levels of expenditure on social security are the results of certain changes made in benefits in the 1970s. The current expansion of military expenditures will have effects on budgets for years from now, as systems ordered today are delivered.

Comparison of Expenditures across Countries

The share of government appears to be smaller in the United States than in most other Western countries (see Figure 2.7), and its relative growth has also been much smaller than in most other industrialized countries. The contrast is more dramatic if we take into account differences in national income. There appears to be a slight tendency for countries

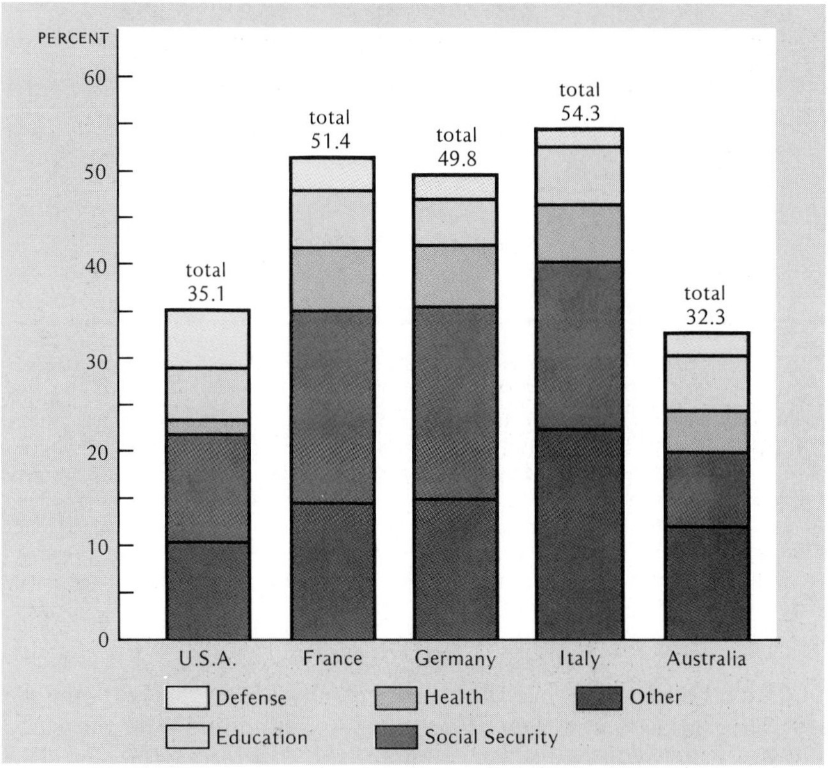

2.7 PUBLIC-SECTOR PROGRAMS AS PERCENTAGE OF GNP IN FIVE COUNTRIES, 1982 In spite of the growth of government in the United States, we see here that compared to four other industrial countries, only Australia has lower expenditures as a percentage of GNP. SOURCE: United Nations, *National Accounts Statistics, Government Accounts and Tables, 1983 Yearbook,* Country Tables 2.3; and *Survey of Current Business,* July 1986, Table 3.14.

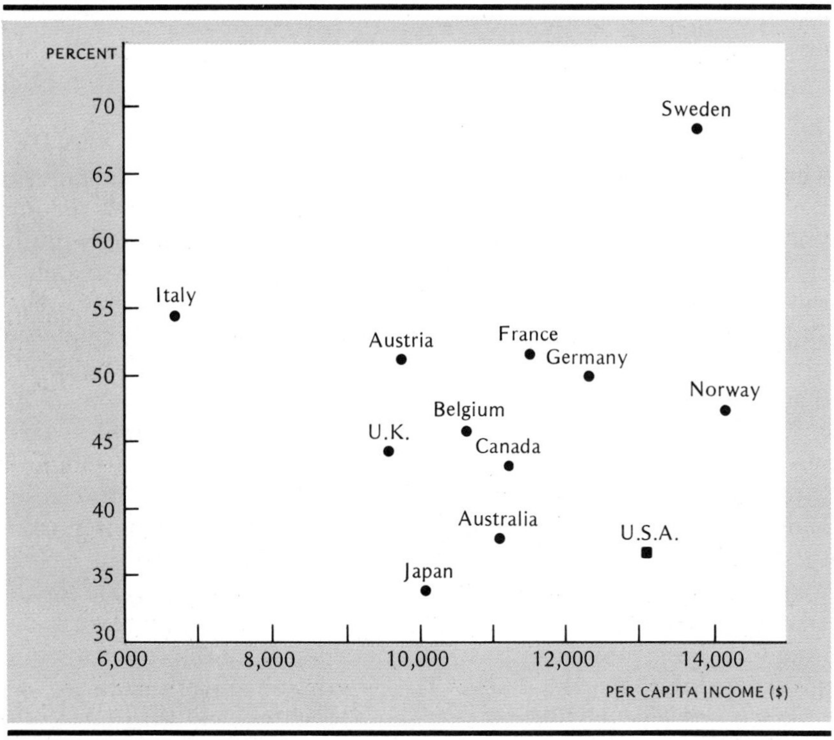

2.8 GOVERNMENT OUTLAYS AS A PERCENTAGE OF GNP, 1982 Compared to other industrial countries with similar per capita income, U.S. government outlays rank rather low as a percentage of national income. SOURCE: United Nations, *National Accounts and Statistics: Government Accounts and Tables, 1983; United Nations Yearbook,* 1986; International Monetary Fund, *International Financial Statistics, 1987.*

with higher per capita incomes to have a relatively large public sector, as Figure 2.8 illustrates. Compared to other industrial countries with similar per capita incomes, the share of public expenditures in the United States is among the lowest. Because defense expenditures play a larger role in the United States, the relative size of nondefense expenditures is particularly low, viewed from this international perspective.[20]

GOVERNMENT REVENUES

Now that we have examined what the government spends its money on, we will briefly survey the methods by which government raises revenue to pay for these expenditures. The government levies a variety of taxes. When the revenues that it receives from taxes are less than its planned

[20] Comparisons across countries always need to be treated with caution. Particular problems are raised by the treatment of public enterprises. The fact that tax expenditures are relatively more important here than abroad may result in an understatement of the "effective" relative size of the public sector in the United States.

expenditures, it must either cut back expenditures or borrow the difference.[21]

Taxes and the Constitution

The issue of taxation was very much in the thoughts of the founders of the Republic. Indeed, the Revolution began as a tax revolt with the Boston Tea Party, which was a protest against the tax on tea, and with the slogan "Taxation without representation is tyranny." The first article of the Constitution provides that "The Congress shall have power to levy and collect Taxes, Duties, Imposts, and Excises, to pay the Debts and provide for the Common Defense and General Welfare of the United States."

Three restrictions were imposed: the government could not levy taxes on exports; "all Duties, Imposts and Excises" had to be "uniform throughout the United States" (referred to as the uniformity clause); and "no capitation or other direct tax shall be laid, unless in proportion to the Census or Enumeration herein before directed to be taken" (referred to as the apportionment clause). (A capitation tax is a tax levied on each person. These taxes are also called head taxes or poll taxes.) The intent of these provisions was to ensure that no group of states took advantage of the other states. The restriction on export taxes, for instance, was enacted because the Southern states were worried lest the Northern states impose a tax on the export of cotton, the burden of which (though uniformly applied) would fall on Southern producers. Similarly, the richer states were worried that the poorer states might force them to pay a disproportionate—from their view—share of the taxes, and thus the only direct tax that was allowed was a uniform head tax.

The writers of the Constitution rightly anticipated that issues of discriminatory taxation of one group of states might split the Union, but they did not fully anticipate the range of instruments by which such discrimination could be effected. Tariffs (taxes on imports) not only raise revenue, but they increase the prices received by domestic producers. The issue of tariffs on goods manufactured in the North—effectively, a net subsidy to Northerners paid for by the South—was one of the most divisive issues during the period preceding the Civil War.

Though the issues may not be so divisive, the conflicts are still present. In 1980, the federal government enacted an unusual excise tax on oil as a result of its decision to phase out price controls on crude oil (which would cause its price to rise to the world price level). The Windfall Profits Tax, so-called because it attempted to capture for the government some of the windfall gains that producers received from the price increase, exempted oil produced on Alaska's Northern Slope. Texas and

[21] In many countries, when there is a gap between expenditures and revenues, the difference is financed by printing money. This is how the Continental Congress financed the revolutionary war. (The expression "not worth a continental" arose from the fact that the currency was not highly valued.)

the other large oil-producing states viewed the tax as discriminatory, in violation of the uniformity clause of the Constitution. The U.S. District Court agreed with them, but upon appeal, the Supreme Court ruled in 1983 that the distinction between "North Slope" oil and other oil was not an arbitrary distinction and that, accordingly, Congress did not violate the uniformity clause.

The constitutional provision restricting direct taxes did, however, prove to be a problem. Congress levied an income tax during the Civil War, and reenacted it in 1894 as a tax on very high incomes. But it was declared unconstitutional by the Supreme Court in 1895. The Court held that the individual income tax was, in part, a direct tax, which the Constitution stipulates must be apportioned among the states according to their population. Widespread criticism of this rule led to a constitutional amendment. The Sixteenth Amendment, ratified in 1913, declares that "Congress shall have the power to levy and collect taxes on incomes, from whatever sources derived, without apportionment among the several states, and without regard to census or enumeration."

The apportionment provision, however, still may restrict Congress's ability to impose some taxes. Several countries impose national property taxes or wealth taxes. But these are likely to be considered direct taxes, and thus precluded in the United States by the apportionment provision.

Federal Taxation Today

The federal government currently relies on five major forms of taxation: (1) the individual income tax, (2) payroll taxes (to finance social security and Medicare benefits), (3) corporate income taxes, (4) excise taxes (taxes on specific commodities, such as gasoline, cigarettes, airline tickets, and alcohol), and (5) customs taxes (taxes levied on selected imported goods).[22] The individual income tax is the single largest source of tax revenue for the federal government, accounting for almost half of government revenues in recent years. In 1986, social security taxes accounted for another 36 percent, the corporation tax 8 percent, and customs and excise taxes 6 percent of government revenue.

Just as there has been a marked shift in the composition of expenditures over the past fifty years, so too there has been a marked change in the source of government revenues. Except for brief periods during the Civil War and again in 1894, the federal government did not impose any income tax on individuals before 1913. As we have noted, such taxes were held unconstitutional until the Constitution was amended in 1913. The individual income tax accounted for 25 percent or less of government tax revenues before the 1940s, when rates were quadrupled to pay for World War II.[23] Since the war, the individual income tax has been the

[22] The estate and gift tax, while it raises less than 1 percent of government revenue, may also have important effects on the economy.

[23] For a historical summary of the major federal taxes, see Joseph Pechman, *Federal Tax Policy*, 5th ed. (Washington D.C.: Brookings Institution, 1987), Appendix A.

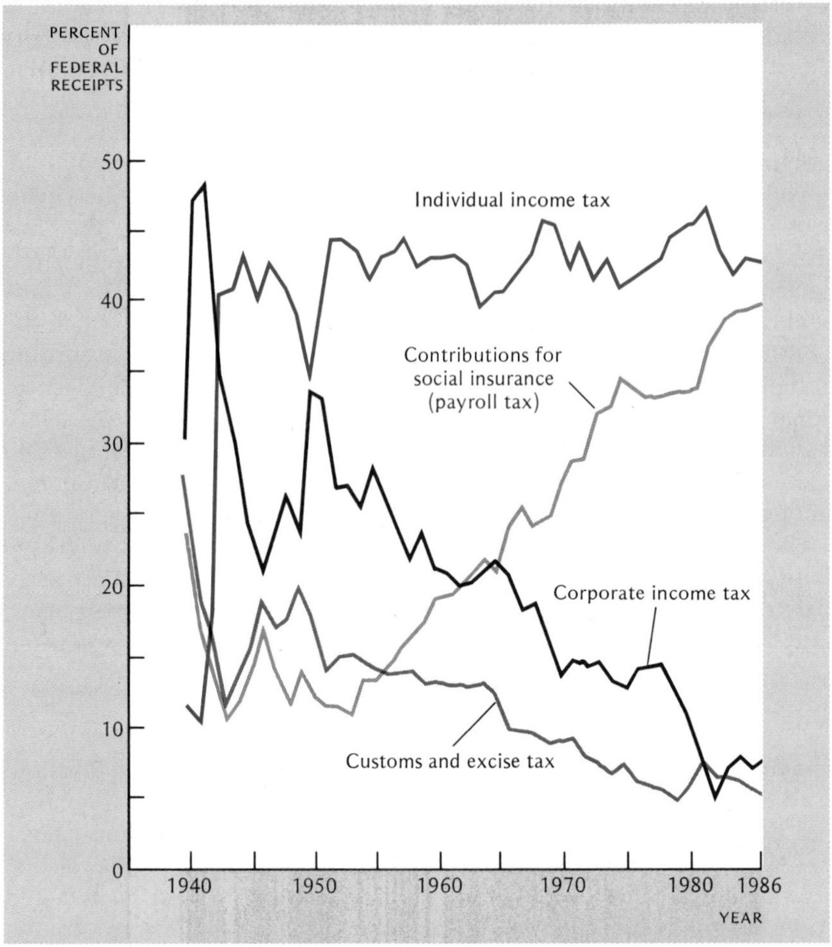

2.9 DISTRIBUTION OF FEDERAL RECEIPTS BY SOURCE The individual income tax and social security taxes on payrolls are today the principal sources of federal revenues. The shares of revenue provided by customs, excise taxes, and the corporation income tax have declined steeply. SOURCE: U.S. Department of Commerce, *National Income and Product Accounts, 1929–1982,* Table 3.2; *Survey of Current Business,* July 1987, Table 3.2

largest single source of federal revenues, as shown in Figure 2.9. The corporation income tax has played a decreasing role, falling from 36 percent of federal revenues in 1927, to 23 percent in 1960, and to 8 percent in 1986. As a result of the Tax Reform Act of 1986, however, corporation tax revenues were estimated to rise to 12 percent of government receipts in 1987.

From 1789 to 1909, the federal government received almost all of its revenues from excise taxes and customs. Today, they are relatively unimportant. On the other hand, the payroll tax, which was introduced by the Social Security Act of 1935, increased from 18 percent of federal revenues in 1960 to an estimated 36 percent in 1987.

State and Local Government Revenues

Unlike the federal tax system, state and local tax systems rely heavily on sales and property taxes. As shown in Figure 2.10, property taxes were their major source of revenue until 1976. Today, sales taxes amount to 23 percent of their total revenue, and property taxes raise 19 percent of revenue. State and local individual income taxes raise only 12 percent of the total, while corporate income taxes raise 3 percent.

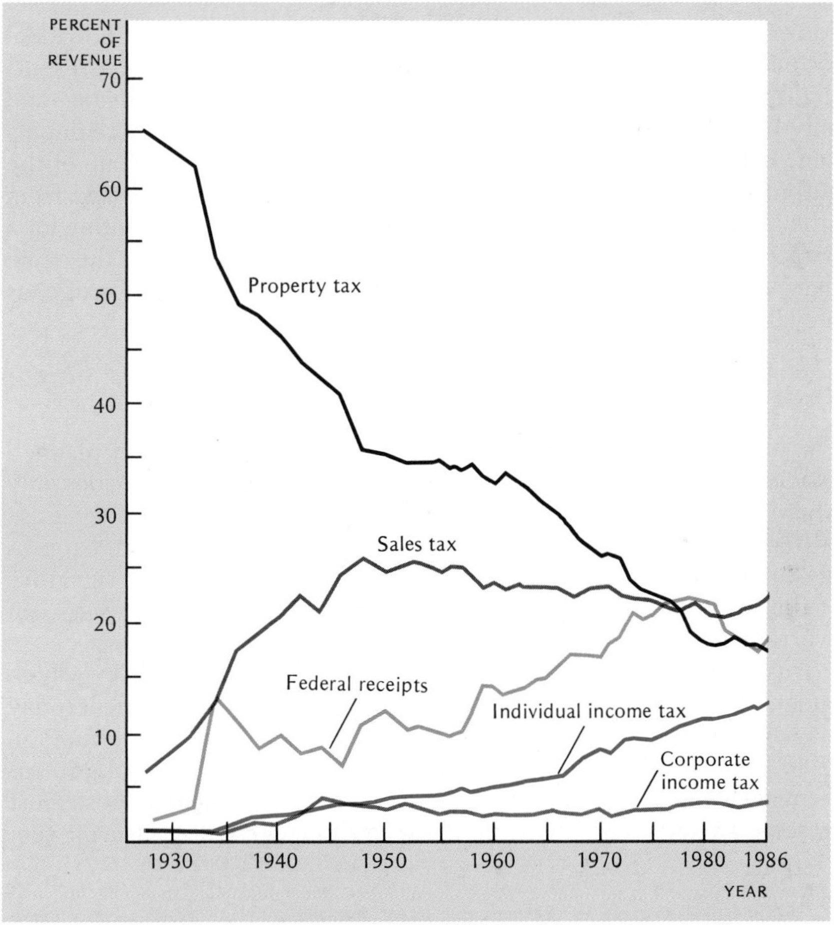

2.10 DISTRIBUTION OF STATE AND LOCAL GOVERNMENT RECEIPTS BY SOURCE We see the declining role played by property taxes in state and local receipts, and the increasing role played by income taxes and revenue grants from the federal government. SOURCE: *Economic Report of the President, 1987,* Table B-80; *Survey of Current Business,* July 1987, Table 3.3.

Competition among states for industry discourages the use of many state and local taxes, especially corporate income taxes. To meet growing demands for state and local services, the federal government has provided increasing aid to state and local governments. Much of this is directed at specific programs like road construction, mass transit, bilingual education, vocational education, and libraries. During the late 1960s and 1970s, the federal government provided substantial unrestricted funds under a program called General Revenue Sharing. In 1986, federal grants to state and local governments provided one-sixth of their revenue.

Comparison of Taxation across Countries

Patterns of taxation differ from country to country. While the individual income tax is less important in most European countries (it represents slightly less than 30 percent of revenues in England and Germany, and only 13 percent in France), taxes on goods and services are more important. For most, the value-added tax (a tax imposed on the value of the output of a firm less the value of goods and services purchased from other firms) is a major source of revenue, in many cases accounting for a sixth of government revenue. Social security taxes make up the same share of government revenues in Japan and, on average, in Europe, as they do in the United States.[24]

THE FEDERAL GOVERNMENT'S BUDGET PROCESS

The federal government, in its yearly budget, looks closely at planned expenditures and anticipated revenues. The Constitution provides only a bare outline for the budget process. Tax bills must begin in the House of Representatives. As with all legislation, enactment of tax and appropriations bills requires a majority vote of both Houses and the signature of the president. The president may veto any bill, and Congress can override his veto by a two-thirds vote.

This description does not adequately reflect the process by which budget decisions are made, nor the central role that the president today plays in formulating the budget.[25] Recall that federal expenditures in 1986 amounted to one trillion dollars. There are thousands of government agencies, most of which claim they need more money. There must be some systematic method of reviewing these needs and ensuring that

[24] In 1984, the last year for which comparable data are available, the share of social security taxes in total tax revenues was 29 percent for the United States, 30 percent for Japan, and 29 percent, on average, for the members of the European Economic Community. Within Europe, the ratio varied widely. For instance, it was 44 percent for France and Holland, but only 18 percent for England. Source: *Revenue Statistics for OECD Member Countries, 1986,* Table 15.

[25] The central role of the president in the budget process is a creature of the twentieth century's large and complex federal government. Before 1921, federal agencies took their requests for funds directly to Congress, and the president had no formal process for reviewing them. See Henry Aaron et al., *Economic Choices 1987* (Washington, D.C.: Brookings Institution, 1986), Ch. 5.

the total amount allocated to the different agencies is roughly commensurate with the revenue raised through taxation. The government agency that is responsible for doing this is the Office of Management and Budget (OMB). OMB formulates a budget, proposing how much each agency will spend, how much will be raised through taxes, and what the deficit or surplus of total spending over total revenues will be. The president sends OMB's proposal to Congress.

Congress's assessment of the nation's priorities often differs markedly from that of the president, particularly when the two are of different parties. The difficulty facing Congress is to come up with an alternative budget. In the past, Congress would take up appropriations for each area separately; that is, it might first pass a defense budget, then a road budget, then a foreign-aid budget, etc. It was difficult, in this process, to ensure that the total expenditures equaled the revenues and that priorities were assessed in any systematic way. Congress attempted to remedy this in 1974 by setting up the Congressional Budget Office and a procedure (with a specified timetable) for formulating a congressional budget. This begins with an initial congressional resolution, calling for an overall level of spending and taxing, and a breakdown by major categories. This serves as a guide to the separate appropriations committees, which consider bills in each of the separate areas. After these bills are passed, Congress then looks at the overall budget again, seeing whether the totals fit within the earlier targets and, if not, deciding whether to change the targets or scale back some programs.

The process is a cumbersome one, but there is no readily apparent alternative, short of delegating more authority to the president, something that Congress, quite rightly in the view of most observers, is reluctant to do.

The concern with the budget process is not only that it is cumbersome, but that it fails to produce a balanced budget. Prior to the Great Depression it was thought that the president should present a balanced budget, except in times of war. The development of Keynesian economics persuaded many that it might be desirable for the government to run a deficit in a recession. As we will see in Chapter 28, deficit spending during a recession can be used to stimulate the economy. But in a nonrecessionary, nonwar year, there is a consensus that the president should propose a balanced budget. While President Reagan was successful in getting a major tax reduction enacted in 1981, he failed to obtain corresponding reductions in expenditures. This led to record deficits, which neither the Congress nor the president professed to want.

Deficit Financing

A deficit in any period is simply the excess of spending during the period over revenues. A deficit is financed by borrowing. The cumulative value of borrowing by a firm, household, or government is its debt.

A firm or household that runs a deficit cannot continue to borrow

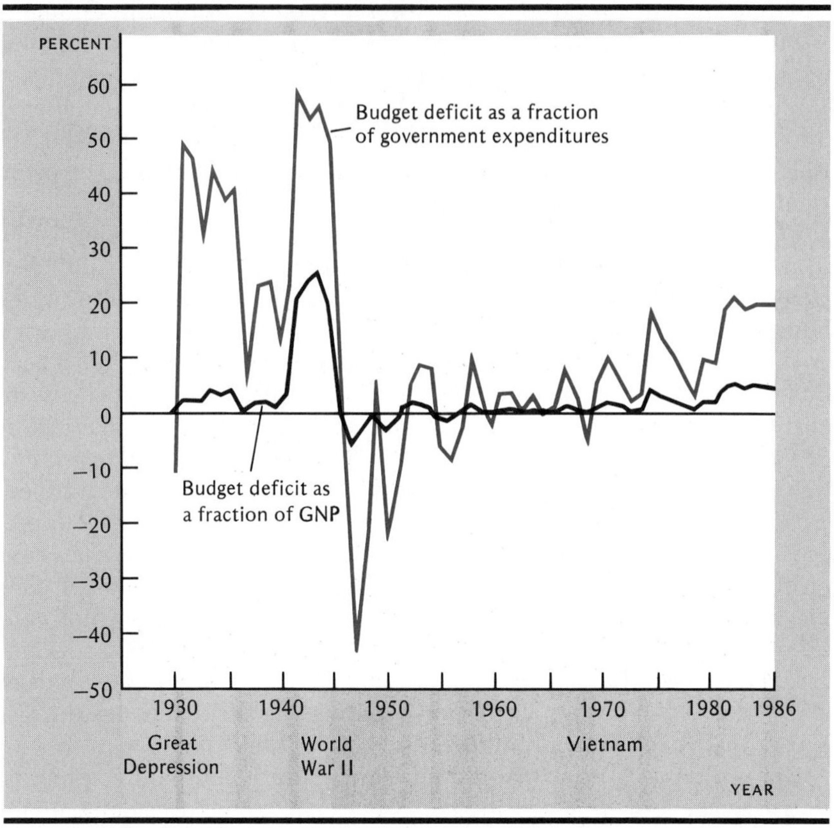

2.11 FEDERAL BUDGET DEFICIT AS A PERCENTAGE OF GNP AND FEDERAL EXPENDITURES Both have increased markedly since 1980. SOURCE: *National Income and Product Accounts, 1929–1982,* Table 3.2; *Survey of Current Business,* July 1987, Table 3.2.

indefinitely, but will be forced into bankruptcy once its debt gets too large. Because of the federal government's ability to tax, and the huge potential revenue sources it can tap, the federal government's deficits do not cause the same kinds of problems that large debts incurred by private firms or individuals would. Lenders will continue to willingly finance the federal government's debt, provided the interest rate is high enough.

In the early 1980s, the size of the federal deficit, both in dollar terms and, more importantly, as a fraction of GNP and of the budget, reached all-time highs (for peacetime); see Figure 2.11. The size of these deficits in the 1980s caused great consternation both in and outside of Washington. There is a concern that the budget deficits contribute to balance of trade deficits and to inflation, that they lead to higher interest rates and lower levels of investment, and that they put an unfair burden on future generations. In order to finance the deficit, the role of the federal government as a *borrower* in U.S. credit markets has been growing. Funds borrowed by the federal government in domestic credit markets, as a percentage of total funds borrowed in U.S. credit markets, rose from 21.2 percent in 1977 to 38.6 percent in 1986.[26] These are funds that have been supplied increasingly by foreigners, as we discuss in Chapter 28 below.

The dollar value of the debt goes up each year by the amount of that year's federal deficit. But the *real* value of the debt also depends very much on inflation. To see what this means, assume you promise to pay someone $100 next year. If the prices of all goods and services rise by 10 percent, next year that person will be able to purchase with $100 the same goods that he could have purchased with $91 this year. The "real value" of what you have to pay him has declined by $9.

Figure 2.12 traces the changes since 1940 in the real value of the federal debt owed to U.S. citizens and foreigners—known as the publicly held federal debt. During the period 1978–1980, when there were

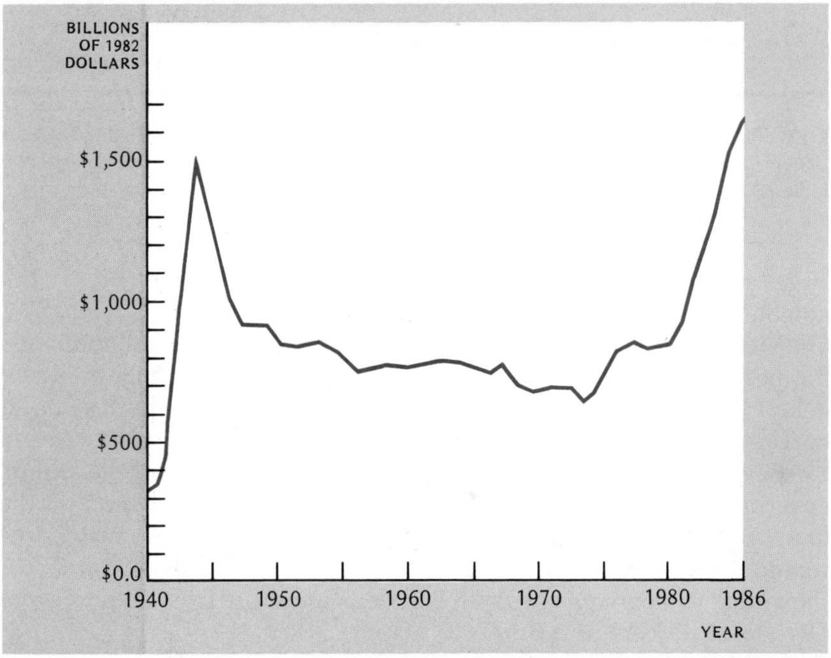

2.12 GROSS FEDERAL DEBT HELD BY PUBLIC, IN 1982 PRICES In real terms, the federal debt held by the public has grown enormously since 1974. Debt held by government agencies, including the Federal Reserve Board and the social security trust funds, is excluded. SOURCE: *Economic Report of the President,* 1987, Tables B-3 and B-73; *Survey of Current Business,* July 1987, Table 7.4.

[26] If we also take into account borrowing undertaken by the private sector with federal assistance or guarantees, the federal borrowing participation ratio in U.S. credit markets in 1986 rose to 42.5 percent. Data are reported in *Special Analysis: Budget of the United States Government, Fiscal Year 1988,* Table F-22.

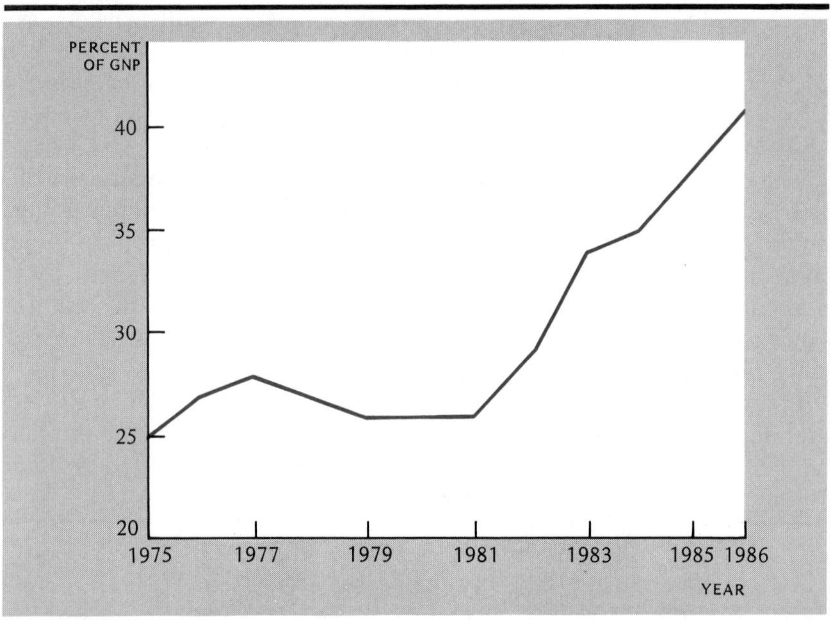

2.13 FEDERAL DEBT AS PERCENT OF GNP The federal debt rose from 25 percent of GNP in 1975 to 41 percent of GNP in 1986. SOURCE: *Survey of Current Business,* July 1987, Table 2.12.

large deficits but high inflation, the real value of the debt fell by $12 billion (in 1982 prices). In real terms, the increase in the debt after 1980 is dramatic. As a result of the high deficits and the fall in the inflation rate, the period 1980–1986 saw a near doubling of the publicly held real debt, from $834 billion in 1980 to $1,525 billion in 1986 (both amounts measured in 1982 prices). To put it another way, in the first six years of the Reagan administration, the total increase in *real* debt of the federal government was nearly equal to the total real debt accumulated over the first two hundred years of this country, including the entire debt required to finance U.S. participation in World War II. Figure 2.13 shows that as a percentage of GNP, federal debt rose from 25 percent in 1975 to 41 percent in 1986.

The increasing debt has cumulative consequences, as the government must pay interest on the debt. By 1986, interest payments reached 13 percent of federal government expenditures.

The Gramm-Rudman Act

In 1985, concern over the mounting debt and popular enthusiasm for balanced budgets led Congress to pass a bill, which President Reagan signed into law, called the Gramm-Rudman Act after its sponsors, Senator Phil Gramm of Texas and Senator Warren Rudman of New Hampshire. The official name of the act is the Balanced Budget and Emergency Deficit Control Act. It was enacted as a desperate attempt to break the deadlock between Congress and the president over levels of spending and taxing. The act specifies annual deficit targets aimed at achieving a balanced budget by 1991. If Congress and the president cannot agree on a budget that falls within each year's deficit target, spending will be cut by an automatic formula, a possibility no one wants to see realized. The act relied on the threat of these automatic cuts to impose congressional and presidential self-discipline in spending and taxing.

However, in 1987, the Supreme Court held as unconstitutional the procedures by which these automatic cuts were to be implemented. In response, Congress enacted alternative procedures, and at the same time postponed until 1993 the target date for balancing the budget.

There are some who have advocated stronger legislation, in particular, a constitutional prohibition on deficit financing except in wartime. Some states have such restrictions (sometimes passed in the aftermath of the state's failure to meet its debt obligations). Critics of a constitutional restriction are concerned that it would impair the government's ability to stimulate the economy when needed. Moreover, they are worried that it would simply encourage the use of budgetary tricks to satisfy the letter of the law, not its spirit.

Impounding Funds

The failure of the president and Congress to come up with a balanced budget is perhaps the most important source of concern over the budgetary process. But it is not the only source of controversy. In recent years, there has been some controversy about the extent of presidential budgetary powers. Though it seems clear that the president has no right to spend funds that Congress does not authorize, there is some debate about whether he has the right *not* to spend funds Congress has authorized him to spend. The question is: Can the president impound funds at his own discretion? By impounding funds, the president could override the wishes of Congress, even if Congress had overridden a presidential veto. President Nixon attempted to impound funds from the Office of Economic Opportunity, which had the responsibility for running many of the federal poverty programs. Allowing the president to impound funds is similar to granting him a line item veto (to veto a particular provision of a law, rather than the whole law). Congress has been unwilling to grant the president these powers.

The Function of Budgets

The budget of the federal government measures the cash flow, the annual receipts and expenditures of the government, just as the income statement of a corporation describes its receipts (sales) and its expenditures. The budget gives a picture of what the government is doing, where its money is going, and where it is coming from.

But in assessing the state of a private corporation, far more important than the cash flow accounts are the capital accounts. These describe the assets of the firm and its liabilities (what it owes to other individuals and firms). The difference between the two is the **net worth** of the firm. If the liabilities of a firm are increasing faster than the assets, its net worth is decreasing; an investor will be concerned about the future well-being of the firm. On the other hand, a firm with a large and increasing debt, but with assets increasing at a rate more than matching these increases in liabilities, is likely to be viewed as being in a strong financial position.

When a business (or a local government) buys a building or a machine, it does not count it as a current expense, and so there is no effect on the firm's net income. The outlay is treated instead as a capital expenditure. When the building or machine is used, a charge against current income is made for the **depreciation,** the decrease in value as it wears out or becomes obsolete. By contrast, the federal government treats the total expenditure as an outlay in the year in which the machine or building is acquired.

When a business sells a machine or a building, it does not change its net income or net worth. It changes only the form in which it holds its assets; its cash holdings increase, its holdings of physical assets decrease. By contrast, when the government sells a building, it treats the receipts just like any other source of income. And so the federal deficit shrinks.

The federal government does not publish a good set of **capital accounts,** which would assess the changes in its assets and liabilities. Professors Robert Eisner of Northwestern University and Paul Pieper of the University of Illinois, however, have estimated the market value of the federal government's tangible assets, financial assets, and financial liabilities. The difference between these assets and liabilities is a measure of net worth. Figure 2.14 shows that the rate of growth of *net* financial liabilities[27] has exceeded that of tangible assets in every year since 1980. As a result, federal net worth has been falling. In 1984, for the first time since 1961, federal liabilities exceeded assets. It should be noted that the government's tangible assets—representing the results of its past investments—decreased in value in real terms in 1981, and they have grown only slightly since then. The deterioration of the federal capital stock—including our highways and bridges—has become a source of concern in recent years.

A complete accounting of the federal government's assets and liabilities should include, of course, not only its buildings, structures, and equipment ("tangible assets") but also "nontangible" assets, the most important of which consist of investments in the future productivity of Americans (what is called "human capital") through public education

[27] That is, financial liabilities less financial assets, or net federal debt.

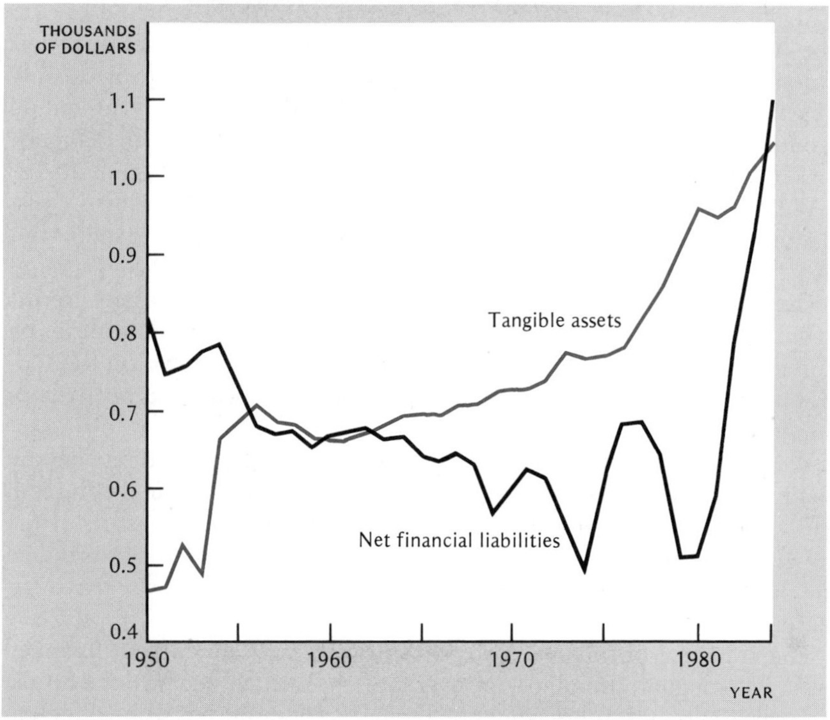

2.14 REPLACEMENT VALUE OF ASSETS AND MARKET VALUE OF NET FINANCIAL LIABILITIES OF THE FEDERAL GOVERNMENT *(1982 dollars)* SOURCE: Data in current dollars are from Robert Eisner, *How Real Is the Federal Deficit?* (New York: Free Press, 1986), Table B.12.

and training programs, and investments in research and development (R&D), which increase the productivity of the entire economy.

The absence of a capital account in the federal budget has some serious implications for economic policy. It creates a systematic bias, particularly in periods of recession when the government faces a large deficit, to cut back on investment expenditures, including investments in human capital and R&D, the consequences of which will not be felt for some time in the future. Similarly, it gives government an incentive to sell more of its land or lease more oil fields, since the sales appear in the current budget as revenue, without an entry to show the cost associated with raising revenue in this way. A capital account would make it clear that the assets of the United States government are thereby decreased.[28]

[28] There is some controversy concerning the construction of capital accounts. The question is: What should be included in the liabilities, what in the assets? The government has the ability to tax, and in this sense it is fundamentally different from a private corporation. In one view, all potential sources of revenues should be included in the asset side. Similarly, there are questions about which commitments of the government should be included as liabilities. Should one, for instance, include future social security obligations as a liability? The figures for net financial liabilities in Figure 2.14 do *not* include social security retirement liabilities.

Playing Tricks with the Data on Government Activities

The budgets of the federal, state, and local governments set out their expenditures and receipts. As we have seen, however, they provide only a partial view of the size of government and the effect of government on economic activity. As a result, one must treat with caution any comparisons of the size of the public sector either over time or across countries.

We have already discussed how tax expenditures may result in misleading conclusions concerning not only the size of the public sector but also the composition of its expenditures. If the federal government wishes to hide the size of its subsidies to business, it provides tax credits to businesses. It hides the extent of its subsidies to states and localities by providing "tax expenditures" in the form of tax deductions on the federal individual income tax for most state and local taxes and tax exemption for interest on state and local bonds.

We have also noted a second method by which the budget may be manipulated: when assets are sold, one records the revenues obtained, while one does not record the cost—the reduction in the assets of the government. Such tricks were important in Reagan's attempt to reduce the deficit. He accelerated, for instance, the sale of off-shore oil and gas leases.

The converse of this is to provide subsidies with no current financial outlay. Loan guarantees are one example; the outlays occur in the future if there is a default. Increasing social security benefits has some effect on current financial outlays, but the primary burden lies sometime in the future (in some later administration). Speeding tax collections by increasing withholding or by increasing penalties for failing to pay taxes in a timely way is another one-time way of reducing a current deficit.

One can decrease the overall size of the public sector (but not the deficit) by setting up independent agencies and enterprises. It makes no real difference whether the post office is a department of the U.S. government or a separate "corporation" receiving a subsidy from the federal treasury. But if it is a department, all of its income and all of its expenditures will be included in the government budget; if it is a separate enterprise, only the deficit (the difference between its expenditures and income) is recorded.

Though these problems provide considerable room for politicians to choose statistics to support their views, the changes in the level and structure of expenditures and taxation in the United States over the past twenty-five to fifty years have been significant enough that there can be little question about the major observations that we have made:

1. The public sector exerts a major and growing influence on the production of goods and the distribution of income in the United States.
2. Social insurance has been the fastest growing category of government expenditures in the past thirty years. Since 1960, the rapid growth in nondefense expenditure by government was largely accounted for by social security, government retirement programs, Medicare, and interest.

3. The individual income tax has become the principal source of federal revenue, and the role of the corporation income tax as a revenue source has dwindled.

SUMMARY

1. The government performs many roles:
   a) It provides the basic legal framework within which we live.
   b) It regulates economic activities. It encourages some activities by subsidizing them and discourages others by taxing them.
   c) It produces goods and provides credit, loan guarantees, and insurance.
   d) It purchases goods and services, including many that are produced by private firms (such as weapons manufacturers).
   e) It redistributes income, transferring income from some individuals to others.
   f) It provides social insurance, for retirement, unemployment, disabilities, and medical care for the aged.
2. The size of the government relative to GNP is much larger now than it was thirty years ago. Much of this is accounted for by increased payments for social insurance.
3. The relative size of the public sector in the United States is smaller than in most Western European countries.
4. The three major areas of government expenditures are defense, social insurance, and education. Together, these accounted for 60 percent of governmental expenditures in 1986.
5. The major source of revenue for the federal government is the individual income tax, followed by the payroll tax, corporation tax, and customs and excise taxes.
6. The major sources of revenue for state and local government are the sales tax, the property tax, and the income tax.
7. The Constitution provides the basic framework for the government of the United States. It provides some restrictions on the taxes that can be imposed, but no effective restrictions on what the government can spend its money on.
8. The federal government attempts, through the budget process, to ensure that there is some balance between expenditures and receipts and that expenditures are allocated according to national priorities. During the Reagan administration, Congress and the president were unable to agree on national priorities, and the result has been massive federal deficits.

KEY CONCEPTS

Privatization
Nationalization
Value added
Income tax
Social security (payroll) tax
Constant dollars
Deficit
Real expenditures
Social insurance
Transfers
Tax expenditures
Excise taxes
Customs duties

QUESTIONS AND PROBLEMS

1. To see what is going on, economists often "adjust" the data to reflect changes in the economy. For instance, in the text, we discussed the adjustments in dollar amounts made to correct for inflation. Another adjustment that is frequently made is to take into account the increase in population. What adjustments might you make in looking at education expenditures? At social security expenditures?
2. In each of the following areas, give one or more examples (where possible) in which the government is involved as a producer; a regulator; a purchaser of final goods and services distributed directly to individuals or used within government:
   a) education
   b) utilities
   c) transportation
   d) credit markets
   e) insurance markets
   f) food
   g) housing
3. In each of the following areas, give an example of a tax expenditure and a conventional expenditure. Explain how the same results could be obtained by converting the tax expenditure into a conventional expenditure:
   a) medicine
   b) housing
   c) education
4. Assume you were president and your planned expenditures exceeded your receipts. Describe some of the tricks you might use to reduce the apparent budget deficit while maintaining current levels of services and transfers (subsidies).

   Assume, on the other hand, that you had run on a platform of keeping the growth in total governmental expenditures down to 3 percent. Once in office, you see, however, that you would like expenditures to rise by 5 percent. How might you do this while appearing to keep your election promises?

3

The Economic Rationale for Government

In the United States, as in most other Western economies, primary reliance for the production and distribution of goods lies in the private rather than the public sector. Those who believe in the private-enterprise system believe that this form of economic organization has certain desirable characteristics; in particular, that it leads to an efficient allocation of resources. This belief is, in fact, one of the oldest tenets of economics. If this is true, then why is government needed? To answer this question we examine the successes and failures of private markets.

THE EFFICIENCY OF COMPETITIVE MARKETS: THE INVISIBLE HAND

In 1776, Adam Smith, in the first major work of modern economics, *The Wealth of Nations,* argued that competition would lead individuals in the pursuit of their private interests (profits) to pursue the public interest, as if by an *invisible hand:*

> . . . he intends only his own gain, and he is in this, as in many other cases, led by an invisible hand to promote an end which was no part of his intention. Nor is it always the worse for the society that it was no part of it. By pursuing his own interest he frequently promotes that of the society more effectually than when he really intends to promote it.[1]

[1] Adam Smith, *The Wealth of Nations* (New York: Modern Library, 1937). Originally published in 1776.

To understand the significance of Smith's insight, we should look at the commonly held views about the role of the government prior to Smith. There was a widespread belief that achieving the best interests of the public (however that might be defined) required an active government. This view was particularly associated with the mercantilist school of the seventeenth and eighteenth centuries; its leading proponent was Jean Baptiste Colbert, the finance minister under King Louis XIV of France. Mercantilists argued for strong government actions to promote industry and trade. Indeed, many European governments had taken an active role in promoting the establishment of colonies, and the mercantilists provided a rationale for this.

Some countries (or some citizens within these countries) had benefited greatly from the active role taken by the government, but other countries, in which the government had been much more passive, had also prospered. Some of those with strong, active governments had not prospered, as the resources of the country were squandered on wars or on a variety of unsuccessful public ventures.

In the face of these seemingly contradictory experiences, Smith addressed himself to the question: Can society ensure that those entrusted with governing society actually pursue the public interest? Experience had shown that while at times governments pursued policies that seemed consistent with the public good, at other times they pursued policies that could not by any reasonable stretch of the imagination be reconciled with it. Rather, those in the position of governing often seemed to pursue their private interests at the expense of the public interest. Moreover, even well-intentioned leaders often led their countries astray. Smith argued that one did not need to rely on government or on any moral sentiments to do good. The public interest, he maintained, is served when each individual simply does what is in his own self-interest. Self-interest is a much more persistent characteristic of human nature than a concern to do good, and therefore provides a more reliable basis for the organization of society. Moreover, individuals are more likely to ascertain with some accuracy what is in their own self-interest than they are to determine what is in the public interest.

The intuition behind Smith's insight is simple: if there is some commodity or service that individuals value but that is not currently being produced, then they will be willing to pay something for it. Entrepreneurs, in their search for profits, are always looking for such opportunities. If the value of a certain commodity to a consumer exceeds the cost of production, there is a potential profit for an entrepreneur, and he will produce the commodity. Similarly, if there is a cheaper way of producing a commodity than that which is presently employed, an entrepreneur who discovers this cheaper method will be able to undercut competing firms and make a profit. The search for profits on the part of firms is thus a search for more efficient ways of production and for new commodities that better serve the needs of consumers.

Notice that no government committee needs, in this view, to decide whether a commodity should or should not be produced. It will be produced if it meets the market test—i.e., if what individuals are willing to pay exceeds the costs of production. Nor does any government oversight committee need to check whether a particular firm is producing efficiently: competition will drive out inefficient producers.

There is a widespread (but not universal) consensus among economists that competitive forces do lead to a high degree of efficiency, and that competition does provide an important spur to innovation. However, during the past two hundred years economists have come to recognize that there are some important instances where the market does not work as perfectly as the more ardent supporters of the free market suggest. The economy has gone through periods in which there have been massive unemployment and idle resources; the Great Depression of the 1930s left many who wanted work unemployed; pollution has choked many of our larger cities; and urban decay has set in on others.

The Two Fundamental Theorems of Welfare Economics

In what sense, then, and under what conditions, do competitive markets lead to economic efficiency? This is a question that has been at the center of much of the theoretical research in economics during the past few decades. The central results are summarized by what are referred to as the two **fundamental theorems of welfare economics.**

FIRST FUNDAMENTAL THEOREM

The first theorem says that under certain conditions, competitive markets lead to an allocation of resources with a very special property: there is no rearrangement of resources (no possible change in production and consumption) such that someone can be made better off without, at the same time, making someone else worse off. There are, to be sure, many other resource allocations that would make one or more individuals better off. But in each of these cases, some individuals would be worse off. Resource allocations that have the property that no one can be made better off without someone else being made worse off are called **Pareto-efficient** (or **Pareto-optimal**) allocations after the great Italian economist-sociologist Vilfredo Pareto (1848–1923). Pareto efficiency is what economists normally mean when they talk about efficiency.

There is a diagrammatic way of representing the Pareto efficiency of the economy. Consider a simple economy with only two individuals, whom we shall refer to as Robinson Crusoe and Friday. Assume that we specify how well off one individual is, and let us call that his level of **utility**. We then ask: Given the level of utility of one individual, how well off can we make the other individual? How high a utility level can he obtain? The curve giving the maximum level of utility that one individ-

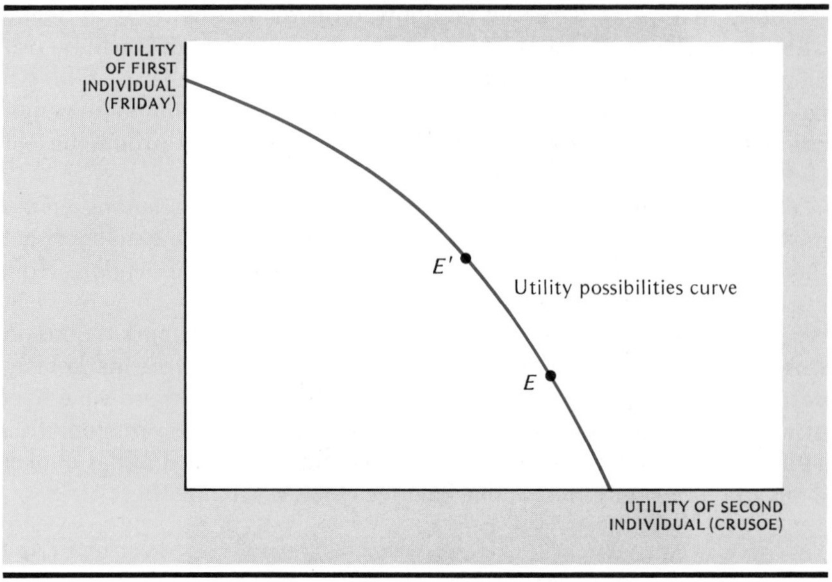

3.1 UTILITY POSSIBILITIES CURVE The first fundamental theorem of welfare economics asserts that the competitive economy attains a point on the utility possibilities curve (*E*). The second fundamental theorem of welfare economics asserts that every point on the utility possibilities curve (such as point *E*′) can be attained simply by redistributing resources from one individual to another (but then allowing the market mechanism to work).

ual can attain, given the level of utility attained by the other, is called the **utility possibilities curve** (see Figure 3.1).

The first fundamental theorem of welfare economics states that, under certain conditions, a competitive economy will attain some point along the utility possibilities curve. The economy will lie along, not under, the colored curve in Figure 3.1.

SECOND FUNDAMENTAL THEOREM

The second theorem states that every point on the utility possibilities curve can be attained by a competitive economy provided we begin with the correct distribution of resources. For instance, assume that initially we were at point *E* in Figure 3.1. By taking away some resources from Crusoe (the second individual) and giving them to Friday (the first individual), we can move the competitive market economy from point *E* to point *E*′.

To say that the economy is Pareto efficient says nothing about how "good" the income distribution is. In a competitive equilibrium Robinson Crusoe might be very well off, while Friday lives in dire poverty (as at point *E*). The statement that the economy is Pareto optimal says only that no one can be made better off without making someone else worse off, that the economy is on its utility posssibilities curve. But the second welfare theorem says that if we don't like the income distribution generated by the competitive market, we need not abandon the use of the competitive market mechanism. All we need do is redistribute the initial wealth, and then leave the rest to the competitive market. Corresponding to E, E', or any other final distribution of utilities that one would like to obtain, there is some initial distribution of resources.

The second fundamental theorem of welfare economics has the remarkable implication that every Pareto-efficient allocation can be attained by means of a **decentralized market mechanism.** In a decentralized system, decisions about production and consumption (what goods get produced, how they get produced, and who gets what goods) are carried on by the myriad of firms and individuals that make up the economy. In contrast, in a **centralized allocation mechanism**, all these decisions are concentrated in the hands of a single agency, the Central Planning Agency, or a single individual, who is referred to as the central planner. Of course, no economy has even come close to being fully centralized, though in the Soviet Union and some of the other Eastern bloc countries, economic decision making is much more concentrated than in the United States and other Western economies. A major thrust of the reforms introduced in the Soviet Union in recent years, however, has been to increase the degree of decentralization.

The second fundamental theorem of welfare economics says that to attain an efficient allocation of resources, with the desired distribution of income, it is not necessary to have a central planner, with all the wisdom an economic theorist or a utopian socialist might attribute to him: competitive firms, attempting to maximize their profits, can do as well as the best of all possible central planners. This theorem thus provides a major justification for reliance on the market mechanism. To put it another way, if the conditions assumed in the second welfare theorem were valid, the study of public finance could be limited to an analysis of the appropriate governmental redistributions of resources.

The reason that the competitive market, under ideal conditions, leads to a Pareto-optimal allocation of resources is one of the primary subjects of study in standard courses in microeconomics. Since we will be concerned with understanding why under some circumstances competitive markets do not lead to efficiency, we first need to understand why competition under ideal conditions leads to efficiency.

The Pareto Efficiency of the Competitive Economy

Competition leads to efficiency because in deciding how much of a certain good to buy, individuals equate the **marginal (additional) benefit** they receive from consuming an extra unit with the **marginal (additional) cost** of purchasing an extra unit, which is just the price they have to pay; and firms, in deciding how much of a good to sell, equate the price they receive with the marginal (additional) cost of producing an extra unit. Hence marginal benefits of consuming an additional unit are equated with marginal costs.

In Figure 3.2 we have depicted the marginal benefit the individual receives from consuming some commodity, say ice cream cones. As the individual consumes more and more ice cream cones, the marginal (extra) benefit he receives from consuming an additional ice cream cone decreases. The marginal benefit curve thus declines. His marginal benefit from the first cone (in dollar terms) is $3; from the second, $2.50, from the third, $2.00; from the fourth, $1.50; from the fifth, $1.00; from the sixth, $0.50, at which point the individual becomes satiated. How many ice cream cones does an individual buy? He buys them up to the point where the marginal benefit of the last ice cream cone just equals its cost—i.e., the price he must pay for it.

If an ice cream cone costs $2.50, the individual will buy 2 cones; if an ice cream cone costs $1.00, he will buy 5 cones. The curve describing the individual's marginal benefits at each quantity of ice cream consumed thus also describes the quantity of the good the individual demands at each price. We thus refer to this curve as the individual's **demand curve.** We form the market demand curve simply by adding up the demand curves for each individual. In Panel C of Figure 3.2, we have drawn the market curve, assuming that there are 1,000 identical individuals. Thus at a price of $2 a cone, each individual demands 3 cones, and market demand is 3,000 cones.

In Panel B of Figure 3.2, we have depicted the marginal (extra) cost a firm incurs as a result of producing an extra unit of the good (making an extra ice cream cone). We have depicted the curve as upward sloping. As the firm produces more and more of a commodity, the cost of producing one more unit increases.[2] In the diagram, the marginal cost to produce the first ice cream cone is $0.50; to produce the second, $1.00; the third, $2.00; the fourth, $3.00.

How many ice cream cones does a firm produce? It produces them up to the point where the marginal cost of the last ice cream cone just equals what the firm receives—i.e., the price of an ice cream cone. If the firm can get $1.00 for selling an ice cream cone, it produces just 2; if it can get $2.00, it produces 3. Thus the curve describing the firm's marginal costs at each quantity of ice cream cones produced also describes the quantity of the good the firm produces at each price. We refer to this curve as the firm's **supply curve.** We form the market supply curve simply by adding up the supply curves for each firm. We depict the market supply curve in Panel C, assuming there are a fixed number (here, 1,000) of identical firms producing.[3] At a price of $2.00 each of the 1,000 identical firms supplies 3 units, so market supply is 3,000 units.

[2] Although this is taken to be the normal case, in some instances the marginal costs may not increase. Industries for which costs neither increase nor decrease are said to have constant costs. There are a few industries where the marginal costs of production may actually decrease with an increase in production.

[3] In the long run, or course, there may be exit or entry into the ice cream industry. As a result, as the price rises, the increase in output is likely to be greater than depicted here, where we have assumed that the number of firms is fixed. In some cases, this long-run supply response of entry and exit of firms can be so strong that the market supply curve is approximately horizontal.

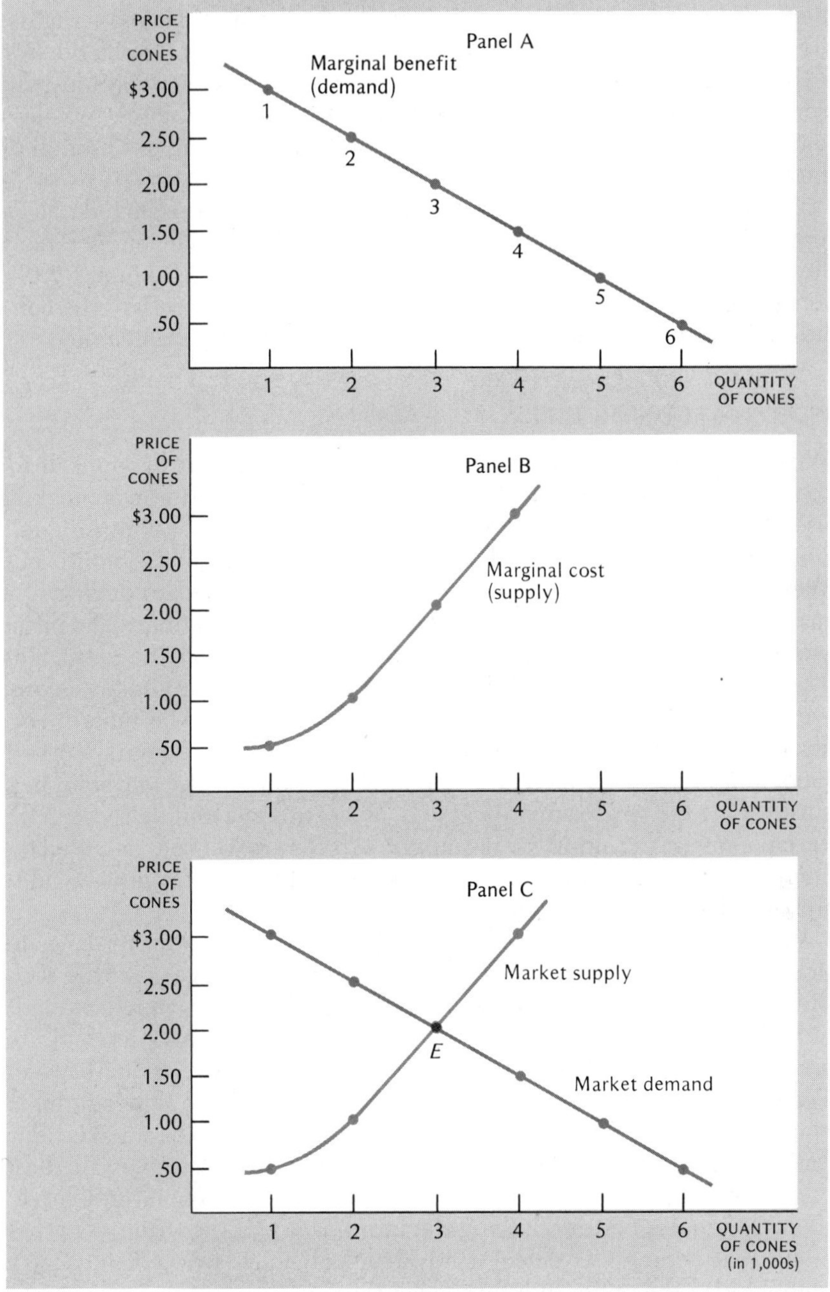

3.2 DEMAND AND SUPPLY OF ICE CREAM CONES Market equilibrium occurs at the point where the marginal benefit of consuming an extra ice cream cone is just equal to the marginal cost of producing an extra ice cream cone.

Efficiency requires that the marginal benefit associated with producing one more unit of any good (the extra benefit resulting from the production of one more unit of the good) equals its marginal cost—that is, the extra cost associated with producing one more unit of the good. For if the marginal benefit exceeds the marginal cost, society would gain from producing more of the good; and if the marginal benefit was less than the marginal cost, society would gain from reducing production of the good.

Market equilibrium occurs at the point where market demand equals supply, point *E* in Figure 3.2C. At this point, the marginal benefit equals the price, and the marginal cost equals the price; both equal \$2.00; hence the marginal benefit equals the marginal cost, precisely the condition we identified earlier as that required for economic efficiency.

INDIFFERENCE CURVE ANALYSIS

We can illustrate the general principle that a competitive economy leads to an efficient allocation of resources in a slightly different way, making use of **indifference curves.** These are curves that trace out the combinations of goods and labor supply among which an individual is indifferent. We will consider the example of an individual who has to decide how many hours he wishes to work. His wage is \$5.00 an hour. Thus if he works ten hours he gets \$50, and if he works forty hours he gets \$200. The relationship between the number of hours he works and his income we call the individual's **budget constraint**. We depict the budget constraint in Figure 3.3. Note that for each increment in hours worked, income increases by \$5. The change in the value of the variable measured along the vertical (income) axis, as a result of a unit increase in the variable measured along the horizontal axis (hours worked), is called the **slope** of the curve. Thus, the slope of the budget constraint is equal to the individual's hourly wage.

In Figure 3.3 we have also depicted the individual's preferences by drawing his indifference curves. Each indifference curve gives the combinations of levels of income and hours worked among which the individual is indifferent. Since income is good and work is bad, by assumption, the indifference curves slope up as shown in the diagram. We have drawn two different indifference curves. The upper indifference curve gives all those combinations for which the individual is indifferent to point *E′*; while the lower indifference curve gives all those combinations for which the individual is indifferent to point *E*. Clearly, the individual is better off along the indifference curve through *E′* than along that through *E*, since at any level of hours worked, income is higher along the upper indifference curve.

Now consider movements along a *single* indifference curve. As we move to the right, increasing the individual's working hours, notice that the amount by which his income must be increased to compensate him for working an additional hour increases. The amount of extra income

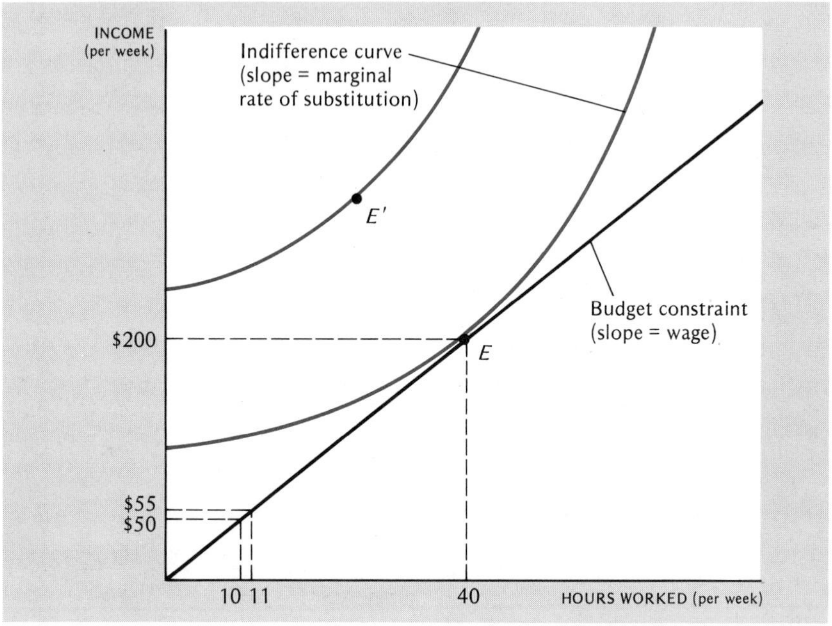

3.3 INDIVIDUAL'S DECISION ON NUMBER OF HOURS TO WORK The individual maximizes his utility at the point where his indifference curve is tangent to the budget constraint, point *E*. At *E* the slope of the budget constraint (the wage) is equal to the slope of the indifference curve, the individual's marginal rate of substitution between leisure and income.

that can just compensate an individual for working an extra hour is called the individual's **marginal rate of substitution** between work and income. Diagrammatically, the slope of the indifference curve gives the individual's marginal rate of substitution.

Through any point, the individual has an indifference curve giving those combinations of income and work among which the individual is indifferent. The individual wishes to be on the highest possible indifference curve; this is just the point of *tangency* between the indifference curve and the budget constraint, point *E*.

At the point of tangency, the slopes of the two curves are the same—i.e. the marginal rate of substitution (the slope of the indifference curve) is equal to the wage.

Consider now a representative firm. The more labor input it hires, the greater its output. The relationship between inputs and outputs is called the firm's **production function** and is depicted in Figure 3.4. In this simple example, labor is the only input. The slope of the production function is called the **marginal product** of labor; it gives the extra output that is produced by an extra hour of labor. Since the firm transforms labor services into goods, economists sometimes refer to the slope of the production function as the **marginal rate of transformation.**

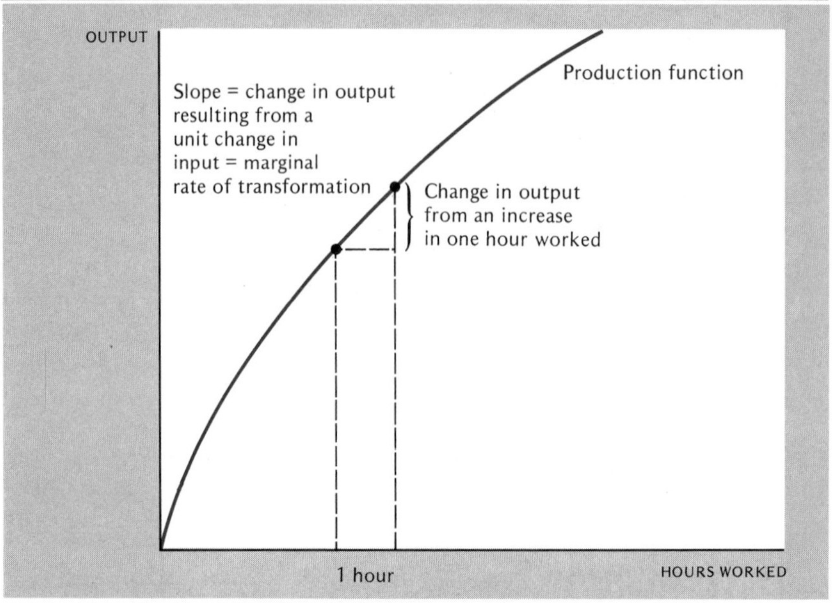

3.4 FIRM'S PRODUCTION FUNCTION The firm produces at the point where the value of the marginal product equals the wage.

The firm wishes to maximize its profits. In deciding how much labor to hire, it compares the extra benefit it receives (the value of the marginal product)[4] with the extra cost (the wage). So long as the value of the marginal product of an extra hour of labor exceeds the wage, the firm continues to hire more labor. In equilibrium, then, the value of the marginal product of labor is just equal to the wage.

Assume, for simplicity, that what is being produced has a price of $1. Then we see that the firm will set the marginal rate of transformation (the marginal product of labor) equal to the wage. But recall that the laborer set his marginal rate of substitution equal to the wage. Thus, in equilibrium, *the marginal rate of substitution equals the marginal rate of transformation.* But this is precisely what efficiency requires. To see why, assume that an individual was willing to give up one hour of leisure, provided he could have 4 ice cream cones. Assume that with one hour of work, 5 ice cream cones could be produced. Clearly, it would be desirable to have the individual work an hour more; he would produce 1 more ice cream cone than he required to leave him just as well off. Conversely, assume in one hour of work, only 3 ice cream cones were produced. Then the individual should work an hour less. By working an hour less, output would be reduced by 3 ice cream cones. The individual

[4] The value of labor's marginal product is just what the firm receives from selling each unit of output (the price) times the number of extra units that are produced with an extra unit of labor (the marginal product of labor, or the marginal rate of transformation).

was willing, however, to give up 4 ice cream cones for an hour's reduction in work. Thus the equality of the marginal rate of substitution and the marginal rate of transformation is required for Pareto efficiency of the economy and is ensured by the competitive market.

Competition and Innovation

The analysis just presented to explain why competitive markets lead to efficiency is not quite the same as Adam Smith's argument. He was also concerned with the incentives for innovation, for taking advantage of new profitable opportunities. As firms compete, those who are most successful may establish temporary monopolies. The threat of competition will still force them to be efficient; they must continue to look for profitable opportunities, lest some other firms grab these opportunities and take their market away. The first fundamental theorem of welfare economics explains why an economy with no technological change, in which all firms are sufficiently small that they have no effect on prices, would be Pareto efficient. But Adam Smith's argument was based on a much broader perspective. Some of the current discussions of the role of the government and the virtues of competition take on this broader perspective rather than the more narrow view reflected in the fundamental theorems.[5]

MARKET FAILURES AS A RATIONALE FOR GOVERNMENT ACTIVITY

The first fundamental theorem of welfare economics asserts that the economy is Pareto efficient only under certain conditions, as we have seen. There are six important circumstances, or conditions, under which the market is not Pareto efficient. These are referred to as **market failures,** and they provide a set of rationales for government activity.

1. Failure of Competition

For the invisible hand to work, there must be competition. In some industries—automobiles, aluminum, photographic film—there are relatively few firms or one or two firms that have a large share of the market. (When there is only one supplier in a market, we say he has a monopoly.) This suggests the absence of strong competition. However, the presence of only a few firms in itself does not necessarily imply the firms are not acting competitively. If there are a large number of *potential* entrants (either domestic or foreign firms), the existing firms may

[5] Sometimes the views come into conflict: to provide the incentives for firms to engage in research and development may require granting temporary monopoly rights—as through the patent system, where a person can obtain sole rights to an invention for a period of seventeen years. This alternative view was stressed by the great Harvard economist Joseph Schumpeter (1883–1950). It has more recently been revived in the work of Richard Nelson and Sidney Winter at Yale (see for instance, their book *An Evolutionary Theory of Economic Change* [Cambridge, Mass.: Harvard University Press, 1982]).

not be able to act monopolistically; as soon as existing firms attempt to reap any monopoly profits, a potential entrant might enter the market and drive down the price.

A second difficulty in ascertaining whether a market is competitive arises from the problem of defining the market. DuPont may have had a monopoly in cellophane or, more widely, in transparent wrapping materials. But there are other wrapping materials (brown paper). These may be sufficiently close substitutes to make DuPont act competitively.

When transportation costs are large, the relevant market may be limited geographically. Though there are many cement companies in the United States, cement customers in Dubuque, Iowa, cannot look to Ohio for a better price on mixed cement. If there is only one cement firm in a particular area, there may be no (or very limited) competition.

Some monopolies are created by the government. The British government gave the East India Company the exclusive right to trade with India. Also, the patent system grants inventors a monopoly over their inventions for a limited period of time.

In other instances, there are barriers to entry arising from what economists refer to as **increasing returns to scale.** These are cases where the costs of production (per unit output) decline with the scale of production. It is less expensive to have one large electrical generator serve a region than to put one in every neighborhood. It thus may be more efficient to have only one generator serving a particular local market. Similarly, it may be efficient to have only one telephone company serving a particular local market, or one water company (imagine the duplication in power lines, telephone lines, and water mains if every other house used a different water or electric company). In industries with increasing returns to scale, new firms that have low output will face much higher costs than those of an established firm with high output.

When a firm has attained its monopoly position as a result of increasing returns to scale, we say that it is a **natural monopoly.** Whether a particular market is characterized by a natural monopoly depends on circumstances. Thus, the development of new telecommunications technologies has led to the elimination of AT&T's natural monopoly over long-distance telephone services.

If entry into and exit from a market were costless, even natural monopolies might be forced to behave competitively by the threat of entry.[6] But governments have seldom relied on this. In the United States, some natural monopolies are regulated. Examples include telephone service and electricity. Other natural monopolies are run directly by the government. Water companies are frequently publicly owned, and there are a number of large, publicly owned electric utilities

[6] This is the view taken, for instance, by William J. Baumol of Princeton University and New York University in his presidential address before the American Economic Association. See W. J. Baumol, "Contestable Markets: An Uprising in the Theory of Industry Structure," *American Economic Review*, March 1982, pp. 1–15. This view has recently been criticized, on the grounds that even if there are very slight entry costs, firms may be able to exercise considerable monopoly power.

(including the Tennessee Valley Authority). In all countries, the post office is public (though there has been a rapid growth in the private provision of many postal services, such as overnight package delivery and parcel post). The United States is unusual, however, in having its telephone services supplied privately. In most countries telephone services are publicly provided.

MONOPOLY PRICING AND THE WELFARE LOSS FROM MONOPOLY

We have noted that under certain circumstances it may be more efficient to have only one firm producing, rather than many. Why is it then that monopolies are generally viewed as bad? The reason is that, if unregulated, monopolies (whether natural or not) will restrict output to attain a higher price.

Because a firm owner seeks to maximize his profits, he produces to the point where the extra revenue he would receive from producing an extra unit is just equal to the extra cost of producing that extra unit (his marginal cost). The extra revenue he receives is referred to as his **marginal revenue.** For a perfect competitor, the marginal revenue is just the selling price. But for a monopolist, the marginal revenue is *less* than the selling price. As the monopolist increases sales, he knows that he must lower his price. The revenue he gains from selling an extra unit is its price *less* the revenue foregone because the expansion in sales lowers the price on *all* units.

Figure 3.5 depicts the marginal revenue curve and demand curve facing a monopolist. In Panel A, we suppose that marginal costs of production are constant at all levels of output. The monopolist operates at Q^*, where marginal revenue equals marginal cost. Clearly output at Q^* is less than at Q_1, where price equals marginal cost. Notice that at Q^*, price, which measures how much individuals value an *extra* unit of the good, exceeds the marginal cost. This is why we say there is a welfare loss from the restriction in output arising from monopoly.

In Panel B, we suppose that marginal costs of production fall as output rises; this is what we mean by *increasing returns to scale.* Since marginal costs are less than average costs, a price set equal to marginal cost, at Q_2, would cause the firm to incur a loss. Q_1 is the highest output at which the firm breaks even since at that output, average cost equals average revenue per unit (price). Whether the Pareto-efficient output is Q_2 or something less depends on how the firm's losses can be financed. In general, we can say only that the efficient output will lie between Q_1 and Q_2.[7] A monopolist, however, would restrict output further, to Q^*. Again, there is a welfare loss arising from this restriction. In Chapter 18, we show how to measure the welfare loss from the restriction in output arising from monopoly.

[7] Chapter 20 describes the precise solution to this problem, known as the Ramsey problem.

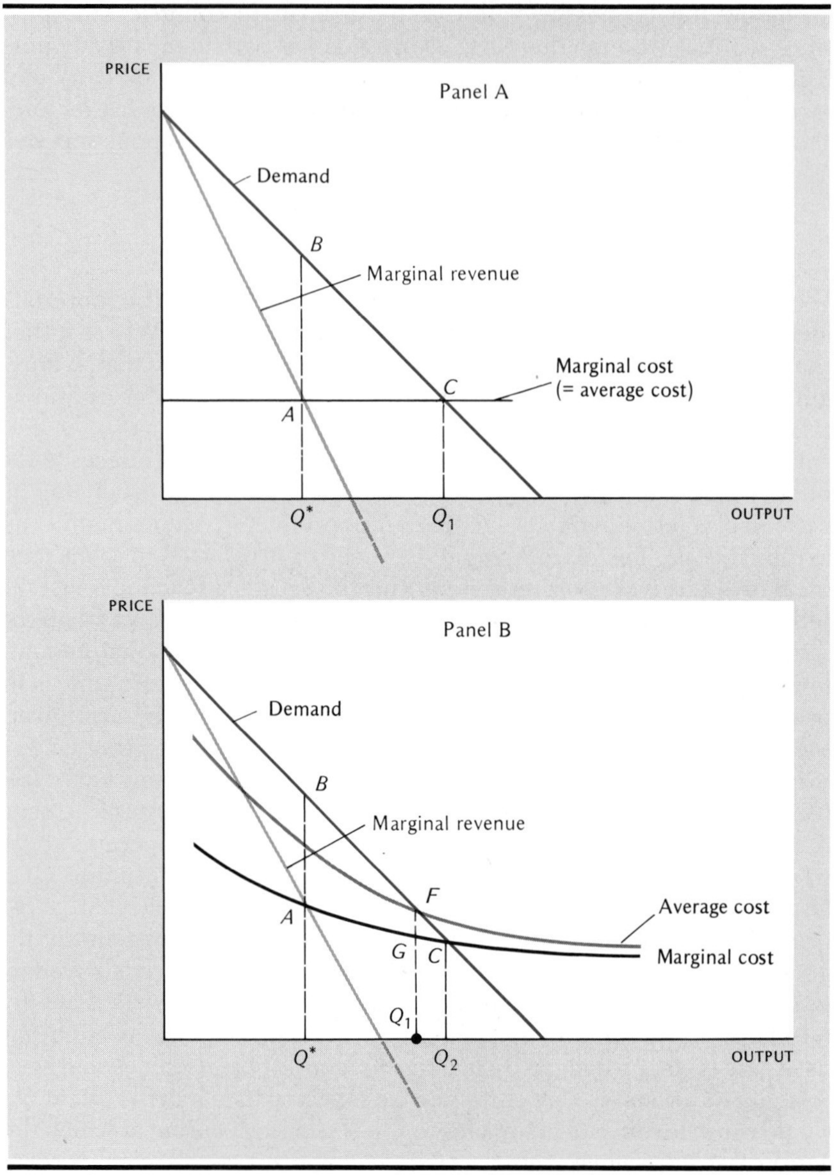

3.5 MONOPOLY PRICING Monopoly output is lower than competitive output, or the output at which profits are zero. There is a resulting welfare loss.

2. Public Goods

There are some goods that either will not be supplied by the market or, if supplied, will be supplied in insufficient quantity. An example on a large scale is national defense; on a small scale, navigational aids (such as a buoy). These are called pure public goods. They have two critical properties: first, it does not cost anything for an additional individual to enjoy the benefits of the public goods. Formally, there is a zero marginal cost for the additional individual enjoying the good. It costs no more to defend a country of one million and one individuals than to defend a country of one million. The costs of a lighthouse do not depend at all on the number of ships that sail past it. Secondly, it is, in general, difficult or impossible to exclude individuals from the enjoyment of the public good. If I put a lighthouse in some rocky channel to enable my ships to navigate safely, it is difficult or impossible to exclude other ships entering the channel from the navigational benefits of my lighthouse. If our national defense policy is successful in diverting an attack from abroad, we all benefit; there is no way we could exclude any single individual from these benefits.

The market either will not supply, or will not supply enough of, a pure public good. Consider the case of the lighthouse. A large ship owner with many ships might decide that the benefits he himself receives from a lighthouse exceed the costs; but in calculating how many lighthouses to put in place, he will look only at the benefits he receives, not at the benefits received by others. Thus there will be some lighthouses for which the total benefits (taking into account *all* of the ships that make use of the lighthouse) exceed the costs but for which the benefits of any single ship owner are less than the costs. Such lighthouses will not be put into place, and that is inefficient. The fact that private markets will not supply, or will supply too little of, public goods provides a rationale for many government activities.

3. Externalities

There are many cases where the actions of one individual or one firm affect other individuals or firms, where one firm imposes a cost on other firms but does not compensate the other firms, or alternatively, where one firm confers a benefit on other firms but does not reap a reward for providing that benefit. Perhaps the most discussed example in recent years has been air and water pollution. When I drive a car that is not equipped with a pollution control device, I lower the quality of the air. (Of course, the effect on air quality if only one person does this may be negligible, but when a large number of individuals do this, the effect is significant.) I thus impose a cost on others. Similarly, a chemical plant that discharges its chemicals into a nearby stream imposes costs on downstream users of the water. They may have to spend a considerable amount of money to clean up the water in order to use it.

Instances where one individual's actions impose a cost on others are referred to as **negative externalities.** But not all externalities are negative. There are some important instances of **positive externalities,** where one individual's actions confer a benefit upon others. If I plant a beautiful flower garden in the front of my house, my neighbors may benefit from being able to look at it. An apple orchard may confer a positive externality on a neighboring beekeeper. An individual who rehabilitates his house in a neighborhood that is in decline may confer a positive externality on his neighbors.

There are a large number of other examples of externalities: an additional car on a crowded highway will add to road congestion, both reducing the speed at which other drivers can travel safely and increasing the probability of an accident. When an additional fisherman starts fishing in a given pond, he may reduce the amount of fish that others will be able to catch. If there are several oil wells drilled in the same oil pool, taking an excessive amount of oil from one of the wells may reduce the amount of oil available for extraction from the other wells.

Whenever there are such externalities, the resource allocation provided by the market may not be efficient. Since individuals do not bear the full cost of the negative externalities they generate, they will engage in an excessive amount of such activities; conversely, since individuals do not enjoy the full benefits of activities generating positive externalities, they will engage in too little of these. Thus, for example, there is a widespread belief that without government intervention of some kind, the level of pollution would be too high. To put it another way, pollution control provides a positive externality, so without government intervention there would be an underprovision of pollution control.

Governments respond to externalities in several different ways. In some cases (mainly involving negative externalities) they attempt to regulate the activity in question; thus the government imposes emission standards for automobiles and imposes regulations for air and water pollution by firms.

Alternatively, the government can attempt to use the price system by imposing penalties (fines) on negative externalities and rewards for positive externalities; individuals can be made to realize the cost they impose and to recognize the benefits they confer upon others. Thus, rather than regulating the level of automobile emissions, the government can impose a charge, proportional to the level of emissions over some critical level. By charging for the use of roads, at least at peak times, the government can make road users aware of the congestion costs they impose on others.

4. Incomplete Markets

Pure public goods and services are not the only goods and services that private markets fail to provide adequately. Whenever private markets fail to provide a good or service, even though the cost of providing it is less than what individuals are willing to pay, there is a market failure that we refer to as **incomplete markets** (a complete market would provide all goods and services for which the cost of provision is less than what individuals are willing to pay). Some economists believe that private markets have done a particularly poor job in providing insurance and loans, and that this provides a rationale for government activities in these areas.

INSURANCE MARKETS

The private market does not provide insurance for many important risks that individuals face, though insurance markets are much better today than they were seventy-five years ago. The government has undertaken a number of insurance programs, motivated at least in part by this market failure. In 1933, following the bank failures of the Great Depression, the government set up the Federal Deposit Insurance Corporation. Banks pay the corporation annual premiums, which provide insurance for depositors against a loss of savings arising from the insolvency of banks. The government has also been active in providing flood insurance. Following urban riots in the summer of 1967, most private insurance companies refused to write fire insurance in certain inner-city areas, and again the government stepped in.

Although the absence of adequate private insurance markets may provide the political justification for public insurance programs, some public insurance programs are designed to transfer resources (perhaps in a disguised way) to the beneficiaries of the program. If their sole or major objective were to provide insurance, they would be designed and paid for in a substantially different manner. For instance, one justification for the government's farm program is that farmers face large risks from price fluctuations, risks against which they cannot obtain insurance.[8] Government programs to stabilize the prices received by farmers reduce these risks. But our farm programs not only stabilize farm prices, they also substantially increase the average income of farmers. Only part of this "gift" to farmers is reflected in the government's budget. The rest is reflected in the higher prices consumers must pay for agricultural products. If the true objective of the price-support program is to stabilize the income of farmers, to reduce the risks that they face, there are ways of doing this more effectively and at less cost. The government might, for instance, simply provide price insurance, at a premium accurately reflecting the costs of providing such insurance.

CAPITAL MARKETS

In recent years, the government has taken an active role not only in remedying deficiencies in risk markets but in ameliorating the effects of imperfect capital markets. Until 1965 it had been difficult for individuals to obtain loans to finance their college education; in that year the government passed legislation providing for government guarantees on student loans. As the program expanded in the 1970s the initial objective, making loans available, became mixed with a second objective, subsidizing education: the interest rates charged were often substantially below market rates.

[8] For the major crops, farmers can obtain some price insurance by trading in futures markets. For a more extended discussion of the distinction between programs aimed at stabilizing farmers' incomes and those aimed at redistributing income to farmers, see D. Newbery and J. E. Stiglitz, *The Theory of Commodity Price Stabilization* (New York: Oxford University Press, 1981).

But this is only one of several government loan programs. The Federal National Mortgage Association provides funds for home mortgages (referred to as Fanny Maes); the government provides loans to farmers; the Export-Import Bank provides loans to businesses engaged in international trade; the Small Business Administration provides loans for small business; and so forth. In each of these cases, there were allegations that access to the credit market was restricted prior to the introduction of the government program.

COMPLEMENTARY MARKETS

Finally, we turn to the problems associated with the absence of certain complementary markets. Suppose that all individuals only enjoy coffee with sugar, that without sugar it tastes bitter and is unpalatable. Assume, moreover, that there was no market for sugar without coffee. Thus an entrepreneur considering whether to produce coffee, given that sugar was not produced, would not do so, because he would realize that he would have no sales. And an entrepreneur considering whether to produce sugar, given that coffee was not produced, also would not do so, since he too would realize that he would have no sales. If, however, the two entrepreneurs could get together, there would be a good market for coffee and sugar. Each *acting alone* would not be able to pursue the public interest, but acting together they could.

This particular example is deliberately quite simple, and in this case coordination (between the potential sugar producer and the potential coffee producer) might easily be provided by the individuals themselves without government intervention. But there are many cases where large-scale coordination is required, particularly in less-developed countries, and this may require government planning. Similar arguments have been put forward as justification for public urban renewal programs. To redevelop a large section of a city requires extensive coordination among factories, retailers, landlords, and other businesses. One of the objectives of government development agencies is to provide that coordination (if markets were complete, the prices provided by the market would perform this "coordination" function).

Great care is required in analyzing the appropriate government response to incomplete markets. There may be good reasons that private producers have failed to provide a particular good or service. There may be large transaction costs associated with providing it. Banks may not make certain categories of loan because the probability of default is so high that to earn the same return as on other loans the bank must charge such a high interest rate that there would be little demand for the loans.

5. Information Failures

A number of government activities are motivated by imperfect information on the part of consumers, and the belief that the market, by itself, will supply too little information. For instance, in 1968, the government passed a Truth-In-Lending bill requiring lenders to inform borrowers of the true rate of interest on their loans. The Federal Trade Commission and the Food and Drug Administration have both adopted a number of regulations concerning labeling, disclosure of contents, etc. At one time, the Federal Trade Commission proposed that used-car dealers be required to disclose whether they had tested various parts of the car, and if so, what the outcome of the test was. These regulations generated a considerable amount of controversy, and under pressure from Congress, the FTC was forced to back down.

Opponents of regulations on information disclosure contend that they are unnecessary (the competitive market provides incentives for firms to disclose relevant information), irrelevant (consumers pay little attention to the information the law requires firms to disclose), and costly, both to government, which must administer them, and to the firms, which must comply with the regulations. Proponents of these regulations claim that, though difficult to administer effectively, they are still useful.

The government's role in remedying information failures, however, goes beyond these simple consumer protection measures. Information is, in many respects, a public good. Giving information to one more individual does not reduce the amount others have. Efficiency requires that information be freely disseminated or, more accurately, that the only charge be for the actual cost of transmitting the information. The private market will often provide an inadequate supply of information, just as it supplies an inadequate amount of other public goods. The most notable example of government activity in this area is the U.S. Weather Bureau. Another example is the information provided to ships by the U.S. Coast Guard.[9]

6. Unemployment, Inflation, and Disequilibrium

Perhaps the most widely recognized symptoms of "market failure" are the periodic episodes of high unemployment, both of workers and machines, that have plagued capitalist economies during the past two centuries. Though these recessions and depressions have been greatly moderated in the period since World War II, perhaps partly because of government policies, the unemployment rate still climbed over 10 percent in 1982; that is low, however, compared to the Great Depression, when unemployment reached 24 percent in the United States.

Most economists take these high levels of unemployment as *prima facie* evidence that *something* is not working well in the market. To some economists, high unemployment is the most dramatic and most convincing evidence of market failure.

[9] The market failures associated with incomplete markets and imperfect information are, in fact, broader than our discussion has indicated. For instance, incomplete risk markets may lead to inefficient levels of investment. For an extended discussion, see B. Greenwald and J. E. Stiglitz, "Externalities in Economies with Imperfect Information and Incomplete Markets," *Quarterly Journal of Economics*, May 1986.

The fact that markets have failed to produce full employment—that there is a serious market failure—does not in itself imply that there is a role for the government to play. One must be able to show, in addition, that there are policies through which the government can improve the functioning of the economy. This has long been a subject of controversy.

The issues raised by unemployment and inflation are sufficiently important, and sufficiently complicated, that they warrant a separate course in macroeconomics. But we shall touch on some aspects of these issues in Chapter 28, where we shall be concerned with the consequences of government deficits and attempt to survey some of the important ways that these macroeconomic considerations affect the design of tax policy.

Relationships among Market Failures

The market failures we have discussed are not mutually exclusive. Information problems often provide part of the explanation of missing markets. In turn, externalities are often thought to arise from missing markets: if fishermen could be charged for using fishing grounds—if there were a market for fishing rights—then there would not be overfishing. Public goods are sometimes viewed as an extreme case of externalities, where others benefit from my production of the good as much as I do. Indeed, much of the recent research on unemployment has attempted to relate it to one of the other market failures.

REDISTRIBUTION AND MERIT GOODS: TWO FURTHER RATIONALES FOR GOVERNMENT ACTIVITY

The preceding sources of market failure resulted in the economy being inefficient in the absence of government intervention—that is, the market economy, if left to itself, would not be Pareto efficient. But, even if the economy were Pareto efficient, there are two further arguments for government intervention. The first is income distribution. The fact that the economy is Pareto efficient says nothing about the distribution of income; competitive markets may give rise to a very unequal distribution of income, which may leave some individuals with insufficient resources on which to live. One of the most important activities of the government is to redistribute income. This is the express purpose of welfare activities, such as Aid to Families with Dependent Children. How we think systematically about issues of distribution is the subject of the next chapter.

The second argument for government intervention in a Pareto-efficient economy arises from concern that the individual may not act in his own best interest. It is often argued that evaluating each individual's welfare by his own perceptions—as with the criterion of Pareto efficiency—provides an inappropriate or inadequate criterion for making welfare judgments. Even if fully informed, consumers may make "bad" decisions. Individuals continue to smoke, even though it is bad for them, and even though they know it is bad for them. Individuals fail to wear seat belts, even though wearing seat belts increases the chances of survival from an accident, and even though individuals know the benefits of seat belts. Many individuals continue to buy sugar-laden breakfast cereals, even though they know that serious questions have been raised concerning the nutritional value of these cereals for their children. There are those who believe that the government should intervene in these cases, where individuals seemingly do not do what is in their own best interest; the kind of intervention that is required must be stronger than simply providing information. Goods that the government compels individuals to consume, like seat belts and elementary education, are called **merit goods.**

The view that the government should intervene because it knows what is in the best interest of individuals better than they themselves do, is referred to as **paternalism.** In contrast to the paternalistic view, many economists and social philosophers believe that the government should respect consumers' preferences. By what right, opponents of the paternalistic role of government ask, can one group of individuals impose their will and preferences over another group? Though there may occasionally be cases that merit a paternalistic role for the government, these economists argue that it is virtually impossible to distinguish such cases from those that do not. And they worry that once the government assumes a paternalistic role, special-interest groups will attempt to use government to further their own views about how individuals should act or what they should consume.

The paternalistic argument for government activities is quite distinct from the externalities argument we discussed above. One might argue that smoking causes cancer, and since individuals who get cancer may be treated in public hospitals or financed by public funds, smokers impose a cost on nonsmokers. This, however, can be dealt with by making smokers pay their full costs—for instance, by imposing a tax on cigarettes. Alternatively, smoking in a crowded room does indeed impose a cost on nonsmokers in that room. But this, too, can be dealt with directly. Those who take a paternalistic view might argue that individuals should not be allowed to smoke, even in the privacy of their own homes, and even if a tax, which makes the smokers take account of the external costs imposed on others, is levied. Though few have taken such an extreme paternalistic position with respect to smoking, this paternalistic role undoubtedly has been important in a number of areas, such as government policies toward drugs (marijuana) and liquor (prohibition), as well as compulsory school attendance.

TWO PERSPECTIVES ON THE ROLE OF THE GOVERNMENT

In Chapter 1, we saw that there are two aspects of the analysis of public-sector activities: the normative approach, which focuses on what the government should do, and the positive approach, which focuses on describing and explaining both what the government actually does, and what its consequences are. We can now relate our discussion of market failures, redistribution, and merit goods to these two alternative approaches.

A Normative Analysis

The fundamental theorems of welfare economics are useful because they delineate clearly a role for the government. In the absence of market failures and merit goods all the government needs to do is worry about the distribution of income (resources). The private enterprise system ensures that resources will be used efficiently.

If there are important market failures—imperfect competition (from, say, increasing returns), imperfect information, incomplete markets, externalities, public goods, and unemployment—there is a presumption that the market will not be Pareto efficient. This suggests a role for the government. But there are two important qualifications.

First, it has to be shown that there is, a least in principle, some way of intervening in the market to make everyone better off without making anyone worse off, that is, of making a **Pareto improvement**. Secondly, it has to be shown that in the attempt to remedy a market failure, the political processes and bureaucratic structures of a democratic society are not likely to interfere with the proposed Pareto improvement.

Thus when information is imperfect and costly, the analysis of whether the market is Pareto efficient must take into account these information costs; information is costly to the government, just as it is to private firms. Markets may be incomplete because of transaction costs, the costs of establishing an additional market; but the government would face costs of establishing markets—for instance, for insurance—and there would be administrative costs of running a public insurance program.

Recent research has established a variety of circumstances under which, assuming that the government has no advantage in information or transaction costs over the private market, the government could, in principle, bring about a Pareto improvement.

The fact that there may exist government policies that would be Pareto improvements does not, however, necessarily create a presumption that government intervention is desirable. We also have to consider the consequences of government intervention, in the form it is likely to take, given the nature of our political process. This distinction, between an ideal government and actual governments, did not play a role in our discussion of the fundamental theorems of welfare economics. There, we showed that in the absence of market failures, not even an ideal government could improve the efficiency with which resources are allocated. Now, in the face of these market failures, we have to understand how governments function if we are to assess whether government action is likely to remedy these market failures.

In the 1960s, it was common to take a market failure, show that a government program could lead to a Pareto improvement (someone could be made better off without making anyone worse off), and conclude that therefore government intervention was called for. When programs were enacted and failed to achieve what they were supposed to, the blame was placed on petty bureaucrats or political tampering. But, as we shall see in Chapters 6 and 7, even if bureaucrats and politicians behave honorably, the nature of government itself still may help explain government's failures.

Public programs—even those allegedly directed at alleviating some market failure—are instituted in democracies not by ideal governments or benevolent despots but by complicated political processes.

A Positive Analysis

The market-failure approach to understanding the role of the government is largely a normative approach. The market-failure approach provides a basis for identifying situations where the government *ought* to do something, tempered by considerations of government failure.

Some economists believe that economists should focus their attention not on normative analysis but on positive analysis, on describing the consequences of government programs and the nature of the political processes.

The popularity of the market-failure approach has caused many programs to be justified in terms of market failures. But this may simply be rhetoric. There is often a significant difference between the stated objective of a program (to remedy some market failure) and the design of the program. Political rhetoric may focus on the failure of markets to provide insurance against volatile prices and the consequences that this has on small farmers, but government agricultural programs may in practice transfer income to large farmers. One may gain more insight into the political forces at work and the true objectives of the programs by looking at how the programs are designed and implemented than by looking at the stated objectives of the legislation.

A few economists take the extreme position that normative analysis is irrelevant. They ask: Of what relevance are statements about what the government should do? Just as one can describe a market equilibrium without referring to how resources "should be" allocated, so too one can describe a political equilibrium without referring to what the government should do. The outcomes depend on the rules of the political process, the incentives facing various participants in the political process, etc. If one fully understands the nature of the government, one fully understands what it is that the governments *will* do. There is little room left over to discuss what the government should do.

Although there is some truth to this view, it is extreme: discussions by economists (and others) of the role that government "should" play constitute an important part of the political process in modern democracies. Legislators recognize that much of the information with which they are supplied comes from those with vested interests; they thus frequently turn to economists for an alternative view of what the government should do. For instance, economists' arguments against tariffs, quotas, and other trade restrictions, though they have not always prevailed, have been important in limiting the scope of trade restrictions.

SUMMARY

1. Resource allocations that have the property that no one can be made better off without someone else being made worse off are called Pareto-efficient allocations.
2. Under certain conditions, the competitive market results in a Pareto-efficient resource allocation. When the conditions required for this are not satisfied, a rationale for government intervention in the market is provided.
3. There are six reasons why the market mechanism may not result in a Pareto-efficient resource allocation: failure of competition, public goods, externalities, incomplete markets, information failures, and unemployment.
4. Even if the market is Pareto efficient, there may be two further grounds for government action. First, the competitive market may give rise to a socially undesirable distribution of income. And second, some believe that individuals, even when well informed, do not make good judgments concerning the goods they consume, thus providing a rationale for regulations restricting the consumption of some goods, and for the public provision of other goods, called merit goods.
5. Though the presence of market failures implies that there may be scope for government activity, it does not imply that a particular government program aimed at correcting the market failure is necessarily desirable. To evaluate government programs, one must take into account not only their objectives but also how they are implemented.

KEY CONCEPTS

Invisible hand
Fundamental theorems of welfare economics
Pareto-efficient resource allocation
Utility possibilities curve
Decentralized market mechanism
Marginal rate of substitution
Production function
Marginal rate of transformation
Marginal cost
Marginal benefit
Returns to scale
Natural monopoly
Marginal revenue
Public goods
Externalities
Incomplete markets
Merit goods

QUESTIONS AND PROBLEMS

1. For each of the programs listed below, discuss what market failures might be (or are) used as partial rationale:
   a) Automobile safety belt requirements
   b) Regulations on automobile pollution
   c) National defense

d) Unemployment compensation
e) Medicare (medical care for the aged)
f) Medicaid (medical care for the indigent)
g) Federal Deposit Insurance Corporation
h) Federally insured mortgages
i) Law requiring lenders to disclose the true rate of interest they are charging on loans (truth-in-lending laws)
j) National Weather Service
k) Urban renewal
l) Post office
m) Government prohibition of the use of narcotics
n) Rent control

2. If the primary objective of government programs in each of these areas is the alleviation of some market failure, how might they be better designed?
   a) Farm price supports
   b) Oil import quotas (in the 1950s)
   c) Special tax provisions for energy industries
3. Many government programs both redistribute income and correct a market failure. What are the market failures associated with each of these programs, and how else might they be addressed if there were no distributional objectives?
   a) Student loan programs
   b) Public elementary education
   c) Public support for universities
   d) Social security

APPENDIX: PARETO EFFICIENCY AND COMPETITIVE EQUILIBRIUM—A DIAGRAMMATIC ANALYSIS

Three conditions are required for Pareto efficiency. Between any two goods, all individuals' marginal rates of substitution must be the same (this is called **exchange efficiency**); all firms' marginal rates of substitution between different inputs must be the same (this is called **production efficiency**); and the marginal rate of transformation between any two commodities must equal the consumers' marginal rate of substitution (this is called **product-mix efficiency**). Here we explain why these conditions are required and how, in the absence of market failures, competitive markets ensure that they will be satisfied.

EXCHANGE EFFICIENCY

Exchange efficiency is concerned with the way a given bundle of goods is allocated between individuals. Consider an economy with a fixed supply of goods (say a fixed supply of apples and oranges). For simplicity, we assume there are two individuals, Robinson Crusoe and Friday. Whatever Crusoe does not get, Friday gets. Thus we can represent all possible allocations in a box (called an Edgeworth-Bowley Box, after two early twentieth-century English mathematical economists), where the horizontal axis represents the total supply of apples and the vertical axis represents the total supply of oranges. In Figure 3.6, what Crusoe gets to consume is measured from the bottom-left corner (*O*), and what

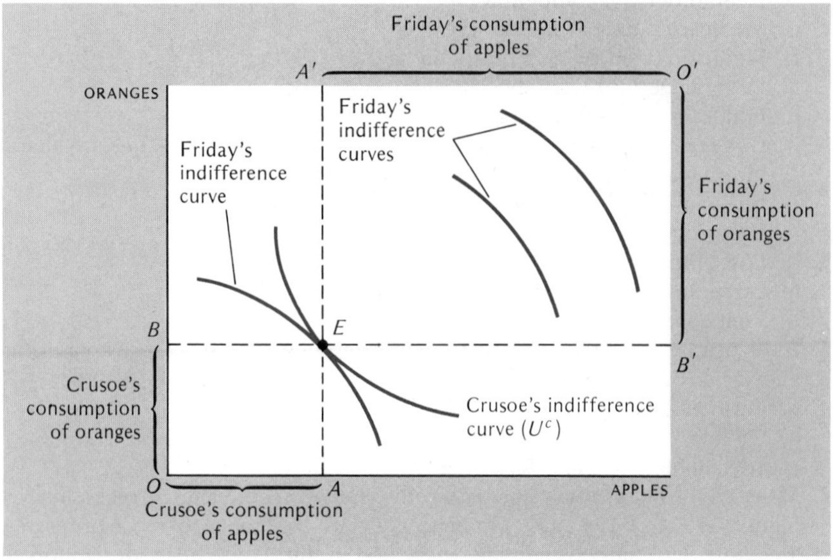

3.6 EXCHANGE EFFICIENCY The sides of this Edgeworth-Bowley Box give the available supplies of apples and oranges. *OA* and *OB* give Crusoe's consumption of the two commodities. Friday gets what Crusoe does not consume, that is, *O'A'* and *O'B'*. Pareto efficiency requires the tangency of the two indifference curves (one such point is at *E*), where the marginal rates of substitution of oranges for apples are equal.

Friday gets is measured from the top-right corner (*O'*). At the allocation denoted by the point *E*, Crusoe gets *OA* apples and *OB* oranges, while Friday gets the remainder (*O'A'* apples and *O'B'* oranges). We then draw Crusoe's indifference curves, such as U^c. We have also drawn Friday's indifference curves. His indifference curves look perfectly normal if you turn the book upside down.

Let us now fix Crusoe's utility. Pareto efficiency requires us to maximize Friday's utility, given the level of utility attained by Crusoe. Thus we ask, given that Crusoe is on the indifference curve U^c, what is the highest indifference curve that Friday can get to? Remember that Friday's utility increases as we move down and to the left (Friday is getting more goods, Crusoe fewer goods). Friday attains his highest utility where his indifference curve is *tangent* to Crusoe's, at *E*. At this point, the slopes of the indifference curves are the same, that is, their marginal rates of substitution of oranges for apples are the same.

Recall from our discussion above that in maximizing their utility subject to their budget constraints, individuals set their marginal rates of substitution (of one good for another, or of income for leisure) equal to relative prices. (In Figure 3.3, the cost in income of another hour of leisure is the foregone hourly wage.) If all individuals face the same relative prices, as they do in competitive markets, they all set their marginal rates of substitution between any two goods equal to the same number. Therefore, in competitive equilibrium, the marginal rates of substitution, say of oranges for apples, will be the same for all individuals: there will be exchange efficiency.

Exchange efficiency, which we have just considered, is about the allocation of a given amount of goods among individuals, and it ignores the problem of production. Efficient production is about the allocation of fixed resources used as inputs in producing goods. Assume that there is a fixed supply of two inputs, say labor and land, which can be used to produce two commodities, apples and oranges. We can again represent the total supply of available resources (here, inputs in producing goods) by a box, such as Figure 3.7. Inputs not used to produce apples will be used to produce oranges; every point in the box represents a particular allocation of inputs between the two commodities.

In Figure 3.7, we have drawn the **isoquants**. An isoquant is the set of all possible combinations of inputs that are just sufficient to produce a given amount of output. We can get the same level of output if we increase the input of labor but decrease the amount of land. We call the slope of the isoquant the *marginal rate of substitution of land for labor;*[10] it gives the extra amount of land required to compensate for a decrease in the input of labor by one unit.

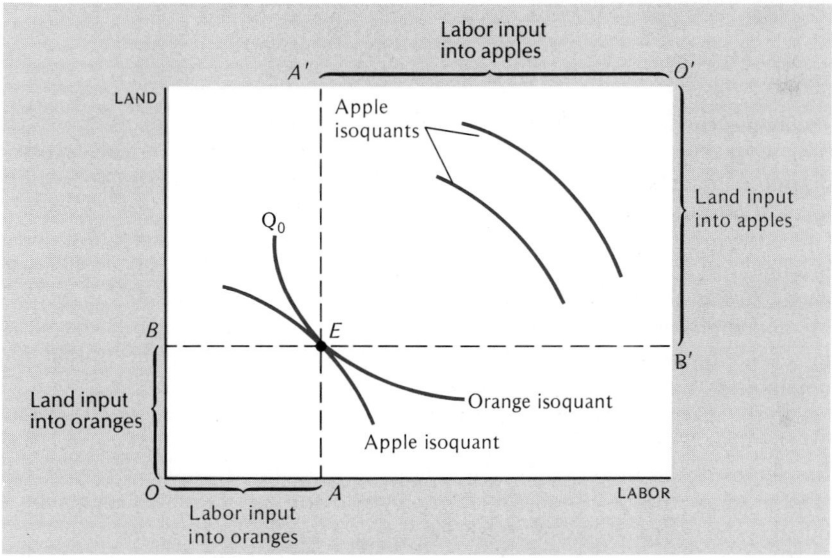

3.7 PRODUCTION EFFICIENCY The sides of this Edgeworth-Bowley Box give the available supply of resources—land and labor. Resources used in the production of oranges are given by *OA* and *OB*; resources not used in the production of oranges are used in the production of apples, *O'A'* and *O'B'*. Production efficiency requires the tangency of the isoquants. At tangency points, such as *E*, the marginal rate of substitution of land for labor is the same in the production of apples and oranges.

[10] Because this marginal rate of substitution depends only on technology, it is sometimes called the marginal rate of *technical* substitution. It is equivalent to the ratio of the marginal product of labor to the marginal product of land. If an extra unit of land increases output by 1, and an extra unit of labor increases output by ½, then if we increase land input by 1, and reduce labor input by 2, output will remain unchanged. Thus the marginal rate of substitution is ½.

Remember again that the quantities of inputs going into apple production are measured from O'. That is why the isoquants for apples have the shape they do; they look perfectly normal if you turn the book upside down. Clearly, production efficiency requires that, for any level of production of oranges, the output of apples is maximized. As we move down and to the left in the box, more resources are being allocated to apple production; hence, isoquants through those points represent higher levels of apple output. If we fix the output of oranges at the level corresponding to isoquant Q_o, it is clear that output of apples is maximized by finding the isoquant that is tangent to Q_o. At the point of tangency, the slopes of the isoquants are the same, that is, the marginal rate of substitution of land for labor is the same in the production of apples as it is in the production of oranges.

We can again see why competitive equilibria will satisfy this condition. At any level of output, each firm will wish to minimize its costs. If a unit of land costs twice as much as a unit of labor, it will hire land only up to the point where land's marginal product is twice the marginal product of labor. In other words, the *marginal rate of technical substitution will be set equal to the ratio of labor's price to land's price.* In competitive markets, all firms face the same prices, and so all firms will have the same marginal rate of substitution between inputs. This ensures production efficiency.

PRODUCT-MIX EFFICIENCY

To choose the best mix of apples or oranges to produce, we need to consider both what is technically feasible *and* individuals' preferences. For each level of output of oranges, we can determine from the technology the maximum feasible level of output of apples. This generates the *production possibilities schedule.* Given the production possibilities schedule, we wish to get to the highest possible level of utility. For simplicity, we assume all individuals have identical tastes. In Figure 3.8 we have depicted both the production possibilities schedule and the indifference curves between apples and oranges. Utility is maximized at the point of tangency of the indifference curve to the production possibilities schedule. The slope of the production possibilities schedule is called the marginal rate of transformation; this tells us how many extra oranges we can have if we reduce production of apples by 1. At the point of tangency, E, the slopes of the indifference curve and the production possibilities schedule are the same, that is, the marginal rate of substitution of oranges for apples is equal to the marginal rate of transformation.

We showed in the chapter why under competition, the marginal rate of transformation will be equal to the relative price of apples to oranges. If, by reducing production of apples by 1, firms can increase the production of oranges by say 1, and sell the oranges for more than the price of apples, profit-maximizing firms will clearly expand production of oranges. We also have shown why under competition consumers' marginal rates of substitution will equal the price ratio. Since both the marginal rates of substitution and the marginal rate of transformation will equal the price ratio, the marginal rate of transformation must equal consumers' marginal rates of substitution. Hence, under ideal competitive markets, all three conditions required for Pareto efficiency are satisfied.

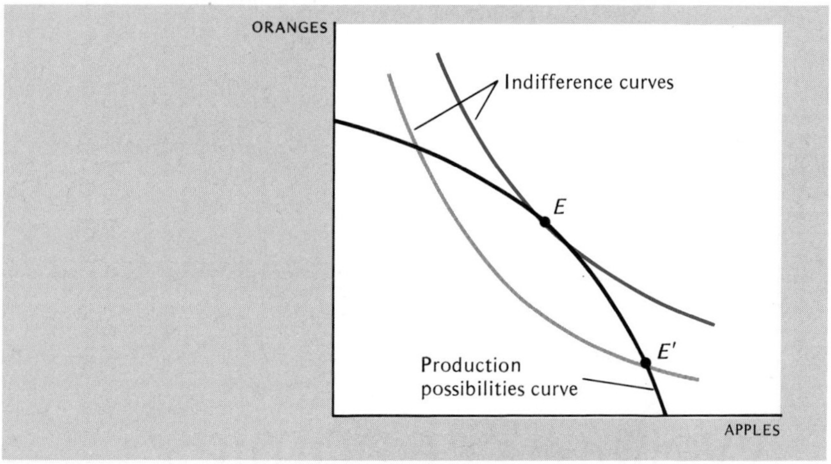

3.8 PRODUCT-MIX EFFICIENCY REQUIRES THAT THE MARGINAL RATE OF TRANSFORMATION EQUAL CONSUMERS' MARGINAL RATE OF SUBSTITUTION In order to reach the highest level of consumers' utility, the indifference curve and the production possibilities schedule must be tangent (point *E*). At any other point, such as *E*′, consumer utility is lower than at *E*.

4

Welfare Economics: Efficiency versus Equity

In the last chapter, we defined *Pareto efficiency*, a condition in which no one can be made better off without making someone else worse off; and we showed that in the absence of market failures, a free market would be Pareto efficient. But even if the competitive economy is efficient, the distribution of income to which it gives rise may be viewed as undesirable. One of the main consequences, and main objectives, of government activity is to alter the distribution of income.

The evaluation of a public program often entails balancing its consequences for economic efficiency and the distribution of income. A central objective of **welfare economics** is to provide a framework within which these evaluations can be performed systematically. Welfare economics is the branch of economics that addresses *normative* questions.

This chapter will show how economists conceptualize the trade-offs between efficiency and equity. In later chapters,[1] we will develop quantitative measures of the welfare effects of policies that change the distribution of income and that may, in the process, cause a loss in efficiency.

EFFICIENCY AND DISTRIBUTION TRADE-OFFS

Consider again a simple economy with two individuals, Robinson Crusoe and Friday. Assume initially that Robinson Crusoe has 10 oranges,

[1]See especially Chapters 10 and 18 through 20.

while Friday has only 2. This seems inequitable. Assume, therefore, that we play the role of government and attempt to transfer 4 oranges from Robinson Crusoe to Friday, but in the process 1 orange gets lost. Hence Robinson Crusoe ends up with 6 oranges, and Friday with 5. We have eliminated most of the inequity, but in the process the total number of oranges available has been diminished. Thus we see a **trade-off** between efficiency—the total number of oranges available—and equity.

The trade-off between equity and efficiency is at the heart of many discussions of public policy. The trade-off is often represented as in Figure 4.1. To get more equity, some amount of efficiency must be sacrificed. Two questions are debated. First, there is disagreement about the nature of the trade-off. To reduce inequality, how much efficiency do we have to give up? Will 1 or 2 oranges be lost in the process of transferring oranges from Crusoe to Friday? For instance, attempting to reduce inequality by progressive taxation is commonly regarded as giving rise to work disincentives, thereby reducing efficiency. But there are disagreements on how large these work disincentives are.

Second, there are disagreements on the relative value to be assigned to a decrease in inequality, compared to a decrease in efficiency. Some people claim that inequality is the central problem of society, and society should simply minimize the extent of inequality, regardless of the efficiency consequences. Others claim that efficiency is the central issue. Still others claim that in the long run, the best way to help the poor is not to worry about how the pie is to be divided but to increase the size

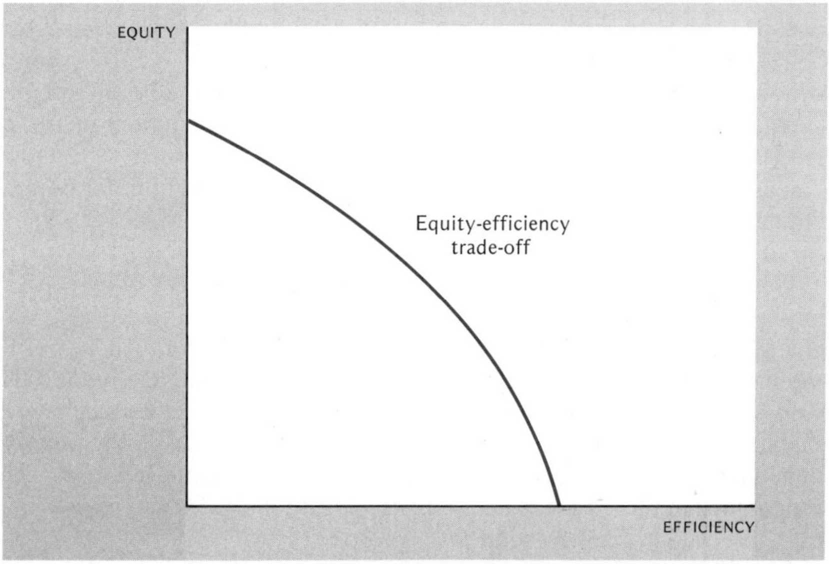

4.1 EQUITY-EFFICIENCY TRADE-OFF To get more equity, some amount of efficiency must, in general, be sacrificed.

of the pie, to make it grow as rapidly as possible, so there are more goods for everyone.

Maximizing efficiency is frequently equated with maximizing the value of national income; a program is said to introduce an inefficiency if it reduces national income, say through discouraging work or investment. And a program is said to promote equality if it transfers resources from someone who is richer to someone who is poorer.

Although this provides a first approximation, economists have devoted considerable attention to assessing the circumstances in which using these measures may be misleading or inapplicable. For instance, one program may make the very poor and the very rich worse off and the middle-income group better off. Has inequality increased or decreased? Suppose the government increased taxes, and squandered the proceeds, but individuals in order to maintain the same standard of living, worked harder and longer than they had previously. National income, as conventionally measured, would go up, but "efficiency"—as we normally think of it—would have decreased.

The measures chosen often have an important impact on policy. A common measure of inequality that has been used during the past twenty-five years is the **Poverty Index,** which measures the fraction of the population whose income falls below some critical level (defined as the level that permits a household to buy the basics in food, shelter, etc., at current U.S. prices). Though there is considerable debate about how this poverty line should be defined, this does not concern us here.

What does concern us is the fact that government officials have often evaluated alternative programs in terms of their effect on the Poverty Index. Thus, assume the government was attempting to choose between two programs, one of which moved some individuals who were just below the poverty line to a level of income just above it, and the other of which increased the income of some very poor individuals, but not enough to move them over the poverty line. The government might be led to conclude that the first project was preferable, since it reduced "measured" poverty; while the second program left the number of individuals below the poverty line unchanged, and had no effect on "measured" poverty.

This example illustrates another feature of most indices: they contain implicit value judgments. Implicitly, the Poverty Index says that changes in the distribution of income among the very poor (those below the poverty line) and changes in the distribution of income among the well off (those above the poverty line) are not as important as changes that move individuals from below the poverty line to above the poverty line. Virtually any measure of inequality contains some implicit value judgments; in recent years economists have been concerned with bringing these value judgments out into the open.

Are there circumstances in which policy evaluations can be made without making value judgments? Economists have identified one important set of circumstances in which this may be done.

Although, as we have noted, most policy changes involve some individuals becoming better off while others are made worse off, occasionally there are changes that make some better off without making anyone worse off. Such changes are referred to as *Pareto improvements.* When there are no further changes that could make someone better off without at the same time making someone else worse off, we say that the resource allocation is *Pareto efficient,* or Pareto optimal.

Assume, for instance, that the government is contemplating building a bridge. Those who wish to use the bridge are willing to pay more than enough in tolls to cover the costs of construction and maintenance. The construction of this bridge is likely to be a Pareto improvement. We use the term "likely" because there are always others who might be adversely affected by the construction of the bridge. For example, if the bridge changes the traffic flow, some stores might find that their business is decreased, and they are worse off. Or an entire neighborhood may be affected by the noise of bridge traffic and the shadows cast by the bridge superstructure.

Frequently on summer days, or at rush hour, large backlogs develop at toll booths on toll roads and bridges. If tolls were raised at those times and the proceeds used to finance additional toll booths or more peak-time toll collectors, everyone might be better off. People would prefer to pay a slightly higher price in return for less waiting. But it is possible that even this change might not be a Pareto improvement: among those waiting in line may be some unemployed individuals who are relatively little concerned about the waste of time but who are concerned about spending more money on tolls.

Economists are always on the lookout for Pareto improvements. The belief that any such improvements should be instituted is referred to as the **Pareto principle.**

"Packages" of changes together may constitute a Pareto improvement, where each change alone might not. Thus, while reducing the tariff on steel would not be a Pareto improvement (since the producers of steel would be worse off), it might be possible to reduce the tariff on steel, increase income taxes slightly, and use the proceeds to finance a subsidy to the steel industry; such a combination of changes might make everyone in the country better off (and make those abroad, the foreign exporters of steel, also better off).

Pareto Efficiency and Individualism

The criterion of Pareto efficiency has an important property upon which we should comment. It is *individualistic,* in two senses. First, it is concerned only with each individual's welfare, not with the relative well-being of different individuals. It is not concerned explicitly with inequality. Thus, a change that led the rich to be much better off but left the poor unaffected would still be a Pareto improvement. Some people, however, think that increasing the gap between the rich and the poor is undesirable. They believe that it gives rise, for instance, to undesirable social tensions. Many less developed countries often go through periods of rapid growth during which all major segments of society become better off; but the income of the rich grows more rapidly than that of the poor. To assess these changes, is it enough simply to say that everyone is better off? There is no agreement on the answer to this question.

Second, it is each individual's perception of his own welfare that counts. This is consistent with the general principle of **consumer sovereignty,** which holds that each individual is the best judge of his needs and wants, of what is in his own best interests.

Consumer Sovereignty versus Paternalism

Most Americans believe strongly in consumer sovereignty; yet there are some important limitations that should be noted. Parents often believe they know what is in the best interests of their children. They believe—and there is some evidence for this—that children are not aware of and/or do not take into account fully all the consequences of their actions; that they are often myopic, paying excessive attention to the short-run pleasures relative to the long-run costs or benefits. They may decide to go to a movie rather than study for an important economics exam, or quit school to earn enough income to buy a car, thus jeopardizing their long-run life prospects. While governments can do little about the first problem, they do try to do something about the second: most states require children to remain at school until they are sixteen years old.

In Chapter 3 we noted that the belief that adults may be shortsighted and need guidance from the government was called *paternalism.* This belief provides the basis for a variety of often controversial government activities, including the provision of certain goods, called *merit goods.*

While there is some presumption that most government programs should be evaluated on an individualistic basis, that is, by noting how different individuals are affected, using their own perceptions of how they benefit from the program, there are some important instances where there is widespread—but not universal—agreement that the desirability of a government program should be judged within a broader perspective, taking explicitly into account a wider range of social objectives. The large number of laws restricting discriminatory practices—fair housing, equal opportunity in employment, etc.—are perhaps the most important illustrations of this.

INCOME DISTRIBUTION

The most severe limitation of the Pareto principle is that it provides no guidance concerning issues of income distribution. Most government programs (when their costs are taken into account) benefit some individuals at the expense of others.

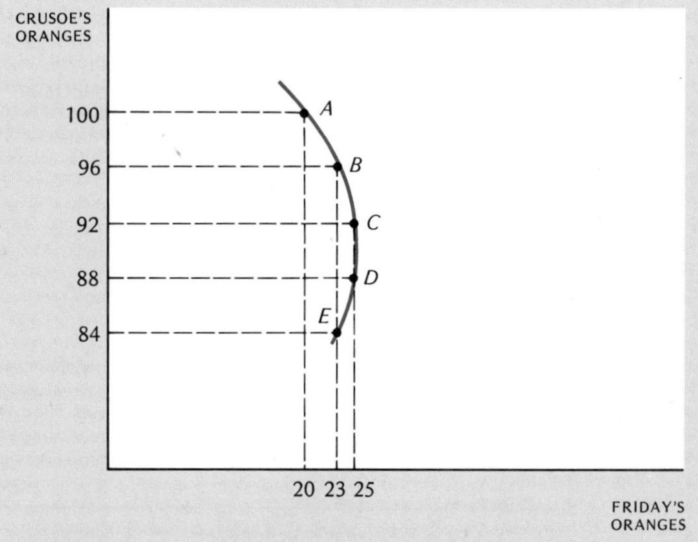

4.2 THE OPPORTUNITY SET The possible combinations of oranges enjoyed by Crusoe and Friday, if, as we attempt to transfer more oranges to Friday, more oranges get lost in the process. Point *D* is Pareto inefficient: Crusoe is better off at *C*, and Friday is no worse off.

The Utility Function and Marginal Utility

To see the nature of the trade-offs, we return to our example of Robinson Crusoe and his friend Friday. Assume now that Crusoe has initially 100 oranges and Friday only 20, as shown by point *A* in Figure 4.2. Assume, further, that as we try to take more oranges away from Crusoe and give them to Friday, we lose more than a proportionate number of oranges. Thus, if we try to take away 4 oranges, Friday gets 3 (point *B*). But if we try to transfer 8 oranges, we lose 3 oranges, so Friday gets only 5 more (Point *C*). The set of possible combinations is called the **opportunity set.** Notice that beyond point *C*, even if we try to take more away from Crusoe, Friday gets no additional oranges (he can only carry a certain number of oranges). We say that a point such as *D* is Pareto inefficient: Crusoe is better off at *C*, but Friday is no worse off. It is even possible that in trying to carry more oranges, he succeeds in carrying fewer. Thus, if he tries to carry 16, he drops all but 3. At *E*, both Crusoe and Friday are worse off than at *C*.

Often changes engendered by a policy are complex. Assume the government increases taxes to supply some public amenity. The individual may work harder (his leisure decreases) and consume less, and from these changes he is worse off; at the same time he is better off because of his access to the public amenity. We summarize these changes in terms of their effect on the individual's welfare, or *utility*. If these changes

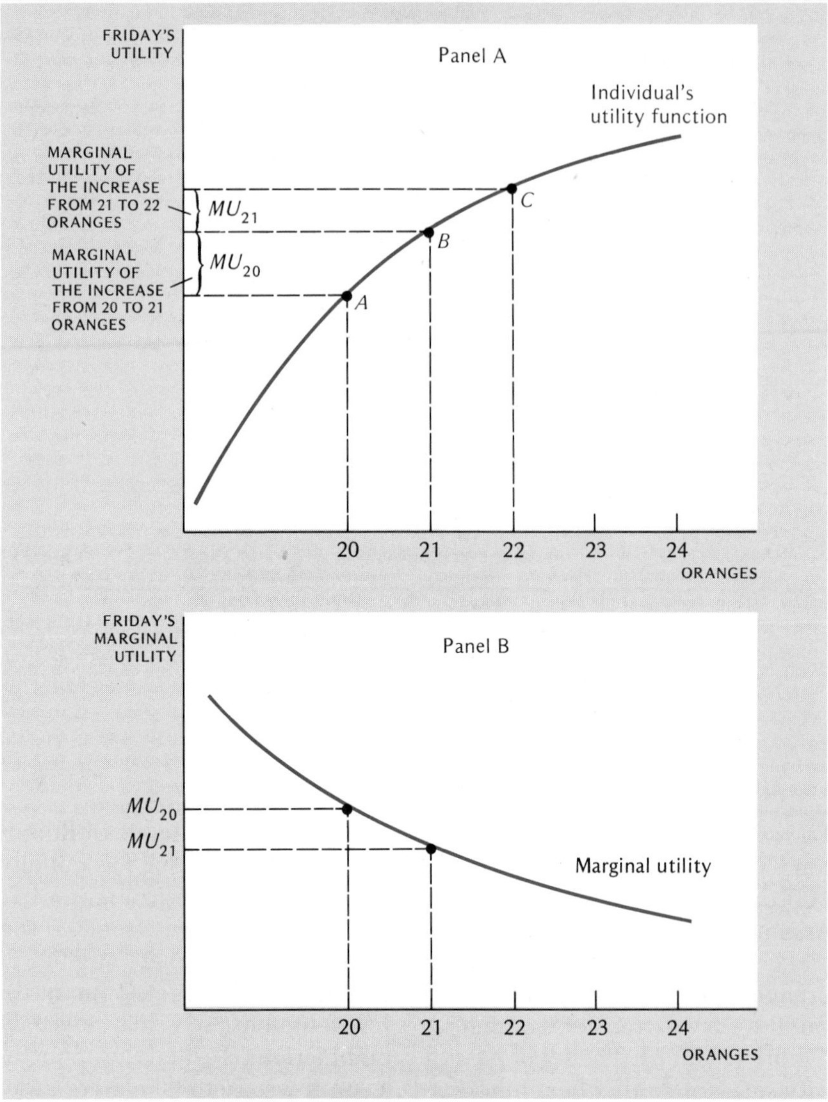

4.3 THE UTILITY FUNCTION AND MARGINAL UTILITY (A) *The utility function.* As we give Friday more oranges, his utility increases, but each additional orange gives him less extra utility. (B) *Marginal utility,* the extra utility he gets from an extra orange decreases as the number of oranges given to Friday increases, corresponding to the decreasing slope of the utility function.

make the individual better off, meaning that he prefers the new situation to the old, we say that his utility has increased.

Thus, as we give Friday more and more oranges, his utility increases. The relationship between the number of oranges and his level of utility we call the **utility function;** it is depicted in Figure 4.3A. The extra utility he gets from an extra orange we call his **marginal utility.** Thus, we have denoted the marginal utility from increasing Friday's oranges from 20 to 21 by MU_{20}, and we have denoted the marginal utility from an increase from 21 to 22 oranges by MU_{21}. In each case, the marginal utility is the *slope* of the utility functions. The slope is the ratio of the change in utility to the change in the number of oranges; more generally, as we mentioned in Chapter 3, the slope of a curve is calculated by dividing the change along the vertical axis by the change along the horizontal axis, when the size of the change along the horizontal axis is small.

Notice that the extra utility in going from 21 to 22 is less than the extra utility Friday receives in going from 20 to 21. This reflects the general principle of **diminishing marginal utility.** As an individual has more of anything it becomes, at the margin, less valuable; that is, the extra gain from having one extra unit of the good becomes smaller. Thus, the slope of the line *BC* is less than that of *AB*. We plot Friday's marginal utility at each level of consumption of oranges in Figure 4.3B.

(Economists are frequently concerned with the extra benefits from shifting one more unit of a resource into one use or into another; they are concerned, in other words, with the marginal benefits. The analysis of the consequences of shifting one unit of a resource from one use to another is referred to as **marginal analysis.**)

By the same token, as we take away oranges from Crusoe, his utility decreases; and as we take away more and more oranges, the extra utility he loses from each additional loss of an orange is increased.

As we transfer oranges from Crusoe to Friday, Friday's utility increases, and Crusoe's utility decreases. This can be depicted by a **utility possibilities schedule,** or **curve.** Recall from Figure 3.1 that the utility possibilities curve gives the maximum utility that one individual (or group of individuals) in the economy can attain, given the levels of utility that the others have. Figure 4.4 depicts the utility possibilities curve for our simple Crusoe-Friday economy.

This is a simple case. Government policy usually affects the utility not just of two individuals but of whole groups of individuals. Government programs are more complicated than simply transferring some oranges from one individual to another. But the utility possibilities curve still provides a good conceptual framework for analyzing government policy.

Pareto Efficiency and the Utility Possibilities Schedule

Consider the utility possibilities schedule shown in Figure 4.5. If resources are not efficiently allocated, the economy will be operating at a point such as *I*, below the utility possibilities schedule. Any change that leaves the economy at a point such as *I′* (above and to the right of *I*) is a Pareto improvement: both groups in society are better off. Any point along the utility possibilities schedule corresponds to a Pareto-efficient or Pareto-optimal resource allocation. No one can be made better off without someone else being made worse off.

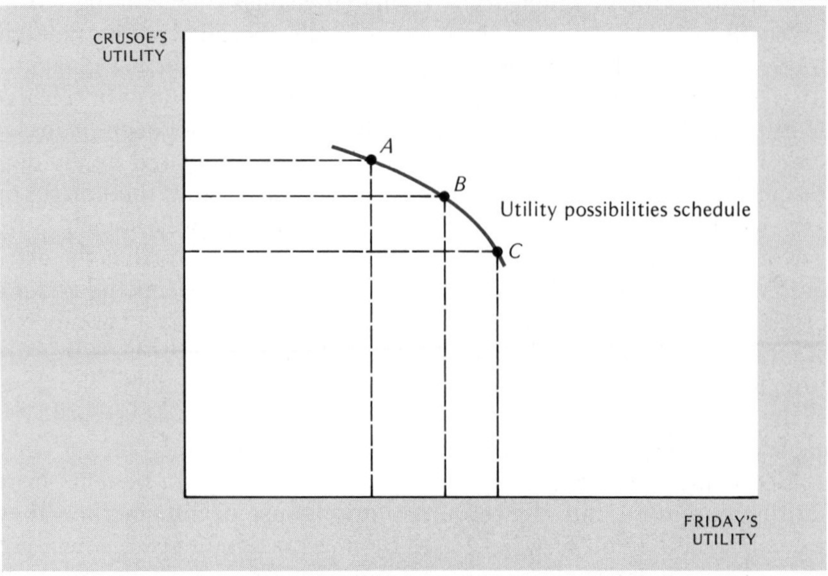

4.4 THE UTILITY POSSIBILITIES SCHEDULE FOR CRUSOE AND FRIDAY In the move from *A* to *B*, and then from *B* to *C*, we take away the same number of oranges from Crusoe. But with each successive transfer of an orange from Crusoe to Friday, the increment to Friday's utility becomes smaller, and the decrease in Crusoe's utility becomes larger. This is because (a) there is diminishing marginal utility, and (b) we have assumed that as government attempts to redistribute more oranges, a larger fraction of the oranges is lost.

Thus, the first question to ask in the evaluation of any public program is, does it represent a movement from an inefficient point, below the utility possibilities curve, to an efficient point, on (or at least closer to) the utility possibilities schedule? Or does it simply represent a movement along the utility possibilities schedule, entailing one individual (or group of individuals) being better off while another individual (or group of individuals) is worse off?

President Reagan seemed to believe that both the 1981 tax cut and the 1986 tax reform would be a movement like the one from *I* to *I′*. Higher-income individuals may have received proportionately larger reductions in their taxes; still he believed that the stimulating effect of the tax cut and tax reform would be so great that all individuals would benefit. On the other hand, the debate over whether current or future social security benefits should be decreased is largely a question of a movement along the utility possibilities schedule, such as the one from *A* to *B*; the trade-off is between the welfare of the current aged and the welfare of the future aged.

Unfortunately, the Pareto principle does not provide any criterion for ranking points, such as *A* and *B*, which lie along the utility possibilities curve. Thus it does not allow us to say whether *A* is preferable to *B* or *B* is

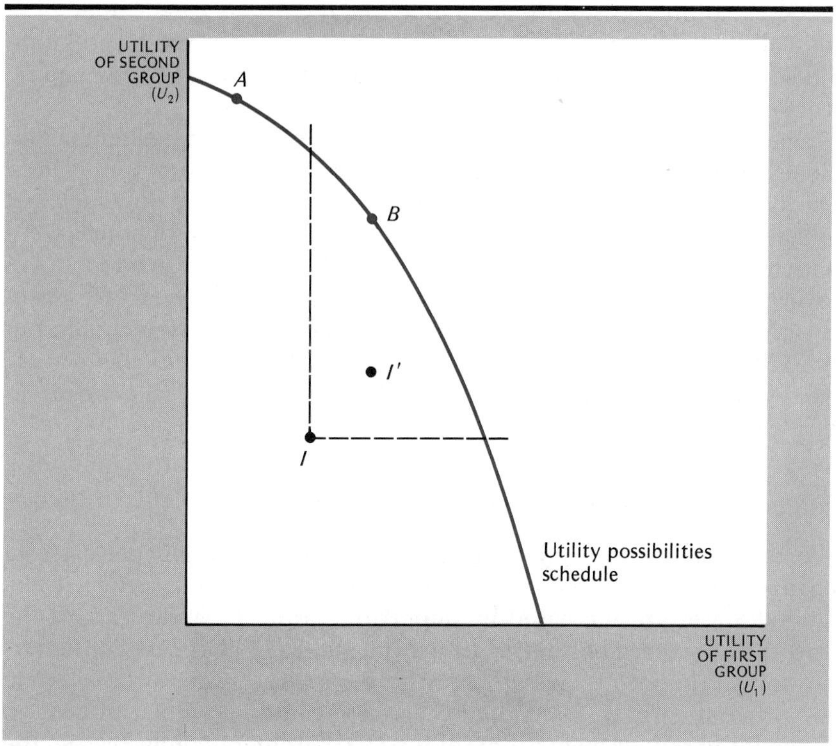

4.5 PARETO IMPROVEMENTS AND THE UTILITY POSSIBILITIES SCHEDULE
Any point on the utility possibilities schedule is Pareto efficient; no one can be made better off without making someone worse off. Movement from *I* to *I′* would be a Pareto improvement. Movement from *A* to *B* would be a movement along the utility possibilities schedule; both points would be Pareto efficient. Movement from *I* to *A* would be a movement from an inefficient point *(I)* to an efficient point *(A)*, but would not be a Pareto improvement, since individual 1 would be worse off.

preferable to *A*. It does not provide us with an answer to the question: Should current social security benefits be cut or future benefits be cut? Indeed, it does not even allow us to make statements concerning movements from points below the utility possibilities schedule, such as *I*, to points on the utility possibilities schedule that do not lie above and to the right of *I*. Thus, though *A* is Pareto efficient and *I* is not, the Pareto principle does not allow us to say whether *A* is preferable to *I* or conversely, whether *I* is preferable to *A*. If a point is not Pareto efficient, we know that there must exist some change that will make everyone better off, but that is all that we know.

Many inefficiencies pose precisely this problem. Consider the example concerning increasing the tolls at a bridge during rush hour to pay for additional toll collectors, which would facilitate the flow of traffic. The value of time saved far exceeds what we would have to pay the toll collectors. The arrangement with fewer toll collectors appears to be below the utility possibilities schedule. But if we increase the number of toll collectors, financing the increase by an increase in the toll, an individual for whom time is not valuable but for whom money is will be worse off.

One of the most famous historical examples of an improvement in efficiency that led many individuals to be worse off occurred in England.[2] During the Middle Ages, each village had common land on which any villager could graze his sheep and cattle. The fact that individuals were not charged for the use of the common land led to excessive utilization (overgrazing). The enclosure of these common lands over the seventeenth and eighteenth centuries led to an increase in productivity; but the villagers who lost the right to graze their cattle and sheep were worse off. The new equilibrium was on (or closer to) the utility possibilities schedule, but the change was not a Pareto improvement.

Pareto Efficiency and the Compensation Principle

We saw earlier that it is frequently possible to design packages of changes that lead to a Pareto improvement. Automobile prices in the United States are increased by import quotas on Japanese cars. If the government were considering lifting the quotas, it could ask consumers how much they would be willing to give up in return for a reduction in the price of cars. If the amount that they would be willing to give up exceeds the reduction in profits of the U.S. automobile industry and the incomes of U.S. autoworkers, then it would appear, in principle, that if we combined the lifting of the quotas with an appropriate tax on consumers we could design a Pareto improvement. We could compensate the automobile producers for the loss of the quota.[3]

In practice, the required compensations are seldom made. When a new highway is built, businesses along the old highway frequently decline, but the owners of the businesses are never compensated. (Occasionally, some attempt at partial compensation is made; those who live in the vicinity of an airport that is about to be constructed, and who find that the value of their property has thereby been reduced, may receive some compensation.)

There are those who believe that, nonetheless, the appropriate criterion for evaluating policies is whether the dollar value of the policy change to those who benefit from it exceeds the dollar value of the loss to those who are made worse off. In these circumstances, the gainers could, in principle, compensate the losers. This principle is referred to as the **compensation principle.** It makes the implicit assumption that a

[2] See G. Hardin, "The Tragedy of the Commons," *Science*, 1986, pp. 1243–47; and M. Weitzman and Jon S. Cohen, "A Mathematical Model of Enclosures," in J. Los and M. Los, *Mathematical Models in Economics* (London and Amsterdam: North Holland, 1974), pp. 419–31.

[3] Estimates by R. Crandall suggest that the Pareto improvement would be substantial. See Crandall, "Import Quotas and the Automobile Industry: The Costs of Protectionism," *Brookings Review*, Summer 1984, pp. 8–16.

dollar's worth of gain to one individual should be weighted the same as a dollar's worth of loss to another.

Critics of the compensation principle point out that if a policy has distributional consequences, these should be explicitly dealt with. One should attempt to quantify the magnitude of the gains and losses to each group; but there is not justification to weighting the gains of the winners equally with the losses of the losers.[4] Society may be more concerned about a decrease of $100 in the income of a poor individual than about a much larger decrease in the income of a rich individual.

The compensation principle tells us that Robinson Crusoe and Friday should not be asked to swap oranges unless, in the process, more oranges become available. In the earlier example, no movement from the original allocation, where Crusoe has 100 oranges and Friday 20 oranges, is desirable, since in the process of redistributing oranges some oranges are lost. On the other hand, any project that increased the total number of oranges would be desirable regardless of its distributional consequences. Thus, a change that increased Crusoe's oranges to 120 and decreased Friday's to 10 would be desirable according to the compensation principle. Since there are now more oranges, Crusoe could, in principle, compensate Friday for the change.

The compensations that would enable some policy change to be a Pareto improvement frequently are not made because it is often difficult to identify either the gainers and losers or the magnitudes of their gains and losses. Suppose, for instance, that we were considering building a new neighborhood park. The people in the neighborhood would be much better off if the park were built. Suppose further that you were the park commissioner, and, by supernatural insight, you knew the tastes of each individual. When you calculated how much better off each would be as a result of the park, you found that the total dollar value of the park (what they would be willing to pay) would be greater than the cost of the park. Some individuals, of course, would value the park much more than others. If you imposed a charge on each individual in accordance with how he would benefit from the park, the park would be a Pareto improvement. By way of comparison, suppose that you cannot distinguish those who would benefit a lot from the park from those who would benefit only slightly (though you still know how much they would value the park in the aggregate). If you imposed a uniform tax on all the houses in the neighborhood to finance the park, the construction of the park would not be a Pareto improvement: there would be some households whose benefits would be less than the tax they would have to pay. Limitations on the information that is available provide an important set of

[4] There are further objections to the compensation principle. There are circumstances in which, if some new policy is instituted, the gainers can more than compensate the losers; but once in the new situation, if the government contemplated a movement back to the original situation, those who gain in returning to the original situation can more than compensate the losers. Thus the compensation principle does not allow us to rank the two situations unambiguously. For an example and further discussion, see R. Layard and A. Walters, *Microeconomic Theory* (New York: McGraw-Hill, 1978), pp. 34–35.

constraints on the kinds of redistribution and compensation schemes that are possible.

The Social Indifference Curve and Income Distribution

The Pareto principle does not, as we have said, allow us to make comparisons between situations where some individuals are better off while others are worse off. Such changes involve questions of income distribution. How do we weight the gains of the winners against the losses of the losers?

As we saw in Chapter 3, the basic tool economists employ when analyzing trade-offs is the indifference curve. Consider an individual making choices between packages containing different combinations of apples and oranges. The individual prefers packages with both more apples and more oranges. He will be indifferent between two packages, one of which has fewer apples than the other, provided it has sufficiently more oranges. Those combinations of apples and oranges among which the individual is indifferent are plotted in Figure 4.6 and trace out his indifference curve. This can be put in a slightly different way. Indifference curves trace out the variety of packages that offer an individual equal levels of utility. The individual has a whole family of indifference curves relating to different levels of utility; in Figure 4.6, for instance, we see all those combinations of apples and oranges that give him the same level of utility as 100 apples and 100 oranges, the curve labeled U_1. We also see all those combinations of apples and oranges that make the individual indifferent to having 200 apples and 200 oranges, labeled U_2.

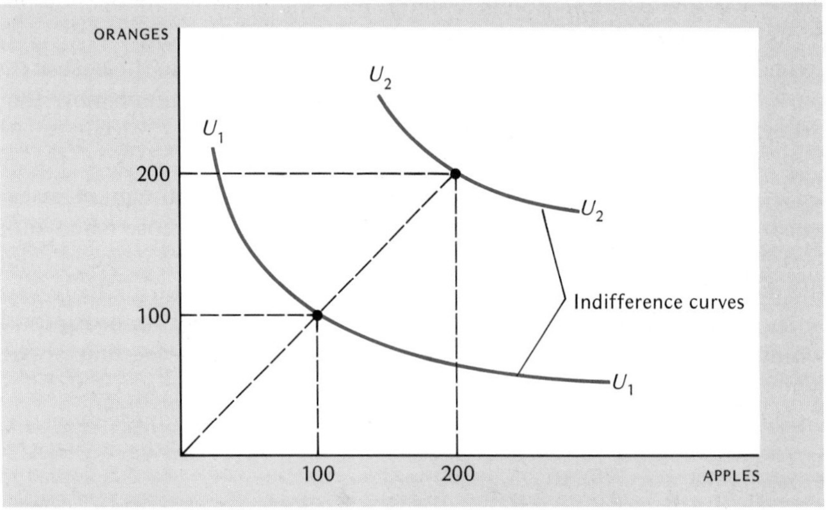

4.6 INDIVIDUAL INDIFFERENCE CURVE An indifference curve gives those combinations of goods among which an individual is indifferent. The individual prefers any point on the U_2 indifference curve to any point on U_1.

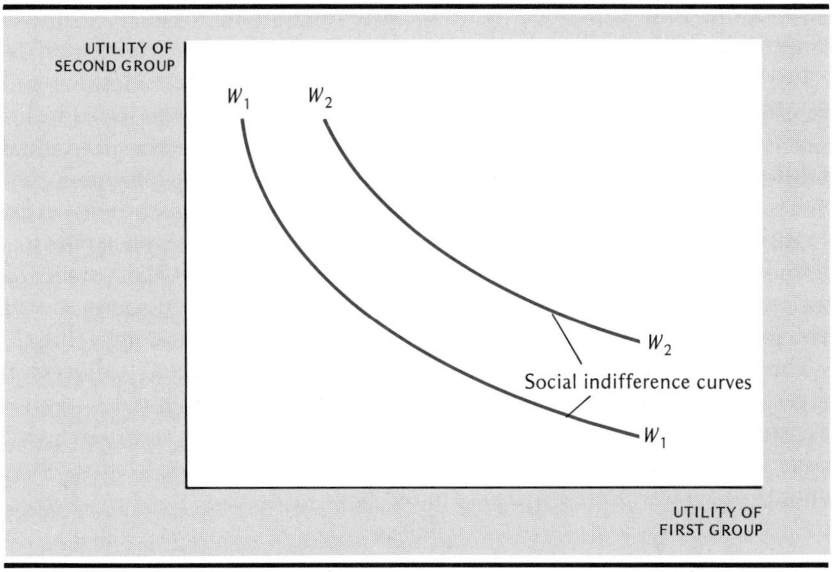

4.7 SOCIAL INDIFFERENCE CURVES A social indifference curve gives those combinations of utilities of group 1 and group 2 among which society is indifferent. Society is willing to trade off some decrease in one group's utility for an increase in another's. Points on the social indifference curve labeled W_2 yield a higher level of social welfare than do points on the social indifference curve labeled W_1.

Clearly utility is higher on the second indifference curve than on the first. The more apples and oranges, the higher the level of utility.[5] For most purposes, we do not need to know by how much utility increases. Indifference curve analysis allows us to ignore the issue of the measurement of utility. All that maters is that if an individual is on a higher indifference curve, his level of utility is higher.

By analogy to the individual's utility function and the individual's indifference curve, we can define the social welfare function and the social indifference curve. Just as individuals derive utility from the goods they consume, so society derives its welfare from the utility received by its citizens. The **social indifference curve** gives those combinations of utilities of different individuals among which society is indifferent. Social indifference curves provide a convenient way of thinking about the kinds of trade-offs society often faces in which one group is made better off and another worse off.

Obviously, society is better off if everyone is better off—this corresponds to the Pareto principle. Thus, in Figure 4.7, all combinations of the utility of Group 1 and Group 2 that are on the social indifference

[5] We represent the utility function mathematically by

$$U=U(c_1,c_2, \ldots),$$

where c_1 is his consumption of the first commodity, c_2 his consumption of the second commodity, etc.

curve labeled W_2 yield a higher level of social welfare than do those combinations on the curve labeled W_1.

Just as there is a simple relationship between utility functions and indifference curves, there is a simple relationship between social indifference curves and social welfare functions. Recall that the individual indifference curve is defined as the set of combinations of goods that yield equal levels of utility to the individual—for which, in other words, the utility function has the same value. The **social indifference curve** is defined as the set of combinations of utility of different individuals or groups of individuals that yield equal levels of welfare to society—for which, in other words, the social welfare function has the same value.

The **social welfare function** provides a basis for ranking any allocation of resources, unlike the Pareto principle, in which we can only say that one situation is better than another if everyone is at least as well off, and someone is better off. The problem, as we shall see, is how to determine what the social welfare function should be.

SOCIAL CHOICES

We have now developed the basic tools with which we can describe conceptually how social choices can be made. First, we identify the **opportunity set,** the set of alternatives that are available to society. We characterize these by the levels of utility that will be obtained by different individuals under the various options that are available. Thus, in Figure 4.8, the initial situation is depicted as point *A*, and alternative projects may move us to points *B*, *C*, *D*, or *E*. Each point describes the utility levels of Robinson Crusoe and Friday. This way of characterizing the options makes clear the trade-offs. After first eliminating the Pareto-inefficient options *(D* and *E)*, that is, the options for which there are alternatives in which at least one person is better off and no one is worse off, we then examine the trade-offs: as we move from *A* to *B* to *C*, Friday becomes better off, while Robinson Crusoe becomes worse off. The question, then, is how do we evaluate these trade-offs?

This is where we make use of social indifference curves. We wish to get to the highest social indifference curve among the options that are available. It is clear in Figure 4.8A that point *B* represents the best option. In moving from *B* to *C*, society's valuation of the losses to Robinson Crusoe exceeds that of the gains to Friday, and such a move is not desirable. On the other hand, the gain to Friday in moving from *A* to *B* is valued more by society than the loss to Crusoe in that move, and hence *B* is preferred to *A* (or *C*).

Obviously, with different social indifference curves, a different option might be preferable. If society has a strong preference for equality, its social indifference curves might look like those in Figure 4.8B, in which case option *C* is preferable.

Social indifference curves thus provide us with a convenient way of conceptualizing social choices.

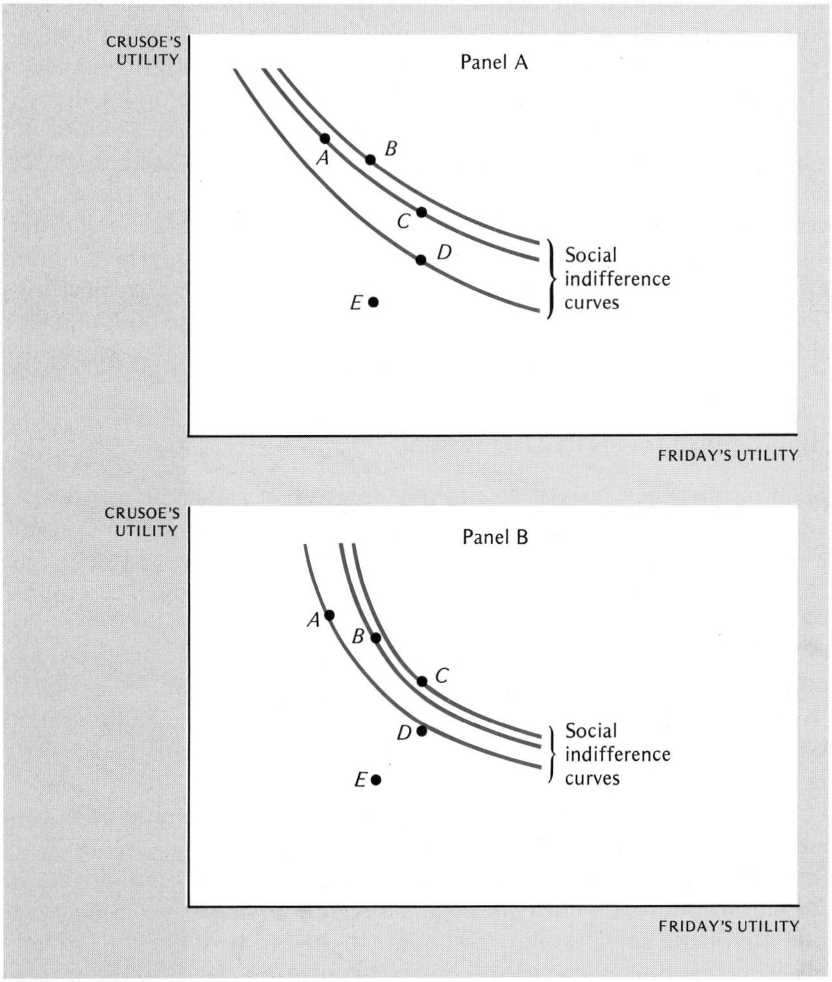

4.8 ALTERNATIVE ASSUMPTIONS ABOUT SOCIAL CHOICE With the social indifference curves shown in Panel A, point *B* is the best option. It lies on the highest social indifference curve. With the social indifference curves shown in Panel B, point *C* is the best option.

Social Choices in Practice

In practice, government officials do not derive utility possibilities schedules, nor do they write down social welfare functions. But they do attempt to identify the effects of government programs on different groups in the population. The impacts are often summarized in terms of their effects on efficiency and equality. The process may be characterized much as we have done it here: the opportunity set is identified, and the trade-offs between efficiency and equality are analyzed; some balancing of the two occurs, which might be reflected in a social indifference curve, now depicting society's attitudes toward equality and efficiency. In some cases, this social indifference curve may be derived from the more basic social indifference curves, representing society's attitudes toward the welfare of different individuals.

We shall encounter numerous examples where choices between equality and efficiency have to be made. For instance, in general, the more effective a tax system is in redistributing income, the greater the inefficiencies it introduces. There is a trade-off between equality and efficiency. There are, of course, important instances of poorly designed tax systems; such tax systems put the economy below its utility possibilities schedule. In such cases, it may be possible to increase both equality and efficiency.

Utilitarianism versus Rawlsianism

Social indifference curves do nothing more than reflect society's attitudes. Thus, a society that was very concerned with equality might not care that Crusoe has to give up 70 oranges for Friday to get 1 orange. So long as Friday was poorer than Crusoe, any sacrifice on the part of Crusoe that makes Friday better off is justified.

On the other hand, a society might care only about efficiency and not at all about equality. Then, of course, no redistribution of oranges from Crusoe to Friday would be justified if, in the process, a single orange were lost. These views have been widely discussed among economists and philosophers.

One of the oldest views holds that society's welfare should be represented simply as the sum of the utilities of different individuals. This view is called **utilitarianism** and was set forth by Jeremy Bentham in the first half of the nineteenth century. Thus, in our simple economy with two individuals, social welfare is the sum of the utility of the two individuals. This function can be expressed in the form

$$W=U_1+U_2.$$

This criterion has the strong implication that society should be willing to give up a little utility of a poor individual for an equal gain in the utility of a rich individual. The trade-off that society is willing to make between the two individuals does not depend on the level of utility of either of the two individuals. That is why the social indifference curve is a straight line (with slope equal to minus one—that is, society is willing to give up one unit of Individual 1's utility for a gain of one unit of Individual 2's utility), as depicted in Figure 4.9A. (Moreover, the trade-off between any two groups or individuals does not depend on the incomes of other individuals in society.)

It is important to emphasize that with a utilitarian social welfare function, society is *not* indifferent to an increase of one orange (or one dollar of income) for Individual 1 and a decrease of one orange (or one dollar of

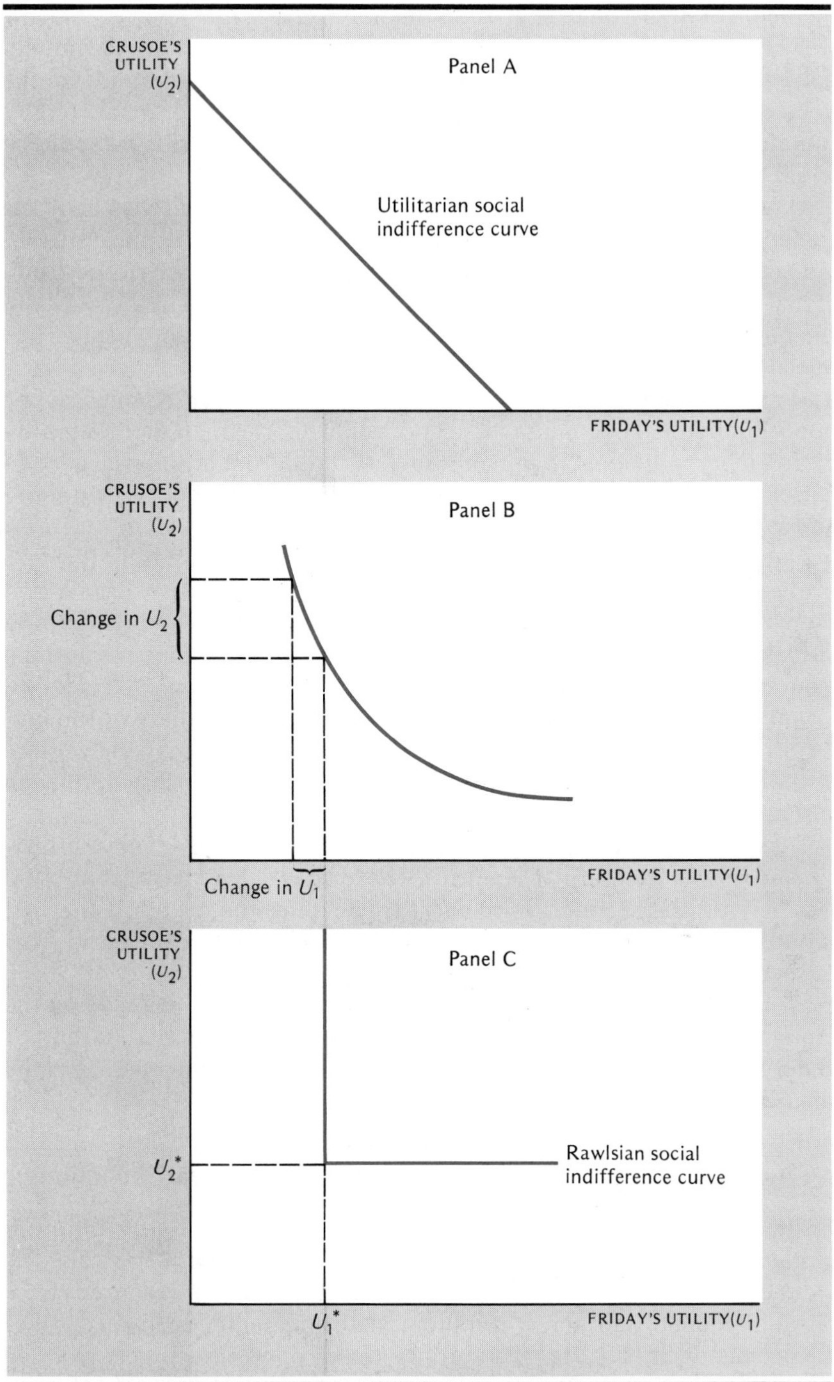

4.9 ALTERNATIVE SHAPES OF SOCIAL INDIFFERENCE CURVES (A) A utilitarian is willing to give up some utility for Crusoe so long as Friday gains at least an equal amount of utility. The social indifference curves are straight lines. (B) Some argue that society requires more than an equal increase in the utility (U_2) of a rich individual to compensate for a decrease in the utility (U_1) of a poor individual. (C) Rawls maintains that no amount of increase in the welfare of the rich can compensate for a decrease in the welfare of the poor. This implies that the social indifference curves are L-shaped.

income) for Individual 2. If Individual 1 has a lower level of income (fewer oranges) than Individual 2, then the increase in utility of Individual 1 from one more orange (one more dollar) will be greater than the decrease in utility for Individual 2. What the utilitarian social welfare function says is that an increase in the *utility* of any individual should be weighted equally.

Many would argue that when one individual is worse off than another, society is not indifferent to a decrease in the utility of the poorer (Individual 1) matched by an equal increase in the utility of the richer (Individual 2). Society should be willing to accept a decrease in the utility of the poor only if there is a much larger increase in the utility of the rich. Social indifference curves reflecting those values are drawn in Figure 4.9B, where they appear not as straight lines but as curved ones; as the poorer individual becomes worse and worse off, the increment in utility of the richer individual that makes society indifferent must be larger and larger (i.e., the slope of the social indifference curve becomes steeper and steeper).

The extreme position of this debate has been taken by John Rawls, a professor of philosophy at Harvard University.[6] **Rawlsianism** argues that the welfare of society only depends on the welfare of the worst-off individual; society is better off if you improve his welfare but gains nothing from improving the welfare of others. There is, in his view, no trade-off. To put it another way, no amount of increase in the welfare of the better-off individual could compensate society for a decrease in the welfare of the worst-off individual. Diagrammatically, this is represented by an L-shaped social indifference curve, as in Figure 4.9C.

Consider a society in which Group 1 has a particular level of utility, U_1^*, and Group 2 has utility level U_2^*, where U_2^* is at least as great as U_1^*. If we increase the second group's utility, keeping the utility of the first group unchanged, we remain on the same social indifference curve; that is, society is no better off. It is not willing to give up any utility of Group 1 for any gain in utility for Group 2. If both groups initially have the same utility level, society's welfare increases only when both Groups 1 and 2 have their welfare increased; and the increase is only equal to the smallest increase on the part of any group.

A Comparison of Utilitarian and Rawlsian Social Welfare Functions

Utilitarian and Rawlsian social welfare functions have very different implications. Since under utilitarianism, an increase in utility by all individuals is valued the same, if we could costlessly transfer resources from one individual to another, we would wish to equate their marginal utility of income. That is, if the extra utility that a poor person gets from an extra dollar of income (his marginal utility) exceeds the loss in utility to

[6] John Rawls, *A Theory of Justice* (Cambridge, MA: Harvard University Press, 1971).

the rich person of losing a dollar (his marginal utility), then total social welfare (the sum of the utilities) will increase by transferring the dollar. If it costs something to transfer resources from the rich to the poor, we stop short of this. On the other hand, with a Rawlsian social welfare function, we continue transferring resources from the rich to the poor so long as we can in the process make the poor better off; we pay no attention to the costs imposed on the rich.

In terms of our earlier example involving transferring oranges from Crusoe to Friday, a Rawlsian would continue to take away oranges so long as Friday gets more oranges. A utilitarian would not go that far. An extreme egalitarian might argue that we should continue to take away oranges from Crusoe so long as Crusoe has more oranges than Friday, whether or not Friday gets more oranges in the process.[7]

As another example of the contrasting implications, consider the treatment of an individual who has lost his leg. Assume that he can be fitted with an artificial leg, and that with the artificial leg he is able to do virtually anything a person with a normal leg can do. Hence, the accident (once the leg is "repaired") leaves his marginal utility of income unchanged, although his total utility at each level of income is reduced. Then a utilitarian would say that society should give the person who has lost his leg a new leg; but having done that, it should give him the same level of income as someone with a natural leg, so that the marginal utility of income is the same for individuals with and without natural legs. A Rawlsian would argue that we should give him enough extra income that the individual would be indifferent between keeping his natural leg and losing his leg, getting a new one, and receiving compensation. The Rawlsian is not concerned with equating marginal utilities but with maximizing the welfare of the worst-off individual (here, the individual who has lost his leg).

Another way of seeing the difference in the implications is the following. Suppose we could either give $1 to someone with an income of $10,000 or $1.05 to someone with an income of $20,000. Which should we do? Assume that all individuals have the same utility function. A Rawlsian has a simple answer: Give it to the individual with the lower income. A utilitarian would ask: Is $1 to the person with an income of $10,000 worth more than $1.05 to the person with an income of $20,000? Because of diminishing marginal utility, it is likely he would give $1 to the individual with $10,000. But now assume we had a choice between $1 to the person with an income of $10,000 and $1 million to the person with $20,000. The Rawlsian answer remains unchanged. In other words, the Rawlsian criterion makes no trade-offs. The utilitarian criterion does. It says that if there is a sufficiently large offsetting gain to those who are already better off, it is worth making them still better off.

[7] The contrasting implications of these three positions can be seen in Figure 4.8. *C* would be chosen by the Rawlsian, since at *C* Friday's welfare is maximized. A utilitarian will choose the point where the sum of the utilities is maximized. An extreme egalitarian might choose *E*, even though both Crusoe and Friday are worse off at *E* than at *C*.

Rawls and Egalitarianism

Rawls's position is not, however, the most egalitarian position taken. There may be changes that make the worst-off person in society a little better off, the richer individuals much better off. By most measures, inequality has increased. Yet Rawls—like a utilitarian—would say such a change is desirable because the poorest individual—the only one he cares about—is better off, while some strong egalitarians would say that such a change is undesirable, since it increases inequality. Similarly, a change that makes the worst-off person worse off would be opposed by Rawls, regardless of what it does to measured inequality. Thus Rawls would oppose a tax increase on the rich if it results in their working less hard, reducing the government's revenue, and thus reducing what it could distribute to the poor, regardless of the effect of this tax increase on inequality.

ASSESSING POLICY ALTERNATIVES

Since many policy changes entail one group's being better off at the expense of some other group, we need to ask how much of a decrease in the welfare of one group we are willing to trade for an increase in the welfare of another group. This is precisely the kind of question that social indifference curves are concerned with, for they provide a convenient way of thinking about the trade-offs facing society.

Deriving Social Welfare Functions

It is possible, of course, for one person to announce what trade-offs he thinks are appropriate, and for another to announce that he thinks a different set of trade-offs is appropriate. We often talk, however, as if there is a social indifference curve for society or for the government. Does this simply refer to the preferences and attitudes of the person in the position of making the relevant decision, or can the social indifference curve be derived from the attitudes and preferences of the citizens making up our society? Unfortunately, whenever there is no unanimity—and there seldom is unanimity on questions of distribution—there is no generally accepted way of "adding together" the preferences of the different individuals in society to arrive at a social welfare function.

Recently, some philosophers and economists have attempted to use an extension of the **contract theory of the state,** or social contract theory, to support their view of the appropriate social welfare function. Social contract theory (originally developed more than 200 years ago by the French philosopher Jean Jacques Rousseau) says that one should view the state as if individuals voluntarily got together for their mutual interest; they sign a "contract" assigning certain rights and powers to the state, in return for which the state provides certain services that, without the state, they could not obtain, or could obtain only at much greater cost. Thus in this view, an "acceptable" tax program must be such that the individual is better off than he would have been in the absence of government. When examined in detail, however, the theory provides little guidance to policy. If one imagines a society with no public roads, no public education, no laws, no police force—no governmentally provided goods of any kind—it is likely that all individuals would be worse off in an individualistic world with no taxes and no state than they are under the present system.

Rawls argues that to arrive at a set of principles for deriving social welfare functions, one must abstract oneself from the selfish interests that would predominate if one knew into what position one were to be born. Thus an individual should arrive at a view of what is "fair" before she knows what her position in society will be. The individual should ask herself, "What would I view as fair behind a **veil of ignorance** where I didn't know whether I would be the daughter of Rockefeller or of a poor woman?" The central point in imagining choices behind the **veil of ignorance** is that one is removing the effects of personal advantages from the analysis. Rawls claims that all individuals would, in that situation, wish society to follow the principle of maximizing the welfare of the worst-off individual, and they would not be willing to make any trade-offs—any changes that would lower the welfare of the worst-off individual would be rejected, no matter how much others might gain.

John Harsanyi of the University of California offers a similar argument for using a utilitarian social welfare function. Behind the veil of ignorance individuals may be thought of as facing a risk, a chance of being a high-income individual and a chance of being a low-income individual. The question of how individuals behave when facing risky situations has been studied extensively; under quite plausible (but still not universally accepted) assumptions, individuals maximize their average utility. If individuals, in choosing among different income distributions (social programs), behave in the same way (behind the veil of ignorance) as they would in choosing among different risks, then it can be shown that social welfare can be evaluated using the utilitarian criterion. Utilitarianism can thus be derived from more basic premises.

INTERPERSONAL COMPARISONS

While many economists object to the social welfare function because there is no persuasive case for arguing that the social welfare function should take on one form (utilitarianism) or another (Rawlsianism), other economists object to the use of social welfare functions on a different basis. Their objection can be seen most clearly in the case of utilitarian social welfare functions, but it holds more generally. With a utilitarian social welfare function, we add up the utility of the different members of society. Because we add Crusoe's and Friday's utility together, we are, in effect, assuming that somehow we can compare *in a meaningful numerical way* their level of utility.

To make **interpersonal utility comparisons,** as a practical matter, however, one must not only assume that utility comparisons are possible but also hypothesize that all individuals have roughly the same utility function. That is, we must postulate that the marginal utility of an extra dollar given to an individual depends only on his income, and that the marginal utility of a dollar given to a richer individual is lower than that given to a poorer individual.

Many economists believe that interpersonal utility comparisons are not meaningful. I may claim that although I have a much higher income than my brother, I am unhappier; not only that, I may claim that I know how to spend income so much better that the extra increment in my utility from a dollar given to me is much greater than the extra increment in utility that he would get from receiving an extra dollar. How could one prove that I was wrong (or right). Because there is no meaningful way of answering the question of whether the increase in utility I get from an extra dollar is more or less than that of my brother, economists argue that there can be no scientific basis for making welfare comparisons.

Moreover, some economists who believe that it may be possible to make interpersonal utility comparisons find the hypothesis that all individuals have approximately the same utility functions unconvincing. Why should we believe that rich individuals get less utility out of an extra dollar than do poor individuals? In fact, some economists have argued that it is reasonable to assume that individuals who have the ability to earn higher incomes (that is, are more productive in translating their labor into wages) also have a higher ability to consume (are more productive in translating their goods into utility).

Since there is no "scientific" basis for making such welfare comparisons, many economists believe that economists should limit themselves to describing the consequences of different policies, pointing out who are the gainers and who are the losers; but that should be the end of their analysis. These economists believe that the only circumstances in which economists should make welfare judgments is when the policy change is a Pareto improvement. Unfortunately, as we have said, few policy changes are Pareto improvements, and hence without making interpersonal comparisons of welfare, economists have little to say.

One can, however, view social welfare functions as providing a convenient way of summarizing the data concerning the effects of a policy change. A concern for equality implies valuing a dollar given to the poor more than a dollar given to the rich. Social welfare functions simply provide a systematic way of evaluating increments in income to individuals at different income levels.

Measuring Inefficiency

In assessing alternative policies, economists have put particular emphasis on economic efficiency. Taxes are criticized for discouraging work effort, monopolies for restricting production and driving up prices. To measure the dollar value of an inefficiency, economists ask: "How much would an individual be willing to give up to have the inefficiency eliminated?" Consider the inefficiency caused by a tax on cigarettes. We ask each individual: How much would he be willing to pay to have the tax on cigarettes eliminated? Say his answer is $100. Thus, eliminating the cigarette tax and imposing in its place a $100 **lump-sum tax** (that is, a tax that the individual would have to pay, regardless of what he did) leaves his welfare unchanged. The difference between the revenue raised by the cigarette tax (say $80) and the lump-sum tax that the individual would be willing to pay is called the **deadweight loss** of the tax. It is the measure of the inefficiency of the tax. Taxes, other than lump-sum taxes, give rise to a deadweight loss because they cause individuals to forego more-preferred consumption in favor of less-preferred consumption in order to avoid payments of the tax. Thus, a tax that raises no government revenue—because individuals completely avoid purchasing the taxed commodity—can have a substantial excess burden.

We can calculate the deadweight loss using compensated demand curves. An ordinary demand curve gives the level of demand for a commodity, say cigarettes, at each price of cigarettes. It shows how demand falls as price increases. Demand normally falls for two reasons. First, at higher prices, individuals substitute other goods (such as alcohol) for cigarettes. Secondly, at higher prices, individuals are worse off, and because they are worse off, they may wish to consume less. A **compensated demand curve** gives the demand for a commodity under the assumption that as its price rises, the individual is given sufficient additional income that his level of utility remains unchanged. If when the individual is given more income (compensated for the price increase), his demand for the commodity is unchanged, then the compensated and ordinary demand curves will exactly coincide. If the individual spends relatively little on the good under consideration, the increase in income required to compensate him for any increase in the price will be small, and hence the compensated and ordinary demand curves will not differ by very much.

Assume the cost of producing a cigarette is c_0, and the tax raises the price from c_0 to $c_0 + t$, where t is the tax per pack. We assume the individual consumes q_0 packs of cigarettes with the tax, and q_1 after the tax has been removed (but replaced by a lump-sum tax that leaves him no better or no worse off than when there was a cigarette tax). We have drawn the compensated demand curve in Figure 4.10. The deadweight loss is measured by the shaded area *ABC*, the area under the compensated demand schedule and above c_0, between the output with and without the tax.

The triangle *ABC* is sometimes called a **Harberger triangle,**[8] in honor of Chicago economist Arnold Harberger, who used such triangles not

[8] See for instance, A. Harberger, "Taxation, Resource Allocation and Welfare," in *The Role of Direct and Indirect Taxes in the Federal Revenue System*, ed. J. Due (Princeton, NJ: Princeton University Press, 1964), reprinted in A. Harberger, *Taxation and Welfare* (Chicago: University of Chicago Press, 1974).

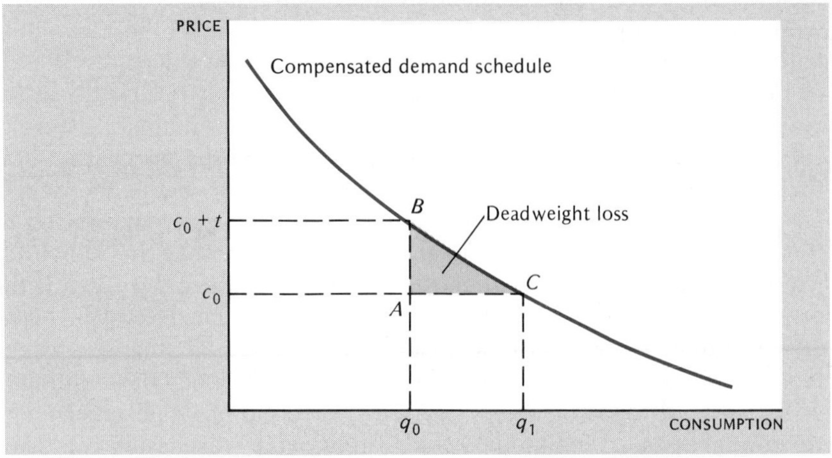

4.10 MEASURING INEFFICIENCIES The area *ABC* measures the deadweight loss, the efficiency loss as a result of a cigarette tax. A lump-sum tax that would have the same effect on the individual's welfare as the cigarette tax would raise an additional revenue of *ABC*.

only to measure the inefficiencies associated with distortionary taxation but also to measure other inefficiencies, such as those associated with monopoly. Why does the Harberger triangle provide a measure of deadweight loss? The price tells us the value of the last unit consumed; that is, at q_0, the individual is willing to trade off $\$p_0 = c_0 + t$ units of "income" (with which he could have purchased other goods) for one more pack of cigarettes. Of course, when the individual has $q_0 + 1$ packs of cigarettes, he will value an additional pack of cigarettes less than when he has q_0 packs, and so the price he is willing to pay will fall.

Assume that initially consumption is 100 packs, and consumption increases by 10 packs when the tax is removed; the tax is 10 cents, and the cost of production is $1.00 per pack. (Tax revenue is 100 packs times 10 cents per pack, or $10.) The individual is willing to pay $1.10 for the first additional pack, $1.09 for the second, $1.08 for the third, etc. If the tax were eliminated, and the price fell to c_0, the cost of production ($1.00 a pack), the total amount that the individual would be willing to pay would be 10 cents times 100 packs = $10 (the amount he saves on the first 100 packs he has purchased, which is equal to the tax revenue); plus 10 cents for the 101st pack (the difference between how much he values the 101st pack and what he must pay), 9 cents for the 102nd pack, etc. Remember, we are calculating how much *more* he would be willing to pay beyond the $1.00 that he will have to pay for each pack. The total he would be willing to pay is thus $10.50. Since the tax raised a revenue of $10, the deadweight loss is 50 cents. This is, of course, just the area under the compensated demand curve and above c_0, between q_0 and q_1.

Making Policy Decisions

The central theme of this chapter has been that most policy decisions entail considerations of both equity (distribution) and economic efficiency; and they often entail a balancing of the two. Few policy changes are Pareto improvements; most entail at least the possibility that some individuals will be worse off. Welfare economics has been useful in providing a framework within which the central issues of equity and efficiency can be systematically discussed. Many of the tools that welfare economists use, such as social welfare functions and the Harberger triangle measurement of deadweight loss, are not without their problems. Still, these tools are a useful way of summarizing and evaluating the effects of alternative policies on efficiency and equity, so long as they are used carefully, with an understanding of their limitations.

SUMMARY

1. Welfare economics—or normative economics—is concerned with criteria for evaluating alternative economic policies. In general, it takes into account both efficiency *and* equity.
2. The Pareto principle is based on individualistic values. It says that changes constituting Pareto improvements should be adopted regardless of what they do to any measure of inequality.
3. The principle of consumer sovereignty holds that individuals are the best judges of their own needs and pleasures.
4. The compensation principle provides one criterion for policy decisions in situations where policy changes make some individuals better off and others worse off, and hence are not Pareto improvements.
5. The social welfare function provides a framework within which the distributional consequences of a policy may be analyzed. It specifies the increase in utility of one individual that is required to compensate for a decrease in utility of another.
6. In the utilitarian social welfare function, social welfare is equal to the sum of the utilities of the individuals in society.
7. In the Rawlsian social welfare function, social welfare is equal to the utility of the worst-off individual in society.
8. The deadweight loss of a tax is a measure of the inefficiency of the tax.
9. As a practical matter, in evaluating alternative proposals we do not, in general, detail the impact each proposal has on each individual in society, but we summarize its effects by describing the impact of the proposal on some measure of inequality (or the impact on some well-identified groups) and describing the efficiency gains or losses. Alternative proposals often present trade-offs between efficiency and distribution; to get more equality one has to give up some efficiency. Differences in views arise concerning the nature of the trade-offs (how much efficiency one needs to give up to get some increase in equality), and values (how much efficiency one should be willing to give up, at the margin, to get some increase in equality).

KEY CONCEPTS

Welfare economics
Trade-offs
Poverty Index
Pareto principle
Consumer sovereignty
Utility functions
Opportunity set
Marginal utility
Diminishing marginal utility
Compensation principle
Social welfare function
Social indifference curves
Utilitarianism
Rawlsianism
Interpersonal utility comparisons
Contract theory of the state
Veil of ignorance
Rawlsian social welfare function
Deadweight loss

QUESTIONS AND PROBLEMS

1. Assume that Friday and Crusoe have identical utility functions described by the following table.

UTILITY FUNCTIONS FOR FRIDAY AND CRUSOE

Number of Oranges	*Utility*	*Marginal Utility*
1	11	
2	21	
3	30	
4	38	
5	45	
6	48	
7	50	
8	51	

Draw the utility function. Fill in the marginal utility data in the table above, and draw the marginal utility function.

2. Assume that there are 8 oranges to be divided between Friday and Crusoe. Take a utilitarian view—assume that social welfare is the sum of the utility of the two individuals. Using the data from Problem 1, what is the social welfare corresponding to each possible allocation of oranges? What allocation maximizes social welfare? Show that it has the property that the marginal utility of an extra orange given to each individual is the same.
3. Now take a Rawlsian view and assume that the social welfare function is the level of utility of the individual with the lowest utility level. Using the data from Problem 1, and again assuming there are 8 oranges, what is the social welfare associated with each allocation of oranges? What allocation maximizes social welfare?
4. Draw the utility possibilities schedule based on the data from Problem 1. Mark the points that maximize social welfare under the two alternative criteria from Problems 2 and 3.
5. Assume that Crusoe's and Friday's utility functions are described in Problem 1. But assume now that initially Crusoe has 6 oranges and Friday 2. Assume that for every 2 oranges taken away from Crusoe, Friday gets only 1, an orange being lost in the process. What does the utility possibilities schedule look like now? Which of the feasible allocations maximizes social

welfare with a utilitarian social welfare function? With a Rawlsian social welfare function?

6. An individual is indifferent among the combinations of public and private goods shown in the following table.

Combination	*Public Goods*	*Private Goods*
A	1	16
B	2	11
C	3	7
D	4	4
E	5	3
F	6	2

Draw the individual's indifference curve. Assuming that the economy can produce 1 unit of public goods and 10 units of private goods, but that it can produce 1 more unit of public goods by reducing its production of private goods by 2 units, draw the production possibilities schedule. What is the maximum production of private goods? The maximum production of public goods? Can it produce 5 units of public goods and 1 unit of private goods? Which of the feasible combinations maximizes utility?

7. Consider an accident like the one cited in the chapter, where an individual loses his leg. Assume that it lowers his utility at each level of income but increases his marginal utility (at each level of income) though only slightly. Show diagrammatically the utility functions before and after the accident. Assume that whether the accident does or does not occur is beyond the control of the individual. Show that if you were a utilitarian, you would give more income to the individual with the accident, but that the level of the individual with the accident would still be lower than that of the individual who did not have the accident. Show the compensation that a Rawlsian would provide.

   Is it possible for a utilitarian to give more to the individual who had experienced the accident than a Rawlsian?

   Under what circumstances would a utilitarian give nothing to an individual who had experienced an accident?

8. For each of the following policy changes, explain why the change is likely or not likely to be a Pareto improvement:
   a) Building a park, financed by an increase in the local property tax rate.
   b) Building a park, financed by the donation of a rich philanthropist; the city acquires the land by exercising the right of eminent domain.[9]
   c) Increasing medical facilities for lung cancer, financed out of general revenues.
   d) Increasing medical care facilities for lung cancer, financed out of an increase in the cigarette tax.
   e) Replacing the system of agricultural price supports with a system of income supplements for poor farmers.
   f) Protecting the automobile industry from cheap foreign imports by imposing quotas on the importation of foreign cars.

[9] The right of eminent domain gives public authorities the right to take property, with compensation, for public uses.

g) Increasing social security benefits, financed by an increase in the payroll tax.
h) Replacing the primary reliance at the local level on the property tax with state revenues obtained from an income tax.
i) Eliminating rent control laws.

In each case, state who the losers (if any) are likely to be. Which of these changes might be approved under the compensation principle? Which of these changes might be approved under a Rawlsian social welfare function?

9. Give some examples where the government seems to violate the principle of consumer sovereignty.
10. Assume you are shipwrecked. There are ten of you in a lifeboat; you know that it will take ten days to reach shore and that there are only rations for ten man-days. How would a utilitarian allocate the rations? How would a Rawlsian? Some people think that even Rawlsian criteria are not sufficiently egalitarian. What might an extreme egalitarian individual advocate? What does Pareto efficiency require?
11. Try to define clearly arguments for the following programs based on merit goods, externalities, and redistribution. Contrast the ways in which considerations of consumer sovereignty would weigh in each of these instances.
    a) Social security
    b) Education
    c) Control of pornography
    d) Public provision of medical care
    e) Public provision of medical care for children

PART TWO

PUBLIC EXPENDITURE THEORY

This part is concerned with the basic theory of public expenditures. Chapter 5 explains what public goods are and describes what it means to have an under- or oversupply of public goods. Chapter 6 describes how the level of expenditures on public goods is determined. We focus in particular on the consequences of majority voting.

Governments both provide and produce goods. Some of the goods they provide are privately produced; some of the goods they produce are sold, just like private goods. Chapter 7 is concerned with the government as a producer. It asks, for instance, whether there are reasons one might expect the government to be less efficient than private firms.

In recent years, governments have taken an increasingly active role in attempting to control the adverse effects of a number of important externalities, including air and water pollution. Chapter 8 explains why market "solutions" to the problems posed by externalities may not be effective and discusses the merits of alternative public remedies.

5

Public Goods and Publicly Provided Private Goods

Few question whether the government should be involved in supplying public goods. How much should be spent on public goods, however, is frequently a matter of heated debate. There are those, for instance, who believe that the public sector is too large, that it spends too much on public goods. Others believe that the nation is insufficiently responsive to public needs that exist in a society of private affluence.

In this chapter we examine in detail two sets of questions:

1. What are public goods and how do they differ from conventional private goods?

2. What do statements such as "There is an undersupply of a public good" or "There is an oversupply of a public good" mean? How can we characterize the efficient level of supply of public goods? To what extent does the efficient level depend on distributional considerations or the system of taxes used to finance the public goods?

DEFINITION OF PUBLIC GOODS

Pure public goods have two critical properties. The first is that it is not *feasible* to ration their use. The second is that it is not *desirable* to ration their use.

Goods for Which Rationing Is Unfeasible

The clearest example of a good for which rationing is not possible is national defense. If, for instance, our national defense achieves its objectives in deterring an attack from the Soviet Union, then all residents of the U.S. benefit; there is no way that any individual could be excluded from the benefits. It is essentially impossible to exclude an individual from the benefits of a national health program, such as polio vaccination, that reduces the incidence of certain epidemics. In some cases of public goods, exclusion is feasible but very costly. For example, it would be very costly to exclude individuals from small local parks; to do so would require that a fence be constructed around the park, which might interfere with the visual enjoyment of the park, and there would have to be someone always on duty to check permits or to collect entrance fees.

The infeasibility of rationing by the price system implies that the competitive market will not generate a Pareto-efficient amount of the public good. Assume that everyone valued national defense, but the government did not provide for it. Could a private firm enter to fill this gap? To do so, it would have to charge for the services it provides. But since every individual believes that he would benefit from the services provided regardless of whether he contributed to the service, he has no incentive to pay for the services *voluntarily*. That is why individuals must be forced to support these goods through taxation. The reluctance of individuals to contribute voluntarily to the support of public goods is referred to as the **free rider problem.**

Two other examples may help illustrate the nature of the free rider problem. One of the methods by which the incidence of some diseases is reduced is through vaccination. Those who are vaccinated incur some cost (discomfort, time, money, risk of getting the disease from a bad batch of the vaccine). They receive some private benefit, in reduced likelihood of getting the disease, but a major part of the benefit is a public good, the reduced incidence of the disease in the community, from which all benefit. In many cases, the private costs exceed the private benefits, but the social benefits—including the reduced incidence of the disease—far exceed the costs. Because of the free rider problem, governments frequently require individuals to become vaccinated.

In many communities, fire departments are supported voluntarily. Some individuals in the community refuse to contribute to the fire department. Yet, in an area where buildings are close together, the fire department will usually put out a fire in a noncontributor's building because of the threat it poses to adjacent contributors' structures. But there have been instances of fires at isolated noncontributors' buildings where fire departments refused to put out the fire. The fire departments were severely criticized. This is an example in which exclusion is feasible; the fire department can withhold its services from those who do not contribute to its support. The fire departments claim that in the absence of such sanctions, everyone would be a free rider. Why should they pay, if they can obtain the service for nothing? Because of the outrage that occurs whenever a fire department refuses to put out a fire, most communities prefer to provide the service to everyone; but to avoid the free rider problem, they require everyone to support it (through taxes).

In some cases, there will be some private provision of public goods, but because of the free rider problem, it will be inadequate. In Chapter 3, we noted that a large ship owner might find it worthwhile to supply some lighthouses, even if he could not charge others for the benefits that they receive from them; but in deciding on how many lighthouses to provide, he would only look at the benefits he himself would receive, not at the total benefits received.

Similarly, my neighbor across the street may enjoy the flowers I plant in front of my house as much as I do, and vice versa; the flowers are a public good; still, I plant them (even though he does not contribute to their support) because of the enjoyment I receive from them. There will, of course, be an undersupply of flowers. When I decide on how much effort to spend on my garden, I balance out the enjoyment I receive with the costs I have to pay. I do not include my neighbor's enjoyment.

It is in the interest of all to agree to be coerced to pay taxes to provide for public goods. In Figure 5.1 we have depicted two utility possibilities

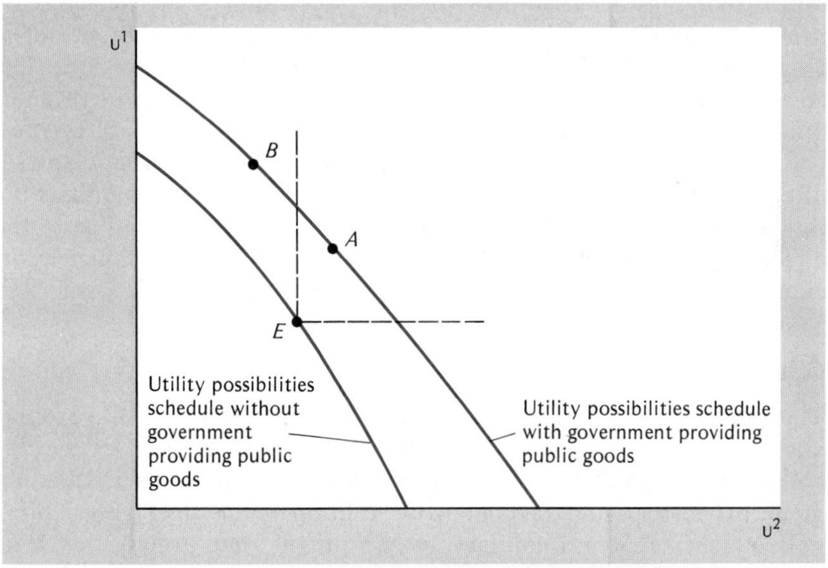

5.1 THE UTILITY POSSIBILITIES FRONTIER The utility possibilities frontier gives the maximum utility attainable by one individual (one group) given the utility level of the second. Without government coercion, the equilibrium may be at a point such as *E*. With government providing public goods (coercing both to contribute), both individuals can be better off than without government provision; at point *A* both are better off than at *E*. But the power of coercion can be used by one group to gain at the expense of another, as at point *B*.

schedules, one drawn under the assumption that the government does not provide public goods and the other under the assumption that it does. Compare point *A* to point *E*. At *A*, with the government providing public goods, everyone is better off than at *E*, where it does not. (Recall the definition of the utility possibilities schedule: it gives—under a particular set of circumstances—the maximum level of utility of one group or individual consistent with the level of utility attained by the others.) But once the power of coercion is granted, unless it is somehow circumscribed, it is clearly possible for some group to take advantage of this power to extract resources from some other group, a situation corresponding to point *B* in Figure 5.1. Thus, granting the government the power to coerce has the potential of making all individuals better off; it also has the potential of making some individuals better off at the expense of others.

Free rider problems arise, of course, in a variety of other contexts. There are often members of a family who fail to pull their own weight; for example, spoiled children who attempt to avoid doing the household errands that have to be done. These children know that it is unlikely that the quantity of the services they receive will be significantly affected by their actions. Somebody else will pick up the slack and make sure everything gets done.

Most of the goods provided within the family are provided in much the same manner that public goods are: individuals normally do not pay for the food they eat at home in the way they would if they were buying it in a restaurant, nor do they get paid for the services they perform. Exclusion is costly, if not impossible, just as it is for public goods. The costs of administering a price system within a family would be prohibitive—imagine charging a family member for each morsel of food he consumed, or each time he made use of a room. As a result, families often face the same kinds of free rider problems that communities do. But while social sanctions (such as parental disapproval) mitigate the effects of the free rider problem within the family, more explicit coercion usually must be employed both at the local and national level.

Goods for Which Rationing Is Undesirable

The second property of a public good is that it is not desirable to exclude any individual: one individual's consumption does not reduce the amount that is available for others to consume. Equivalently, the marginal cost of supplying the good to an additional individual is zero. If the government creates a military establishment that protects us from attack, it protects all of us; national defense costs are essentially unaffected when an additional baby is born or an additional individual immigrates to the United States. This is in sharp contrast to private goods. If I am sitting on a chair, I deprive others of being able to sit on that chair. If I eat an ice cream cone, you cannot eat the same ice cream cone. It is important to distinguish the marginal cost of producing the good from the marginal cost of an additional individual enjoying the good. It costs more to build more lighthouses, but it costs no more for an additional ship to make use of a lighthouse when sailing by.

IMPURE PUBLIC GOODS

National defense is one of the few *pure* public goods, satisfying both conditions: the impossibility and undesirability of exclusion. Lighthouses provide another example of an almost pure public good: it is difficult (but not impossible) to exclude those who do not contribute to the support of the lighthouse from enjoying its benefits. The lighthouse owner could, of course, turn off his light upon the approach of a noncontributing ship, provided that there was not, at the same time, a contributing ship in the vicinity. In nineteenth-century England there were, in fact, some private lighthouses. But the marginal cost of an extra ship receiving the benefits of the lighthouse is zero.

Many goods have one or the other property in varying degrees. For instance, exclusion may be feasible but undesirable. This is the case of an uncrowded road, for which a toll can be levied. But the toll would restrict the use of the road, even though there are no significant costs associated with its use. In other cases, exclusion may be feasible but costly. For instance, some communities provide water free of charge; though it is possible to install water meters, the costs exceed the benefits. (The marginal costs associated with supplying water to an extra household are small, though not zero.)

Figure 5.2 shows the ease of exclusion along the horizontal axis, and the (marginal) cost of an additional individual using the commodity along the vertical axis. The lower left-hand corner represents a pure public good, where the cost of exclusion is prohibitive and the marginal cost of an additional individual enjoying the good is zero. The upper right-hand corner is a pure private good, where the cost of exclusion is low and the marginal cost of an additional individual using the commodity is high.

In the diagram are several "impure" cases. The marginal cost of usage of an uncongested road is close to zero, but there is a cost of exclusion (the toll collectors, and the loss in time to pay the toll). For a congested road, on the other hand, there may be a large social marginal cost associated with an additional individual using the road.

Most of the time, firemen are not engaged in fighting fires but are waiting for calls. Protecting an additional individual then has little extra cost. Only in that rare event when two fires break out simultaneously will there be a significant cost to extending the protection to an additional individual. On the other hand, the costs of excluding an individual from the services of the fire department are relatively low.[1]

[1] There may be disagreements about precisely where a particular program should lie. We have represented public health programs as being close to pure public goods. A program that results in the elimination of some disease (such as polio) from the population benefits everyone in society; it would not be

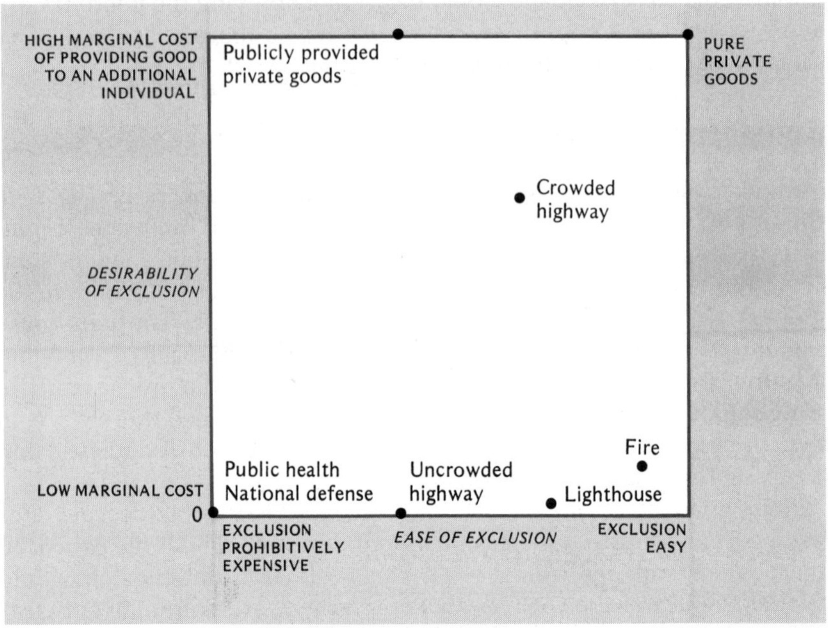

5.2 PURE AND IMPURE PUBLIC GOODS Goods differ in the ease and desirability of exclusion.

Inefficiencies from the Private Provision of Public Goods

As we have noted, it is possible to charge for many goods for which the marginal cost of an additional person enjoying them is (close to) zero. These goods can be provided privately. The argument for public provision is that it is more efficient to have them publicly provided.

When there is no marginal cost to an additional individual using the good, then, as we have said, it should not be rationed. But if it is to be privately provided by a firm, the firm must charge for its use; and any charge for its use will discourage individuals from using it. Thus when public goods are privately provided, an *underutilization* of these goods will result.

This is illustrated in Figure 5.3 for the case of a bridge. We have drawn the demand curve for the bridge, describing the number of trips taken as a function of the toll charged. Lowering the toll results in increased demand for the bridge. The capacity of the bridge is Q_c; for any demand below Q_c, there is no congestion and no marginal cost associated with use of the bridge. Since the marginal cost of usage is zero, efficiency requires that the price for usage be zero. But clearly, the revenue raised by the bridge will then be zero.

feasible or desirable to exclude any individual from the benefits. On the other hand, the public health service provides other services that are like private goods—e.g., the provision of yellow fever vaccinations, which benefits primarily those who travel internationally.

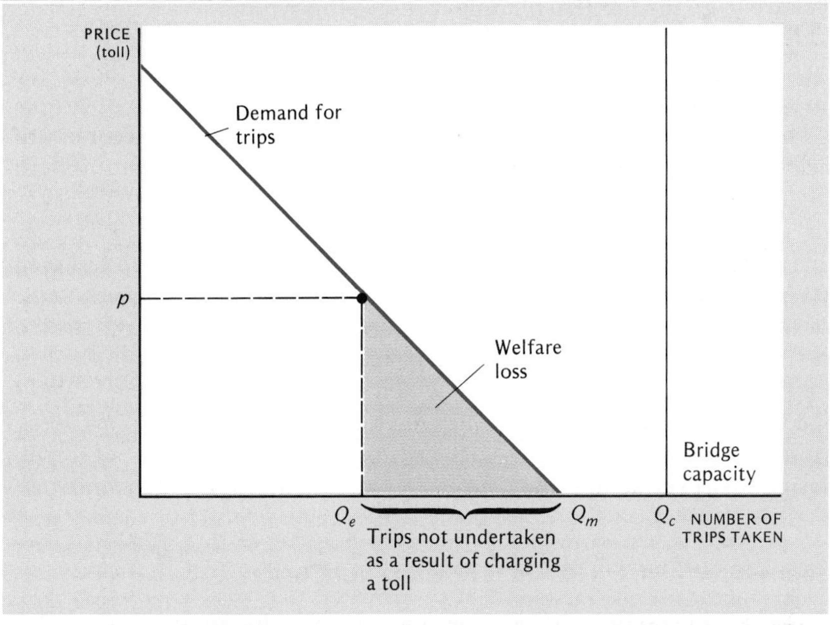

5.3 BRIDGES: GOODS WHERE EXCLUSION IS POSSIBLE BUT NOT NECESSARILY DESIRABLE It is feasible to charge a toll for crossing a bridge, but if the capacity of the bridge is large enough, it is not desirable to do so. The shaded area provides a measure of the welfare loss from charging a toll of p.

Exclusion is, however, feasible: a private firm could construct the bridge and charge any toll it desired. It might, in particular, be possible for it to charge a toll that would more than cover the cost of construction. But whenever it charges a toll, the usage of the bridge will be reduced, and some trips, the benefits of which exceed the social cost (zero), will not be undertaken. We can measure the loss in welfare by the shaded triangle in Figure 5.3. This is referred to as the *deadweight loss*. To see this, we recall that the points on the demand curve measure the individual's marginal willingness to pay for an extra trip at different quantities. Assume a price, p, was charged for the use of the bridge. The number of trips taken would then be Q_e. At Q_e, the individual's marginal willingness to pay (the price he is willing to pay) for an extra trip is just p. The cost of providing an extra trip is zero. The welfare loss from not taking the trip is the difference between what he is willing to pay (his marginal benefit) and the marginal cost; thus the welfare loss is just p. At slightly higher levels of usage, the loss is still the marginal willingness to pay, but this is now smaller. To find the total welfare loss, we simply add up the welfare loss associated with each of the trips *not* taken as a result of charging the toll. At a zero price, Q_m trips are taken. At a price of p, Q_e trips are taken. Hence, the toll results in $(Q_m - Q_e)$ trips not being taken. The loss in welfare from the first trip not taken is, of course, p; the loss in welfare from the last trip not taken is zero (his willingness to pay for one additional trip at Q_m is zero). The *average* welfare loss from each trip not taken is thus $p/2$; and the total welfare loss is $p\ (Q_m - Q_e)/2$, the area of the shaded triangle in Figure 5.3.[2]

This argument suggests that goods for which the marginal cost of provision is zero should be freely provided, regardless of whether it is feasible to charge for them. Occasionally, there may be a small marginal cost for using the public good, in which case the individual should be charged only the marginal cost. These **user charges** will not be sufficient to cover the total cost of the public good. The revenue required to pay for the public good must be raised in some other way. Although most of the taxes used to raise revenue entail significant costs, the argument for the public provision of goods for which user charges could be levied is that the costs associated with charging for their use—the welfare losses from reduced consumption— are *greater* than the costs associated with raising the revenue in some other way, such as through the income tax.

Goods for Which Exclusion Is Feasible but Costly

There are, of course, costs associated with exclusion for private goods as well as for public goods; that is, there are costs associated with running the price system. For example, the checkout clerks at grocery stores and the collectors of tolls along toll highways and at toll bridges are part of the administrative costs associated with operating a price mechanism. But while the costs of exclusion are relatively small for most private goods, they may be large (prohibitive) for some publicly provided goods.

Even when there is a marginal cost associated with each individual using a good, if the costs of running the price system are very high, it may be more efficient simply to provide the good publicly and finance the good through general taxation.

We illustrate this in Figure 5.4, where we have depicted a good with constant marginal costs of production, c. (It costs the firm $\$c$ to produce each unit of the good.)[3] However, to sell the good entails certain **transaction costs**. Transaction costs include all the costs required to complete an economic transaction, such as the costs of the checkout clerk at a grocery store or salespeople. Transaction costs raise the price to p^*. Assume now the government supplied the good freely. This eliminates the transaction costs, and the entire lightly shaded area *ABCD* is saved. There is a further gain as consumption increases from Q_e to Q_o, since individuals' marginal valuations exceed the marginal costs of production. The heav-

[2] Recall from Chapter 4 that this is only an approximation for the deadweight loss. The correct calculation entails using, as we did in Figure 4.10, the *compensated* demand schedule, not the ordinary demand schedule. However, if the fraction of income spent on traveling across the bridge is negligible, the two demand curves differ by very little.

[3] We assume, moreover, that the demand curve does not shift significantly as we raise taxes.

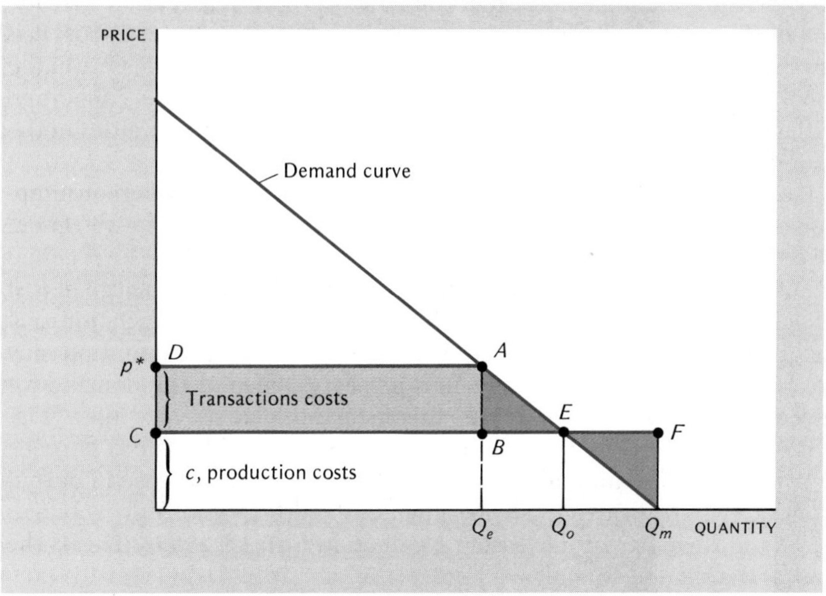

5.4 TRANSACTION COSTS When transaction costs are sufficiently high, it may be more efficient to supply the good publicly than to have the good supplied by private markets.

ily shaded area *ABE* measures the gain. On the other hand, if individuals consume the good until the marginal value is zero, in expanding consumption form Q_o to Q_m, the marginal willingness to pay is less than the cost of production. This is obviously inefficient. To decide whether the good should be provided publicly, we must compare the savings in transaction costs plus the gain from increasing consumption from Q_e to Q_o with (1) the loss from the excessive consumption of the good (the shaded area EFQ_m in Figure 5.4), plus (2) the loss from the distortions created by the taxes used to raise the revenue required to finance the provision of the good.

The high costs of private markets providing insurance has been used as one of the arguments for the public provision of insurance. For many kinds of insurance, the administrative costs (including the selling costs) associated with providing the insurance privately are more than 20 percent of the benefits paid out, in contrast with the administrative costs associated with public insurance, which (ignoring the distortions associated with the taxes required to finance the social insurance programs) are usually less than 10 percent of the value of the benefits.

PUBLICLY PROVIDED PRIVATE GOODS

Publicly provided goods for which there is a large marginal cost associated with supplying additional individuals are referred to as **publicly**

provided private goods. Though the costs of running a market provide one of the rationales for the public supply of some of these goods, it is not the only rationale. Education is a publicly provided good. One of the usual explanations given for public provision of education is concerned with distributive considerations; many feel that the opportunities of the young should not depend on the wealth of the parents.

If a private good is freely provided, there is likely to be overconsumption of the good. Since the individual does not have to pay for the good, he will demand it until the point where the marginal benefit he receives from the good is zero, in spite of the fact that there is a real marginal cost associated with providing it. In some cases, such as water, satiation may be quickly reached, so that the distortion from overconsumption may not be too large (Figure 5.5A). In other cases, such as the demand for certain types of medical services, the distortion may be very large (Figure 5.5B). Again, the welfare loss can be measured by the difference between what the individual is willing to pay for the increase in output from Q_e (where price equals marginal cost) to Q_m (where price equals zero) and the costs of increasing production form Q_e to Q_m. This is the area of the shaded triangles in Figure 5.5.

Rationing Devices for Publicly Provided Private Goods: Uniform Provision

It is likely, then, that some method for controlling consumption of publicly provided private goods will have to be used. Any method restricting consumption of a good is called a **rationing system.** Prices provide one rationing system. We have already discussed how user charges may be used to limit demand. Another commonly employed way of rationing publicly provided goods is to supply the same quantity of the good to everyone. Thus, typically, we provide a uniform level of education to all individuals, even though some individuals would like to have more and some less. (Those who would like to purchase more may be able to purchase supplemental educational services on the private market, such as tutoring.) This, then, is the major disadvantage of the public provision of private goods; it does not allow for the adaptation to differences in individuals' needs and desires as does the private market.

This is illustrated in Figure 5.6, where we have drawn the demand curves for two different individuals. If the good was privately provided, Individual 1, the high demander, would consume Q_1, while Individual 2, the low demander, would consume the much smaller quantity Q_2. The government chooses to supply each individual with a quantity that is somewhere in between, Q^*. At this level of consumption, the high demander is consuming less than he would like; his marginal willingness to pay exceeds the marginal cost of production. On the other hand, the low demander is consuming more than the efficient level; his marginal willingness to pay is less than the marginal cost. (But since he does not

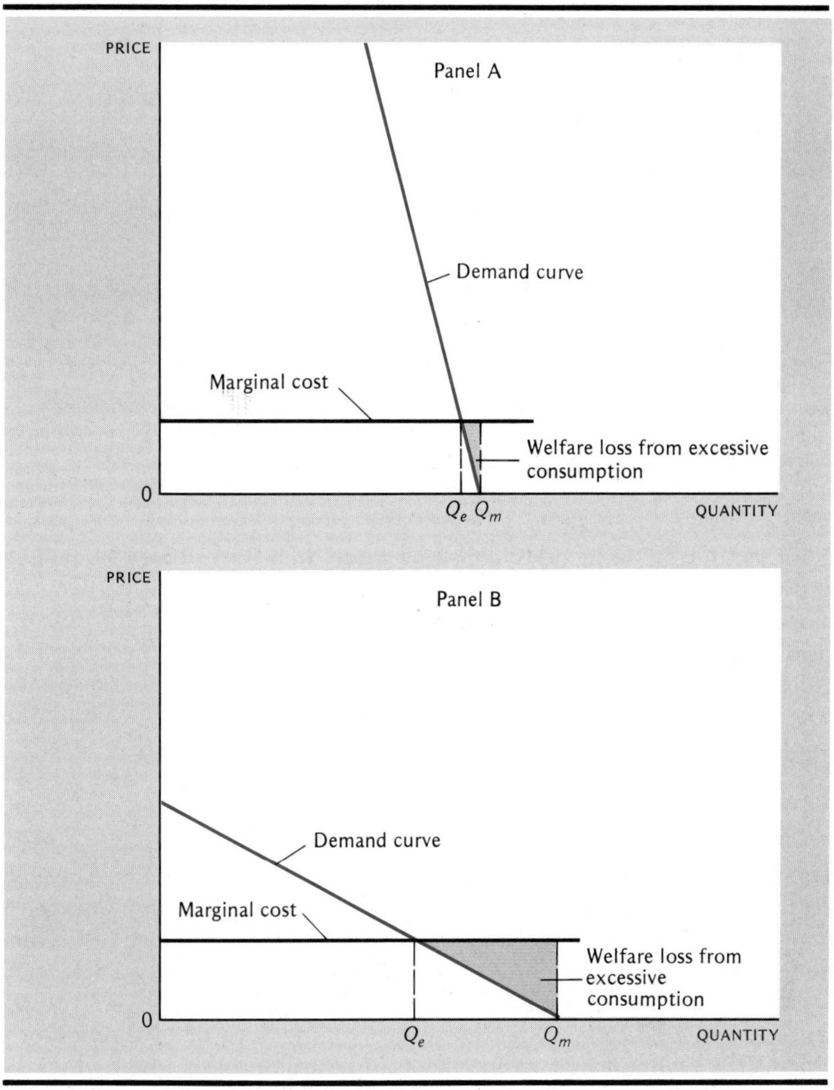

5.5 DISTORTIONS ASSOCIATED WITH SUPPLYING GOODS FREELY (A) For some goods, such as water, supplying the good freely rather than at marginal costs results in relatively little additional consumption. (B) For other goods, such as certain medical services, supplying the good freely rather than at marginal costs results in extensive overconsumption.

have to pay anything for it, and still values the good positively, he, of course, consumes up to Q^*.)

For certain types of insurance (say, social security for retirement), the government provides a basic, uniform level. Again, those who wish to purchase more can do so, but those who wish to purchase less cannot. The distortion here may not, however, be very great; if the uniform level provided is sufficiently low, then there will be relatively few individuals

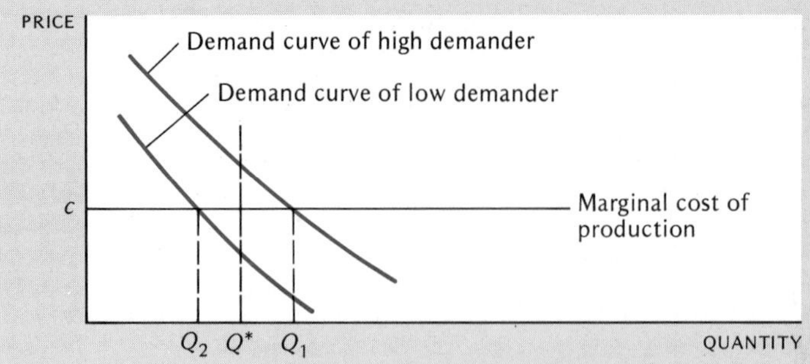

5.6 DISTORTIONS ASSOCIATED WITH UNIFORM PROVISION When the publicly provided private good is supplied in equal amounts to all individuals, some get more than the efficient level and some get less.

who are thereby induced to consume more than they otherwise would, and the savings in administrative costs that we referred to earlier may more than offset the slight distortion associated with the uniform provision of the basic level of insurance. On the other hand, the system of combining public and private provision may significantly increase total transaction (administrative) costs over what they would be if only the public sector or private sector took responsibility.

Queuing as a Rationing Device

The second method of rationing that is commonly employed by the government is queuing: rather than charging individuals money for access to the publicly provided goods or services, the government requires that they pay a cost in waiting time. This allows some adaptability of the level of supply to the needs of the individual. Those who have a stronger demand for medical services are more willing to wait in the doctor's office. It is claimed that money is an undesirable basis upon which to ration medical services: Why should the wealthy have a greater right to good health than the poor? Queues, it is argued, may be an effective device for discriminating between the truly needy (who are willing to wait in line) and those who are less needy of medical care. But queues are a far from perfect way of determining who is deserving of medical care since those who are unemployed or retired, but are not so needy of medical care, may be more willing to wait in the queue than either the busy corporate executive or the low-paid worker holding down two jobs. In effect, we are replacing willingness to pay as a criterion for allocating medical services by willingness to wait in the doctor's office. There is, in addition, a real social cost to using queuing as a rationing device—the waste of time spent queuing; this is a cost that could be avoided if prices were used as a rationing device.

THE CHANGING BALANCE BETWEEN PUBLIC AND PRIVATE PROVISION

Many of the goods that are publicly provided could be provided either publicly or privately. Often they are provided both publicly and privately. The balance between public and private provision differs from country to country and has changed frequently over time.

The changing balance between private and public provision is partially related to changing technologies. The development of cable television makes it easier to charge for the use of television. Computers have lowered the administrative costs associated with many collection systems. For instance, it is now feasible to charge more for the use of subways at peak hours. Each car and each busy corner could conceivably be equipped with electronic devices to measure roadway use by individuals during peak hours, much as telephone use is now measured. Such a scheme was actually introduced on an experimental basis in Hong Kong in 1985.

The changing balance is also related to changes in the standard of living (income per capita). Children's swings are provided in public parks, and, in addition, individuals privately purchase swings for their backyards. The advantage of public provision is that the swings are more fully utilized. Private swings are not used for most of the day. The advantage of private provision is that it saves on transportation costs. If the cost of transportation (including the value of the time it takes to go to the public park) increases relative to the cost of the swing, one might expect a shift toward private provision.

Albert Hirschman of the Institute for Advanced Study at Princeton has suggested that these changing patterns are the consequences of changes in tastes.[4] He argues that there are periodic swings in the balance between private and public consumption. As individuals find disappointment or incomplete satisfaction in what they obtain in their private lives, they turn their attention to public service and to the public provision of goods and services. But their anticipations about the satisfaction that they can obtain in the public sphere are, in turn, unfulfilled, and in their disappointment they turn again to the private market.

EFFICIENCY CONDITIONS FOR PUBLIC GOODS

A central question of concern is how large the supply of public goods should be. What does it mean to say that the government is supplying too few or too many public goods? In Chapter 3 we provided a criterion that enables us to answer this question; a resource allocation is Pareto efficient if no one can be made better off without making someone else worse off. There we established that Pareto efficiency in private markets

[4] A. O. Hirschman, *Shifting Involvements* (Princeton, NJ: Princeton University Press, 1981).

requires, among other criteria, that the individual's marginal rate of substitution is equal to the marginal rate of transformation.

In contrast, *pure public goods are efficiently supplied when the sum of the marginal rates of substitution (over all individuals) is equal to the marginal rate of transformation.* The *marginal rate of substitution* of private goods for public goods tells how much of the private good each individual is willing to give up to get one more unit of the public good. The sum of the marginal rates of substitution thus tells us how much of the private good all the members of society, together, are willing to give up to get one more unit of the public good (which will be jointly consumed by all). The *marginal rate of transformation* tells us how much of the private good must be given up to get one more unit of the public good. Efficiency requires, then, that the total amount individuals are willing to give up—the sum of the marginal rates of substitution—must equal the amount that they have to give up—the marginal rate of transformation.

Let's apply this efficiency condition to national defense. Assume that when we increase our production of guns (national defense) by one, we must reduce our production of butter by one pound (the marginal rate of transformation is unity). Guns used for national defense are a public good. We consider a simple economy with two individuals: Crusoe and Friday. Crusoe is willing to give up one-third of a pound of butter for an extra gun. But his one-third pound alone does not buy the gun. Friday is willing to give up two-thirds of a pound of butter for an extra gun. The total amount of butter that this small society would be willing to give up, were the government to buy one more gun, is

$$1/3 + 2/3 = 1.$$

The total amount they would *have* to give up to get one more gun is also 1. Thus, the sum of the marginal rates of substitution equals the marginal rate of transformation; their government has provided an efficient level of national defense. If the sum of the marginal rates of substitution exceeded unity, then, collectively, individuals would be willing to give up more than they had to; we could ask each of them to give up an amount slightly less than the amount that would make them indifferent, and it would still be possible to increase the production of guns by one unit. Thus they could all be made better off by increasing the production of the public good (guns) by one.

Demand Curves for Public Goods

In Chapter 3 we described a market equilibrium for a private good (ice cream cones) as the intersection of a demand and a supply curve (see Figure 3.2). We showed that at this point, the marginal benefit of producing an extra unit was equal to the marginal cost. That is why the market equilibrium was Pareto efficient.

We can use a similar apparatus to describe the efficient level of production of public goods. We can derive each individual's demand curve for public goods in the same way we can derive his demand curve for private goods.

Individuals do not buy public goods. We can, however, ask how much they would demand if, for each extra unit of the public good, they had to pay a given amount. This is not a completely hypothetical question, for as expenditures on public goods increase, so do individuals' taxes. We call the extra payment that an individual has to make for each extra unit of the public good his **tax price.** In the following discussion, we shall assume the government has the discretion to charge different individuals different tax prices.

Assume that the individual's tax price is p, that is, for each unit of the public good, he must pay p. Then, the total amount the individual can spend, his *budget constraint,* is:

$$C+pG=Y,$$

where C is his consumption of private goods, G is the total amount of public goods provided, and Y is his income. The budget constraint shows the combinations of goods (here, public and private goods) that the individual can purchase, given his income and his tax price. We represent the budget constraint in Figure 5.7A by the line BB. Along the budget constraint, if government expenditures are lower, consumption of private goods is obviously higher. The individual wishes to obtain the highest level of utility he can, consistent with his budget constraint. In Figure 5.7A we have also drawn the individual's indifference curves between public and private goods. The individual is willing to give up some private goods if he gets more public goods. The quantity of private goods he is willing to give up to get one more unit of public goods is his marginal rate of substitution. As he gets more public goods (and has fewer private goods), the amount of private goods he is willing to give up to get an extra unit of public goods becomes smaller—that is, the individual has a diminishing marginal rate of substitution. Graphically, the marginal rate of substitution is the slope of the indifference curve. Thus as the individual consumes more public goods and fewer private goods, the indifference curve becomes flatter.

The individual's highest level of utility is attained at the point of tangency between the indifference curve and the budget constraint, point E in Panel A. At this point, the slope of the budget constraint and the slope of the indifference curve are identical. The slope of the budget constraint tells us how much in private goods the individual must give up to get one more unit of public goods; it is equal to the individual's tax price. The slope of the indifference curve tells us how much in private goods the individual is willing to give up to get one more unit of public goods. Thus at the individual's most preferred point, the amount that he

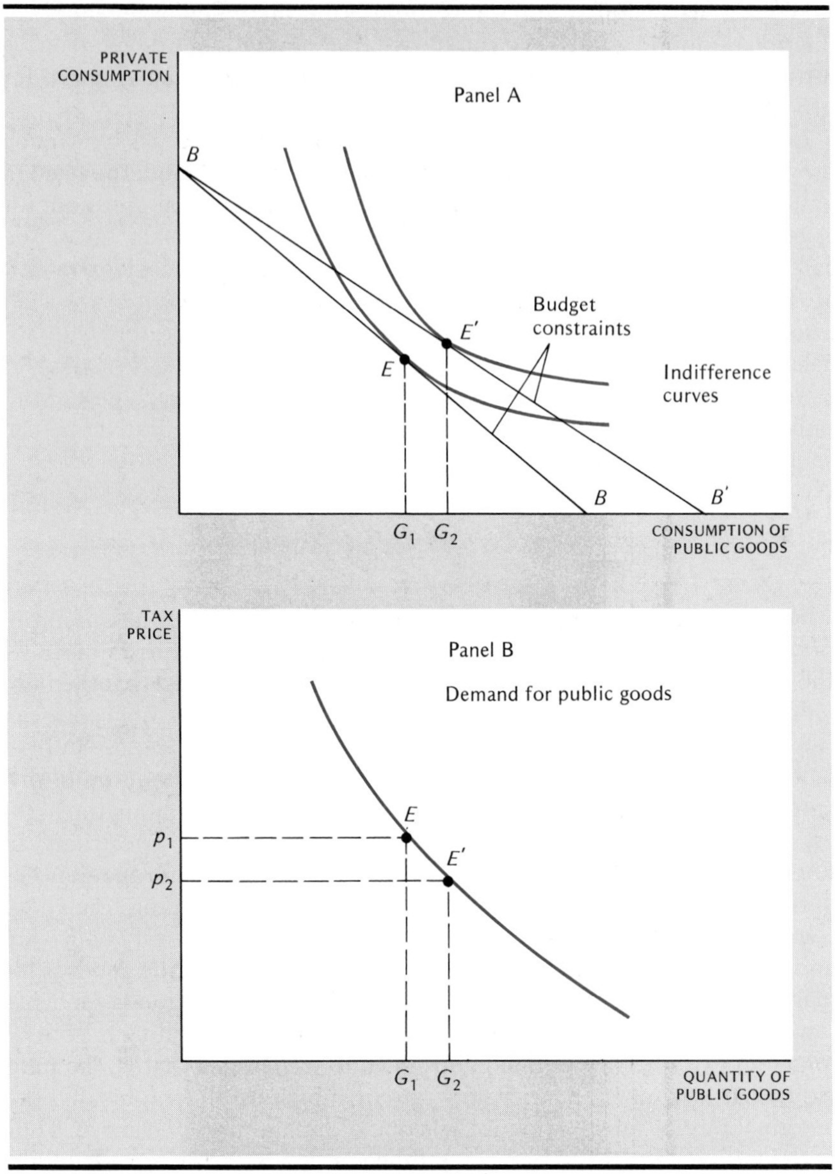

5.7 DEMAND CURVE FOR PUBLIC GOODS The individual's most preferred level of expenditure is the point of tangency between the indifference curve and the budget constraint. As the tax price decreases (the budget constraint shifts from *BB* to *BB'*), the individual's most preferred level of public expenditure increases, generating the demand curve of Panel B.

is *willing* to give up to get an additional unit of public goods is just equal to the amount he *must* give up to get one more unit of the public good. As we lower the tax price, the budget constraint shifts out (from *BB* to *BB'*), and the individual's most preferred point moves to point E'. The individual's demand for public goods will normally increase.

By raising and lowering the tax price, we can trace out a demand curve for public goods, in the same way that we trace out demand curves for private goods. In Figure 5.7B we have plotted the demand curve corresponding to Panel A. Points E and E', from Panel A, show the quantity of public goods demanded at tax prices p_1 and p_2. We could trace more points for Panel B by shifting the budget constraint further in Panel A.

We can use this approach to trace out the demand curves for public goods of Crusoe and Friday. Then we can add them *vertically* to derive the aggregate demand curve in Figure 5.8. Vertical summation is appropriate because a pure public good is necessarily provided in the same amount to all individuals. Rationing is infeasible and is also undesirable, since one individual's usage of the public good does not detract from any other individual's enjoyment of it.

The demand curve can be thought of as a "marginal willingness to pay curve." That is, at each level of output of the public good, it says how much the individual would be willing to pay for an extra unit of the public good. (Remember, the tax price for the public good faced by the individual is set equal to his marginal rate of substitution, which simply gives how much of the private good he is willing to give up for one more unit of the public good.) Thus, the vertical sum of the demand curves is just

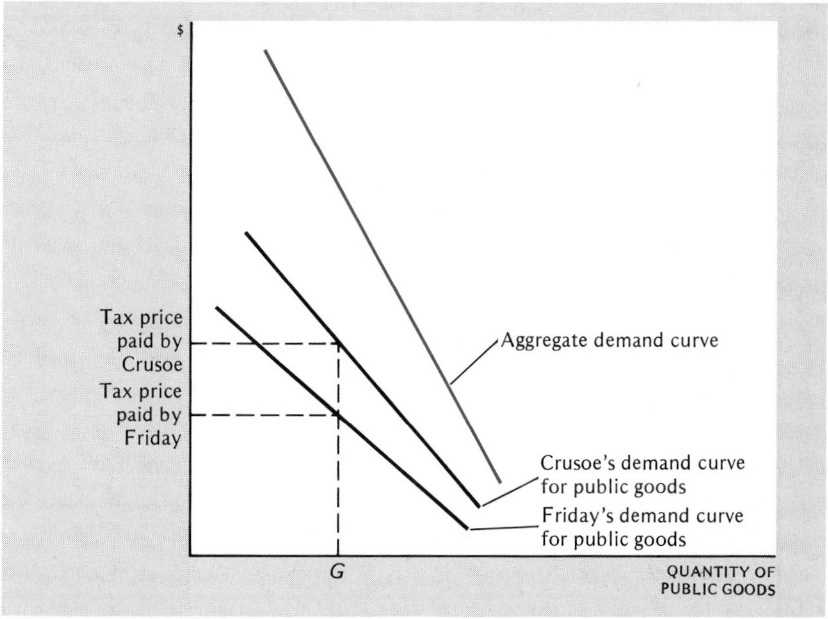

5.8 AGGREGATE DEMAND FOR PUBLIC GOODS Since at each point on the demand curve the price is equal to the marginal rate of substitution, by adding the demand curves vertically we obtain the sum of the marginal rates of substitution, the total amount of private goods that the individuals in society are willing to give up to get one more public good. The vertical sum thus can be thought of as the aggregate demand curve for the public good.

the sum of their marginal willingnesses to pay, that is, it is the total amount that all individuals together are willing to pay for an extra unit of the public good. Equivalently, since each point on the demand curve of an individual represents his marginal rate of substitution at that level of government expenditure, by adding the demand curves vertically we simply obtain the sum of the marginal rates of substitution (the total marginal benefit from producing an extra unit). The result is the aggregate demand curve shown in Figure 5.8.

We can draw a supply curve just as we did for private goods; for each level of output, the price represents how much of the other goods have to be foregone to produce one more unit of public goods; this is the marginal cost, or the marginal rate of transformation. At the output level where the aggregate demand is equal to the supply (Figure 5.9), the sum of the marginal willingnesses to pay (the sum of the marginal rates of substitution) is just equal to the marginal cost of production or the marginal rate of transformation. Since at this point, the marginal benefit from producing an extra unit of the public good equals the marginal cost, or the sum of the marginal rates of substitution equals the marginal rate of transformation, the output level described by the intersection of the aggregate demand curve and the supply curve for public goods is Pareto efficient.

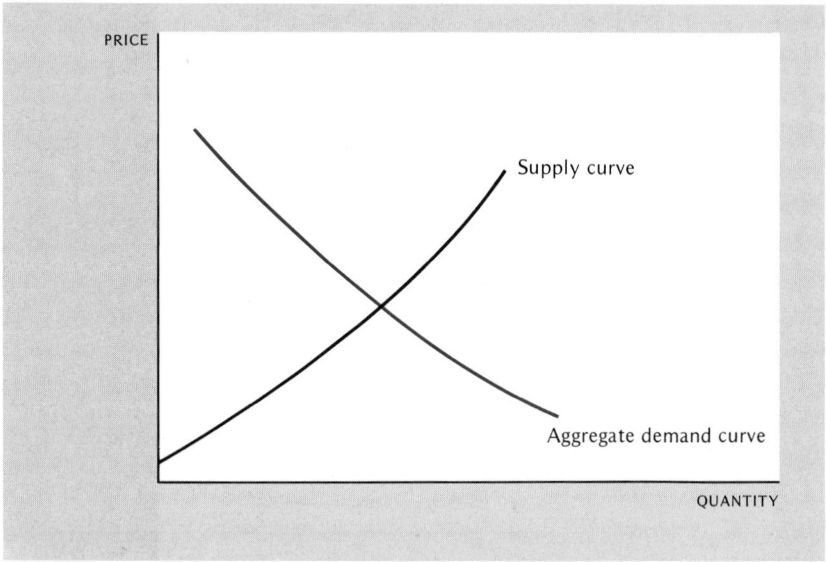

5.9 EFFICIENT PRODUCTION OF PUBLIC GOODS An efficient supply of public goods occurs at the point of intersection of the demand curve and the supply curve. The aggregate demand curve gives the sum of what all individuals are willing to give up, at the margin, to have one more unit of public goods (one more gun), while the supply curve gives the amount of other goods that have to be given up to obtain one more unit of the public good.

Though we constructed each individual's demand curve for public goods in a manner analogous to the manner in which we could construct his demand curve for private goods, there are some important distinctions between the two. In particular, while market *equilibrium* occurs at the intersection of the demand and supply curves, we have not provided any explanation for why the equilibrium supply of public goods should occur at the intersection of the demand curve we have constructed and the supply curve. We have only established that if it did, the level of production of the public good would be Pareto efficient. Decisions about the level of public goods are made publicly, by governments, and not by individuals; hence, whether production occurs at this point depends on the nature of the political process, a subject we discuss at length in the next chapter.

Moreover, while in a competitive market for private goods, all individuals face the same prices, but consume different quantities (reflecting differences in tastes), a public good must be provided in the same amount to all affected individuals, and we have hypothesized that the government could charge different tax prices for the public good. One way of thinking about these prices is to suppose that each individual is told beforehand the *share* of public expenditures that he will have to bear. If some individual has to bear 1 percent of the cost of public expenditures, then an item that costs the government $1.00 costs him 1¢, while if an individual has to bear 3 percent of the cost of public expenditures, then an increase in public expenditures by $1.00 costs that individual 3¢.

Finally, we should emphasize that we have characterized the Pareto-efficient level of expenditure on public goods corresponding to a particular distribution of income. As we shall see in the next section, the efficient level of expenditure on public goods generally depends on the distribution of income.

Pareto Efficiency and Income Distribution

Recall from our discussion of Chapters 3 and 4 that there are many Pareto-efficient resource allocations; any point on the utilities possibilities schedule is Pareto efficient. The market equilibrium in the absence of market failures corresponds to just one of those points. By the same token, there is not a unique Pareto-optimal supply of public goods. The intersection of the demand and supply curves in Figure 5.9 is one of these Pareto-efficient levels of supply, but there are others as well, with different distributional implications.

To see how the efficient level of public goods depends on the distribution of income, assume the government transferred a dollar of income from Crusoe to Friday. This would normally shift Crusoe's demand for public goods (at any price) down and Friday's up. In general, there is no reason why these changes should exactly offset each other, so that the aggregate level of demand will normally change. With this new distribution of income, there is a new efficient level of public goods. But efficiency is still characterized by the sum of the marginal rates of substitution equaling the marginal rate of transformation. To put it another way, each point on the utilities possibilities schedule may be characterized by a different level of public goods, but at each point the sum of the marginal rates of substitution equals the marginal rate of transformation.

The fact that the efficient level of public goods depends, in general, on the distribution of income has one important implication: one cannot separate out efficiency considerations in the supply of public goods from distributional considerations. Any change in the distribution of income, say, brought about by a change in the income tax structure, will thus be accompanied by corresponding changes in the efficient levels of public-goods production.[5]

Limitations on Income Redistribution and the Efficient Supply of Public Goods

Governments, in evaluating the benefits of a public program, often seem to be particularly concerned with the question of *who* benefits from the program. They seem to *weight* benefits that accrue to the poor more highly than benefits that accrue to the rich. Yet the previous analysis suggested that one should simply add up the marginal rates of substitution, the amounts that each individual is willing to pay at the margin for an increase in the public good, treating the rich and the poor equally. How can these approaches be reconciled?

In Chapter 4, we showed how we could trace out the utility possibilities schedule simply by taking away resources from one individual and giving them to another. Recall our parable of the Robinson Crusoe economy, where in the process of transferring oranges from Crusoe to Friday some of the oranges are lost. In the U.S. economy, we use primarily the tax system and welfare system to redistribute resources. Not only are the administrative costs of running these systems large, but they have important incentive effects—for instance, on individuals' savings and work decisions. The fact that redistributing resources through the tax and welfare systems is costly implies that the government may look for alternative ways to achieve its redistributive goals; one way is to incorporate redistributive considerations into its evaluation of public projects.

[5] Some economists have suggested that decisions concerning the efficient level of public-goods production and distribution of income can be separated; for instance, there is a view that concerns about the distribution of income should be reflected in tax schedules and welfare programs, but that decisions concerning the supply of public goods can and should be made quite independently of such considerations. There are some cases where the decisions can be separated (see Atkinson and Stiglitz, *Lectures in Public Economics* [New York: McGraw-Hill, 1980] or L. J. Lau, E. Sheshinski, and J. E. Stiglitz, "Efficiency in the Optimum Supply of Public Goods," *Econometrica* 46 [1978]: 269–84), but these are indeed special.

Distortionary Taxation and the Efficient Supply of Public Goods

The fact that the revenue raised to finance public goods is raised through taxes, such as the income tax, which have important effects on incentives, has some important implications for the efficient supply of public goods. The amount of private goods that individuals must give up to get one more unit of public goods is greater than it would be if the government could raise revenue in a way that did not entail these incentive effects and that was not costly to administer.

We can define a **feasibility curve**, giving the maximum level of private-goods consumption consistent with each level of public goods, for our given tax system. The tax system introduces inefficiencies, so this feasibility curve lies inside the production possibilities schedule, as in Figure 5.10.

The amount of private goods we have to give up to obtain one more unit of public goods, taking into account these extra costs, is called the marginal **economic rate of transformation,** as opposed to the marginal **physical rate of transformation** we employed in our earlier analysis. The latter is completely determined by *technology*, while the marginal economic rate of transformation takes into account the costs associated with the taxes required to finance increased public expenditure. Thus we replace the earlier condition that the marginal physical rate of transformation must equal the sum of the marginal rates of substitution with the

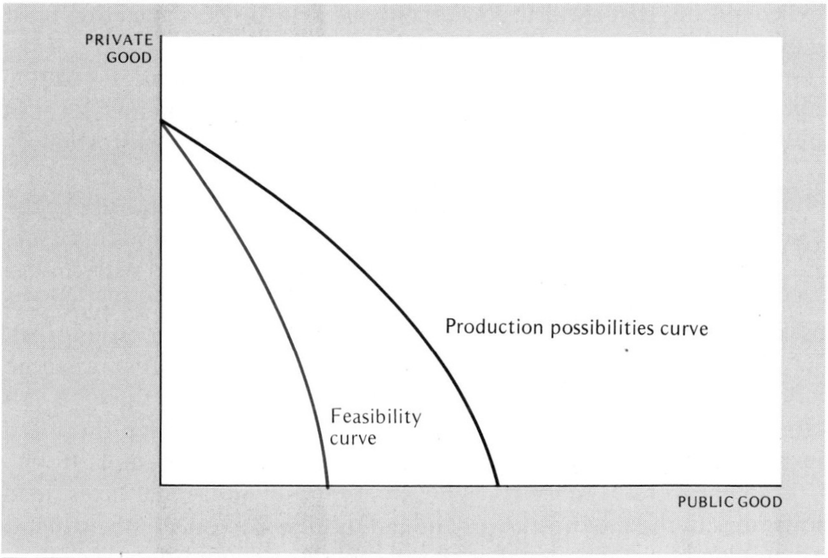

5.10 THE FEASIBILITY CURVE The feasibility curve gives the maximum output (consumption) of private goods for any level of public goods, taking into account the inefficiencies that arise from the taxes that must be imposed to raise the requisite revenue. The feasibility curve lies below the production possibilities schedule.

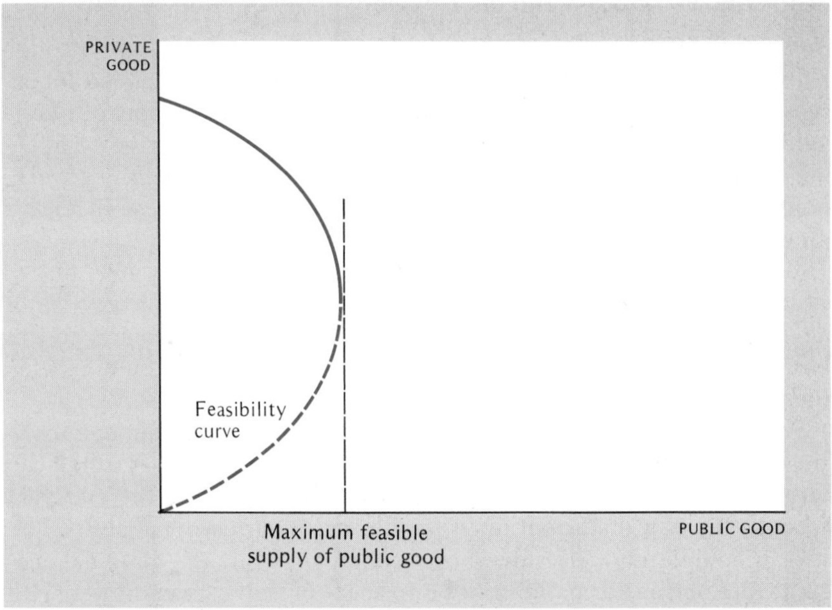

5.11 THE LAFFER CURVE Raising tax rates beyond some level may so decrease incentives that output, and tax revenues, are actually reduced. There is then a maximum feasible level of government expenditure.

new condition, that the marginal economic rate of transformation must equal the sum of the marginal rates of substitution.

Since it becomes more costly to obtain public goods when taxation imposes distortions, normally this will imply that the efficient level of public goods is smaller than it would have been with nondistortionary taxation.

Indeed, it appears that much of the debate in recent years about the desirable level of public goods provision has centered around this issue. There are those who believe that the distortions associated with the tax system are not very great, while there are others who contend that the cost of attempting to raise additional revenues for public goods is great. They *may* agree on the magnitude of the social benefits that may accrue from additional government expenditures, but disagree on the costs.

In Figure 5.11 we have drawn a feasibility curve in which there is a maximum level of public goods that can be provided; attempts by the government to raise more revenue, by imposing additional taxes, lead individuals to reduce their effort and induce firms to reduce investment, and thus lead to a lower level of private-goods consumption *and* a lower level of tax revenue (and hence government expenditure). This curve has been popularized in recent years as the Laffer curve, after Arthur Laffer of the University of Southern California, although the possibility of the effect the curve describes had been noted by others earlier. It has provided one of the bases of what has come to be called **supply-side economics,** which claims that reducing tax rates would increase tax revenues. Although this is clearly theoretically possible, there is no evidence that this is a relevant concern at current tax rates, as we shall see in Chapter 19.

EFFICIENT GOVERNMENT AS A PUBLIC GOOD

One of the most important public goods is the management of the government: we all benefit from a better, more efficient, more responsive government. Indeed, "good government" possesses both of the properties of public goods we noted earlier: it is difficult and undesirable to exclude any individual from the benefits of a better government.

If the government is able to become more efficient and reduce taxes without reducing the level of government services, we all benefit. The politician who succeeds in doing this may get some return, but this return is only a fraction of the benefits that accrue to others. In particular, those who voted against the politician who succeeds in doing this gain as much as those who worked for his election, and the individual who did not vote, who attempted to free ride on the political activities of others, benefits as much as either.

SUMMARY

1. This chapter has defined an important class of goods, pure public goods. They have two critical properties:
   a) It is impossible to exclude individuals from enjoying the benefits of the goods.
   b) It is undesirable to exclude individuals from enjoying the benefits of the goods, since their enjoyment of these goods does not detract from that of others.
2. While there are a few examples of pure public goods, such as national defense, for most publicly provided goods exclusion is possible, although frequently costly. Imposing user charges may result in the underutilization of public facilities.
3. Private markets either will not supply or will provide an inadequate supply of public goods.
4. The problem with voluntary arrangements for providing public goods arises from individuals trying to be *free riders*, of simply enjoying the benefits of the public goods paid for by others.
5. For publicly provided private goods, some method of rationing other than the price system may be used; sometimes queuing is used, while at other times the good is simply provided in fixed quantities to all individuals. Both of these entail inefficiencies.
6. Pareto efficiency requires that a public good be supplied up to the point where the sum of the marginal rates of substitution equals the marginal rate of transformation. Different Pareto-efficient levels of consumption of the public good will be associated with different distributions of income.

7. The basic rule for the efficient level of supply of public goods must be modified when there are costs (distortions) associated with raising revenue and redistributing income.
8. Efficient management of the government is a public good itself.

KEY CONCEPTS

Pure public goods
Exclusion
Free rider problem
User charges
Tax price
Transaction costs
Publicly provided private goods
Uniform provision
Rationing system
Marginal physical rate of transformation
Marginal economic rate of transformation
Feasibility curve
Laffer curve

QUESTIONS AND PROBLEMS

1. Where should each of the following goods lie in Figure 5.2? Explain why each is or is not a pure public good. Where applicable, note instances where the good is both publicly and privately provided:
   a) College education
   b) A local park
   c) Yosemite Park
   d) Sewage collection
   e) Water
   f) Electricity
   g) Telephone service
   h) Retirement insurance
   i) Medicine
   j) Police protection
   k) TV
   l) Basic research
   m) Applied research
2. What happens to the efficient allocation between public and private goods as an economy becomes wealthier? Can you think of examples of public goods, the consumption of which would increase more than proportionately to the increase in income? Less than proportionately to the increase in income?
3. The government rations a variety of publicly provided private goods and impure public goods (in which there is congestion) in a variety of ways. Discuss how each of these are rationed, and consider the effect of alternative rationing systems:
   a) Public higher education
   b) Health services in the U.K.
   c) Yellowstone National Park

   What happens to a publicly provided good in which congestion can occur (such as a highway or swimming pool on a hot, sunny day), but in which no direct rationing system is employed?
4. To what extent do you think differences in views between those who believe there should be less spending on public goods and those who believe there should be more spending can be attributed to differences in judgments concerning the marginal cost of public goods, including the increased distortions associated with the additional taxes required to finance public goods? What are other sources of disagreement?
5. What implications might the fact that efficient government is a public good have for the efficiency with which governments function?

APPENDIX: AN ALTERNATIVE EXPOSITION OF PUBLIC GOODS EFFICIENCY—THE LEFTOVER CURVE

In this appendix we provide an alternative, diagrammatic exposition for the basic efficiency condition for public goods:

$$\text{Sum of marginal rates of substitution} = \text{Marginal rate of transformation.}$$

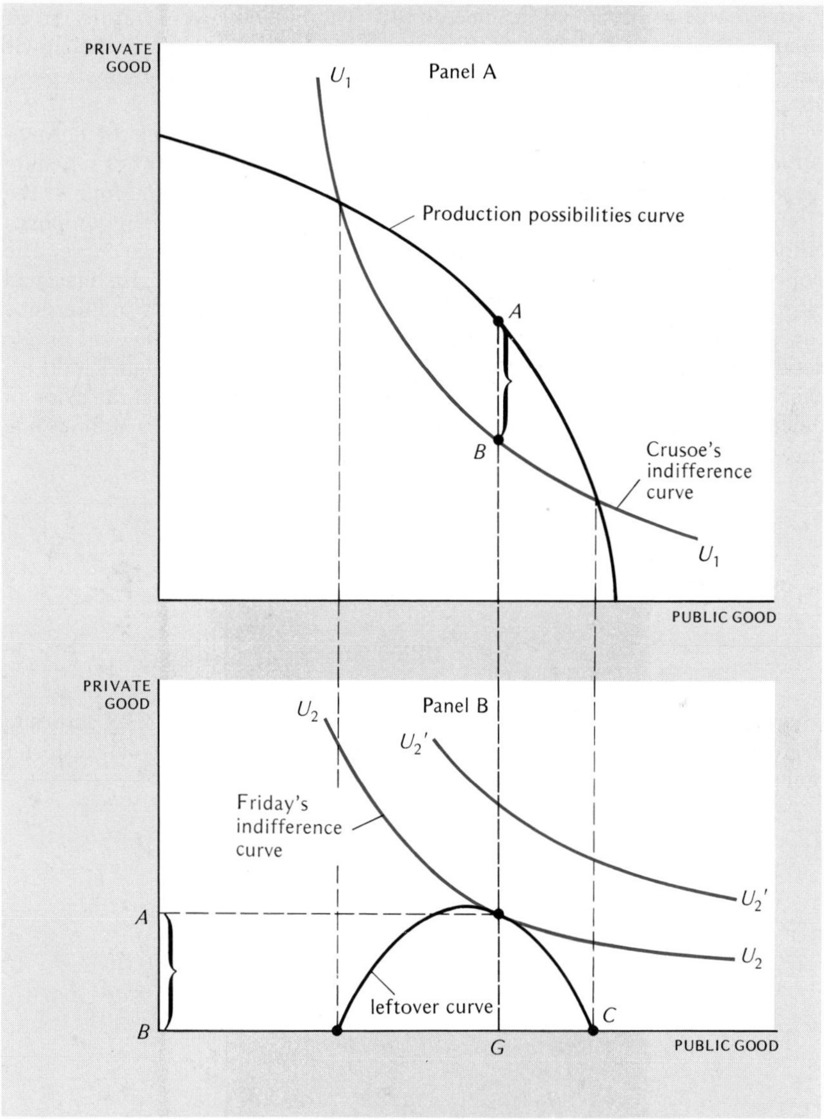

5.12 DETERMINATION OF THE EFFICIENT LEVEL OF PRODUCTION OF PUBLIC GOODS (A) If the level of public goods is *G*, and the first individual is to get level of utility U_1, then the distance *AB* represents the amount of private goods left over for the second individual. (B) The second individual's welfare is maximized at the point of tangency of his indifference curve and the "leftover" curve.

In Figure 5.12A we have superimposed Crusoe's indifference curve on the production possibilities schedule. If the government provides a level of public goods G, and wishes, at the same time, to ensure that Crusoe attains the level of utility associated with the indifference curve U_1 drawn in the figure, then the amount of private good that is "leftover" for Friday is the vertical distance between the production possibilities schedule and the indifference curve. Accordingly, we call the (vertical) difference between the two the leftover curve. This leftover curve is plotted in Figure 5.12B. We now superimpose on Figure 5.12B Friday's indifference curves. The highest level of utility he can attain, consistent with the production possibilities schedule, and consistent with the prespecified level of utility of Crusoe, is at the point of tangency between his indifference curve and the leftover curve.

There is a simple way to express this tangency condition. Since the leftover curve represents the difference between the production possibilities schedule for the economy and the first individual's indifference curve, the slope of the "leftover" curve is the difference between the slope of the production possibilities schedule and the slope of the first individual's indifference curve. The slope of the production possibilities schedule is, as we just saw, the marginal rate of transformation, while the slope of the first individual's indifference curve is his marginal rate of substitution. If G is the optimal level of public goods, the leftover curve must be tangent to the second individual's indifference curve. Hence Pareto efficiency of the economy requires that the slope of the leftover curve be equal to the slope of the second individual's indifference curve—that is,

$$MRT - MRS^1 = MRS^2$$

or

$$MRT = MRS^1 + MRS^2,$$

where MRT stands for the marginal rate of transformation and MRS^i stands for the ith individual's marginal rate of substitution. The marginal rate of transformation must equal the sum of the marginal rates of substitution.

6

Public Choice

The supply of conventional goods is determined by market forces. Equilibrium occurs at the intersection of the demand and supply curves. As we saw in Chapter 3, these market forces ensure that what is produced reflects the tastes of consumers. In contrast, the supply of public goods is determined through a political process. This chapter is concerned with two sets of questions:

1. What can we say about how the level of public-goods expenditure is determined in a democratic society, such as the United States, where such decisions are made by majority voting (or by elected representatives who are chosen on the basis of a majority vote)? How accurately are the preferences of the citizens reflected? Is the supply Pareto efficient? If not, are expenditures on public goods too high or too low?

2. Are there better democratic procedures for determining the level of public goods? Are there procedures that better reflect the preferences of the individuals in society? It is often alleged that the government acts in an inconsistent manner, making a series of choices and decisions that appear to be incompatible. Is this a reflection of incompetence on the part of government officials, is it a consequence of particular aspects of the political process in the United States, or is this an *inevitable* consequence of democratic decision making?

These questions bring us to the border between political science and economics. Our concern is understanding economic aspects of the political process. Traditional political science has been particularly concerned with the role of special-interest groups and how various political institutions and groups in society exercise "political power." Our focus is somewhat more abstract. We say nothing about particular institutions, and little about interest groups. Nor do we discuss the influence of particular individuals, of a Ronald Reagan or a Franklin D. Roosevelt, on the outcomes of the political process. We are concerned with questions such as: How can we explain the tendency in the United States for both political parties to move toward the center, with the consequence that voters are presented with relatively little choice? How successfully can we predict, on the basis of economic variables alone, the outcomes of elections and the voting patterns of the elected representatives?

We begin our discussion with an analysis of how the political process for determining the level of public goods differs from market mechanisms.

PRIVATE MECHANISMS FOR ALLOCATING RESOURCES

The market economy provides a simple and effective method for determining the level of production of *private* goods: the price system. It provides incentives for firms to produce goods that are valued, and it provides a basis for allocating the goods that are produced among the various consumers. We often speak of the important role that prices play in conveying information: from consumers to producers, concerning the value they attach to different commodities, and from producers to consumers and from one producer to another, concerning the costs of production and the scarcity of these commodities.

Equilibrium in private markets is determined at the intersection of the demand curve and the supply curve. When, for one reason or another, the demand for some commodity increases, the demand curve shifts up, the price rises, and this induces firms to produce more. Thus, information about a change in individuals' tastes is conveyed, through the price system, to firms. Similarly, when, for one reason or another, it becomes less costly to produce some commodity, the supply curve for that commodity will shift down, the price will fall, and individuals will be induced to shift their consumption toward the commodity that is now cheaper. Again, the price system has conveyed information about the change in technology from the firm to consumers. Indeed, one of the central results of modern welfare economics, as we pointed out in Chapter 3, is that in a competitive economy, the resulting resource allocations are efficient.[1]

[1] It is important, however, to bear in mind the many caveats to this basic result that we discussed in Chapter 3. In particular, the simple heuristic argument concerning the informational role played by prices in efficient production needs to be treated with some caution. Traditional analysis makes very strong and unrealistic assumptions concerning the nature of the information that is available to the various agents in society. When more realistic informational assumptions are made, the welfare theorem needs to be qualified.

PUBLIC MECHANISMS FOR ALLOCATING RESOURCES

Decisions about resource allocations in the public sector are made in quite a different manner. Individuals vote for elected representatives, these elected representatives in turn vote for a public budget, and the money itself is spent by a variety of administrative agencies. There is thus a major difference between how an individual decides to spend his own money and how, say, Congress decides to spend the public's money. A congressman, when he votes, is supposed to reflect the views of constituents, not just his own views. In deciding how to vote, he faces two problems: first he must ascertain what the views of his constituents are; secondly, since these views are likely to differ, he must decide how much weight to assign to various positions.

The Problem of Preference Revelation

While individuals may express their views about the desirability of one private good versus another by a simple action—they decide either to buy the good or not—there is no comparably effective way that individuals can express their views about the desirability of one public good versus another.

Federal elections of senators and representatives convey only limited information about voters' attitudes toward specific public goods; at best, they convey a general notion that voters prefer more or less government spending. At the state and local levels, voters are sometimes asked to approve specific appropriations (often bond issues for provision of highways and mass transportation). But even then, the information obtained is limited; if an individual voted for what is in his own best interest, it would simply indicate that he believed that his gain from the public program exceeded its cost to him. If a majority voted for the program, it would mean that this is true for at least half the voters, but not that the sum of the benefits exceeded the costs.

Economists have also worried, in those circumstances where individuals are asked what their preferences are, whether they would *truthfully* reveal their preferences. Is there any way in which individuals could be induced to reveal truthfully their preferences concerning public goods?

The decision maker in private decisions knows his own preferences. The decision maker in public decisions has to ascertain the preferences of those on whose behalf he is making the decision. This is the first important difference between public and private resource allocations.

The Problem of Aggregating Preferences: Reconciling Differing Views

Even if all individuals correctly and honestly reveal their preferences, the politician must have some way of putting the information together to make a decision. In the private market, the firm does not have to balance the claims and interests of one group against those of another. If an individual is willing to pay a price for the commodity that exceeds the marginal cost of production, it pays the firm to sell the commodity to the individual. Decisions are made on an individual basis. In contrast, in the public sector, decisions are made collectively—when a politician votes to increase the expenditure on some public good, it is not as if he has to pay for the good himself. His vote is intended to represent the interest of his constituents, but their opinions are not likely to be unanimous. Some individuals would like more military spending, others less. Some individuals would like more expenditures on welfare, others less. How should the politician vote in the face of such conflicts?

One view says that the politician should realize that in the case of pure public goods, such as defense, efficiency requires that sum of the marginal rates of substitution equal the marginal rate of transformation. But even if the politician realizes this, it will be of only limited help. It will help him avoid Pareto-inefficient outcomes. But it will not tell him how to select among alternative Pareto-efficient allocations. Issues of income distribution are central to most public policy debates.

Another view sees the politician as an individual acting in his self-interest (just as consumers and producers act in their own self-interest). The politician is interested in staying in office. The "price" he pays (or receives) for voting one way or another on budgetary issues is a loss (or gain) in votes. (This assumes, of course, that there is some significant relationship between how the politician votes on particular budgetary matters and how citizens vote in the next election.) What implications this hypothesis has for the voting behavior of politicians is a question we shall soon investigate.

But even when a particular representative decides about his position on a specific issue, other representatives are likely to have differing views. The problem of reconciling differences arises whenever there must be a collective decision. Popular political discussions often refer to what the "people" want. But since different people want different things, how, out of these divergent views, can a social decision be made? In a dictatorship, the answer is easy: it is the preferences of the dictator that dominate. But in a democracy, there is no such easy resolution. A number of different voting rules have been suggested, among them unanimity voting, simple majority voting, and two-thirds majority voting. Of these, perhaps the most widely employed rule for decision making in a democracy is majority voting.

MAJORITY VOTING

The majority voting rule says that, in the choice between two alternatives, the alternative that receives the majority of votes wins. The alternatives can be thought of as two different levels of expenditure on some public good, or the decision to undertake one project, say, building a new swimming pool, rather than another, say, building a new set of tennis courts.

How the Typical Taxpayer Casts His Vote

We first analyze the *preferences* of the voter. We shall assume that he casts his ballot on the narrow grounds of self-interest: he evaluates the benefit he receives from any new government program and compares it with the extra cost he has to bear. Thus, in Figure 6.1A, as the government increases its expenditures on public goods, the individual gets some extra benefit (the *marginal utility* of an additional expenditure on public goods). The *marginal cost* he has to bear depends on the tax structure. Assume, for instance, that the tax burden is shared equally among 100 individuals. Then, if the government spends $1,000 more on public goods, his extra tax is $10; his *marginal cost* (in utility terms) is the marginal utility of each dollar (which he would otherwise spend on the consumption of private goods) times his incremental tax ($10).

If the government is spending very little on public goods, the marginal utility of the public good is very high; as the government spends more and more, the marginal utility of the public good diminishes. At the same time, as the government spends more on public goods, individuals have fewer private goods. Thus the marginal utility of private goods increases, so the marginal cost (in utility terms) of the public good (the foregone consumption of private goods) increases. Since the marginal benefits from public goods are diminishing, and the marginal costs are increasing, the *net marginal benefit*—the marginal benefit minus the marginal cost—while positive for low values of government expenditures, is negative for high values of government expenditures. To put this another way, the individual's utility increases initially with increased government expenditures (there is a positive net marginal benefit) but eventually decreases. The level of government expenditures most preferred by the individual is obviously that level at which utility is maximized, or where the *net* marginal benefit is zero. This is the point in Figure 6.1A where marginal benefit equals marginal cost (remember, *net* marginal benefits is the *difference* between marginal benefits and marginal costs). In Figure 6.1B, we plot the level of utility as a function of government expenditures (taking into account the extra taxes that must be paid as public expenditures increase). The point G^* at which marginal benefit equals marginal cost corresponds to the point where utility is maximized.

There are three factors that determine an individual's attitudes toward public-goods expenditure. First, some individuals may simply like public goods more than others. Some individuals may get a great deal of pleasure out of public parks, while others never use them. Secondly, individuals' incomes differ. For individuals who are poor, the marginal utility of private goods will be higher than for wealthy individuals. Poor individuals will be less willing than the wealthy to give up a

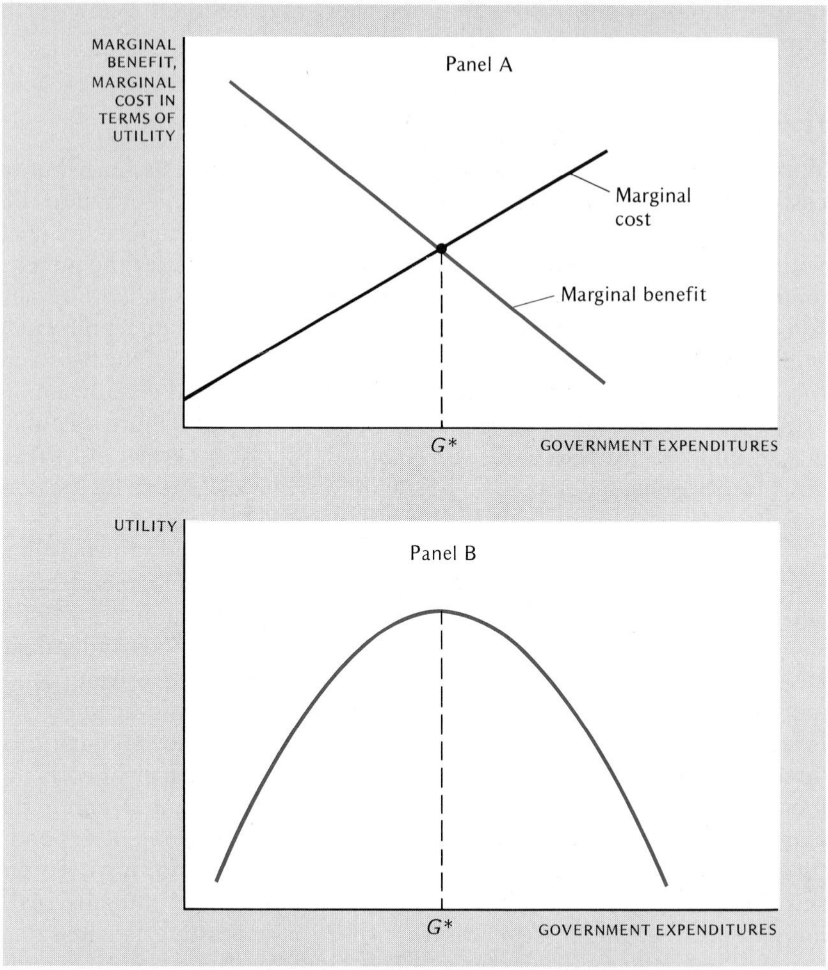

6.1 INDIVIDUAL'S EVALUATION OF THE DESIRABILITY OF INCREASED GOVERNMENT EXPENDITURES Panel A shows the change in an individual's utility (his marginal benefit) as he is provided with an additional dollar of government services, and the loss in utility (his marginal cost) as he has to bear a part of their cost. As public expenditure increases, the marginal benefit of increased expenditures decreases, and the marginal cost (of foregone private expenditures) increases. Panel B shows the level of his utility at each level of government expenditure. His utility is maximized at G^*, where the marginal benefit equals the marginal cost. G^* is the individual's most preferred level of expenditures, given the tax structure, which specifies by how much his taxes increase as public expenditure increases.

dollar of private goods to get a given increment in public goods. Because they have fewer private goods, the marginal utility of public goods may be higher for them as well, but under normal conditions, the increase in their marginal utility of private goods exceeds that for public goods; more generally, at any level of expenditure on public goods the marginal

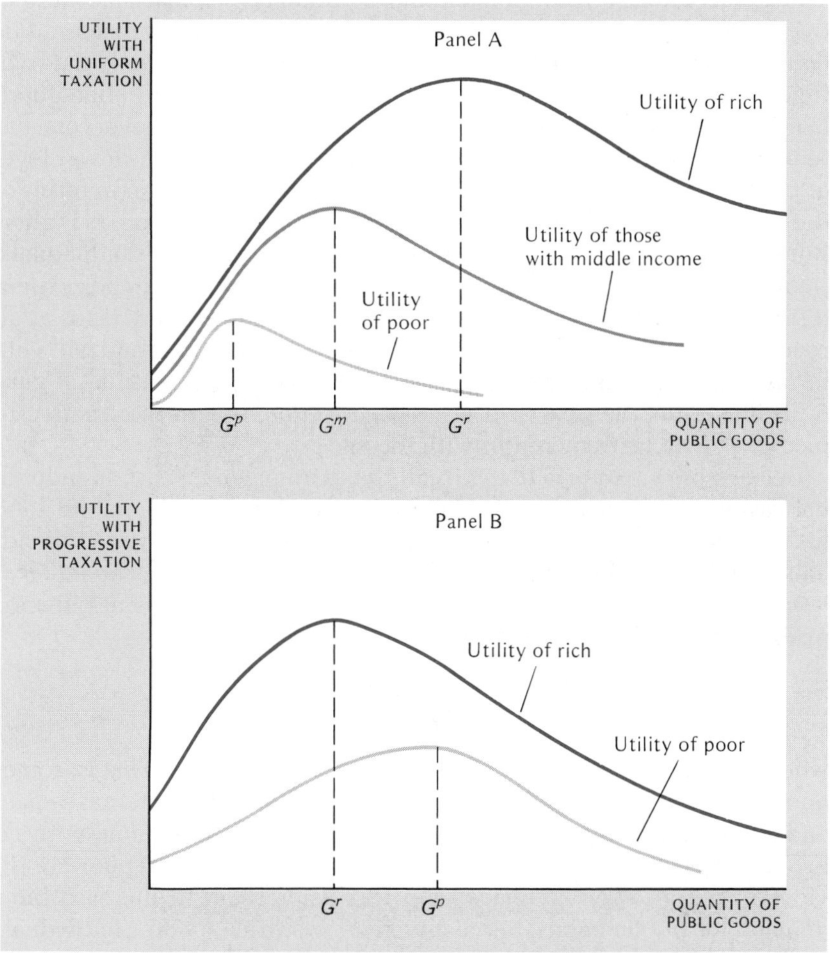

6.2 UTILITY LEVELS AS A FUNCTION OF GOVERNMENT EXPENDITURES (A) With uniform taxation (where everyone has to pay the same amount), the higher the income, the more government spending is preferred. G^p is the most preferred point of the poor, G^m of those with middle income, and G^r of the rich. With uniform taxation, the marginal cost (the marginal utility of the private goods foregone) is higher for the poor. (B) With progressive taxation, the marginal cost to the poor of additional expenditures on public goods may be relatively little, and hence their demand for public goods may be high. The level of expenditures on public goods that maximize their utility may exceed that of the rich.

rate of substitution—how many units of private goods they are willing to sacrifice for a unit increase in public goods—is smaller for poorer individuals. As a result, with uniform taxation, rich individuals will prefer higher levels of expenditures on public goods, as illustrated in Figure 6.2A.

These statements are not inconsistent with the observations that poor individuals often seem to demand more public goods; this is because of the third determinant of individuals' attitudes toward increased public expenditure—the nature of the tax system, which determines what fraction of the additional costs associated with the increased public-goods expenditures each individual has to bear. With a tax where everyone has to pay the same amount, a poor individual is likely to prefer a lower level of public-goods expenditure, since the marginal cost to him (in terms of the foregone utility from the private goods he has to give up) is higher. But if the poorer individuals have to pay less than the richer individuals, then poor individuals may prefer a higher level of public-goods expenditure. Obviously, an individual who does not have to pay taxes at all receives only benefits from increased public expenditures and will vote for as high a level of expenditure on public goods as is feasible. Figure 6.2B illustrates the case of *progressive taxation,* where the fraction of income paid in taxes increases with income.

Recall from Chapter 5 that we call the extra payment that an individual has to make for each extra dollar of expenditure on the public good his **tax price.** Thus, with uniform taxation, in an economy with N individuals, the tax price facing each individual is $1/N$. With *proportional taxation* (where everyone pays the same percentage of his income), the tax price for an individual whose income is Y_i, is

$$\frac{Y_i}{\overline{Y}} \cdot \frac{1}{N},$$

where $\overline{Y}$ is the average level of income in the population. That is, someone whose income is average pays exactly $1/N$th of the total taxes paid and faces exactly the same tax price as before. An individual with no income pays no taxes and thus has a tax price of zero.[2] Thus poorer individuals face a lower tax price, and this leads them to increase their demand for public goods; but at any given tax price, poorer individuals prefer a lower level of expenditure on public goods than wealthy individuals. These two effects offset each other, so that it is possible with proportional taxation that poorer individuals prefer either higher or lower levels of public expenditures than do richer individuals..

In Chapter 5, we showed how to derive the individual's demand curve for public goods. The demand curve shows how an individual's most preferred level of public goods varies as his tax price varies.

Figure 6.3 shows the effect of differences in income on an individual's demand for public goods. First, Panel A shows the lower budget con-

[2] This formula for the tax price may easily be derived. Let t be the tax rate. Total government income is

$$t \cdot N \cdot \overline{Y},$$

since total national income is average income, $\overline{Y}$, times the number of individuals. This must equal government expenditure,

$$t \cdot N \cdot \overline{Y} = G \quad \text{or} \quad t = \frac{G}{N\overline{Y}}.$$

If government expenditure increases by a unit, the *tax rate* must increase by $1/N\overline{Y}$. The tax paid by an individual with income Y_i is just tY_i, and so his incremental tax—his tax price—is just $Y_i/N\overline{Y}$.

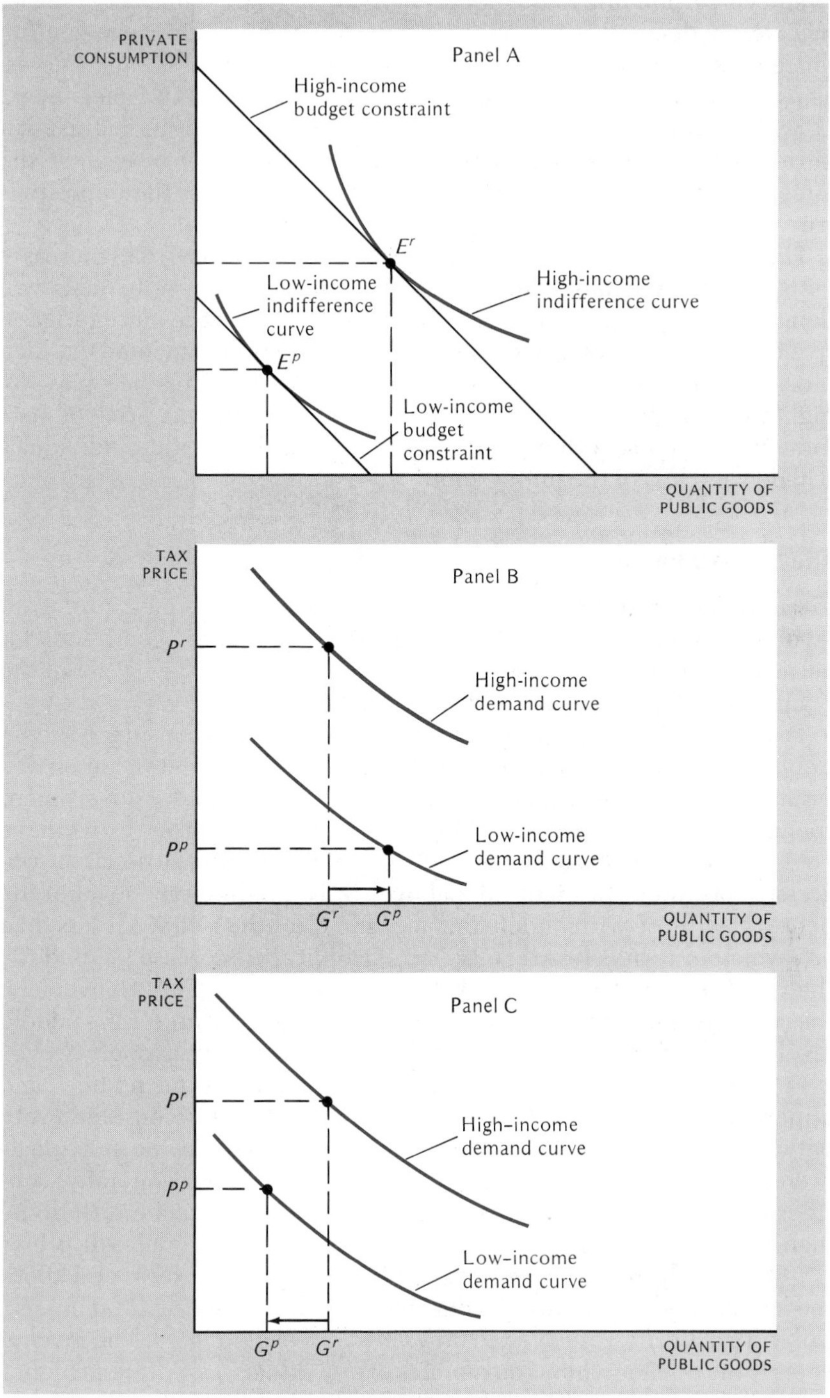

6.3 EFFECT OF DIFFERENCES IN INCOME ON DEMAND FOR PUBLIC GOODS (A) If all individuals face the same tax price (so that their budget constraints have the same slope), low-income individuals will normally demand a lower level of public goods. If individuals with lower incomes have a lower tax price, their demand for public goods may be higher (as in Panel B) or lower (as in Panel C).

straint corresponding to the poorer individual. At the same tax price, he will clearly demand fewer public goods: points E^p and E^r represent the tangencies between the budget constraints and indifference curves. Thus the poorer individual's demand curve, illustrated in Panels B and C, will always be below that of the rich. But the poorer individual will normally face a lower tax price. In Panel B this effect outweighs the effect of having a lower demand, while in Panel C, just the opposite is true.

The more the demand for the public good (at any tax price) increases with income, the more likely it is that high-income individuals will demand more of the public good. On the other hand, the more progressive the tax system, that is, the higher the proportion of income that rich individuals pay in taxes *relative* to that which poor individuals pay, the higher the tax price of rich individuals *relative* to the tax price of poor individuals; and accordingly, the more likely it is that rich individuals will demand less of the public good.

The Median Voter

We have now described how each voter decides on his most preferred level of expenditure in the simple case of a single public good. Individuals will differ on their most preferred level. What can we say about the equilibrium that results when these individuals vote?

To analyze the majority voting equilibrium, we first consider a simple example, where there are three individuals with different incomes. We assume that the wealthier the individual is, the more government spending he or she prefers. (This will generally be true, as we have noted, for uniform taxation, but not necessarily for proportional or progressive taxation.) In Figure 6.2 above, G^p is the preferred level of the poor, G^m of those with middle income, and G^r of the rich. G^p is less than G^m, which in turn is less than G^r. As expenditures increase beyond G^p, the poor's utility declines. Thus the poor prefer G^m to G^r. Conversely, the rich, while preferring G^r to either G^m or G^p, clearly prefer the middle level of expenditure, G^m, to the low level preferred by the poor, G^p.

First, consider a vote between G^p and G^m. Both the middle- and upper-income individuals vote for G^m, so G^m wins. Now consider a vote between G^m and G^r; clearly both the middle- and low-income individuals prefer G^m to G^r, so G^m again gets 2 out of 3 votes. More generally, consider G^m against any other level of expenditure lower than G^m. Both the high-income individual and the middle-income individual will prefer G^m. Conversely, for any level of expenditure slightly in excess of G^m both the low-income and middle-income individuals will prefer G^m. Thus, G^m can win a majority vote over all other levels of expenditure. The **median voter** is the one for whom the number of individuals who prefer a higher level of expenditure (the number of individuals who have a higher income) is exactly equal to the number of individuals who prefer a lower level of expenditure (the number of individuals who have a lower income). The result we have just obtained is general: the *majority voting equilibrium level of expenditures is the level that is most preferred by the median voter.*[3]

To find out who the median voter is and therefore what the level of expenditures on public goods will be, we arrange individuals in order by the level of expenditures they most prefer. For each level of government expenditure we can ask what fraction of individuals prefer the government to spend less. The median voter is that voter for whom exactly half prefer the government to spend less (and correspondingly, exactly half prefer the government to spend more).

The median voter may have an income that is above or below *average* income. We calculate the average income by taking the total income and dividing it by the number of individuals. Assume that wealthier individuals demand more public goods. Then if all individuals vote, the median voter is the individual who has the median income. In Figure 6.4 we have depicted the distribution of income, which gives the percentage of the population at different income levels. As we have drawn it, the income distribution is not *symmetric*—that is, there are many more people who have very low incomes than have very high incomes. The few people with very high incomes raise the average level of income, so with this kind of income distribution, the individual with a median income has a lower income than the average income.

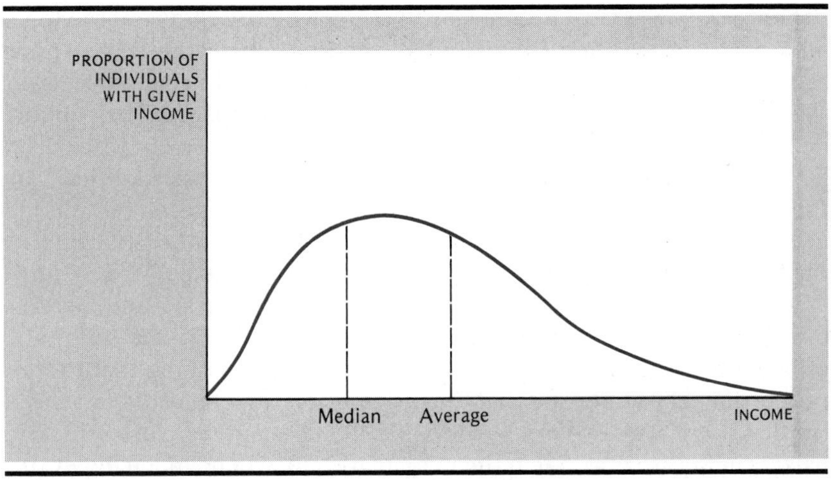

6.4 RELATIONSHIP BETWEEN AVERAGE AND MEDIAN INCOME With a distribution of income which is skewed to the right, the median is much less than the average. The median income is the income such that 50 percent have incomes below that number, 50 percent have incomes above that number. In a skewed distribution, the very large incomes of the very rich increase the average, resulting in the average exceeding the median.

[3] Provided a majority voting equilibrium exists. We shall see that such an equilibrium may not exist.

The median voter theory implies that if there is a redistribution of income within a community, so that the income of the median voter increases, then the demand for public goods in the community will rise even though the average income remains the same.

Similarly, the median voter theory says that a change that leaves the demand for public goods of the median individual unchanged will leave the equilibrium expenditure on public goods unchanged, regardless of what happens to the demand for public goods by other individuals. For instance, in the discussions leading up to the Tax Reform Act of 1986, it was proposed to eliminate the deductibility of state and local taxes for purposes of the federal income tax. This would have reduced the demand for state and local goods by all individuals who itemize their deductions. But in most states, the median voter does not itemize his deductions; thus the median voter theory would have predicted that this change would leave the level of expenditures on public goods at the state and local level unchanged.

The Inefficiency of the Majority Voting Equilibrium

Since the median voter determines the level of expenditure, to ascertain whether there is too much or too little expenditure on public goods we need only examine how he votes, and contrast that with the conditions for efficiency discussed in Chapter 5. The median individual is assumed to compare only the benefits he receives with the costs that he bears. His benefits are lower than total social benefits (which includes all the benefits that accrue to others), but so are his costs. Whether there is too much or too little expenditure on public goods depends thus on whether his share of total (marginal) costs is less than or greater than his share of total benefits.

Consider first the example where all individuals are identical, and there is uniform taxation. Then, if there are N individuals, the individual's private benefits are $1/N$ of the total benefits, and his costs are $1/N$ of the total costs. The majority voting equilibrium is efficient.

Now consider a case where all individuals obtain the same marginal benefit from the public good; the median individual's private assessment of benefits is $1/N$ of total marginal social benefits. Assume that there is proportional taxation, and that the distribution of income is very skewed (so that there are few very wealthy individuals, and many poor individuals, as in Figure 6.4). Then the median income will be much lower than the average income, so that with a proportional income tax, the tax price of the median individual will be very low. He will bear a small share of the total costs. Because his private marginal benefits represent $1/N$ of the total social marginal benefits, but his private marginal costs are less than $1/N$ of the total social marginal costs, there will be an oversupply of the public good. This argument is strengthened if the tax system is progressive, so that low-income individuals pay a smaller proportion of their income in taxes than do higher-income individuals.

This argument for the oversupply of public goods assumes that the marginal benefits of the public good do not differ much by income. But there are some publicly provided goods whose marginal benefits may rise with income. Thus, higher-income individuals may value more highly public television, or public support for the arts. Because the median voter's marginal valuation of these benefits is *less* than 1/*N*th that of total social marginal benefits of the public good, there may be an undersupply of such goods, even though the median voter pays less than 1/*N*th the total marginal social costs of the good.

The Voting Paradox

A more widely discussed limitation of majority voting is the possibility that there does not exist an equilibrium. This problem was noted as early as the eighteenth century by a famous French philosopher, Condorcet, and may be seen in the following simple example, where there are three voters and three alternatives, denoted A, B, and C.

Voter 1 prefers A to B to C
Voter 2 prefers C to A to B
Voter 3 prefers B to C to A

Assume we vote on A versus B. Voters 1 and 2 vote for A, so A wins. Now we vote on A versus C. Voters 2 and 3 prefer C to A, so C wins. It appears that C should be the social choice. C wins against A, which wins against B. But let us now have a direct confrontation between C and B. Both Voter 1 and Voter 3 prefer B to C. This is referred to as the **voting paradox,** or the paradox of cyclical voting. There is no clear winner. B beats C and C beats A but A beats B.

If we employ majority voting, then it is clear that it may be very important to control the agenda. Assume we structure the election as first a contest between A and B, and then the winner of that contest against C. Clearly, C could win that election. But suppose instead we structured the election as first a contest between B and C, and then the winner of that contest against A. A would win that election. Finally, suppose we structured the election as first a contest between A and C, and the winner of that election against B. Then clearly B would win. Thus the winner of each of these elections is determined solely by the order in which the pair-wise comparisons were made.

Note, too, that if the individuals realize there is going to be a particular sequence of votes, they may wish to vote strategically. That is, in the first round of the vote, Voter 1 may not vote his true preferences on, say, A versus B, but think through the *consequences* of that for the eventual equilibrium. He may vote for B, even though he would prefer A, knowing that in a contest between C and B, B will win, while in a contest between A and C, C might win. Since he prefers B to C, he votes initially for B.

Single-Peaked Preferences and the Existence of a Majority Voting Equilibrium

The voting paradox does not always arise. Indeed, earlier, we showed that, in voting on the level of public goods, there was a well-defined majority voting equilibrium, which corresponded to the preferences of the median voter. What distinguishes those cases where an equilibrium exists from those where it does not?

In Figure 6.2, we plotted the level of utility as a function of the level of expenditure on public goods. There, each individual has a single peak to his preference profile. This property of **single-peakedness** is enough to guarantee the existence of a majority voting equilibrium. Note that the peak need not be "interior" but could lie on the "end," so that preferences such as those in Figure 6.5A are also consistent with single-peakedness.

On the other hand, preferences such as those illustrated in Figure 6.5C are not consistent with single-peakedness. Both 0 and G_1 are (local) peaks. Unfortunately, such examples arise naturally in considering many public choice problems.

For instance, consider the problem of an individual's attitudes toward expenditures on public education. If the level of expenditure on public education is below a certain minimum level, a rich individual may prefer to send his children to private schools. If he does this, any increase in expenditure on public schools simply increases his taxes; he gets no direct benefits. Thus his utility decreases with government expenditures up to a critical level at which he decides to send his children to public school. For increases beyond that level, he derives some benefit. Of course, beyond some point, the increases in taxes more than offset the benefits. For this individual, a high level of expenditure is preferred to no expenditure, but no expenditure is preferred to an intermediate level of expenditure. There may be no majority voting equilibrium in this case.

Although preferences for a *single* public good (with no private-good option, unlike education) are usually single-peaked, when we have to rank choices involving more than one public good, those rankings are seldom single-peaked.[4] To obtain single-peakedness, we have to restrict ourselves to voting on one issue at a time.[5]

Equally important, there will not be a majority voting equilibrium for most distribution issues.[6] This can be seen most clearly in considering the structure of income taxation. Suppose we are voting among three income tax schedules that are designed to raise the same amount of revenue. For simplicity, we shall assume there are three groups of individ-

[4] See G. Kramer, "On a Class of Equilibrium Conditions for Majority Rule," *Econometrica* 41 (1973): 285–97.

[5] See S. Slutsky, "A Voting Model for the Allocation of Public Goods: Existence of an Equilibrium," *Journal of Economic Theory* 11 (1975): 292–304.

[6] See D. K. Foley, "Resource Allocation and the Public Sector," *Yale Economic Essays* 7 (1967): 45–98.

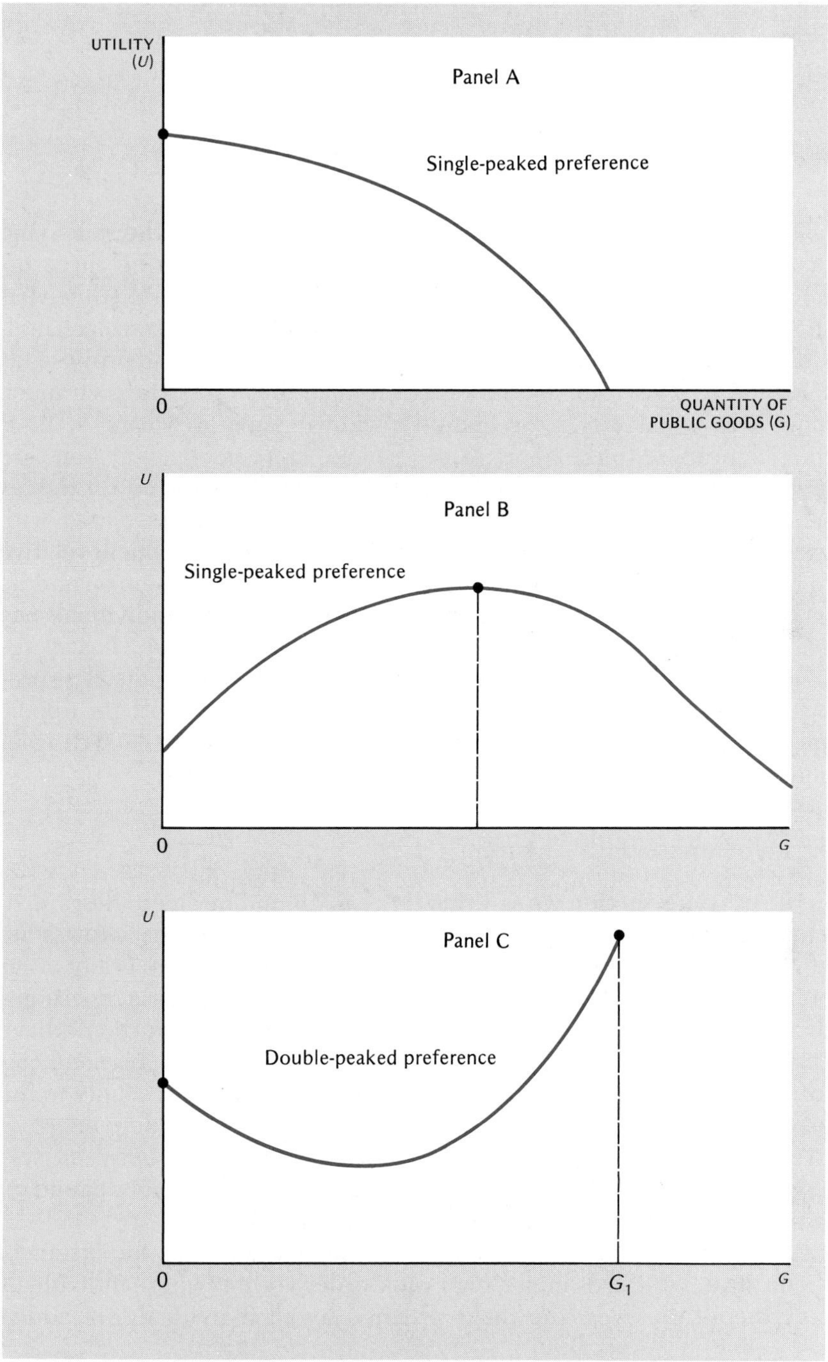

6.5 SINGLE-PEAKED AND DOUBLE-PEAKED PREFERENCES With single-peaked preferences (Panels A and B), there always exists a majority voting equilibrium. Without single-peakedness (Panel C), there may not exist a majority voting equilibrium.

Table 6.1 ALTERNATIVE TAX SCHEDULES

Fraction of Income Paid in Taxes	*A*	*B*	*C*
Poor	20%	18%	17%
Middle	20%	18%	21%
Rich	20%	24%	22%

uals with equal numbers: the poor, the middle class, and the rich—and that they vote in solid blocks. Assume we are considering three tax schedules, denoted by A, B, and C, in Table 6.1. Tax schedule A is strictly proportional; it takes the same fraction of income from each individual. The poor and the middle class then get together and propose tax schedule B. This reduces the taxes they pay but taxes the rich much more heavily. Clearly, tax schedule B will win a majority over A. Now, the rich propose to the poor: "Since you are more needy, why don't we lower your taxes somewhat more; at the same time, we'll adjust the tax schedule at the upper end, to reduce the inequities associated with excessive taxation." Thus they propose tax schedule C, which, relative to B, lowers the taxes on low and high income and raises them on middle income, so that now both the middle- and upper-income individuals pay a larger proportion of their income in taxes than do the poor. Clearly, tax schedule C wins a majority over B. Now, however, the middle class proposes we go back to straight proportional taxation. Since both the upper- and middle-income individuals prefer schedule A, A defeats C. We again get a cyclical pattern of voting.[7]

Arrow's Impossibility Theorem

In the previous section we saw that there might not be an equilibrium to a majority voting political process. This is clearly an unsatisfactory state of affairs. A natural question to ask, then, is whether there is any other political mechanism, any other set of rules for making social decisions, that will eliminate this problem. The political mechanism should have certain other desirable properties: it should, for instance, be nondictatorial (with a dictator, the decisions of society correspond simply to the preferences of the dictator). The outcome should be independent of irrelevant alternatives; that is, if we have to make a choice between, say, a swimming pool and a tennis court, the outcome should not depend on whether there is a third alternative (a new library).

A number of alternative rules have been examined, for instance, requiring a two-thirds majority or rank-order voting (where individuals rank the alternatives, the ranks assigned by all individuals are added

[7] If we restrict the set of tax schedules over which voting occurs, for instance to tax schedules with an exemption level and a fixed marginal tax rate (these are called flat-rate tax schedules), there may be a majority voting equilibrium. See T. Romer, "Individual Welfare, Majority Voting, and the Properties of a Linear Income Tax," *Journal of Public Economics* 4 (1975): 163–85.

together, and the alternative with the lowest score wins). All of those examined fail to meet one or the other criterion. The quest for an ideal system came to an end with the findings of Nobel Laureate Kenneth Arrow of Stanford. He showed that there was no rule that would satisfy all of the desired characteristics. This theorem is referred to as **Arrow's impossibility theorem**.[8]

Arrow's impossibility theorem has one further interesting and important implication. We often hear expressions such as: "The government should do such and such . . .," "It is the responsibility of the state to . . .," "The government seems to be acting in an inconsistent manner . . .," or "Why doesn't the government determine its priorities and then act upon them?" This language personifies the government, treats the government as if it were an individual. Language is important: although we all know that the government is not a single individual, speaking of it as if it were, we are frequently led to believe that it is. We come to expect that government should act consistently like a rational individual. But Arrow's impossibility theorem suggests that, short of granting some individual dictatorial powers, one should not expect the government to act with the same degree of consistency and rationality as an individual. In subsequent chapters, we shall often talk of the "government." But in doing so, we do not wish to personify it, to treat it as if it were a single individual, to ascribe to it more wisdom than the individuals who compose it have. The caveats that we have raised throughout this and the next chapter must be constantly borne in mind.

Further Results on Voting

We have noted that with single-peaked preferences, there always exists a majority voting equilibrium, while if this condition is not satisfied, one cannot, in general, find *any* voting system that has the desired properties. There has been a long quest for conditions that are not as restrictive as single-peakedness and under which some voting system will work. The strongest result to date is that of two young Princeton economists, Andrew Caplin and Barry Nalebuff. They asked: Assuming that we could overturn existing policies only with a vote of x percent, what is the *smallest* value that x could be to ensure an equilibrium, that is, to avoid cyclical voting patterns? Clearly, with majority voting (x=50 percent), cyclical voting can occur. With unanimity, no Pareto-efficient allocation could be overturned (since any alternative would have to hurt someone, and he could, by assumption, veto it). Hence, cyclical voting will not arise with unanimity. Caplin and Nalebuff have shown that so long as preferences of the voters do not differ too much, a voting rule of 64 percent will ensure that there will be no cyclical voting.[9]

[8] See K. Arrow, *Social Choice and Individual Values*, 2nd ed. (New York: Wiley, 1963).

[9] A. Caplin and B. Nalebuff, "On the 64% Majority Rule," *Econometrica,* forthcoming.

In the example we discussed earlier in which there was no majority voting equilibrium, we saw the importance of the control of the agenda. We also saw that, in general, it is beneficial for individuals to vote strategically, that is, to vote not according to their true preferences, but to take into account how the outcome of the current vote will affect the final outcome. These results turn out to be general: just as Arrow established that there does not exist any way of adding together the preferences of different individuals to satisfy all of the desired characteristics, it has been shown that there does not, in general, exist any voting system[10] in which individuals will always vote their true preferences.

The Two-Party System and the Median Voter

We noted earlier that an elected representative bears a negligible fraction of the costs of, and receives a negligible fraction of the benefits from, an increase in government expenditure. What can economic theory say about how he should vote? A natural supposition is that the politician wishes to stay in office and that, accordingly, he wishes to maximize his votes, given the position taken by his rival. A vote-maximizing voting strategy can easily be defined as follows: Assume there are two parties "R" and "D." Party R takes the position of Party D as given. Focusing on a single issue, the level of expenditure, denote by G_R the "position" (that is, the level of public expenditure advocated by the party) of Party R and by G_D the "position" of Party D. For each value of G_D there is an optimal (i.e., vote-maximizing) position for G_R.

Under the hypothesis that each party seeks to maximize its vote given the position of its rival, what will each party do? Let G_m be the preferred level of expenditure of the median voter. Suppose Party D chooses $G_D > G_m$. Then if Party R takes a position between G_m and G_D, it will get all the voters who prefer an expenditure level less than or equal to G_m, and some who prefer slightly more. Thus Party R gets over 50 percent of the votes and wins. In response, Party D will choose a position, G_D', between G_m and G_R, which wins against G_R. But then Party R chooses a position, G_R', between G_D' and G_m. The process continues until both parties stand for the same position: that of the median voter (G_m). (See Figure 6.6.)

This result is consistent with the widely observed allegation that with our two-party system voters get no choice: both parties take a "middle-of-the-road" position. This is precisely what the theory predicts.

There are, however, some important limitations of the theory that need to be borne in mind. First, we noted earlier that, in general, there may not exist a majority voting equilibrium. There does if individuals have single-peaked preferences. In the present context, this requires that we should be able to arrange issues along a single dimension—for

[10] A voting system is any set of voting rules by which a group of individuals tries to reach a decision —for instance, by dropping from consideration the alternative with the lowest number of votes or by giving individuals several votes, and allowing them to assign as many as they like to each alternative.

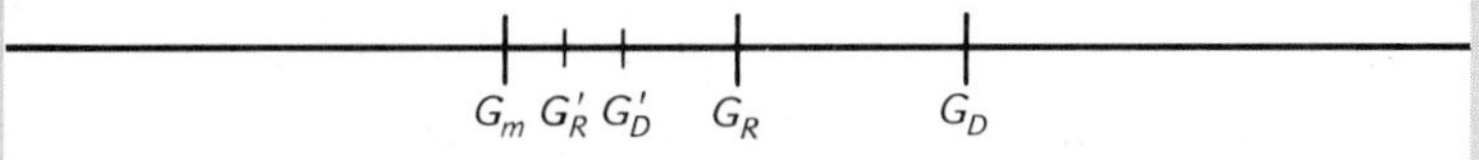

6.6 TWO-PARTY SYSTEM If both parties in a two-party system try to maximize their votes, taking the position of the rival as fixed, in equilibrium both parties will adopt the position of the median voter.

example, conservative-liberal. If, however, there are a variety of dimensions—some individuals are liberal on some issues and conservative on others—then the median voter is not well defined, and there may be no equilibrium to the political process.

Secondly, we have ignored questions of participation in the political process. There are costs associated with being actively involved in it; as a voter, there are costs associated with becoming informed and voting. These costs are sufficiently great relative to the perceived benefits that slight changes in the weather, making it slightly less pleasant to go outside to vote, have significant effects on voter participation. In particular, voters whose preferences are near the median have little incentive to be active politically, particularly if they believe that the political process will reflect their preferences anyway. Thus, it may be in the interests of those who are more extreme to attempt to pull their party away from the center. This tendency for greater political activism at the extremes may partially offset the median-directed tendencies noted earlier.

POLITICS AND ECONOMICS

The discussion of the political process in the preceding section differs markedly from the kind of analysis one might typically find in a political science course. There, one might discuss the roles of special-interest groups and political institutions. A full discussion of the relationship between economic theories of the political process and other theories would take us beyond the scope of this book. In the following pages, we touch on some economic interpretations of certain political phenomena.

Why Do Individuals Vote?

In the previous section, we observed that in many elections voter participation rates are low, and that they are sensitive to such chance occurrences as changes in the weather. The reason for this, as we have noted, is that the benefits of voting are low—there is little chance of affecting the outcome. The alternatives may differ so little that the outcome is inconsequential, and, though the costs of voting are relatively low, they are not low in relationship to the benefits. Indeed, in a fully rational calculation, no one would vote: the probability that an individual's vote would make a difference to the outcome (since in most cases the individual cares only about whether his candidate wins or loses, not the magni tude of the win or loss) is essentially zero. Yet individuals do vote.[11]

This paradox is resolved, in a somewhat tautological manner, simply by assuming that individuals get utility out of voting or more generally out of participation in the political process. More to the point, individuals do give money to charity; they are brought up to believe that it is good to be considerate of others (and that more is entailed by this than simply the view that it is in the individual's self-interest to be considerate of others). So, too, considerable time and energy are devoted to inculcating into our children notions of civic responsibility, and among these civic responsibilities is the responsibility to be an informed voter.

The same considerations imply that when the individual votes, he may not act in the narrowly self-interested manner that we have assumed in our discussion so far. Individuals may vote for closing some loophole in the income tax system because it would result in a more equitable distribution of the tax burden, even though their personal tax liability might thereby be increased.

Elections and Special-Interest Groups

The models we have discussed in the preceding sections have assumed that all individuals are well informed about the consequences of all alternatives under consideration, all individuals vote, and they cast their votes on the basis of the implications that each alternative has for their own (private) welfare.

There are many who believe that this does not provide an adequate description of the political process. Although constitutionally each person has one vote, some votes seem more effective than others. The outcome of the political process, in this view, reflects the political power of special-interest groups.

Assessing the validity of these views is beyond the scope of this chapter. We limit our discussion here to a more narrow set of questions: What can economic theory say about the kinds of interest groups that are likely to be effective? And how can we reconcile the effectiveness of special-interest groups with the fact that each individual does, in the United States, have only one vote?

The answer to these questions is related to our discussion in the previous chapter of the public interest as a public good. We saw there that the efficient management of the public sector was a public good. Simi-

[11] In U.S. presidential elections since 1932, between 51 percent and 63 percent of the voting age population has voted. In elections of U.S. representatives to Congress, participation has been somewhat lower (33 percent to 59 percent) (*Statistical Abstract*, 1987, p. 243). In local school board elections, often less than 10 percent of the eligible voters vote.

larly, choosing elected officials who are competent and who reflect values similar to our own is a public good.

At the same time, we should note that the free rider problem may not be as serious in small groups as it is in large. Thus it is easier to form an interest group of a small number of steel producers to attempt to persuade Congress to restrict steel imports than it is to form an interest group of the large number of steel users who would be adversely affected by such restrictions. *Each* of the producers has more to gain than each of the consumers has to lose, though the aggregate gains of producers may, in fact, be less than the aggregate losses to consumers.

Trade unions have long recognized the nature of the free rider problem, and that is why they have sought closed shops, forcing all workers to support the activities they believe to be in the collective interests of workers. But once they have this power, they can attempt to use it not only at the bargaining table but also in the political arena, where they act as a special-interest group.

The Power of Special-Interest Groups

How are interest groups able to exercise power? There appear to be at least three mechanisms. First, we noted before that individuals have little incentive to vote or to become informed concerning the issues. Interest groups can attempt to lower the costs of voting and information, particularly for those voters who are likely to support them. They do so by making information (obviously supporting their own views) readily available; and they often assist directly by providing transportation, child care, etc., on polling day.

Secondly, we noted the difficulty that politicians have in obtaining information about the preferences of their constituents. There is no simple demand revealing mechanism for public goods as there is for private goods. Interest groups attempt to provide such information. Politicians may lack the technical information required to make informed political decisions—for example, they may not know the consequences of continued imports of cheap foreign steel. Interest groups are a primary source of information, and it is through providing information that they often exercise influence.

The third mechanism is through direct and indirect bribery of the politician. Direct bribery does not occur often, at least in most jurisdictions in the United States. (Presumably, this may not be due to the purity of our politicians so much as to the costs associated with being caught.) But indirect bribery is important: special-interest groups provide financial and other forms of support for politicians who support their interests. Again, this is important because voters must be informed of the positions taken by a candidate, and providing voters with information is costly. Voters must be persuaded that the benefits of voting warrant their going to the trouble of voting, and their private costs must be reduced through providing assistance in going to the polls. We earlier hypothesized that we could explain politicians' behavior by their wish to stay in office; they increase the probability of reelection by maximizing the number of people who are likely to vote for them. Politicians realize that what is of concern is how their stands on particular issues affect the number of individuals who will actually vote for them as opposed to their opponents. They must take into account all the effects, including the increased opportunity to get in touch with the voters, that the additional support of a special-interest group provides.

The Altruistic Politician?

An alternative view says that many politicians do not behave in as self-interested a way as we have assumed throughout this chapter. Just as individuals behave altruistically as private citizens, and give to charity, so too do they behave as public citizens, in their capacity as elected officials. In our society considerable status and respect is accorded to public statesmen and public service. Effective government depends on the quality of these civil servants.

Although there is some grain of truth in this "noneconomic" view, three qualifications should be noted. First, while the majority voting theory provided clear predictions concerning the outcome of political processes, no such clear predictions emerge for a political process that depends on some political leader's views of the public interest. Indeed, it was precisely the seeming capriciousness of the actions taken by political leaders (whether or not allegedly in the public interest) that led Adam Smith to suggest that there was a better way that the public interest might be served: by each individual pursuing his private interest. Unfortunately, though Adam Smith's invisible hand may work well for most goods, it does not work well for public goods.

Secondly, there is the selection problem. So long as not all individuals running for office are disinterested, the voters must select between those who are and those who are not. If voters believe that it is better to be a "disinterested" public statesman than a selfish politician, then self-interested politicians will all attempt to resemble a disinterested public statesman. How is the voter to choose among them on the basis of the limited information he normally has available?

Thirdly, there are those who contend that there is no such thing as disinterested behavior in pursuit of the public interest, or at least it is such a rarity as not to be the basis of an adequate theory of the public sector. Even if individuals do not act in their own selfish interest, they act in their "class interest," in the interests of those with whom they have associated for life. They are often indeed not conscious of acting in this way.

Unfortunately, we cannot test the validity of these alternative views. There is, perhaps, some truth in all of them: many politicians do, undoubtedly, act in their self-interest, and the simple "voter" maximization model we have discussed here does provide some insights into their behavior. Not all politicians, however, act consciously in their self-interest; some, undoubtedly, believe that they are acting for the public good. But it is not clear what this means—that is, what interpretation is to be associated with "acting in the public good" when there are alternative views of what is in the public interest, and there is (by Arrow's impossibility theorem) no simple way of consistently resolving these differences. What is clear is that, with the perspective of hindsight, many politicians who claimed to be acting in the public good have advocated and instigated policies that later appear to most observers not to have been in the public interest.

The Persistence of Inefficient Equilibrium

Though there are no general propositions concerning the nature of the resource allocations that emerge when the political process is dominated by special-interest groups, most economists believe that when special-interest groups manage to impose trade restrictions or to obtain subsidies for themselves, the resulting resource allocations not only violate generally accepted standards of equity and fairness but also are frequently inefficient. That is, the resulting resource allocations generally result in the economy being below the utility possibilities frontier: there are alternative allocations that could make everyone better off.

Why, in the face of this, do individuals not get together and propose one of these Pareto-dominating alternatives, to which, presumably, all would agree? There is no universally agreed-upon answer to this puzzle. Several "partial" answers may be suggestive.

First, as we have already seen, the public interest is a public good. Since the efforts to maintain a good government must come from private individuals, there will be an undersupply of this (as any other) privately provided public good.

Secondly, many of the distributive implications of public programs undertaken at the behest of special-interest groups are far from obvious —and this is deliberately so. It is unlikely, for instance, that the American voters would deliberately vote to transfer resources (give a public gift) to *rich* rice farmers. For these individuals to receive a transfer at the public expense, they must be included in a broader-scale program, of which they are an almost accidental beneficiary. Thus, rich rice farmers become advocates of federal aid to rice farmers, singling out, in their public rhetoric, the benefits that would accrue to poor rice farmers from such a program. A Pareto improvement might, for instance, entail giving each rice farmer a fixed sum, which would leave him free to move into some other occupation where his productivity might be higher. But though such direct grants could be structured to make everyone better off, they would expose the true distributive implications of the program, that is, that most of the benefits accrue not to the poor rice farmers, but to the rich. Since this would likely weaken political support for the program providing subsidies to rice farmers, this Pareto improvement would not receive the backing of rich rice farmers.

ALTERNATIVE SCHEMES FOR DETERMINING THE LEVEL OF PUBLIC GOODS

Since there is a strong presumption that current political processes lead to inefficiencies, the question naturally arises as to whether there are some better schemes. Arrow's impossibility theorem suggests that we are likely to encounter difficulties. We now discuss two proposals that have been put forward for arriving at efficient allocations.

Lindahl Equilibrium

The first is called the Lindahl solution, after the great Swedish economist Erik Lindahl, who first proposed it in 1919.[12] It attempts to mimic, as far as possible, the way that the market works in providing private goods. Market equilibrium for private goods is described by the intersection of the demand and supply curves. All individuals face the same price. The sum of the quantities they demand is equal to the sum of the quantities supplied by firms.

One of the ways that we characterized the efficient level of public goods was the intersection of the aggregate demand curve (formed by adding vertically each individual's demand curve) with the supply curve. The demand curves are generated by asking the individual how much of the public good he would demand if he were to pay so much for each unit produced; that is, in Figure 6.7 if the first individual faced a tax price of, say, p_1, he would demand G^*.

The Lindahl equilibrium is just the intersection of the demand curve for public goods with the supply curve. The Lindahl equilibrium is obviously efficient. In the Lindahl equilibrium all individuals enjoy the same quantity of the public good but differ in their tax prices. In the diagram, the Lindahl equilibrium occurs at G^*, and the first individual pays a tax price of p_1 and the second a tax price of p_2.

The Lindahl equilibrium is Pareto efficient; but we noted earlier that there were, in fact, a whole range of Pareto-efficient resource allocations, in some of which one individual is better off, in others of which another is better off. Almost by definition, there cannot be unanimity about which, among these points, is preferred. The Lindahl equilibrium picks one of the Pareto-efficient points; but individuals who are disadvantaged by this particular Pareto-efficient point will not agree to the use of this mechanism for determining the allocation of public goods;

[12] E. Lindahl, "*Positive Lösung, Die Gerechtigkeit der Besteuerung*," translated as "Just Taxation—A Positive Solution" in *Classics in the Theory of Public Finance*, R. A. Musgrave and A. T. Peacock, eds. (New York: St. Martin's Press, 1958).

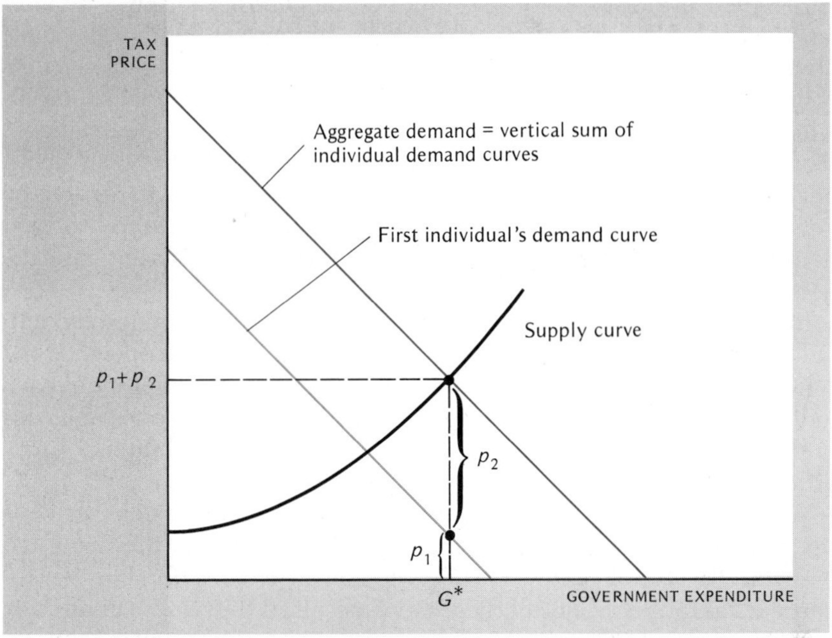

6.7 LINDAHL EQUILIBRIUM The intersection of the aggregate demand curve (formed by adding vertically the individual demand curves) and the supply curve yields a Pareto-efficient allocation.

indeed, they would prefer Pareto-inefficient allocations so long as the level of utility they obtain is higher.

The most telling criticism of the Lindahl solution is that *individuals do not have an incentive to tell the truth because their tax price increases as their stated demand does.* That is, the higher their stated demand (given the demand statements of others), the higher the equilibrium expenditures on public goods will be. Higher expenditures on public goods necessitate, of course, higher equilibrium tax prices. The demand curves that are used in the Lindahl analysis were drawn under the hypothesis that individuals face a given tax price; they believe that nothing they say will alter what they have to pay per unit of public expenditure. But if they understand the Lindahl mechanism, they will realize that what they say does alter what they have to pay per unit of public expenditure, and thus they will not truthfully reveal their demands. The question to which we now turn is, are there mechanisms that induce individuals to be honest about their preferences?

New Revelation Mechanisms

We noted earlier that one of the essential problems with public goods is that of preference revelation. In acquiring private goods, individuals reveal their preferences for different private goods. There was no similar mechanism for revealing preferences for public goods. The most obvious political mechanisms either link the individual's statements concerning his attitudes toward the public good to what he must pay, in which case they result in an undersupply (since each individual believes that his statements will have a negligible effect on the supply but a non-negligible effect on what he must pay, he has an incentive to say that he gets a negligible benefit), or they do not link what he has to pay to what he says, in which case he will have every incentive to exaggerate the benefits.

Recent research has focused on designing simple rules whereby individuals will truthfully reveal their preferences. The rule specifies the relationship between the level of public goods, the tax liability of each individual, and the statements each individual makes concerning his preferences for public goods. (The rule should have the further property that the resulting resource allocation is Pareto efficient).

Several economists have proposed alternative mechanisms that have the desired properties of inducing individuals to reveal the truth and ensuring Pareto efficiency.[13] There is, however, considerable controversy about the relevance of these mechanisms. If they are so good, why are they not used? Unfortunately, they also have some serious problems. To induce individuals to reveal the truth, each individual must believe that he can have a distinct effect on the outcome, on the equilibrium level of public goods expenditure. The administrative costs of running these schemes may be large. Moreover, the mechanisms are sensitive to collusion. They have the property that it pays each individual to reveal truthfully his preferences; but if two or more individuals can get together and coordinate their announcements, they can usually gain by making announcements that are not truthful.

The search for *better* mechanisms for revealing preferences thus continues. Many economists are not sanguine about whether practicable alternatives to existing political mechanisms exist.

VALUES AND COMPETENCE

Most of this chapter has been concerned with the political mechanisms by which the levels of public goods are determined. The political mechanism provides a means by which conflicts of values concerning what the government should do with respect to public goods are resolved.

Although conflicts of value are central to many political debates, these are not the only sources of disagreement. In the elections for the local commissioner of sewers, for instance, there is seldom controversy over whether or not clean waste is desirable, although occasionally there is controversy about what are acceptable levels of pollution. Rather, each contestant claims that he or she will be a more efficient manager. That is,

[13] The appendix to this chapter discusses these in more detail.

public officials play an important role in determining the level of outputs that can be obtained from any given level of inputs. The efficiency of the public sector depends on the competence of public management, and this in turn depends on the competence of the elected officials (on their ability to choose, for instance, good bureaucrats, or their ability to design programs that attain desired objectives). Unfortunately, voters have only limited information on the basis of which to make judgments concerning competency.

SUMMARY

1. The majority voting equilibrium, when it exists, reflects the preferences of the median voter.
2. The majority voting equilibrium does not, in general, result in an efficient supply of public goods; there may be either an undersupply or an oversupply.
3. The majority voting equilibrium exists if preferences are single-peaked.
4. Preferences for a single public good will usually be single-peaked. Preferences will not be single-peaked if: (a) there is more than one public good, and the vote is taken over packages, rather than over a single good at a time; (b) voting is over a publicly provided private good, for which there exists a private alternative, such as education; (c) voting is over distributional questions, such as the structure of the income tax schedule.
5. A majority voting equilibrium may not exist when preferences are not single-peaked. That is, if there are three alternatives—*A*, *B*, and *C*—*A* may be preferred by a majority over *B*, *B* by a majority over *C*, and *C* may be preferred by a majority over A.
6. Arrow's impossibility theorem demonstrates the impossibility of finding an alternative, nondictatorial political mechanism that resolves this problem of majority voting and that satisfies certain other properties that one would desire of any political mechanism (such as the independence of irrelevant alternatives).
7. In a two-party system, there will be a convergence of positions of the two parties toward that of the median voter.

KEY CONCEPTS

Preference revelation	Voting paradox
Aggregating preferences	Single-peaked preferences
Tax price	Arrow's impossibility theorem
Median voter	Lindahl equilibrium

QUESTIONS AND PROBLEMS

1. Assume that some individual's marginal valuation of public goods increases. What does this do to the Pareto-efficient level of public expenditures? If this individual is not the median individual, what will happen in a two-party system to the equilibrium level of expenditure on public goods? If the equilibrium was originally Pareto efficient, will it still be?

2. Assume that all individuals have identical preferences but some individuals are wealthier than others. Assume there is a single public good and a single private good. (a) Show diagrammatically how you derive the demand curve for the public good, as a function of the tax price charged the individual. (b) Assume that the demand function is of the form

$$G=kY/p,$$

where k is a constant (less than one), Y is income, and p is the tax price. This says that when income doubles, the demand for public goods doubles, but when the tax price doubles, the demand is cut in half. If the tax price is proportional to the individual's income (as with proportional taxation), how will the demand for public goods differ among those with different incomes?
3. Assume instead there is uniform taxation, so that all individuals face the same tax price. Recall that along each individual's demand curve, the price equals the marginal rate of substitution. Thus,

$$MRS=p=kY/G,$$

the marginal rate of substitution is proportional to income. Assume that income is symmetrically distributed, so that mean income equals the median. Explain why the majority voting equilibrium will be Pareto efficient. Assume now that income is not symmetrically distributed, but rather is skewed toward higher incomes, as in Figure 6.4. Will the majority voting equilibrium still be efficient? Will there be an under- or oversupply of public goods?
4. Demand curves are said to be *income elastic* if the demand for the good increases *more* than proportionately with income. For instance, with the demand curve

$$G=kY^2/p$$

the demand for public goods increases with the *square* of income. Draw the marginal rate of substitution as a function of income (for a fixed level of expenditure on public goods). Assume income is symmetrically distributed. What is the relationship between the average value of the marginal rate of substitution and the marginal rate of substitution of the median individual? What does this imply about the equilibrium supply of public goods under majority voting with uniform taxation?
5. In the text, we suggested that for well-off individuals, with uniform taxation, preferences for education were not single-peaked. Why might preferences for local parks and for urban public transportation systems (buses and subways) also not be single-peaked?
6. Is the median voter always the voter with the median income? Give examples.
7. How might the majority voting model be used to explain the growth of government expenditures?
   a) Should changes in median or average income better explain increases in the demand for government services?

b) What should be the effect of an increase in the costs of producing public good caused by government inefficiency? Would it make a difference if the increase in cost is a result of government paying above-market wages (wages higher than those paid comparable workers in the private sector)? (Does your answer to the last question depend on whether the median voter is a government employee?)
c) Why might you expect that, if income per capita remains the same but the number of individuals in the economy increases, the demand for public goods would increase?

8. One popular voting scheme is rank-order voting, where individuals assign a rank (1, 2, 3) to the possible alternatives; the assigned ranks are then added up, and the alternative with the lowest sum wins. Consider a choice among four alternative ways of spending public funds (a library, a ski slope, a swimming pool, a garbage dump). Can you construct an example in which the outcome (the most preferred alternative) is, say, a library, if the vote is among the first three alternatives, while the outcome is a ski slope if the vote is among all four alternatives? This voting scheme thus violates the principle that the chosen outcome should be independent of irrelevant outcomes (the garbage dump was not chosen in either situation).

APPENDIX: NEW REVELATION MECHANISMS

In this appendix, we describe a simple procedure which induces individuals to reveal truthfully their demands, provided there is no collusion among individuals. Everyone is asked to give his demand curve for public goods, just as in the Lindahl equilibrium. As before, the equilibrium will be at the intersection of the aggregate demand (formed by adding vertically the demand curves of each individual) and the supply curve. For simplicity, we continue to assume that the marginal cost of production of the public good is constant, so the supply curve is horizontal. But now, there is a different rule for determining the individual's tax liability.

We first add up the demand curves for *all other* individuals (vertically). The aggregate demand curve of all *others* intersects the supply curve at G_0 in Figure 6.8. This is what the level of public goods would be if the individual said that he got no value out of the public good. He is told that for each unit beyond G_0 that the government produces, he will have to pay the difference between the marginal costs of production and the aggregate valuation (demand) of all others. If the equilibrium entailed an output of $G_0 + 1$, the individual would have to pay *AB*, the distance between the marginal cost curve and the others' aggregate demand curve.

The individual is in a position to determine the level of public goods simply by his announcement of how much they are valued to him. Clearly, he will try to increase *G* to the point where the marginal cost to him of increasing *G* is equal to his marginal benefit. This can be seen in two alternative ways. First, in Figure 6.8B, we have plotted the marginal cost to the individual from each additional unit of production beyond G_0, given others' demands. Since his marginal cost is the difference between the cost of production and others' demand, the marginal cost of the $G + 1^{st}$ unit is equal to *AB*. In Panel B we have also drawn the individual's demand curve; the individual will wish point G^* to be chosen, where *his* demand curve intersects *his* marginal cost curve.

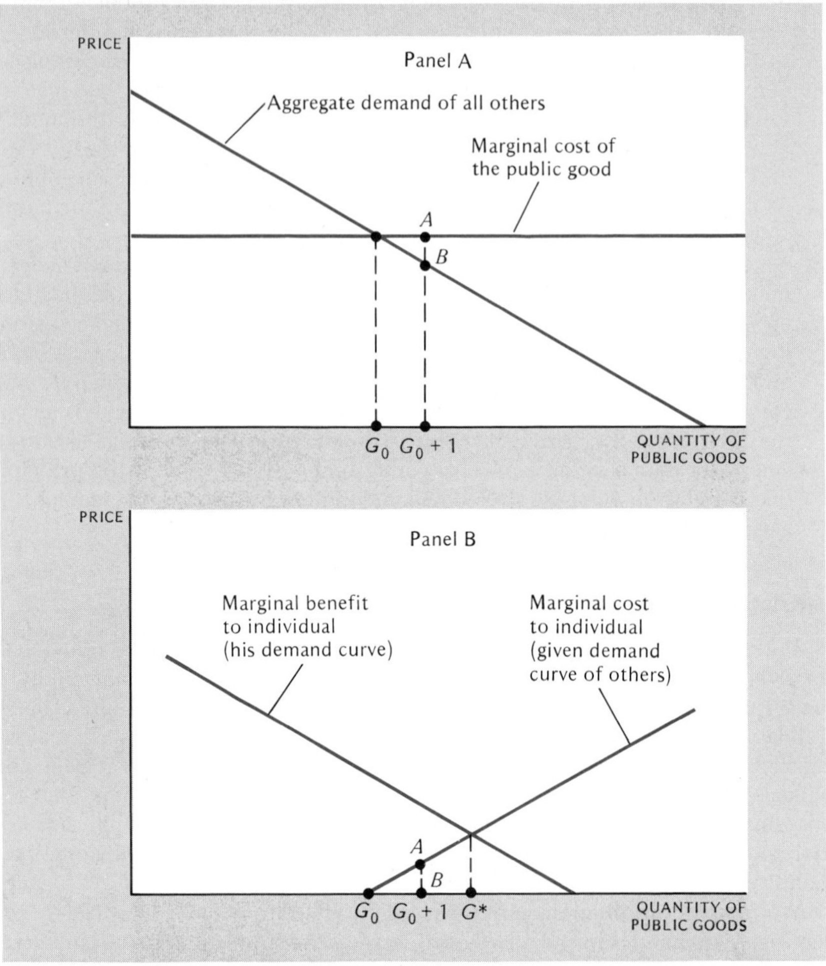

6.8 NEW REVELATION MECHANISM Panel A shows the aggregate demand of all but one individual for the public good (the sum of their marginal valuations) and the marginal cost of production. If the last individual placed no value on the public good, the level of production of the public good would be G_0, where the sum of the marginal valuations equals the marginal cost. As the level of expenditure increases beyond G_0, the last individual is required to pay, for each additional unit, the difference between the aggregate (marginal) valuation of all others and the marginal cost. Thus, if $G_0 + 1$ is produced, he must pay the amount denoted by *AB*. Panel B shows, at each level of output, the *marginal* cost that the (last) individual must pay for each extra unit of output. Thus, to have the economy go from producing G_0 to producing $G_0 + 1$ requires that he pay *AB*. Panel B also shows the last individual's marginal valuation of the public good (his demand curve). The individual's most preferred level of expenditure is where his marginal benefit from increased expenditures (given by his demand curve) exactly equals his marginal cost, that is G^*. The individual will thus be induced to reveal truthfully his demand.

We now show that each individual has an incentive to reveal honestly his demand for public goods, and that the equilibrium is Pareto efficient. To see this, we look at the individual's budget constraint. The individual faces a budget

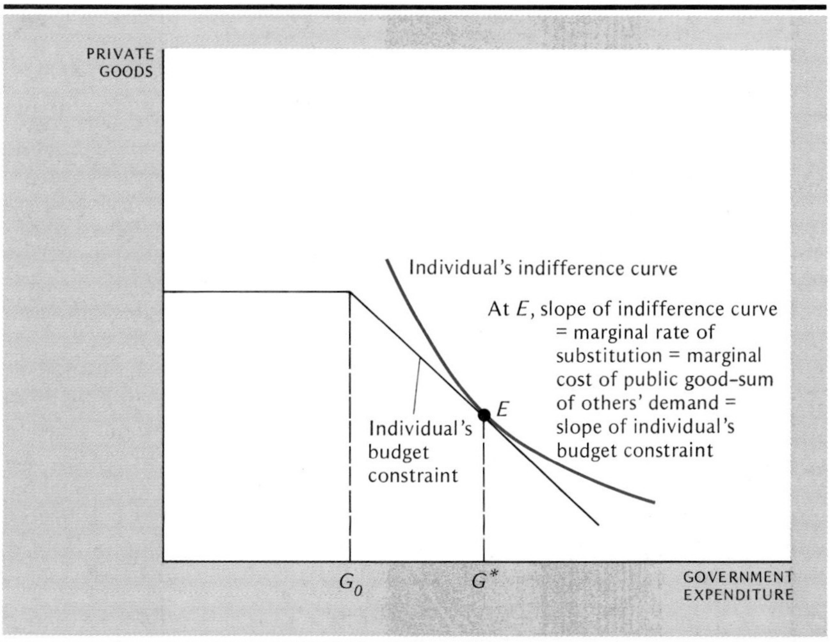

6.9 CHOICE OF OPTIMAL G BY INDIVIDUAL If the individual must pay the difference between marginal cost and others' demands, and others have honestly revealed their demands, the level of public goods will be Pareto efficient.

constraint as depicted in Figure 6.9. The extra amount that the individual has to give up for each extra unit of public goods beyond G_0 is the marginal cost minus the others' aggregate demand (marginal valuation). Thus he sets his marginal rate of substitution equal to the marginal cost minus the others' aggregate demand, point E in Figure 6.9. It is clear that the individual has no incentive to misrepresent his preferences. If he asked for any level of public goods other than G^* he would be worse off.

Assume now that each individual honestly announces his demand curve. Recall that in constructing the demand curve, the tax price for each individual (the slope of his budget constraint) was set equal to the individual's marginal rate of substitution. Hence, when the demand curves are added vertically, the sum of the marginal rates of substitution are just the sum of the tax prices, and that equals the marginal cost (the marginal rate of transformation):

$$MRS_1 + MRS_2 + \ldots = MC.$$

In other words, each individual's marginal rate of substitution is equal to the marginal cost of the public good minus the sum of the marginal rates of substitution of others (the sum of their tax prices). For instance, for the first individual,

$$MRS_1 = MC - (MRS_2 + MRS_3 + \ldots).$$

But this is exactly the point we described earlier, where the marginal cost to the individual of further increases in government expenditure (which equaled the marginal cost of production minus the sum of others' demand prices at the given quantity) equaled the marginal benefit to the individual (his marginal rate of substitution). We have just shown that by honestly revealing his demand curve, the individual maximizes his own utility, and the allocation of resources to public goods will be Pareto efficient.

In the text, we noted that in spite of the attention that revelation mechanisms such as the one we have just described have received from economic theorists, there is considerable controversy about their relevance. We noted several objections to them, their possibly high administrative costs and the fact that they are susceptible to collusion. There are further problems.

Like the Lindahl equilibrium we described earlier, these mechanisms ensure that the condition for a Pareto-efficient allocation—that the sum of marginal rates of substitution equals the marginal rate of transformation—is satisfied. But some individuals might prefer another, Pareto-inefficient allocation that gives them a higher level of utility. Hence, it is not obvious that they would agree to a decision to adopt this mechanism, knowing that they would thereby be disadvantaged. Finally, the mechanisms do not, in general, guarantee a balanced budget. Although the sum of the marginal valuations (marginal rates of substitution) does equal the marginal cost, the total amount paid may well differ from the total costs of the public good.

7

Public Production and Bureaucracy

In Chapter 2, we saw that government had a central role in production. It both produces goods itself and it affects the production decisions of private firms, through taxes, tax expenditures, subsidies, and regulations.

In Chapter 3, we discussed some of the rationale for these activities, the kinds of market failures that lead to government interventions in the production decisions of firms. But how does the government decide on the form that the intervention should take? Should it take over the industry? Should it regulate the industry? Should it encourage good behavior through subsidies? Should it discourage bad behavior through fines?

We also discussed in Chapters 3 and 5 an important category of goods, public goods (and publicly provided private goods), which the government takes responsibility for supplying. But the fact that the government pays for the good does not mean that the government necessarily produces the good. It may purchase the good (the buoy) or the service (running the hotels in the National Parks) from private firms. What are some of the factors that go into those decisions?

Today, while government production looms large in the United States —with almost a sixth of the labor force working for the government—it is still small compared to that in many other countries. But the past decade has witnessed a large international movement to decrease the role of the government in production. This is partly motivated by an increasingly widespread perception that the government is an inefficient producer.

The Center for Policy Studies of the University of Michigan periodically does a survey in which it asks, "Do you think people in the government waste a lot of money we pay in taxes, waste some of it, or don't waste very much of it?" In 1958, 43 percent thought that the government wasted a lot of it. Two decades later, this had increased to 77 percent. We wish to know if these perceptions are justified and if there are reasons to *expect* government bureaucracies to be less efficient than the private sector.

This chapter is divided into five parts. In the first, we *describe* some of the more important public production activities. In the second, we discuss briefly the *rationale* for government involvement in the production of private goods. In the third, we treat other means that the government may use to affect production of private goods. In the fourth, we discuss alternative arrangements for the provision of public goods. In the fifth, we discuss the major argument against government production, namely the inefficiency of the government.

PUBLIC ENTERPRISES AND PRODUCTION IN THE UNITED STATES

In the United States, government is involved in the production of both public goods and private goods. Public production occurs at the federal, state, and local levels. In addition, however, the government (both at the federal, state, and local levels) contracts with private firms to supply goods and services, both directly to itself and to individuals. In this section we discuss the role of the government in production of private and public goods, and of private firms in supplying services to the government.

Table 7.1 shows the array of arrangements that are found in the United States. There are publicly produced private goods, like electric-

Table 7.1 THE VARIETY OF ARRANGEMENTS BY WHICH GOODS ARE PRODUCED AND PAID FOR

	Who Pays?	
Who Is the Producer?	*Private Sector (80% of GNP)*	*Public Sector (20% of GNP)*
Public Sector (12% of GNP)	Some electricity Rail	Education Police protection
Private Sector (88% of GNP)	Toothpaste Most housing	Most hospital services Garbage collection (in some communities) Air Force airplanes Army tanks

Most, but not all, goods produced in the public sector are financed by it. The government also pays for many goods produced by the private sector, especially hospital services and defense equipment. Percentages are for 1986. SOURCE: *Survey of Current Business,* July 1987, Tables 3.15 and 6.1.

ity and railroads; there are publicly produced goods that are publicly provided, free of charge, like education; and there are privately produced goods that are publicly provided—the government typically buys its airplanes and tanks from private firms. Of course, most goods in the United States are private goods that are privately produced.

Even this catalogue does not adequately describe the wide variety of arrangements by which goods are paid for and produced in the United States. Medicare is paid for by the government, but the government does not directly hire the doctors; the decision as to which doctor to hire is left to the individual. In the case of garbage collection, even though the community may contract out to a private firm, the individual homeowner is not given a choice of garbage collection services.

Public Production of Private Goods

There are six major areas in which the federal government produces private goods. For these goods, exclusion is possible (and the government does in fact charge for most of these goods and services) and the extra costs of providing the goods and services to an additional individual are significant. In most of these areas, government production coexists with private production.

1. *Postal Service.* This is one of the few activities that is constitutionally mandated. The delivery of first-class mail is the one area (besides printing money) in which the government maintains an exclusive monopoly. But there has been extensive competition in recent years in other areas of mail delivery. The United Parcel Service now delivers more parcels than does the Post Office; there are scattered local delivery firms; and a number of companies are now actively competing in the express-mail delivery service. Electronic mail delivery promises to be another area of active competition in the near future.

2. *Electricity.* In 1985, 22 percent of the electricity in the United States was produced by publicly owned utilities.[1] Some government production is a by-product of its responsibility for controlling rivers; a joint product with flood control is the production of hydroelectric power. The federal government also took an active role in the electrification of the rural parts of the United States (through the Rural Electrification Authority).

3. *Railroads.* Until recently, the United States was one of the few countries in which virtually all railroads were private enterprises. (The government had, however, given extensive subsidies to help establish the railroads, through land grants.) But for a variety of reasons, during the period after World War II, the railroads increasingly found themselves in difficult economic straits, and a number of them went into bankruptcy. The federal government responded to the impending crisis by establishing two enterprises: Amtrak, the national passenger railroad

[1] *Statistical Abstract of the United States, 1987,* p. 554.

company, and Conrail, a consolidation of the bankrupt Penn Central and a number of other railroads in the Northeast. After a massive infusion of public funds, Conrail was sold to private investors in 1987 (with the government recouping only a fraction of what it had spent); its sale for $1.65 billion amounted to the largest stock offering in U.S. history. President Reagan also proposed to end subsidies to Amtrak and sell off all its assets, which, it was estimated, would return $1 billion.

4. *Insurance.* The government is involved in a variety of insurance programs, including, among others, flood insurance, crime insurance, insuring bank deposits (the Federal Deposit Insurance Corporation), disability insurance and life insurance (social security), unemployment insurance, and credit insurance. Many of these insurance programs arose because private firms failed to provide what was perceived to be adequate insurance coverage for certain risks. (In some cases, however, the market failed to provide the insurance because at the premiums that reflected the true risks, demand for the insurance was insufficient. In these cases, government-provided insurance is really a scheme for providing hidden subsidies.)

5. *Banking and Credit.* In almost every major industrialized country, there is a central bank that serves as a bankers' bank and plays an active role in regulating and controlling the banking industry; this central bank is a government enterprise. The United States is no exception to the pattern, with the Federal Reserve System serving as the central bank in the United States. The governors of the Federal Reserve Board are appointed by the president, with the approval of Congress. The reason that in most countries the central bank is governmentally controlled is that the central bank's control of the money supply, availability of credit, and interest rates is thought to have a critical effect on the performance of the economy as a whole, on levels of inflation, unemployment, and the balance of payments. These are among the major responsibilities of any government. Accordingly, most governments are reluctant to leave these matters in the hands of the private sector.

Though the Federal Reserve Board's activities can be viewed as primarily regulating the banking system and controlling the money supply, the federal government is involved in a large number of other activities in the credit market. Indeed, we noted in Chapter 2 that a substantial fraction of new loans involve the federal government, either directly through one of its agencies, or as a guarantor of the loan.

In many countries, governments have taken an even more active role in allocating credit, by nationalizing all banks. These countries maintain that by allocating credit, banks have a dominant position in determining both who controls (manages) the nations' resources and how those resources get allocated; they believe that these central decisions should not be in private hands, which will only pursue their own narrow self-interest. Later, we shall evaluate this claim, as well as the counterclaim that government credit programs are particularly vulnerable to pressures from special-interest groups. Whenever a borrower is charged less than the market rate of interest, there is a subsidy; since it is difficult for outsiders to evaluate the risks associated with any borrower, it is difficult to ascertain the magnitude of the subsidy. Also, in many countries, the resulting opportunities for corruption and inefficiencies are difficult to control. Interestingly enough, France, after nationalizing most of its banks after World War II (and the remaining private banks after the Socialist Mitterand government was elected in 1981), began privatizing its banks late in 1986.

6. *Land and Resource Management.* The federal government is the largest land owner in the United States, owning 32 percent of the country. This percentage is much higher for some regions than for others; the federal government owns 5 percent or less of the land outside the western states, but 60 percent of all the land in the West.[2] Much of this land is used to produce timber or for grazing, and under some of it there are vast mineral resources. Although the federal government has the responsibility of *managing* these enormous resources, it has for the most part not actually engaged in production, other than providing national parks and recreational areas; it leases the land to private firms and individuals to extract the oil, to mine the coal, to fell the timber, and to graze their cattle. Beginning in 1981, the Reagan administration increased significantly the rate at which this land was sold or leased to private individuals, reducing the amount of land under direct federal management. These initiatives have been the subject of considerable controversy.

The role of government in the production of private goods is greater in most other countries. Among the industries that are frequently nationalized, besides railroads, banking, insurance, and electric power, are steel, coal, and telecommunications.

Public Production of Public Goods and Publicly Provided Private Goods

Much of public production is associated with providing public goods (like defense) and what we referred to in Chapter 5 as publicly provided private goods (like education). The analysis of Chapter 5 showed only that government must finance public goods, not that it needs to produce them. The decisions about whether to produce a good publicly and whether to provide it (finance it) publicly should be viewed separately. For instance, the government is actively involved in the production of national defense, but the military purchases most of its equipment (its airplanes, guns, ships, etc.) from private firms. And it frequently hires private contractors to manage public facilities. In the years 1983–1985, the Department of Defense used nearly one-half of its budget to pay private contractors.[3]

[2] *Statistical Abstract of the United States, 1987*, p. 183.
[3] *Statistical Abstract of the United States, 1987*, pp. 318, 320.

Though some local communities are involved in the production of private goods, like electricity and water, which they sell to their citizens, most of what is produced by local governments is again provided directly (and freely) to the citizens: waste disposal, garbage collection, police protection, fire protection, and most important of all, education.

ADMINISTERING PUBLIC LAWS AND PROGRAMS

Perhaps the most important "production activity" of the government is administering public laws and programs. After individuals have voted for their elected representatives, and these representatives have legislated public programs, the public programs have to be administered: detailed regulations have to be promulgated, procedures for applying for funds have to be developed, applications have to be reviewed, checks have to be sent out, etc. No matter how well-intentioned a program may be, if it is badly designed, inequities and inefficiencies will result. We refer to those collectively responsible for the administration of government programs as the government bureaucracy. Figure 7.1 represents, in a schematic way, the links between the electorate and the public programs designed to provide services to the electorate.

Changing Patterns in Government Production

The United States has not experienced dramatic changes in the role of government production such as have occurred in many European countries over the past fifty years. In the United Kingdom after World War II, the government nationalized the steel and coal industries and completed the nationalization of the railroads. In France, there were two waves of nationalizations, one after World War II and another after the election of a Socialist government in 1980. But this was followed in 1986 and 1987 by a privatization movement, in which many of the nationalized industries (including some that had been in the public sector for decades) were sold off to private investors.

The issue of government control of production has not been a particularly heated political issue in the United States, and the changes that have occurred have occurred gradually. The government's direct involvement in railroads occurred only after the bankruptcy of several private railroads (though its involvement through regulation and, as mentioned earlier, land grants dates back more than 100 years). Similarly, though the government is now extremely active in providing credit, this has not come about suddenly, by nationalizing the banking system, but gradually, by providing a variety of special loan programs aimed at meeting particular needs.

Still, the question of the appropriate role of government in production remains widely debated: Would some of the services that the government presently produces (such as education) be better produced by pri-

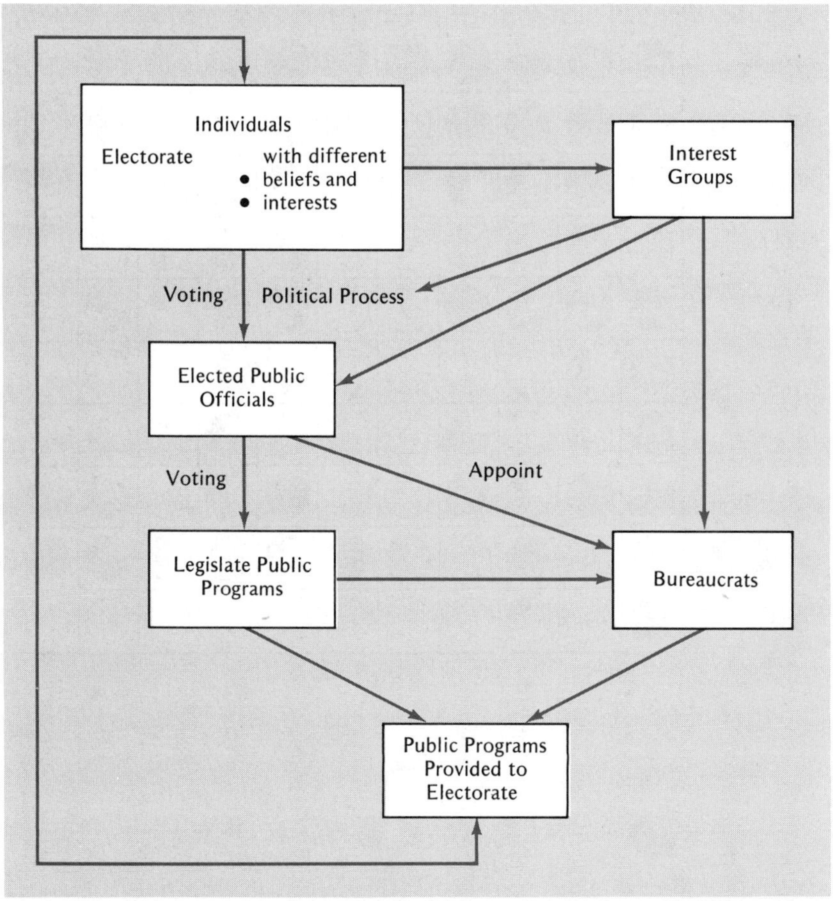

7.1 LINKS BETWEEN THE ELECTORATE AND THE PUBLIC PROGRAMS DESIGNED TO PROVIDE SERVICES TO THE ELECTORATE (1) The electorate elects public officials. (2) The public officials legislate programs and appoint bureaucrats to administer public programs. (3) The bureaucrats provide the services to the electorate, within the context of the programs that have been legislated. (4) Interest groups exert influence at all stages.

vate firms? Are there other services (such as telephones) currently privately produced that might be better produced by a government enterprise? What should be the role of private insurance companies in insuring the medical expenses of the aged?

Figure 7.2 shows the different levels of public ownership in different industries in different countries. It is apparent that government's direct role in production is far less in the United States and Japan than in most European countries.

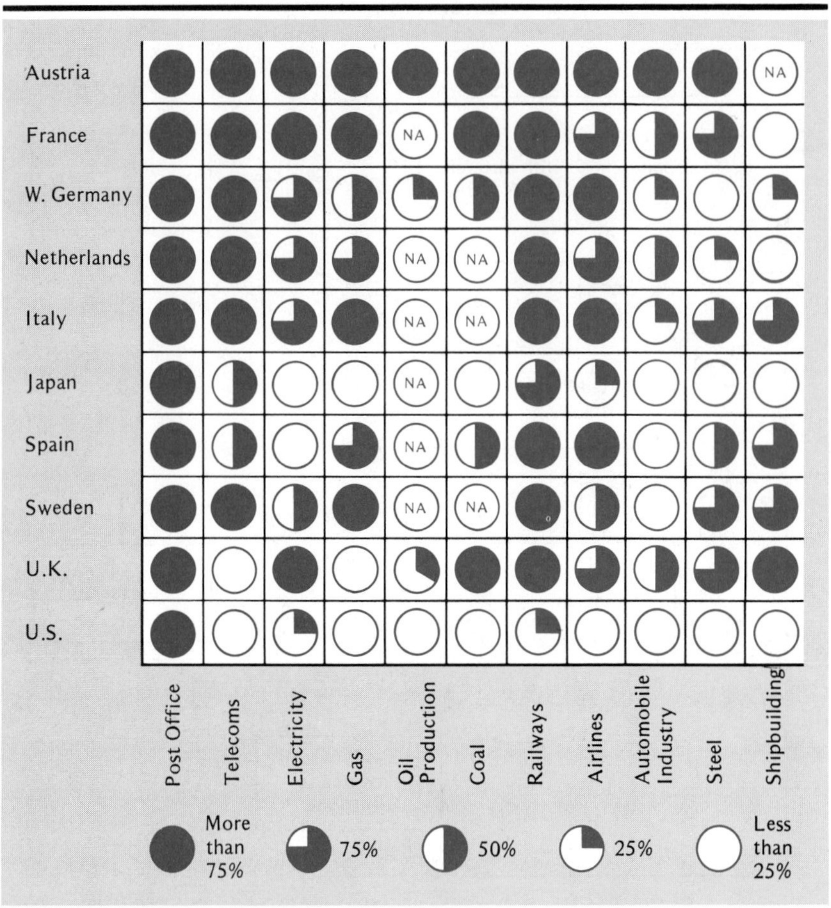

7.2 LEVELS OF PUBLIC OWNERSHIP IN DIFFERENT INDUSTRIES IN DIFFERENT COUNTRIES SOURCE: *Financial Times,* December 10, 1986, based on *AMEX Bank Review.*

THE RATIONALE FOR GOVERNMENT PRODUCTION OF PRIVATE GOODS: MARKET FAILURES

The most widely heard argument for government control of production of private goods is that private firms pursue the maximization of profits of the owners, and not the welfare of the nation. To assess the validity of this argument, we must return to the basic discussion of Chapter 3. Private firms, in pursuing their narrow self-interest (profit maximization) in competitive markets, can be thought of as pursuing the public interest. The fact that competitive firms, maximizing profits, lead the economy to an efficient allocation of resources means that there is not necessarily a conflict between the pursuit of private interests (profit maximization) and what is in the public interest. However, when market failures occur, firms' pursuit of profit maximization might not result in an efficient resource allocation.

Natural Monopoly

The most important market failure that has led to public production arises when markets are not *competitive*. As we saw in Chapter 3, a common reason that markets may not be competitive is the existence of increasing returns to scale; that is, the average costs of production decline as the level of production increases. In that case, economic efficiency requires that there be a limited number of firms. Industries where increasing returns are so significant that only one firm should operate in any region are referred to as **natural monopolies**. Examples of natural monopolies include telephones, water, and electricity.

The major cost associated with delivering water is the network of pipes. Once pipes have been installed, the additional costs of supplying water to one extra user are relatively insignificant. It would clearly be inefficient to have two networks of pipes, side by side, one delivering to one home, the next to a neighbor's. The same is true of electricity, cable TV, and natural gas.

We represent the average cost curve and the demand curve for a natural monopoly in Figure 7.3. Since the average costs of production decline as the level of production increases, it is efficient to have only one firm. In the case depicted, there is a whole range of viable outputs (where the firm makes a profit). The maximum viable output (without subsidies) is Q_1, where the demand curve intersects the average cost curve.

In these situations, we cannot rely on the kinds of competitive forces that we discussed earlier to ensure that the industry is efficient. Efficiency requires that price equal marginal cost (and quantity is Q_0). But if the firm charges a price equal to marginal cost, it will suffer a loss, since marginal cost is lower than average cost for industries with declining average cost.

One common recommendation in this situation is for the government to provide a subsidy to the industry and insist that the firm charge a price equal to the marginal cost. Such a policy is sometimes referred to as "first-best." It ignores, however, the question of how the revenues required to pay the subsidy are to be raised; it assumes, in particular, that there are no distortions associated with raising this revenue. Moreover, it assumes that the government knows the magnitude of the subsidy that will enable the firm to be viable.

In practice, most governments have *attempted* to make such industries pay for themselves. (They may also be concerned with the equity of making general taxpayers pay to subsidize a private good that is enjoyed by only a portion of the population, or enjoyed by different individuals to different extents.) Thus they have insisted on government-managed natural monopolies operating at the intersection of their demand curve

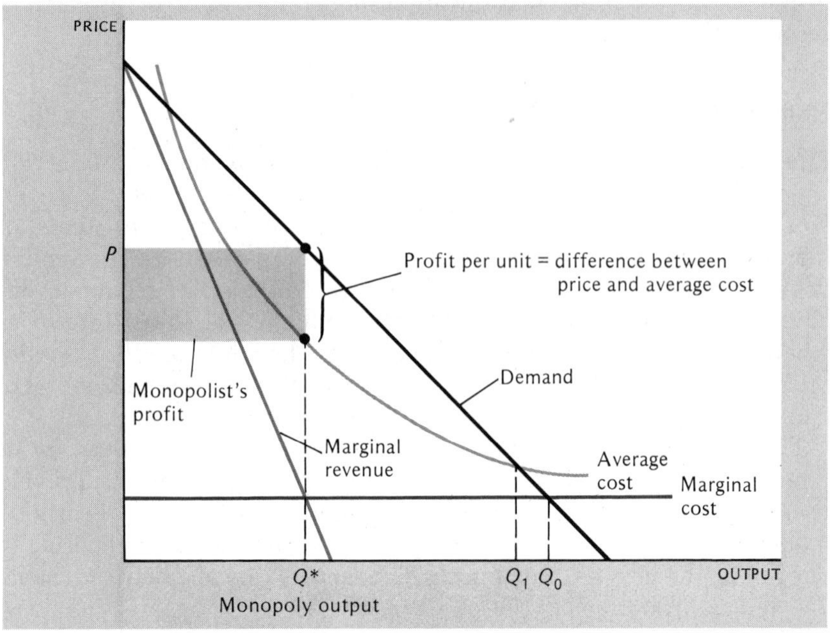

7.3 NATURAL MONOPOLY With no sunk costs and potential entry, a natural monopolist would operate at Q_1, the lowest price consistent with at least breaking even. With sunk costs, the price will be higher. The monopolist unconcerned with the threat of entry operates at Q^*, where marginal revenue equals marginal cost.

and their average cost curves (Q_1 in the figure). This is called the zero profit point, and this policy is sometimes referred to as a second-best policy.

This zero-profit point is precisely the point where natural monopolies may operate, under the assumption that there is effective potential competition. Assume a firm tried to charge a price that exceeded the average cost of production. If it were easy to enter (and exit) from an industry, a firm that tried to capture a profit for itself would instantaneously be threatened with entry by other firms willing to provide the given service or commodity at a lower price. New firms could come in and provide the services or commodities at a profitable price, without worrying unduly about the reactions of the original firm.[4] Thus the presence of a single firm in an industry does not, in itself, imply that the firm can exercise monopoly power. So long as there are potential entrants, that single firm must charge a price equal to average cost. The market allocation does

[4] In the recent literature in industrial organization, markets with decreasing average costs but no sunk costs, in which price is maintained at a level equal to average costs, are referred to as contestable. See W. J. Baumol, J. Panzar, and R. Willig, *Contestable Markets and the Theory of Industrial Organization* (New York: Harcourt Brace Jovanovich, 1982). For a simple exposition of the theory of contestable markets, see W. J. Baumol, "Contestable Markets: An Uprising in the Theory of Industry Structure," *American Economic Review* 72 (1982): 1–15.

not correspond to the first-best policy we described earlier: price equals average costs, not marginal cost. But this allocation does correspond to the second-best situation, in which the government does not provide subsidies to industries.

EFFECTS OF SUNK COSTS

All of this changes when there are **sunk costs**. Sunk costs are costs that are not recoverable upon the exit of the firm. Most research and development expenditures represent sunk costs. But a building that can be costlessly converted into another use does not represent a sunk cost. An airplane, which can easily be sold to another airline, does not represent a sunk cost.

Why are sunk costs so important? They create an essential asymmetry between a firm that is established in an industry, and those that are not. The potential entrant is not in the same position as the firm already in the industry, for the firm already in the industry has expended funds that it cannot recover. In deciding whether to enter, a firm does not look at the level of current profits and prices, but at what prices and profits will be *after* entry. Even if prices currently are considerably above average costs (so profits are large), a potential entrant may well believe that the firm already in the industry will respond to entry not by exiting the industry but by lowering its price; at the lower price, entry no longer is profitable. Moreover, when sunk costs are important, entrants will not be able to recover all the expenditures they make upon entry. Thus they will be reluctant to take the gamble that the current firm will either exit or leave its prices at their currently high levels; and they probably will not enter the industry. Accordingly sunk costs act as a barrier to entry and allow the established firm a degree of monopoly power that it could not exercise in the absence of the sunk cost.

Since virtually all natural monopolies entail important sunk costs, the government cannot simply rely on the threat of potential competition. The fact that a single firm controls a consumer's telephone service, his water, or his electricity gives rise to concern: the monopolist is in a position to exploit the consumer. The consequences of this were seen in Chapter 3, and are reproduced in Figure 7.3. The monopolist who is unconcerned about entry by other firms charges a price that maximizes his profits, the price where the extra revenue (the marginal revenue) he gets from selling an additional unit is equal to the extra costs (the marginal costs). His profit per unit of output is the difference between the price he charges and the average costs.

THE CASE OF MULTI-PRODUCT AND NATURAL MONOPOLIES

So far, we have focused our attention on a natural monopoly producing a single commodity. If the industry is not to be subsidized, it must charge a price in excess of marginal cost.

On what principle should prices be set when the natural monopoly produces several commodities? Prices, on average, will still need to exceed marginal cost (if the firm is to break even). Should, for instance, the ratio of the price to marginal cost be the same for all the firm's products? Should higher charges on some services be used to subsidize other services?

The U.S. Postal Service, for instance, imposes uniform charges for delivering mail, even though the marginal cost of delivering mail to a rural household in North Dakota may be much higher than the cost of delivering a letter in Chicago. If the post office is to break even, there must be a **cross subsidy**, a subsidy from one user (product) to another user (product).

The issue is obviously a very political one; the elimination of cross-subsidies will adversely affect some groups. When pricing decisions are made politically, these groups will attempt to persuade those in charge to lower the prices they face (implicitly raising prices to others).

The analysis of pricing decisions involves both efficiency and distributional considerations. Economists have been particularly concerned with the efficiency costs of politically determined pricing policies. When prices are raised on some service, the consumption of that service declines, but a 1 percent price increase for some goods reduces demand more than a similar price rise for other goods. Goods for which demand is more sensitive to price increases are said to be price-elastic. In Figure 7.4A we have drawn an inelastic demand curve, for which a change in price does not result in very large change in consumption, while in Figure 7.4B the demand is very elastic; a change in price results in a large change in consumption.

If a natural monopoly is to break even (without government subsidies), it obviously must charge a price in excess of marginal cost. If the government increased price above marginal cost by the same percentage for all commodities, clearly consumption of goods with elastic demand would be reduced by more than those with inelastic demand. Under some circumstances it can be shown to be desirable to charge prices such that consumption of every good is reduced by the same percentage (from what it would be if price equaled marginal cost). If the government wishes to do this, it should increase the price (above marginal costs) more for commodities whose demand is inelastic than for commodities whose demand is elastic.[5]

[5] This policy will minimize the deadweight loss resulting from price exceeding marginal cost. The problem of how to set prices for a multi-commodity public monopoly was first solved in 1956 by Marcel Boiteux, who served as the director of Electricité de France, the government agency responsible in France for producing electricity. For an English translation, see "On the Management of Public Monopolies Subject to Budgetary Constraints," *Journal of Economic Theory* 3 (1971): 219–40. This question of the determination of prices for different commodities turns out to be equivalent to a rather similar question posed some twenty-five years earlier by the great British economist Frank Ramsey. He asked: If the government must raise a given amount of revenue by distortionary taxation, how should it raise the revenue? Should it, for instance, charge a uniform tax on all commodities, so that the ratio of the price to marginal cost would be the same for all commodities? Would there then be no relative distortions? Ramsey showed that, as plausible as that might seem, it was not the correct answer; it was preferable to charge a higher tax on a commodity whose demand was inelastic. Both Ramsey and

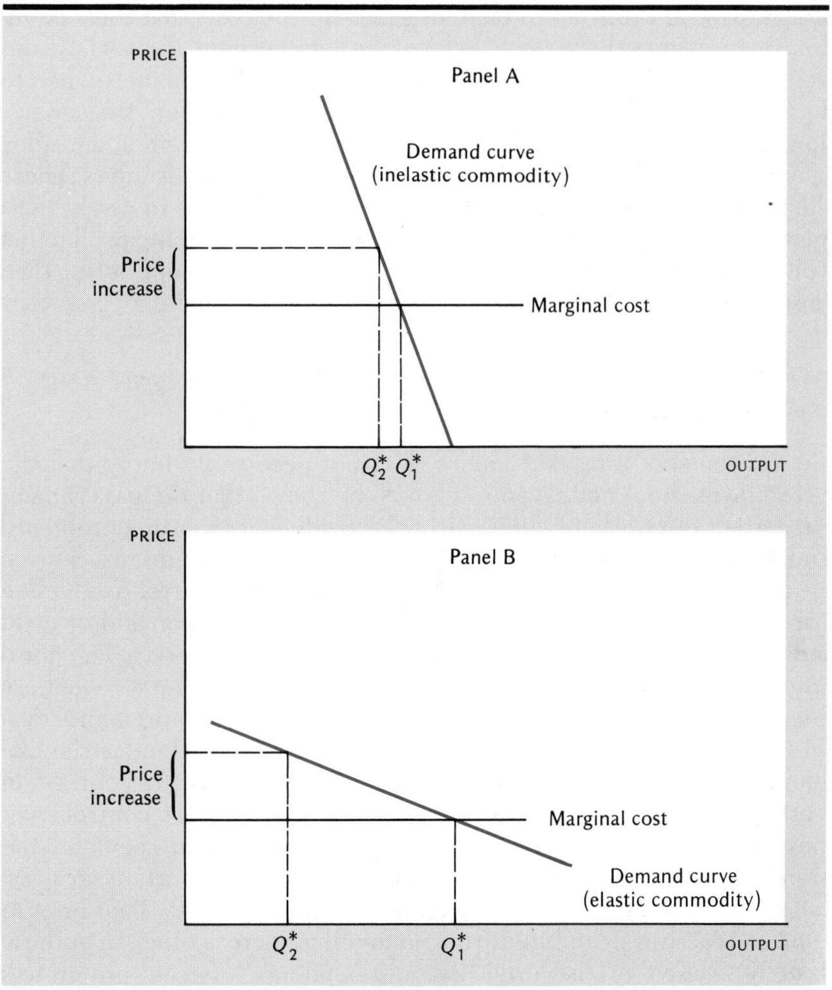

7.4 PRICING IN A MULTI-COMMODITY NATURAL MONOPOLY (A) With an inelastic demand, an increase in the price above marginal cost results in a relatively small decline in output. (B) With an elastic demand, an increase in price above marginal cost results in a large decline in output.

Public Production and Other Market Failures

Though natural monopolies provide the clearest class of market failures giving rise to public production, advocates of public production cite

Boiteux ignored the distributional issues that are central to most of the political debate. These were introduced into the analysis by M. Feldstein, "Distributional Equity and the Optimal Structure of Public Prices," *American Economic Review* 62 (1973): 32–36 and (in the context of taxation) by P. Diamond and J. Mirrlees, "Optimal Taxation and Public Production," *American Economic Review* 61 (1971): 261–78, and by A. B. Atkinson and J. E. Stiglitz, "The Structure of Indirect Taxation and Economic Efficiency," *Journal of Public Economics* (1972): 97–119 and "The Design of Tax Structure: Direct versus Indirect Taxation," *Journal of Public Economics* 6 (1976): 55–75. See also below, Chapter 20.

others: private firms fail to take into account the costs that their pollution imposes on others; they fail to take into account the social gains from employment (and thus may replace men with machines, when to do so is not socially desirable); they fail to take into account the congestion costs associated with locating in a crowded urban area; and they attempt to take advantage of uninformed and unwary consumers. These allegations are serious, but unfortunately, it is difficult to assess their quantitative importance, or the extent to which public production would alleviate these problems, or at least alleviate them better than appropriately designed regulatory and tax-subsidy policies.

OTHER WAYS FOR GOVERNMENT TO RECONCILE PRIVATE AND SOCIAL INTERESTS: REGULATION AND TAXATION

The existence of a market failure does not necessarily imply that the government should intervene. It has to be shown that the government can correct the market failure, without introducing offsetting problems. And when government does intervene, public production may not be the appropriate remedy. Rather than attempting to control production directly, it may try to do so indirectly, by using regulation and/or taxes and subsidies to encourage firms to act in the public interest. The question is not so much which policy is the correct one but rather what are the circumstances under which each of these is the appropriate policy.

In the Unted States, regulation has been used to control industries like telephones and electricity, in which there is a single firm. In contrast, in most other countries, the government has taken direct control over these industries. In the United States, the government regulates the prices the firm can charge, it mandates that it provide certain services, and it prohibits the firm from engaging in certain activities. Thus prior to 1983, AT&T was prohibited from competing in areas other than those directly related to the provision of telephone services, but it was required to provide telephones to everyone who was willing to pay the fees set by the government. Even if the telephone company lost money in providing telephone service to a remote farmer, it was required to do so.

The government also uses tax policy to encourage what it views to be socially beneficial actions. To encourage the hiring of disadvantaged teenagers during the summer, the government provides a tax credit. In many other countries, the government provides generous tax subsidies to those firms locating in areas where there is high unemployment.

Those who advocate regulation and taxation as remedies for market failures believe that they have three major advantages over public ownership. First, they allow for a more consistent and efficient national policy. Assume it is desirable to locate firms in some area with high unemployment. Because of this, nationalized firms are often told to locate in these areas. It is, however, better to provide a general subsidy, with those firms for whom the move to the areas has the least cost taking advantage of the subsidy, than to impose the burden simply on those firms that happen to be nationalized.

Second, the utilization of tax and subsidy schemes allows a clearer estimate of the costs associated with pursuing the given objective. It may be desirable to reduce the level of pollution, but how much is it worth? It may be desirable to locate the firm in an area where there is high unemployment, but how much is it worth? It is often difficult to ascertain the additional costs of government enterprises following these objectives; providing direct government subsidies brings the costs of pursuing these alternative objectives more into the open and thus allows a more rational decision concerning whether the costs are worth the benefits.

Third, there is a widespread belief that incentives for efficiency are greater with private firms, even if regulated. The evidence for this greater efficiency, and the reasons for it, are discussed below.

Advocates of public production claim that these indirect control mechanisms are not completely effective; private firms have more information than the regulators and are able, through one means or another, to get the regulators to work in the interests of the regulated. Moreover, the government may have a multiplicity of objectives. Some argue this is particularly true for activities like education and defense, where, in addition, it is difficult to ascertain the "quality" of what is being produced.

Finally, the use of regulation (and tax or subsidy schemes) often has resulted in large distortions, as firms attempt to use their superior information to get the upper hand over the regulators and to take advantage of any improperly designed regulatory provisions. There is a widespread belief, for instance, that utility regulations have led to excessive investment by utilities.

Those who advocate no (or very weak) controls believe that proponents of regulation are correct in their view that publicly owned enterprises are inefficient. They also agree with critics of regulation that regulations result in inefficiencies, and that regulation frequently serves the interest of the regulated or of special-interest groups. They go further in arguing that there is no reason to believe that public enterprises act in the "public interest" (rather than in the interests of special-interest groups or of the managers and workers of the public enterprises). In recent years, for instance, there have been frequent complaints of pollution and sex discrimination against public enterprises and governmental agencies.[6] (The relevant question, of course, is whether such complaints are more or less frequent than in similarly situated private firms.)[7]

[6] See E. S. Savas, *Privatizing the Public Sector,* (Chatham, NJ: Chatham House Publishers, Inc., 1982), p. 86.

[7] An interesting reflection of this dichotomy between the actions of public enterprises and "social interests" is the recent attempt by the Socialist government in Greece, headed by Andreas Papandreou (formerly chairman of the economics department of the University of California, Berkeley), to "socialize" the public enterprises.

More generally, those who believe that the government should not intervene in the market believe that any slight advantages that might exist from the possibly improved congruence between firms' actions and social objectives resulting from either public ownership or regulation are small compared to the inefficiencies arising from public ownership or regulation.

ALTERNATIVE ARRANGEMENTS FOR THE PRODUCTION OF PUBLICLY PROVIDED GOODS

We emphasized earlier that though there is a link between the public provision of a good or service and public production of that good or service, the link is not inevitable. Governments can, and do, contract with private firms for the production of publicly provided goods.

Contracting for the Production of Public Services

Governments have increasingly relied on the private sector for data processing (record keeping).[8] Some security services and fire protection services (such as at airports) are contracted out to private firms, and there have even been several instances of privately run prisons.

In a few cases, the government has gone one step further: it has turned over responsibility for what is normally a publicly provided good to a private firm. Although almost all roads and bridges in the United States are public, there are some exceptions: the Ambassador Bridge and Detroit-Windsor Tunnel linking Detroit, Michigan, with Windsor, Ontario, is a private, for-profit enterprise. In Italy (where the government has taken a more active role in many areas) the major limited-access inter-city highway network was built and operated by private, for-profit companies, which obtain their revenues by charging tolls.[9]

Though recent years have seen an increase in contracting out of public services with the private sector, there are some services for which private production does not seem well-suited. It may be difficult to specify precisely the characteristics of the product or service that is to be provided and to ensure that the desired "quality" is maintained. While it is possible to contract for the delivery of a specific tank or plane, it would be difficult for the government to contract with a private firm to "provide for the national defense." (It should be recalled, however, that the Revolutionary War was partially fought with Hessians, hired mercenaries. In effect, the government, even from the beginning, had contracted out for the production of defense services.) Education, as

[8] "Privatization in the United States: Cities and Counties," National Center for Policy Analysis, Policy Report No. 116 (Dallas, TX: NCPA, June 1985), p. 7.

[9] See Robert W. Poole, Jr., "Privatization of Transportation Infrastructure," *Transportation Quarterly* 38 (April 1984), p. 203.

mentioned earlier, is an activity about which there has been considerable debate concerning suitability of private production. Could local governments write a contract with private schools to produce the kind of education the community wishes? Would it have to supervise what is done so closely that it might as well take direct control to ensure that the desired "quality" is maintained?

Critics of contracting out point to other difficulties. In many cases, there are relatively few bidders, in which case there may be high profits for the winning bid for a contract. (In recent bidding for off-shore oil and gas leases, the average tract on which bids were received had less than two bidders.) This problem is exacerbated by the long-term nature of many projects, such as the development of a new airplane. The winner in the first round (initial planning stage) may have a decided advantage over other firms in subsequent stages of development. Thus, competition becomes increasingly thin, to the point where it may become ineffective. Indeed, the winning bidder may then be in a position to insist on the government paying it more than its original bid; the delays and costs associated with going to another contractor induce the government to comply with the contractor.

Moreover, if there is uncertainty concerning the cost of delivering on the contract, the contractor must be compensated for bearing the risk, again raising the cost to the government. (In such situations, the government often responds with a cost-sharing contract; but such contracts seriously erode the contractor's incentives to provide the services efficiently.)

Finally, in recent years there have been widespread allegations of corruption in contracting, particularly for municipal services. Recent multimillion dollar scandals include towing contracts and traffic violations contracts in New York. Not surprisingly, the union of government employees has been a vehement opponent of contracting out, publishing two books, *Government for Sale*[10] and *Passing the Buck.*[11] Defenders of contracting out, while acknowledging the human interest aspect of these anecdotes, deny their quantitative significance, and contend that these problems can be alleviated with properly designed contracting procedures.

The importance of the problems we have noted varies from situation to situation.[12] There are some local services, such as refuse collection, for which these problems do not appear to be significant and for which contracting out is not uncommon.

[10] John D. Hanrahan, *Government for Sale: Contracting-Out—the New Patronage,* American Federation of State, County, and Municipal Employees, 1977.

[11] American Federation of State, County, and Municipal Employees, 1983.

[12] Recently, David Sappington of Bell Communications Research and Joseph Stiglitz have proved a theorem referred to as the *fundamental privatization theorem,* establishing conditions under which an appropriately designed procedure for contracting out can be used to ensure not only efficiency, but also that all the government's distributional objectives (including no excess profits for the contractor) can be attained. See D. Sappington and J.E. Stiglitz, "Privatization, Information, and Incentives," *Journal of Policy Analysis and Management,* 6 (1987): 567–82.

Voucher Schemes

Many advocates of private production of publicly provided goods argue not only that there should be private production but also that the decision about which private producer should be involved should be left to the individual, and not decided by government. Individuals should be given a **voucher** that allows them to purchase the good or service from a list of approved sellers meeting certain standards that the government establishes. Proponents of schemes for educational and housing vouchers have been particularly vocal. They argue that the individual benefiting from the services is in a better position, and has greater incentives, to judge and monitor the quality of what is being provided than a government agency. They also argue that the competition among alternative providers will enhance the quality and reduce the cost of the services being provided.

The critics of educational vouchers have been concerned that the full range of public objectives that motivated the establishment and growth of the public school system in the United States will not be satisfied; they worry, for instance, that voucher schemes may lead to greater social stratification. And they are not convinced that parents are in a better position to judge what is in the best educational interests of their children than are professional educators. Needless to say, the issue remains a source of contention.

ARE PUBLIC ENTERPRISES LESS EFFICIENT?

A major ground of comparison between public and private enterprises is that of inefficiency. Stories of government waste, bureaucratic red tape, rigid regulations, and obtuse regulators abound in the popular press.

In 1984 a presidential panel entitled "Private Sector Survey on Cost Control," headed by New York industrialist J. Peter Grace, completed an eighteen-month study. It made 2,500 recommendations to eliminate government waste that could save $424.4 billion over three years, 27 percent of which could be achieved simply by administrative action. Among the administrative failures cited were the following:

• The Pentagon bought standard screws (available in any hardware store for 3 cents) for $91 each. The panel attributed this to lack of competitive bidding and estimated the total loss from this practice to be $7.3 billion.

• Federal employees use 64 percent more sick time than private-sector employees in nonmanufacturing industries. The panel attributed this to sick-leave policy and estimated that the loss over a three-year period was $3.7 billion.

• Replacing out-of-date computers (average age 6.7 years, twice that in the private sector) would save $6.5 billion.

• Improving the Department of Defense inventory management (the present system generates 6 million pounds of computer output annually) would save $6.1 billion.

• Correcting government mailing lists, which sometimes repeat the same address 29 times, would save $96 million.

• The Veterans Administration spends $61,250 per bed to build nursing homes, almost four times the costs of a major private-sector nursing home operator.

• The General Services Administration employs 17 times as many people and spends 14 times as much on management costs as a private-sector company managing comparable space.

Many of the recommendations for eliminating waste were really recommendations for eliminating hidden subsidies to particular groups in the population. Among these:

• The total savings (over a three-year period) from eliminating subsidies for electric power are estimated at $19.8 billion.

• The government is required by law to pay "prevailing wages" on federal construction projects. The law prevents both outside contractors and smaller, more competitive contractors from undercutting large, established local builders. The three-year cost of this practice is estimated to be $5.0 billion.

• Congressional resistance to closing unneeded military bases adds $3.1 billion to the budget over a three-year period.

• Legislation prohibiting competitive bidding on moving household goods to Alaska or Hawaii increases moving costs by up to 26 percent.

The Grace panel's study confirms inefficiency in the public sector. But the government does not have a monopoly on inefficient practices. One could of course find similar anecdotes concerning inefficiencies in private firms, of the difficulties in collecting money from insurance firms, of bureaucratic red tape in banks. There are incompetent people in all walks of life, and competent people make mistakes. The question is, is there any evidence to suggest that waste is greater in the public sector that in the private sector?

Comparison of Efficiency in the Public and Private Sectors

Unfortunately, there have been few systematic studies of the relative performance of the public and private sectors, and these have to be interpreted with some caution. On the negative side are such findings as:

• Public housing projects cost about 20 percent more to produce than comparable private housing.[13]

• Public garbage collection costs about 50 percent more than private garbage collection.[14]

[13] R. Muth, *Public Housing* (Washington, D.C.: American Enterprise Institute, 1973).

[14] E. S. Savas, *The Organization and Efficiency of Solid Waste Collection* (Lexington, MA: D. C. Heath, 1977).

• The cost of privately produced (but publicly financed) fire protection in Scottsdale, Arizona, was approximately 47 percent less than the cost of publicly produced fire services provided to comparable communities.[15]

• A study of contractor-provided school bus transportation in Indiana showed that it was generally 12 percent less costly than equivalent district-provided transportation.[16]

• A Department of Defense study of contracting out for support services found cost savings of 22 percent.[17]

• A U.S. Department of Housing and Urban Development funded study, using a data base of some 120 Southern California jurisdictions, found that contractor provision was significantly less expensive for seven of eight services studied, the one exception being payroll processing.[18]

But not all studies show that government enterprises perform more poorly than private. In Canada, there are two major rail systems, one private and one public; one recent study concluded that there was no significant difference in the efficiency of the two systems.[19]

While some studies show higher hospital costs in government hospitals, others show lower costs. And in state-run liquor stores, Sam Peltzman of the University of Chicago found that prices were 4 to 11 percent lower than those charged by private retailers.[20]

While administrative costs of the social security administration are less than 2 percent of the benefits paid, private insurance companies frequently spend as much as 30 to 40 percent of the amount provided in benefits in administrative and sales costs. One study compared the number of administrators to teachers and researchers in public and private institutions of higher education, and found that there were almost

[15] R. Ahlbrandt, "Efficiency in the Provision of Fire Services," *Public Choice* 16 (1973). A more recent study confirmed those findings. See *Alternatives to Traditional Public Safety Services* (Berkeley, CA: Institute for Local Self-Government, 1977).

[16] Robert A. McQuire and Norman T. Van Cott, "Public vs. Private Activity: A New Look at School Bus Transportation," *Public Choice* 43 (1984). Similar findings (with cost savings of up to 50 percent have been obtained for urban bus transportation. See James L. Perry and Timlynn T. Babitsky, "Comparative Performance in Urban Bus Transit: Assessing Privatization Strategies," *Public Administration Review*, Jan./Feb. 1986, and Edward K. Morlock and Philip A. Viton, "The Comparative Costs of Public and Private Transit," in *Urban Transit: The Private Challenge to Public Transit*, Charles Lave, ed. (Cambridge, MA: Ballinger Publishing Co., 1985).

[17] U.S. Department of Defense, "Report to Congress on the Commercial Activities Program," March 1984.

[18] See Barbara J. Stevens, ed., *Delivering Municipal Services Efficiently: A Comparison of Municipal and Private Service Delivery*, Report prepared by Ecodata, Inc., June 1984.

[19] D. W. Daves and L. R. Christensen, "The Relative Efficiency of Public and Private Firms in a Competitive Environment: The Case of Canadian Railroads," *Journal of Political Economy* 88 (1980): 958–76.

[20] Cotton Lindsay, "A Theory of Government Enterprise," *Journal of Political Economy*, October 1976. L. G. Hrebinia and J. A. Alutto, "A Comparative Organizational Study of Performance and Size Correlates in Inpatient Psychiatric Departments," *Administrative Science Quarterly* 18 (1973). Sam Peltzman, "Pricing in Public and Private Enterprises: Electric Utilities in the United States," *Journal of Law and Economics* 14 (1971). Perry and Babitsky, "Comparative Performance in Urban Bus Transit," report that publicly owned systems managed by private contractors performed no more efficiently or effectively than publicly owned, publicly managed systems. Their study emphasizes the importance of appropriately designing contractual arrangements.

50 percent more administrators in private schools than in public schools.[21] Moreover, some studies have found marked improvements in productivity in the public sector in recent years. One study, by the Office of Personnel Management, covering 65 percent of federal employees, showed that productivity had increased at an annual rate of 1.4 percent between 1967 and 1978, slightly higher than the rate of productivity increase in the private sector.[22]

The same ambiguity in findings has been noted on an international basis. While the major British nationalized enterprises have suffered (often huge) losses, many of the French national enterprises have been quite profitable.

One difficulty encountered in such studies is determining "comparabilities": costs for garbage collection in communities in which houses are close together might differ significantly from costs for garbage collection in communities in which houses are far apart. Communities that elect to use private services may be different, in some important way, from communities that elect to use public services.

Those enterprises that are run by the government may differ systematically from those that are privately run. Many of the public enterprises in Britain today became public enterprises as a result of bankruptcy: the government intervened to stop the plants from closing by taking over the firms. These firms are government enterprises because they were running at a loss; they are not running at a loss because they are government enterprises.

An example of the caution necessary in evaluating studies comparing public and private performance is provided by the recent study of private versus public schools headed by University of Chicago sociologist James Coleman. He found not only that students in private schools performed better but that such schools were as racially mixed as public schools.[23] However, students attending the private schools had chosen to go there; they (or their parents) had expressed a commitment to education (in their willingness to spend money on it); and the school had the option of rejecting students who failed to perform or were disruptive. Hence even if one finds that private school students do perform better, one cannot infer that converting any public school system into a privately managed one would improve performance.

Though there is only scattered evidence that public bureaucracies are less efficient than private firms, the belief that this is so is widespread. Instances of public incompetence are very much in the public eye; instances of private incompetence do not draw comparable attention.[24]

Still, it is worth noting that several studies indicate a reasonably high

[21] Lorraine E. Prinsky, "Public vs. Private: Organizational Control as Determinant of Administrative Size," *Sociology and Social Research* 62 (1978).

[22] See Nancy Hayward and George Kuper, "The National Economy and Productivity in Government," *Public Administration Review* 38 (1978) and U.S. Office of Personnel Management, *Measuring Federal Productivity,* February 1980.

[23] Most students in private schools attend inner-city Catholic schools.

[24] Instances of "large" private failures also receive considerable attention. The huge cost overruns on nuclear power plants (with final costs frequently being more than ten times the originally estimated

level of "consumer satisfaction" with government bureaucracy. A Harris survey of those who had had some nonroutine dealings with a federal government agency found that 46 percent found the experience "highly satisfying" while an additional 29 percent found it "only somewhat" satisfying. A University of Michigan study found comparable levels of satisfaction, while an Ohio State University study found high satisfaction levels from about 60 percent of the respondents. These studies (in which individuals evaluate a specific experience) should be contrasted with surveys of general impressions of government efficiency. A Gallup poll study found that two-thirds of those interviewed thought bureaucrats do not work so hard as the interviewees themselves would in governmental jobs and that the government employs too many individuals.[25] On the other hand, in a CBS/*New York Times* poll in January 1985, only 38 percent of those interviewed agreed that it would be a good idea to cut the salaries of all federal civil service employees; 50 percent thought it would be a bad idea.

SOURCES OF INEFFICIENCY IN THE PUBLIC SECTOR

One of the traditional arguments in favor of government control of production is that it would be more efficient than private production. There are problems of coordination among private firms that will frequently lead to excessive investment at one time or in one industry and insufficient investment in another.[26] The government (in this view) is in a better position to plan for the orderly development of an industry. These concerns have been particularly important for less developed countries, and for industries requiring heavy investments. Some economists, such as John Kenneth Galbraith of Harvard University, believe that more planning is required. The prevalent view today among American economists about both the merits and the necessity of government planning (at least as it has turned out in practice) is somewhat skeptical. On the other hand, it is pointed out that extensive planning goes on within private firms. On the other hand, there is concern about the ability of government to plan well.

Why should public enterprises in fact behave much differently than private ones? Until 1987, over half the shares of British Petroleum were owned by the British government. Yet, at least in its day-to-day operations, it looked little different from any other multinational oil company.

---

cost) are only partially attributable to changing government regulations. Losses of over a billion dollars by financial giants such as Bank of America have also drawn attention in recent years.

[25] George H. Gallup, *The Gallup Poll: Public Opinion, 1972–77* (Wilmington, DE: Scholars Resources, 1978) and *The Washington Post*, October 1978, p. 16.

[26] The French government pioneered in the use of what is called indicative planning, in which information about production plans is shared among firms but they are left to make their own decisions. In recent years, however, even this limited form of government planning has not been extensively employed.

Though there may be important differences in how a small firm that is operated by its owner functions and how a large corporation does, what difference does it make if there are private shareholders or if there is a single shareholder, the government? Some contend that managers of public enterprises may behave in much the same way that managers of large private enterprises do. In both cases, managers have a large amount of discretion, allowing them to pursue their own interests, often at the expense of the public interest (in the case of public enterprises) or shareholder interests (in the case of private enterprises). Recent payoffs, called "green-mail," out of the corporate purse to those attempting to take over a firm have confirmed these views; these payments, as well as the provisions that management has attempted to put into their corporate charters making take-overs more difficult, have preserved management's prerogatives, but at the expense of shareholders.

Though there are thus some important similarities between large corporations and public enterprises, there remain some important differences. The main difference that economists emphasize is incentives, both organizational and individual.

Organizational Incentives

Government enterprises differ from private enterprises in two important ways: they do not need to worry about bankruptcy, and they usually do not have to worry about competition.

BANKRUPTCY

One source of differences in incentives facing public and private enterprises has to do with the threat of bankruptcy that private firms face, in contrast with the ever-present possibility of subsidies from the government for public enterprises.

The possibility of bankruptcy is an important one; it provides a limit to the magnitude of the losses that an inefficient management can generate in a private enterprise, and a natural mechanism for the replacement of inefficient management teams. It imposes a budget constraint on the firm. In a competitive market, even a generous manager cannot pay his workers much more than the prevailing wage without risking the possibility of bankruptcy.

In contrast, government enterprises often run large deficits over extended periods of time. In Britain, for instance, the cumulative deficits of the British Steel Corporation during the period since nationalization have been massive. Between 1976 and 1983, the company's net losses amounted to £4.3 billion, which is equivalent to approximately $500 for the average British household of four. The possibility of public subsidies has, it is argued, made managers of public enterprises less resistant to union wage demands; in many countries, wages of public enterprises are considerably in excess of wages for corresponding workers in the private sector. The same is true more generally for public employees in the United States. Federal wages for males have been 15 percent above wages for comparable workers in the private sector; females' wages have been 21 percent higher.[27]

COMPETITION

A second difference between public and private enterprises arises from the absence of competition facing most public enterprises. Competition plays several important roles. First, competition provides the opportunity for choice. Consider the government agency responsible for issuing license plates: frequently the agency fails to take into account the value of time used waiting in line to obtain the license plate. Since that cost does not appear in the agency's budget, while the costs of additional personnel that might be required to reduce waiting times is included, there is an incentive to reduce costs in this way (which actually increases the total social costs of providing the service).

Individuals might be willing to pay more for the service, but they are not offered the opportunity of choice. When there is competition, individuals can reveal their preferences by their acts of choice. The presence of choice *forces* firms to come to terms with the costs imposed on those outside their agency as a result of bureaucratic processes. Thus a bureaucratic insurance firm, which requires extensive paperwork in order to obtain a claim, might find itself losing customers to a less bureaucratic firm. The public bureaucracy behaving in the same way will not receive the same signal.

Albert O. Hirschman of the Institute for Advanced Study at Princeton has called this method of communicating preferences (through an act of choice) "exit," as opposed to "voice" (the expression of views through the political process). When individuals have no choice, voice is the only option available, and voice may be an ineffective method of inducing bureaucracies to act efficiently. Thus competition provides a check, a limitation on the inefficiencies associated with public enterprises.[28]

More positively, competition provides an incentive structure: competing enterprises, in their attempt to attract clients, try to find a mixture of services that best meets customer needs. More generally, competition provides a *basis for comparison*. When there is only one agency issuing license plates, it may be difficult to ascertain whether or not the agency is being efficient. Those who are responsible for manag-

[27] Sharon P. Smith, "Pay, Pensions, and Employment in Government, *American Economic Review*, May 1982, p. 275. See also Paul N. Courant, Edward M. Gramlich, and Daniel L. Rubinfeld, "Public Employee Market Power and the Level of Government Spending," *American Economic Review*, December 1979, pp. 806–17.

[28] A. O. Hirschman, *Exit, Voice and Loyalty: Responses to Decline in Firms, Organizations, and States* (Cambridge, MA: Harvard University Press, 1970). The book contrasts the economist's solution to poor performance—"exit," taking one's business elsewhere—with the political scientist's emphasis on "voice," working within the organization to improve it.

ing the agency are more knowledgeable about the technology of issuing license plates than outsiders. But when there are several agencies engaged in similar activities, one has a basis for comparison. One can see that one agency has a lower cost than another, and one is then in a position at least to ask why.[29] Even when the comparison of performance is not made explicitly, it is made implicitly by the market and is reflected in the firm's profitability. Competition implies that those firms that are efficient and are able to deliver the kinds of goods and services consumers desire will grow and expand, and that those that are inefficient will decline. These rewards and punishments are meted out by the market in an impersonal way; managers know this and have a strong incentive to promote efficiency and to be innovative in developing products and services that better meet the needs of consumers.

Individual Incentives

Another important difference between the private and public enterprises lies in the incentive structures facing government employees.

RESTRICTIONS ON SALARY STRUCTURE

Managers in public enterprises seldom have pay structures that are as closely related to profits as managers of large private enterprises. For a government enterprise to pay its president, say, five times the salary of the president of the United States is probably unacceptable. How important this restriction is is a question of some debate. It may affect the quality of the individuals it succeeds in hiring, and it may affect the effort the manager exerts. But there are those who claim that managers do the best they can, and financial reward is only part of what motivates individuals; and there are those who argue that there is little evidence that managers make much difference anyway.[30]

TENURE

A second important difference is the ease with which individuals can be fired. It is very difficult to be fired from government jobs. This attribute of security is often cited by potential employees as one of the more desirable features of government employment. Prior to the current civil service system, federal employees served at the whim of the president; part of the spoils of winning the election was the right to appoint one's supporters to government jobs. Today, the only political appointments are the secretaries of each of the departments, and those who serve

[29] See B. Nalebuff and J. E. Stiglitz, "Prizes and Incentives: Towards a General Theory of Compensation and Competition," *Bell Journal* 14 (1983): 21–43.

[30] In an often-quoted study, Lieberson and O'Connor showed that changes in management had little significant effect on the performance of the firm. See S. Lieberson and S. F. O'Connor, "Leadership and Organizational Performance: A Study of Large Corporations," *American Sociological Review* 37 (1972): 117–30. See also G. Salanick and J. Pfeffer, "Constraints on Administrator Discretion: The Limited Influence of Mayors on City Budgets," *Urban Affairs Quarterly* 12 (1977): 475–98.

immediately under them (the undersecretaries, assistant secretaries, and deputy assistant secretaries). Though the intent of the civil service legislation was to establish a professional administrative system, immune from political pressures, this protection from being fired for political reasons also entails considerable protection from being fired for incompetency.

The combination of the limitations on rewards for good performance and the absence of punishments for bad performance undoubtedly plays an important role in explaining bureaucratic behavior. At the same time, the government may attract to itself individuals who value security highly and who do not view the absence of high rewards as much of a loss, since they would not attain a high salary in the private sector anyway. Changes in the reward structure for these individuals might not elicit a marked change in their behavior.[31]

THE BUREAUCRACY

Over the years, various branches of the civil service have developed different reputations. While some, such as the National Park Service, have developed a positive public image, there is a general view of the federal bureaucracy as entailing inefficiency, lack of innovativeness, inflexibility, blind attention to following routines, and endless red tape.

In this section, we discuss how bureaucracies differ from other kinds of organizations and how we can explain certain aspects of bureaucratic behavior.

Differences between Administrative Activities and Other Production Activities

Earlier, we cited several studies comparing public and private enterprises undertaking similar activities, such as garbage collection. It is important to remember, however, that a large fraction of government activity is very much different from these kinds of production activities. Much of government activity is administrative, or "white" collar. It may be that many of the problems we associate with bureaucracies arise not because they lie within the public sector but because of the nature of the duties of bureaucrats.[32] In the economists' typical model of a production activity, there is a well-defined notion of what the worker is supposed to do, inputs can be observed, outputs can be observed, and there is a well-

[31] This slightly exaggerates the lack of rewards within the bureaucratic structure: individuals can still be promoted. But the possibilities of promotion become limited in periods in which the growth of government is restricted. Though this may happen in private enterprises as well, private-sector individuals who find their promotion possibilities limited leave to go to other firms; whereas the security of tenure within the civil service and the relatively high pay of those in the public sector make their exit to private firms relatively unattractive. In these circumstances, incentive problems may become particularly severe.

[32] These differences have been emphasized in the work of J. Hannaway, "Supply Creates Demands" *Journal of Policy Analysis and Management* 7 (1987): 118–34.

defined relationship between inputs and outputs.[33] None of these conditions holds for much of the administrative activity within the public sector. The differences between administrative activity and production activity also account for the limited use of incentive pay structures. It may not be possible to design effective incentive structures where it is difficult to measure performance.

DIFFICULTIES IN MEASURING PERFORMANCE

There are some difficulties in measuring the performance of firms in the private sector. The manager of the firm may claim that though current profits are low, the firm has taken decisions that are aimed at maximizing the long-run profitability of the firm. Nevertheless, the criterion of profitability is clear. In the case of public-sector agencies, however, it is far more difficult to ascertain whether the agency has been successful. Did students do better as a result of federal aid to education for the poor? How does one measure this: does one use reading scores? What are valid tests? And how can one distinguish the contribution of one particular public program from all the other changes that are going on in the environment at the same time? In the last few years, these problems have been of considerable concern and have given rise to attempts to develop systematic evaluation procedures for public programs.

Where outcomes cannot be evaluated precisely, performance is more likely to be judged on the basis of procedures and process: how well the manager follows the present routines and how successful he is in dealing with the bureaucracy.

MULTIPLICITY OF OBJECTIVES

The difficulty of assessing the success of a government official is exacerbated by the multiplicity of objectives associated with most public programs. While profit maximization is the clear objective of private firms, public agencies have to worry about a variety of distributional considerations. The legislation setting up a program frequently lists a number of objectives without specifying how trade-offs are to be made. Individuals inside and outside the bureaucracy may differ on how those trade-offs should be made. To some it may be far more important to make sure that everyone who is entitled to some government program gets access to it than it is to make sure than someone who is not entitled to a government program is denied access. Critics of government programs tend to focus only on the latter. But any attempt (with given administrative resources) to cut back on one type of error increases the number of errors of the other type.

[33] There has been an extensive recent literature dealing with the special problems that arise when inputs cannot be observed but outputs can. See, for instance, J. E. Stiglitz, "Incentives, Risk, and Information: Notes towards a Theory of Hierarchy, *Bell Journal of Economics and Management Science,* Autumn 1975, pp. 552–79.

A third characteristic of many government programs that makes them ill-suited for the use of conventional incentive structures is that the relationship between the efforts of the manager and the success of the program is very tenuous. This is particularly true of the newer government programs. The objectives of many of the measures enacted under President Johnson's "Great Society" program were clear: to reduce, if not eliminate, the extent of poverty in the United States. But the "technology"—how this was to be done—was (and to a large extent remains) unclear. The fact that in bureaucracies there was no clear relationship between inputs and outputs was noted by C. Northcote Parkinson:

> It is a commonplace observation that work expands so as to fill the time available for its completion. . . . Granted that work (and especially paper work) is thus elastic in its demands on time, it is manifest that there need be little or no relationship between the work to be done and the size of the staff to which it may be assigned. . . . Politicians and taxpayers have assumed with occasional phases of doubt that a rising total in the number of civil servants must reflect a growing volume of work to be done. Cynics, in questioning this belief, have imagined that the multiplication of officials must have left some of them idle or all of them able to work for shorter hours. But this is a matter in which faith and doubt seem equally misplaced. The fact is that the number of the officials and the quantity of the work to be done are not related to each other at all. . . .[34]

Parkinson went on to announce Parkinson's Law, which describes the law of growth of public organizations. It was predicated on two hypotheses: "An official wants to multiply subordinates, not rivals; and officials make work for each other."

What Do Bureaucrats Maximize?

Economists begin with the presumption that individuals act in their own self-interest. Thus, to understand the behavior of bureaucracies, one must ask, What is it in the interests of the bureaucrats to do? In the preceding section we argued that, for a variety of reasons, bureaucrats are not given incentive structures in which their pay is related very closely to their performance. The question then is, What do bureaucrats seek to maximize? One answer is provided by W. A. Niskanen, a member of the Council of Economic Advisers in the Reagan administration and a former vice-president of the Ford Motor Company.

He postulated that bureaucrats seek to maximize the size of their agency. Bureaucrats are concerned with "their salary, the perquisites of office, public reputation, power, patronage," all of which are related to

[34] From C. Northcote Parkinson, "Parkinson's Law," *The Economist*, November 1955, reprinted in E. Mansfield, *Managerial Economics and Operations Research* (New York: W. W. Norton, 4th ed., 1980).

the size of their agency. In this view, the bureaucrat attempts to promote the activities of his bureau in many of the same ways that a firm attempts to increase its size. He *competes* with other bureaucrats for funds. Bureaucratic competition replaces market competition.[35]

What implications does the Niskanen hypothesis have for the behavior of the bureaucrat (and the bureaucracy)? How does a bureaucrat succeed in increasing his share of the overall budget? There are several mechanisms, and understanding them gives some insights into a number of the well-known characteristics of bureaucracies.

INCREASING THE SIZE OF THEIR AGENCY

Bureaucrats seek to provide desired services. To this extent, bureaucratic competition serves a healthy function. But the direct clientele of the bureaucrat are not the citizens, who receive the services, but the congressmen and congresswomen who vote for the appropriations. Government bureaucrats tend to be particularly attuned to the desires of those congressmen and congresswomen who serve on the committees and subcommittees that oversee the government agency. Thus some of the alleged bureaucratic inefficiencies are not really inefficiencies arising from the bureaucracy but legislative (congressional) inefficiencies: the bureaucracy is simply responding to the desire of Congress to extend special favors to certain special-interest groups.

It is when there is little competition among bureaucracies that the bureaucrats' interest and the public interest may diverge most markedly. Niskanen argues that there has been an increasing centralization (and hence decreasing competition) within the bureaucracy.[36] But the attempts to "rationalize" the bureaucracy, to ensure that two government agencies do not perform duplicative functions, has the disadvantage that it reduces competition.

If we view a bureaucrat as a monopolist who provides some service, and we postulate that the bureaucrat wishes to maximize the size of his agency, then we can obtain a clear prediction concerning what the

[35] W. A. Niskanen, Jr. *Bureaucracy and Representative Government* (Chicago: Aldine, 1971), p. 38. It should be emphasized that the bureaucrat does not necessarily view himself as pursuing his own selfish interest. The navy admiral who pushes for more aircraft carriers believes that he is doing what is in the national interest, but so does the air force general who pushes for more bombers, and the army general who pushes for more land-based missiles. These individuals come to believe in the worth of the activities in which they are engaged. It should be emphasized that the bureaucrats often have a multiplicity of objectives: they may not only wish to increase the size of their department but also their discretion; and they may also wish to avoid risks. See W. Niskanen, "Bureaucrats and Politicians," *Journal of Law and Economics*, December 1975, pp. 617–43, and Jane Hannaway, *Managed Managers: Signals and Signalling in Administrative Systems* (New York: Oxford University Press, 1988).

[36] Sam Peltzman has criticized this centralization hypothesis as an explanation for the growth of bureaucracy. He compares economies with different degrees of centralization and argues that there is no systematic relation between that and bureaucratic growth. There are other variables that affect bureaucratic size and growth, and it is, unfortunately, difficult to account for all of them. The question is, other things being equal, does an increase in centralization lead to more bureaucratic growth? See S. Peltzman, "The Growth of Government," *Journal of Law and Economics*, October 1980, pp. 209–88. See also D. North, " The Growth of Government in the United States: An Economic Historian's Perspective," *Journal of Public Economics* 28 (1985), pp. 383–99.

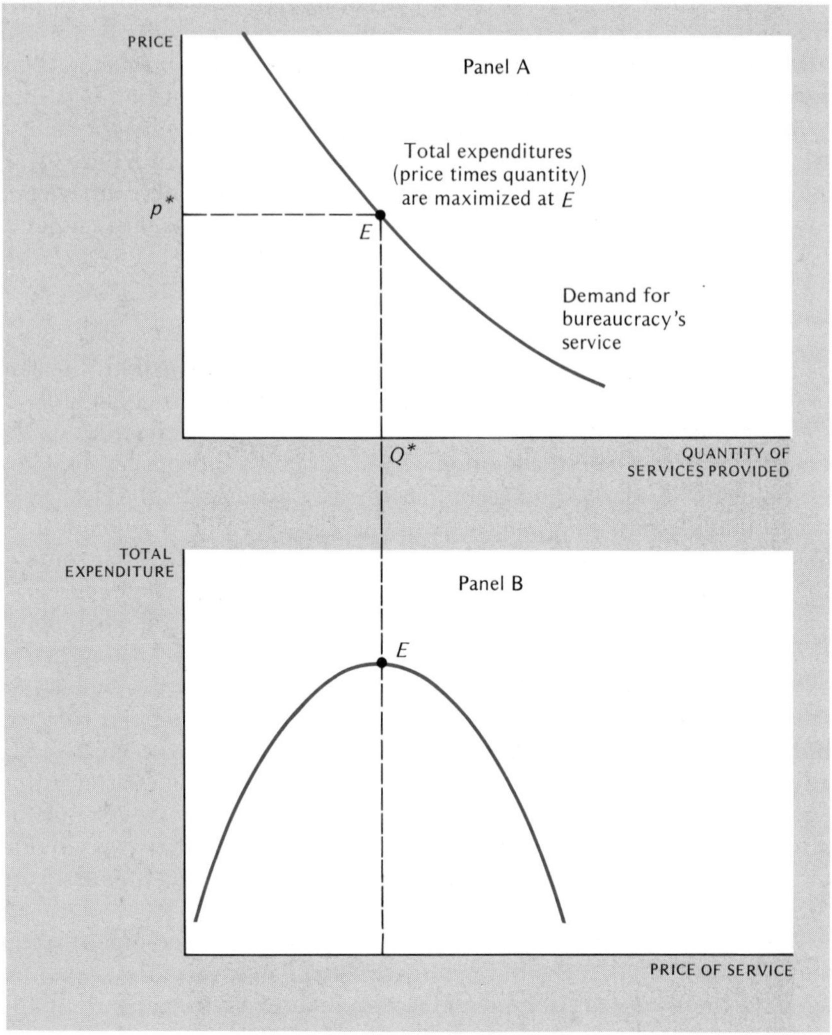

7.5 MAXIMIZING A BUREAUCRACY'S SIZE As the price of the service increases up to p^*, total expenditure increases. To maximize revenue, the bureaucrat sets the price of the bureaucracy's service at the point of maximum expenditures, *E*.

bureaucrat should do. If the demand for the service of the bureaucracy is inelastic over some ranges as the price of the service is increased, total expenditure (price times quantity) increases (see Figure 7.5). In Figure 7.5B we have plotted the total expenditure on the public service as a function of the price charged. Expenditure is maximized at the point *E*.[37]

[37] Technically, this is the point where the elasticity of demand is equal to unity. The elasticity of demand, it will be recalled, gives the percentage change in demand resulting from a one percent change in price.

$$\text{Elasticity of demand} = \frac{\%\text{ change in demand}}{\%\text{ change in price}}$$

As the price of the service increases up to p^*, total expenditure increases. The bureaucrat maximizes his revenues at point *E*. If the bureaucrat could charge what he liked for the public service, and if he wished to maximize expenditures by the public on the services he provides, he would charge price p^*. But the bureaucrat cannot arbitrarily choose a price to charge. The price for the service provided by the bureaucrat is simply the costs per unit of the service delivered. If he wishes to increase the price, he can do it only by decreasing efficiency. If the bureaucrat were a perfect monopolist, he would increase the degree of inefficiency until the price (costs per unit of delivered service) were increased to p^*.

Several factors are critical in enabling the bureaucrat to do this. First there must be an absence of competition. If there were competition, some other bureaucrat could offer to perform the services at lower costs. Second, the technology must be ambiguous, so that it must be difficult to ascertain whether or not the bureaucrat is being inefficient. How many pieces of paper should a paper processor process per minute? Since this is likely to vary markedly from task to task, no outside standard can readily be set.

IMPERFECT INFORMATION AND BUDGETS

Finally, the bureaucrat often has an important *informational advantage* over legislators. Congressmen usually have limited information concerning what it should cost to perform various services. They do not know how much it should cost to produce a new missile system. At times, when bureaucrats are competing against each other or when the costs of some program seem excessively high, bureaucrats will tend to underrepresent the costs. They know that once the program has been initiated, they will be able to obtain the necessary supplemental funds required to complete it. Military procurement has been particularly marked by cost overruns. At other times, there may be an incentive to exaggerate the costs required to perform some task; the extra resources can then be diverted to some other use.

Indeed, one of the great concerns of a bureaucrat is that it come to be believed that he can do his job at a lower cost. A bureaucrat who failed to spend his entire budget would be in danger of having his budget cut the next year. This is what gives rise to what are called "spend-out problems"—problems using up the congressional appropriation during the final months (days) of the fiscal year.

The bureaucrat can not only misrepresent the benefits and costs associated with his activities, he can also take actions that *affect* those benefits and costs. In particular, it is common for an agency to be given an overall budget; this is the major instrument of control over the agency.

Thus, demand is elastic if a one percent increase in the price causes a more than one percent reduction in demand, so that total revenue (the product of price times quantity) is reduced. Demand is inelastic if the quantity demanded is not very sensitive to price. In Figure 7.5, the demand curve is inelastic in the price range between 0 and p^*, and elastic at prices above p^*.

The agency, though, may enjoy some discretion within that budget. In particular, the bureaucrat may use this discretion to pursue his own goals (whatever those are) rather than those of the legislators. The threat of cutting back on some part of the expenditure is sometimes employed by public agencies to increase their overall budgets. Thus when the National Park Service had its budget cut, it eliminated its expenditure for lighting the Statue of Liberty in hopes that the ensuing public outcry would lead to a restoration of its budget.

Finally, the bureaucrats may exercise influence over the size of their budgets by presenting a limited set of alternatives. The military may claim that only two types of defense systems are feasible, one very ineffective but costing very little, and the other costing a great deal. (Although there may well be others, these are claimed to be "inferior" in one way or another.) By refusing to present details of the alternatives, they force a vote between two extremes, hoping in doing so to get the high level of expenditure. By controlling the agenda in this way, they may seek to increase the size of the budget.[38]

Bureaucratic Procedures and Risk Aversion

The bureaucrat's desire to increase the size of his budget seems to provide an explanation of many aspects of bureaucratic behavior. There are other aspects of bureaucratic behavior that can best be explained by another important aspect of the incentives facing bureaucrats. Though bureaucrats' pay may not be closely and directly related to their performance, in the long run their promotion is at least partially dependent on observed performance.

A bureaucrat can absolve himself of responsibility for mistakes by following certain bureaucratic procedures that ensure that all of his actions are reviewed by others. Although this process of group decision making also reduces the claims the individual can make for any success, the bureaucrats seem willing to make this trade-off. We say they are **risk-averse.** This is what gives rise, in part, to the nature of bureaucracies: everything must pass through the appropriate channels (red tape).

Two other factors contribute to the prevalence of bureaucratic procedures. First, many of the costs associated with engaging in risk-averse activities are not borne by the bureaucrats themselves. Rather, they are borne by society as a whole, through the taxes required to pay the extra personnel. Further costs are imposed on those dealing with the bureaucracy in the form of delays, paperwork, etc. (Indeed, there are those who claim that the bureaucrats may actually enjoy the bureaucratic process.)[39]

[38] See R. Filimon, T. Romer, and H. Rosenthal, "Asymmetric Information and Agenda Control: The Bases of Monopoly Power in Public Spending," *Journal of Public Economics,* February 1982, pp. 51–70.

[39] There are alternative, more psychologically or sociologically based theories of why bureaucrats behave bureaucratically.

Second, the prevalence of set routines that must be followed entailing the approval of any proposal by several different individuals is not only a consequence of bureaucrats pursuing their own self-interest. It follows naturally from the **fiduciary** relationship between government bureaucrats and the funds they allocate. That is, government bureaucrats are not spending their own money. They are spending public resources. It is generally accepted that an individual should have less discretion—should take greater care—in spending the money of others than he might in spending his own money. Again, what is implied by taking greater care is that certain routines are followed; these routines ensure that the funds are spent not according to the whim of any single individual. They also serve the function of reducing the possibility of corruption. Since many individuals must give approval, it is usually not in the power of any individual to give a contract at an above-market price and thus receive a kickback.

Two examples of routines are the use of cost-benefit analyses and environmental impact statements. The intention of following such procedures is clear. On the other hand, because the data on which an assessment can be firmly established are rarely available, the studies often become *pro forma* exercises with predictable outcomes. Occasionally they serve as the basis for attempts by opponents of the project to delay the project; by delaying the project, the opponents hope to increase the costs to the point where the project is no longer economically feasible. There is a social loss in these delaying practices.

Reform of the Bureaucracy

Though reforms might improve the incentives facing bureaucrats, these reforms might themselves have disadvantages that outweigh the benefits. Consider the Civil Service Law, which protects civil servants from being fired. It was originally instituted to eliminate the spoils system, in which the winner of the election was entitled to appoint those who would be responsible for administering public programs. The protection from dismissal, combined with the rigidities in the pay scale, means that individuals may have relatively little reward for performing well, and relatively little punishment for performing badly, so long as performance is above a certain minimal level of competence. Though the elimination of job protection might have a beneficial effect on incentives, few advocate this as a resolution to the incentive problem, because a politicizing of the administrative process would almost inevitably result. There may be, however, reforms in the pay structure and promotion systems that would enhance incentives.

In some cases, the introduction of competition—establishing competing bureaus performing similar tasks—might have a beneficial effect. Recall our earlier discussion where we suggested that one of the major differences between public and private enterprises arises from the absence of competition facing most public enterprises. It is often alleged that monopolies in the private sector are also frequently characterized by inefficiencies, bureaucratic red tape, etc. Indeed, Daves and Christensen, in their comparison of private and public railroads in Canada, conclude that "any tendency toward inefficiency resulting from public ownership has been overcome by the benefits of competition . . . that the oft-noted inefficiency of government enterprises stems from their isolation from effective competition rather than their public ownership *per se*."[40] To what extent competition can be extended in the public sector remains a question of continuing debate.[41]

Finally, there are those who believe that the inefficiencies we have noted are an inevitable consequence of our constitutional system. Harvard political scientist M. P. Fiorina has argued:

> To have an impact a structural reform must change incentives . . . but those structural reforms which would significantly change the incentives facing congressmen and bureaucrats will stand little chance of adoption. . . . The political forces underlying existing equilibria will understandably block any structural reform capable of destroying these equilibria. Unfortunately, such equilibria arise from fundamental features of our constitutional system; only structural reforms aimed at that level can make much of a difference.[42]

SUMMARY

1. In the United States, the government has played an important role in production in several sectors, though its role is far more limited than in most other countries.
2. While most European governments have taken over direct control of natural monopolies, in the United States they are regulated. Whether regulation works effectively in the public interest is a question of some debate.
3. There is some limited evidence that governments are less efficient than private enterprises in providing comparable services. Though there are some problems with contracting out, it remains a viable alternative to public production for many goods and services.
4. Government enterprises differ from private enterprises in two important ways:
   a) While private enterprises maximize profits, government enterprises may pursue other objectives. The government may, however, be able to use tax and subsidy policies as well as regulations to affect employment, wage, location, and other policies of private enterprises, just as it could if it controlled the enterprise directly.
   b) Public enterprises face different incentives. Some of the differences in incentives arise from the absence of competition and the absence of the possibility of bankruptcy. The limited use of pay incentives and the

[40] D. W. Daves and L. R. Christensen, "Relative Efficiency of Public and Private Firms."

[41] Some claim, for instance, that the rivalry between the different branches of the military has been beneficial, while others argue that the competition has prevented them from working together in the national interest.

[42] M. P. Fiorina, "Flagellating the Federal Bureaucracy," *Society* 20 (March/April 1983), pp. 66–73.

greater degree of job security may provide part of the explanation of the differences in individuals' behavior.
5. The behavior of the bureaucracy (and individual bureaucrats) plays an important role in determining not only the efficiency with which public goods are provided but what goods are provided and to whom they are provided.
6. Bureaucrats face limited financial incentives for performing well; part of this is a result of problems inherent in measuring performance, the uncertain technologies in providing public goods, and the multiplicity of objectives. Bureaucratic behavior may be partly understood in terms of bureaucrats' desire to increase the size of the bureaucracy. Bureaucratic red tape and reliance on routines are partly explained by bureaucrats' aversion to risk.

KEY CONCEPTS

Bureaucracy	Regulation
Nationalized industry	Sunk costs
Privatization	Cross-subsidy
Public enterprise	Voucher
Indirect control	Risk aversion
Natural monopoly	Fiduciary

QUESTIONS AND PROBLEMS

1. In recent years there has been extensive privatization of public enterprises. The U.S. government has sold Conrail, the French government sold off many of its banks, and the British government has partly sold off its telephone services. In each of these cases, outline the major arguments in favor of and against privatization. Do you feel differently about the three cases? Why?
2. Under the Reagan administration, the Department of Interior greatly increased the rate at which it leased offshore oil and gas. This had the effect of significantly reducing the prices that the government received for these leases. (Though the leases are sold by auction, on more than two-thirds of the tracts there was only a single bidder.) Discuss the distributional and efficiency consequences of this policy.
3. The post office claims that one of the reasons it cannot provide services as cheaply as private firms is that it is required to provide services to rural areas but it cannot charge them more than the urban areas. The private companies "skim" the low-cost markets. (Effectively, the urban areas are subsidizing the rural areas.) Discuss the efficiency and equity consequences of this kind of cross-subsidization.

   Some have argued that if it is desirable, as a matter of national policy, to subsidize rural post offices, the subsidies should be paid out of general tax revenue, not by the other users of the postal system. Discuss the advantages and problems of such an alternative subsidy scheme.
4. There are many private security firms, and many large housing developments have police protection provided by such private firms. Yet few towns contract out their police department. Why do you think this is so? What would be the advantages and disadvantages of doing so? Recently, however, many communities have contracted to have their prisons run by private firms. What advantages or problems might you anticipate from this?

5. The military buys most of its equipment from private contractors but does not use private contractors to man its ships or fly its airplanes. What differences in the nature of the services provided might account for these differences?
6. There have been recurrent proposals for education voucher schemes, in which the government provides a voucher that can be used to purchase education either from a public provider (the local town) or a private provider. The GI Bill effectively provided such vouchers for veterans of the Korean War and World War II. More recent proposals have focused on vouchers for disadvantaged children. What do you see as the advantages and disadvantages of these voucher schemes? Are there some circumstances (some kinds of educational services) for which vouchers seem more attractive?

8

Externalities

In the past two decades, the government has taken an increasingly active role in ensuring the quality of the environment. In early 1987 Congress passed a multi-billion dollar clean water bill, over President Reagan's veto. Legislation restricting automobile emissions has been passed, and standards for admissible levels of air and water pollution by manufacturers have been established. Before any offshore oil wells are drilled, the environmental impact must be assessed. Stringent regulations for the disposal of toxic chemicals have also been imposed.

Government activity in this area has clearly had some beneficial effect. There has been a noticeable improvement in the quality of air in major industrial cities such as Pittsburgh and Gary since the passage of the Air Pollution Control Act of 1962. Lakes such as Lake Erie, which once faced the prospect of becoming so polluted that much marine life would be extinguished, have been saved. Still, problems remain: on some days Los Angeles is blanketed by smog in spite of stringent California regulations on air pollution. Dangerous poisons from chemical dumps have threatened many communities, and the question of whether the Environmental Protection Agency was lax in enforcing the law became a political issue in 1982. Acid rain still threatens some of our major forests, and because acid rain created by U.S. pollutants falls on Canada as well, it has been a sore point in U.S.–Canada relations for several years. Many claim that still more stringent laws are thus required if we are to ensure the quality of the environment for our descendants.

Others claim that the costs of many of these attempts to control pollution exceed the benefits, and that the present system of government regulation is both unfair and inefficient.

Air and water pollution are two examples of a much broader range of phenomena that economists refer to as **externalities,** one of the market failures we saw in Chapter 3. Whenever an individual or firm undertakes an action that has an effect on another individual or firm for which the latter does not pay or is not paid, we say there is an externality. This chapter explains what economists mean by externalities, the means by which private markets deal with externalities, the limits of these private mechanisms, and therefore, why government action may be required. Finally, we ask, given that government action to control externalities may be warranted, what is the best method of dealing with them? Should the government impose direct regulations, as it has done in the case of automobile emissions? Alternatively, should it subsidize private expenditures to control pollution, as many industry spokespeople advocate? Or should it simply impose a charge for pollution?

EXTERNALITIES: SOME DISTINCTIONS

Economists distinguish among several categories of externalities. Some externalities have a beneficial effect on others and are referred to as **positive externalities;** others have a detrimental effect and are referred to as **negative externalities.** A firm that pollutes the air is imposing a negative externality on all individuals who breathe the air and on all firms whose machines wear out more rapidly in the presence of polluted air.

The beekeeper confers a positive externality on the owner of the neighboring apple orchard: as a result of pollination, the greater the number of bees, the more apples in the apple orchard. And the apple orchard confers a positive externality on the beekeeper. The more trees in the apple orchard, the more honey will be produced by the bees. The action of each individual has a direct benefit on the other for which no compensation is received.

Some externalities are generated by *producers,* others by *consumers.* While most air pollution today is industrial, the major source in Victorian England was home coal fires. An individual who smokes in a nonventilated room causes a negative externality that is keenly felt by nonsmokers. A firm that pollutes a river causes an externality both to consumers who live downstream and to producers whose plants are located downstream. The externality may both lower the profits of the downstream firm and result in its raising its prices.

Some externalities, like those that affect the quality of air, are environmental and thus affect everyone who makes use of the environment. Others are more direct. If I leave garbage strewn over my lawn, only my immediate neighbors experience the externality.

There is a particularly important class of externalities referred to as

common resource problems. The central characteristic is that there is a pool of scarce resources to which access is not restricted. Consider a pond popular with fishermen. The difficulty of catching a fish depends on the number of other fishermen. Each fisherman imposes a negative externality on the other fishermen.

An important example is oil pools. Oil is usually found in large pools beneath the ground. To obtain access to a pool, all one needs to do is to buy enough land to drill a well and equipment for the drilling. Of course, the more oil that one well takes out of the pool, the less there is for others to take. The total extra oil obtained as a result of drilling an extra well may, in fact, be negative; drilling an extra well reduces the pressure, and this may reduce the amount of oil that can be extracted from the pool. Again, there is a marked difference between the private returns to drilling a well and the social returns.

THE CONSEQUENCES OF EXTERNALITIES

Whenever there are externalities, resource allocations will not be efficient. Levels of production as well as expenditures directed at controlling the externality will be incorrect. Consider, for instance, a firm that could, by expending resources, reduce its level of pollution. There would be a large social benefit; but there is no private incentive for the firm to spend this money.

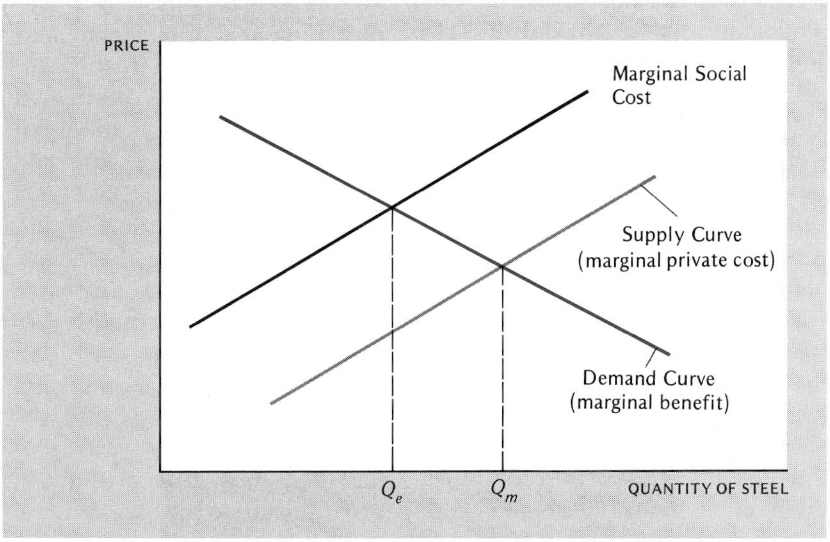

8.1 EXCESSIVE PRODUCTION OF GOODS YIELDING NEGATIVE EXTERNALITIES The presence of a negative externality means that marginal social costs exceed marginal private costs, and the market equilibrium will entail an excessive production of the commodity. Q_m is market equilibrium, Q_e is the efficient level of output.

The level of production of negative externality-generating commodities will be excessive. Figure 8.1 shows conventional demand and supply curves. We argued earlier that, in the absence of externalities, the resulting market equilibrium, Q_m, was efficient. The demand curve reflected the individual's marginal benefits from the production of an extra unit of the commodity, and the supply curve reflected the marginal costs of producing an extra unit of the commodity. At the intersection of the two curves, the marginal benefits just equal the marginal costs. Now, with externalities, the industry's supply curve will not reflect marginal *social* costs, only marginal private costs—those borne directly by the producers. If the expansion of steel production increases the level of pollution, there is a real cost to that expansion in addition to the costs of the iron ore, labor, coke, and limestone that go into the production of steel. But the steel industry fails to take the cost of pollution into account. Thus Figure 8.1 also shows the marginal social cost curve, giving the total extra costs (private and social) of producing an extra unit of steel. This cost curve lies above the industry supply curve. Efficiency requires that marginal social cost equal the marginal benefit of increasing output: production should occur at Q_e, the intersection of the marginal social cost curve and the demand curve. The efficient level of production is lower than the market equilibrium level.

Similarly, in the common resource problem, marginal social benefits are less than marginal private benefits. Consider a lake in which the total number of fish caught increases with the number of fishing boats, but less than proportionately, so that the number of fish caught per boat decreases as the number of boats increases. The marginal social benefit of an additional boat is thus less than the average catch of each boat, as shown in Figure 8.2; some of the fish that the additional boat catches would have been caught by some other boat. The private return to an additional individual deciding whether to purchase a boat is simply the average return (once they are on the lake, all boats catch the same number of fish) which is much more than the marginal social return. Thus, while the private market equilibrium entails average returns equal to the cost of a boat (assumed to be constant), social efficiency requires that the marginal social return be equal to the cost of a boat.

There is thus a presumption that when there are externalities, the market equilibrium will not be efficient.

PRIVATE SOLUTIONS TO EXTERNALITIES

One way that the private sector can deal with externalities without the aid of direct government intervention is to **internalize** the externality by forming economic units of sufficient size that most of the consequences of any action occur *within* the unit.

Let us see how this applies to another example we gave earlier, the positive externality between beekeeping and apple orchards. This

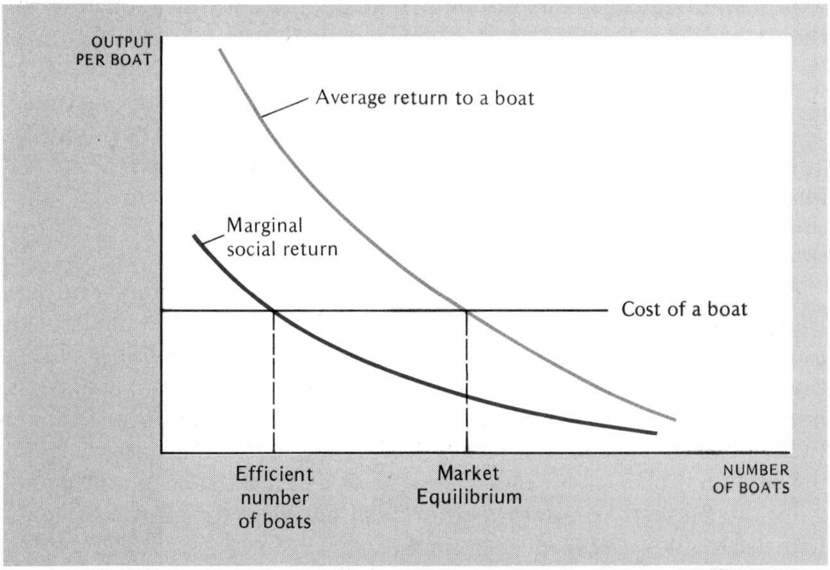

8.2 COMMON RESOURCE PROBLEM LEADS TO EXCESSIVE FISHING The extra output of an additional boat is less than the average output. There will be an excessive number of boats.

externality may be internalized by having the owner of the apple orchard also become the beekeeper. It will work, of course, only if the apple orchard is sufficiently large that the bees stay in this one apple orchard.

The Coase Theorem

Externalities arise, as we have noted, when individuals do not have to pay for the full consequences of their actions. There is excessive fishing in a common pool because individuals do not have to pay for the right to fish. Externalities can frequently be dealt with by the appropriate assignment of **property rights.** Property rights assign to a particular individual the right to control some assets and to receive fees for the property's use. It was because no one had the property rights controlling access to an entire oil pool that too many wells were drilled. When the oil pool is controlled by a single individual, he has an incentive to make sure that the correct number of wells is drilled. Since economic efficiency is enhanced by having a single firm control the entire pool, any firm could buy the land over the pool from its present owners (at what they would have received from selling the oil) and wind up with a profit. In this view, no outside intervention would be required to ensure that an efficient pattern of property rights emerged.

Even when property rights for a common resource are not assigned to a single individual, the market may find an efficient way of dealing with the externality. Owners of oil wells frequently get together to **unitize** their production, thus making it less likely that too many wells are drilled.[1] And fishermen using the same grounds may get together to devise mutually agreed upon restrictions to prevent excess fishing.

The assertion that whenever there are externalities, the parties involved can get together and make some set of arrangements by which the externality is internalized, and efficiency ensured, is referred to as the **Coase theorem.**[2]

For instance, when there are smokers and nonsmokers in the same room, if the loss to the nonsmokers exceeds the gains to the smokers, the nonsmokers might get together and "bribe" (or, as economists like to say, "compensate") the smokers not to smoke. If the smokers are in a nonsmoking compartment of a train, and the restriction on smoking (which can be viewed as an externality imposed on the smokers by the nonsmokers) takes away more from their welfare than the nonsmokers gain, the smokers will get together and "compensate" the nonsmokers in order to allow themselves to smoke.

Of course, the determination of who compensates whom makes a great deal of difference to the distributive implications of the externality; smokers are clearly better off in the regime in which smoking is allowed unless the smokers are paid not to smoke, compared to the regime in which smoking is banned unless they compensate nonsmokers.

Social Sanctions

The example of the externality associated with smoking can be used to illustrate another mechanism for the control of externalities: social sanctions and the inculcation of social values. The Golden Rule can be thought of as an attempt to deal with externalities: "Do unto others as you would have them do unto you." Its converse is also important: Do not do unto others as you would not have them do unto you.

This may be roughly translated into the language of economics as "Do cause positive externalities," and "Do not cause negative externalities." As children, we are all made aware of the fact that some of our actions—such as talking loudly at the dinner table—have effects on others, for which we do not have to pay, at least directly, in the form of monetary compensation. There are, however, other sanctions that may be applied. Parents try to induce their children to behave in "socially acceptable ways" (including not generating negative externalities and conferring positive externalities). Although this socialization process does succeed

[1] Under unitization, the development of an oil or gas reservoir is put under a single management, with proceeds distributed according to a formula specified in the unitization agreement. This unitization is not done to reduce competition (it occurs even among small oil companies who take the price of oil as given, unaffected by their actions) but to increase efficiency.

[2] R. H. Coase, "The Problem of Social Cost," *Journal of Law and Economics* 3 (1960): 1–44.

in avoiding many negative externalities at the level of the family, it is less successful in dealing with many of the kinds of externalities that arise in modern society: even the threat of a $200 fine for littering may be insufficient to induce some individuals to clean up after themselves in a public park. It is not possible to rely solely on social mechanisms for limiting externalities.

Failures of Private Solutions

If the arguments asserting that private markets can internalize externalities are correct, is there any need for government intervention? And if these arguments are correct, why is it that cooperative agreements have failed to take care of so many externalities?

There are basically three reasons that government intervention is required. The first has to do with the public-goods problem we discussed in Chapter 5. Many (but far from all) externalities entail the provision of a public good, such as clean air or clean water: in particular, it may be very costly to exclude anyone from enjoying the benefits of these goods. Where nonsmokers get together to compensate smokers for not smoking, it pays any individual nonsmoker to claim that he is almost indifferent to letting others smoke. He will attempt to be a free rider on the efforts of other nonsmokers to induce the smokers not to smoke.

The problems of arriving voluntarily at an efficient solution are exacerbated by the presence of imperfect information. The smokers will try to persuade the nonsmokers that they require a lot of compensation to induce them not to smoke. In any such bargaining situation, one party may risk the possibility of not arriving at a mutually advantageous agreement, in order to get more out of those bargains that are made.

Problems may arise even in cases where markets are well established. Consider the problem of an oil pool, the land above which is owned by several individuals. Though efficiency can be obtained by unitization, if all but one of the landowners unitize, it may not pay the last owner to join. He knows that production on the unitized portion will be reduced, thus enabling him to increase his production. He will only join if he receives more than a proportionate share of the revenues. But each small owner may believe he can gain by holding out to be the last to join the unitization agreement (or to sell to a large firm attempting to purchase all the small owners). Thus states have found it necessary to pass legislation requiring unitization.

The second reason for government intervention concerns transaction costs. The costs of getting individuals together to internalize these externalities voluntarily is significant. The provision of those organizational services itself is a public good. Indeed, the government may be looked upon as precisely the mechanism that individuals have set up to reduce the welfare losses from externalities.

The third reason that currently markets may not deal adequately with externalities is that the set of property rights that have been established often give rise to inefficiencies. Many of the existing property rights have been established not through legislation but through what is called the common law. When one individual imposed an externality on another, the injured individual brought suit against the first individual. Sometimes these suits were successful, sometimes they were not. Over the years, a set of implicit property rights and rules has been established that defines in a fairly clear way those situations in which an individual suffering an externality can bring suit with some hope of success, and where he cannot. For instance, if a nonsmoker develops a cough as a result of some smokers smoking in the same compartment of a train in which he sits, he cannot sue the smokers with much hope of success. If an individual throws garbage on his neighbor's lawn, the neighbor has a reasonable chance of success in a suit. If an individual burns leaves on the corner of his lot so that the wind blows smoke into his neighbor's house, causing smoke damage to the house, the neighbor has *some* chance of a successful suit.

Some have argued that how property rights get assigned is less important than that there be well-defined assignments. In the examples given above, with well-defined property rights, the party that would have suffered from the externality could have bribed the other party if it was worth it to him, assuming that one of the other problems, such as transaction costs, to which we have already referred, did not occur.

The advantages of using the government as a vehicle through which externalities are dealt with are that it saves on transaction costs (an additional organization to deal with each type of externality does not have to be created) and it avoids the free rider problems typically associated with public goods. Among disadvantages of using the government are those we encountered in Chapters 6 and 7: the political mechanism is a far from perfect means for allocating resources, since it is subject to manipulation by special-interest groups. Further, any regulations and rules devised in the public sector have to be enforced by a bureaucracy with all of the limitations noted earlier.

PUBLIC REMEDIES FOR EXTERNALITIES

There are four broad categories of public-sector remedies for externalities: the government can impose fines; it can subsidize expenditures to reduce negative externalities; it can impose regulations to restrict the negative externalities imposed by one group on another; or it can attempt to define, through the legal system, a set of property rights that discourages negative externalities.

Before comparing the merits of these alternative remedies we should first dispel the common fallacy, which asserts that we should never allow an individual or firm to impose a negative externality on others. For example, it is sometimes asserted that a firm should never be allowed to pollute the air and water. In the view of most economists, such absolutist positions make no sense. There is, indeed, a social cost associated with pollution (or any other negative externality), but the cost is not infinite; it is finite. There is some amount of money that people would be willing to receive in compensation for having to live in a community with dirtier air or dirtier water. Thus we need to weigh the costs and benefits associated with pollution control just as we need to weigh the costs and benefits associated with any other economic activity. The problem with the market is *not* that it results in pollution; there is, indeed, a socially efficient level of pollution. The problem instead is that firms fail to take into account the social costs associated with the externalities they impose—in this case, pollution—and as a result, there is likely to be an excessively high level of pollution. Since the government cannot eliminate pollution entirely, its task is to help the private sector achieve the socially efficient level of pollution, to make individuals and firms act in such a way that they are induced to take into account the effects of their actions on others.

In the ensuing discussion we shall focus our attention on pollution externalities. The arguments, however, extend in a straightforward way to other categories of externalities.

Fines

Most economists favor the use of fines as a way of remedying the inefficiencies associated with negative externalities: a pollution charge should be imposed on those who pollute the air or water.

The basic principle involved in the imposition of fines (charges) for controlling externalities is simple: in general, whenever there is an externality, there is a difference between the social cost and the private cost, and between the social benefit and the private benefit. A properly calculated fine presents the individual or firm with the true social costs and benefits of his actions.

Taxes (which can be thought of as fines) and subsidies designed to ameliorate the effects of externalities, to make marginal private costs equal to marginal social costs, and to make marginal benefits equal to marginal social benefits are called **taxes.**[3]

Consider the example, discussed earlier, of a steel firm polluting the air. We showed that because the firm was concerned only with its private marginal costs, not the social marginal costs (the two differing by the marginal costs of pollution), output of steel would be excessive. By charging the firm an amount equal to the marginal cost of pollution, the marginal private costs and marginal social costs are equated. In Figure 8.3 we have assumed that the amount of pollution is proportional to the level of output, and the marginal cost of each unit of pollution is fixed; hence by imposing a fixed charge per unit of output, equal to the mar-

[3] A. C. Pigou, a great English economist of the first half of this century, argued persuasively for the use of corrective taxes in his book *The Economics of Welfare* (London: Macmillan, 1918). These taxes are sometimes called Pigovian taxes in his honor.

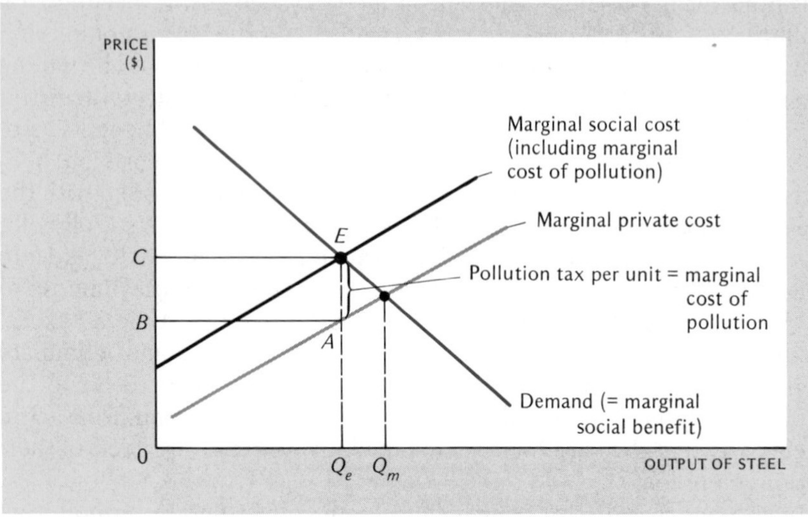

8.3 MARKET EQUILIBRIUM WITH AND WITHOUT FINES In the absence of a tax on pollution, firms will set price equal to marginal private cost. There will be excessive production (Q_m). By setting a tax equal to the marginal pollution cost, efficiency is obtained.

ginal social cost of pollution, the firm will be induced to produce the socially efficient level of output. In the figure, the distance *EA* represents the pollution tax per unit output, and the area *EABC* represents the total pollution taxes paid.

Fines also ensure that the firm spends a socially efficient amount on pollution abatement. Assume that there is a given, known marginal social cost imposed on others by each unit of pollution (measured, say, by the number of particles added to the air per unit of time). It is costly to reduce pollution; at any given level of production, it costs more to reduce pollution more. We assume that the *marginal* cost of pollution control is also rising. This is depicted in Figure 8.4, where we measure along the horizontal axis the *reduction* in pollution (from what it would be if the firm spent nothing on pollution abatement). Efficiency requires that the marginal social benefits associated with further pollution abatement expenditures just equal the marginal social costs, point P^* in the diagram. If the firm is charged a fine, f^*, equal to the marginal social cost of pollution, the private firm will undertake the efficient level of expenditure on pollution abatement. (It also should be clear that firms will undertake the pollution abatement in the least costly—most efficient—manner possible; this may entail not only direct expenditures for pollution control devices but changes in the input mixes and other alterations in the production process.)

Similarly, in those situations where there is a *positive* externality, the government should impose subsidies. There are a few instances where the government does subsidize the consumption of some commodity

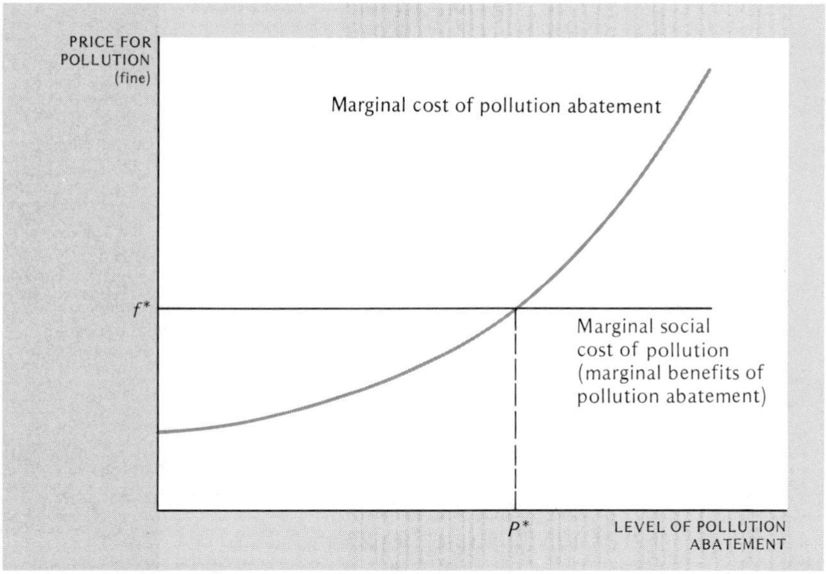

8.4 EFFICIENT CONTROL OF POLLUTION The efficient level of pollution can be attained either by charging firms a fine of f^* per unit of pollution (say, measured by the number of particles added to the air) or by imposing a regulation that firms have a pollution abatement level P^*.

(often through the tax system) because it believes this will result in a positive externality. For instance, expenditures for the restoration of historical buildings receive extremely favorable tax treatment. This is presumably on the grounds that we all benefit from the preservation of our national heritage. In Figure 8.5 we depict a situation where the price does not correctly reflect the true marginal social benefit of an extra unit of the commodity. The marginal social benefit exceeds the price, because, for instance, some individuals may reap some benefits from a given individual's purchase of the commodity. In the diagram we have assumed that there is no externality associated with the production of the commodity, so that the marginal private costs equal the marginal social costs. In the absence of a government subsidy, market equilibrium will entail price equaling marginal cost, and there will be too little consumption of the commodity in question. If the government subsidizes the consumption of the commodity, by the difference between the marginal social benefit and the marginal private benefit, then marginal private benefit (including the subsidy) will equal the marginal social benefit, and consumption of the commodity will be increased to the socially efficient level.

We noted earlier, in the discussion of pollution externalities, that since the firm in question was likely to receive a negligible direct benefit from pollution abatement (most of the benefits accruing to those who live in the vicinity of the plant), it had little incentive to spend money on

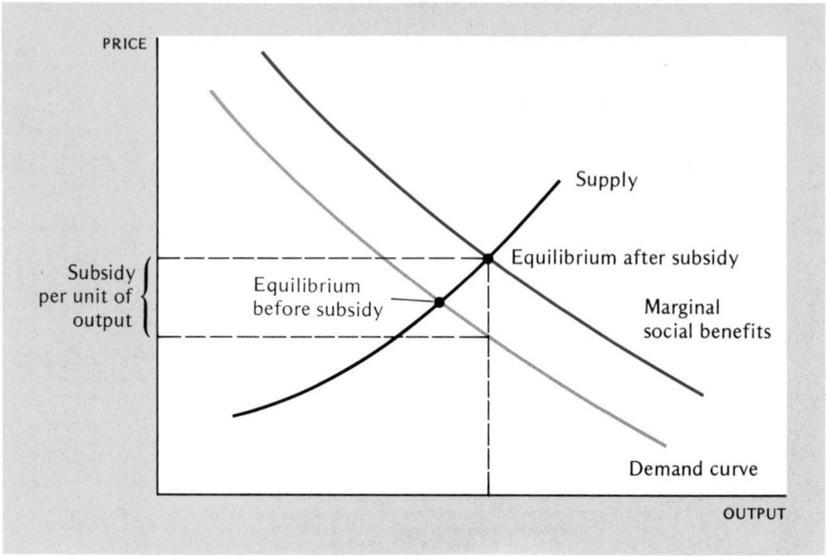

8.5 EQUILIBRIUM WITH AND WITHOUT SUBSIDIES IN THE PRESENCE OF POSITIVE EXTERNALITIES If there are positive externalities associated with consumption of the commodity, there will be too little consumption of it. This can be corrected by imposing a subsidy on its use.

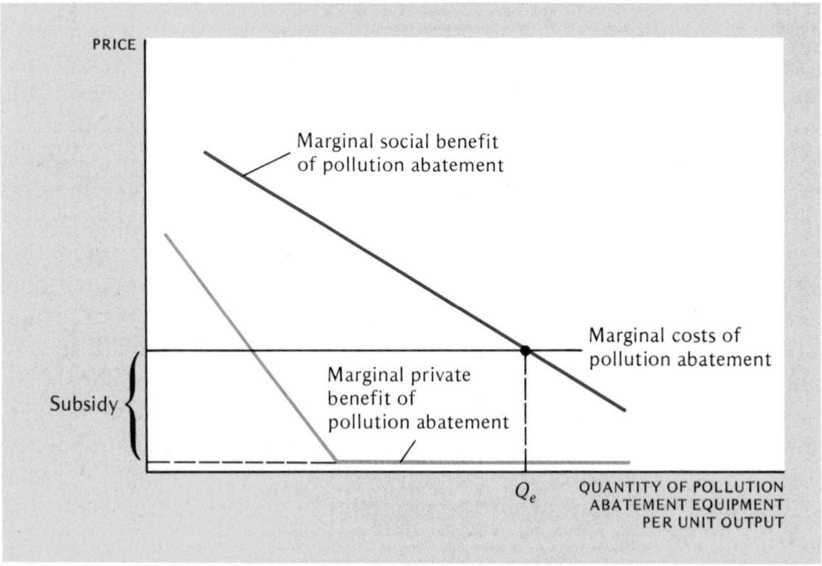

8.6 POLLUTION ABATEMENT SUBSIDIES By subsidizing the purchase of pollution abatement equipment (by the difference between marginal social benefit of pollution abatement and marginal private benefit), an efficient level of expenditure on pollution abatement can be attained.

pollution abatement. There was, from a social point of view, too little expenditure on pollution abatement. Rather than taxing pollution, the government could subsidize pollution abatement expenditures. By providing a subsidy equal to the difference between the marginal social benefit of pollution abatement and the firm's marginal private benefit, the efficient level of pollution abatement expenditures can be attained. This is illustrated in Figure 8.6. (Note that the marginal cost of pollution depicted in Figure 8.4 is directly related to the marginal benefit of pollution abatement depicted in Figure 8.6. While in Figure 8.4 we assumed a fixed marginal social cost of pollution, and hence a fixed marginal social benefit from pollution abatement, in Figure 8.6, as pollution decreases, the marginal social benefit from further pollution abatement decreases. Either case may hold in a real situation.)

This remedy does not, however, attain a socially efficient resource allocation. The reason is simple: the total marginal social costs of producing steel include the costs of the government subsidies for pollution abatement. Firms fail to take this into account in deciding on the level of production. Thus, as before, the marginal social cost of steel production exceeds the marginal private cost. The pollution abatement subsidy reduces the marginal social cost of output (from the dashed line to the solid black line in Figure 8.7). But it also reduces the marginal private costs. There is still an excessive level of production of steel, as illustrated by point Q_s in Figure 8.7.[4]

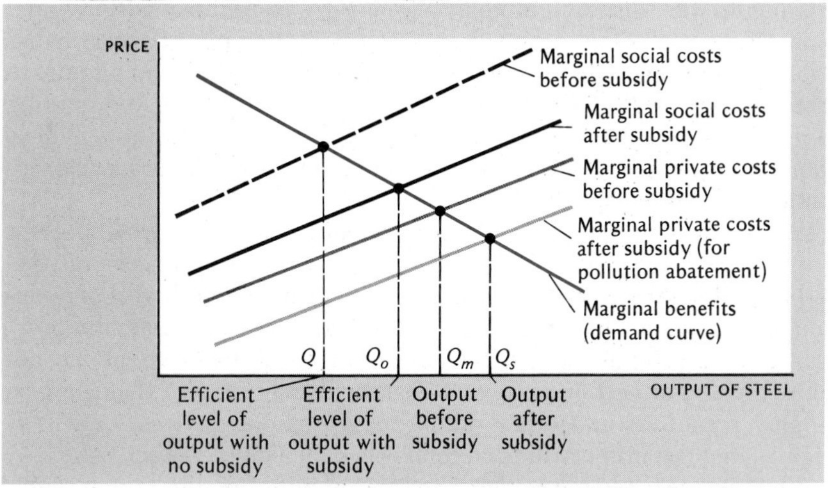

8.7 MARKET EQUILIBRIUM WITH POLLUTION ABATEMENT SUBSIDIES Even after the pollution abatement subsidy, the equilibrium level of output of steel is still inefficient; the firm fails to take into account the extra costs of public subsidies for pollution abatement associated with increased output of steel as well as the marginal social cost of any remaining pollution.

[4] If the level of pollution of a firm cannot be directly monitored, a desirable policy would entail a subsidy for expenditures on pollution abatement combined with a tax on output. The tax on output (if set at the appropriate rate) reduces the level of output to the socially efficient level.

The reason that polluters prefer subsidies for pollution abatement to fines is clear: profits under the former system are higher than under the latter. The distributional consequences are not limited to the polluting firms and their shareholders. Because output will be smaller under the system of fines, prices will be higher, and consumers of the products of the polluting firm will be worse off. On the other hand, those who have to pay the taxes to finance the subsidies for pollution abatement are clearly better off under the system of fines. It should be emphasized, however, that the choice between subsidies and fines is not just a distribution issue. When both systems are feasible (and ignoring monitoring costs) the system of fines results in a Pareto-efficient resource allocation, while the system of subsidies for pollution abatement does not; that is, in principle, there is a set of taxes that could be imposed on different individuals or firms who benefit from the use of the fine system, the proceeds of which would be distributed as compensatory payments to the polluting firms. This would make all individuals and firms better off than they are under the subsidy-for-pollution-abatement scheme.

Regulation

Rather than using either fines for pollution or subsidies for expenditures on pollution abatement, the government has generally employed regulations in its attempt to restrict negative externalities. It has set emission standards for automobiles. It has put forth a detailed set of regulations relating to the disposal of toxic chemicals. It requires airlines and railroads to set aside certain designated areas for nonsmokers. It has imposed laws requiring oil companies with wells in the same oil pool to unitize their production. It imposes restrictions on fishing and hunting to reduce the inefficiencies associated with excessive utilization of these common resources. These examples illustrate the myriad forms that regulation may take.

In the case of pollution, we should distinguish between two important classes of regulations: those in which the level of pollution is monitored and firms are proscribed from exceeding a certain critical level of pollution, and those in which the government regulates the production process—known as input regulations. For instance, the government may not allow the use of certain grades of coal; or it may require that the firm employ scrubbers and other pollution abatement devices; or it may require that the firm construct a smokestack of a given height.

When it is feasible to regulate the level of pollution directly, it seems preferable to input regulation. What society is concerned with is the level of pollution, not how the pollution is produced. The firm is likely to know better than the government the best ways of reducing the level of pollution (how to reduce the level of pollution at least cost). Yet the government has relied heavily on input regulations since in some cases it may be easier to monitor inputs than to measure the level of pollution. But this does not provide the full explanation: the choice of regulatory method has also been influenced by political considerations, as we shall see later.

Comparison between Regulations and Fines

The comparison between the use of *regulations* and *fines* corresponds to the comparison between the use of direct controls (a command system) and prices in running the economy. In Chapter 3 we showed how a price system could be used (in the absence of externalities) to implement an efficient resource allocation. Not only is the competitive equilibrium Pareto efficient, but every Pareto-efficient allocation can be sustained through a competitive price mechanism, provided the appropriate transfers are made. Of course, the same resource allocation could have been attained simply by the government imposing it through a set of commands. In situations where there are no monitoring costs, and where all the costs and benefits associated with pollution and pollution control are known, the government can accomplish with regulation anything it can accomplish through fines. Thus if social efficiency requires that no more than so many units of pollutants be added to the air per ton of steel produced, the government can impose this as a regulation rather than setting a level of fines that induces the socially efficient level of pollution.

When input regulations alone are used, the regulator can attain the efficient level of expenditures on pollution abatement. But the efficient level of production of the polluting commodity cannot be obtained (except in the extreme case where efficient pollution abatement entails the elimination of all pollution). Thus regulation has the same deficiency that subsidies for pollution abatement have, but to a lesser extent. In Figure 8.8 we have depicted the regulations as bringing marginal private costs near but still not equal to marginal social costs, so that there is still overproduction of the polluting commodity.

NONLINEAR FINE SCHEDULES

A nonlinear fine schedule entails having a fine that depends on the level of pollution. The simplest such system is depicted in Figure 8.9. There, the fine for levels of pollution up to some critical level P^* is low, but for pollution levels in excess of that critical level, the fine per unit of pollution is high. Ideally, one might like to confront the firm with the entire marginal social cost of pollution schedule, as depicted in Figure 8.9. Then, at each level of pollution, the firm would face the true marginal social cost. The two-level fine schedule depicted in the figure may be thought of as an approximation of the marginal social cost function. If it should turn out that the pollution control technology results in a very low level of pollution, then the approximating schedule will have resulted in an excessive expenditure on pollution control; if it should turn out that the pollution control technology results in a very high level

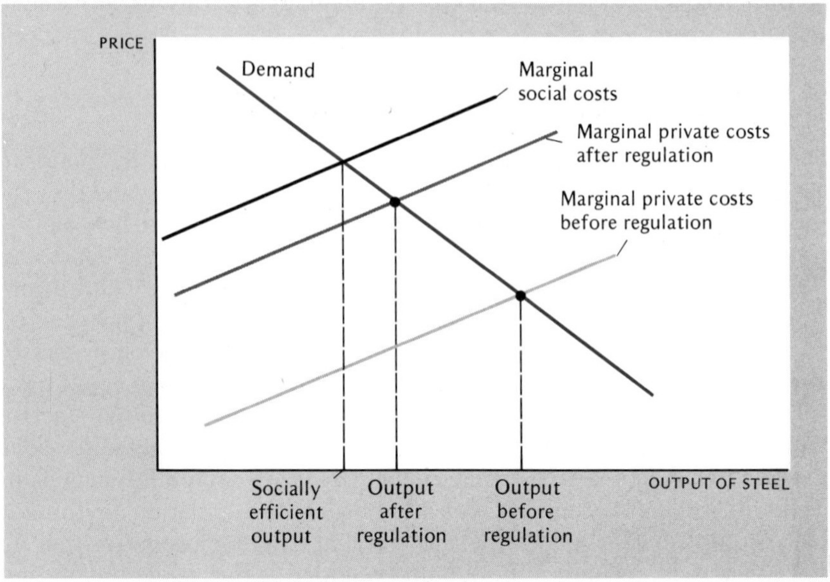

8.8 EFFICIENCY WITH REGULATION ON POLLUTION ABATEMENT Even with regulations on pollution abatement, there will not be an efficient level of output. So long as some pollution remains, firms fail to take into account the social cost of the allowed pollution.

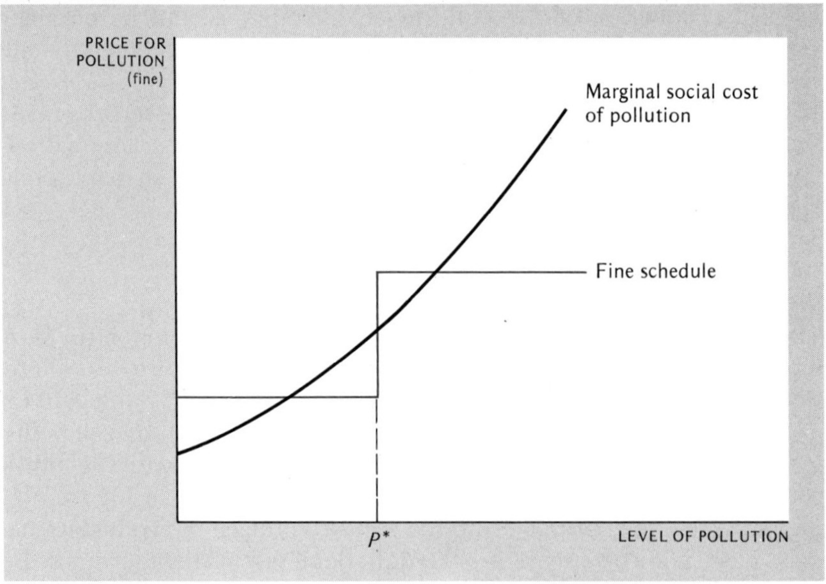

8.9 REGULATIONS AND NONLINEAR FINES A regulatory scheme can be viewed as a limiting case of a fine scheme, where the fine for levels of pollution in excess of P^* is so large that no firm will pollute in excess of P^*.

of pollution (because pollution control is very expensive), then the approximating schedule results in too little expenditure on pollution control.

One possible schedule entails a zero fine up to some critical level, and then an infinite fine beyond that, making levels of pollution greater than P^* impossible. This is essentially a regulation against pollution above the level of P^*. Thus the distinction between fines and regulations is not a clear one. A regulation can be viewed as equivalent to a limiting case of a nonlinear fine system.

Choice among Fines, Subsidies, and Regulations

So far, our discussion has established that in the presence of negative externalities, Pareto-efficient resource allocations can be attained by a system of fines but not by regulations or subsidies. On the other hand, the different systems have distinctly different distributive effects. Firms (and their consumers and workers) are more adversely affected by fines than by regulation, and benefit from subsidies. Though those who gain from the use of a system of fines might, in principle, be able to compensate those who lose, in fact the compensations are seldom made. The potentially large differences in the distributive impacts of the different programs are largely responsible for the controversies that have arisen over the appropriate system of pollution control. But there are other issues as well: (1) the alternative methods have different transactions costs associated with implementing them; (2) different information is required for their efficient implementation; (3) they differ in how well they perform in the presence of variability or uncertainty about costs and benefits; and (4) they may differ in the ease with which they can be politically manipulated to serve special-interest groups.

TRANSACTION COSTS

Regulation and fine schemes require different kinds of monitoring on the part of the government. Under both schemes it is not in the interests of a steel company to announce how much pollution it is creating. Nor is it in the interests of any of the users of steel (to the extent that the market is competitive), since any fines imposed as a result of excessive pollution or any expenditure on pollution-control devices mandated by regulations are simply passed along to the user. And while it may be in the interests of consumers collectively to monitor, if monitoring is costly none will be willing to do it. We have a classic public-good problem. The burden of monitoring must fall upon the government. Simple regulatory schemes require only that the government ascertain whether a firm has exceeded a certain threshold level of pollution. This may be much less costly than determining with any precision the exact level of pollution, as a system of fines requires.

Equally important, different externality control systems require different information for their implementation. It is perhaps reasonable to assume that the government has a fair estimate of the marginal social costs associated with pollution. But it is likely that the government is not well informed about the technology of pollution abatement and control, at least not as well informed as are private firms. This is particularly true in those cases where the pollution control devices have not yet been developed. Neither side has very good information: both are simply making guesses, but since producers know more about the technology of their industries than does the government, their guesses are likely to be more accurate. The private producers have no incentive to reveal their information to the government; rather, they have every reason to try to persuade the government that the technology for pollution abatement will be extremely hard to develop, so that it will be impossible to satisfy stringent regulations. If the government does impose stringent regulations but allows firms several years to develop the requisite technology, they may not have an incentive to comply: they may believe that, when the deadline arrives, if the new technology has not been developed, it is unlikely that the government will shut down the industry.

The information required to achieve an efficient level of pollution via regulation is even greater than the discussion until now has suggested. If firms have different costs associated with pollution abatement, the efficient level of pollution abatement will differ from firm to firm. To set efficient levels of pollution control, then, the government must know the cost functions of *each* firm in the economy. Since government's knowledge of firms' cost functions is heavily dependent on information provided by the firm, firms clearly have an incentive to "fudge" the data.

Note, moreover, that if in the regulatory scheme the government errs in its judgment concerning the costs of pollution control, the resulting level of pollution will be inefficient. If the government underestimates the costs of pollution control and sets stringent regulations, firms may spend a considerable amount of resources to comply with the regulations. At the margin, the cost of compliance will exceed the marginal social benefit. In a competitive economy, these costs will be passed along to the users of the product.

The system of imposing fines does not suffer from the same informational requirements. The government need ascertain only the marginal social costs of pollution. Then the firms decide whether the costs of the pollution control devices exceed the benefits of the pollution control as measured by the penalties imposed for failing to control pollution. There is no longer any gaming between the industry and the government. Of course, if the government incorrectly estimates the marginal social costs of pollution, then inefficiencies will arise, under either a system of fines or a regulatory system.

The costs of pollution control (and the benefits) may vary from place to place, from time to time, and from firm to firm. The *marginal* social benefit of pollution control may be quite different in Los Angeles (which is faced with a severe smog problem) from what it is in Montana. The cost of pollution control may be markedly different for one kind of coal than for another. In principle, either a set of regulations or a set of fines should recognize these differences. There should thus be a different set of regulations for each different set of circumstances, or a different level of fines for each community, firm, and date. The informational requirements to implement such a detailed scheme are clearly enormous. In practice, this has resulted in broad sets of regulations that are not adapted well to varying conditions. In localities where there is a belief that the marginal social cost locally is greater, these general regulations are supplemented by local regulations. Thus California has far more stringent regulations on automobile pollution than does the rest of the country, because of the tendency for particulate matter to combine with moist air off the Pacific Ocean to produce smog.

By the same token, if the marginal social costs of pollution vary from situation to situation, then the appropriate fine should vary. Governments seldom have the requisite information to adapt the fine schedule to all of the varying situations. As a result, sometimes the fine may be too high, sometimes it may be too low.

The nature of the variability in costs and benefits plays an important role in the choice between regulatory schemes and fines. If costs of pollution control vary but benefits are certain, fines are preferable to regulations. Firms that are subject to fines will adjust the level of pollution control to the efficient level; regulations will not allow this adjustment. If benefits vary but costs don't, the two systems are equivalent. The fine system will result in a fixed level of pollution, sometimes too high, sometimes too low, just as with a regulatory system. The consequences of a fine are no different from those of a regulatory system in which the government fixed the level of permissible pollution.

When both costs and benefits vary, matters are more difficult. There are circumstances in which regulations may be preferable to fines. This can be seen most easily in cases where lower levels of marginal social costs of pollution are associated with lower levels of marginal costs of pollution abatement. If they decrease just the right amount, then the optimal amount of pollution will be the same in the situation with high marginal social costs of pollution as it is in the situation with low marginal social costs. In that case, a regulatory scheme could attain these results. With a system of fines—where the level of fines was fixed and did not vary with the marginal social costs of pollution—too much pollution would sometimes result (when the marginal cost of pollution abatement was low) and too little pollution would result at other times.

Since the costs of regulations to the firms are not insignificant, the extent of regulations is a politically charged subject. The form of the regulations that emerge is affected not only by the economic costs (as estimated by a dispassionate observer) but by the power of the various interest groups affected by the regulations. A politically powerful interest group may be able to stave off a set of regulations that would have been imposed had the group been weaker.

More interestingly, a group that is without the political power to stave off some regulations may be strong enough to extend the regulations to rivals, for whom it is not appropriate. This happened in the coal industry. Eastern and midwestern coal is dirty (high sulfur), while western coal is clean. Thus, specifying a maximum level of admissible pollution, or requiring scrubbers only on dirty coal, would give western coal an advantage over eastern coal—as well it should, given that there was an additional social cost of using eastern coal. But when the Clean Air Act Amendment of 1977 was passed, the eastern coal producers teamed up with the environmentalists to lobby for the scrubbers for western coal as well.

There is a widespread feeling among economists that regulatory systems are more susceptible to such political manipulation than are systems of fines.

Problems with Compensation

But while the fine system may be Pareto efficient, not all individuals are better off under the fine system than under the two alternative regimes —subsidies or regulations. In principle, however, those who are better off could more than compensate those who are worse off. The difficulty is that this compensation is seldom paid; in many cases it is difficult to identify individually those who should be compensated.

Similar problems arise more generally in determining the appropriate compensation for externalities. Consider, for instance, a steel mill that pollutes the neighboring air. Those who live nearby are clearly worse off as a result of the pollution. But if the steel mill existed before they purchased their houses, the price they paid for their house would have reflected the fact that the air was polluted; they paid less for their house than they otherwise would have. The person who suffered was the owner of the house at the time that the steel mill was constructed (or at the time it was announced that the steel mill would be constructed). In most cases, it would be impossible to find that individual (years may have passed since the steel mill was constructed). Alternatively, suppose that the house was not constructed until after the mill was. In that case, the person who might have been hurt was the owner of the land. But it may be that the gain in value to his land from its proximity to the mill exceeded the loss from the pollution. When the value of an asset (like land) increases or decreases to reflect the surrounding amenities (the cleanliness of the air, the proximity to jobs), we say that the value of these amenities is **capitalized.**

It is not only consumers of the products of the pollution industry, owners of capital in the polluting industry, and breathers of air near the polluting firm who are affected by the system of pollution control. Workers may be affected as well. Imposing a system of fines may result in some plants closing down. Workers at those plants may become unemployed. They bear the costs of finding other jobs. If costs of finding another job and of moving were negligible, these individuals may not be very adversely affected; but in many instances, these costs are significant, and unemployment compensation only partially reduces the burden imposed upon them. Thus in principle, if a system of fines were to be adopted, these individuals should be compensated.

Because of the difficulties in implementing compensation, compensation is seldom made. Thus the choice of the system by which the effects of externalities are remedied has a direct bearing on the welfare of different individuals. The firms whose profits will be reduced by fines or regulations will oppose them; to them, the fact that fines are Pareto efficient is of little concern. They contend that since imposing a fine lowers the return to previously invested capital, it is "unfair" to those who have invested their capital in the polluting industry to make them bear the full burden of the change in society's attitudes toward pollution.

Legal Remedies for Externalities

There is one great advantage of employing the legal system to deal with externalities. Rather than relying on the government to ensure that externalities do not occur, the injured party, who has a direct, vested interest, bears the responsibility for enforcement. This is obviously informationally more efficient, since presumably the injured party is more likely than the government to know that an injury has occurred.

For this to be effective, however, a well-defined and consistent set of property rights has to be established. Thus the legal system could not be used to deal with the externalities that we noted were associated with common resources; by definition, no one had the right to exclude others from the use of these resources, and it was this that gave rise to the externalities. The process by which property rights have been established through the judicial system on a case-by-case basis has not resulted in the establishment of a consistent and well-defined set of property rights that can deal with the whole array of externalities that arise in modern society. It has, however, two important advantages over the alternative approach to defining property rights, through legislation. It is not as sensitive to interest-group pressures, and the full complexity of the range of externalities that occur in practice often is best brought out through a judicial process.

The judicial process for dealing with externalities has five limitations. First, there are large transaction costs associated with any litigation. Of course, it is not clear whether these are large in comparison to the administrative costs of enforcing a regulatory or fine system. For many externalities, the losses involved may simply be too small to be worth dealing with under any system. Since those costs are borne publicly in regulatory or fine schemes, but privately with judicial enforcement, the decision on whether to attempt to eliminate the externality is made efficiently under the judicial enforcement scheme but inefficiently under the other schemes.

Second, since those generating externalities know that litigation is expensive, they may be inclined to generate their externality just up to the point where it pays the injured party to sue—which obviously gives rise to considerable inefficiencies. One way of dealing with this is to impose multiple damages similar to the system of triple damages in antitrust cases; there, when a firm has been shown to have behaved in a noncompetitive way and to have caused, as a result, a loss of profits to his rival, the firm must pay the injured party three times the amount of losses that are deemed to have been sustained. Applied to pollution, this plan would make sure that firms will not induce externalities the losses from which are greater than one-third the cost of litigation.

Third, frequently there is some uncertainty about the extent of the injury, and there is also often some ambiguity about the outcome of most suits. If litigation costs are large, the uncertainty acts as a further deterrent to individuals using the court system to deal with externalities.

Fourth, the high litigation costs and uncertain outcome of the litigation process imply that there is, in effect, differential access to legal remedies, which conflicts with our usual notion of justice.

Finally, in many cases there is a large number of injured parties; no single individual sustains a sufficiently large loss of welfare to make it worth his while to sue, but the injured parties as a class suffer sufficiently large losses that it would more than compensate them for suing. Once again, there is a free rider problem. It pays any one individual to let the others file suit; and if they are successful, he can file suit on his own using the previous findings as precedents. This will greatly reduce his litigation costs (indeed, usually there will be an out-of-court settlement).

The legal system has attempted to deal with this important free rider problem by establishing a category of suits called **class-action suits.** A lawyer files a suit on behalf of the entire class of injured individuals. If he is successful he collects his fee from all of those within the class, all those who have benefited from the judicial decision. There is not universal agreement about how well this system works; in particular, none of the injured individuals is usually in a position to monitor the legal expenses, and these expenses often seem to be unduly large (or at least so the injured parties claim; the lawyers claim that the high level of legal expenses arises from the particular nature of the cases).

In short, the legal system does provide a framework that can deal with certain categories of externalities. It provides an important remedy for some of those externalities not adequately dealt with through one of the alternative means discussed in this chapter; but the limitations of the judicial process are sufficiently important that it cannot be relied upon to deal with a number of the more important externalities.

SUMMARY

1. Externalities are actions of an individual or firm that have an effect on another individual or firm for which the latter does not pay or is not paid.
2. Sometimes, economic efficiency can be attained without resorting to government intervention by establishing sufficiently large economic organizations that the externalities can be internalized. Alternatively, they may be resolved through cooperative action by individuals.
3. There are some strong incentives for private markets to eliminate any inefficiencies arising from externalities. The assertion that they do is called the Coase Theorem.
4. There are several important limitations on these private solutions to externality problems. We have emphasized two in particular: public-goods problems and transaction costs.
5. There are four methods by which the government has attempted to induce individuals and firms to act in a socially efficient manner: fines, subsidies, regulation, and the judicial system.
6. When there is good information about the marginal social cost of the externality (pollution), and the fines can be adjusted to reflect those costs, then a fine system can attain a Pareto-efficient outcome. Subsidies to pollution abatement and regulation of the pollution process, while enabling the efficient level of pollution abatement to be attained, will result in excessive production of the pollution-generating commodity. In principle, the gainers under the fine system could more than compensate the losers, but in practice, these compensations are seldom made. Thus, the choice of the system for controlling externalities has important distributional consequences.

KEY CONCEPTS

Positive externalities	Property rights
Negative externalities	Coase theorem
Common resources	Corrective taxes
Internalizing externalities	Capitalization
Unitization of oil fields	Class-action suits

QUESTIONS AND PROBLEMS

1. Make a list of the positive and negative externalities that you generate or that affect you. For each, discuss the advantages and disadvantages of each of the remedies discussed in the text.
2. An important class of externalities to which attention has recently been directed are called *information externalities.* The information produced by one individual or firm generates benefits for others. The success of an oil well

on one tract of land increases the likelihood of oil being found on an adjacent tract, and hence increases the value of that tract. Can you think of other examples of information externalities? What are the likely consequences of information externalities for the efficiency of resource allocations? Discuss the possibilities of private market solutions to these problems.

3. Explain why subsidies for pollution abatement equipment, even if they result in an efficient level of pollution abatement, will not result in an efficient resource allocation. Under what circumstances can regulations lead to an efficient resource allocation?
4. Assume there are two types of communities in the United States, those in which there is a high benefit of pollution control and a high cost of pollution control; and those in which there is a low benefit of pollution control and a low cost of pollution control. Assume that the government must set either uniform regulations (a uniform level of pollution control) or a uniform fine for pollution. Show diagrammatically that a regulatory scheme may be preferable to a system of fines. How does your answer change if communities in which there is a high marginal cost of pollution control happen to be communities in which there is a low marginal benefit; and communities with a low marginal cost of pollution control happen to be communities in which there is a high marginal benefit?
5. Zoning laws, which restrict how individuals can use their land, are sometimes justified as a means of controlling externalities. Explain. Discuss alternative solutions to these externalities.
6. What is the externality associated with an additional individual driving on a congested road? How do tolls help alleviate this externality? How should the toll be set?
7. Show diagrammatically that in the situation in which the marginal social costs of pollution increase whenever the marginal costs of pollution abatement also increase, a system of regulations may be preferable to a system of fines (when neither can adjust to the varying circumstances). In each case, show the deadweight loss resulting from the inability to vary the fine or the permissible amount of pollution.

PART THREE

EXPENDITURE PROGRAMS

In this part, we show how the theoretical models we developed in previous chapters can be used to analyze a variety of public expenditure programs: national defense, health care, education, welfare, and social insurance. These particular programs were chosen for two reasons. They are among the most important programs: in terms of dollars spent they account for more than two-thirds of federal expenditures as well as of total public expenditures in the United States. And the examination of these particular programs brings out most of the critical issues in expenditure analysis; other programs can be analyzed using the basic framework and tools of analysis that we develop here. The first two chapters are devoted to explaining our basic approach to the analysis of public expenditures: Chapter 9 develops a general framework, while Chapter 10 shows how the benefits and costs of different government programs may be quantified. Chapters 11–15 then apply this framework.

9

The Analysis of Expenditure Policy

The framework for the analysis of public expenditure we will set up in this chapter is intended to provide guidelines. It is not a simple formula that can be applied blindly to all problems but rather a list of considerations that should be raised. Some of these may be more relevant to certain government programs than to others. The kinds of questions we are ultimately interested in addressing are:

Why is there a government program in the first place?

Why does the government program take on the particular form that it takes?

How does the government program affect the private sector?

Who gains and who loses as a result of the government program? Are the gains greater than the losses?

Are there alternative programs that are superior to current government programs (that is, in which all individuals can be made better off)? Are there alternative programs that have different distributional consequences but that at the same time achieve the primary objectives of the program? What are the impediments to the introduction of these alternative programs?

We begin by breaking down the analysis of public expenditures into eight steps: (1) the need for a program; (2) market failures addressed by the program; (3) workable alternatives to the program; (4) efficiency consequences; (5) distributional consequences; (6) equity-efficiency trade-offs; (7) program evaluation; and (8) the political process.

NEED FOR PROGRAM

It is often useful to begin the analysis of a public program by investigating the history of the program and the circumstances under which it arose. Who were the individuals or groups who pressed for its passage, and what were the perceived needs that it supposedly addressed?

For instance, when the bill establishing the social security program was passed in 1935, the United States was in the midst of the Great Depression. Up to that time few employers provided adequate pensions for their employees, and the private market for annuities (insurance policies that provide individuals with a given annual income from retirement until death, regardless of how long they live) was undeveloped; many individuals had failed to save adequately for their retirement, and many of those who had saved had found their savings wiped out by the stock market crash in 1929. The failure to have adequate savings was not as irrational and improvident as it appears to us today; in those days, many individuals continued to work until they died. They needed life insurance to look after their family after their demise but not pensions for themselves. But in the Great Depression, many of these individuals lost their jobs and had no unemployment insurance. It was widely felt that society had to make some provision for them and that it was preferable to do so on a systematic basis rather than just to solve the immediate problems of the time.

MARKET FAILURES

The second step in the analysis of public programs is to attempt to relate the need, the source of demand, to one or more of the market failures discussed in Chapter 3: imperfect competition; public goods; externalities; incomplete markets; and imperfect information. In addition, we saw in Chapter 3 that even if the economy is Pareto efficient, there are two further arguments for government intervention: first, there is no reason to suppose that the distribution of income emerging from the market economy will be socially equitable; and second, some individuals believe that evaluating each individual's welfare by his own perceptions provides an inappropriate or inadequate criterion for making welfare judgments. There are merit goods, which the government should encourage, and merit bads, which the government should discourage or prohibit.

In some cases, the nature of the market failure is obvious: national defense is a pure public good, and as we argued earlier, in the absence of public provision, such goods will always be in undersupply. In other cases the answers are not so obvious, and there may not be agreement among economists about the nature of the market failure. Some economists believe that education is a public good. But most economists argue that it is essentially a private good and that to find an explanation for its public provision one must look elsewhere: at the distributive consequences of public provision or at education as a merit good, essential for the functioning of a democratic society.

The fact that there is a demand for the public provision of some good or service does not in itself imply that there has been a market failure. Currently, there is widespread concern about the rising cost of medical services. This has led some groups to demand that the government take a more active role in providing health care. There are a number of explanations for the rise in health care costs, one being that health care is a service industry: In most recent years there has been a sharp increase in the price of all services relative to manufacturing goods. Some economists argue that although there have been market failures in health care, there is no reason to presume that greater government intervention would improve things. Others believe that government programs (including Medicare) have made things worse, both by increasing the demand for limited medical resources and by reducing the pressure for cost controls because the government pays most of the cost. Similarly, while some economists view as evidence of market failure the fact that individuals cannot obtain complete insurance coverage for their health risks, others believe that the reason the market does not provide complete coverage is that with it, individuals have no incentive to economize on health expenditures. Thus the government has found that it too has been forced to insist that individuals pay some portion of their health care expenditures.

In short, some of the demands for public provision arise from an inadequate understanding of the market and of the possibilities that the government has for making things better. Identifying whether there is or is not a market failure is an essential step in identifying the appropriate scope for government action.

ALTERNATIVE FORMS OF GOVERNMENT INTERVENTION

Once a market failure has been identified, a variety of government actions might address the problem. The three major categories of action are public production; private production with taxes and subsidies aimed at encouraging those activities the government wishes to encourage and discouraging those activities it wishes to discourage; and private production with government regulation aimed at ensuring that firms act in the desired way.

The consequences of any government program are critically dependent on the exact nature of the program. Thus if the government decides to bear responsibility for production, it still must decide on how the output is to be allocated. It can charge for the good at market prices; it can charge for the good at something approximating the cost of production, as it typically does for electricity; it can charge for the good, but the charges can be much less than the cost of production, as it typically does for higher education; it can provide the good freely and uniformly, as it does for elementary school and secondary school education; or it can allocate the good or service in some corresponding way to a perceived need or benefit. In countries like Britain, where medicine is provided freely, it is obviously not provided equally to all individuals. Needs differ. The decision as to who gets how much of the available supply of medical services is left to doctors (operating within guidelines set up by the government, in consultation with them).

Similarly, if the good is to be privately produced, the government must decide whether to: (a) contract directly for the commodity but retain responsibility for distributing the good; (b) provide a subsidy to producers, with the hope that some of the benefits will be passed on to consumers through lower prices; or (c) provide a subsidy to consumers. And if some form of subsidy is desired, it must be decided whether it should be provided through the tax system or through a direct grant. If a subsidy is granted, the terms have to be decided upon—e.g., how restrictive eligibility standards should be. All of these possible forms of government action are observed.

Higher Education: An Example

Consider higher education. It is publicly produced: every state has its own system of universities, colleges, and junior colleges. Though direct aid to private universities is limited in the United States, in other countries (such as Canada) it is common, and granted on the basis of the number of students enrolled. In the United States the federal government provides considerable aid to research universities through a variety of programs of support for basic and applied research. Most federal support to higher education, however, takes the form of support to the consumers: the students. Though there have been no general programs of support, there have been two major selective programs. First, since World War II a large number of veterans have attended colleges and universities at government expense; the enticement of this support has been credited as a major attraction for enlistment in the armed forces. Second, federal loans and federally guaranteed loans have been available, particularly to lower- and middle-income individuals, often at subsidized rates.

In recent years there has been extensive discussion of two new programs. The first is to allow individuals, in computing their income taxes, to deduct their educational expenses from their income, or to get a tax credit against their educational expenses. The second is educational vouchers: all individuals would be given a certificate entitling them to, say, $4,000 of education at an approved institution, either public or private. We will discuss education in detail in Chapter 15.

The importance of identifying alternative programs cannot be overestimated. Frequently, new programs can be devised that attain the objectives of older programs at less cost and more effectively. "Social innovation" is no less important than technological innovation.

The Importance of Particular Design Features

The detailed provisions of a program, for instance the precise statements concerning eligibility standards, are often crucial in determining the success of the program, its distributional impact, and its efficiency consequences. If the eligibility standards for some government subsidy program, for instance, are defined too broadly, a disproportionate share of the funds may go to those who are not in need. In addition, distortions arise as individuals alter their behavior in an attempt to satisfy the eligibility standards.

Fairness and efficiency require making a number of distinctions that, though clear in principle, are difficult to administer in practice. The distinction between those who are hungry and those who are not is an important one, but to devise a program to provide food for the hungry requires some easy way of identifying who the hungry are. Too narrow a definition will result in many of those who are needy not receiving aid. Again, a broad set of eligibility standards will result in many individuals who are not needy receiving aid, much to the objections of other taxpayers who are having to contribute to the support of these individuals. Thus because of the impossibility of identifying perfectly those who are truly deserving of aid, there is a trade-off, when designing regulations, between two types of errors: denying aid to those who are deserving and granting aid to those who are not deserving (see Figure 9.1). Different

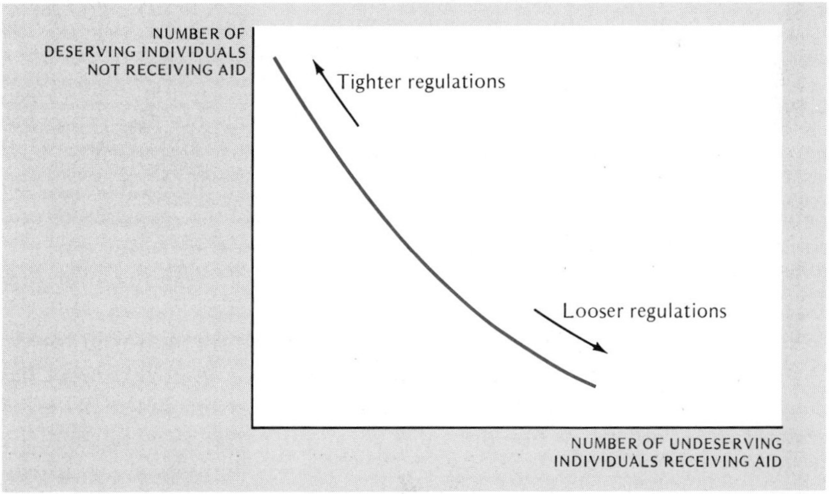

9.1 THE TRADE-OFF IN DESIGNING REGULATIONS When eligibility standards are loose, many individuals who are undeserving will qualify for aid. When standards are tight, many deserving individuals will not qualify for aid.

individuals may differ in their judgments concerning the importance of these two kinds of errors.

EFFICIENCY CONSEQUENCES

Having identified a number of alternative programs, the next step in the analysis is to evaluate them. This entails identifying the efficiency and distributional consequences of the program and assessing the extent to which alternative programs can meet the objectives of public policy.

Government programs may result in inefficiencies both in the production of a good or service and in levels of consumption. In Chapter 7 we suggested that whether the government decides to produce a good or service itself, decides to purchase the good or service from private firms but distribute it itself, or decides to have private firms produce it and market it subject to government regulation may have an important effect on the costs associated with producing and delivering the given good or service.

We also suggested that when consumers had an element of choice, the competition among providers was likely both to increase the efficiency with which the goods or services were provided and to make what was produced more responsive to the needs and desires of consumers. These arguments are less persuasive if consumers have limited information concerning the product they are purchasing (such as medical care) or if consumer concern about costs is reduced because the government pays whatever the individual spends, up to some limit.

Private-Sector Responses to Government Programs

One of the central features of a mixed market economy like that of the United States is that the government has only a limited degree of control over it. The private sector may, for instance, react to any government program in such a way as to undo many of its alleged benefits. When the government increases social security benefits, the welfare of the aged may not increase in the long run by the full corresponding amount; individuals may be induced to reduce their own savings for retirement, and children may be induced to provide less support for their aging parents. Public support may thus "crowd out" private support, although not generally on a dollar-for-dollar basis.

Another area where it is critical to take private-sector responses to government programs into account is agriculture. The government has long been concerned with the magnitude of fluctuations in the prices of agricultural products. When output is very low, prices rise enormously; and when output is very high, prices fall. Farmers know this, and it provides them with an incentive to put into storage crops whose storage costs are low (like wheat and rice) when the price is low and to sell out of storage when the price is high. This reduces the magnitude of the price fluctuations. It also serves a very useful social function: transferring resources from periods in which they are less valuable (when the price is low) to periods in which they are more valuable (when the price is high). But since storage is not costless, the price fluctuations are not eliminated. The government has been concerned about the magnitude of these price fluctuations. It has attempted to stabilize the prices farmers receive for their crops further by guaranteeing to farmers a minimum price. These programs reduce the incentive for the private sector to store commodities on its own and result in the government having to pay for the storage of enormous amounts of such commodities as butter, cheese, milk, and wheat.

There are further repercussions of the government program: the reduction in risk makes it more attractive to grow crops whose prices are stabilized; the increased output depresses the prices, and to maintain them at their previous average levels necessitates further expenditures by the government and programs to restrict production (paying farmers not to produce). Our example illustrates the importance of considering not only the immediate consequences of a government program but the long-run consequences, after all producers and consumers have adjusted their behavior.

Income and Substitution Effects and Induced Inefficiency

For many programs, it is useful to distinguish between **substitution effects** and **income effects.** Whenever a government program lowers the price of some commodity, we say that there is a substitution effect. The individual substitutes the cheaper good for other goods. Tuition subsidies for higher education have a substitution effect: individuals substitute education for other goods they might have spent their money on. On the other hand, grants to individuals that make them better off but do not alter the prices at which they can purchase different commodities have an income effect; the individual changes his expenditure pattern because he is better off. In many cases, there is both an income effect and a substitution effect, and both alter the individual's behavior. Normally, however, it is only the substitution effect that we associate with an *inefficiency.*

To see this, assume that the government gave an individual food stamps to buy \$10 worth of groceries every week. Prior to this, the individual's budget constraint appeared as in Figure 9.2. By giving up \$1 of groceries the individual could acquire \$1 more of other goods. The food stamp program shifts his budget constraint up. If the individual now wants to consume more than \$10 worth of groceries, he still must give up \$1 of other goods for each extra dollar of groceries consumed. There is no substitution effect. There is, however, an income effect. But the effect on food consumption is the same as giving the individual an equivalent amount of income (except in the case where the individual would

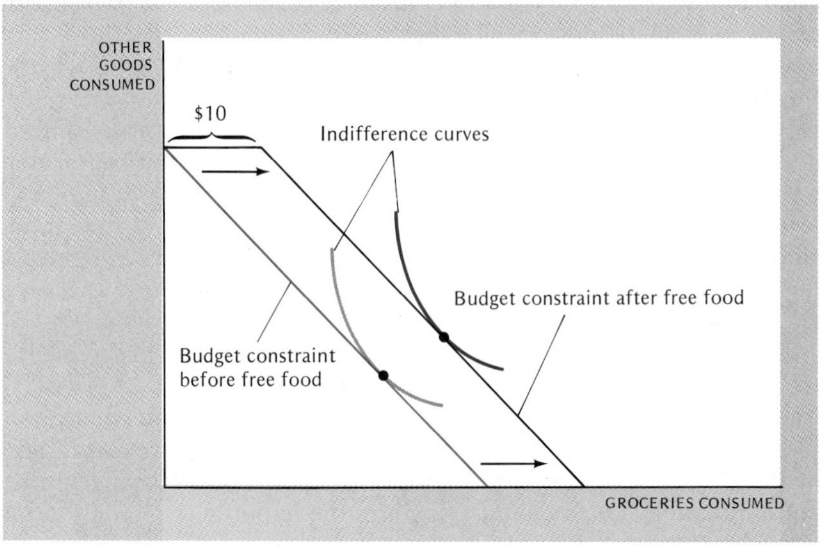

9.2 INCOME EFFECT Giving free food has an income effect but no substitution effect: its effects are identical to giving an individual extra income.

prefer to consume less than $10 worth of food each week). The food stamp program has altered his behavior; he consumes more food than he previously did. But the increase in his consumption of food is less than $10. And because there is no substitution effect, there is no inefficiency associated with this food stamp program.[1]

Assume, in contrast, that the government had said that it would pay for 10 percent of the first $100 of food purchased; that is, the maximum payment that the government would make to any individual is still $10. This lowers the cost of food for expenditures up to $100. The new budget constraint appears as in Figure 9.3. Now, provided consumption of food per week is less than $100, there is a substitution effect.

The reason we say that this program results in an inefficiency is that we can design an alternative program that leaves the individual just as well off but costs less. This can be seen in Figure 9.3. The true cost of the food—the amount of other goods that society must somehow give up to obtain an extra unit of food—remains unchanged: for each additional dollar of food consumed, society must give up $1 worth of other goods. The magnitude of the subsidy is the difference between what the individual has to pay and what society has to forego; it corresponds to the vertical distance between the before-subsidy budget constraint and the after-subsidy budget constraint at the equilibrium level of consumption

[1] The food stamps simply increase his effective income by $10. Thus the extent to which he increases his consumption of food depends only on his income elasticity of demand, which specifies the percentage increase in his consumption of food as a result of a 1 percent increase in his income, at a fixed set of prices.

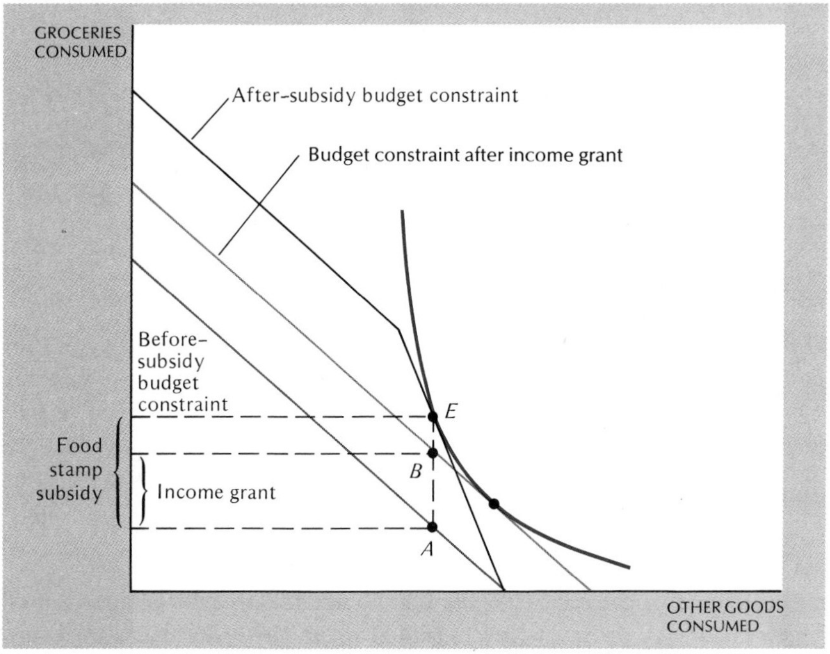

9.3 SUBSTITUTION EFFECT When the magnitude of the subsidy depends on the amount of food consumed, there is a substitution effect and a resulting inefficiency. The poor individual could have been made just as well off with an income grant (or an equivalent food grant) of *AB*. *BE* measures the cost of the inefficiency.

of groceries, the distance *AE*. In Figure 9.3 we have also drawn a budget constraint for a food stamp program of the type first analyzed, where the individual simply gets a grant of a fixed amount for expenditure on food. We have chosen the size of the fixed amount to be given so that the individual is just as well off as he is with the alternative program. Again, the cost of the program is represented by the vertical distance between the before-subsidy and after-subsidy budget constraints. But note that now the size of the required subsidy *(AB)* is smaller.

The reason for this is simple enough: when individuals have to pay the full price of food at the margin (that is, when they have to pay \$1 for \$1 more worth of groceries), they value the increased consumption of groceries by precisely what they have to forego in other consumption goods. But when individuals are given a 10 percent subsidy, they then purchase groceries up to the point where they value \$1 worth of groceries at 90 cents, which is the cost to them of the \$1 worth of groceries.

It is important to distinguish between income and substitution effects. In some cases, the government may wish to encourage or discourage some economic activity; in that case, it may want a large substitution effect. Thus, if there is a belief that poor individuals do not attach sufficient importance to housing, and the government wishes to improve the quality of housing they purchase, then a program in which the government pays a fraction of housing expenditures (which has, as a result, a substitution effect) will be more effective than a flat housing grant, which (unless it is very large) has only an income effect.

On the other hand, if the government is primarily concerned with how well off different individuals are, then programs that do not alter *marginal incentives* are preferable; such programs do not cause the inefficiencies we noted were associated with the substitution effect.

DISTRIBUTIONAL CONSEQUENCES

Different individuals are likely to receive different benefits from any particular government program. But it is not always easy to ascertain who really benefits from a given program. We emphasized in our discussion of the efficiency consequences of public programs the importance of identifying the private-market responses to the government program. These responses are equally important in identifying the distributional consequences.

Consider, for instance, the Medicare program, under which government finances most medical care for the aged. The aged clearly benefit greatly from the program; but to some extent, the federal aid substitutes for money that the elderly's families would have contributed, and to that extent, the true beneficiaries of the program are not the elderly but their children.

Similarly, there has been considerable concern that, at least in the short run, federal subsidies for private housing for the poor simply increase the price of housing; the true beneficiaries are the slum landlords, not the poor.

Who benefits from a new subway system? At first glance, one is inclined to give the obvious answer: subway riders. But this may be incorrect. Those who own houses or apartments near the subway will find that their houses and apartments are more sought after; the increased demand for these houses and apartments will be reflected in the rents that the owners can charge (and hence in the market value of the houses and apartments). The commuter who owns no real estate finds that he is better off because of the better subway service, but worse off because of the higher rents, and the two effects are likely to cancel. The true beneficiaries are the property owners near the subway lines.

These examples illustrate once again the importance of taking into account the full effects of the government program, including its effects on market prices. We illustrate the effect of a government subsidy in Figure 9.4. There we have drawn the demand and supply curves for housing. In the short run (Panel A), the supply of housing is assumed to be very inelastic: it takes some time before new housing can be constructed. Assume the government passed a general subsidy for housing, the effect of which is to increase the demand for housing (the demand curve shifts up). Note that in the figure, almost the entire subsidy is

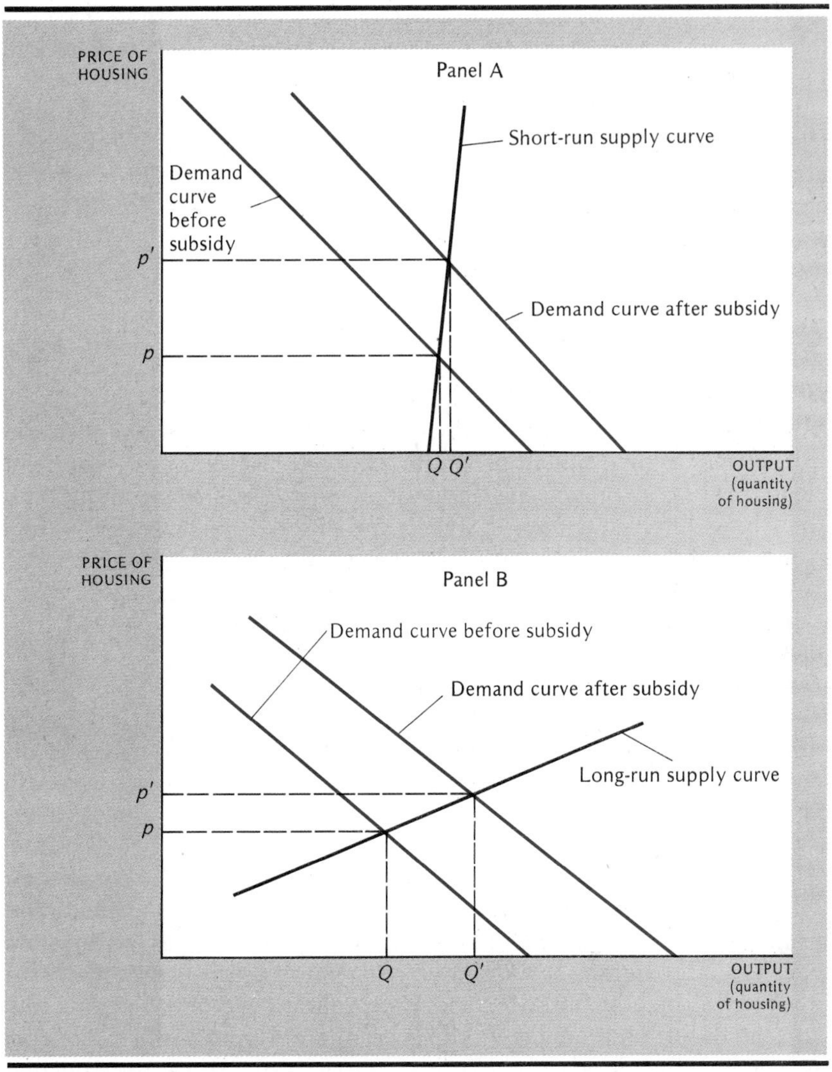

9.4 SHORT-RUN AND LONG-RUN INCIDENCE OF EXPENDITURE PROGRAM (A) In the short run, a subsidy may increase price more than quantity. Thus landlords may benefit from a housing subsidy given to help the poor acquire better housing. (B) In the long run, the output response will be large and the price response smaller.

reflected in the increased price of housing; there is very little increase in the actual level of housing services provided. In the long run, of course, the supply response is likely to be larger; hence in Figure 9.4B we have drawn a fairly flat long-run supply curve, showing that a small percentage increase in the price, given enough time, elicits a fairly large increase in the supply of housing. In the short run, the beneficiaries of housing are the current owners of houses; renters find that virtually their entire subsidy is reflected in higher rents (the shift from p to p'). In the long run, however, renters are better off as the quantity of housing supplied (the shift from Q to Q') outweighs the price increase.

When those who benefit from a government program are different from those that the program was intended to help, we say that the benefits have been *shifted*, or that the *actual incidence* (those on whom the benefits actually fall) is different from that intended one. Considerable research in recent years has been devoted to determining the actual incidence of government programs.

Evaluating the Distributional Consequences

As we have noted, different individuals receive different benefits from any particular government program. Although it is obviously not possible to identify how much *each* individual benefits, it may be important to know how different groups in society are differentially affected. Which groups we focus on may vary from program to program, and benefits may vary within a particular income group. Thus, a program of rebates for heating-oil expenditures for those whose income falls below a particular level obviously benefits the poor more than the rich, but it benefits some poor (those who consume a lot of heating oil, those who live in the Northeast) more than others (those who live in the Sunbelt). If the variability of consumption of heating oil among the poor is very large, this may be viewed as an unfair way of helping the poor, unless those who consume a lot of heating oil are viewed to be particularly deserving of assistance.

In other cases, we may attempt to identify how producers are affected differentially. This is typically the focus of analysis in the evaluation of programs aimed at aiding particular industries, such as government loans to a large defense contractor or agricultural price supports. In still other cases, such as the social security program, we may be concerned with the differential impact on the present elderly versus the impact on the young—the elderly of the future. We refer to these as the **intertemporal distribution effects**—distribution effects over time—of the program. In still other cases, we may wish to identify the regional impact or the impact on cities versus suburbs, or urban versus rural areas.

When the benefits of a program accrue disproportionately to the poor (they receive more than their contribution to the costs of the program through the tax system), we say that the distribution effect of a program is **progressive.** If the benefits accrue disproportionately to the rich we say that it is **regressive.**

There are often controversies about who are the real beneficiaries of a program, and the perspective one obtains on its distributive impact is determined in large part by the group one is focusing on. For instance, government support for higher education is often viewed as enabling the children of the poor to go to college, and thus is viewed to have a positive redistributive impact. But, on closer examination, children of the middle- and upper-middle-classes are more likely to avail themselves of a higher education and whatever government support for it they can obtain. Thus the net benefits accrue disproportionately to the children of middle- and upper-middle-class individuals, and in this perspective, state support appears to be regressive. Moreover, it is not clear that parents' income provides the appropriate focus of attention; the beneficiaries of education are not the parents but the children; it is the children who will receive higher wages as a result of the increased level of education.

Let us contrast the distributional consequences of direct state support for universities (allowing them to charge a low tuition) with those of a loan program for students. Those who avail themselves of higher education will, on average, have a much higher income than those who do not. A loan program may thus be more progressive than the current system, where even low-wage high-school dropouts are called upon to provide some support for higher education.

This example makes clear that one's view of the distributional impact of a government program depends not only on what groups one focuses upon but also on the available alternatives to a given program. The relevant choice is seldom this program versus no program but one type of program versus another. Thus, the present state system of aid to higher education *may* be more progressive than a totally private education system; but its distributional impact may look less favorable when contrasted with a system of loans for higher education.

Fairness and Distribution

Political discussions commonly focus on the equity of various proposals, with each side claiming that its proposals are more fair. Notions of fairness are, unfortunately, not well defined; different individuals may have conflicting views of what is fair. The middle-class family that loves children but has decided for financial reasons to limit the number of children that they have to two may feel that it is unfair for them to have to support someone else's child simply because that other person has refused to use modern birth control methods. The family that has saved $40,000 to put a child through college may feel that it is unfair that they are not entitled to receive a government grant or loan, when their next-door neighbors, with the same income (who have put nothing aside for their children's education) enjoy expensive vacations every winter and are entitled to a government grant.

The unmarried person and the family with both spouses working may both think it unfair that their expected returns from social security are so much lower than those of an individual whose spouse does not have a job outside the home. But an individual whose spouse does not work outside the home may feel that it is fair that he receive more, since his family has not had the benefit of a second income.

EQUITY-EFFICIENCY TRADE-OFFS

Because of the ambiguities associated with using the term *fair*, we try to avoid it; rather, we focus our analysis simply on identifying the impact of programs. In many expenditure programs, trade-offs exist between the objectives of efficiency and equity (redistribution of income to the needy). It may be possible to design a more progressive expenditure program, but only at some cost. An increase in social security benefits may be desirable from the perspective of certain distributional goals, but the increased benefits may lead to earlier retirement, and the higher taxes required to finance them may decrease work incentives. Higher unemployment compensation may provide increased income to some who are among the most needy, but unemployment insurance may make an individual feel disinclined to find another job.

Disagreements about the desirability of different programs often arise from disagreements, not only about values—the relative importance of equity versus efficiency considerations—but also about the nature of the trade-offs, how much loss of efficiency would result from an attempt to change the structure of the benefits of some program to make its distributional impact more progressive.

Figure 9.5 shows the equity-efficiency frontier for some hypothetical program and the indifference curves for two individuals. In Panel A, Scrooge is much less willing to give up efficiency for a gain in equity than is his brother, Spendthrift. E_1 represents the point on the trade-off curve that is optimal as Spendthrift sees it, while E_2 is optimal from the point of view of Scrooge. Not surprisingly, Scrooge chooses a point with higher efficiency but lower equity than does Spendthrift. Thus in Panel A, the source of the disagreement about policy is a difference in the values held by the two individuals.

On the other hand, in Panel B we have depicted a situation where the differences about policy arise from differences in judgments concerning the nature of the trade-off. Scrooge thinks that to get a slight increase in equity one must give up a lot of efficiency. On the other hand, Spendthrift thinks that one can get a large increase in equity with just a slight loss in efficiency.

For instance, if the main reason that unemployed individuals do not obtain jobs is that there are no jobs available, then the size of unemployment insurance may have little effect on search. But if unemployment insurance has little effect on job search, there is not much trade-off between efficiency and equity, and the frontier is consistent with Spendthrift's perceptions; if job search is very sensitive to unemployment compensation, there is a significant trade-off, and the equity-efficiency frontier is consistent with Scrooge's perceptions.

It is important to emphasize that the equity-efficiency trade-off is encountered repeatedly in the evaluation of the detailed provisions of any government program. The decision to charge tolls on a bridge means that those who benefit from the bridge (that is, those who use it)

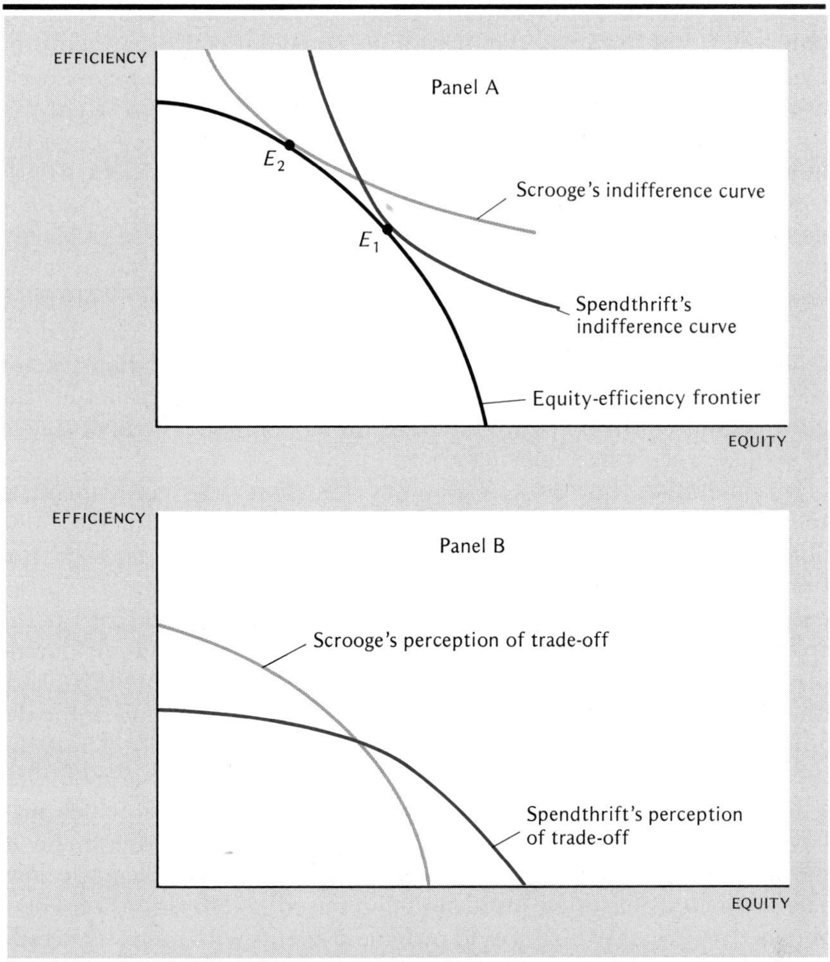

9.5 SOURCES OF DIFFERENCES IN VIEWS CONCERNING PUBLIC PROGRAMS (A) Scrooge and Spendthrift have the same perceptions concerning trade-offs but differ in values. (B) Scrooge and Spendthrift differ in their perception of the nature of the efficiency-equity trade-off.

have to bear its costs. To many people, this is desirable for equity reasons; it is unfair to make someone who does not drive over the bridge pay for it. But there is an efficiency cost in money and time: the wages of toll collectors and the time of motorists. Moreover, if some drivers are discouraged from using the bridge (when it is below capacity), there is a further efficiency loss from under-utilization.

PROGRAM EVALUATION

The discussion so far has focused on two bases for evaluating public programs: their effect on economic efficiency and their effect on distribution. Government policy may be concerned with a broader range of objectives. For instance, the government may be concerned with the extent to which individuals of different racial, ethnic, and class backgrounds are mixed together in schools. It may be concerned not just with the income of the poor but with the physical appearance of the housing in which they live. When these alternative objectives are fairly well defined, the government can still make use of a variety of instruments for attaining them; in particular, it can still make use of private producers, by imposing regulations on them, or by setting standards that have to be met for individuals or firms to be eligible to receive subsidies. Thus the government has specified that institutions receiving federal grants must comply with certain affirmative action regulations. If the government decided to institute a program of housing grants for the poor, it could insist on basic standards for anyone providing housing to individuals receiving a housing grant.

In some cases, however, it may be difficult for the government to specify clearly (and in advance) all of its objectives, or to articulate these objectives in the form of a set of regulations or standards. There is, furthermore, a concern about the extent to which these regulations will be enforced. There is widespread belief that private producers, in the absence of well-articulated and enforced regulations, will simply pursue profit-maximizing behavior, regardless of alternative objectives that they may affirm. There is an argument, in such circumstances, for the government to assume direct responsibility for the activity. Similarly, there is a concern that whenever the government finances an activity, it will almost inevitably impose a set of regulations, some of which may have adverse effects, particularly on economic efficiency; thus, many of the alleged efficiency advantages of private production may be lost. These concerns have, for instance, been raised in discussions of school voucher programs, which would provide students with funds that could be used at any school, private or public.

POLITICAL PROCESS

In a democracy, many individuals and groups are involved in the design and adoption of any public-expenditure program. These individuals have various objectives and various beliefs about how the economy works. The program that eventually is adopted is a compromise among their views. The compromise that emerges will probably not resemble the views of any one individual and may seem to be inconsistent with any single set of objectives. If two chefs disagree about the appropriate liquid to add to a sauce, one arguing that lemon juice should be added and another that cream should be added, the compromise solution of adding a little of both may be disastrous, with results inconsistent with any culinary objective.

The study of the political process by which a particular expenditure program was adopted may be insightful for two reasons. First, we may be able to understand why the program looks the way it does. We discussed earlier the government program to stabilize farmers' prices. There is a market failure that this program addresses: the inability of individuals to obtain insurance for many of the important risks they face, including that associated with the variability of prices.[2] But a closer examination of the program suggests that if that were the only objective of the program, it would be designed in a quite different way. Rather, one of the clear objectives of the program is to transfer resources (income) to farmers from the rest of the population. Yet if that is the objective, there are more efficient ways of transferring resources to the farmers; outright grants would be preferable to the present program. But *if* the objective were made explicit, if the transfers were made conspicuous, it is not clear that they could get approved. Voters in urban districts might strongly oppose them, while they do not oppose the present form of inefficient subsidies, simply because they are not fully aware of the nature of the transfers.

Particular provisions of public programs are likely to have strong distributional consequences for particular groups in the population. If one group can be suitably organized, it will attempt to induce the political process to adopt provisions that are to its benefit. In Chapter 8 we discussed the regulations providing for scrubbing the smoke emitted from burning coal. These regulations may have an enormous effect on the relative demand for hard (or western) coal and bituminous coal and hence on the incomes of both miners and coal producers in different parts of the country. The shape of environmental legislation and regulation may be affected as much by these particular distributional consequences as by overall efficiency considerations.

This brings us to the second reason why it is important to study the political process by which expenditure programs get adopted. Some programs may be more influenced by political pressures than others. An example is a program with an elaborate set of technical regulations and a variety of detailed provisions. Such a program may be subject to pressure to have those regulations that favor certain well-defined interest groups. When technical expertise is required, it may be difficult to get impartial technical advice. Those who are capable of providing the information often have a vested interest in the outcome. Generals in the armed forces may have the most information about the military strengths of the United States and its potential enemies, but by virtue of their training and their positions, they look at the world from a particular perspective. Even if they do not take positions from a narrowly self-interested point of view but really believe that they are making their recommendations on the basis of the public interest, the nature of their advice may be very much the same as if they were acting out of self-

[2] Futures markets now enable the farmer to divest himself of some of the risks associated with price variability.

interest. Thus it is not surprising that we see a navy admiral arguing for aircraft carriers while an air force general pushes for bombers.

Accordingly, in evaluating alternative policies, one needs to take into account the political process, what the legislation might look like after it has been subjected to the political process, and what the consequences of the program will be, knowing that it will be administrated by bureaucrats, probably not unlike those administering other government programs, and subject to the same kinds of incentives.

SUMMARY

There are eight major elements in the analysis of public-expenditure programs:

1) identifying a need, the source of demand for the government program;
2) identifying a market failure (if it exists) and ascertaining whether what is at issue is a concern for (the consequences of) the present distribution of income or the provision of a merit good;
3) identifying alternative programs that might address the perceived problems, noting in particular the importance of particular design features for the determination of the consequences of the program;
4) identifying the efficiency consequences of alternative programs;
5) identifying the distributional consequences of alternative programs;
6) identifying the trade-offs between equity and efficiency considerations;
7) identifying the extent to which alternative programs achieve public policy objectives; and
8) identifying how the political process affects the design and implementation of public programs.

KEY CONCEPTS

Income effect	Intertemporal distribution effects
Substitution effect	Regressive
Merit good	Voucher
Incidence	Shifting

QUESTIONS AND PROBLEMS

1. Explain how the following actual design features have an important effect on the consequences of government programs:
   a) The income ceiling for eligibility for food stamps is reduced by expenditures on housing.
   b) Until recently, whether an individual between sixty-five and seventy was eligible for social security benefits depended on his income calculated on a month-by-month basis.
   c) An ex-spouse becomes eligible for social security benefits only if she has been married for at least ten years.

   Can you think of other instances where particular design features have seemingly unintended consequences?
2. Who may be the actual beneficiaries of the following government program or proposed programs; that is, taking into account how individuals respond to

the government program, who are those who are actually better off as a result of the program?

a) Medicare
b) housing subsidies for the poor
c) education loans.

Can you think of other instances where those who actually benefit from the program may be different from those the program seemingly intended to benefit?

3. In Chapters 11–15, we will use the framework that we have discussed in this chapter to analyze several different government programs. Before reading those chapters, see if you can answer the following questions for each program:
   a) What were the original sources of demand for the program? What perceived need was the program intended to address?
   b) What are the market failures?
   c) What are the possible forms of government intervention? Are there particular design features that have had, or currently do have, an important effect on the effectiveness of the program?
   d) What are the major efficiency consequences of the program?
   e) Does the program entail any effective redistribution of income?
   f) Are there important instances of trade-offs between equity and efficiency in the design of the program?
   g) What are some alternatives for meeting the objectives of the program? To what extent might they do a better job—e.g., by reducing distortions and increasing the equity of the programs?
   h) How has the political process affected the nature of the present program?

10

Cost-Benefit Analysis

The preceding chapter set out the basic framework for the analysis of government expenditure policies. In many cases, the government wants more than a qualitative analysis; it needs a quantitative analysis. It needs to know whether a particular project should be undertaken, whether the benefits exceed the costs.

Should the government build a bridge and, if so, of what size?

Should the government construct a dam and, if so, of what size?

Should the government institute more stringent regulations for inflammability of mattresses?

Should the government institute more stringent regulations for licensing drugs?

Should the government extend the Washington, D.C., subway system?

Should the government declare certain portions of the Cape Cod seashore a national park?

These are all examples of particular projects (regulations, actions) upon which the government must decide. The government must also make decisions concerning entire programs. Should manpower training programs, which attempt to train unskilled and unemployed workers for better jobs, be terminated or extended? What has been the value of their benefits relative to their costs? Has the bilingual education program, which provides native-language instruction to those for whom

English is a second language, been successful—that is, have its benefits exceeded its costs? This chapter describes how the government goes about making these evaluations.

Before doing this, however, it is instructive to consider how a *private* firm makes decisions concerning which projects to undertake.

PRIVATE COST-BENEFIT ANALYSIS

Private firms constantly have to make decisions whether to undertake some investment. We can characterize the procedures they follow in four steps.

1. Identify the set of possible projects to be considered. If a steel firm wishes to expand its production capacity, there may be a number of ways it can do this. There may be alternative technologies available for smelting iron ore, and there may be a number of alternative specialized forms of steel that can be produced. The first stage is then a listing of the various major alternatives.

2. Identify the full consequences of each of these alternatives. The firm is primarily concerned with its inputs and outputs. Thus the firm will determine the labor, iron ore, coal, and other materials required for each production alternative; it will assess the quality of steel that will be produced under each alternative; it will determine the quantity of various wastes that will be produced.

3. Assign a value to each of the inputs and outputs. The firm will have to estimate the costs of various kinds of labor (with various skills) over the lifetime of the plant; it will have to estimate the costs of other inputs, such as coal and iron ore. It will have to estimate the prices at which it can sell the steel (which will depend on the quality of the steel produced, which may in turn vary from project to project). And it will have to estimate the costs of disposing of wastes.

4. Add up the costs and benefits to estimate the total profitability of the project. The firm will undertake the project with the highest profit (the maximum difference between benefits and costs)—provided, of course, that profits are positive (taking appropriate account of the opportunity costs, the return the firm's resources could obtain elsewhere). If profits for all contemplated projects are negative the firm will undertake no project; it will invest its funds elsewhere.

Present Discounted Value

The procedure described above seems simple and straightforward. Only one part requires some elaboration. The benefits and costs of the steel mill occur over an extended period of time. Surely the firm is not indifferent when it comes to choosing between receiving a dollar today or receiving one in twenty-five years. How are the benefits and costs that accrue at different dates to be valued and compared?

The basic procedure employed by economists (and businesspeople) is based on the premise that *a dollar today is worth more than a dollar tomorrow*. If the firm receives \$1 today, it can take it down to the bank, deposit it, and have (if the rate of interest is 10 percent) \$1.10 at the end of the year. Thus \$1 today is worth \$1.10 next year. The firm is just as well off receiving \$1 today as \$1.10 next year. If the firm invests the \$1.10 it will have at the end of the following year \$1.21. Accordingly, the firm is indifferent between receiving \$1 today and \$1.21 in two years' time.

To evaluate projects with receipts and expenditures in future years, it multiplies those receipts and payments by a **discount factor**, by a number (less than one) that makes those future receipts and payments equivalent to current receipts and payments. The discount factor is smaller the further into the future the benefit is received. The discount factor for payments in one year is just $1/1+r$, where r is the rate of interest (in our example $r = .10$, so the discount factor is $1/1.1 = .9$); for payments in two years' time it is just $1/(1+r)(1+r) = 1/(1+r)^2$ (in our example it is $1/1.21$). The value *today* of \$100 to be received two years in the future is thus \$100/1.21 = \$82.60. We then add up the value of what is to be received (or paid out) in each year of the project. The sum is called the **present discounted value** of the project, often abbreviated as PDV. If R_t is the *net* receipts from the project in period t, and r the rate of interest, then if the project lasts for N years, its PDV is given by

$$\text{PDV} = R_0 + \frac{R_1}{1+r} + \frac{R_2}{(1+r)^2} + \frac{R_t}{(1+r)^t} \cdots \frac{R_N}{(1+r)^N}$$

Table 10.1 provides an illustration of how this might be done for a hypothetical steel mill lasting five years. (Most steel mills last much longer than that; this makes the calculations more complicated, but the principle is the same.) For each year, we multiply the net receipts of that year by the discount factor for that year. Notice the large difference between undiscounted profits (\$1,000) and discounted profits (\$169). This difference is likely to be particularly large for long-lived projects entailing large initial investments; the benefits for such projects occur later in time (and are therefore worth less) than the costs, which occur earlier in time.

Table 10.1 HYPOTHETICAL CALCULATION OF PROFITABILITY FOR A FIVE-YEAR STEEL MILL

Year	*Benefits (Receipts)*	*Costs*	*Net Profits*	*Discount Factor*	*Discounted Net Profits*
1		3,000	−3,000	1	−3,000
2	1,200	200	1,000	$1/1.1 = .909$	909
3	1,200	200	1,000	$1/(1.1)^2 = .826$	826
4	1,200	200	1,000	$1/(1.1)^3 = .751$	751
5	1,200	200	1,000	$1/(1.1)^4 = .683$	683
Total	4,800	3,800	1,000		169

The government goes through basically the same procedures in evaluating a project. There are, however, two critical differences between social and private cost-benefit analyses.

1. The only consequences of a project that are of concern to the firm are those that affect its profitability. The government may be concerned with a much broader range of consequences. It may be concerned with the ecological effects of some dam; it may be concerned with the impact of the dam on the recreational uses to which the river can be put.

2. The firm uses market prices to evaluate what it has to pay for its inputs and what it receives for its outputs. There are two instances in which the government might not use market prices in evaluating projects: (a) In many cases market prices do not exist because the outputs and inputs are not sold on the market. There are not market prices for clean air, for lives saved, or for the preservation of wilderness in its natural state. (b) In other cases, market prices do not represent true marginal social costs or benefits. Recall from Chapter 3 that in the absence of market failures, market prices do reflect marginal social costs and benefits. Accordingly, in the absence of market failure, the government should also use market prices in evaluating its projects. Government action is required, however, precisely because there is some market failure, and the prices the government uses to evaluate its projects must reflect these market failures. Thus if the government is concerned about unemployment, it may not view the individual's wage as a true measure of the marginal social cost of employing that individual. If the government believes that capital markets are not working well, it may not wish to use the market rate of interest in discounting future benefits and costs.

Valuing Nonmarketed Commodities

In this section, we consider some of the problems associated with the evaluation of nonmarketed commodities.

CONSUMER SURPLUS

We begin with an example where, in principle, the government could charge a price. The government is considering building a bridge. It can charge a toll for the use of the bridge. For each level of the toll, there will be a certain demand for usage of the bridge. Assume that the minimum feasible size of the bridge is such that at a zero price, there is excess capacity, as depicted in Figure 10.1. Thus, the price the government should charge (since the marginal cost of using the bridge is then zero) is zero; but clearly, the *value* of the bridge is positive; the bridge enables individuals to save time, and they would be willing to pay for its use. The question is, how much is it worth?

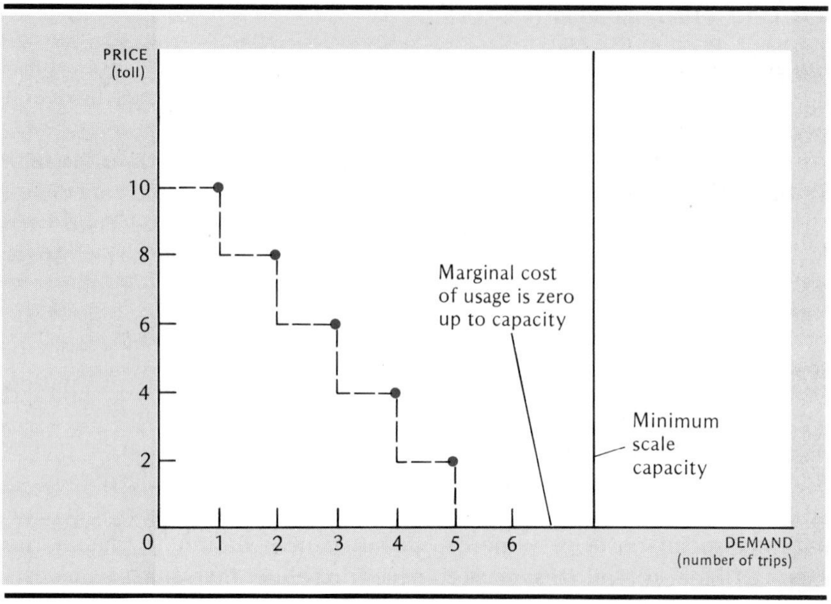

10.1 CALCULATION OF CONSUMER SURPLUS Even at minimum scale, the capacity exceeds the demand at zero price. It still may be desirable to construct the bridge if the consumer surplus (area under the compensated demand schedule) exceeds the costs of construction.

How much better off are individuals as a result of the construction of the bridge? First we construct a **compensated demand curve**, as shown in Figure 10.1. The compensated demand schedule traces out the demand for any commodity as we lower the price when, at the same time, we take away enough income from the individual so that he is no better off at the lower price than he was at the higher price. To see this, think of asking an individual how much he would be willing to pay to use the bridge once, then how much *extra* he would be willing to pay to use the bridge twice, and so on. By asking these questions we are able to trace out the compensated demand curve. We call it the compensated demand curve because at each question, we are asking the individual to compare his welfare when the bridge was not available with the new situation, when he can use the bridge once, twice, thrice, etc. The level of welfare of the individual is thus kept fixed at the level it was prior to the construction of the bridge. The area under the demand curve between 0 and, say, 5 units clearly gives the total amount that the individual would be willing to pay for 5 units. If the total number of trips taken on the bridge at a zero price is 6, the area under the demand curve gives the total amount that he would be willing to pay for 6 trips and still be just as well off as he was when there was no bridge.

The compensated demand curve needs to be distinguished from the ordinary demand curve. Usually as we lower the price of a commodity, the individual is better off; as we raise the price of a commodity, the individual is worse off. Thus at each point along the ordinary (or uncompensated) demand curve, the welfare of the individual is different. Along the compensated demand curve, however, as we change prices we continuously take away or give income to an individual, to leave him at a fixed level of welfare. If an individual's demand for a commodity (e.g., the number of trips he takes over the bridge) does not depend on his income, then his compensated demand curve and his ordinary demand curves coincide. Otherwise, the two differ as a result of the "income effect" associated with taking away or giving income as compensation.[1]

The gain as a result of the bridge construction is the area under the compensated demand curve, and is called the **consumer surplus.** In our example, this may easily be calculated. For the first trip, individuals are willing to pay $10; for the second, only $8 (additional); for the third, $6; for the fourth, $4; and for the fifth, $2. They are willing to pay nothing additional for more than 5 trips. If they were asked, What would you be willing to pay to have unlimited use of the bridge?—i.e., How much could we charge you and leave you just as well off as you were before the bridge was built?—the answer would be $30, which measures the benefit of the bridge to a particular individual. A similar calculation can be performed for all other users of the bridge. The total benefit of the bridge is the sum of the consumer surpluses of all users. The bridge should be built if these benefits exceed the costs.[2]

INFERENCE PROBLEMS

A central problem in social cost-benefit analysis is, as we have noted, that many of the costs and benefits are not marketed. Though for some commodities produced by the government—such as electricity—there are well-established market prices (which still may not reflect marginal social costs or benefits), there are not markets for lives saved, for clean air, or for unpolluted rivers.

How is the government to value the savings in lives resulting from a better program of drug regulation, or tighter standards for mattress inflammability, or seatbelt requirements? How is the government to value the savings in time or comfort provided by a new subway system? How is the government to value cleaner air? These are not easy ques-

[1] There has been some controversy concerning the empirical significance of the "income effect." See, for instance, R. Willig, "Consumer's Surplus Without Apology," *American Economic Review* 66 (1976): 589–97 and J. Hausman, "Exact Consumer's Surplus and Deadweight Loss," *American Economic Review* 71 (1981): 662–76, for two opposing views. Whether economists "should" ignore the income effect or not, in practice, they sometimes do, because of difficulties in quantifying the magnitude of the income effect.

[2] This discussion abstracts from a number of other considerations that will be the subject of discussion below, including the assessment of who benefits and who pays the costs.

tions, but techniques have been developed (in some cases they are rather controversial) that provide answers. These techniques entail making inferences about individuals' evaluations from market data and from their observed behavior in other contexts.

VALUING TIME

The old adage "time is money" describes the view taken by most economists in evaluating the savings in time resulting from an improved transportation system, such as a better subway system or road network. The typical approach is to attempt to ascertain the wage rate of those who use the transportation system; under certain ideal conditions, the wage provides a measure of an individual's evaluation of his own time. In simple economic models, an individual is pictured as making a choice between the amount of leisure and the amount of work that he undertakes. As a result of giving up one more hour of leisure, he gets an increase in consumption goods equal to his hourly wage. In equilibrium, he is indifferent when choosing between giving up one more hour of leisure and increasing his consumption by an amount equal to his hourly wage, or reducing his work (increasing his leisure) by an hour and decreasing his consumption by an amount equal to his hourly wage. Thus his wage provides a monetary valuation of his time. If a faster subway reduces commuting time by twenty minutes, and the wage is $9 an hour, the value of the time saved is $3. We calculate the value of time saved by each individual and add to obtain the total value of time saved.

There are some who claim that this provides an overestimate of the value of time: many individuals would like to work more at their wage rate but are unable to find additional employment at that wage; the job restricts the number of hours that they can work. The individual's valuation of his leisure is thus fairly low; the compensation that would be required for reducing an individual's leisure by one hour is, in this view, much less than the wage that the individual receives.

There are others who claim that the wage may provide an underestimate of the value of leisure for some individuals and an overestimate of the value of leisure for other individuals. They point out that, for instance, professors have chosen a relatively low-wage job relative to other options available to them because of the great nonmonetary benefits associated with the job. The value of their leisure exceeds the wage they receive. On the other hand, the wage of the coal miner or the garbage collector includes some compensation for the unattractive features of those jobs and hence represents an overestimate of the value of leisure.

VALUING LIFE

Probably no subject in public cost-benefit analysis has engendered so much emotional discussion as economists' attempts to place a monetary value on life. As distasteful as such a calculation may seem, it is necessary, in a variety of circumstances, for governments to face up to this problem. There is virtually no limit to the amount that could be spent to reduce the likelihood of an accident on a road, to reduce the likelihood of someone dying from some disease, etc. Yet at some point a judgment must be made that the gain from further expenditures is sufficiently small that such additional expenditures are not warranted. An individual who otherwise would not have may die as a result of this decision. Yet we cannot spend 50 percent of our national income on transportation safety or 50 percent of our national income on health.

There are two methods that have been used for estimating the value of life. The first is the *constructive method*—that is, we estimate what the individual would have earned had he remained alive (until his "normal" age of death). To do this, we extrapolate his employment history, comparing it to individuals in similar positions. Some argue that this method provides an overestimate of the economic value of the individual. If one believes that individuals' incomes correspond to their marginal products—what they have added to the production of society—then this method reflects the loss of national income as a result of the death of this individual. At the same time, it does not make any allowance for what it costs society to sustain this individual. His projected income, for instance, might be the result in part of training he would have received at some date in the future. Society has saved itself those educational expenditures, and this ought to be netted out of the loss to society from the death of the individual. The problem is that there seems to be no clear way of determining precisely how much of an individual's expenditures ought to be subtracted to provide an estimate of the economic value of life.

More importantly, this method fails to distinguish between the value of life and the livelihood that goes with it. It thus suggests that after retirement, an individual's life has a zero value, since there is no loss of earnings. This seems clearly wrong.[3]

There is an alternative, indirect method that does recognize the natural desire to live longer. In some occupations, there is a much higher chance of death than in others. For instance, the accident rates for coal miners are higher than for college professors, and the death rate for those who work in asbestos factories and who operate jackhammers is much higher than for clerical workers. Individuals who undertake riskier occupations normally require compensation for undertaking these additional risks. By choosing the riskier occupation, they are saying that they are willing to face a higher chance of death for a higher income while they are alive. The second method calculates the value of life by

[3] The method is also beset by a number of technical problems. For instance, the results are very sensitive to the discount rate employed, and there is no agreement about what this should be. For an early critique of this method and one of the first developments of the second, indirect method, see T. Schelling, "The Life You Save May Be Your Own," reprinted in T. Schelling, *Choices and Consequences* (Cambridge, MA: Harvard University Press, 1984).

looking at how much extra income individuals need to compensate them for an increase in the chance of death. There is considerable controversy, however, about this second method just as there is about the first method. There are those who believe that it provides a gross underestimate of the value of life; they argue that individuals are not well informed concerning the risks they face.[4] Also, for well-known psychological reasons, individuals attempt to ignore what information they do have concerning the riskiness of their jobs.[5]

As controversial as the estimates of the value of life may be, it is likely that they will continue to be useful in the evaluation of projects that affect the likelihood of death. There appears to be no alternative if we are to evaluate projects in which a change in death probabilities is a significant consequence. Whether, for instance, there should be higher standards for air quality may depend on the value assigned to the resulting reduction in mortality.

COST EFFECTIVENESS

An alternate procedure that is widely employed when the benefits of some project are hard to evaluate is called **cost-effectiveness analysis.** An objective is taken as given, and the question is simply: What is the most effective way to achieve this objective? Assume that we wish to avoid the problems associated with valuing lives while helping the government assess a variety of ways of reducing highway deaths. We could calculate the costs associated with each of several methods of accomplishing the same goal. Or we might simply show the marginal costs associated with incremental reductions in the death rate under each method, and leave it to the legislators to determine which point along the curve should be chosen (and therefore what method of improving traffic safety should be chosen).

When the Occupational Safety and Health Administration considered standards for noise pollution, it did a cost-effectiveness study, calculating how many extra workers would be protected from hearing loss as a result of alternative standards. It then calculated the cost associated with each standard. From this information, it calculated the marginal gross and net costs (taking into account the fact that hearing losses reduce productivity) associated with different levels of protection, as depicted in Figure 10.2. The curve shows that there are significant extra costs of trying to protect additional individuals from hearing loss.[6] On the basis

[4] Several studies have attempted to estimate the magnitude of workers' misperceptions and suggest that they may not be too large. See, for instance, W. K. Viscusi, *Risk by Choice: Regulating Health and Safety in the Workplace* (Cambridge, MA: Harvard University Press, 1983).

[5] This is sometimes referred to as "cognitive dissonance." For an application of these psychological concepts to economics, see G. Akerlof and W. T. Dickens, "The Economic Consequences of Cognitive Dissonance," *American Economic Review* 72 (1982): 307–19.

[6] From J. R. Morrall III, "Exposure to Occupational Noise," in *Benefit-Cost Analyses of Social Regulation*, ed. James C. Miller III and Bruce Yandle (Washington, D.C.: American Enterprise Institute for Public Policy Research, 1979).

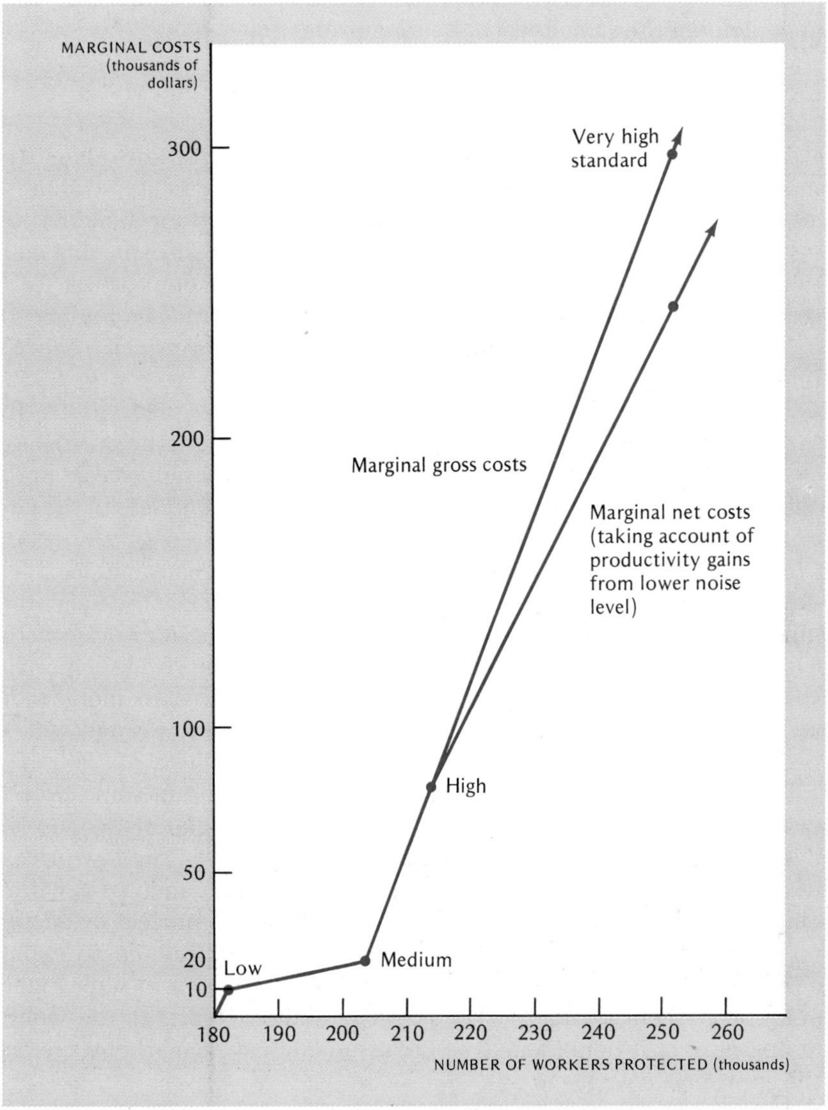

10.2 COMPARISON OF ALTERNATIVE STANDARDS FOR OCCUPATIONAL NOISE EXPOSURE Higher standards cost more and protect more workers from hearing loss. SOURCE: J. R. Morrall III, "Exposure to Occupational Noise," in *Benefit-Cost Analyses of Social Regulation,* ed. James C. Miller III and Bruce Yandle (Washington, D.C.: American Enterprise Institute for Public Policy Research, 1979).

of this, one study concluded, "an effectively administered hearing-protector program could provide most of the benefits at much lower cost in comparison with an industrywide engineering-only noise standard. . . . an 85-decibel hearing-protector standard [has] the relatively reasonable marginal cost of about $23,000 per hearing impairment avoided. . . ." In ordinary English, the study recommended the use of ear plugs rather than the drastic changes in plants and equipment that would be required to implement the same level of hearing protection.

SHADOW PRICES AND MARKET PRICES

Whenever there is a market failure, market prices may not reflect true marginal social costs or benefits. In such circumstances, economists attempt to calculate the true marginal social costs or benefits, for instance, of hiring an additional worker or importing or exporting additional goods; they call these "social prices" or "shadow prices." The term **shadow price** is used to remind us that these prices do not really exist in the market but that they are the true social prices, reflected imperfectly in the market price.

The most difficult part of calculating the shadow prices is tracing through the full consequences of a government action in the presence of a market failure. Disagreements often arise among economists about the nature of the market failure and thus about the consequences of the government action.

For instance, some economists have argued that because, in most less developed countries, unemployment is high, the marginal social cost of hiring an individual is very low. But hiring an unemployed worker in the urban sector may induce workers to migrate from the rural sector. The social cost of hiring labor in the urban sector will then include the reduced output in the rural sector, and so the shadow wage will be higher than it would be in the absence of migration.

It is, of course, unlikely that a bureaucrat working in some project evaluation office will be able to trace out the full consequences of undertaking a project. He cannot ascertain the appropriate "shadow prices" to use. Thus in some countries in which cost-benefit analysis is widely employed, the minister of planning may instruct his project evaluators on what shadow wage to use. (He may tell them, for instance, to assume a shadow wage that is 80 percent of the market wage for unskilled labor and 120 percent of the market wage for skilled labor.) In the United States, most cost-benefit analysis has assumed that the market wages are the appropriate wages to use.

DISCOUNT RATE FOR SOCIAL COST-BENEFIT ANALYSIS

In our discussion of private cost-benefit analysis, we noted that a dollar next year or the year after was not worth as much as a dollar today. Hence, income to be received in the future or expenses to be incurred in the future had to be discounted. In deciding whether to undertake a project, we look at its present discounted value. The discount factor private firms use is $1/1 + r$, where r is the rate of interest the firm has to pay. The question is, what discount rate should the government use? The discount rate used by the government is sometimes called the **social**

discount rate. The central question of concern is the relationship between this and the interest rate faced by consumers, on the one hand, and producers, on the other.

For evaluating long-lived projects, such as dams, the choice of the discount rate is crucial: a project that looks very favorable using a 3 percent interest rate may look very unattractive at a 10 percent rate. If markets worked perfectly, the market interest rate would reflect the opportunity cost of the resources used and the relative evaluation of income at different dates. But there is a widespread belief that capital markets do not work well. Moreover, taxes may introduce large distortions. Thus it is not clear which of the various market rates of interest, if any, should be used: for instance, should it be the rate at which the government can borrow, or should it be the rate at which the typical taxpayer can borrow?

Although no consensus has been reached among economists at a practical level, there is some agreement about the principles. First, one needs to consider how a project will affect the economy, and to whom the benefits (and costs) will accrue. This is often a subject of controversy. A government project might, for instance, displace ("crowd out") a private project that otherwise would have been undertaken. Then the *net* reduction in consumption in the period in which the project is undertaken will be much different from the direct costs; it will, in general, be much smaller; and the *net* increase in consumption in subsequent periods will likewise be much smaller.

If the individuals who benefit from the project are the same as those who pay the costs, we can simply use their *marginal rate of substitution,* how they are willing to trade off the reduction in current consumption for gains in future consumption. Since their marginal rate of substitution will be directly related to the rate of interest at which they can borrow and lend, in this case we can use that market rate of interest for evaluating costs and benefits in different periods. It is important to remember that what we are discounting is the *net* change in consumption in each period; this may differ markedly from the *direct* costs or returns to the project in each period, since the project will affect private investment and savings.

If the public project displaces a private project of the same size, then the net cost of the project is zero. If both the public and private projects yield all of their returns in the same period, then we can easily decide whether to undertake the project: we should undertake it if its output exceeds that of the private project; or equivalently, if its rate of return exceeds that of the private project. In this view, which, not surprisingly, is called the **opportunity cost view,** it is the producer's rate of return that should be used in project evaluation.

Unfortunately, however, in most cases, even if the public project displaces a private project, the returns accrue at different dates, and to different individuals for the public project than for the private project.

More generally, in the case of most long-lived projects, those who benefit from a project often are not those who paid its costs; subsequent generations receive the benefits while the current generation pays the costs. And it is precisely for these long-lived projects that the choice of a discount rate is so important. In these situations, we have to have some way of evaluating the gains and losses at different dates, to different generations.

One approach is to use a social welfare function (Chapter 4) to evaluate the gains and losses to these different generations, that is, the trade-off between individuals of different generations. We can then talk about society's marginal rate of substitution of one generation's income for another's, just as we can talk of an individual's marginal rate of substitution of consumption in one period for another. The question is: What is the relationship between *society's* marginal rate of substitution and the market rate of interest? The answer depends on how successful the government has been in adjusting the intergenerational distribution of income to reflect society's judgments concerning the appropriate intertemporal distribution.[7]

In the absence of an active government policy, most economists believe that the intergenerational distribution of welfare generated by the market does not have any optimality properties; they believe, in other words, that there will not be any systematic relationship between the market rate of interest and society's marginal rate of substitution between this generation's consumption and that of the next generation.[8] Using the market rate of interest may result in too high a discount rate, or too low a discount rate.[9]

Disagreements arise among economists both about the impact of the project being evaluated and about the extent to which the government has used other policy instruments to bring about the appropriate intergenerational distribution of income, and, consequently, how increments to income of different generations should be valued. For instance, some

[7] Several economists have argued that parents take into account the welfare of their children in making their savings-bequest decisions. In this view, then, in equilibrium, the marginal rate of substitution between their consumption and their children's is simply related to the rate of interest (if they give up one unit of consumption today, their children can get more than one dollar; the amount extra is just the return on their investment; in equilibrium, they must be indifferent when choosing between consuming one more unit today and postponing consumption, giving the extra consumption to their children). In this view, the social rate of discount can be directly calculated from the market rate of interest, in exactly the same way that it can for a short-lived project affecting a single generation. Indeed it should be noted that if the government decides to transfer more resources to the next generation, parents will decide that they need to transfer less; the change in bequests just offsets the government's action. This argument that public savings are a perfect substitute for private saving requires that there are no limitations on borrowing, all individuals know that they will have children, and all have the same number of children. For a discussion of this view, see R. Barro, "Are Government Bonds Net Wealth?" *Journal of Political Economy* 82 (1974): 1095–1117.

[8] We sometimes refer to this marginal rate of substitution as the **social rate of time preference.**

[9] Even if there is "crowding out," it may not be appropriate to use the producer rate of interest (the rate of interest facing firms) in the absence of an active and effective government policy to redistribute income across generations. If, however, the government imposes a full set of optimal commodity taxes and subsidies, it should use the rate of interest faced by producers. There is considerable controversy, however, over whether these special cases provide much guidance for policy purposes.

economists are particularly concerned about the extent to which public projects displace (or "crowd out") private projects. These economists tend to argue for using the rate at which firms can obtain financing.

Several of the issues we have discussed are illustrated by the cost-benefit analysis of a hydroelectric project on the Middle Snake River in the Pacific Northwest, which was conducted in the early 1970s.[10] Four alternative projects were considered. They differed in scale, in location, in the output of electricity they would generate, in their effects on fish and wildlife and on flood control, and in the extent of the recreational facilities they would provide. Which project was desirable turned out to depend critically on two factors: the discount rate and the evaluation of the effects on the environment. While at a 3¼ percent interest rate several of the plans looked viable, at a 9 percent interest rate only one of the projects had a positive present discounted value—and this was not the project that would have been selected at the lower interest rate.

While a market value can be assigned to the value of the fish, it is more difficult to determine the value of "natural wilderness." John Krutilla argued that the Middle Snake canyon

> may have few, if any, close substitutes. Morever, if the present environment is adversely altered, its reproduction is not possible. In short, while rare phenomena can be reduced in supply, they cannot be expanded by the works of man. They represent irreplaceable assets not subject to reproduction. Now if the supply is thus fixed but the demand for the services of this asset increases, it is an irreplaceable asset with an increasing annual benefit.[11]

He estimated that when the cost of the loss of the free-flowing character of the river was included in the analysis—and the benefits and costs discounted at 9 percent—none of the projects had a positive present discounted value.

Nevertheless, the Federal Power Commission licensed one of the four projects. Environment economist Lawrence Hines argued that that decision was not cost effective:

> Adding 1,700 megawatts of thermal output instead of hydroelectric output to the Pacific Northwest grid would have an inappreciable effect upon power rates in that region. But adding a dam to the Middle Snake would involve a transcendent aesthetic change. There is no doubt about which is the greater cost.

Curiously enough, benefits of the project turned out to depend on two events that were not anticipated at the time these evaluations were conducted. The enormous increase in the price of energy resulting from

[10] I have drawn heavily on L. G. Hines, *Environmental Issues* (New York: W. W. Norton, 1973). For a fuller discussion, see Chapter 7 of his book.

[11] J. V. Krutilla, *Testimony before the Federal Power Commission on the Middle Snake Issue* (Washington, D.C.: Mimeographed, 1970), p. 29.

the oil crises in 1973 and 1979 vastly increased the price of electricity. But while demand for electricity was forecasted to rise rapidly, it failed to do so, so that by the late 1970s and early 1980s there was considerable excess capacity. The cost-benefit analysis completely ignored the inevitable uncertainties associated with any long-lived project.

THE EVALUATION OF RISK

The most common mistake in trying to cope with the uncertainties of the benefits and costs of a project is to argue that in the face of risk, the government should use a higher rate of discount. Recall that the discount rate relates the value of a dollar at one date to its value at a later date. To see how increasing the discount rate may lead to absurd results, consider a project that, at termination, requires an expenditure (an automobile has to be towed to the junk yard). Assume that there is some uncertainty about the magnitude of that cost. We would normally think that this uncertainty would make the project less attractive than if we knew for sure what the termination costs were. But consider what happens if we use a higher discount factor to offset the risk: the present value of those costs is reduced, and the project looks more, not less, attractive. To use a higher discount rate confuses the evaluation of income at different dates with the evaluation of risk; these are two separate issues.

To evaluate risks, economists introduce the concept of **certainty equivalents.** Assume there is some risky prospect. Next year the output of the project may be worth $0 or $100; there is a fifty-fifty chance of each outcome. The *average* value is just $50 (½ × $100 + ½ × $0 = $50). If we dislike risk, however, we would clearly prefer a project whose return was a certain $50. In fact, we would prefer a project with a smaller average value, so long as the risk was smaller. If we would be indifferent in choosing between the risky project with an average value of $50 and a perfectly safe project with a value of $45, we would say that $45 is the certainty equivalent of the risky project with an average value of $50. We could, alternatively, have said that there is a 10 percent **risk discount factor**—i.e., we deflate the average value by 10 percent to obtain the certainty equivalent. To evaluate risky projects, then, we simply take the present discounted value of the certainty equivalents.[12]

Thus risky projects have to earn a higher return than safe projects with the same certainty equivalent to be acceptable. The extra amount a risky project must earn to compensate is its **risk premium.**

We illustrate the procedure in Table 10.2, for a five-year project. We have assumed that the initial investment in the first period is certain, and hence the risk discount factor is 1. The benefits that accrue in years 2, 3, and 4 are increasingly uncertain, and hence larger risk discount factors

[12] This methodology is not perfectly general. It requires that we be able to separate the analysis of risk at one date from that at other dates. For most practical purposes, however, it is sufficiently general.

Table 10.2 EXAMPLE OF COST-BENEFIT ANALYSIS FOR RISKY INVESTMENT

Year	*Expected Net Benefit*	*Risk Discount Factor*	*Certainty Equivalent Net Benefit*	*Time Discount Factor (10 percent interest rate)*	*Discounted Value of Certainty Equivalent Net Benefit*
1	$−100	1	$−100	1	$−100
2	100	.9	90	.91	81.90
3	100	.8	80	.83	66.40
4	100	.75	75	.75	56.25
5	−50	1.5	−75	.68	−51
Total	150		70		53.55

are used in each of those years. The final year, the project is scrapped; there are large costs associated with the termination of the project. (Consider the problem of what to do with a nuclear power plant when its useful life has come to an end.) But these costs are uncertain. Hence its certainty equivalence exceeds the $50 expected cost. (In contrast, had we employed a higher time discount rate to take account of risk, these uncertain scrapping costs would not have weighed very heavily on our cost-benefit calculation.)

To obtain the certainty equivalent value at each date, we multiply the expected net benefit by the risk discount factor. Then to obtain the present discounted value of the certainty equivalent net benefit at any date, we multiply it by the time discount factor. To obtain the present discounted value of the certainty equivalent net benefit for the entire project, we add up the discounted certainty equivalent net benefits for the life of the project.

How should the government evaluate the risks associated with various projects? In some cases, such as the risks associated with electricity generation, it can look to how private markets value risks. But for risks for which there is no comparable private project, matters are more difficult. Some, such as a flood control project, serve to *reduce* the risks individuals face, and for these projects, the risk premium is negative. Individuals are willing to pay something to reduce the risk of flood. Since the government can spread risks over the entire population, when the project neither serves an insurance function (reducing the risks individuals would otherwise face) nor provides a return that is correlated with income from other sources (that is, the return to the project is neither particularly high nor particularly low when the economy is, say, healthy), the government should employ no risk premium.

DISTRIBUTIONAL CONSIDERATIONS

The benefits of any given public project are not uniformly distributed across the population. Some projects, such as a dam, have benefits that are limited geographically. Other projects, such as the bilingual education program and jobs retraining program, are directed mainly at the poor. The government is clearly concerned about the impact of its programs on the distribution of income. How are these effects to be taken systematically into account, and how can they be quantified?

Two procedures are commonly employed. One is to attach different weights to benefits accruing to different individuals, and the other is simply to compare measures of inequality with and without the program.

Distributional Weights

The procedure for introducing social (distributional) weights into social cost-benefit analysis is straightforward. We divide the population into income groups; for example, the lowest quartile (one-fourth) of the population, the second quartile, etc. We then assess the magnitude of the net benefits (benefits minus costs) that accrue to each of the groups. Next, we determine social weights to be attached to each group. Thus if we attach a weight of 1 to the first quartile, richer individuals get smaller weights. We then multiply the benefits by the weights, to obtain "weighted benefits." Adding these up over all groups yields the net weighted benefit of the project. Note that a project could have a negative net unweighted benefit and a positive net weighted benefit, as illustrated in Table 10.3. Thus the attractiveness of a project may depend critically on how the weights are assigned to different groups.

Table 10.3 WEIGHTED SOCIAL COST-BENEFIT ANALYSIS: AN EXAMPLE

Quartile of the Population	*Net Benefit*	*Social Weight*	*Weighted Social Net Benefit*	*Alternative Social Weight*	*Alternative Weighted Social Net Benefit*
1	100	1	100	1	100
2	+50	.5	25	.9	45
3	−50	.25	−12.5	.7	−35
4	−200	.125	−25	.55	−110
Total	−100		87.5		0

Economists often relate these evaluations to their views of the rate at which the marginal utility of income diminishes. It is generally hypothesized that each additional dollar that an individual obtains increases his welfare, but by smaller and smaller increments. Under this hypothesis, and the additional hypothesis that each individual's utility function is approximately the same, an extra dollar given to a poor individual is worth more than an extra dollar given to a rich individual. How much more depends on how rapidly marginal utility diminishes. In Figure 10.3A the utility function is almost a straight line; the marginal utility of income for a rich individual is almost the same as that for a poor individ-

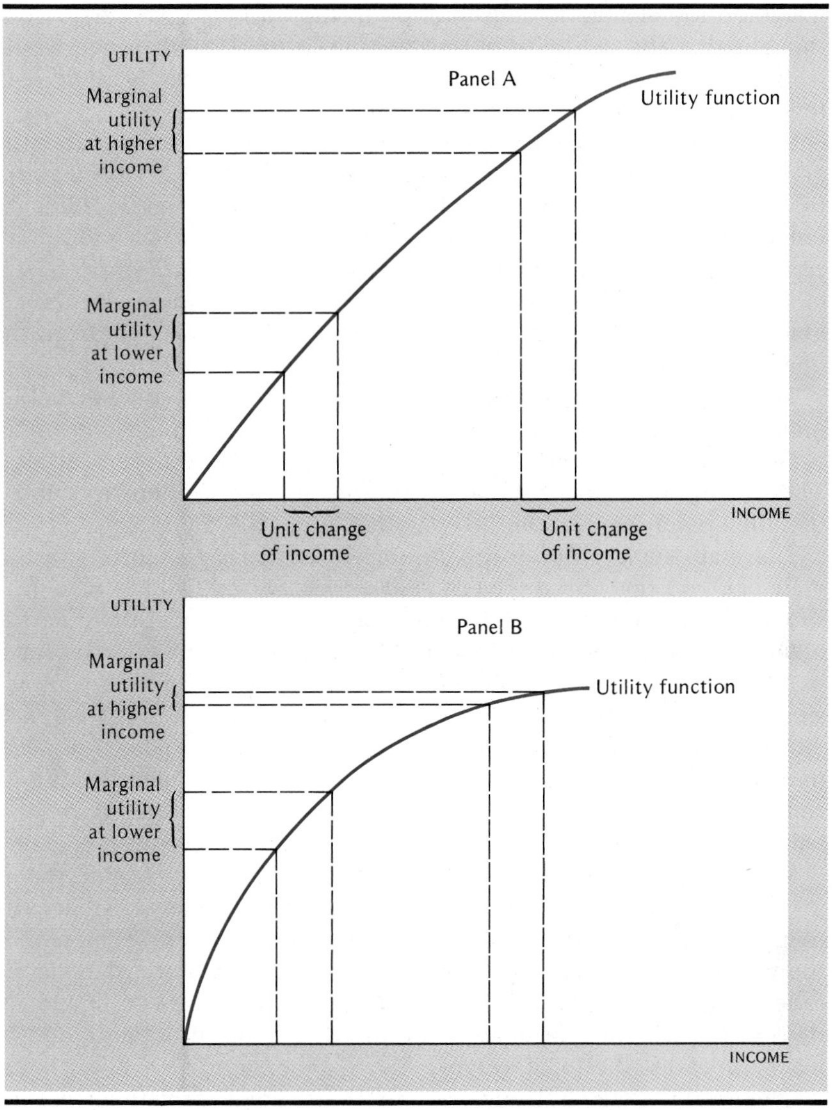

10.3 TWO ASSUMPTIONS ABOUT MARGINAL UTILITY (A) Marginal utility does not change much with a change of income. (B) There is rapidly diminishing marginal utility of income.

ual. On the other hand, in Figure 10.3B the utility function is very curved, so that the marginal utility of income for a rich individual is much less than that for a poor individual. The percentage by which marginal utility decreases as a result of 1 percent increase in income is referred to as the *elasticity* of marginal utility; if this were 1, and skilled workers had a 10 percent higher income, then one would weight the *change* in consumption of skilled workers by 10 percent less than one weighted the change in consumption of the unskilled workers. If one thought that the elasticity of marginal utility was 2, then one would weight the change in consumption of the skilled workers by 20 percent less than that of the unskilled.

Many economists have argued that a "reasonable" number for the elasticity of marginal utility of income is between 1 and 2. They attempt to infer the elasticity of marginal utility from observing individuals' behavior in various circumstances—in particular, their behavior under risk. The greater the elasticity of marginal utility, the more worried individuals are about losses of income. Hence they will buy more insurance. One can make inferences about the degree of risk aversion from the quantities of insurance purchased at different premiums.

There are some who claim that in the actual cost-benefit calculation one should ignore distributional considerations, although one might want to report separately how the project affects different groups. There are others who insist that distributional considerations are central to public-policy evaluation.

There are some grounds for the former position. Supporters of this view contend that if the government wishes to redistribute income it should do so directly. Recall from Chapter 5 that in determining the efficient level of expenditure on a public good there were circumstances in which distributional considerations were shown to be irrelevant; we simply calculated the sum of the willingness to pay of each of the individuals. We did not weight the willingness to pay of a poor individual more than that of a rich individual. But when the government's ability to redistribute income through nondistortionary means is limited, the distributive effects of a government project should be taken into account.

Moreover, there are many public projects (generally not pure public goods) whose object is deliberately to redistribute welfare. In that case, to ignore the distributional consequences in an assessment seems to miss the whole point of the project or program. Thus a major argument for federal support of education is its positive distributive consequences; therefore a cost-benefit analysis of an educational program ought to make use of distributional weights.

One need not take a strong stand on this issue: it is relatively easy to calculate the costs and benefits corresponding to any relevant set of welfare weights assigned to different groups.

The Effect of Public Programs on Measures of Inequality

The second basic approach to incorporating distributional considerations in program evaluation is to ascertain the effects of the program on the distribution of after-tax and after-subsidy income (or welfare). To assess the impact, we need some way of measuring inequality. In the following pages we describe some of the alternative ways that are frequently employed.

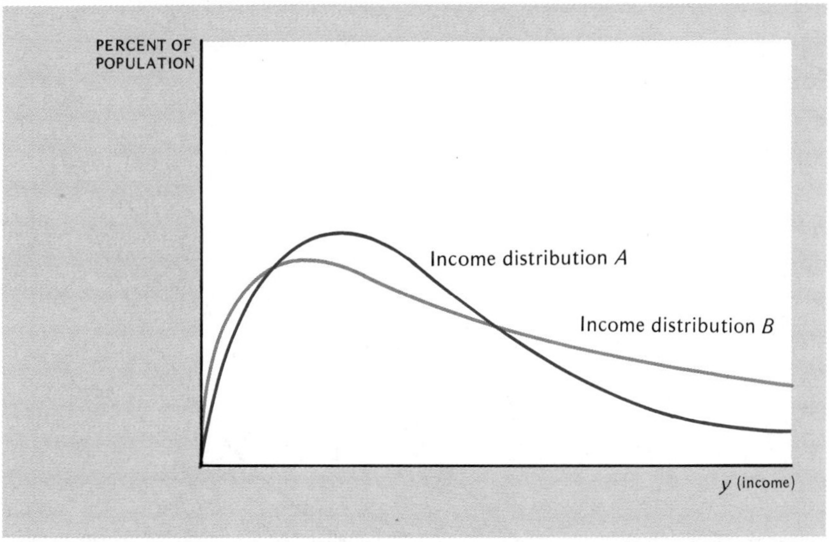

10.4 MEASURES OF INCOME DISTRIBUTION The income distribution specifies the fraction of the population at each income level. Income distribution *B* is more unequal than income distribution *A*, since there is a higher probability of having a very high or a very low income and a smaller chance of having an "average" income.

One way is depicted in Figure 10.4, where we show the proportion of the population at various income levels. With complete equality, of course, everyone would have the same income; a distribution with a high percentage of individuals with a very low income and a higher percentage with a very high income is, naturally, more unequal than one in which the income is concentrated in the middle. Thus, in Figure 10.4 the income distribution marked *B* is more unequal than that marked *A*.

LORENZ CURVES

Another way of describing the income distribution is depicted in Figure 10.5. We rank individuals from the lowest to the highest. We add up the income of the poorest 1 percent of the population, the poorest 2 percent, the poorest 3 percent, etc. We then calculate what percentage of the total income this poorest 1 percent has, what percentage the poorest 2 percent has, etc. We plot these numbers in Figure 10.5. The curves plotting the percentage of national income earned by the various income groups within the population are known as **Lorenz curves.** If there were complete equality, the poorest 5 percent would have 5 percent of the national income. With a great deal of inequality, the poorest 5 percent would have a negligible percentage of national income. Curve

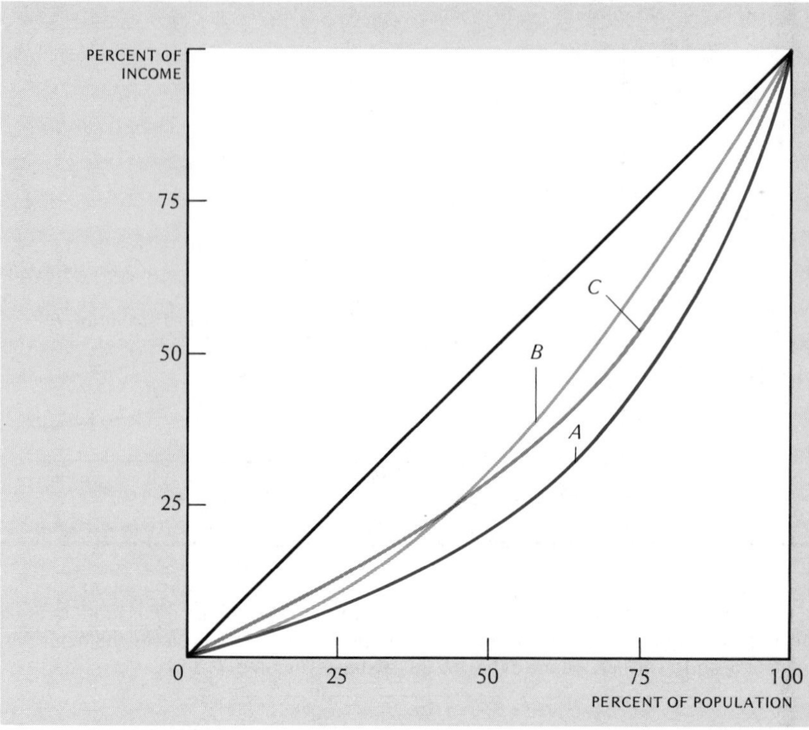

10.5 THE LORENZ CURVE The Lorenz curve gives the cumulative percentage of the total income accruing to the lowest percentiles of the population. *A* corresponds to a more unequal distribution than *B*, since with *A*, the poorest groups have a smaller percentage of total income. Lorenz curves frequently cross. It is not clear whether *B* or *C* is more equal.

A represents a very unequal distribution, while curve *B* represents a fairly equal income distribution.

More generally, we say that if one Lorenz curve lies inside that of another, the distribution of income corresponding to the second is less equal than the distribution corresponding to the first.[13] Unfortunately, just as we saw earlier that the Pareto principle provides insufficient guidance for most policy purposes, ascertaining whether one Lorenz curve lies inside another is often only of limited usefulness, for two reasons. The first is that frequently the criterion is not satisfied. That is, one Lorenz curve crosses the other (*B* and *C* in Figure 10.5). When two Lorenz curves cross, we cannot say which curve represents a more equal distribution of income. By some measures of inequality, *B* is more unequal than *C*; by other measures, *C* is more unequal than *B*. Equally important, we often are called upon to make trade-offs between inequality and mean income. How much is society willing to pay for a reduction

[13] See A. B. Atkinson. "On the Measurement of Inequality," *Journal of Economic Theory* 2(1970):244–63 for a more extensive discussion of the concept of greater income inequality.

in inequality? These are quantitative questions, requiring a numerical measure of inequality. If one Lorenz curve lies inside another, we can say that one income distribution is more equal than another, but this provides no quantitative measure of the difference.

GINI COEFFICIENT

One commonly used measure of the difference between income distributions is the Gini coefficient. The closer to the diagonal that a Lorenz curve is, the more egalitarian is the distribution of income. We can measure the distance from the diagonal by the area between the curve and the diagonal.[14] Twice that area is called the Gini coefficient. When the area is 0, the Gini coefficient is 0, and there is no inequality; when the area is ½, all of the income is concentrated in the wealthiest individual, and the Gini coefficient is 1. Thus the Gini coefficient must lie between 0 and 1. For the United States and most other developed countries, the Gini coefficient is around .3 (and has not changed much in recent decades).[15]

THE POVERTY INDEX

Another measure that is commonly employed in policy analysis is the percentage of the population that falls below the poverty line. The poverty line is defined as some "minimal" subsistence level of income. Exactly what that means, of course, is not clear, since individuals at the poverty line in the United States have incomes that far exceed the average level of income of individuals in most poorer countries.

The poverty index has a number of peculiar properties. It does not pay any attention to the extent to which individuals are below the poverty line, or the extent to which they are above the poverty line. It simply counts the fraction of the population that lies below a particular level. Some economists are concerned that all too often government policies are more directed at reducing a particular measure of poverty than at reducing poverty itself; thus, the use of the poverty index induces governments to focus attention on moving those just below the poverty cutoff level to just above it. This is, of course, the most cost-effective way of reducing the measure of poverty, but it may do little to ameliorate real concerns about those with low incomes.

SUMMARY

1. Cost-benefit analysis provides a systematic set of procedures by which a firm or government can assess whether to undertake a project or program and,

[14] Note that the area of the entire square in Figure 10.5 is 100% × 100%, or just one. The area below the diagonal is thus .5.

[15] See U.S. Congress, Joint Economic Committee, Subcommitte on Trade, Productivity, and Economic Growth, *Poverty, Income Distribution, the Family and Public Policy,* December 19, 1986.

when there is a choice among mutually exclusive projects or programs, which one to undertake.

2. Private cost-benefit analysis entails determining the consequences (inputs and outputs) associated with a project, evaluating these using market prices to calculate the net profit in each year, and, finally, discounting profits in future years to calculate the present discounted value of profits.
3. Social cost-benefit analysis involves the same procedures as private cost-benefit analysis, except that a broader range of consequences is taken into account, and the prices at which inputs and outputs are evaluated may not be market prices, either because the inputs and outputs are not marketed (so market prices do not exist) or because market prices do not accurately reflect marginal social costs and benefits due to a market failure.
4. When the government makes available a good or service that was not previously available (e.g., constructs a bridge across a river) or provides a public good, the value of the project to an individual is measured by the consumer surplus it generates; this is the area under the (compensated) demand curve.
5. The government has to make inferences (based on market data or observed behavior) concerning the valuation of nonmarketed consequences—e.g., lives and time saved.
6. The rate of discount used by the government to evaluate projects may differ from that used by private firms.
7. To evaluate risky projects, the certainty equivalent of the benefits and costs needs to be calculated.
8. Distributional considerations may be introduced into evaluations, either by weighting the benefits accruing to different groups differently or by assessing the impact of the project on some measure of inequality.

KEY CONCEPTS

Discounting, discount factor
Present discounted value
Compensated demand curve
Shadow prices
Consumer surplus
Cost effectiveness
Crowding out
Social discount rate
Intergenerational distribution
Certainty equivalent
Risk discount factor
Risk premium
Distributional weights
Lorenz curve
Opportunity cost
Gini coefficient

QUESTIONS AND PROBLEMS

1. Consider a project that costs \$100,000 and yields a return of \$30,000 for five years. At the end of the fifth year, there is a cost of \$20,000 to dispose of the waste from the project. Should the project be undertaken if the discount rate is 0? 10 percent? 15 percent? The interest rate at which the net present discounted value of the project is zero is referred to as the *internal rate of return* of the project.
2. Assume there is uncertainty about the costs of disposing of the waste: there is a fifty-fifty chance that they will be \$10,000 and \$30,000. Discuss how this uncertainty affects the cost-benefit calculation, if the government is *risk-neutral*, that is, it requires no risk premium to compensate it for bearing risk; if it is very *risk-averse*, that is, if it requires a large risk premium to compensate it for bearing risk.

3. Assume now that there are two groups in the population. Each contributes equally to the cost of the project, but two-thirds of the benefits accrue to the richer group. Discuss how this alters the cost-benefit calculation. Under what circumstances will the decision to undertake the project be altered?
4. Assume that the government has a choice now between undertaking the project described in problem 1. and undertaking a larger project. If it spends an additional $100,000, returns will be increased by $25,000 per year and disposal costs in the final year will increase by $20,000. Which project should be undertaken if the discount rate is 0? 10 percent? 15 percent? In the case where there are two groups in the population, how are your answers affected if two-thirds of the incremental benefits go to the poor (with the incremental costs being shared equally, as before)?
5. Discuss why, under each of these circumstances, a social cost-benefit analysis might differ from a private cost-benefit analysis: (a)the unemployment rate is 10 percent; (b)the government has imposed a tariff on the importation of textiles; (c)the government has imposed a quota on the importation of oil; (d)the government has imposed a tax on interest income; (e)the government has imposed price controls on natural gas; (f)the government has regulated airlines, so that prices exceed the competitive levels.
6. For each of the following projects, what benefits or costs might be included in a social cost-benefit analysis that might be excluded from a private cost-benefit analysis: (a)a hydroelectric project; (b)a steel mill; (c)a chemical plant; (d)a project to improve car safety; (e)a training program to improve the skills of minority workers in a firm? How might your answers be affected by changes in legislation (e.g., concerning manufacturers' liabilities for automobile accidents, legislation imposing fines on polluters, etc.)?

11

Health Care

Overall U.S. expenditures on health care have risen from 5.9 percent of GNP in 1965 to 10.8 percent in 1986. The rise in health-care spending, adjusted for general price inflation, reflects increases in per capita use of medical services (52 percent), medical price increases in excess of overall price inflation (30 percent), and population growth (18 percent).[1] Government's share in total health-care expenditures has been about 41 percent in every year since 1974, up from 26 percent in 1965.

Was it a coincidence that the increase in overall spending and in the prices of medical services occurred at the same time that government increased its sharing of financing, or did the increased government financing of health care "cause" the increase in total expenditures and in the cost of medical services? Or was the increased role of government a response to these higher medical costs? Are we spending too much on health? And are we getting as much "health" as we can for what we spend? Do we have an equitable system for the provision of medical services?

These questions have been at the center of a political debate during the past decade. The 1965 enactment of **Medicare** (health care for the aged) and **Medicaid** (health care for the poor) committed the government to provide a minimum standard of health care for all citizens, but there is concern that even today, some gaps remain, most notably for the unemployed. There is also concern with the rapid rise in hospital costs. Since 1967, the first full year of Medicare and Medicaid, these have increased at almost twice the rate of inflation.

[1] *Health Care Financing Review*, Spring 1986, p. 35.

Improvements in medical technology have meant that it is now possible to keep individuals alive who previously would have died. Kidney dialysis, heart valve bypass surgery, even organ transplants have become, if not routine, at least common. But many of these medical procedures are extremely expensive. Families find it almost impossible to deny their elders the advantages of these medical wonders, even if it imposes huge financial stresses. And the financial burden in turn imposes an enormous emotional strain both on those facing the medical expenditure and on their families. Such *catastrophic* medical expenses also became a major source of political debate during the final years of the Reagan administration.

There is more of a consensus that there exists a problem with the provision of medical services in the United States than there is about what that problem is, or how it should be remedied. There are those who advocate more extensive government programs. But support for a system of universal national health insurance or federally provided medical care (along the lines of that provided in many other countries, including the United Kingdom) has considerably weakened in recent years. This is partly because the large federal deficits have made the introduction of any major expenditure program look unattractive. Even apart from the current concerns about the federal deficits, support may have waned because the huge increase in costs of existing federal medical programs has led to a general wariness about whether the government could contain the costs of any new program within any reasonable level.

For example, spending under the Medicare hospital insurance program has surpassed the original projections made in 1965 by fourfold in constant dollars.[2] Today there is a widespread concern that in the not too distant future, unless Medicare taxes are raised, there will be a crisis in Medicare. The principal source of funding for Medicare hospital insurance is a payroll tax that is administered as part of the social security tax but whose proceeds go into the Medicare Hospital Insurance Trust Fund.[3] The Social Security Administration has projected the revenues to be received from this tax and compared them to the projected expenditures. Ignoring changes in either benefits or taxes, a projected deficit of $3 billion in 1990 will grow to a deficit of $35 billion by 1995. Based on these estimates, the Hospital Insurance Trust Fund will be insolvent in 1994.[4] The impending crisis will be caused both by the rising costs of medical care and by the rising proportion of the population that will be over sixty-five, and thus eligible for Medicare.

The rise in public and private spending for health care is not unique to the United States. Data on health-care expenditures as a percentage of gross domestic product—a measure of national income similar to gross

[2] *Economic Report of the President,* 1985, p. 129.

[3] In 1987, the hospital insurance tax rate was 2.9 percent of wages of up to $43,800. This was part of the overall social security tax of 14.3 percent.

[4] Alicia Munnel, "Paying for the Medicare Program," *New England Economic Review,* January/February 1985, pp. 46–61.

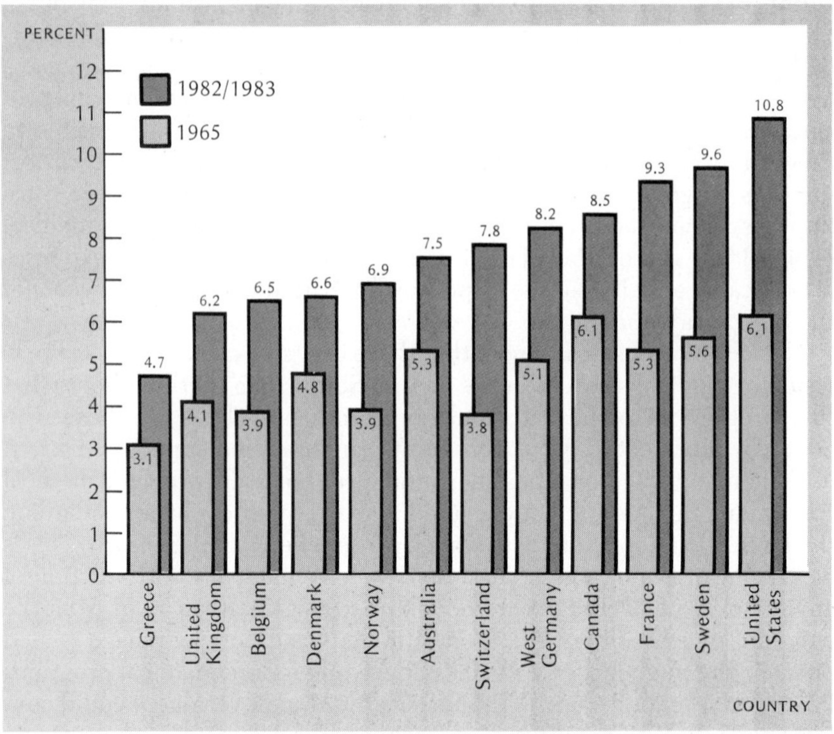

11.1 TOTAL HEALTH EXPENDITURES AS A SHARE OF GROSS DOMESTIC PRODUCT: SELECTED COUNTRIES, 1965 AND 1982/1983 SOURCE: Health Care Financing Administration, Office of the Actuary; Data from the Division of National Cost Estimates.

national product—for twelve industrialized countries are shown in Figure 11.1. Between 1965 and 1982/1983, five of these countries had increases in the share of income spent on health care of more than 70 percent. Large increases occurred both in countries where the role of government was fixed and where it was changing, in countries in which the role of government was small and in which it was large. As a result of these increases, other countries share, to a remarkable degree, many of the same policy debates on health-care financing and management that confront the United States.

AN OUTLINE OF U.S. GOVERNMENT MEDICAL PROGRAMS

The federal government has played a role in medical expenditures for a long time. For instance, since 1948 the Hill-Burton construction grants have provided federal support for the construction and renovation of hospitals.

The increasing role of government in financing health care is shown in Figure 11.2. Panel A shows the dramatic increase in both state and local

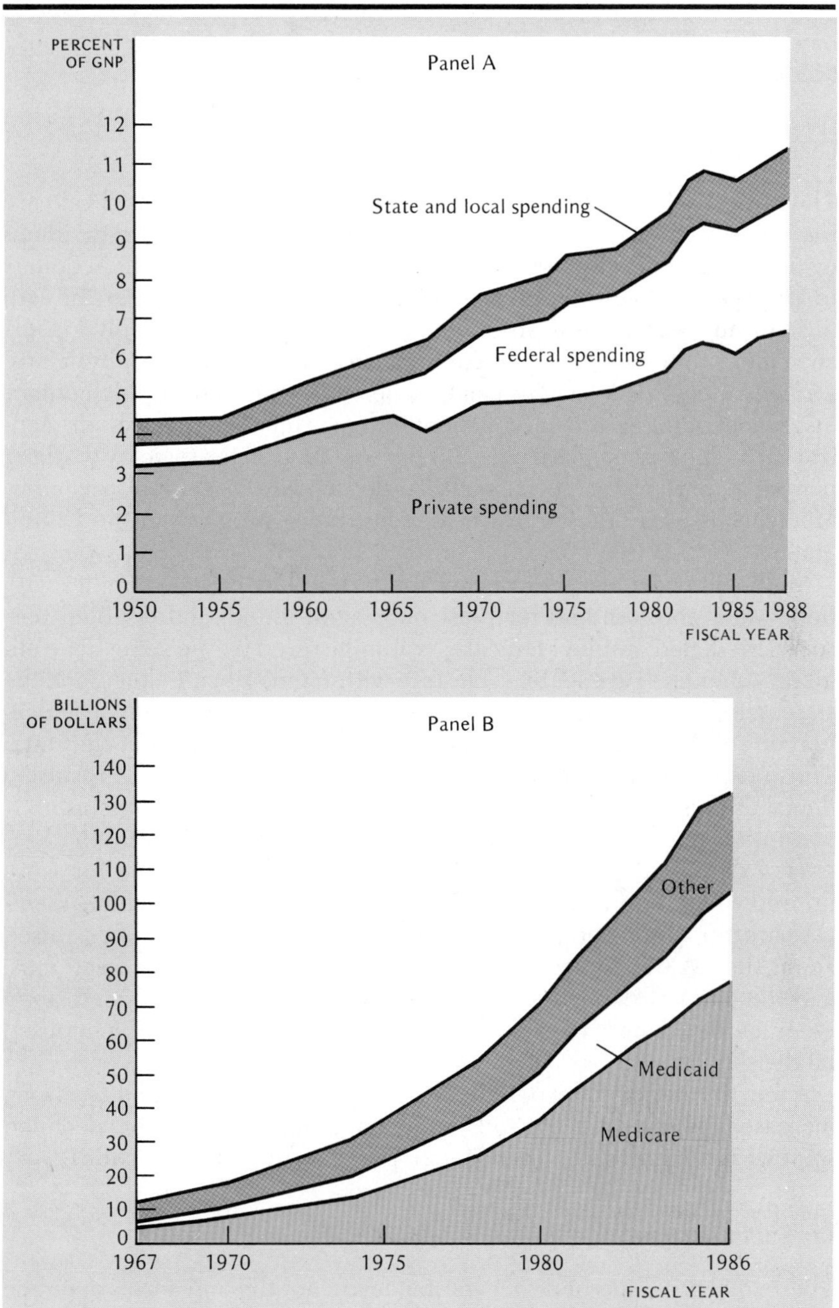

11.2 RISING EXPENDITURES ON HEALTH CARE Panel A shows national health expenditures by source of funds as a percentage of GNP. (The bump after 1982 reflects the 1982 recession, when GNP fell but health-care spending did not.) Panel B shows how federal dollars for health are spent. Medicare accounts for most of the growth in federal outlays. SOURCE: *Health Care Financing Review,* Vol. 7, No. 1, p. 3; Vol. 7, No. 3, p. 6; *National Income and Product Accounts of the United States, 1929–1982,* pp. 171–81.

expenditures and federal expenditures, while Panel B shows that today most of the federal expenditures are accounted for by two programs, Medicare and Medicaid.

Direct Assistance

The largest of the programs is **Medicare,** which provides medical care for those over sixty-five and certain disabled persons. All individuals over sixty-five are eligible for Medicare: a person with a million dollars in savings and investments receives the same benefits as a person with little or no wealth. Medicare is composed of two parts—hospital insurance and supplementary medical insurance, which pays for physicians' services. Recipients have to make some contribution to supplementary insurance, but it is far from sufficient for covering the costs of their medical care. The rest comes from a 2.9 percent payroll tax (paid by working people as part of the social security tax) and from general revenues. Medicare is today the largest health insurance program in the United States.

Medicaid provides medical care for certain low-income families with dependent children and for most poor aged, blind, and disabled persons.[5] Medicaid, unlike Medicare, is administered by the states. The eligibility standards are set by each state within federal guidelines, and the states and local communities are required to provide between 20 and 50 percent of the funds, depending on the per capita income of the state. These expenditures too have grown at a rapid rate, and the resulting demands on local and state resources have posed serious problems.

Another major government medical program is that run by the Veterans Administration. The **VA hospitals** provide medical care for those injured while serving in the armed forces, as well as also providing medical care for other veterans. In recent years, concern has been raised about the VA's ability to continue to provide medical care to veterans, and the costs of doing so. As those who fought in World War II grow older and need more medical care, increasing demands will be imposed on the system.

A fourth category of expenditures, for **medical research and teaching,** increased rapidly in the 1950s and 1960s but in real terms declined somewhat during recent years (by 20 percent from 1975 to 1986).[6]

Tax Expenditures

These four programs of direct assistance are not the only forms of public support for health care. There are, in addition, two major categories of indirect government assistance arising from the tax treatment of employer-financed health insurance and of medical expenses exceeding a certain level.

[5] Census estimates show that in 1983, 46 percent of the poor (defined relative to the poverty level) were Medicaid beneficiaries, down from a peak of 64 percent in 1976.

[6] Using the medical care price index.

If an employer pays for the health insurance of his employee, the expenditure is not treated as taxable income by the employee, nor does it enter the base for the payroll tax. It is as if the government simply allowed the individual to deduct all of his expenditures on health insurance in computing his taxable income.[7] Obviously, this greatly encourages employer expenditures on health insurance. The extent to which it reduces the effective cost of health insurance depends on the individual's marginal tax bracket—that is, on how much extra tax he would have had to pay if the firm had simply given him the extra income rather than spending it on health insurance. Assume, for instance, that the firm is currently spending $1,000 on health insurance for an employee who is in the 28 percent marginal bracket—that is, if his income increases by $1,000, his taxes increase by $280. Accordingly, if the firm had paid the worker the $1,000 directly, his taxes would have gone up by $280. Economists call the $280 a **tax expenditure** because it is the same as if the government taxed income fully but then gave the individual a (tax-free) grant of $280 for each $1,000 that he spent on medical insurance. The estimated federal income tax expenditure on **employer-financed medical insurance** amounted to $23 billion in 1987.

The second major category of indirect assistance, or tax expenditure, for health is the **income tax deduction for medical expenses.** Under the new tax law passed in 1986, only medical expenses in excess of 7.5 percent of an individual's income can be deducted, a less-generous allowance than the 5 percent floor under the previous tax law. The estimated tax expenditure for 1987 in this category is $3 billion, or only about one-eighth of the tax subsidy for insurance.

Tax expenditures encourage both health insurance purchases and medical expenditures. They effectively lower the price the individual must pay for insurance, as depicted in Figure 11.3. The employer is concerned only with the total cost of compensation, what it costs him to employ a worker. Consider an insurance policy that the individual who is in the 28 percent marginal tax bracket feels is worth only $72 but that costs $95. It is worthwhile for the individual's firm to provide the policy, for by offering it, the firm can reduce wages by $100 ($72 after taxes is equivalent to $100 before taxes), and the policy costs only $95. The tax system effectively reduces the price of hospital insurance by 28 percent. Even if the insurance company is very inefficient and spends considerable resources to administer the program, it still pays the firm to provide the insurance.

Insurance also encourages individuals to consume more medical services than they otherwise would and to be less concerned about the cost of medical care, since they have to pay a relatively small proportion of medical expenses. Thus government tax expenditures, by increasing the

[7] Individuals, however, are not allowed to deduct their medical insurance premiums; it is only insurance that is paid for by the employer that receives favorable treatment. In the Tax Reform Act of 1986, favorable treatment of health insurance costs was extended to self-employed persons, but their deduction is limited to 25 percent of health insurance premiums.

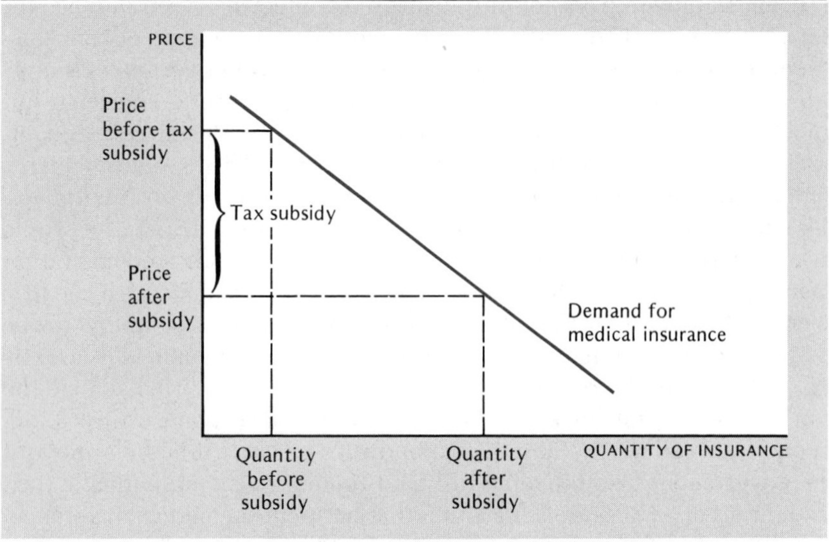

11.3 EFFECTS OF TAX POLICY ON DEMAND FOR MEDICAL INSURANCE The subsidy of medical insurance through the tax system increases the demand for medical insurance.

level of insurance coverage, lead to higher expenditures on medical services.

How significant these effects are is an area of active research.[8] Their impact depends partly on the impact of insurance on competition among health-care providers, as we will see in later sections of this chapter, and partly on how elastic the demand curve for health care is. If the demand curve is very inelastic—if most medical expenditures are not voluntary but are dictated by the health condition—the effect of tax expenditures on the demand for health care is very small. If the demand is elastic, as in cosmetic surgery, where the medical service provided is not essential to the well-being of the individual, then lowering the effective price to the consumer can have a substantial effect.

The price elasticity of hospital care has been estimated at about .7 by Martin Feldstein, who served as Chairman of the Council of Economic Advisors from 1982 to 1984.[9] This means that if an insurance policy covers 90 percent of hospital costs, the effective price of medical services is reduced by 90 percent. Accordingly, the demand for hospital services will rise by 63 percent (.7 x 90). Other studies have obtained lower price elasticities, between .2 and .7, implying that an insurance

[8] See Mark Pauly, "Taxation, Health Insurance, and Market Failure in the Medical Economy," *Journal of Economic Literature,* June 1986, pp. 629–75.

[9] Martin Feldstein, "Hospital Cost Inflation: A Study in Nonprofit Price Dynamics," *American Economic Review* 61 (1971):853–72. See also R. Rosett, and L. Huange, "The Effect of Health Insurance on the Demand of Medical Care," *Journal of Political Economy* 81 (1973):281–305.

policy covering 90 percent of hospital costs increases demand by 18 to 63 percent.

There is concern not only about the efficiency consequences of our tax expenditures—that is, the excessive consumption of medical services that is induced, but also about their equity. Tax benefits are clearly larger for those at higher marginal tax rates, that is, for wealthier individuals. It is estimated that in 1983, the tax benefit resulting from exclusion of employer contributions from the taxable incomes of employees was $622 per household in the $50,000 to $100,000 income range, and $83 per household in the $10,000 to $15,000 range. This was in part because average employer contributions were nearly five times as large for the former as for the latter.[10] The unemployed and those at low-paying jobs with few or no benefits obviously do not enjoy the tax expenditures associated with employer-provided medical insurance.[11]

Employer-provided medical insurance is a significant and growing source of financing for health care. Employer contributions for private health insurance premiums in 1983 were twice the level of ten years earlier in constant dollars. Today, about 80 percent of private health insurance is purchased through the workplace.

RATIONALE FOR GOVERNMENT'S ROLE IN HEALTH-CARE FINANCING, PROVISION, AND REGULATION

As we discussed in Chapter 3, there are two broad sets of reasons that may justify government activity in the marketplace. First, there are market failures that cause the private market not to be Pareto efficient. Examples of market failures in the health care market are imperfect competition among suppliers, imperfect information among consumers, and externalities. Second, inequality provides another justification for government intervention. A private market for health care could be Pareto efficient and yet provide no services to members of the population who were uninsured and too poor to pay for those services.

Inequality and Government Financing of Medical Services

The most important explanation for the increased role of the government in subsidizing medical services arises from the concern about the

[10] Cited in *Health Care Financing Review*, 1986 Annual Supplement, p. 116. Ginsburg, P., *Containing Medical Costs Through Market Forces*, Congressional Budget Office (Washington, D.C.: U.S. Government Printing Office, May 1982).

[11] Prior to 1983, the tax expenditures were so regressive that total federal expenditures (including tax expenditures) per capita on high-income individuals actually exceeded those on middle-income individuals, even though direct expenditures (i.e., through Medicare and Medicaid) were considerably lower on a per capita basis for upper-income groups. In fact, expenditures per capita on the middle-income group were lower than those on any other group. (See Gail R. Wilensky, "Government and the Financing of Health Care," *American Economic Review*, May 1982, p. 205.) The reduction in marginal tax rates and the increase in the minimum expenditure required for tax deductibility of medical expenses have somewhat reduced the importance of tax expenditures for health care after 1986.

consequences of income inequality. There is widespread belief that no individual, regardless of his income, should be denied access to adequate medical care. If choices have to be made, they should be made on the basis not of wealth but of other attributes, like age, or the likelihood of success of the operation, or perhaps random selection. This view holds that medical services are different from clothes, movies, automobiles, and most other commodities. Just as the right to vote should not be subjected to the marketplace (individuals are not allowed to buy and sell their votes), and just as when there was a draft, individuals were not allowed to buy their way out of their military obligations (though during the Civil War they were), the right to live—access to medical services—should not be controlled by the market. The view that there are goods and services, such as health care, whose availability to different individuals should not just depend on their income, is known as **specific egalitarianism.**[12]

Not all economists agree about whether medical services should be treated differently than other commodities. Many hold that they should not: those who have more money and want to spend it on getting health care should be allowed to do so. Those who hold this view often point out that the relationship between medical care and life (death) is very weak; that other factors, such as smoking, drinking, food, and particularly education, seem to play an equally, if not more, important role in determining an individual's life span and health status.[13] In Britain, the government provides free medical care to all individuals and has done so since shortly after World War II, yet there do not seem to have been marked reductions in class differences in infant mortality, maternal mortality, or overall life expectancy.

Still, a third view—toward which many Western democracies seem to be gravitating—is that everyone should have the right to a certain minimal level of care. The provision of Medicaid can be thought of as reflecting that view. At the same time, those who hold this view are often concerned with the consequences for economic efficiency of alternative methods of ensuring that everyone has access to a certain minimal level of medical care.

Market Failures

Though the concerns we have just sketched out provide part of the explanation for the current role of the government, there are also important market failures that may provide grounds for government

[12] J. Tobin, "On Limiting the Domain of Inequality," *Journal of Law and Economics* 13 (1970): 263–77.

[13] For an articulation of this view, see V. R. Fuchs, "From Bismarck to Woodcock: The 'Irrational' Pursuit of National Health Insurance," Chapter 13 of *The Health Economy* (Cambridge, MA: Harvard University Press, 1986), pp. 257–71, or V. Fuchs, *Who Shall Live? Health Economics and Social Choice* (New York: Basic Books, 1975).

intervention of one form or another. Thus there are different explanations for different categories of federal expenditures.

Medical research, like other forms of research, is often close to a pure public good. While some innovations, like drugs, can be patented, most discoveries are not patentable, and even when they are, it may be questionable whether it is desirable to do so. The increased prices for these drugs may result in a decrease in their utilization. And there is considerable concern over whether a disproportionate fraction of private research expenditures goes to attempting to invent around a patent—to come up with a drug that is just as good as the patented drug but is not covered under the existing patents.

There are externalities associated with certain diseases, particularly contagious diseases. These may make it desirable to have regulations concerning quarantining and compulsory vaccinations and provide part of the rationale for the Public Health Service.

The expenditures on veterans' medical benefits can be viewed as a delayed form of compensation; though the government provides relatively low salaries to those who serve in the military, it provides medical insurance extending beyond the period of service. This insurance seems particularly justified in connection with service-related medical needs.[14]

The tax deductibility of medical expenses is justified on the grounds that the appropriate basis of taxation is some measure of ability to pay. Medical expenses reduce an individual's ability to pay (if they are involuntary). Thus income minus medical expenditures (in excess of some given fraction of income) may provide a better measure of ability to pay than does income alone. To put it another way, the tax system tries to offset the "unjust tax" imposed on individuals by fate, in the form of medical expenditure. Medicare could be justified partly on the basis of the failure of the market to provide adequate insurance for the elderly.

Why Medical Markets Do Not Satisfy the Standard Conditions for Well-Behaved Competitive Markets

Underlying these specific market failures and public remedies are more general failures in the health-care market. Unlike the markets described in competitive market theory, health care is characterized by imperfect information and imperfect competition. To review, standard competitive market theory makes several critical assumptions:

a) There are many sellers, each of which is seeking to maximize its profits.

b) The commodity that is being bought and sold is homogeneous.

[14] The principle that employers should be responsible for injuries to workers while on the job has been extended to most workers in the private sector. Employers are required to provide "workers' compensation insurance."

c) The buyers are well informed: they know the prices and qualities being sold by all vendors.

d) The consumers are the buyers; they pay the full cost of what they consume.

Under these conditions, if a firm discovers a better way of producing some commodity, it simply lowers its price, stealing customers away from other producers. Production is always efficient, and prices always reflect the production costs of the most efficient producers.

When these conditions are not satisfied, inefficient producers may survive, and prices may exceed costs of production. For instance, if there is a monopolist, he charges a price at which marginal revenue equals marginal costs. Since marginal revenue is less than price, the monopolist's charges will exceed his (marginal) costs of production.

When the commodity is heterogeneous and individuals are not perfectly well informed, then it is difficult for an individual to tell whether a lower price signals a better buy or a lower-quality commodity. And when consumers are uninformed about prices, firms may be able to increase their prices above the competitive level with only a limited loss of customers. Unfortunately, none of the conditions required for a well-functioning competitive market is satisfied in medical markets, as we see in Table 11.1.

Table 11.1 DIFFERENCES BETWEEN MEDICAL MARKETS AND STANDARD COMPETITIVE MARKETS

Standard Competitive Markets	*Medical Markets*
Many sellers	Only limited number of hospitals (outside of major cities)
Profit-maximizing firms	Most hospitals are not-for-profit
Homogeneous commodities	Heterogeneous commodities
Well-informed buyers	Ill-informed buyers
Direct payments by consumers	Patients cover only a fraction of costs

IMPERFECT INFORMATION

While there is some presumption that the consumer is reasonably well informed when he purchases a car or a TV (and there are a number of sources from which he can readily obtain information), when individuals go to a doctor, what they are buying, in large measure, is the doctor's knowledge or information. The patient must rely on the doctor's judgment about what medicine is required, whether an operation is advisable, etc. It is far more dificult to appraise various doctors than to appraise various television sets. This is one reason that the government has long taken a role in licensing doctors and regulating the drugs they can administer to their patients.[15] Beginning in 1985, the government created peer review organizations to assess doctors' performance and to

[15] Kenneth Arrow has emphasized the importance of imperfect information in medical markets. See K. J. Arrow, "Uncertainty and the Welfare Economics of Medical Care," *American Economic Review* 53 (1963): 941–73.

disqualify from Medicare reimbursements those who were deemed inadequate.

LIMITED COMPETITION

Imperfect information has the effect of decreasing the effective degree of competition.[16] A firm selling a standard commodity, like a Zenith television, knows that it can attract customers away from other stores by lowering its price. Customers can easily ascertain where they are getting the best value for their money.

By contrast, potential patients who see a doctor with lower prices than his competitors may infer that he is not in great demand and is therefore trying to attract more customers; but the lack of demand for his services may suggest to them that he is not a good doctor.

By the same token, the heterogeneity of medical services makes price and quality comparisons difficult and thus inhibits the effective dissemination of information. My neighbor may have been pleased with the medical treatment that he obtained from his doctor, but if his medical problems are different from mine, that is no assurance that I will be pleased. And if I hear that one doctor charges more than another doctor, to evaluate whether one is a better buy I have to know precisely what services were performed.

The practices of the medical profession may compound the inevitable limitations of competition resulting from imperfect information. Doctors used not to be allowed to advertise. In other contexts, restrictions on advertising have been shown to raise prices (because they inhibit competition). Thus, several states now allow advertising for eyeglasses, and in those states, there has been a dramatic decrease in the price of eyeglasses.

There are other measures by which doctors can attempt to restrict price competition. It has been suggested, for instance, that "lowering fees might provoke one's colleagues to deny a surgeon hospital privileges or seek to damage his reputation."[17]

The fact that doctors often need to consult with each other and that they share hospital facilities (and often other interests) may also reduce competitive pressures. As Adam Smith put it, perhaps too strongly, in *The Wealth of Nations*, "People of the same trade seldom meet together, even for merriment and diversion, but the conversation ends in a conspiracy against the public, or in some contrivance to raise prices."

Moreover, there is also limited competition among hospitals. Most smaller communities have only a few hospitals. In the event of an emergency, the individual seldom is in a position to choose from among many. And even when there is time to make a choice, the choice is made not by the individual but by his doctor.

[16] See, for instance, S. Salop, "Information and Monopolistic Competition," *American Economic Review*, May 1976, pp. 240–45.

[17] V. Fuchs, *Who Shall Live?*

For an ordinary commodity, for which the consumer directly pays the full price, it can be taken for granted that the consumer believes that the benefits of the commodity are at least as great as its cost. Health care differs from an ordinary commodity in that consumers are insulated from cost considerations at the point of consumption, partly through prepaid private insurance, and partly through government insurance and entitlement programs. As shown in Table 11.2, consumers today prepay (directly or through their employers) 32 percent of the cost of health care in the form of private insurance premiums. Another 41 percent of health-care costs are paid by government. That leaves only 27 percent of the money spent on medical care coming from direct payments by consumers.[18] As shown in the table, this percentage has fallen consistently since 1973, when it was 37 percent.

Table 11.2 SOURCES OF FUNDS FOR PERSONAL HEALTH-CARE EXPENDITURES

	Patient Direct	*Private Health Insurance*	*Federal*	*State and Local*	*Other**
1973	37.4%	24.0%	23.7%	12.5%	2.5%
1983	27.2	31.9	29.7	10.1	1.1
1985	26.8	31.6	31.2	9.3	1.2
1988	26.6	31.8	32.0	8.6	1.1

*Spending by philanthropic organizations and industrial in-plant health services.
Source: Health Care Financing Review, Spring 1985, Table 9.

The fact that so much of medical expenditures is paid by third parties reinforces our earlier conclusion that medical markets are likely to be characterized by limited competition. Not only does the consumer worry that the doctor charging a lower price is providing a lower-quality service, he is likely not to care much about getting a less-expensive doctor; if insurance pays 90 percent of his doctor bills, a doctor who charged 30 percent less would save the patient only 3 percent—hardly enough to compensate him for his extra anxiety.

MALPRACTICE SUITS

Another consequence of the fact that consumers are uninformed purchasers is that they are frequently disappointed with what they have purchased. In the case of an individual who purchased a bad brand of TV, this does not have significant consequences. But in the case of medicine, an individual who believes that the doctor has provided him with

[18] These figures on the overall sources of funds disguise the fact that the share of out-of-pocket costs varies a great deal among consumers (depending on their insurance plan) and among kinds of health expenditures. For example, only 9 percent of national hospital costs are paid directly by consumers, compared to 28 percent of doctors' fees and 50 percent of nursing home costs.

inappropriate medical care can sue, and in recent years there has been a rash of such malpractice suits. These greatly encourage the doctor to provide excessive care.

The doctor can be sued if he fails to prescribe some drug, even though the probability of its having a beneficial effect is low. If he fails to administer some test, even if the costs relative to the information it yields are high, he can be sued. Since most of the costs of the test or drug are borne by a third party (the insurance company), he has every incentive to administer the test or to prescribe the drug, even though an informed patient would have been unwilling to do so if he had to pay for the test or drug himself.

Both the number of malpractice suits and the size of settlements in the United States have increased rapidly in recent years. The number of malpractice lawsuits per 100 physicians doubled between 1979 and 1983, and tripled in that period for obstetricians/gynecologists. At the same time, the average medical malpractice jury verdict also rose dramatically. Figure 11.4 shows that in constant 1986 dollars, the average medical malpractice jury verdict increased from $423 thousand in 1975 to more than $2 million in 1986.

These malpractice suits have increased the cost of malpractice insurance. To illustrate the impact of malpractice suits on insurance costs,

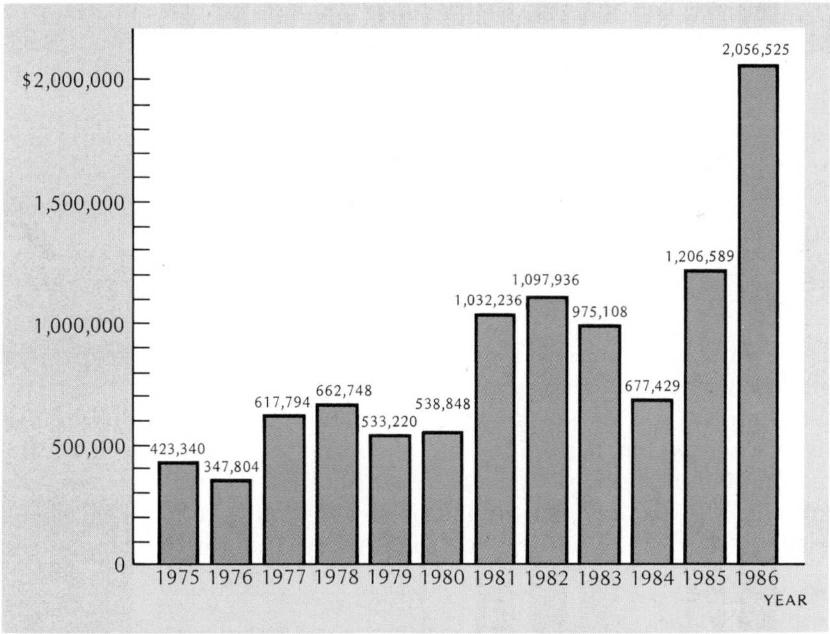

11.4 AVERAGE MEDICAL MALPRACTICE JURY VERDICT (Constant 1986 dollars) In medical malpractice cases, average jury verdicts were almost five times larger in 1986 than in 1975. SOURCE: U.S. Department of Justice, Tort Policy Working Group, *An Update on the Liability Crisis* (Washington, D.C.: U.S. Government Printing Office, 1987), pp. 36–37.

suppose that the number of lawsuits against an insurance company doubles over some period, and the average damage award (or out-of-court settlement) doubles as well. Then, assuming all other factors held constant, the insurance company in a competitive market would have to increase its premiums fourfold. Since malpractice insurance is a cost to the providers of medical care, the increase in insurance premiums has contributed to the increase in health-care costs in recent years.

The fear of malpractice suits induces doctors to prescribe treatments and tests that they might not otherwise have ordered, increasing medical costs by an amount estimated to be between $15 and $40 billion in 1983.

Doctors and insurance companies claim that lawyers are abusing the legal system. They also note that the jury system that makes awards is far from perfect, and that there may be a tendency to overcompensate (since jurors' sympathies are more likely to reside with the injured party than with an impersonal insurance firm). Lawyers claim that malpractice suits are necessary to insure that doctors take appropriate care, and that without such a system, those who are injured will not be adequately compensated. Economists focus their attention on trade-offs. While a system that limits malpractice suits (or the magnitude of awards) might result in some individuals not being adequately compensated for their injuries, it might also increase economic efficiency. It would reduce excessive legal expenditures, which now amount to approximately one dollar for every dollar (net of legal fees) received by plaintiffs in such cases.[19] It would also reduce the excessive expenditures designed to forestall such suits.

The rise in malpractice awards and the resulting rise in malpractice insurance premiums have caused many states to amend their laws.[20] Whether the changes enacted so far will be sufficient remains an open question.

ABSENCE OF PROFIT INCENTIVE

The final difference betwen medical markets and standard competitive markets is the absence of a profit motive: the vast majority of hospitals in the United States are not-for-profit institutions. They view their objective, not as minimizing the cost of delivering medical care (or maximizing profits), but as maximizing the quality of the medical care they can provide. The consequences of the absence of profit incentives have been exacerbated by the manner in which they were traditionally reimbursed

[19] These data are based on all tort cases in 1985. In addition to malpractice, tort law includes product liability cases and accident insurance cases. Data are from U.S. Department of Justice, Tort Policy Working Group, *An Update on the Liability Crisis* (Washington, D.C.: U.S. Government Printing Office, 1987), p. 52.

[20] For example, eight states set caps on noneconomic damages in 1986, sixteen states limited the liability of "deep-pocket defendants" (defendants who, although they merely share in the finding of fault, may be required to pay all the damages if their codefendants are unable to pay), and nine states limited the size of attorneys' fees by imposing fee scales or by requiring courts to review fee agreements.

for their expenses by government and by private insurance companies: in most cases, hospitals were paid whatever they charged.

Recently, there has been an increase in the market share of for-profit hospitals. The market share of for-profit hospitals in all nonfederal hospitals rose from 4 percent in 1960 to almost twice that in the mid-1980s. Several large for-profit hospital chains, such as Humana, have achieved a reputation not only for efficiency but for innovativeness as well.[21] Concerns that the incentive provided by the profit motive are incompatible with the provision of quality medical care have not been realized. The distinction we made in Chapter 7 between production of a good or service and its financing is an important one. Medicare has, for instance, made sure that the elderly have better access to medical care. The issue of who should provide the hospital services (whether government-run, not-for-profit institutions, or profit-making hospitals) is, to a large extent, separable from the issue of financing health care.

CONSEQUENCES OF DIFFERENCES BETWEEN HEALTH CARE AND OTHER MARKETS

These differences between health care and other markets that we have just described mean that the medical market may behave quite differently from markets where competition is more effective, where consumers are well informed, where they pay directly for what they get, and where producers are driven by the profit motive. For instance, conventional competition theory would predict that an increase in the supply of doctors would lower the price of medical services. During the past decade the number of doctors has almost doubled; it has increased much faster than demand, yet prices have not fallen. The consequence is extensive underemployment of many doctors, particularly surgeons. As long as a decade ago, Victor Fuchs, one of the nation's leading health economists, cited as evidence for a "surgeon surplus" a comprehensive detailed study of one surburban New York community, in which the typical surgeon had a work load that was only one-third of what experts viewed as a full schedule. (These results were consistent with calculations for the state and country as a whole, dividing the number of operations by the number of surgeons.) Indeed, some have argued that increasing the number of surgeons leads to an increase in the number of operations rather than a lowering of price.[22]

Questions of whether an operation is advisable or necessary are, of course, debatable. Most doctors do not recommend operations simply to increase their own income. But in making a professional judgment about whether an operation is desirable, the amount of time that they have on their hands and the pressure from other patients who may need the operation more has an important effect. And the "customers" with lim-

[21] Most notably, in the implanting of an artificial heart in 1986 in their Louisville, Kentucky, hospital.

[22] V. Fuchs, *Who Shall Live?* and W. McClure, "Buying Right: The consequences of glut," *Business and Health*, Sept. 1985, 43–46.

ited information are likely to have surgery if their surgeon recommends it.[23]

HEALTH INSURANCE

To many people, the major problems with the medical industry relate to insurance. Although an efficient private market for health insurance was slow to develop (major medical insurance covering large medical risks did not become widely available until after World War II), with the encouragement of the tax laws we described earlier, the majority of those working were covered by insurance by the early 1960s. This still left some important gaps: the unemployed, the poor, the aged, and those suffering catastrophic illnesses. Medicare and Medicaid were enacted to remedy the problems of the aged and the poor so that today 85 percent of the population is covered, either by public programs or by private plans. There have been recurrent proposals to provide some kind of health coverage for the unemployed, though there is none in place now. And most medical insurance policies have limits on their coverage, so that certain catastrophic illnesses are not covered.

The Importance of Health Insurance

The basic objective of insurance is to reduce the risks that individuals have to bear, to shift them to those who are more willing (i.e., in a better position because of risk pooling and diversification) to bear these risks.

Consider an individual who faces a 10 percent probability of having an accident that will cost him $1,000 in medical services. We say his average (or "expected") medical expenditures are $.10 \times \$1{,}000 = \$100$. Without insurance an individual with a $10,000 income faces a 10 percent chance of having only $9,000 to spend on goods other than medicine. If he has the accident, he may find it difficult to meet his house payments, his car payments, etc. Most individuals do not like facing such risky prospects; we say that they are *risk-averse.* They would prefer paying an insurance company $100 every year, whether or not they have an accident, and having the insurance company pay the costs of an accident if it occurs. If there were no administrative costs, the insurance company would, on average, break even with an annual premium of $100. But most individuals are willing to pay considerably more than $100 to have the insurance company assume the risk. In a competitive insurance market, insurance will be provided at a premium that allows an insurance company to just break even, taking into account administrative costs; thus, if administrative costs amount to 10 percent of the average payout, the insurance premium will be $110. A very risk-averse individual

[23] Although seeking second opinions before undergoing surgery may improve matters, it is far from a solution. In a community in which there is a larger supply of physicians, "standard practice"—the conditions under which operations are recommended—adjusts.

would have been willing to pay, say, $150 to have the insurance company assume the risks for him. The difference—$40—is the perceived gain from insurance coverage.

The magnitude of the gain from insurance depends on the size of the risk and the extent to which it can be anticipated. For instance, most pregnancies, though very costly, are planned; they do not represent an unpredictable risk. It is only the complications that sometimes attend pregnancy that give rise to a risk.[24]

The Consequences of Health Insurance

Though insurance performs an important role in reducing the risks an individual faces, it has another important consequence: insurance encourages the individual to spend more on medical services than he otherwise would. In the preceding example, we treated a health insurance plan as if it provided a fixed payment if an accident or illness occurred. But in most existing medical insurance plans, the precise payment depends not just on the accident the individual suffers or the diagnosis of his health, but also on the amount he actually spends on medical care.

If an individual knows that his insurance company will pay 80 percent of the cost of staying in the hospital an extra day, he may decide to stay in an extra day, though he really doesn't need to. And he will not object much if the hospital charges $300 a day for a room rather than $200, knowing that the extra charge will cost him only $20 a day. His doctors will not hesitate to administer a very expensive drug even if it has a low probability of providing relief, because they know that their patient will not have to pay the bill. These costs are spread throughout the insurance pool and are negligible to the individual.

Thus the provision of insurance leads individuals to purchase medical services to the point where the marginal return is far less than the marginal social cost of these services. They purchase medical services until the marginal return is equal to their private marginal cost, the extra amount they have to pay, which is a small fraction of the total extra costs.

We illustrate this in Figure 11.5, where we have drawn an individual's demand curve for medical services conditional on his having some particular illness. The horizontal axis can be interpreted as either the quantity or quality of services. At a lower price, the individual demands more and better medical services. We have also drawn the marginal cost of

[24] Many standard insurance policies cover the standard pregnancy costs but exclude complications, precisely the kind of risk that should be insured. Similarly, routine doctor's visits are both small in cost and fairly predictable in occurrence. The costs of administering an insurance program to cover such costs far exceed the benefits from any slight risk reduction. It is inefficient to insure such risks, but as a result of the subsidy to employer-provided insurance through the tax system, such costs often are covered by insurance. Suppose the administrative costs for insuring routine medical needs are 20 percent. Then the effect of a subsidy in excess of 20 percent of premiums is to make it cheaper (after taxes) to pay one's medical care bills via insurance than to pay them directly (see Pauly, "Taxation, Health Insurance, and Market Failure," p. 638).

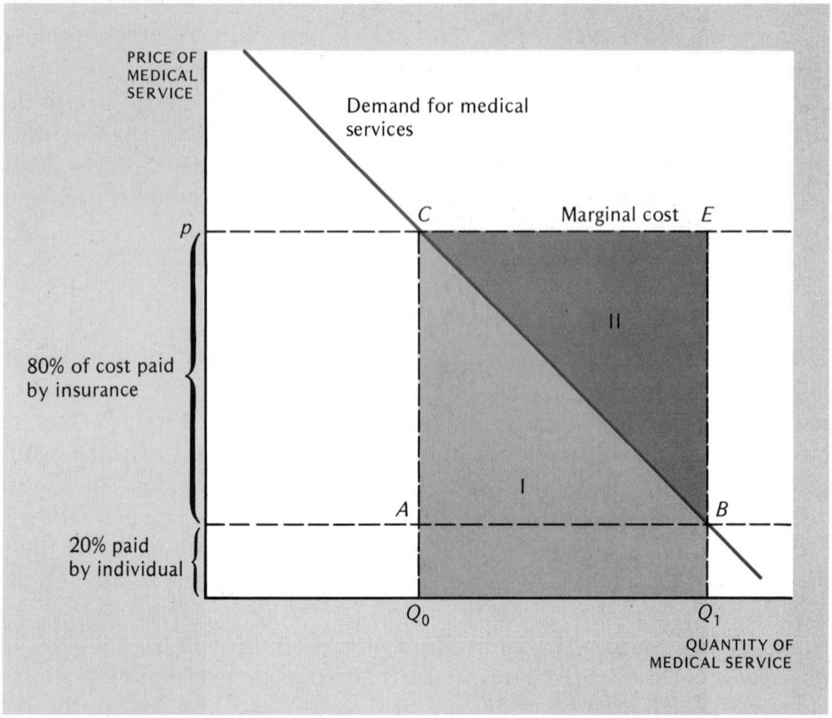

11.5 INSURANCE AND THE COST OF MEDICAL SERVICES Insurance lowers the cost of medical services to individuals and increases demand.

providing extra (higher-quality) medical services. For simplicity, we have assumed that these costs are constant. But the individual who has insurance coverage does not have to pay the entire marginal costs, only a fraction of the marginal costs. As before, assume the insurance policy pays 80 percent of his hospital costs. Then the marginal price he pays is only 20 percent of the value of the resources he uses. This induces him to increase his demand from Q_0 to Q_1. But what is of particular concern is that the value of the extra services consumed is less than the marginal costs; hence it is inefficient to supply Q_1. The gray area labeled I measures the extra amount the individual would be willing to pay for an increase in output from Q_0 to Q_1. The extra cost of the increase, including that paid by the individual and the insurance firm, is the rectangle Q_0Q_1EC under the cost curve from Q_0 to Q_1, which is the sum of areas I and II. The extra costs exceed the extra benefits by the colored triangle II. The magnitude of this distortion depends again on the price elasticity of medical services. If Feldstein's estimate of a price elasticity of hospital services of .7 is correct, a policy where the insurance company pays 80 percent of the costs increases expenditures by more than 50 percent.

Notice how the effect of the tax expenditure for insurance (illustrated in Figure 11.3) interacts with the effect of insurance on the consumption of medical services (Figure 11.5). The tax treatment of health insurance has resulted in an excessive purchase of insurance, and the purchase of insurance has resulted in excessive consumption of medical care. The first distortion thus aggravates the second distortion.

The fact that the rapid growth of insurance coverage and the rapid increase in health-care expenditures have occurred contemporaneously in the United States suggests to some that the provision of insurance has indeed been a major factor contributing to the growth in expenditures. Ninety-one percent of hospital expenses and 72 percent of physicians' fees are today paid by insurance companies and the government—by parties other than those receiving the medical services. But the fact that there has been substantial growth in expenditures in some countries where there has not been a corresponding increase in insurance coverage casts doubt on the view that insurance is the sole or even a major culprit. Other factors that are generally believed to have contributed to the growth of health-care spending relative to GNP are the rapid development of new technologies to treat disease and the lack of competition among health-care providers to hold down costs and increase productivity.

Moral Hazard

The effect of insurance on behavior is sometimes called the problem of **moral hazard.** The term *moral hazard* arises from the view that it would be immoral for an individual to undertake an action for the sole purpose of obtaining the receipt of an insurance benefit. It would, for instance, be immoral for an individual to set fire to his house simply to collect his fire insurance. But though such actions might be widely held to be immoral—and indeed are illegal—there is a much broader category of incentive issues, such as the care the individual should take to prevent a fire. The term moral hazard has come to refer to this broad range of incentive effects.

Insurance affects not only the quantity and quality of medical care that individuals purchase when sick, as just discussed. It also may affect their "health maintenance" activities. Because individuals do not have to pay all the costs of an illness, they may take insufficient care to prevent it. Would individuals smoke less, or drink less when they drive, if they had to bear all the economic consequences of their actions?

Insurance firms are, of course, aware of the incentive effects of insurance. They may stipulate, for instance, that the insured install sprinkler systems to reduce the likely damage of a fire, even though the benefits to the insured—given that he has good insurance protection—are less than its costs. But there remain many important actions about which the insurance firm can do little—it cannot make sure, for instance, that the insured does not smoke in bed.

There is no perfect solution to the moral hazard problem. The better the insurance coverage, the weaker the normal economic incentives for efficiency; the worse the insurance coverage, the stronger the incentives. One must strike a balance. The balance will entail limited coverage. Individuals will not be insured for 100 percent of the costs, for that completely eliminates all incentives; but they will be insured for some of the cost for all large risks. (Efficiency requires that on small risks and predictable costs, there should be no insurance.)

Some of the moral hazard problems can be reduced by greater monitoring to ensure that unnecessary medical expenditures are not undertaken. But whether the increased costs of improved monitoring are worthwhile is another matter. Some of the increased costs associated with medical insurance have been a consequence of misguided attempts to improve monitoring. For instance, to ensure that only relatively serious operations are covered, some policies have covered only operations occurring in the hospital. But the consequence of this provision has been to increase the number of minor operations occurring in hospitals, operations that could have been conducted in the doctor's office at much less expense.

REFORMS IN THE PROVISION AND FINANCING OF HEALTH CARE

There is more agreement that something should be done about the health-care system in the United States than there is about what should be done. The proposed reforms attempt to address problems in two areas: reducing medical costs and ensuring that all individuals have access to adequate medical care.

Reducing the Extent of Insurance Coverage

Many economists believe that the moral hazard problem resulting from the extensive provision of insurance is the central factor explaining the rise in medical costs and expenditures. Private markets, in providing insurance, recognize the critical role of moral hazard; they deal with it by providing only limited insurance coverage—for instance, by insisting on what are called **co-insurance** clauses, where the purchaser of the insurance still must pay a significant fraction of the costs. Critics of governmental policy claim that in designing the Medicaid and Medicare programs, insufficient attention was paid to the problem of moral hazard, and that more extensive co-insurance requirements should be introduced. Moreover, the special tax treatment of employer-financed health insurance programs has led to excessive provision of private health insurance; removing these tax subsidies would reduce the level of private insurance and again induce individuals to pay more attention to costs.

Those who believe that the demand for medical services is fairly price-inelastic but that the demand is affected greatly by what physicians prescribe believe that requiring individuals to pay even 20 percent or 25 percent of the costs will not go a long way to resolving the problems facing the industry.

Reforming the Manner in Which Hospitals Are Reimbursed

Critics of the Medicare and Medicaid programs and the major private insurance firm, Blue Cross–Blue Shield, claim that the way that reimbursements—e.g., for hospital expenses—were originally determined left little incentive for efficiency. These reimbursements were based on costs of the hospital, up to some maximum determined by the charges of all hospitals in the previous year. There was no incentive in this system for the hospital to reduce its costs below the maximum reimbursable level. If, in contrast, the fees for different services—the treatment of different diseases—were fixed, each hospital would have an incentive to lower the costs of providing the service, since it could keep any costs savings as profit. This is, of course, the kind of incentive that works in other markets for firms to devise less expensive ways of providing goods and services. Such a system was introduced into the Medicare program in 1983. Under the new system, based on diagnosis-related groups (DRGs), a hospital receives a predetermind fixed payment based primarily on a patient's diagnosis, irrespective of the actual costs incurred.[25] For example, the reimbursement for care of a mild heart attack patient is fixed at the time he enters the hospital, and does not depend on his length of stay. This system imposes a strict budget on the hospital beyond which it will incur losses. This is a drastic change in the method of reimbursing hospitals, and it has put hospitals into what Princeton University health economist Uwe Reinhardt calls "DRG shock."[26] Advocates of this new system believe it will provide hospitals with a strong incentive to get more health-care benefit per dollar, while critics worry that it will adversely affect the quality of medical care. Hospitals may refuse to provide for under-reimbursed diagnoses. They may also be encouraged to discharge patients prematurely because, while they may be able to be reimbursed for a return stay, they could not be reimbursed for an extended stay. There is evidence suggesting that the 500 or so DRG prices currently in use are still too crude to account accurately and fairly for the mix in the severity of illnesses treated by individual hospitals.[27]

[25] The diagnosis-related groups (DRGs) method of reimbursement was developed by researchers at Yale University in the 1970s. Eighty-three major categories of diagnoses were identified, and these were further subdivided according to surgical procedures and patient age. Medicare began phasing in the prospective compensation system based on DRGs in October 1983, but it was not yet fully in effect in 1987.

[26] Uwe Reinhardt, "Assuring Access, Quality, and Efficiency in the Delivery and Financing of Hospital Services," Princeton University, Mimeograph, 1985.

[27] Reinhardt, "Assuring Access, Quality, and Efficiency." He cites, for example, S. D. Horn, P. D. Sharkey, A. F. Chambers, and R. A. Horn, "Severity of Illness within DRGs: Impact on Prospective Payment," *American Journal of Public Health*, October 1985, pp. 1195–1200, showing that severity-adjusted DRGs differ by as much as 35 percent from the crude DRGs now in use.

Supporters of the programs to provide better incentives for cost saving reply that the supervision of hospitals, both by governmental agencies and by the doctors who use the hospitals, is sufficiently great to limit extensive abuse, and they point to the success of several chains of private for-profit hospitals in lowering the costs of providing certain services.

The fact that most hospitals are not-for-profit reduces the force of some of these concerns but also suggests that the range of incentives for improving efficiency may be limited, even with a system that is effective in reducing costs in for-profit hospitals.

Preliminary evidence suggests that the new system, while not without its problems, has been remarkably effective in reducing costs, and that the worst fears of its critics have not materialized. Still, the new system, while it may limit the rate of increase of Medicare expenditures, does not directly affect many of the other problems facing the health-care sector.

Regulation of Physicians

Some individuals believe that costs can be contained by regulating the amount a doctor can charge for certain services. It may be difficult to devise a scheme that both contains costs and maintains quality. The time (and associated care) it takes a doctor to perform a given procedure is variable; if the public program lowers his reimbursement for some service, he may simply spend less time performing it. If there are some services for which the reimbursement is high relative to the minimum time required to perform that service, doctors may perform more of those services. If the fees provided by public insurance are lower than those offered for similar services in the private market, only low-quality doctors may opt to work for those covered by public insurance. The problems of organizing a national health insurance system on the basis of a fee for services were sufficiently formidable that when the United Kingdom established its system, it chose to reimburse general practitioners on the basis of the number of patients served rather than the number of services performed, and it put specialists on salary.[28]

Another partial approach is to regulate the tests that a doctor can order. In 1987, Blue Cross–Blue Shield issued detailed guidelines for the use of medical tests. The insurance company will withhold payment for tests that are deemed unnecessary under the guidelines.

Changing the Organization of the Medical Industry

Those who believe that it is the doctor who primarily determines the kinds of medical services to be consumed believe that the appropriate

[28] See R. Zeckhauser and C. Zook for a good discussion of why regulations are likely to be ineffective as a means of cost control. "Failures to Control Health Costs: Departures from First Principles," in *A New Approach to the Economics of Health Care*, ed. M. Olson (Washington, D.C.: American Enterprise Institute for Public Policy Research, 1981), pp. 87–116.

remedy entails improving the entire set of incentives facing the doctor. They believe that we should be concerned with the provision of health, not the provision of medicine. To do this efficiently requires undertaking certain preventive procedures. Health maintenance organizations (HMOs) provide comprehensive medical care on the basis of a fixed periodic prepayment. Unlike insurance companies, HMOs directly provide health services, in addition to ensuring payment for medical services performed by outside organizations. Doctors are normally on salary. Advocates believe that these organizations create better incentives than traditional medical services to provide "health" in an efficient way, i.e., to provide preventive medicine where it pays, and combine outpatient and inpatient services in the appropriate manner. This is because an HMO gains financially if the cost of meeting its contractual obligations falls below its prepaid revenues.

Health economist Uwe Reinhardt summarizes results for a controlled experiment that compared health-care utilization under an HMO and under traditional fee-for-service medicine.[29] This study randomly assigned 1,580 patients to fee-for-services physicians of their choice, or to an HMO. In addition to the randomly assigned HMO enrollees, the study followed the utilization patterns of persons already enrolled with the HMO.

Table 11.3 presents some of the findings of the study. The study found

Table 11.3 COMPARATIVE DATA ON HEALTH-CARE UTILIZATION: HMO VERSUS FEE-FOR-SERVICE

Insurance Plan	*Use of Hospital Services (per 100 members)*		*Use of Ambulatory Services (per 100 members)*	*Imputed Annual Expenditures Per Person[4] (in 1983 dollars)*
	Admissions	*Days*	*Face-to-Face Physician Visits*	
HMO, experimental[1]	8.4	49	4.3	$439
HMO, control[2]	8.3	38	4.7	469
Fee-for-service[3]				
free	13.8	83	4.2	609
25%	10.0	87	3.5	620
95%	10.5	46	3.2	459
deductible	8.8	28	3.3	413

[1] Persons assigned under the experiment to the HMO.
[2] Persons already in the HMO on a voluntary basis.
[3] There were several types of fee-for-service policies under the experiment: (a) completely free care, (b) co-insurance at 25 percent, (c) co-insurance at 95 percent, and (d) a flat deductible beyond which care was free. The maximum annual out-of-pocket expenditure was limited in proportion to income and did not exceed $1,000.
[4] Includes services procured outside the HMO plan.
Source: Uwe Reinhardt, "Health Maintenance Organizations in the United States: Recent Developments and Performance," Princeton University, Mimeograph, 1987, Table 3.

[29] Uwe Reinhardt, "Health Maintenance Organization in the United States: Recent Developments and Performance," Princeton University, Mimeograph, 1987.

that patients in the HMO tended to use substantially fewer hospital services (40 percent) than did patients under fee-for-service contracts and that, therefore, their annual health-care costs were substantially lower (25 percent) than those of groups treated under the traditional system. HMO patients also tended to receive relatively more preventive care than did patients under fee-for-service care.

The study also assessed the effect of differences in the use of health services on health status. For most participants without serious health problems prior to entering the study, the reduction in use of services under HMO care did not trigger adverse effects on health. For high-income persons with serious health problems prior to the experiment, HMO care actually produced significantly superior health status results relative to fee-for-service participants. The opposite, however, was obtained for low-income enrollees with serious health problems prior to entering the experiment. The investigators speculated that this adverse outcome may reflect differences in the patients' ability to cope with the more formal organizational structure of HMOs.

In the last fifteen years, HMOs have been encouraged under federal law, and they have been experiencing rapid growth. In 1970, enrollment in HMOs was only 6 million. By the end of 1985, membership in HMOs and similar prepaid medical plans reached 30 million Americans, or 13 percent of the population, of whom 1 million were Medicare beneficiaries. Since 1982, the federal government has contracted with HMOs to deliver comprehensive care to aged persons electing to join an HMO. From the viewpoint of the aged, the advantage of joining an HMO is that it obviates the need for the cost sharing they must bear under the traditional Medicare contract. The disadvantage, of course, is that choice of hospitals and doctors is limited and long-established doctor-patient relationships may have to be broken. It is as yet too early to assess the impact of these government initiatives on costs of Medicare and on patient satisfaction.

Extending Benefits to the Uninsured

Finally, there are those who believe that the most significant problem is that some individuals cannot now obtain adequate medical services. Within ten years of being established, Medicare and Medicaid had proven their ability to guarantee *access* to medical services to the poor. While prior to these programs the poor (those with income under $4,000) had 20 percent fewer doctor visits per year per person, with these programs they have had 20 percent more visits.[30]

[30] The fact that they avail themselves of doctors even more than do those with higher incomes is not completely surprising: the cost is lower (both the direct cost, what they pay, and the indirect cost, the value of the time spent). Moreover, poor nutrition and other conditions may increase medical needs. Finally, the poor include a disproportionate number of the elderly, who have higher medical needs. For a more extensive discussion, see K. Davis and C. Schoen, *Health and the War on Poverty: A Ten-Year Appraisal* (Washington, D.C.: Brookings Institution, 1978).

But there remain some important gaps. Medicaid has never covered more than two-thirds of the poor; stricter eligibility standards in recent years have reduced even that number. In 1983, when unemployment peaked, 11 million people who had employer-provided insurance lost that coverage. According to census estimates, 15 percent of the population was not covered by health insurance and was not eligible for government assistance.[31] Lack of coverage has meant lack of care in some instances and reliance on uncompensated care, for instance, through charity and bad-debts care. Hospitals were able to provide unreimbursed care until the early 1980s because they could raise their charges to insured patients by enough to cover the cost.[32] But they may not be able to do this under the more competitive environment that exists today. If a hospital seeks to load extra charges into its prices to cover uncompensated care, it is likely to lose business to other hospitals that do not. The gaps in medical insurance coverage have motivated some within Congress (such as Senator Kennedy) to advocate a system of universal national health insurance. Currently such proposals are receiving little support, partly because of concern about the huge federal deficit.

Covering Catastrophic Medical Expenses

The one gap in coverage that has received enormous attention in recent years is that for catastrophic illnesses. Medicare and private health insurance will usually pay only a fraction of the costs of expensive, new techniques, such as kidney dialysis, heart surgery, and organ transplants that have become almost routine. For example, Medicare provides full coverage of hospital costs (after a deductible) for only the first 60 days of an illness; and it covers at most 100 days of nursing home care, whereas the average stay for all nursing home patients is 456 days.[33] There is very little private insurance for either nursing homes or long-term personal care at home.

The number of families who suffer "catastrophic" out-of-pocket medical costs depends, of course, on the definition of catastrophic. The most useful definition for our purposes is one that allows us to identify medical costs that are so high that they force individuals or families to significantly lower their standard of living, now or in the future. Such a definition allows appropriate comparisons across households and captures, at the same time, an intuitive sense of catastrophe. One reason-

[31] Lack of coverage is not spread evenly among the population. The study showed that 23 percent of blacks and 22 percent of Hispanics were not covered, compared to 14 percent for whites. See Alicia Munnell, "Ensuring Entitlement to Health Care Services," *New England Economic Review*, November/December 1985, Table 2.

[32] Hospitals provided an estimated $6.2 billion in uncompensated care in 1982. For a discussion of the access of the uninsured to medical care, see K. Davis and D. Rowland, "Uninsured and Underserved: Inequities in Health Care in the United States," *Milbank Memorial Fund Quarterly/Health and Society*, 60 (2): 1983, 149–176.

[33] Moreover, only nursing home care that was immediately preceded by hospitalization is eligible for payment by Medicare.

able definition of "catastrophic" is out-of-pocket expenses in excess of a fixed figure, say $2,000 in 1987 dollars, plus 10 percent of household income.[34] Using this definition, the Department of Health and Human Services has estimated that about 2.4 percent of American households headed by someone under age sixty-five incur catastrophic medical expenditures each year. For households where the head is aged sixty-five or older, the percentage is 7 percent.[35] As the U.S. population ages, the percentage of those facing catastrophic expense will rise steeply unless insurance coverage expands to meet the need.

As part of his State of the Union message in 1987, President Reagan proposed an expansion of Medicare's coverage of hospitalization and related expenses, to be financed by an increase in Medicare premiums paid by the elderly. The proposal has been criticized by both conservatives and liberals. Some maintain that it represents an encroachment on the private sector. Others believe that it does not go far enough, since it would not pay for catastrophic expenses for those not covered by Medicare, nor would it cover long-term nursing care costs, the single largest medical expenditure for the elderly. But even those who would like to see nursing home coverage included are worried about the expense. Whatever view one takes, however, the rising political concern with coverage of catastrophic health expenses makes some form of government action likely.

SUMMARY

1. Though decisions about health are difficult, resource allocations—choices among alternative uses of funds—must be made. Economic analysis may be useful in making those decisions in a systematic and consistent way.
2. National expenditures on medical services, the prices of medical services, and public expenditures on medicine have all risen rapidly in recent years. Medical expenditures represent the third largest category of public expenditures, after defense and education. The government now pays more than two-fifths of all health expenditures.
3. The four major public programs are Medicare, Medicaid, health care for veterans, and public support for research and development. In addition, there are two major categories of tax expenditures: employer-financed health insurance and tax deductibility of medical expenses exceeding a certain level.
4. The health care industry is characterized by several market failures:
   a) Uninformed consumers;
   b) Limited competition;
   c) Externalities, associated with contagious diseases; and
   d) Non-profit-maximizing behavior.
5. Many economists believe that the rapid increase in medical costs arises from

[34] A simple percentage of income threshold is not satisfactory because, for extremely low-income households, it would define as catastrophic the expense levels associated with routine health-care costs. A flat percentage of income rule thus confuses the problem of lack of insurance coverage with the problem of poverty (the lack of income).

[35] U.S. Department of Health and Human Services, *Catastrophic Illness Expenses*, 1986, Table 2.1.

the extensive growth of private insurance plus government programs that cover medical expenses.

6. Those who believe that the medical market is competitive believe that if individuals have to bear a larger fraction of the costs, and if hospitals are reimbursed in a way that provides them with an incentive to be efficient and to reduce costs, costs will be reduced.
7. Some of those who believe that the market is not competitive believe that costs should be controlled by regulation. Most economists, however, are skeptical about the likely success of regulation in a market as complex as that for medicine. Many believe that a change in the methods by which medicine is delivered—in particular, the more extensive use of health maintenance organizations—is the most hopeful way of reducing medical costs.
8. There is concern that there are still some large gaps in coverage, particularly for the unemployed and for catastrophic expenses.

KEY CONCEPTS

Medicare	Moral hazard
Medicaid	Third-party payment
Tax expenditures	Diagnosis-related groups
Co-insurance	Health maintenance organizations
Specific egalitarianism	Catastrophic medical expenses

QUESTIONS AND PROBLEMS

1. In what ways is the purchase of medical services similar to the purchase of a car? In what ways is it different?
2. We have noted that there are extensive disagreements about what should be done about how medical care is provided in the United States. To what extent are these differences due to differences in judgments concerning how the market for medical services functions? Be specific. To what extent are these differences due to differences in values?
3. Consider the "market failures" that arise in medical markets and the proposals currently being debated for altering how medical care should be provided in the United States. Discuss the extent to which each of the proposals is aimed at remedying particular market failures.
4. During the past twenty-five years there has been a decline in community-run hospitals and an increase in private (for-profit) hospitals. Are there reasons that hospitals should be particularly well- or badly suited to being run publicly? What do you think accounts for these trends?
5. Critics of malpractice suits claim that they have contributed significantly to the rise of medical costs and argue for legislation that would limit the size of awards, limit lawyers' fees, or otherwise discourage such suits. Many lawyers are concerned that any such legislation would impair the rights of those injured by malpractice to be justly compensated for the damages they have incurred. Discuss the equity-efficiency trade-offs. What do you think should be done?
6. Assume that medical expenditures are fully deductible from taxes. Show diagrammatically the effect on the demand for medical services. If the elasticity of demand with respect to price is .7, what is the effect of deductibility on an individual in the 15 percent marginal tax bracket; in the 28 percent marginal tax bracket; in the 33 percent marginal tax bracket?

12

DEFENSE

Defense expenditures represent the largest single item of government spending, constituting 28 percent of the federal government's budget in 1986. In addition to military spending by the Department of Defense ($266 billion in 1986), official figures for defense spending include expenditures by the Department of Energy on atomic energy defense. Though only a tiny part of total defense expenditures ($7 billion, or 2.6 percent), atomic energy defense expenditures constitute 70 percent of the Department of Energy's budget.

Not included in official defense figures, shown in Figure 12.1, are veterans' benefits ($29 billion in 1986) and military retirement ($16 billion), which represent deferred compensation for those who previously served in the armed forces.[1] Much (but not all) of the $4 billion spent on space research is also motivated by military considerations. Using this broader measure, defense spending today represents over 30 percent of the federal budget.

Military expenditures, both in real terms and as a percentage of GNP, have varied markedly over time. Following the Vietnam War, there was a steep reduction in military expenditures. Military expenditures began to increase under the Carter administration and were further increased under President Reagan. As Figure 12.1 illustrates, real expenditures reached an all-time high for peacetime during the Reagan administra-

[1] We would also like to make a further adjustment for retirement pay to former civilian workers in the Department of Defense. We do not do this because of lack of data.

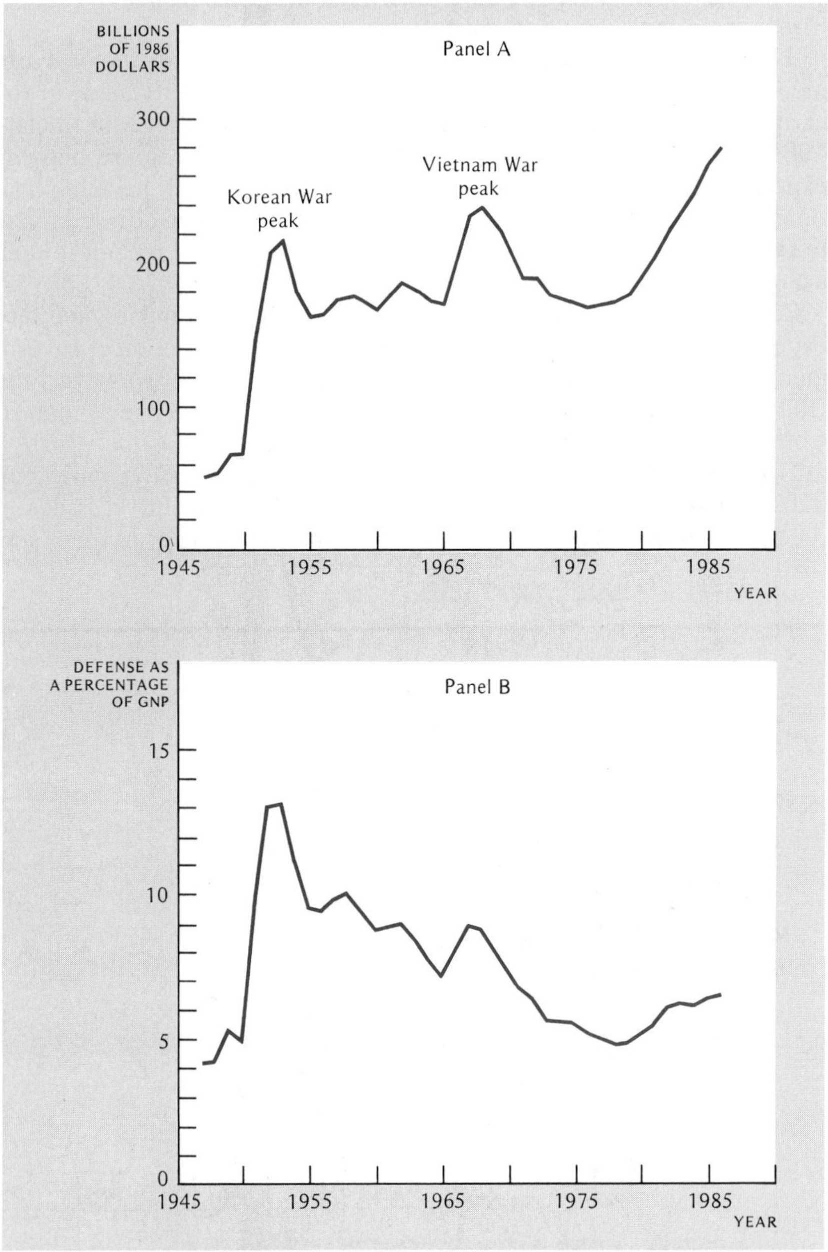

12.1 U.S. DEFENSE EXPENDITURES Panel A shows national expenditures on defense in constant 1986 prices (using GNP deflator). Panel B shows defense expenditures as a percentage of GNP. SOURCE: *National Income and Product Accounts, 1929-1982,* Tables 1.1, 3.15; *Survey of Current Business,* July 1987, Tables 1.1, 3.15.

tion, but as a percentage of GNP they were still smaller than during the Eisenhower and Kennedy administrations.

Because a large fraction of military expenditures is for the procurement of new defense weapons systems, the commitments made in the early 1980s will have implications for defense expenditures in the late 1980s. And because these new military systems will require ongoing expenditures in maintenance and in personnel, they will have implications for defense budgets into the 1990s. Even if it were decided today to reduce military expenditures, it might take several years before such a changed policy could have significant effects.

Compared to spending by most other Western countries, military expenditures in the United States are large, both as a fraction of government expenditures and as a fraction of national income. However, the United States percentage is not large relative to the Soviet Union or China, as Figure 12.2 demonstrates.

The issue of whether we are spending enough (or too much) on defense has been one of the most hotly contested political issues in recent years. A 1985 Gallup poll showed that 46 percent of those sur-

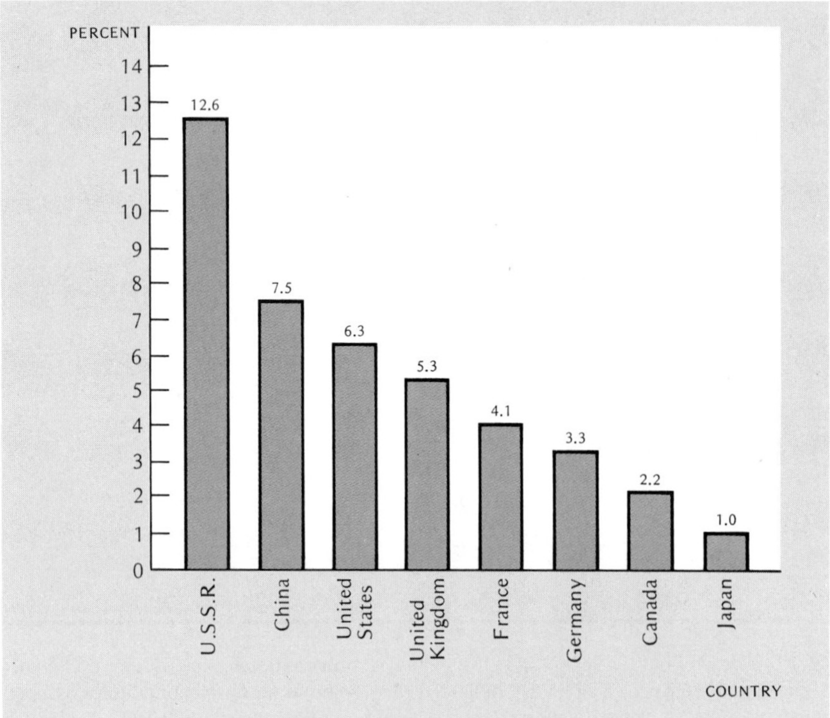

12.2 MILITARY EXPENDITURE AS A PERCENTAGE OF GNP, 1984 SOURCE: U.S. Arms Control and Disarmament Agency, *World Military Expenditures and Arms Transfers, 1986,* Table 1.

veyed thought we were spending too much on defense, the highest level of support for reduced spending since 1971, when 50 percent thought it excessive. There are also controversies about whether we are allocating our defense dollars in the best way possible. There have been frequent accusations of inefficiency against the military.

Defense is one of the few examples of a pure public good. In our discussion of the theory of public goods, we suggested that we could decide on how much should be spent on some public good simply by asking individuals for their marginal willingness to pay, how much extra benefit they get out of additional expenditures on a particular public program. Unfortunately, this will not do for defense. Most of us simply do not know how much more protection we buy by spending an extra dollar on defense. We rely on military experts for an assessment of the benefits yielded by further expenditures. But the experts have a natural bias in favor of increased expenditures for the services for which they are responsible.

We rely on experts for judgments concerning the costs of a particular program (say, for a weapons system), for judgments concerning what the program, if successful, would do, and for judgments concerning the responses of others (the Russians) to any action we take. Of course, even if the experts could provide a reliable estimate of the number of lives a particular program would save in a particular contingency, and a reliable estimate of the likelihood of different contingencies, it would not be sufficient to provide a quantitative assessment of the value of a program: we have to know how to place a monetary value on lives. Even if one is not loath to do this, it is at best hard to come up with a number upon which there is widespread agreement. And, the survival of our nation and our way of life are at stake; the difficulties of assigning monetary values to these should be obvious.

Still, economics has an important contribution to make to the analysis of defense expenditures. We discuss three sets of issues here. We first discuss the organization of our defense expenditures, how decisions are made and goods and services are procured; we next discuss cost-effectiveness analysis, how different programs aimed at similar objectives can be compared. We conclude the chapter with some remarks on the most difficult question of all: how do we decide how much defense expenditure is enough?

THE ORGANIZATION OF DEFENSE

Those responsible for decisions concerning military expenditures and how the government obtains the goods and services it needs have an important effect on the efficiency with which defense dollars are spent. In this section we address three questions:

What should be the role of civilian versus military experts in shaping defense policy?

How have military procurement practices contributed to inefficiency?

How should the military obtain the personnel it needs?

Civilian Control

There has been a continuing controversy over the extent to which there should be civilian involvement in military decision making.

Several arguments have been put forth in support of greater civilian control. The first is that each branch of the armed forces seems to pursue its own interests. The navy may place greater emphasis on obtaining more aircraft carriers than on obtaining transport ships (the primary benefit of which is to make the army more effective).

Even within each of the forces, established interests may resist new developments that detract from their power. For instance, though the navy recognized the value of Polaris missiles, many of the admirals were afraid that an increased expenditure on Polaris missiles would decrease other naval expenditures, and this initially led them to have limited enthusiasm for the new system. It was Secretary of Defense Robert McNamara who pushed for an increase in the rate of delivery of Polaris missiles, from three to ten Polaris submarines a year.

The limited coordination between the services has often worked to the detriment of the United States. A famous example of this occurred during the Spanish-American War. The capture of Santiago was delayed four weeks because the army commander, General Shafter, and the naval commander, Admiral Sampson, could not agree on a joint plan of action.[2] In more recent years, failure of the navy and air force to agree on specifications for new aircraft has led to greatly increased costs.

Though the Joint Chiefs of Staff, consisting of a representative from each of the services, attempt to overcome these problems through coordination, they have had limited success. Each of the chiefs feels loyalty toward his own service. General LeMay, while chairman of the Joint Chiefs of Staff, put it this way in testimony before Congress: "I make no claim to objectivity. It is well known that I am partial to air power as a defensive arm of our country. However, I have been and shall continue to be as fair to the other services as my experience will permit."[3]

The staff of the Joint Chiefs has the further problem that upon the completion of the term of service with the Joint Chiefs, they return to the service from which they came. Their chances of promotion undoubtedly depend to some extent on how well they have served their own service.

Thus, the advocates of civilian control believe that only a strong Secretary of Defense can perform the vital role of objectively evaluating the merits of alternative requests for funds. Those who oppose civilian con-

[2] See F. E. Chadwick, *Relations of U.S. and Spain, the Spanish-American War* (New York: Scribner's Sons, 1911).

[3] General Curtis E. LeMay, *America Is in Danger* (New York: Funk and Wagnalls, 1968), p. xii.

trol believe that civilians lack the expertise and experience with which to make such military judgments.

Concern about the organization of defense decisions culminated in a new law that took effect on October 1, 1986, giving the Chairman of the Joint Chiefs of Staff greater power, and making him the principal military adviser to the President, the Secretary of Defense, and the National Security Council. The new law attempted to reduce duplication among the military services and to give more authority to the commanders of the field forces. Previously, army, navy, marine, and air force commanders reported to the chiefs of each of their own services on administrative and budget matters and to the field commander on war plans and operations.

Though the reorganization has far from ended bureaucratic squabbles —Reagan's Secretary of Defense, Caspar Weinberger, for instance, attempted to insist that the Chairman (Admiral William J. Crowe, Jr.) only provide advice to the National Security Council through him, while the Secretary of State, George Schultz, a member of the National Security Council, insisted he had the right to receive the Chairman's advice directly—it holds the prospect for better, more coordinated decision making.

Defense Procurement

As we noted in Chapter 7, the Defense Department purchases a large fraction of its goods from private contractors. Most of these purchases are not made in a conventional competitive market, in which there are many suppliers and many buyers. There is one large buyer—the United States government. There are a few (and often only a few) potential suppliers: for aircraft, for instance, Lockheed, Boeing, and McDonnell-Douglas compete against each other.

To ensure that it obtains the best price, the government usually resorts to competitive bidding; different contractors tell the government the price at which they are willing to deliver, say 1,000 tanks of a given specification, and the government purchases the tanks from the lowest bidder. Frequently, however, there are major **cost overruns**—that is, the costs exceed what the producer originally estimated these costs to be. Sometimes the contract between the government calls for these costs to be shared by the government and the private contractor; such contracts are called **cost-sharing contracts.** Even when the contract does not explicitly call for sharing the costs of the overrun, the government may absorb all or a significant fraction of the additional costs. The contractor may claim that the cost overruns are a result of changes in the design specification; such changes almost always accompany the development of a new weapon, particularly when the development occurs over a period of several years, and it is frequently difficult to ascertain the extent to which the cost overruns are in fact a result of the design changes. In other cases, the private contractor simply says that he cannot complete the contract without further funds; the government then has the choice of losing all that it has already spent or negotiating a settlement with the contractor. And even if the government were to sue the contractor for breach of contract, the delays in the development and deployment of the weapons could be very costly.

The military has been greatly criticized for its procurement procedures. The prevalence of cost overruns means the public, or its representatives in Congress, seldom has an accurate view of the cost of a ship, a defense system, a tank, etc., at the time it makes a commitment to purchase them. It also means that the government seldom knows whether it has, in fact, let out the contract to the lowest-cost producer;[4] all that it knows is that it let out the contract to the firm that bid the lowest.

What are the reasons for these cost overruns? In the case of new weapons, errors in estimating costs are common. But why should there be a bias in these errors? That is, why should there be a systematic tendency to underestimate the costs? Part of the reason has to do with the competitive bidding process; potential contractors know that they have to produce a low bid to win. The system of cost sharing (implicit or explicit) means that there is relatively little penalty associated with bidding too low. There is, however, a penalty associated with bidding too high, particularly when other firms are bidding low (using, say, their most optimistic estimates of costs): the high-bidding firm will fail to get the contract. Moreover, most of the technical expertise, the ability to judge the reasonableness of the estimates, resides in those who have a vested interest in the outcome—the defense contractors who are bidding and the military officers who would like to have the best possible defense system for their service branch.

The system of cost sharing has a further disadvantage in addition to reducing the penalty for under-bidding: the winner of the contract has little incentive to be efficient. Indeed, some contracts are of a cost-plus form; that is, the government pays whatever it costs to develop the weapons plus, say, 10 percent. Such contracts provide incentives to be inefficient; the more the firm spends, the more it gets from the government.

Why does the government engage in cost-sharing contracts, with all their obvious disadvantages? Why, even when there are not explicit provisions for cost sharing, does the government agree to pay at least part of the cost overruns?

Part of the reason for cost sharing is the uncertainty inherent in the development of a new weapons system. The best that a firm can do, as we have said, is to provide an estimate of these costs. If there were a **fixed-fee contract** (a contract where the contractor got paid a fixed amount, regardless of the eventual cost), the contractor would have to

[4] Notice that at the time the cost overruns occur, what limited competition there was before the contract was let no longer exists: it would, in general, be costly or impossible for the government at that point to turn to other potential suppliers.

bear considerable risk; even if he were very efficient, there is some chance that he would encounter difficulties in the development of the system that would increase his costs way beyond the fixed fee he would receive, in which case he might incur an enormous loss. If firms (or their managers) are *risk-averse* and insist on being compensated for bearing risks, they will all put in high bids, representing their estimate of the actual costs plus a fee for bearing the risk. The government is in a better position to bear the risk. By agreeing to a cost-sharing contract, it absorbs much of the risk, but at the same time it reduces the incentives for efficiency.

Though this provides an important rationale for cost-sharing contracts, some critics of the Pentagon argue that other forces are at work when the government agrees to pay all or part of a cost overrun. A large number of military officers upon their retirement from the armed forces take up positions in private industry, and in particular with defense contractors. Critics say that this provides an incentive for these officers to be accommodating to the requests of the defense contractors.

Supporters of the current system, though admitting that it is far from perfect, point out that there is a healthy level of competition among defense contractors and that this competition provides at least some limit to the extent of inefficiency. Any contractor who performed persistently worse than other firms would find itself having difficulty obtaining contracts.

The Draft versus the Volunteer Army

The government frequently has obtained labor for its military services in a way quite different from that by which other employers obtain labor: it forces young men to serve in the armed forces. Most countries resort to the draft during war, and many countries (for instance, Greece and Switzerland) employ the draft also in peacetime. In the aftermath of the Vietnam War, the draft was abandoned in the United States and an all-volunteer army was established.

The fact that individuals are forced to go into the armed forces means that the salary paid to these individuals is less than the "market" wage for that kind of activity. The draft can thus be viewed as a tax levied on selected individuals in the population. The tax is inequitable and introduces inefficiencies. It is inequitable because it is only levied upon a selected group within the population, able-bodied males between the ages of eighteen and twenty-six. And not all individuals within this group are selected. During the early years of the Vietnam War, individuals could obtain exemptions if they attended school or if they were in certain occupations. There was a strong bias in these exemptions: more sons of the middle class obtained them than those of the poor.

The draft introduced two inefficiencies. For some individuals, the opportunity cost—in terms of foregone wages—of going into the military was much smaller than for others. (That is, their productivity in other occupations was much lower.) Markets serve the important function of allocating workers of different abilities to their most productive uses. The draft does not take into account individuals' opportunity costs. The effective tax on some individuals is thus much higher than on others.

Secondly, the draft may result in the military not taking into account full costs of the alternative programs. Because the draft makes manpower less expensive than it would be if the required high wages were paid to recruit workers, the military may not make the appropriate trade-offs between the use of men and machines.

But those who favor the draft and oppose the volunteer army put forward several arguments. First, they are concerned with the inequities associated with a volunteer army. Since the poor (with limited alternative opportunities) will be attracted into the army, the burden of a war will fall more upon the poor. Holders of this view maintain that certain rights and obligations should not be distributed according to the market place. We referred to this view in the last chapter as *specific egalitarianism*. The duty to fight and risk dying for one's country is one of these obligations.

Secondly, critics of the volunteer army are concerned with the effectiveness of the armed forces. If only those with low opportunity costs serve, the quality of the armed forces is likely to be low. There is an obvious solution to this problem: any employer faces a similar problem and responds by increasing the wage to the point where he has an applicant pool with a sufficiently large number of good applicants that he can obtain the quality he wishes. But if Congress is so shortsighted that it fails to allocate enough funds for military wages, our national defense may suffer from the low quality of personnel.

These concerns about the quality of the military were particularly strong in the early days of the volunteer army, but in recent years (abetted partly by high youth unemployment rates during the early 1980s) the quality of volunteers has increased substantially.

COST-EFFECTIVENESS ANALYSIS

One of the ways by which the Defense Department has attempted to increase the efficiency of how the defense dollar is spent is to employ cost-effectiveness analysis. This entails a detailed comparison of alternative ways of achieving the same objective. Cost-effectiveness analysis was popularized by Robert McNamara, who was Secretary of Defense under presidents Kennedy and Johnson. Many military officers objected to cost-effectiveness analysis because they believed that military judgments concerning the relative merits of alternative defense programs could not be reduced to a simple (or even complicated) set of economic calculations.

One example of cost-effectiveness analysis is provided by economist

William Kaufman, of M.I.T. and the Brookings Institution. The problem he considered was how best to prepare for a Soviet offensive directed simultaneously at central Europe and the Persian Gulf. He estimated that it might be necessary to deliver 800,000 tons of material to the two theaters within thirty days. He also estimated that the current airlift capacity was no more than 200,000 tons. The 1984 budget requested fifty C-5B aircraft at a cost of $6.4 billion. This could increase capacity by about 70,000 tons, leaving a shortfall of 530,000. Kaufman argued that a more cost-effective method of delivering the material would be the construction of fast sealift ships. He calculated that thirty-two such ships, combined with the eight already available, could deliver the full 800,000 requirement within thirty days.[5]

Similarly, there are alternative ways of ensuring a **second-strike capability,** the ability of the United States to retaliate after a surprise attack against us. We could construct a new MX missile system, or we could expand our submarine-based Polaris missile system. For each missile system, we can estimate the number of such missiles that would be destroyed in a first strike by the Soviet Union. We could then calculate the cost—per megaton of second-strike capacity, say—for each alternative. The one that is lower is the more cost-effective.

Multiple Objectives

In many cases, however, a given weapons system serves multiple objectives. The airlift capacity would be of particular value in delivering small amounts of tonnage to a distant theater on short notice. But Kaufman claims "that this is hardly an argument for expanding the current airlift force. The same effect can be achieved by forces deployed in Europe and the Arabian Sea and prepositioned equipment in the two theaters—both of which already exist—combined with current airlift."

A similar issue arose in discussions concerning the air force's proposed B-70 bomber. This was intended to replace the B-52 as the principal United States bomber. Its major mission was to drop nuclear bombs on predesignated targets. McNamara argued that the same objective could be accomplished at less cost by missiles; and indeed, he contended that missiles had certain advantages: they required less time (fifteen to thirty minutes, as opposed to two to three hours) to reach most targets, and the bombers are more vulnerable on the ground than either Minutemen missiles in underground silos or mobile missiles like those in the Polaris submarine.

No two defense systems are ever identical, and proponents of the bombers claimed that they could perform other functions better than the missiles. In particular, the air force generals who advocated the B-70 bomber claimed that the bomber had a reconnaissance potential that

[5] W. W. Kaufman, "The Defense Budget," in J. A. Pechman, *Setting National Priorities* (Washington, D.C.: Brookings Institution, 1983).

missiles did not have. This would enable the more effective destruction of Soviet missiles remaining after our initial strike. Assuming that the B-70 enabled the destruction of all intercontinental ballistic missiles, it would still not be able to destroy the submarine-launched missiles. Thus, from buying the B-70s, the net reduction in deaths would be small: under one set of assumptions (in which the United States struck first) the number of Americans killed would be reduced from between 60 and 90 million to between 45 and 75 million; under another set of assumptions, if the Soviet Union struck first, the number of Americans killed would be reduced from between 80 and 150 million to 70 and 135 million. Thus McNamara claimed that even under the most "favorable" conditions, the B-70 bomber's secondary mission had limited value, not worth the $10 to $15 billion estimated cost.

Alternative Scenarios

These examples illustrate the kind of analysis that is essential in assessing the value of a weapons system. An important part of this analysis involves the consideration of alternative scenarios—e.g., an attack on one front with conventional weapons with some warning, an attack on one front with no warning, an attack on two fronts with conventional weapons, or a nuclear attack. We then attempt to ascertain how, say, a new weapons system or increased expenditure on naval ships would affect the outcomes in each of these scenarios. For instance, we might calculate for a new missile system the additional second-strike capacity (that is, the megatons of deliverable nuclear weapons) we would have after an attack by the Soviet Union. Or we might calculate the additional number of troops that we could deliver overseas in thirty days after the outbreak of a one-front war as a result of purchasing so many air transport planes.

Thus one defense system may be more effective in one scenario, another in another. Spending more (purchasing both systems) may increase our defense capabilities, but that is hardly an answer: we need some assessment of the likelihood of alternative scenarios and the consequences under each of the additional defense expenditures. On the basis of this, one may be able to make some judgments about how much is enough.

Trade-offs in Allocating Defense Dollars

Cost-effectiveness analysis can be used to help ensure that defense dollars are not wasted. But there are many decisions where it is of only limited usefulness. A question that arises repeatedly is how much of our defense budget should be spent in preparation for conventional wars. We can obtain greater protection against conventional attacks (by increasing, say, our expenditures on conventional weapons) at the expense of decreasing our protection against a nuclear attack. For a given amount of resources, we cannot, in general, obtain more of one type of protection without sacrificing some amount of the other kind of protection. Different individuals may prefer different points on this feasibility locus depending on their judgments concerning the likelihood of the two types of wars.

Some Problems in Allocating Defense Expenditures

ENDS VERSUS MEANS

Quite often in defense discussions there is a confusion between ends and means. Acquiring various weapons systems should not be viewed as an end in itself but as a means of attaining certain defense objectives—e.g., the destruction of a certain fraction of the Russian arsenal in the event of a first strike by the Soviet Union. In this calculation, the least expensive missile is not necessarily the most effective. Assume, for instance, that Polaris submarine-based missiles are twice as expensive as land-based missiles but that, in a first strike, 75 percent of the land-based missiles are destroyed, while none of the Polaris missiles are destroyed. In order to have one land missile available after the strike, we need to construct four missiles. Hence, the "effective" cost of the submarine-based missile is half that of the land-based missile.

FULL COST ACCOUNTING

Another error frequently encountered in defense analysis is the failure to account for all the costs of a defense system. These include not only the research and development costs but personnel and the expenditures required to maintain the defense system.

Without this full cost information, it is difficult to make efficient choices. There may be a bias in favor of projects with low capital costs but high maintenance and personnel costs.

TECHNOLOGICALLY DRIVEN INNOVATION

There is a strong desire by many in the military establishment to have the most modern weapons. This appears almost as an end in itself. New defense systems are developed to take advantage of technological breakthroughs, and old weapons may be discarded simply because more advanced weapons systems might be available.

Economists argue that newer equipment is not necessarily more cost-effective. The question of whether or when to phase out old technologies and adopt new ones should be related to the overall objectives of defense. Newer equipment may not be as reliable and may require more maintenance expenditures.

The final question to which we turn—How much should we spend on national defense?—is an even more difficult question to answer than the question of how to allocate a given defense budget.

Are we spending too much on national defense? Spending more money on defense *may* increase the probability of survival in the event of an attack and *may* decrease the likelihood of an attack.

We are concerned here with how to make judgments concerning how much to spend on defense in a systematic way. This is the traditional choice between guns (national defense) and butter (other goods) represented by the production possibilities schedule, as illustrated in Figure 12.3. One can obtain more national defense, but only at the expense of sacrificing other goods. An indifference curve represents combinations of guns and butter that society is indifferent in choosing among. Society is willing to sacrifice some butter for more defense. As we give up more butter, we require larger and larger increments in defense to leave us indifferent. Higher indifference curves (giving more guns and butter) obviously represent higher levels of welfare. The highest level of welfare that is attainable is at point *E*, where the indifference curve is just tangent to the production possibilities schedule.

This is a good way of thinking about the trade-offs that society must face. Unfortunately, it is not very helpful in answering the question of how much is enough. To apply this analysis to defense spending, we have to know how much extra protection we get from increased military spending.

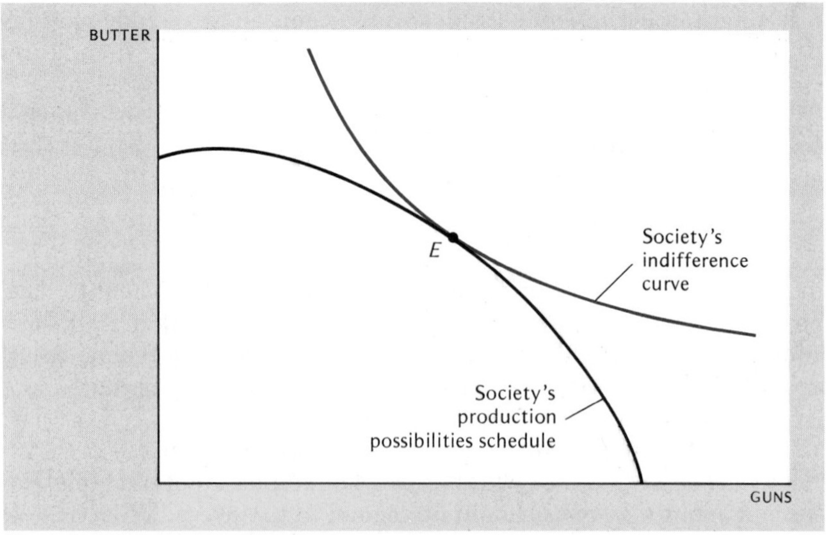

12.3 SOCIETY'S PRODUCTION POSSIBILITIES SCHEDULE Society can only obtain more defense (more guns) by giving up other goods (butter).

The Value of Marginal Analysis

In allocating a *given* defense budget, one needs to consider the effect of the expenditures on various defense objectives. In evaluating whether we should spend more on defense, we similarly need to know how much *extra* "protection" we get from an extra expenditure of $1 billion.

The following example, provided by Charles Hitch, who was Assistant Secretary of Defense in the Kennedy-Johnson administration, illustrates the role of marginal analysis.[6] Assume each missile has a 50 percent probability of success in killing its target. We have 100 targets that we would like to destroy. If we sent 100 missiles at the targets, we would "achieve an expectancy of 50 kills, 200 missiles—75 kills, 300 missiles —87 kills," as depicted in Figure 12.4. There are clearly very strong diminishing returns. Each target can be destroyed only once, and some of the additional missiles will land on an already destroyed target. While the first 100 missiles give us 50 kills, increasing the number of missiles from 400 to 500 increases the number of kills by only 3. We need to ask

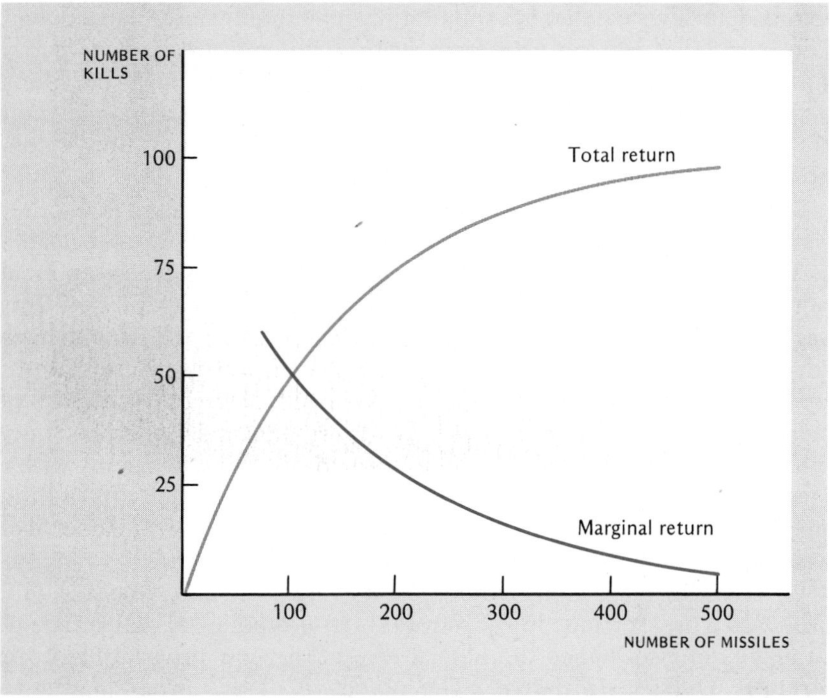

12.4 THE ROLE OF MARGINAL ANALYSIS IN DEFENSE The relevant question is not whether we should have 500 missiles or no missiles, but how many extra kills we get from each additional missile. There may be sharply diminishing returns.

[6] From C. J. Hitch, *Decision Making for Defense* (Berkeley: University of California Press, 1966), pp. 50–51.

ourselves not whether it is worth the cost of 500 missiles to get 97 kills but whether it is worth the cost of 100 additional missiles to get 3 extra kills.

This kind of analysis is not easy. But by relating the expenditures to the objectives, and by showing what one gets from additional expenditures, one can hope to make more rational decisions concerning how much is enough.

In making these assessments, however, one set of considerations is particularly hard to evaluate: deterrence.

Deterrence and the Arms Race

The calculations described above are all made on the basis of a given size of enemy forces (current plus projected increases). But an essential aspect of defense analysis is that the behavior of our enemies is affected by our military expenditures, in two important ways. First, if we spend more, then they are likely to spend more; the net gain in our advantage cannot be calculated assuming that they do not respond at all. It is even possible that increased expenditures result in our net advantage being reduced: for every dollar we spend, they may spend more than a dollar. The belief that we can gain from further expenditures is thus partly based on the assumption that the Soviet Union will not be able or willing to fully match our expenditures. This is, of course, debatable: while their national income is much smaller than ours, their ability to suppress consumption of their citizens is greater than ours.

But there is also the belief that the Soviets will be affected in another way by our military strength: they will be less likely to undertake hostile actions. Thus the probabilities of the different scenarios, a conventional war or a nuclear war, will be affected by our military capabilities. This has played an important role in recent military debates. Those who have advocated increased military spending have argued that an enhanced second-strike capability reduces the likelihood of an attack. Critics of increased military spending have argued that once one has assured oneself of a very high probability of effectively destroying the enemy with a second-strike capability, further increments to that capacity have little additional deterrent value; they believe that given our current arsenal of weapons, further increments have little value.

President Reagan, in his famous "Star Wars" speech in March 1983, proposed a basic change in U.S. strategy, from a policy of deterrence to strategic defense (hence the official title of the new program, **SDI**, or **Strategic Defense Initiative**). The objective of this program was to develop weapons systems that would protect against a nuclear attack, thus rendering nuclear weapons "impotent and obsolete." As one commentator put it, "the promise of 'assured survival' would displace the threat of 'assured destruction.'"[7] Whether it is feasible to develop such a

[7] Joshua M. Epstein, *The 1987 Defense Budget* (Washington, D.C.: The Brookings Institution, 1986), p. 11.

weapons system, or whether hopes of such a system border on science fiction, remains a subject of considerable scientific controversy.

In the meanwhile, there is concern that these increased expenditures might actually increase the likelihood of an attack. Assume Russia believed that in ten years' time, we would have constructed a defensive system that would make us invulnerable, and that they would not be able to develop a corresponding system for another fifteen years. Russia could believe that it would then be in the interests of the United States to attack during the period during which they were vulnerable but we were not. But then, Russia, anticipating this, would have every incentive to launch a preemptive strike, before our defense capacity is put into place.

More positively, some view SDI as part of a long-range bargaining ploy. Russia will try to match the U.S.; because of their fundamentally weaker economy, they will find it difficult to do so, and, it is hoped, this will induce them to bargain for meaningful arms reductions. Partly for this reason, the possibility of such agreed-upon arms reductions has looked more hopeful in recent years. A major step was taken in 1987, when the United States and Russia agreed to withdraw all short- and medium-range missiles from Europe.

Economists have relatively little to say about many of these critical questions on defense strategy. They can analyze "rational" responses, using a technique of analysis called game theory, originally explored by economist Oskar Morgenstern of Princeton and by mathematician John von Neumann, of the Institute of Advanced Studies. But there are no assurances that the Soviet Union will respond rationally to our actions. There are disputes about what motivates the leaders of the Kremlin and what they believe are the intentions of the United States. Recent failures and inconsistencies in U.S. foreign policy make Russia's anticipations of our future actions particularly problematic. It is largely because these responses play such a critical role in the assessment of the benefits that accrue from alternative defense policies that economists have made only a limited contribution to the debate over how much is enough.

SUMMARY

1. Advocates of greater civilian control of the Department of Defense are concerned with the lack of coordination among the services and the biases in decision making that result when excessive reliance is placed on experts with vested interests.
2. In choosing among alternative uses of defense funds, cost-effectiveness analysis is useful in ensuring that the best weapons systems are employed to attain given objectives.
3. Frequently, however, there is a multiplicity of objectives. We need to ascertain the marginal benefit of additional funds spent in different ways assuming different scenarios and different objectives.
4. In evaluating alternative weapons systems, it is important not to confuse means with ends and to take full account of the long-run costs (including maintenance and personnel) associated with each weapons system.

5. The procurement systems often employed by the military entailing cost-plus contracts may have contributed significantly to high costs.
6. The draft can be viewed as a selectively imposed tax. Though there are both equity and efficiency arguments in favor of the volunteer army, there are some who believe that a volunteer army is inequitable.
7. In evaluating alternative defense programs, it is important to focus on the extra benefits attained from an extra expenditure—to employ, in other words, marginal analysis.

KEY CONCEPTS

Civilian control	Cost-sharing contracts
Deterrence	Fixed-fee contract
Cost overrun	Full cost accounting

QUESTIONS AND PROBLEMS

1. Assume the government has decided to install a missile system designed to provide a second-strike capability with 100 missiles. It is now considering whether to increase the number to 110. Assume you are on the congressional committee that must approve the increased expenditure. List some of the questions you might ask to ascertain whether the increased expenditures are desirable.
2. Should military officers and defense department officials be proscribed from working for private defense contractors for a period of several years after termination of their governmental service?
3. In what ways is the purchase of a hammer by the military different from the purchase of an MX missile system? How does this affect government procurement policies in these two areas?
4. In what ways is the purchase of a hammer by the military different from the purchase of labor services? How does this affect government procurement policies in these two areas?
5. "The problems of defending our country have become so technical and complex that they should be left to the military experts. The government should simply decide how much it wishes to spend on defense and leave the problem of allocating the expenditures to the military." Discuss.

13

Social Insurance

Although modern governments have long taken some responsibility for providing for the needy, during the past fifty years this has come to be viewed as one of the primary functions of government. In 1986, social insurance and welfare expenditures represented more than one-third of the federal government's budget. But social security differs from most government programs in that it has its own **earmarked** payroll tax. The revenues from this tax go into special trust funds that finance benefit payments. Social security was originally designed to be self-financing, that is, revenues from the payroll tax were intended to cover outlays.

Of the major social insurance programs, by far the largest is Old Age, Survivors', and Disability Insurance (OASDI), enacted in 1935. This is usually referred to as social security and is intended to provide a basic standard of living to the aged, the disabled, and their survivors. As Table 13.1 indicates, in twenty-three years this program has more than tripled in *real* terms, going from 55 billion (in 1986 dollars) in 1963 to 197 billion dollars in 1986. The second largest program, Medicare (technically, social security includes both the Medicare and OASDI programs), provides medical care for the aged and was discussed in detail in Chapter 11. Unemployment insurance, also enacted in 1935, is intended to provide income to individuals during short-term spells of unemployment (as its name suggests). Other social insurance programs include workers' compensation, which provides money to individuals who are injured on the job, disability benefits for veterans, retirement benefits for railroad

Table 13.1 EXPENDITURES IN MAJOR SOCIAL INSURANCE PROGRAMS

	Real Expenditures (billions of 1986 dollars)	
	1963	*1986*
Social Security (OASDI)	55.4	196.9
OASI	51.0	176.1
Disability Insurance	4.5	20.8
Unemployment Insurance	12.0	19.1
Medicare	—	77.4

Source: National Income and Product Accounts 1929–1982, Table 3.15; *Survey of Current Business,* July 1987, Table 3.15.

workers, and funds for coal miners suffering from black lung. Until 1984, government employees were not included in the social security program. There are separate retirement programs for civilian and military employees, which should probably be viewed as deferred compensation rather than as social insurance programs.

In many ways, social insurance programs provide insurance to individuals against particular risks that they face, just as private insurance does. Thus Medicare covers medical expenditures of the aged, just as a private health policy would. Social security is designed to replace a part of the income lost due to retirement or disability; private insurance policies exist that meet the same need. There is one important difference: with private insurance there is a close relationship among the payments of the individual, the risks he faces, and what he receives. Thus the premium for a private health insurance policy depends on factors affecting the health condition of the individual, such as his age. The amount that an individual receives back from an *annuity* (a private insurance policy providing a certain income every year after the individual reaches, say, sixty-five) on average is effectively just what he puts in (plus accumulated interest). This is not true of social insurance. Social insurance programs provide insurance *and* redistribute income. Confusion between these two roles has been a major impediment in the evaluation and reform of social insurance programs. In this chapter we shall discuss the major issues facing the social security (OASDI) insurance program.

THE STRUCTURE OF THE SOCIAL SECURITY SYSTEM

The social security retirement program is the largest government program aimed at providing for the elderly, as illustrated in Figure 13.1. It is financed by a payroll tax that is paid both by employees and their employers. In 1987, the combined tax rate was 14.3 percent on the first $43,800 of income. The base rises as average earnings increase, and the rate is scheduled to rise to 15.3 percent by 1990 (see Table 13.2). According to the law, half the tax is paid by employees and half by their employers; but most economists believe that this is simply a legal fiction.

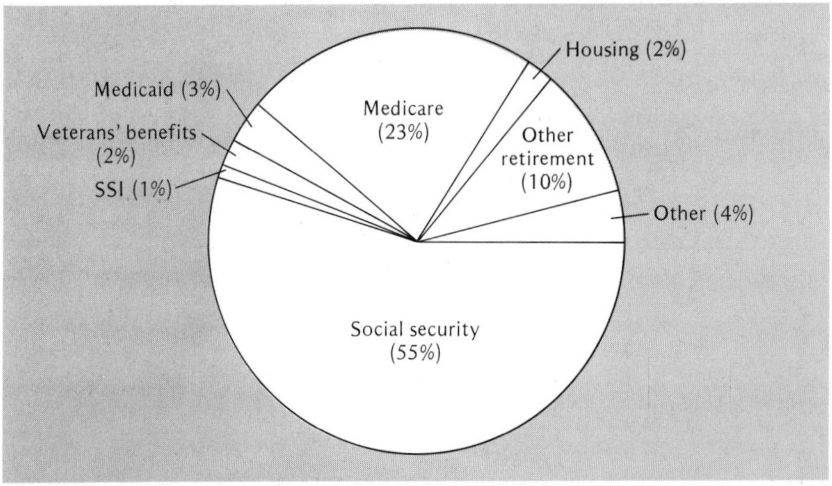

13.1 FEDERAL OUTLAYS BENEFITING THE ELDERLY: FISCAL YEAR, 1985
About 78 percent of federal spending for the elderly is in the form of social security and Medicare benefits. SOURCE: U.S. Senate, Special Committee on Aging, *America in Transition: An Aging Society,* 1984–1985, p. 94.

The consequences of the tax are *essentially the same* as they would be if the individual were responsible for paying all of it. What difference should it make who mails the check to the government?[1]

The system is organized on a **pay-as-you-go basis**; the payroll taxes of those working today pay for the benefits received by the elderly today. By contrast, a pension system in which each age group's pension is supported by its own contributions is called a **fully funded system**. Private pension systems are normally fully funded; while they are working, individuals contribute to a fund that is then used to provide for their pensions in retirement. In any year, of course, the social security system may take in more or less than it pays out. The difference is added to (or taken out of) the social security trust fund. There are separate trust funds for old age and survivors' insurance, for disability insurance, and for Medicare. For the first two decades of its existence, social security revenues exceeded benefits; by 1970, the trust funds amounted to more than $40 billion. But in the past fifteen years, payments have exceeded revenues; by 1983, the **OASDI** fund was essentially depleted, and the Medicare insurance fund was rapidly on its way to depletion. Legislative changes in 1983 attempted to put social security back on a sound financial footing. Whether it succeeded will depend on the accuracy of its

[1] Employers are concerned only with their total labor costs, including any employment taxes; employees are concerned only with their net after-tax income. The government's revenue is simply the difference between the two, and it makes little difference who the government says is paying the tax. For a more extensive discussion, see Chapter 17.

Table 13.2 SOCIAL SECURITY TAX RATES AND BASE HAVE INCREASED RAPIDLY OVER THE PAST FIFTY YEARS

Employers and employees each pay these taxes. Tax rates include the OASDI tax as well as the Medicare tax (5.7 percent and 1.45 percent, respectively, in 1987, summing to the tax rate of 7.15 percent shown).

	Maximum Annual Taxable Earnings	*Tax Rate for Employer and Employee, Each*	*Maximum Tax Payment by Employer and Employee, Each*
1937	$ 3,000	1.0%	$ 30.00
1950	3,000	1.5	45.00
1951	3,600	1.5	54.00
1954	3,600	2.0	72.00
1955	4,200	2.0	84.00
1957	4,200	2.25	94.50
1959	4,800	2.5	120.00
1960	4,800	3.0	144.00
1962	4,800	3.125	150.00
1963	4,800	3.625	174.00
1966	6,600	4.2	277.20
1967	6,600	4.4	290.40
1968	7,800	4.4	343.20
1969	7,800	4.8	374.40
1970	7,800	4.8	374.40
1971	7,800	5.2	405.60
1972	9,000	5.2	468.00
1973	10,800	5.85	631.80
1974	13,200	5.85	772.20
1975	14,100	5.85	824.85
1976	15,300	5.85	895.05
1977	16,500	5.85	965.25
1978	17,700	6.05	1,070.85
1979	22,900	6.13	1,403.77
1980	25,900	6.13	1,587.67
1981	29,700	6.65	1,975.05
1982	32,400	6.7	2,170.80
1983	35,700	6.7	2,391.90
1984	37,800	7.0	2,646.00
1985	39,600	7.05	2,791.80
1986	42,000	7.15	3,003.00
1987	43,800	7.15	3,131.70
1988–89	*	7.51	*
1990–99	*	7.65	*
2000 & later	*	7.65	*

* The maximum taxable earnings will automatically increase with growth in average wages.
Source: Social Security Bulletin, Annual Statistical Supplement, 1986, pp. 24, 27.

projections of future wage increases and employment growth; if its projections are correct, then OASDI funds (taken together) are projected to remain in balance over the next fifty to seventy-five years.[2]

[2] H. Ballantyne, "Actuarial Status of the OASI and DI Trust Funds," *Social Security Bulletin,* July 1986, p. 5.

It should be emphasized that the trust fund is not like pension funds. With a private pension fund, the employer is supposed to set aside enough money while the worker is working to pay the benefits that have been promised. On the other hand, with social security, current benefits are financed by the current social security (payroll) taxes, plus any surplus of revenues over benefits in previous years, which have been accumulated in the trust fund. The trust fund is simply a buffer stock, to ensure, for instance, that if the economy went into a recession, causing revenues to decline, the system would still be able to meet its obligations.

Individuals are eligible to receive benefits at the age of sixty-two. However, if they wait to retire until sixty-five, they receive a higher payment. Payments are not increased if retirement is postponed beyond sixty-five. The amount of payments depends on the contributions of the individual; in general, the greater the contributions, the greater the receipts, although the relationship is a complicated one.[3]

The concept of **replacement rates** is sometimes used to assess the magnitude of social security benefits. The replacement rate is defined as the *ratio* of the social security benefit to pre-retirement income. A replacement rate of unity means that an individual who retires would suffer no loss in income, assuming there were no private pensions. Replacement rates in 1983 were close to one (and in some cases exceeded 1) for low-income workers with an uninsured spouse, but were much less than unity for high-income workers, as Table 13.3 shows.

The amount of payments also depend on the number of dependents of the worker. For instance, an individual with average yearly earnings of $8,000 who retired at age sixty-five in 1965 would receive a monthly social security check of $480 if he was single, but if he had a wife who had never worked, he would receive $720, or 50 percent more.[4]

Table 13.3 REPLACEMENT RATES, 1983

Earnings Each Year	*Unmarried Worker*	*Worker with Uninsured Spouse Aged Sixty-Five*
Half-time Minimum Wage	.9	1.35
Full-time Minimum Wage	.63	.95
Average Covered Earnings	.46	.69
Maximum Taxable Earnings	.26	.39

Source: L. H. Thompson, "Social Security Reform Debate," p. 1429. Data describe a sixty-five-year-old worker retiring in 1985.

[3] However under the 1983 law, benefits of those who retire between sixty-five and seventy will gradually rise, so that by the year 2000, the present discounted value of benefits for a retiree will be the same regardless of the age of retirement. (For a definition of present discounted value, see Chapter 10.)

[4] For workers who reached sixty-five in 1988, the basic benefit was 90 percent of the first $280 of the worker's average indexed monthly earnings (AIME), plus 32 percent of AIME between $280 and $1,691, plus 15 percent of AIME over $1,691. For individuals who reach age sixty-two after 1990, to be eligible for full benefits of OASDI, an individual must have worked at least ten years. Fewer years of work are required for individuals who were born earlier.

Originally, the social security system covered only a fraction of the working population, with agricultural workers, the self-employed, government employees, and employees of nonprofit institutions excluded. Over the years, the coverage has been extended so that today, the only employees not covered are federal employees hired before 1984 and a few categories of employees of state and local governments.

Until 1983, social security payments were tax-exempt. Now, 50 percent of the benefits are taxable for individuals with more than a $25,000 income (or married couples with an income in excess of $32,000). The tax proceeds flow into the social security trust funds.

The growth of the system can be represented in several different ways. The number of beneficiaries of Old Age and Survivors' Insurance has increased from 3.5 million in 1950 to 33.2 million in 1985; this is a reflection of the general increase in population, of an increased proportion of elderly people within the population, of earlier retirements by the elderly, and of the broadening coverage. The number of beneficiaries of disability insurance increased from less than 1 million in 1960 to 4.7 million in 1980, though tighter eligibility standards reduced the number to 4 million in 1985.

While the beneficiaries of OASDI increased ten-fold in thirty-five years, the benefits increased *forty-fold* in real terms, from less than $5 billion in 1950 (in 1985 dollars) to $183.3 billion in 1985.

There has been a concomitant increase in taxes. As shown in Table 13.2, employers and employees together paid a maximum amount of tax of just $60 per worker in 1937, which is equivalent to $620 in 1987 dollars. By 1987, the maximum tax payment had risen ten-fold, to $6,263. Since Medicare was enacted in President Johnson's administration, a small part of the social security tax (currently one-fifth of it) has gone to pay for Medicare.

SOCIAL SECURITY, PRIVATE INSURANCE, AND MARKET FAILURES

Prior to 1935, private markets provided life insurance but not retirement insurance. Few firms provided much in the way of pensions.

The Great Depression caused a crisis: there were many aged thrown out of work who had little prospect of being rehired and no means of support. The social security system was intended to ensure that all of the aged had at least a minimal level of support.

In the past thirty-five years, however, there have been marked improvements in private markets. Pension coverage expanded rapidly in the 1950s when large manufacturers adopted pension plans. While in 1950, only twenty-five percent of nonagricultural workers in the private sector were covered by private pensions, by 1979, 55 percent were covered. In the early 1980s, pension coverage declined to 50 percent as the number of jobs in manufacturing declined and the poorly covered service sector grew.[5] The government has taken steps to ensure the financial soundness of private pension programs.[6] But these private insurance policies still are deficient in several respects.

High Transaction Costs

To provide for their retirement, individuals can purchase **annuities** from private firms. Annuities pay a fixed amount every month from some age (usually sixty-five or seventy) until the individual dies, no matter how long he or she lives. Under most private annuity programs, however, the expected rate of return obtained does not appear to be very good—far lower than market rates of interest. This is partly because of high administrative costs (including in many cases substantial commissions for the salespeople). While administrative costs for social security are less than 2 percent of benefits paid, private insurance companies spend one dollar in administrative costs, dividends (profits), and taxes for every two dollars in benefits paid.[7] The trade-offs between reducing costs and increasing the scope for individual choice are clear: it is administratively less expensive to provide a uniform retirement program for all individuals than to have a large number of competing programs available, among which the individuals can choose. So long, however, as the level of retirement benefits is relatively low, few individuals are being forced to save more for retirement than they would like; hence, there is no significant welfare loss from the provision of a reasonably low level of benefits. This argument does not hold, however, if the retirement benefits are substantial.

Lack of Indexing: The Inability of Private Markets to Insure Social Risks

A major difference between private insurance policies and the social security program is that social security benefits are indexed; they increase with inflation. The closest private policies have come to indexed benefits are annuities whose benefits were linked with the performance of the stock market. When these insurance policies were introduced, it was thought that they would provide a hedge against inflation; the stock market would go up with prices in general. As it has turned out, however, between 1974 and 1982 the stock market failed to keep pace with inflation.

[5] *The Pension Gamble: Who Wins? Who Loses?*, Hearings before the Special Committee on Aging, U.S. Senate, 99th Congress, First Session, Serial no. 99–5, June 14, 1985, pp. 85, 126.

[6] The government not only regulates private pensions but provides insurance to ensure that workers receive the promised pensions. A number of large defaults on the private pension schemes have threatened the financial viability of the federal insurance program. The program run by the U.S. Pension Guaranty Corporation had a deficit of $1.3 billion in 1985.

[7] Charles T. Goodsell, *The Case for Bureaucracy* (Chatham, N.J.: Chatham House Publishers, 1983), p. 52.

The risks of inflation are an example of an important class of risks referred to as **social risks.** These are risks that society as a whole faces. It is difficult for any private insurance firm to bear such risks. Aside from exceptional circumstances such as war, the deaths of different individuals are "independent" events. The firm that insures a large number of individuals can predict fairly accurately the number of individuals that will die each year. But if there is a war, the number may be much larger. Thus, most insurance policies exclude the coverage of death in a war. Similarly, if a policy insured against inflation, it would find that if the inflation rate increased much faster than it had expected, it would bear a loss on all of its policies; it might well find that it was not able to meet all these commitments at the same time. As a result, there is no market for insurance against inflation.

There are two major distinctions between the ability of the government and that of private firms to provide insurance for social risks. First, the government is in a position to meet its obligations by raising taxes. Secondly, the government can engage in risk sharing across generations. The costs of a war, for instance, can be shared by the current generation and future generations; through reducing investment during the period of war and through subsequently imposing taxes on the young for the benefit of the old, the costs of the war can effectively be shared by the generation that is working during the period of war and by subsequent generations. If the economy experiences a particularly bad episode of inflation this decade, it can transfer some of the burden of that onto younger, working generations.

As important as intergenerational risk sharing may be in practice, it has provided little of the official rationale for social insurance programs.

Adverse Selection, Differential Risks, and the Cost of Insurance

A third major problem with private insurance arises from the fact that different individuals have different life expectancies. Consider life insurance, which provides a fixed payment to the insured person's survivors after his death. (Thus, life insurance is actually death or survivors' insurance.) A firm selling a life insurance policy does not want to insure people who are likely to die; if it knows that they are likely to die, it will insist on charging a high premium. For someone over the age of sixty-five or someone with a heart condition, these premiums may be particularly high. On the other hand, for private insurance firms selling an annuity, the concern is just the opposite: they only want to insure people who are unhealthy, who are likely to die soon. Since women live longer than men, insurance companies in the past charged women lower life insurance premiums but higher premiums for annuities.

To the extent that differences in individuals' life expectancies can easily be identified, economic efficiency requires that private insurance firms will have to charge premiums reflecting them. There are those who believe that this is unfair: if someone is unlucky enough to have bad health, it is bad enough, but to charge him a higher premium for his life insurance is adding insult to injury.

If private insurance firms cannot discriminate among individuals of different risks, quite another problem arises. In competitive equilibrium, the premiums must reflect the *average* risk of those who purchase the policy (for life insurance or annuity, this corresponds to the average life expectancy). But this means that good risks are in effect subsidizing the poor risks. With annuities, those who die young subsidize those who live a long time; with life insurance, those who live a long time subsidize those who die young. This means, in turn, that good risks, on average, get back less from the insurance company than they put in. To them, insurance is a bad gamble. But if such individuals are not very risk-averse, they will not buy insurance. When the best risks no longer purchase insurance, the premiums must increase. This process, by which only the worst risks purchase private insurance, is called **adverse selection**.[8] Adverse selection may provide part of the explanation for high premiums charged for annuities. The government, however, can force all individuals to purchase the insurance, and thus avoid the problem of adverse selection. In doing so, it is engaging in some redistribution; good risks are paying more than they "ought to"; bad risks less than they "should."

Moral Hazard and Social Security

There is another reason why private insurance firms often offer only limited insurance. Insurance may reduce the individual's incentive to avoid the insured-for event; we referred to this as **moral hazard** in Chapter 11.

Individuals, in contemplating making provisions for their eventual retirement, face two important sources of risk.[9] The first is that they do not know how long they might live after retirement. An individual who did not buy an annuity would have to husband his resources carefully; he would have to worry about the possibility that he will live longer than average. In insuring this risk, no significant moral-hazard problem arises. But a moral-hazard problem does arise in the second risk, for which social security provides insurance: individuals do not know how well they will be able to work at the age of sixty-two or sixty-five or seventy. Some individuals are healthy and their skills have not become obsolete; they continue to work well beyond seventy. Others are incapable of working; they become disabled. But many individuals are in an in-between state at sixty-two or sixty-five; they are not medically disabled, but they are finding it increasingly difficult, or less enjoyable, or less productive, to work. When they are younger, individuals like to pur-

[8] For a more extended analysis of the effects of adverse selection in insurance markets, see M. Rothschild and J. E. Stiglitz, "Equilibrium in Competitive Insurance Markets," *Quarterly Journal of Economics* 90 (1976): 629–50.

[9] Other than the risk of inflation, which we have already discussed.

chase insurance against the possibility that they will fall in this gray area, not so disabled as to qualify for a medical disability but not so well that they can easily continue working. Social security provides that insurance: it enables an individual who wishes to retire at sixty-two to do so. But the better the "insurance"—the larger the fraction of working income that social security replaces—the weaker the incentive to work; with full replacement, even an individual who is in perfect health and is highly productive might be induced to retire. This is the central moral-hazard problem associated with social security.

The failure of the private market to provide complete insurance should not be viewed as a capricious consequence of rapacious insurance companies trying to exploit the hapless consumer, but rather as a rational response to a critical economic problem, of providing at least some incentives to the insured. To the extent that this provides an explanation of the limitations of insurance provided by the private market, there is no reason to believe that the government can do any better: the trade-offs between risk reduction and incentives remain the same. In other words, concerns about the moral-hazard problem provide a limitation on the extent of insurance that can or should be provided, privately or publicly.

Retirement Insurance as a Merit Good

Even where there are good insurance markets, there remains a rationale for government action: if society believes that it cannot countenance an older individual suffering because he has failed to make adequate provision for his retirement years, and if a number of individuals fail to make adequate provision for their retirement on their own, there is an argument for *compelling* individuals to do so. For those who do make provision for their retirement may feel that it is unfair that they should have to bear the burden of those who could have made adequate provision for their retirement but simply had insufficient foresight to do so. In this view, retirement insurance (and life insurance) are merit goods that a paternalistic government forces on the individual for his own good. But they are different from many other merit goods, because much of the costs of the individual's failure to purchase the good are borne by others. However, to the extent that this provides the rationale for social insurance, it suggests only that the government should require individuals to obtain insurance, not that the government should require that individuals purchase the insurance from the government itself.

PROBLEMS FACING THE SOCIAL SECURITY SYSTEM

In 1983 the social security system was in a crisis, for the second time in five years. The program was running out of funds. The trust fund reserves that had been accumulated were virtually depleted, and anticipated revenues could not cover expected outlays. Though there was a short-term problem, the long-term problems were even greater. The long-term deficit—the difference between expected revenues and expected benefits—was according to some estimates well over one trillion dollars.[10] One pessimistic projection suggested that to cover current commitments for social security and health benefits would necessitate raising the payroll tax to 48 percent, while even optimistic projections suggested that the tax rate would have to be increased to 18 percent.[11]

There were three possible solutions: social security taxes could be increased, its benefits could be reduced, or funding from general tax revenues could be directed to finance the social security system. All three prospects seemed unattractive. To reduce benefits seemed unfair to those who were counting on social security for their retirement; it was as if the government was reneging on a promise. Social security taxes were already scheduled to increase, and further increases seemed politically unpalatable. Using general tax revenues was opposed by many in principle and as a practical matter did not help much, since there already was a large budget deficit that had to be dealt with. Ronald Reagan appointed a presidential commission, headed by the former chairman of the Council of Economic Advisers, Alan Greenspan, to offer a set of recommendations to solve the problem. Before we turn to these, let us first examine the causes of the problem.

The Causes of the 1983 Crisis in Social Security

Because the social security program is funded on a pay-as-you-go basis, the financial viability of the system depends on the ratio of those working to those retired. During the past twenty-five years, there have been three marked changes. First, life span has increased. Those who reached age sixty-five in 1930 could expect to live to age seventy-seven; by 1950 women could expect to live to age eighty-eight while men could expect to live to age eighty-one. Second, birth rates have fallen; the average woman now has fewer than two children. Finally, labor force participation of men over sixty-five (the percentage of those who work) has dropped dramatically, from 45 percent in 1950 to 20 percent in 1980.

The consequences of these changes, as Figure 13.2 shows, is a marked increase in the fraction of the population sixty-five and over, from less than 7 percent when social security was enacted, to 12 percent today; and the ratio is expected to increase to more than 20 percent within fifty years. Even more marked has been the change in the ratio of those working to social security beneficiaries. Figure 13.3 shows how it has

[10] This was about the size, at the time, of the entire privately held national debt. The estimate depended on a number of assumptions concerning the rate of interest, productivity changes, and demographic (that is, population) changes, as we shall see below. The Social Security Administration provided a range of estimates. Under alternative assumptions, the deficit was projected to be even larger. For a discussion of the alternative assumptions, see L. H. Thompson, "The Social Security Reform Debate," *Journal of Economic Literature*, December 1983, pp. 1425–67.

[11] Michael Boskin, *The Social Security System* (New York: Twentieth Century Fund, 1984).

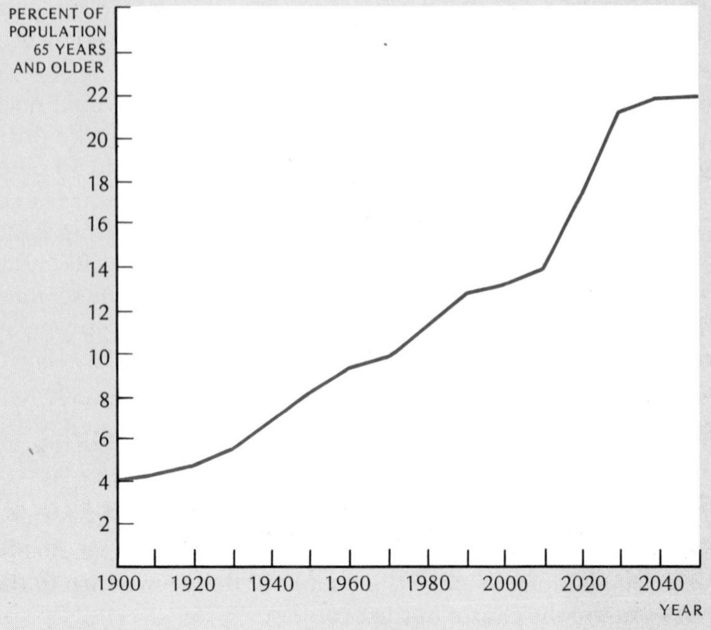

13.2 GROWTH OF THE OLDER POPULATION, ACTUAL AND PROJECTED
SOURCE: U.S. Senate, Special Commitee on Aging, *America in Transition: An Aging Society, 1984–1985*, p. 11.

declined from 16.5 in 1950 to slightly more than 3 today; further declines to 2 are expected over the next fifty years.

There is another important determinant of the viability of the system. The payments to the old are related to their wages. They increase with inflation. If the wages of the young (adjusted for inflation) increase, then their income is larger, relative to the receipts of the beneficiaries. Over the past fifty years, wages have increased faster than inflation, reflecting the continuing rise in productivity. But during the past decade, there has been a slowdown in the rate of increase in productivity, and, correspondingly, real wages have failed to rise.

The future viability of the system depends on whether the trends of recent years are continued. If productivity increases remain low, if birth rates remain low, and if people continue to live longer, then the obligations to those who will retire in twenty-five years will be large relative to income of the working population at that time: the system may be in for trouble.

Though the ratio of social security beneficiaries to those working has increased—and will continue to increase—markedly, the same demographic changes that place a higher burden on the working may make them better able to bear this burden: they will have fewer children to

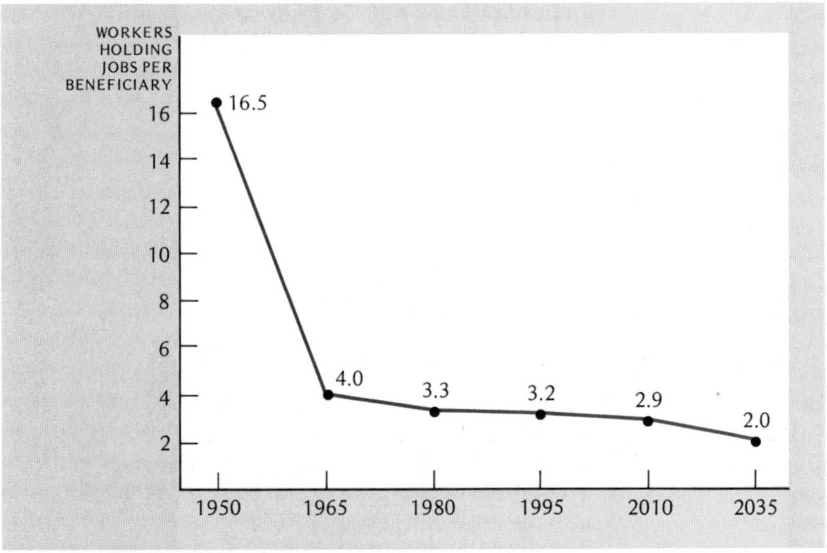

13.3 WORKERS PER SOCIAL SECURITY BENEFICIARY There has been a marked decline in workers per social security beneficiary. SOURCE: *The New York Times,* February 4, 1983.

support.[12] Still, to support the aged may require large increases in the tax rate, and these may have significant (and deleterious) effects on the economy.

The problems facing the United States are similar to those facing many European countries. Indeed, in many European countries, expenditures on social security are not only much larger than in the United States, but they have grown more rapidly, as we see in Figure 13.4. As a result, payroll taxes (earmarked, as in the United States, for social security) are high: 35 percent in the Netherlands and 25 percent in Italy, for instance. There has been increasing concern within these countries about the incentive effects of such high tax rates (particularly when combined with high income tax rates).

The 1983 Response to the Crisis in Social Security

The financial viability of the social security system posed a political dilemma. The solution proposed by the presidential commission headed by Alan Greenspan did not involve a careful balancing out of the trade-offs, either those involving efficiency or equity considerations; rather, it entailed a mixture of "quick fixes" and long-run compromises. The

[12] The net effect is that while in 1960 there were 91.5 individuals either under nineteen or over sixty-five, for every 100 individuals between twenty and sixty-five, by the year 2000 this will be reduced to only 70.5.

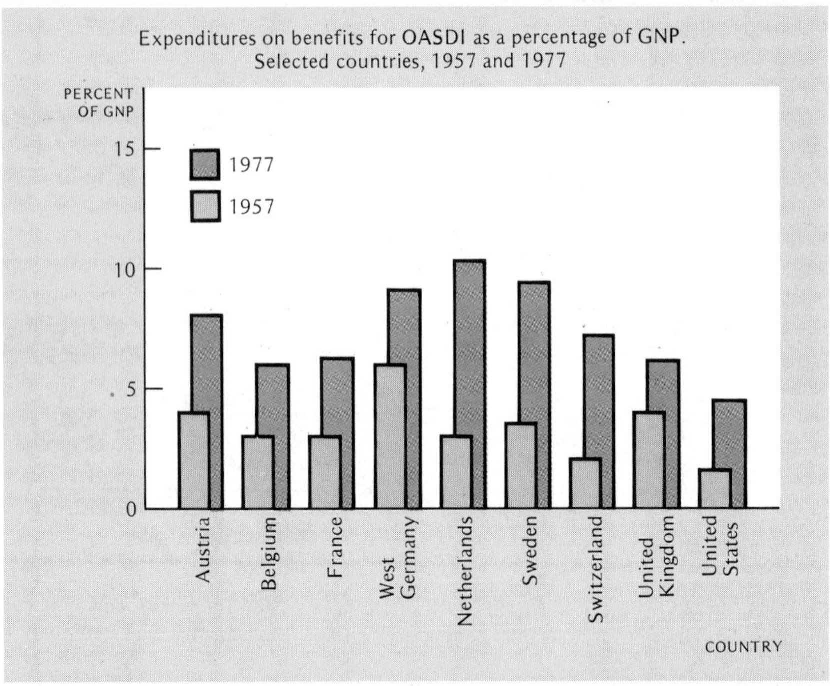

13.4 EXPENDITURES ON BENEFITS FOR OASDI AS A PERCENTAGE OF GNP —SELECTED COUNTRIES, 1957 AND 1977 Expenditures in the U.S. are less (as a fraction of GNP) than in other countries. Data for Belgium and France do not include disability benefits. SOURCE: *Social Security in Europe: The Impact of an Aging Population* (Washington, D.C.: Government Printing Office, 1981).

means by which the short-run problems were alleviated included: postponing a scheduled cost-of-living increase, accelerating scheduled increases in social security taxes, extending social security coverage to new federal employees, and (perhaps most controversial) taxing social security benefits of high-income individuals. The extension of coverage increases revenues more in the short run than in the long run; the effect of such a change on the long run depends on whether these individuals will be getting back more than they are putting in; if they do, then it exacerbates the long-run problem.

In addition, to improve the long-run viability of the system, the retirement age will be raised gradually from sixty-five to sixty-seven.[13] That decision involves two trade-offs. Implicitly, there was a decision concerning the intergenerational distribution of income. It entailed a decision to place the burden of the adjustment on future generations. (Note that even prior to this decision, while current recipients were receiving

[13] Under the 1983 legislation, after the year 2000 retirement benefits will still be available for individuals who retire between the ages of sixty-two and sixty-seven, but there will be a greater benefit reduction for electing to retire early.

a large net transfer from the government, future recipients could expect to pay a large transfer *to* the government over their lifetimes. It is interesting that many younger economists thought this unfair.)

Secondly, it entailed a judgment about the insurance-incentive trade-offs. The individuals who will be particularly disadvantaged by the change in the retirement age are those who find working at sixty-five particularly difficult. The younger generation is, in effect, receiving less insurance against this prospect. On the other hand, this should have the effect of reducing the distortions associated with productive individuals being induced to retire earlier than they otherwise would. Proponents of this change argued that if sixty-five was the appropriate retirement age thirty years ago, then the changes in health—which result in individuals living longer—suggest that today the retirement age should be somewhat higher.

Current Equity Issues in the Design of Social Security

Social security is a combination of a (forced) retirement savings program, an insurance program, and a redistribution program. Looked at simply from the perspective of a savings and insurance program, fairness would dictate that the returns received by different individuals correspond to their contribution. Any insurance program entails, of course, some individuals (those for whom the insured-against event occurs) receiving more than they contribute. Here, in this context, we would expect that those who live longer, or who need to retire earlier, would receive more than they contribute. Fairness here means only that the "expected" receipts for any individual correspond to his contributions.

If one looked at social security from the perspective of a redistribution program, however, one would assume that fairness dictates that there be transfers to those who are less well-off; the poor should get back more than they contribute.

INTERGENERATIONAL EQUITY

The current social security system represents a transfer of resources from the current young to the current old, a transfer for which they may not be subsequently compensated. A single, middle-income male who retired in 1970 can expect to receive, on average, by the time he dies, a net transfer of more than $25,000; for those retiring in 1980, the transfer is estimated to be slightly smaller, $24,000. Those of later generations will pay more than they get back: a single male retiring in the year 2010 will pay over his lifetime $69,000 more than he gets back, and for someone retiring in the year 2020 (someone who is thirty in 1985), the difference *will have increased to $88,000.*[14]

[14] All numbers represent present discounted values, valued in real 1980 dollars, at age sixty-five. See M. Hurd and J. B. Shoven, "The Distributional Impact of Social Security," *National Bureau of Economic Research Working Paper* No. 1155, June 1983. Similar results are reported in M. Boskin, *Too Many Promises: The Uncertain Future of Social Security* (Homewood, IL: Dow Jones, Irwin, 1986).

Social Insurance (Ch. 13)

Is this **intergenerational redistribution** desirable? The question of transferring income from the current working generation to the current elderly entails an analysis of the same issues involved in redistribution at one point in time. During the past fifty years, there has been a marked increase in the standard of living of most Americans. If this continues, a redistribution of income from the current working generation to the current aged is equitable, since the current working generation, over their lifetime, will in any case (even after this distribution) still be better off than the current aged. But during the past ten years there has been a marked slowdown in the rate of productivity growth; in some years there have even been decreases in per capita income. If this more recent pattern continues, the grounds for redistributing income from the current working generation to the current aged are much weaker. The problem is that it is impossible to predict with any reliability what will happen to per capita incomes over the next fifty years.

INTRAGENERATIONAL DISTRIBUTION

A second set of issues concerns the distributive effect of social security *within* a generation. At the present time, all retirees get back considerably more than they put in. One of the objectives of the social security system was to provide a minimal level of income even to the poorest. The social security system has succeeded in greatly reducing poverty for those over sixty-five. Using the standard poverty index, in 1959, 35 percent of those over sixty-five were in poverty; by 1985 this was reduced to 12.6 percent.[15]

The social security system transfers different amounts to aged individuals in different circumstances. The ratio of the amount received to the amount contributed is higher for low-income individuals than for high-income individuals. At the same time, the actual amount transferred—the size of the social security bonanza—is largest for the better off. For married retirees in 1979, the average lifetime transfer (the difference between what they receive and what they contribute) for those in the poorest quarter of the population was $34,042, while for the richest quarter it was one-third greater, almost $46,000.[16] Although all the current retirees have benefited from social security, "to them that have, more shall be given." The ratio of receipts to benefits also differs markedly according to marital status, and whether both the husband and wife worked or only one worked.

A particularly vexing problem in the design of the social security system is the treatment of married versus single individuals. Consider two individuals, Bob and Joe, who had the same income when they worked

[15] *Money, Income, and Poverty Status of Families in the U.S.*, 1983 (Washington, D.C.: U.S. Department of Commerce, Current Population Report Series, P–60, No. 154), p. 22.

[16] All expressed in present discounted value terms.

and thus paid the same amount in social security taxes. Bob is married, but his wife never worked outside the house. Joe is not married. The total amount that Bob will receive is much greater than the amount that Joe will. Why, single individuals ask, should they be asked to support married couples? One proposal for addressing this seeming dilemma, as well as several other of the problems facing social security, is the Personal Security Account.

PERSONAL SECURITY ACCOUNTS

The Personal Security Account proposal was put forward by several prominent young economists, Michael Boskin and John Shoven of Stanford and Laurence Kotlikoff of Boston University, as a way of remedying some of these inequities. We noted earlier that the social security system combines a transfer program and insurance-retirement program. Essentially, their proposal separates these two functions. Each individual would have his own account. The government would provide an inflation-indexed return on tax contributions. The level of insurance benefits would be determined on an actuarial basis that would provide all families with identical rates of return on their contributions. The contributions would be used to purchase five separate categories of insurance policies: (1)old-age benefits for household heads and their spouses; (2)survivor benefits for spouses; (3)survivor benefits for children; (4)disability benefits; and (5)old-age health insurance.[17]

If the benefits of these insurance programs did not provide a retired individual with a level of income considered adequate by society, then they would be supplemented by direct transfers, with amounts based on the individual's circumstances. These transfers would be financed by general tax revenues.

Such a proposal would eliminate the seemingly capricious patterns of transfers that characterize the present social security system. It would also enable the system to be put on a sounder financial footing.

Current Efficiency Issues

Concern has been expressed that the current social security system interferes with economic efficiency in two important ways: it reduces capital formation and it induces early retirement.

SAVINGS

The provision of social security reduces what individuals need to save for their retirement. There is a widespread belief that as a result the national savings rate is lowered. As a result of this reduction in savings, there is less capital formation, and this may have a deleterious effect on

[17] The proposal was presented to the National Commission on Social Security Reform, August 29, 1982.

the growth in productivity. Future generations will be worse off. Some critics of social security, such as Martin Feldstein, claim that it may have reduced capital accumulation in the United States by as much as one-third.[18] They attribute at least some of the marked differences in growth rate between Japan and the United States to differences in savings rates, and much of the difference in savings rates in turn is attributed (in their view) to the differences in social security systems: Japan makes very limited public provision for the aged.

Supporters of social security, though admitting the theoretical possibility that social security may have depressed savings, doubt the quantitative importance of this effect. They point out, for instance, the marked growth of pension funds that occurred after the introduction of social security. One explanation for this is that social security enables individuals to retire earlier; but because it does not fully replace earnings, individuals are induced to save on their own account to make up the difference. Moreover, supporters of our current social security system contend that to the extent that there is a depressing effect on savings, the government can, through other actions, offset these effects. It can stimulate investment, for instance, by investment tax credits. By reducing government deficits it can ensure that a larger fraction of savings goes into private capital formation rather than into the holding of government debt. Feldstein believes that the social security system's depressing effects on savings are so large that no other government actions can fully offset them. Finally, those who believe that international capital markets work reasonably well argue that while social security may have reduced savings, it should not have any significant effect on investment or capital accumulation. Thus, the social security system may contribute to the increase in America's indebtedness to foreigners, but it cannot be blamed for the decrease in productivity.

EARLY RETIREMENT

Social security also has an effect on labor supply: it induces individuals to retire earlier than they otherwise would. We noted above the large decline in the labor force participation of those over sixty-five during the past two decades; this has occurred at exactly the same time that there has been a large increase in social security benefits. (During the period 1970–1972, real social security benefits were increased by 28 percent; in the period between 1968 and 1976, real benefits increased over 50 percent.) Michael Hurd of the State University of New York at Stony Brook and Michael Boskin of Stanford University argue that the

[18] There is considerable controversy concerning Feldstein's results, involving a number of technical issues. Different studies have obtained different results. S. Danziger, R. Haveman, and R. Plotnick ("How Income Transfers Affect Work, Savings and the Income Distribution," *Journal of Economic Literature*, September 1981) conclude in their survey that the transfer programs (in which the effect of social security is dominant) "...have depressed annual private savings by 0-20 percent relative to their value without these programs, with the most likely estimate lying near the lower end of this range."

decline in labor force participation was, indeed, due largely to the real increase in social security benefits.[19]

Earlier, we pointed out that government programs have both income effects and substitution effects. Inefficiencies are associated with substitution effects. Both of these effects arise in the case of social security. The large transfer of resources to the elderly has an income effect; the elderly take some of this increased income in the form of extra leisure: early retirement. In addition, however, there is a substitution effect, because social security changes the return to working.

There is, however, considerable controversy about the size, and even direction, of the substitution effect. As individuals work longer, their total contributions to social security increase, since they are taxed on their additional income. Their benefits per year are also increased. The question is, do they increase *enough* to compensate for the increased payments? At present the adjustment is not enough, but as a result of the reform act of 1983, by the year 2008, on average, there will be a full adjustment. And in recent years, there has been an effect encouraging workers to stay on: the magnitude of social security benefits depends on individuals' contributions in previous years. In 1937 their contributions were limited to the first $3,000 of their income; in 1987 they were made up to $43,800. Thus the way social security benefits are calculated means that an individual with, say, a $40,000 income may now experience a significant increase in benefits by staying at work an additional year or two.[20]

Note that there is a distortion of the labor-leisure choice whether individuals are subsidized or taxed. The fact that some individuals are subsidized and some taxed does not result in the distortions netting out: the total distortion is not simply related to the average value of the marginal subsidy or tax.

Some of this distortionary effect is an inevitable consequence of the provision of retirement insurance. We could reduce the distortion, but only by, in effect, providing less insurance. There is not agreement about whether such a change is desirable. But part of the distortion in labor supply is related to how the social security system treats earnings

[19] There is, however, some controversy about these results. One survey by Olivia S. Mitchell and Gary S. Fields concluded, "Clearly, no empirical conclusions can be drawn about the effects of Social Security on retirement," while Danziger, Haveman, and Plotnick ("Income Transfers") argue that social security has been at most responsible for one-half of the decline in labor force participation by older men since 1950 (a reduction in total work hours in the economy of 1.2 percent). See O. S. Mitchell and G. S. Fields, "The Effects of Pensions and Earnings on Retirement: A Review Essay," in *Research in Labor Economics,* vol. 5, ed. Ronald G. Ehrenberg (Greenwich, CT: JAI Press, 1982), pp. 115–55.

[20] Some economists have argued that the relationship between benefits and taxes is so loose (and so complicated) that individuals simply treat the social security system as a tax-transfer system; thus, in their decision about how much labor to supply, they take account of the payroll taxes they pay but not of any incremental benefits they receive. For a discussion of the whole set of issues, see M. Feldstein, "Facing the Social Security Crises," *Public Interest* 47 (1977): 88–100; A. B. Laffer and R. D. Ranson, "A Proposal for Reforming the Social Security System," in *Income Support Policies for the Aged,* ed. G. S. Tolley and R. Burkhauser (Cambridge, MA: Ballinger, 1977); A. Munnell, *The Future of Social Security* (Washington, D.C.: Brookings Institution, 1977); and A. Blinder, R. Gordon, and D. Wise, "Reconsidering the Work Disincentive Effects of Social Security," *National Tax Journal* 33 (1980): 431–42.

of those between sixty-five and seventy. Individuals who continue working after sixty-five are entitled to receive social security benefits, but for every two dollars they earn, above a certain amount, they lose one dollar of benefits, in effect, a 50 percent tax on earnings. In addition, high-income individuals are subject to personal income tax on half of their social security benefits. As a result, a sixty-six-year-old with a high income from investments could face an effective marginal tax rate of 83 percent on his wage income—and this does not include state and local income taxes. Such an individual has little incentive to continue working.

ALTERNATIVE PERSPECTIVES

In this chapter, we have viewed the social security program mainly as an insurance and savings program. It is, of course, more than this: it is also a transfer program. Some economists (notably Joseph Pechman of the Brookings Institution) think of it primarily as a transfer program. To them, the link between the payroll tax and the social security system is of no substantive significance; there is (in general) no reason to tie particular programs to particular revenue sources.

For others, the link between the two is important, for three reasons. Many of the early advocates of social security believed that it was important that individuals believe that they are getting what they paid for, that there was not a public handout. Many individuals would find it demeaning to take a public handout. (Thus the confusion in the present system —between the different functions of social security, its role in insurance and savings, and its role in transfers—is viewed to be an advantage.) Moreover, if individuals perceive themselves as "purchasing" retirement benefits with their social security contributions, the distortions of the labor supply associated with the payroll tax will be reduced.

Others have been concerned that the political process might lead to excessively generous social security programs; some check on these redistributive programs is required. Having a clearly identified tax that must be raised when social security benefits are raised provides such a check.

SUMMARY

1. The market failures that give rise to the government provision of social insurance include the failure to provide insurance for many of the most important risks facing individuals, the high transaction costs associated with the private provision of insurance, the failure to provide insurance against social risks, and the problem of adverse selection when markets cannot differentiate among individuals with different risk.
2. The social security retirement program serves three functions: it is a forced savings program, an insurance program, and a transfer program.
3. The social security program has an effect on labor supply (through its effect on early retirements) and on capital formation (through its effect on savings). There is dispute about the significance of these effects.

4. Changes in birth rates and life expectancy, in labor force participation among the aged, and in the rate of growth of productivity all contributed to recent financial crises facing the social security system.

KEY CONCEPTS

Earmarked tax	Pay-as-you-go basis
Transaction costs	Adverse selection
Replacement rates	Intergenerational equity
Social risks	Intragenerational distribution
Indexing	Moral hazard
Annuity	

QUESTIONS AND PROBLEMS

1. For each of the major aspects of the social security program (retirement insurance, survivors' insurance, disability insurance) describe the market failures that gave rise to the program or that might be used to justify its continuation. Assume you were asked to design a program that was to address only one of the market failures. For as many market failures as you can, describe an alternative program to the present system and explain its advantages and disadvantages over the present one.
2. List the risks against which the social security program provides insurance. In which of these instances do you think providing insurance affects the likelihood of the insured-against event occurring?
3. What are the theoretical reasons that social security might be expected to decrease savings? Are there any theoretical reasons why social security might be expected to increase savings? Why might a tax on interest income lead to later retirements? Under what circumstances might such a tax be desirable?
4. Discuss the equity and efficiency effects of the following recent and proposed changes in the social security system and, where appropriate, provide alternative reforms directed at the same objective:
   a) terminating support of children of deceased workers at age nineteen, whether they are in school or not;
   b) tougher standards for eligibility for disability payments;
   c) increasing the age for eligibility for social security benefits;
   d) increasing benefits for those who retire later so that they receive the same expected present discounted value of benefits, regardless of age of retirement;
   e) exempting those over the age of sixty-five from paying social security taxes.
5. To what extent could the purposes of the social security program be served by a law that required individuals to purchase retirement insurance from a private firm? Discuss difficulties with such a proposal, and what kinds of regulations might be required to avoid these difficulties.
6. Do you think social security benefits, unemployment benefits, or disability payments should be treated like ordinary income for purposes of the income tax?

14

Welfare Programs and the Redistribution of Income

There is consensus among Western democracies that no individual should be allowed to go hungry, go without housing, or go without any of the other basic necessities of life simply for want of income. The view that it is the responsibility of the federal government to provide these basic necessities dates in the United States to Franklin Roosevelt's New Deal.

In 1964, President Johnson launched his War on Poverty. He believed that it was the responsibility of the government not only to care for the needy, but to eliminate the root causes of poverty.

We call programs that **transfer** cash and consumption goods to the poor **public assistance** or **welfare programs**. The payments are called **transfer payments**. Responsibility for welfare traditionally resided at the state and local levels, but the federal government has taken on an increasingly large role in financing public assistance. Even today, however, the states and localities administer most welfare programs and finance nearly one-fourth of their cost. In 1985, combined federal and state outlays for public assistance were $132 billion.[1]

[1] The $132 billion figure includes $16.2 billion for education programs and $5.4 billion for low-income veterans, which we did not classify as public assistance in Figure 2.4. Executive Office of the President, *Up from Dependency, Supplement 1: The National Public Assistance System* (Washington, D.C.: U.S. Government Printing Officer 1986), Vol. 1, pp. 12–16.

There are two types of welfare programs. The first type provides cash benefits, which the recipients are free to use as they wish. The principal cash programs are **Aid to Families with Dependent Children** (AFDC), which provides funds to families in which there is no earner, and **Supplemental Security Income** (SSI), which provides funds to aged and disabled individuals with low incomes (it supplements social security benefits).

The second type of program provides benefits for specific purposes. **Medicaid** provides free medical care to low-income individuals. The housing and energy assistance programs provide subsidized housing and energy.[2] These benefits are called **in-kind benefits** (as distinguished from cash benefits). In some cases, the government actually provides the goods (as with public housing, public health clinics, and free cheese and butter to the poor), but in most cases the individual purchases the commodities from private sellers, with the government paying all or part of the cost (as with Medicaid or food stamps).

In the twenty years from 1965 to 1985, welfare expenditures in real terms increased four-fold—see Figure 14.1. The most striking increase in welfare expenditures occurred in Medicaid, which accounted for 30 percent of welfare expenditures by 1972 and 40 percent by 1985. As a percentage of gross national product, welfare expenditures rose from 1.2 percent in 1965 to approximately 3 percent in each of the years 1981 to 1985. Most of this increase was accounted for by an increase in the number of recipients. AFDC beneficiaries increased from 4.3 million in 1965 to 10.8 million in 1985; food stamp recipients from 400 thousand to 19.9 million; and SSI recipients from 2.7 to 4.2 million. The Medicaid program, which was just starting in 1965, grew to about 22 million beneficiaries in the mid-1970s, a level at which it has remained since then. While the number of welfare recipients rose, the magnitude of transfers per recipient did not increase in real terms. By contrast, social security benefits—in real terms—have increased by two-thirds since 1965.[3]

These programs, designed to transfer income to the poor, have been the subject of considerable controversy. There are those who believe that their structure has weakened incentives of the poor to seek employment, and that they have contributed to the breakup of families and to a sense of dependency among the poor. On the other hand, there are those who believe that the level of support is too small, that it is not sufficient to allow the poor to break out of the vicious circle of poverty. For instance, because of their low income, they obtain low levels of nutrition, housing, and education, and this leads to a low level of productivity; and the low level of productivity in turn results in their receiving low wages.

[2] As we noted in the previous chapter, the Medicare and social security programs can be thought of as being partially transfer (income redistribution) and partially social insurance programs. The government typically classifies veterans' disability and pension payments as transfer payments. It is more appropriate to think of these payments as deferred compensation for military service, and hence we do not include those expenditures here.

[3] See *Social Security Bulletin, Annual Statistical Supplement*, 1986, Tables 176 and 206.

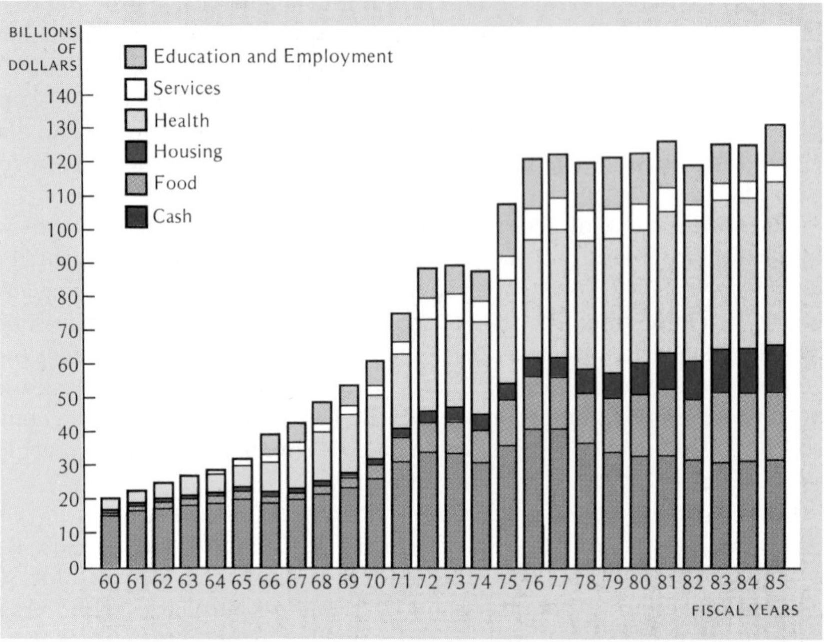

14.1 TOTAL SPENDING FOR PUBLIC ASSISTANCE BY FUNCTION In constant 1985 dollars, these amounts include federal and required state outlays. SOURCE: Executive Office of the President, Office of Policy Development, *Up from Dependency,* Supplement 1, The National Public Assistance System, Vol. 1: An Overview of the Current System, December 1986.

As usual, there are efficiency and equity issues: What are the distortions associated with such transfers? Are there provisions of the current system that exacerbate the inefficiencies? How effective has the present system been in reducing inequality? Could we achieve the same distributional objectives at lower cost with an alternative welfare system? These are among the questions we will address in this chapter.

WELFARE PROGRAMS AND SOCIAL INSURANCE

In our discussion, we distinguish between welfare programs and social insurance; the latter include social security and Medicare and were the subject of Chapters 11 and 13.

The distinction, however, is not a clear one. We noted in the previous chapter that most of the social security programs do entail considerable redistribution; they combine insurance and transfer programs.

Moreover, welfare programs can be thought of as insurance against the kinds of contingencies that we, or our children, might face: "There, but for the grace of God, go I." If one did not know whether one was going to enter the world poor or rich, one might well want the government to provide some "insurance" against the possibility of the former occurring—i.e., one might want the government to increase the welfare allocations, the consumption of the poor, at the expense of the rich. It is in this sense that programs aimed at income redistribution can be viewed as insurance programs.

CASH VERSUS IN-KIND REDISTRIBUTION

Three dollars out of every ten that are transferred through welfare are provided in the form of subsidized food, housing, and energy, and four dollars out of every ten are transferred as free medical care. Only three out of ten dollars are transferred as cash (see Figure 14.1), although many people may believe that it would be preferable for the government simply to provide all welfare in cash. The present system is criticized on three grounds:

1. It is administratively costly: each of the programs has to be run separately; several different agencies have to determine the eligibility of each individual for each program. Eligibility standards determine who is qualified to receive aid under the given program. These eligibility standards are based primarily on income, but adjustments for family size and other circumstances are generally made. (Programs that provide aid to particular groups of individuals are called **categorical aid** programs. When income is a major element in determining eligibility, the programs are said to be **means-tested**.)
2. It introduces inefficiencies in resource allocations when there are substitution effects; and when there are not substitution effects, the consequences are not different from those of a direct transfer of income.
3. It is inappropriate for the government to attempt to distort individuals' consumption decisions.

In the following sections, we examine in detail the last two sets of criticisms.

Inefficiencies from In-Kind Redistributions

Consider food stamps, one of the more rapidly growing programs. Initiated on a pilot basis in 1961, the program was formally established by the Food Stamp Act of 1964. In constant 1986 dollars, federal outlays grew from $99 million in 1964, to $5.4 billion a decade later, to $11 billion in 1985. The number of recipients increased from 400,000 in 1964 to 20 million in 1985. (See Figure 14.2.)

To get food stamps, one has to have a sufficiently low net income (income minus certain allowable deductions). A family of four with an income below $14,000 in 1986 could in some cases receive some food stamps. In 1986, the maximum value of food stamps that could be received (by someone with zero net income) was $271 per month, but

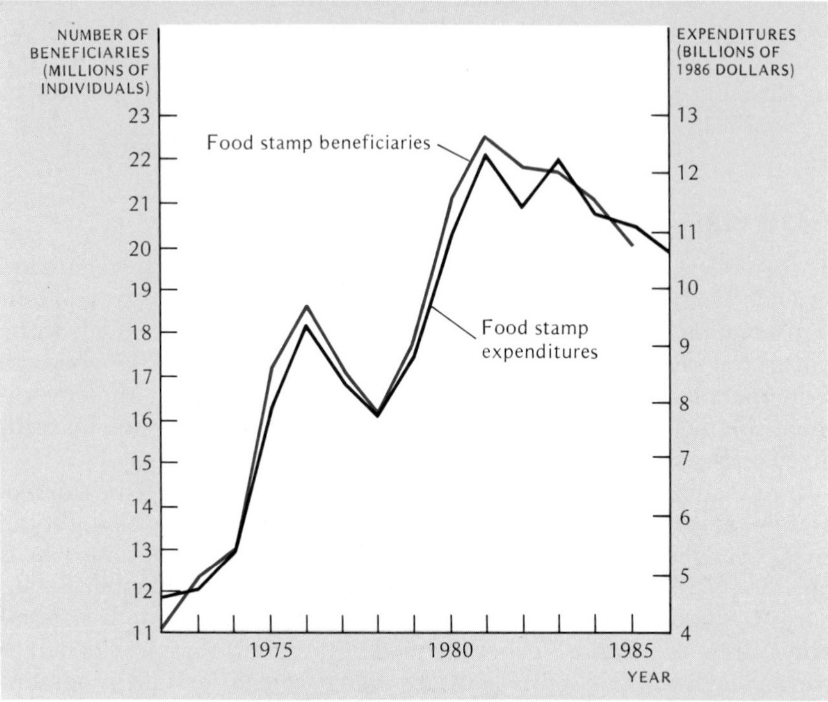

14.2 THE FOOD STAMP PROGRAM, 1972–1986 There has been rapid growth in the food stamp program. (The data do not include beneficiaries in Puerto Rico after 1982, and that accounts for the drop shown in the figure for that year.) SOURCE: *Social Security Bulletin, Annual Statistical Supplement,* 1986, Table 206. Data for the food price deflator are from *Economic Report of the President 1987,* Table B–55.

the average benefit received per recipient was only $45.[4] The food stamp allotment is supposed to enable the individual or family to maintain a healthful diet, but whether it is adequate to do that is controversial.

To see the effects of the food stamp program, we have drawn an individual's budget constraint in Figure 14.3 before the food stamp program and after it. For simplicity, we consider an individual who initially had $1,000 and now receives $100 in food stamps. His new budget constraint is parallel to the old. If he consumed only food, his consumption of food would go up by $100. For every dollar less he spends on food, he

[4] Both the amount received and the eligibility standards are adjusted annually for changes in the cost of living. The amount received is the difference betwen 30 percent of an individual's net income (after allowance for certain expenses) and the cost of a nutritionally adequate diet ($271 per month for a four-person household in 1986), provided the individual meets certain eligibility standards. To be eligible, a family (without anyone aged sixty or older) must have less than $2,000 in disposable assets and a gross income below 130 percent of the poverty guidelines for the household size. To calculate net income, the following deductions from income for households without an aged individual are made: (a) 18 percent of earned income; (b) a standard deduction, which in 1986 was $99; (c) child-care expenses, with a limit of $160 a month; and (d) total shelter costs including utilities in excess of 50 percent of income (after subtracting the above deductions), limited to $149. If there is an aged individual, a further allowance is made for medical expenses, and there is no limit on the deduction for shelter costs. From *Social Security Bulletin, Annual Statistical Supplement,* 1986, p. 60.

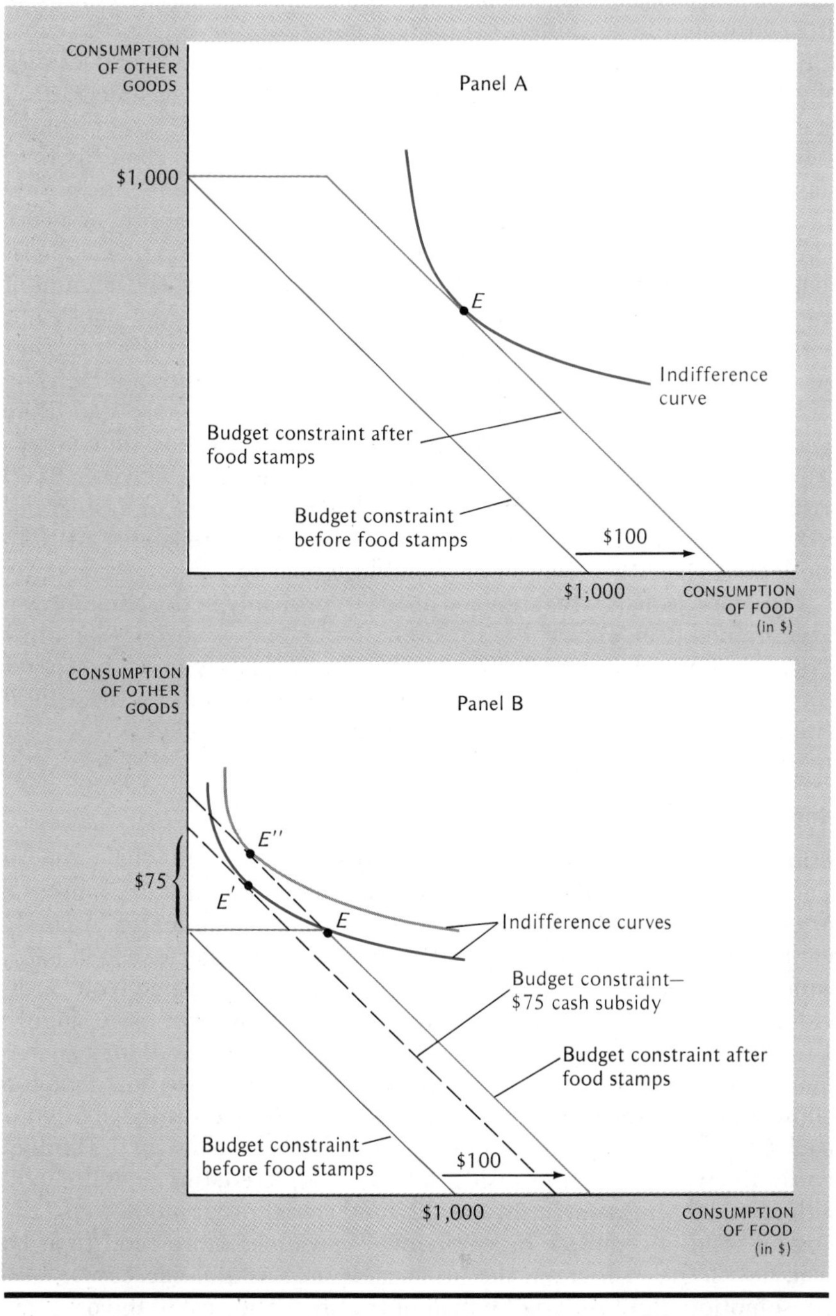

14.3 THE EFFECT OF FOOD STAMP PROGRAMS (A) If the individual consumes more than his food stamp allotment, there is no substitution effect, just an income effect; the food stamp program is in effect no different from a $100 cash subsidy. (B) This individual purchases no food beyond his food stamp allotment. If he were given a $100 cash subsidy, he would consume less than $100 in food. A cash subsidy would make the individual better off. Alternatively, the government could give the individual a $75 cash subsidy, and he would be just as well off.

has one dollar more to spend on other goods. Notice that a cash subsidy at $100 would have shifted his budget constraint in exactly the same way, except that with the cash subsidy he could have consumed $1,100 of other goods; with the food subsidy, he can still only consume $1,000 of other goods.

In Figure 14.3A the individual consumes more food than his food stamp allotment. There is then no substitution effect, only an income effect. The effect of the program is identical to a cash subsidy of $100. The $100 of food stamps increases his consumption of food by much less than $100. In Figure 14.3B the individual consumes just the amount of the food stamp allotment. We have also drawn the budget constraint with a $100 grant. The individual would have consumed less food, but he would have been better off. There is a clear substitution effect: the fact that food is free induces individuals to consume more than they would if they had to pay for it. But there is an efficiency cost: individuals are worse off than they would have been if they had been given a $100 cash grant. To put it another way, if we had given a smaller cash grant, $75, the individual would have been just as well off receiving $100 in food stamps, and the government would have saved $25.

Those individuals who are very poor are probably in the situation we have depicted in Figure 14.3B: their food stamps exceed what they would have purchased with a cash grant. Individuals who are better off consume more food and receive fewer food stamps. Thus for these individuals there is no substitution effect, only an income effect.

Inefficiencies from Subsidized Food Stamps

Prior to 1979 the food stamp program worked differently. All families of a given size were entitled to the same allotment of food stamps, but the price they paid for the food stamps depended on their income. A family with zero income would pay nothing; as income increased, families would pay a larger fraction of the value of the stamps. Effectively, individuals were allowed to purchase food below the market price. Figure 14.4 shows the individual's budget constraint before and after such a food stamp program. In this example, the food stamp program depicted allows him to purchase food stamps valued at $200, at a price of 50¢ for each $1 of food stamps. In Figure 14.4A, we have also drawn the budget constraint with a flat cash subsidy of $60; as depicted, this gives the individual exactly the same utility as the food stamp program. Because the cost of food is reduced, the individual consumes more food than he would with the cash grant; the program is successful in increasing food consumption. But this is an inefficient transfer. The cost of the program is the difference between what the individual pays for food and the market cost of the food consumed. Since the individual consumes $150 of food, he receives a $75 subsidy. The cash subsidy, which shifts the budget constraint up in parallel, would leave the individual just as well off but would cost the government less. In our example, a $60 cash subsidy

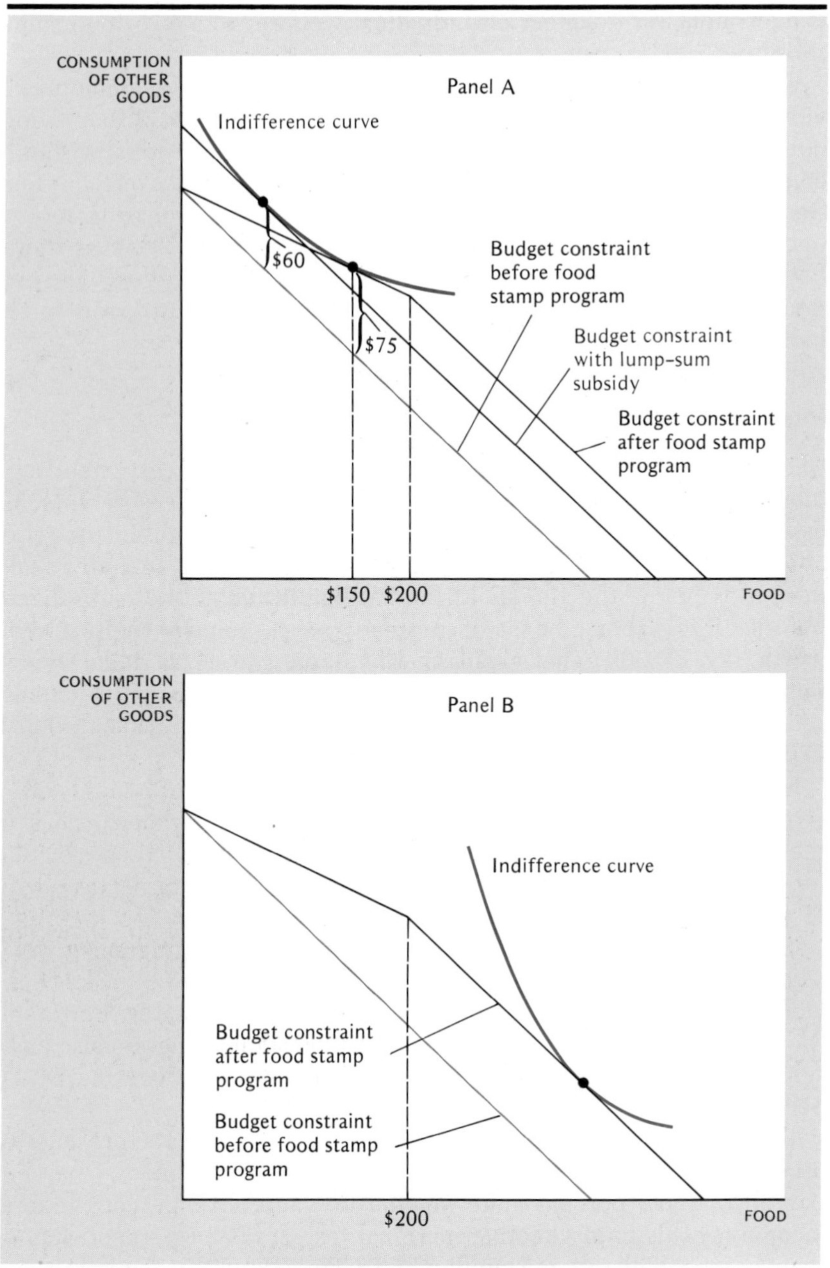

14.4 THE EFFECT OF A FOOD STAMP PROGRAM WHERE FOOD STAMPS HAVE TO BE PURCHASED In Panel A there is a substitution effect; in Panel B there is only an income effect. Up to $200 worth of food, the individual has to give up only 50¢ for each $1 of food. He must give up $1 of other goods for each dollar's worth of food beyond $200.

is equivalent (in its effect on individual welfare) to a $75 food stamp subsidy.

Figure 14.4B depicts a situation in which the maximum amount individuals can purchase with food stamps is sufficiently small that it does not meet the individual's entire food desires. If the individual wishes to consume more than $200 worth, he must pay the full price once his food stamps run out. Now, since the marginal cost of purchasing food is unchanged (the *slope* of the budget constraint is the same as it was before the food stamp program), there is only an income effect. The program's effects are no different than if $100 were transferred to the individual.

Incentive Effects of Eligibility Standards

The differing welfare programs, with differing eligibility standards, often result in distortions in individuals' incentives to work. In some cases, such as in most housing programs, as the individual's income rises above a certain threshold, he becomes ineligible. If an individual's income is below the threshold, he is eligible for public (subsidized) housing; if it is above, he is not. Assume that the value of the subsidy is worth, say, $1,000. That means that by earning an extra dollar, which puts him above the threshold, the individual's real income is actually reduced by $999. Effective tax rates above 100 percent make it foolish to work an extra hour.

Even when there are not rigid thresholds, the extent of benefits often is reduced as income increases. This has the same effect that a tax has. In the food stamp program, the allotment of food stamps decreases by $30 for each $100 increase in income. This is an effective marginal tax rate of 30 percent.

Note that the food stamp program alone has an unambiguously deleterious effect on work incentives. The food stamp program makes individuals better off; it has an income effect: since individuals are better off, they wish to consume more leisure. The food stamp program also has a substitution effect; it reduces the marginal return to working by 30 percent.

This is bad enough, but its effects are compounded by the presence of other taxes in the system. Thus, if the individual has to pay a 7 percent payroll tax, a 2 percent state income tax, and a 15 percent federal income tax, his total effective marginal tax rate is 54 percent, higher than for most high-income families and a likely deterrent to effort.[5]

We should note, however, that one of the results of the Tax Reform Act of 1986 was to remove most families in poverty from the federal income tax rolls.

[5] We should actually include the employer's social security tax as part of the tax paid by the individual; this would raise the effective marginal tax rate to in excess of 60 percent. On the other hand, if the social security benefits to which the individual is entitled increase as a result of his increased income, the net tax would be lower. For most young individuals the value of the incremental social security beneifts is negligible.

FOOD STAMPS AS A HOUSING SUBSIDY

The eligibility standards for welfare programs may affect not only individuals' work incentives, but other aspects of consumption as well. In the food stamp program, for instance, families are allowed to make a deduction for housing expenditures in calculating their net income that will determine their food stamp allotment. Thus, an increase in expenditure on housing may increase their food stamps. The net cost to the family of increasing its housing expenditures by $100 may be considerably less than $100. It is as if the government were subsidizing housing. Indeed, for a family consuming more food than its food stamp allotment, the only substitution effect associated with the food stamp program is on housing; there is no substitution effect on food.

Should the Government Interfere with Individuals' Free Choices?

Critics of in-kind welfare payments criticize these programs for being paternalistic. In the view taken in the previous section, if providing in-kind subsidies does alter behavior from that associated with a transfer system, it causes an inefficiency; the same levels of utility of recipients could be attained at lower cost to the government. But there is another view that this is precisely what the government is attempting to do: it wants to ensure that the money that is transferred is spent on "good" uses, on housing, food, and medicine. What society cares about, in this perspective, is not so much the welfare of the recipients as the outward manifestations of poverty, the slums, malnutrition, etc., that result from it. Some economists find this paternalistic view of the government objectionable; they argue that it violates the principle of consumer sovereignty. Others point out that one of the main objectives of many of these programs is to improve the welfare of the children of the poor; cash grants may not be as effective in doing this as certain in-kind benefits.

Earlier, we encountered the view, called specific egalitarianism, that contends that society may have views not only about the distribution of purchasing power in general but about access to particular goods, services, and rights. The right to a minimal level of medical care, food, and shelter ought to be viewed as a nontransferable right.

Housing

One form of in-kind aid that has recently become the subject of considerable attention is housing. Federal housing programs began with efforts during the Great Depression to provide temporary shelter for families in financial distress. Today there are more than 1.2 million units of public housing; poor families rent these housing units at subsidized rates. Many of the public housing facilities—high-rise buildings in urban centers—have been labeled "storehouses of the poor" and have been accused of breeding crime and social decay. While construction costs have been high, many local authorities have found it impossible to maintain them adequately. In one infamous incident, St. Louis decided it was better to level its Pruit-Igoe project with dynamite than to try to maintain the facility. In fact, in recent years there has been a net decline in the number of public housing units; 5,000 more units were abandoned than were constructed.

One remedy that has been under serious consideration for a number of years is a housing voucher scheme. Poor families would not be concentrated together in public facilities but would be provided with subsidies to obtain private housing. There have been a number of experimental studies to determine how effective such a voucher scheme would be and how best to design it.

Earlier, concern that the poor could not afford adequate housing led many communities to pass rent control acts. But such legislation has proved to be counterproductive: the supply of rental housing has decreased as landlords have not been able to obtain the returns on their investments that they could have obtained elsewhere.[6]

During the mid-1980s, concern focused on the plight of the homeless. While some of these were very poor families, others were individuals who had previously been institutionalized for mild mental disorders, but seemed ill equiped to care for themselves.[7] In 1986, Congress passed legislation providing a half billion dollars of aid for the homeless.

CATEGORICAL VERSUS BROAD-BASED AID

A second major controversy has been associated with whether aid should be given to all poor or only to the poor falling into certain categories. Thus the Supplementary Security Income Program transfers income only to the aged or disabled poor, and AFDC, which was created in 1935 to give aid to poor widows with children, transfers income only to single-parent families with dependent children. Some states also offer an AFDC-Unemployed Parent Program (AFDC-UP) for two-parent families with an unemployed parent, but there are stringent restrictions on eligibility and the program is very small—less than 5 percent of the total AFDC Program in 1984.

Categorical aid (whether in-kind or cash) is more expensive to administer than broad-based aid, primarily because of costs associated with ascertaining eligibility for the program. For instance, in recent years, administrative costs per beneficiary for the Supplemental Security Income Program have averaged three and one-half times more per beneficiary and seven times more per dollar of benefit payments than administrative costs for the Old Age and Survivors' Insurance Program.

[6] There is some suspicion that some communities, such as Princeton, New Jersey, may use rent control as a means of discouraging rental properties.

[7] The program of releasing from mental institutions those who did not represent any threat to society and who could probably take care of themselves was referred to as *deinstitutionalization*.

Efficiency and Equity Issues

Besides considerations of administrative costs, there are two efficiency issues and one equity issue that arise in comparing categorical versus broad-based aid. Categorical aid may have the effect of inducing individuals to fall into the benefited category; it may have a distortionary effect. This is not true of social security: individuals do not become older faster simply to take advantage of the program. But there are allegations that AFDC has contributed to the breakup of families; the departure of a low-wage father may increase total "family" income by making it eligible for AFDC.[8] During the past decade, there has been a marked increase in the number of children born in families without a father. Whether there is a causal connection remains a subject of dispute.[9]

The major advantage that categorical aid has over broadly based programs is that, under certain circumstances, it can provide more effective redistribution, with less loss in efficiency. It can enable the targeting of aid to the most needy, who, at the same time, will not have adverse incentive responses. We have repeatedly emphasized the trade-offs between equity and efficiency considerations in the design of redistribution programs. Providing a high level of basic income through a transfer program that then declines as the individual's income from wages or other sources increases may discourage work. This will normally imply that a lower level of redistribution is more desirable for individuals whose response to incentives is large than for individuals whose response to wage incentives is small (e.g., those over seventy).

Figure 14.5 depicts a relationship between the magnitude of redistribution and the loss in output for two different groups (the working population and the aged). The greater the redistribution, the greater the loss in output. But because the loss in output for the aged is smaller (for each increase in the extent of redistribution), it is desirable to have a more redistributive program for the aged. By having different programs for groups with different characteristics, one can obtain a more effective redistribution of income.

There is an equity argument against categorical programs. There are those who believe that the government should not discriminate in favor

[8] A recent study estimated the gap between welfare benefits of one-parent families and incomes of young black men. In 1983, the combined AFDC and food stamp benefit for an AFDC family averaged $4,741. This figure was higher than the income reported in that year for 62 percent of black men aged twenty to twenty-four, and 29 percent of black men aged twenty-five to thirty-four. While these figures reflect in part the high national unemployment rate in 1983, comparison of these figures with data for earlier years suggests that a significant number of men cannot provide income high enough to maintain a family at above welfare levels. See Frank Levy and Richard Michel, "Work for Welfare: How Much Good Will It Do?" *American Economic Review*, Vol. 76, May 1986, pp. 399–404.

[9] For instance, the illegitimate birth rate (births per 1,000 unmarried females) almost tripled from 1940 to 1982, from 7.1 to 19.4 (*Statistical Abstract of the United States*, 1986, p. 62). But whether this increase is due to welfare, or to other causes, is more problematic. Professors David Ellwood and Larry Summers of Harvard concluded, on the basis of a variety of evidence, that the impact of welfare on family structure was slight. They found, for example, that variations in benefit levels across states were not associated with corresponding variations in divorce rates, illegitimacy rates, or percentages of children in single-parent families. See D. Ellwood and L. Summers, "Poverty in America: Is Welfare the Answer or the Problem?," in *Fighting Poverty: What Works and What Doesn't*, eds. Sheldon Danziger and Daniel Weinberg (Cambridge, MA: Harvard University Press, 1986), pp. 78–105.

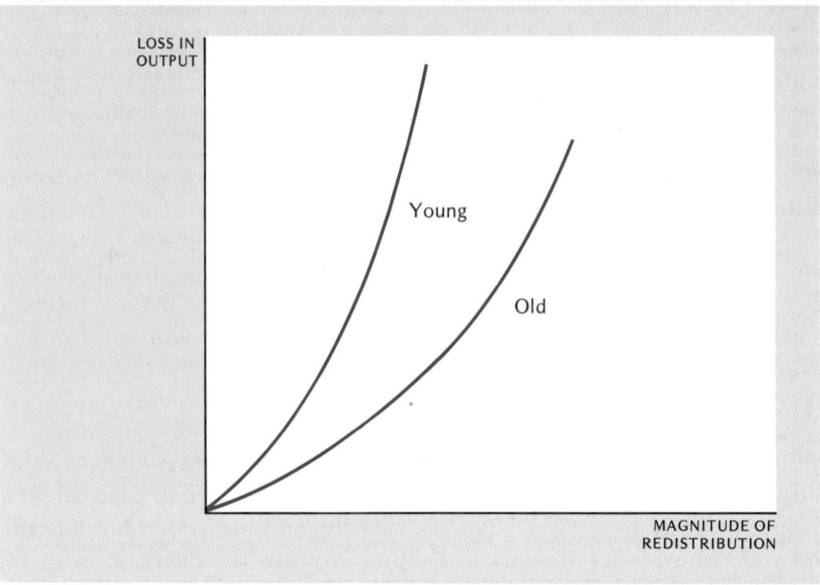

14.5 THE ADVANTAGE OF CATEGORICAL PROGRAMS The loss in output for any given increase in equality may differ across different groups. This may make it desirable to design redistributive programs aimed at different groups.

of or against particular groups in the population. Two individuals who are equally poor should receive the same amount from the government, whether they are young or old. There should not be "favored" categories, such as single-parent households or the aged. Admittedly, older individuals may have more medical expenses, and one might want to adjust the transfers to take this into account; but this is already effectively done through Medicare. On the other hand, many object to means-tested programs, whether categorical or not, because they are believed to be demeaning to recipients.[10]

The Negative Income Tax

There are many who believe that the present system of categorical aid and in-kind aid should be replaced by a single cash-based welfare system, which should be integrated into the income tax system. The proposal has been called the **negative income tax**.

All individuals would be required to file a tax return, but just as only individuals above a critical threshold would have to pay income taxes, those below that critical threshold level would receive a check from the government. Consider a tax regime in which everyone receives a check from the government of, say, $1,000 per year but then pays to the government, say, one-third of each dollar that he earns. Those with an

[10] As a result, many who are eligible do not take advantage of the benefits, and thus the programs are less successful in attaining their objectives.

income of less than $3,000 would receive something net from the government; those with an income greater than $3,000 would pay to the government more than they receive. Those who favor this system argue not only that it is administratively simpler but that it is less demeaning than the present system, which forces individuals to present evidence to several agencies concerning their low income. Furthermore, advocates claim that the implicit tax rate associated with the present tax system either discourages work or encourages dishonesty. Since an individual's eligibility for benefits declines markedly with an increase in income, the net increase in his consumption from an increase in income may be very limited. As a result, in some types of work, such as household services, the practice of not reporting income is very widespread. It is debatable, of course, whether switching to a negative income tax would alter this.

There were a large number of studies conducted in the 1960s and 1970s to ascertain the effect of our current system of welfare and proposed reforms on work effort and to quantify the associated inefficiencies. There is more of a consensus that effects on work effort are small for SSI, food stamps, and housing asistance[11] (of the order of magnitude of 0.1 percent for SSI, 0.3 percent for food stamps, and housing assistance) than there is for AFDC.[12] The magnitude of the welfare losses is also a subject of debate. We discuss how these welfare losses are measured in greater detail in Chapter 18, and we discuss the effect of welfare programs on labor supply in Chapter 19.

Supporters of the negative income tax also argue that its further advantage is that it allows individuals to spend money in a way that reflects their own preferences; it does not distort their expenditure patterns in the way that the present welfare system does with in-kind aid.

Though the idea of a negative income tax has received widespread support, it has faced one serious problem: to provide what is viewed by many as a minimal level of support requires a high marginal tax rate. The present system, as we have said, entails a high effective tax rate on the very poor. Switching to a negative income tax would lower the tax rate on these individuals but increase the tax rate on middle-income individuals. Not only would this be politically unpopular, but there is a view that it might have serious incentive effects. Advocates of the present system claim that (1) incentive effects among many of the recipients of welfare in our present system are relatively small; a significant fraction of the recipients are individuals, like the aged and disabled, who would not enter the labor force or work much even if the implicit tax rate were reduced; (2) incentive effects on middle-income individuals may be large; (3) the recipients of welfare are much less productive than those in the lower-middle-income ranges who would face an increase in mar-

[11] S. Danziger, R. Haveman, and R. Plotnick, "How Income Transfers Affect Work, Savings and the Income Distribution," *Journal of Economic Literature*, September 1981, p. 996.

[12] For instance, J. Hausman ("The Labor Supply," in *How Taxes Affect Economic Behavior*, ed. J. H. Aaron and J. Pechman [Washington, D.C.: Brookings Institution, 1981], pp. 27–72) obtains estimates thirty-seven times as large as those obtained by R. Moffitt, "An Economic Model of Welfare Stigma," Rutgers University mimeo, 1980.

ginal tax rates under the negative income tax proposals; and (4) since there are many more individuals in these lower-middle-income ranges than there are poor individuals on welfare, we should be particularly concerned with the incentive effects of such a change in tax structure.

A very limited form of negative income tax is provided under current law through the earned income tax credit. Enacted in 1975, this credit applies only to low-income workers who have children, and it is refundable, that is, individuals with low incomes actually receive a check from the government. The credit is 14 percent of wage income up to a maximum of $800. The credit is reduced by 10 percent of income in excess of $9,000. Thus, a single individual with one child and with an income of $11,000 receives an earned income credit of $600[13] and faces a marginal tax rate (under the federal income tax) of 25 percent—a 15 percent "official" rate plus the 10 percent from the reduction in the earned income credit. When combined with payroll and state taxes, such a low-income individual may well face an effective marginal tax rate of 30 percent.

HOW EFFECTIVE HAS OUR PRESENT WELFARE SYSTEM BEEN IN REDUCING POVERTY?

How effective have the major transfer programs of the past two decades been in decreasing inequality? Answering this question is not as easy as it might seem. It depends on what one measures.

The official measure of poverty is the number of people below the **poverty line**, which the government calculates to be the income level that affords a minimally decent level of consumption. The line depends on household size, and is updated yearly to maintain its purchasing power based on changes in the consumer price index. In 1986 dollars, the poverty line ranged from $5,360 for a single person to $11,000 for a family of four.

By the official measure, 19 percent of the population was poor when the War on Poverty was declared in 1964.[14] The poverty rate declined to 11 percent in the 1970s. The high unemployment in 1982–1983 and the cutback in welfare payments during the Reagan administration resulted in a marked increase in the poverty rate. It rose to 15 percent in 1982–1983, and edged down to 14 percent in 1985–1986. When in-kind transfers are included, the poverty rate is reduced by about two percentage points in each year.

There is a consensus that transfer programs have significantly reduced the number of Americans below the poverty line, though the social security program has played a more important role than the cash welfare programs. In order to measure the impact of these programs on poverty,

[13] The credit is reduced from $800 by ($11,000−$9,000)×10 percent.

[14] The official income concept includes all cash income, but takes no account of in-kind benefits (food stamps, Medicaid, etc.).

a recent study estimated the number of Americans whose incomes from private sources—*before transfers*—fell below the poverty level. The percentage of these pre-transfer poor persons taken out of poverty by all transfers was 46 percent in 1983—with 34 percent attributable to cash social insurance, 9 percent attributable to in-kind public assistance, and only the remaining 3 percent attributable to cash public assistance.[15] Nearly all of the elderly pre-transfer poor received transfers, but 40 percent of the nonelderly pre-transfer poor households received no cash transfers. And many of those who did receive transfers did not obtain enough to lift their households above the poverty line.

The Paradox of Unchanged Inequality

While the poverty programs have been at least partially successful in moving people from below the poverty line to above the poverty line, there has not, somewhat paradoxically, been any decline in the overall degree of inequality (as measured, say, by the Gini Coefficient (discussed in Chapter 10), or by the fraction of total income received by the lowest fifth of the population.)[16] The transfer-redistribution programs seem merely to have offset an increase in the before-tax/before-transfer inequality in income. The forces that have led to this increase in before-tax/before-transfer inequality are complex and not well understood.

One question that has been raised is the extent to which the government programs have *caused* the increase in before-tax/before-transfer inequality. If, for instance, individuals are induced to retire early as a result of social security, there will be more individuals in the population with zero before-tax/before-transfer incomes. The government programs may also have contributed to the formation of low-income households: older people with low income previously may have lived with their children; with the higher social security payments, they may decide to live on their own. In the data, the number of households with low income has increased. But these individuals may well be better off than when they were living with their children.

This example also raises another question concerning the effectiveness of government redistribution programs: the extent to which they have substituted for private transfers. The elderly formerly received more income from their children. If for each extra dollar that social security gives an elderly person his children feel they can reduce what they give him, the net beneficiary of the social security program is not the elderly but the younger individuals who are supporting them. (From

[15] Sheldon Danziger, Robert Haveman, and Robert Plotnick, "Antipoverty Policy: Effects on the Poor and the Nonpoor," in *Fighting Poverty: What Works and What Doesn't*, eds. Sheldon Danziger and Daniel Weinberg (Cambridge, MA: Harvard University Press, 1986), Table 3.6.

[16] Throughout the period from 1947 to 1983, the bottom fifth of the population received approximately 5 percent of all income. But the sources of this income changed substantially. The share of the income of the bottom fifth which came from earnings fell from 70 percent in 1959, to 50 percent in 1969, to 42 percent in 1983. Government transfers represented 45 percent of the total income of this group in 1983. See Levy and Michel, "Work for Welfare: How Much Good Will It Do?," p. 399.

this perspective, then, what is at issue is not so much the level of support for the elderly, but rather whether there should be individual or collective responsibility for their support, and the economic and social consequences of alternative arrangements).

A factor that has undoubtedly contributed to the change in the before-tax income distribution is the change in the fraction of the population over age sixty-five (which we discussed in the previous chapter). Their needs (apart from medical, which are taken care of by Medicare) may well be less than those of an individual with four children, two of whom are going to college. A sixty-five-year-old individual who is living alone and receives $10,000 may be (from a material point of view) no worse off than a family of six with four children and an income of $25,000. The data, unfortunately, do not make adjustments for these differences in circumstances, and economists disagree about how this should best be done. It is worth noting, however, that inequality among families of the same composition is smaller than inequality among the population as a whole.

Most economists would argue that one ought to focus on inequality in lifetime incomes; there are systematic variations in earnings over an individual's lifetime; the individual's income usually begins low, increases over his middle years, and then declines again as the individual goes into retirement. There may be, in addition, short-term fluctuations: the individual may, for instance, go through a short period of unemployment; a self-employed individual's income will normally go down as the economy goes into a recession. But individuals use savings to smooth out these variations in their income to provide for periods in which their anticipated consumption will exceed their anticipated income (such as retirement, or during the years in which their children go to college). Focusing on the inequality of income in any particular year exaggerates the true extent of inequality in our society.

Finally, we should note that income may not provide the only index of inequality. Better nutrition and better medical care among the poor will be reflected in better health. During the past decades there have been marked changes in the differences in some important health indicators between the poor and the rich. One study showed that indeed mortality rates (the probability of dying in a given year) increased with income; this is explained by adverse diet, lack of exercise, and increased stress.[17] Another study concludes, "Strong evidence suggests...that reductions in mortality have been concentrated disproportionately in the lower income classes."[18] Moreover, access to medical care now no longer seems to be strongly dependent on income. Ten years after the introduction of Medicare and Medicaid, the average number of physician visits per person per year for all groups was 5.1: for those with an income

[17] R. Auster, I. Leveson, and D. Sarachek, "The Production of Health, An Exploratory Study," *Journal of Human Resources*, Vol. 4, Fall 1969, pp. 411–36.

[18] K. Davis and C. Schoen, *Health and the War on Poverty* (Washington, D.C.: Brookings Institution, 1978).

under $5,000 it was 6.0, and for those with an income over $15,000 it was 4.9.[19]

Poverty among Children

These statistics on the failure of our welfare system to eliminate poverty or reduce inequality have probably not been as influential as the findings concerning children.

More than one out of every four children is born into poverty, a figure that has increased dramatically in the last decade.[20] Much of this poverty is attributed to the high birth rate among unmarried teenagers, particularly minority teenagers. In 1980, for instance, 9.5 percent of minority teens and 4.5 percent of white teens gave birth,[21] a rate that was higher than that of most other developed countries and of many of the less developed.[22] Of these, half were unmarried. There is increasing concern that there is a cycle of poverty from which it is hard to escape.

Indices other than income probably provide more convincing evidence of the shortcomings of our welfare system. Infant mortality (the likelihood that a child will die in the first year of its life) is greater for blacks in Chicago than for infants in Cuba or Costa Rica. The United States ranks fourteenth among all countries in infant mortality.[23]

Recent Reform Initiatives

The growing dissatisfaction with our welfare system led President Reagan to make welfare reform a major theme of his 1986 State of the Union Message. Concern has focused particularly on what some see as the formation of an "underclass" inured to poverty and welfare. In December 1986, a White House working group recommended: (1) a greater role for state and local government in designing their own experimental welfare programs, in lieu of federal programs; (2) the replacement of some in-kind benefits by cash benefits; and (3) a requirement that individuals receiving public assistance who are able to work should do so (if jobs exist).[24]

There has long been some support for proposals to require those on

[19] Source: National Center for Health Statistics, Health, United States, 1976–1977, DHEW (HRA) 77-1232 (GPO, 1977), p. 265.

[20] From a report of the American Public Welfare Association, reported in *Education Week*, December 3, 1986.

[21] From K. A. Moore, *Facts at a Glance* (Washington, D.C.: The Urban Institute; Statistics compiled from the National Center for Health Statistics, 1983). For a fuller discussion, see Diane Scott-Jones, "The Family," in *Contributions of the Social Sciences to Educational Policy: 1965–1985*, eds. J. Hannaway and Marlaine E. Lockheed (Berkeley: McCutchan Publishing Corporation, 1986).

[22] Alan Guttmacher Institute, *Teen-age Pregnancy: The Problem That Hasn't Gone Away* (New York: Alan Guttmacher Institute, 1981).

[23] From Children's Defense Fund, *A Children's Defense Budget. An Analysis of the FY 1987 Budget and Children.* Reported in *Phi Delta Kappan*, November 1986. On the other hand, the data provided in Chapter 11 suggests that Medicaid and Medicare have enabled much greater access to medical care by the poor.

[24] Executive Office of the President, *Up From Dependency: A New National Public Assistance Strategy*, 1986.

welfare who can work to do so, and a few states have such requirements in effect. If individuals cannot obtain jobs in the private sector, it is argued that the government should provide them with jobs. Welfare programs requiring work are sometimes referred to as **workfare**. Proponents claim that the work requirement will be an inducement for those who can to get off the welfare rolls. Opponents of workfare contend that the work requirements are demeaning, that relatively few of those on welfare, other than mothers with young children, can work, and that it is not socially desirable to require mothers with young children to work. Moreover, they worry about the administrative problems of running a workfare system. Will those who are hired by the public sector, because they fail to obtain employment in the private sector, really be gainfully employed? Will they learn work habits that will make it even more difficult for them to be gainfully employed in the future? What will their public employer do if they fail to perform, or to show up for work? Can our society countenance seeing such individuals starving? (Supporters of workfare suggest that such individuals could still be supported by welfare, but at a sufficiently reduced level to provide them incentives to perform well; and that any form of employment is better preparation for entering the work force in a gainful way than welfare dependency.)

There is a consensus that if workfare programs are to be successful, they must be accompanied by training and educational programs. In New Jersey, for instance, a first-time mother on AFDC (usually a young, unemployed high-school dropout) has a four-in-ten chance of remaining on welfare for periods lasting ten years. If educational and training programs are successful in removing even 15 percent of these people from the welfare rolls, these programs will more than pay for themselves.

Proponents of welfare reforms, such as workfare, argue that what is at stake is more than just a reduction in the costs of our welfare system. Individuals' self-respect depends on being contributing members of society. The loss of self-respect, as well as some provisions in many states that make the receipt of AFDC conditional on the *absence* of an adult male in the house, contribute to the breakdown of families. And the breakdown of families contributes to the perpetuation of poverty, a vicious circle that many see as one of America's most important long-run problems.

The trade-offs—between ensuring that all those who need assistance obtain it and ensuring that those who do not need it do not get it, between providing an adequate safety net, particularly for children whose poverty is in no sense a consequence of their own actions, and an appropriate set of work and family incentives—are likely to continue to be a source of public discussion for years to come.

SUMMARY

1. Public assistance provides cash and in-kind benefits to the poor. Expenditures for in-kind transfers have grown rapidly in recent years, but cash assistance (as a percentage of government expenditures) has fallen.

2. The in-kind redistributive programs have several disadvantages: (a) They are administratively costly. (b) In some cases, they have only an income effect (i.e., they have the same effect as a transfer of cash); in other cases, they have a substitution effect, and in those cases, the government could make the poor better off at less cost through a cash subsidy. (c) The effect of many eligibility standards is to discourage work and, when compounded with payroll and state income taxes, can result in very high marginal tax rates. (d) The structure of eligibility standards provides unintended results; for instance, the food stamp program subsidizes the consumption of housing. (e) They are paternalistic.
3. Categorical programs have similar disadvantages: (a) They are administratively costly. (b) They are viewed by some as inequitable, since individuals with the same income may be treated differently. (c) They are sometimes distortionary, as individuals attempt to qualify for subsidies. However, when groups differ in their labor-supply responses (or other responses) to government programs, the government may be able to obtain a higher degree of redistribution, for the same loss of inefficiency, by providing categorical aid.
4. The negative income tax is a proposal to integrate the welfare programs with the income tax system. It would provide only cash subsidies and would eliminate the present programs of categorical aid. The main concern is whether it could provide an adequate "minimum" standard of living to the very poor, without at the same time imposing very high marginal tax rates on middle-income individuals.
5. The transfer programs of the past two decades have reduced the number of individuals in poverty, and they have had some effect in reducing measures of overall inequality. At the same time, however, there has been an increase in the extent of before-tax/before-transfer inequality.

KEY CONCEPTS

Transfers
Aid to Families with Dependent Children
Supplemental Security Income
Negative income tax
In-kind benefits
Categorical aid
Means tests
Eligibility requirements
Specific egalitarianism
Poverty line
Workfare

QUESTIONS AND PROBLEMS

1. It has sometimes been suggested that the government should restrict the use of food stamps to "healthy" foods. Discuss the merits of this proposal. Assuming that it would be easy to distinguish between "healthy" and "unhealthy" foods, describe the effect of such a restriction on an individual's consumption of the two kinds of foods.
2. Consider a welfare program (such as housing) with an eligibility standard that requires that an individual's income be below some threshold level. Draw the individual's budget constraint with and without the subsidy (put labor on one axis, consumption on the other).
3. Consider a welfare program (such as food stamps) with benefits that decrease as an individual's income increases. Draw the individual's budget constraint

with and without the subsidy. (Put hours of work on the horizontal axis, and income on the vertical axis.) Use the diagram to illustrate how work incentives are reduced and how a fixed dollar subsidy could lead the individual to the same level of utility at lower dollar cost.

4. There have been proposals for the use of government subsidies to help poor individuals purchase private housing (just as the government's food stamp program helps them purchase food). Discuss the merits of the private versus public provision of housing.
5. Several different proposals have been put forward concerning how housing subsidies should be provided. Discuss the merits of: (a) the government's paying a given fraction of the family's housing expenditures, up to some maximum, with the percentage depending on the family's income; and (b) the government's paying a fixed dollar amount of housing allowance, the amount depending on the family's income. In both cases, discuss the appropriateness and consequences of adjustments to reflect the family's expenditures on medicine; on food.
6. Assume you were particularly concerned with the welfare of children. How would this affect the kind of welfare programs you might support or how you might design your welfare programs?

15

Education

Some of the most heated political controversies in recent years have revolved around education, the third largest single item of expenditure in the public sector, behind national defense and social security. The debates have involved how education should be financed and how it should be produced. Should the federal government take a larger role in the financing of education? Should there be public support for private schools? Should tuition be charged at state universities? How should the funds that are available be allocated between remedial education for the disadvantaged and accelerated education for the gifted?

Underlying the debate are the following basic questions: What is the most efficient way of providing for the education of America's youth? What should be the relative roles of government and the private sector in the production and financing of education? What are the trade-offs between equity and efficiency? Are we spending enough (or too much) on education, and are we spending it well?

Concern that all is not well with American education has reached a crescendo in recent years, with reports from the Secretary of Education, the Carnegie Forum on Education and the Economy, and the National Governors' Association, among others, criticizing the state of American schooling. Just as the Soviet success in 1957 in launching the first man-made satellite (Sputnik) before an American satellite was launched was attributed to deficiencies in our schools and therefore provided a spur to education, particularly in the sciences, so the loss of America's competitive edge today has again been at least partly attributed to the failure of our educational system. The mathematics skills of U.S. eighth graders appear to be lower than those of nine of the twelve major industrialized countries with which they were compared.[1] The Japanese not only score higher than we do, but they spend far more time in school than our students do.[2]

There are other indications of problems. While scores on standardized tests for college-bound seniors, such as the Scholastic Aptitude Test (S.A.T.) and the American College Testing (A.C.T.) test, have recovered slightly from the lows they hit in the early eighties, they still remain below the levels of fifteen years ago.[3] Between 1964 and 1982, students' performance declined on fifteen of twenty-three examinations used to determine admissions to graduate and professional schools.[4]

Not surprisingly, there is more agreement that something is wrong than about what should be done, or who should take responsibility for doing it. In this chapter we address a few of the recent proposals for reforms in our educational system. We review the present structure of American education and survey some of the arguments for why education should be publicly provided.

THE STRUCTURE OF EDUCATION IN THE UNITED STATES

Traditionally, elementary- and secondary-school education has been the responsibility of local communities. They financed it (usually with property taxes), hired the teachers, and determined the curriculum. The states have taken an increasing role in financing education; in 1978–1979 for the first time, revenues from state sources exceeded revenues from local sources (as we see in Figure 15.1). Federal support for education, mostly for special programs such as aid to schools where there are a large number of disadvantaged children, also increased in the 1960s and 1970s, so that by 1980, it represented almost 10 percent of total financing for public elementary and secondary schools. Since then, federal financing has declined, to a point where by 1985 the federal govern-

[1] National Center for Educational Statistics, *Second International Mathematics Study* (Washington D.C.: U.S. Department of Education, 1985).

[2] For instance, in the United States, the school day is typically about six hours, and the school calendar 180 school days; and of the six hours, only 50 percent to 60 percent are spent on instruction (N. Karweit, *Time-On-Task: A Research Review* [Baltimore: Center for Social Organization of Schools, Johns Hopkins University, 1983]). In Japan, the school year is 240 to 250 days a year, students typically go to school almost seven hours a day and three and one-half hours on Saturday, and they spend 85 percent of their time on instruction. (D. P. Schiller and H. J. Walberg, "Japan: A Learning Society," *Education Digest*, October 1982). Beyond this, a sizable fraction attend after-school programs (about 75 percent of fourth, fifth, and sixth graders).

[3] The average S.A.T. verbal score was 445 in 1973; in 1986 it was 431; the average math score was 481 in 1973, in 1986 it was 475. (In 1980 the two scores reached 424 and 466, respectively.) The average A.C.T. was 19.2 in 1972–1973, 18.3 in 1982–1983, and 18.8 in 1985–1986. (From *Education Week*, October 1, 1986 p. 4.) The S.A.T. is taken mainly in the East and West coasts; the A.C.T. is more common in the Midwest and South.

[4] Clifford Adelman, *The Standardized Test Scores of College Graduates, 1964–1982* (Washington, D.C.: U.S. Government Printing Office, 1985); for a fuller discussion of these issues, see Joe Nathan, "Implications for Educators of Time for Results," *Phi Delta Kappan*, November 1986, pp. 197–201.

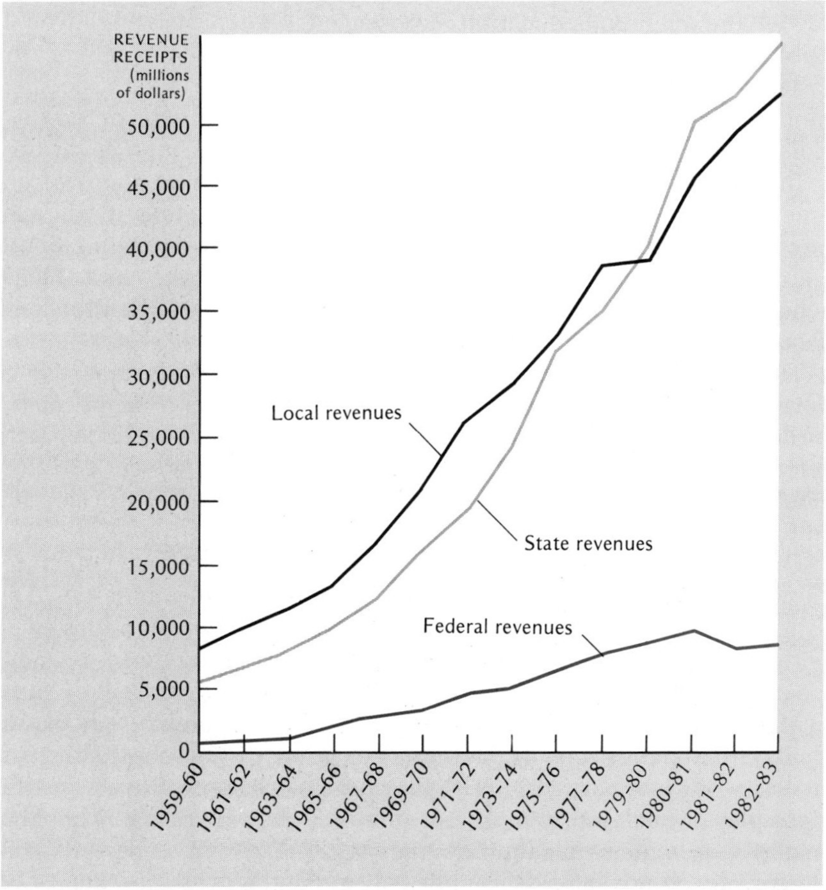

15.1 REVENUE RECEIPTS OF PUBLIC ELEMENTARY AND SECONDARY SCHOOLS There has been a steady increase in the relative role of state support for public education. SOURCE: *Digest of Education Statistics,* 1985–1986, Table 69, p. 80.

ment provided only 6.5 percent of the funds.[5] There is, however, a great deal of variability, both in the role of the federal government and in the role of the state. While in recent years, the federal government has provided approximately a sixth of the funds for primary and secondary schools in Mississippi, it has provided less than 5 percent of the funds in Wyoming. States provided on average slightly more than half of the nonfederal funds, but this varied from 100 percent in Hawaii (where there are no local school districts), to slightly less than a third in Nebraska, and slightly less than a tenth in New Hampshire.

At the same time, the states have taken an increasingly active role in setting certain minimum standards—the number of days students must

[5] From a Report of the Secretary of Education, reported in *Education Week,* February 18, 1987, pp. 1, 18–21.

be in school per year, the lowest age at which children may drop out of school, the minimum education requirements for teachers employed in public schools (they often specify not only that the teachers, for instance, have a college degree, but also that they have taken a specified number of courses in education). They also play a role in the determination of the curriculum. Many states require courses in American history in the eleventh grade and adopt certain approved lists of textbooks, from among which the local community must select the books it will use. Seven states—Arkansas, Georgia, Kentucky, New Jersey, Ohio, South Carolina, and Texas—have made provisions for state takeovers of local school districts when there is "academic bankruptcy"—when the local school districts fail to meet certain minimal standards.

The federal government has not attempted to impose standards or curricula. But following the Supreme Court decision of *Brown v. Board of Education* in 1954, in which the court ruled that so-called separate but equal educational facilities for blacks and whites were not constitutional, the federal government has taken an active role in promoting integration.

One of the consequences of local control is that many rich communities have spent far more on education than most poor communities. The range in educational expenditures per student has been enormous, even within a single state, with rich districts spending two, three, or more times the amount spent in poor districts.

More than 87 percent of all elementary- and secondary-school students attend public schools. Of those who go to private schools, the vast majority (63 percent) go to Catholic parochial schools. Private institutions play a much more important role in higher education. Though a majority of higher education degrees at the bachelor's, master's, and doctor's levels are earned at public colleges and universities, almost 60 percent of first professional degrees are earned in private universities.

In the 1970s the federal government took an increasingly active role in providing aid to higher education, not to institutions but directly to students, mainly in the form of low-interest loans. There were, however, significant cutbacks during the Reagan administration.

Federal Tax Subsidies to Private and Public Schools

The personal income tax may have important effects on the demand for public and private education. Expenditures of state and local communities for education (as well as for other purposes) are implicitly subsidized because state and local taxes (other than sales taxes) are deductible on federal income tax returns, and interest on state and local bonds is exempt from federal taxation. This means that if my community taxes me $1,000 to support public schools, the cost to me is far less than $1,000. If I am in the 33 percent marginal tax bracket (so that I pay 33 percent of each additional dollar of taxable income to the federal gov-

Table 15.1 ESTIMATED TAX EXPENDITURES ON EDUCATION, 1988 *(in millions of dollars)*

Subsidy to public education from deductibility of state and local taxes and tax exemption of interest on state and local bonds		$ 9,337
Subsidies to private education		
Deductibility of interest on state and local student loans and exclusion of interest on state and local debt for private educational facilities	$ 630	
Deductibility of charitable contributions for educational purposes	1,225	
Tax exemption of employer-paid educational assistance	25	
Subtotal		1,910
Total Subsidies		$11,247

Source: Calculated from *Special Analyses, Budget of the United States Government,* Table G-2: "Revenue Loss Estimates for Tax Expenditures, by Function," 1986.

ernment), then by deducting $1,000, my federal taxes are reduced by $330. The *net* cost to me of $1,000 on public education is only $670. In contrast, if I spend $1,000 on private education, it costs me $1,000 that I could have spent elsewhere.[6]

The total value of tax expenditures for education in 1988 was estimated to be approximately $11 billion, as Table 15.1 shows. Most of these expenditures arose from the deductibility of state and local taxes from federal income tax. Since the value of the tax deductions is greatest for higher-income individuals, this form of support for education is, in effect, *regressive;* that is, it benefits higher-income individuals and higher-income communities more than lower-income ones.

At the same time, the tax system serves to discourage private expenditures on education.[7] If I spend $1,000 in tuition to send my child to a private school, not only do I pass up the already-paid-for public education, but the expenditure is not even tax-deductible. Furthermore, the return to the education, which occurs later in the form of higher wages, is taxed. The tax system thus discourages private spending on education.

WHY IS EDUCATION PUBLICLY PROVIDED AND PUBLICLY FINANCED?

The public role in the provision of education has been so pervasive in the United States that it is generally taken for granted. In some other countries, however, while the government may provide funds to educa-

[6] This example assumes that I itemize my deductions rather than claiming the standard deduction. Only individuals with large deductible expenses (such as interest on a home mortgage) itemize. See Chapter 21 for a more detailed discussion.

[7] But the tax deductibility of gifts to private schools (which are treated as charities) strongly encourages private education.

tional institutions, much of the education itself is provided by private, particularly religious, schools.

Is There a Market Failure?

Education is not a pure public good. The marginal cost of educating an additional child is far from zero; indeed, the marginal and average costs are (at least for large school districts) approximately the same. And there is no difficulty in charging an individual for use of this service.

Those who seek to justify public education in terms of a market failure focus on the importance of externalities; it is often claimed, for instance, that there are important externalities associated with having an educated citizenry. A society in which everyone can read can function far more smoothly than a society in which few can read. But there is a large private return to being able to read, and even in the absence of government support, almost all individuals would learn this and other basic skills. Indeed, most individuals would go far beyond that. The question is, given the level of education that individuals would privately choose to undertake were there no government subsidy, would further increases in education generate any significant externalities? There is no agreement concerning the answer, but the case for government support based on these kinds of externalities seems, at best, unproved.[8]

There may be other important externalities associated with education. Public education may have played an important role in integrating new immigrant groups into American culture. Public education may have been essential in making the melting pot work. The benefits of this accrued not only to individuals but to the nation as a whole.[9]

Distribution

The primary justification for public support of education arises from concern about the distributional implications of the private financing of education. Richer individuals will want to spend more on the education of their young, just as they spend more on cars, homes, and clothes. There is a widespread belief that the life-chances of a child should not depend on the wealth of his parents or the happenstance of the community in which his parents live. The prospect of upward mobility, that one's children will be better off, has provided much of the political support for public education and may have played an important role in the political stability of the United States. The immigrants who came to the United States at the turn of the century, though poor, did not feel per-

[8] See, for instance, D. M. Windham, "Economic Analysis and the Public Support of Higher Education: The Divergence of Theory and Policy," in *Economic Dimensions of Education*, A Report of a Committee of the National Academy of Education, May 1979.

[9] There are other externalities associated with the educational process: students learn from each other; good students may learn more from being with other good students than from being with bad students. These externalities have important consequences for questions like: Should students be ability-tracked? Should special schools be set up for the very able? These questions are important, not only in discussing how public schools should be organized but in assessing proposals for more parental choice, particularly through public support of private schools.

manently disadvantaged: they had hopes for their children's prospects. Those prospects, however, often depended on access to good schools.

Imperfect Capital Markets

These concerns about "equity" may explain why the government has taken an active role in providing education at the elementary- and secondary-school levels, but they do not fully explain the role of the government in higher education. If capital markets were perfect, individuals for whom education is beneficial, for whom the return to education exceeds the cost, have an incentive to borrow to finance their higher education. But private lenders are not, for the most part, willing to lend to finance education, and hence those without funds of their own (or their parents') would be denied access to higher education without some assistance from the government. There are good explanations for this: banks are concerned about the difficulty of getting repaid. The substantial difficulties that the government has had in getting loans to students repaid is consistent with these concerns.

Most public support for higher education has taken the form of free, or at least subsidized, education in state universities and colleges. More recently, however, the federal government has attempted to attack the problem directly, by making available grants and loans (often subsidized) and by guaranteeing loans (so that private lenders are willing to extend credit) for higher education.

CURRENT ISSUES

The concern for equality of opportunity has led to almost universal agreement that the government should play some role in the provision of education. Less certain is what its role should be. Currently, it ties both the production and financing of grade-school and high-school education together. If students wish to receive public support, they must go to public schools. They can choose to go to private schools, but they receive little, if any, public support. The issues currently facing education include:

Should this link between production and financing be broken? Should there be public support for private schools?

How much should be spent on public schools?

How should the funds that are available for public elementary and secondary schools be allocated among competing uses?

How much and what kind of support should be provided for higher education?

There are those who believe that a greater reliance on the market (private production) would result in greater efficiency, with little loss (and possibly a gain) in equity, while others believe that the loss in equity would be substantial. In the following sections we review some of the central arguments and proposals for reform.

How Should Public Educational Funds Be Allocated?

Every school district faces the problem of how it should allocate its educational budget. It can allocate more funds for special education, for remedial classes for the disadvantaged, or it can allocate more funds for accelerated classes for the gifted. As we allocate more funds to any one individual, there is some increase in that individual's productivity. This is the return to education.

If we wished to maximize national output, if efficiency alone were our goal, we would allocate funds so that the extra increase in productivity from spending an extra dollar on one individual would be the same as the extra increase in productivity from spending an extra dollar on another. If very able individuals not only reach a higher level of productivity than others at each level of education but also benefit more from education, so that the *marginal* return to education is higher, such a policy entails spending a greater amount on the education of the able than on that of the less able. To some this seems unfair; these individuals believe that the government should ensure that there is equality of expenditure in public education. But when educational expenditures are equalized, those who are more able—or who have home backgrounds that give them an advantage—will still be better off. Accordingly, there are some who believe that government should engage in **compensatory education;** it should attempt to equalize not input (expenditure) but output (achievement). It should attempt to compensate for the background disadvantages facing some groups in our society. One of the major federal programs is directed specifically at encouraging local communities to provide such compensatory education.

As we allocate more and more funds (of a fixed budget) to the less able, and less and less to the more able, total output falls, since the marginal return to education (under our assumption) for the less able is smaller than for the more able. There is thus a trade-off between efficiency and equality, as depicted in Figure 15.2A. What point one chooses on this locus depends on one's values, on how one is willing to trade off efficiency versus equality.

There are some who maintain, however, that the trade-off curve does not look as in Figure 15.2A but as in Figure 15.2B; that is, some movement toward compensatory education may actually increase national output. In this view, those who are advantaged have a higher output than the disadvantaged at each educational level, but the *marginal* return to further education for the more able is actually lower than for the less advantaged. This implies that we can get both more efficiency (higher output) and more equality by having at least some degree of compensatory education. Unfortunately, there is little empirical evidence to support one view versus the other.

Note that the differences in the education-productivity relationship between one individual and another may be the result either of differences in innate ability or differences in environment (home back-

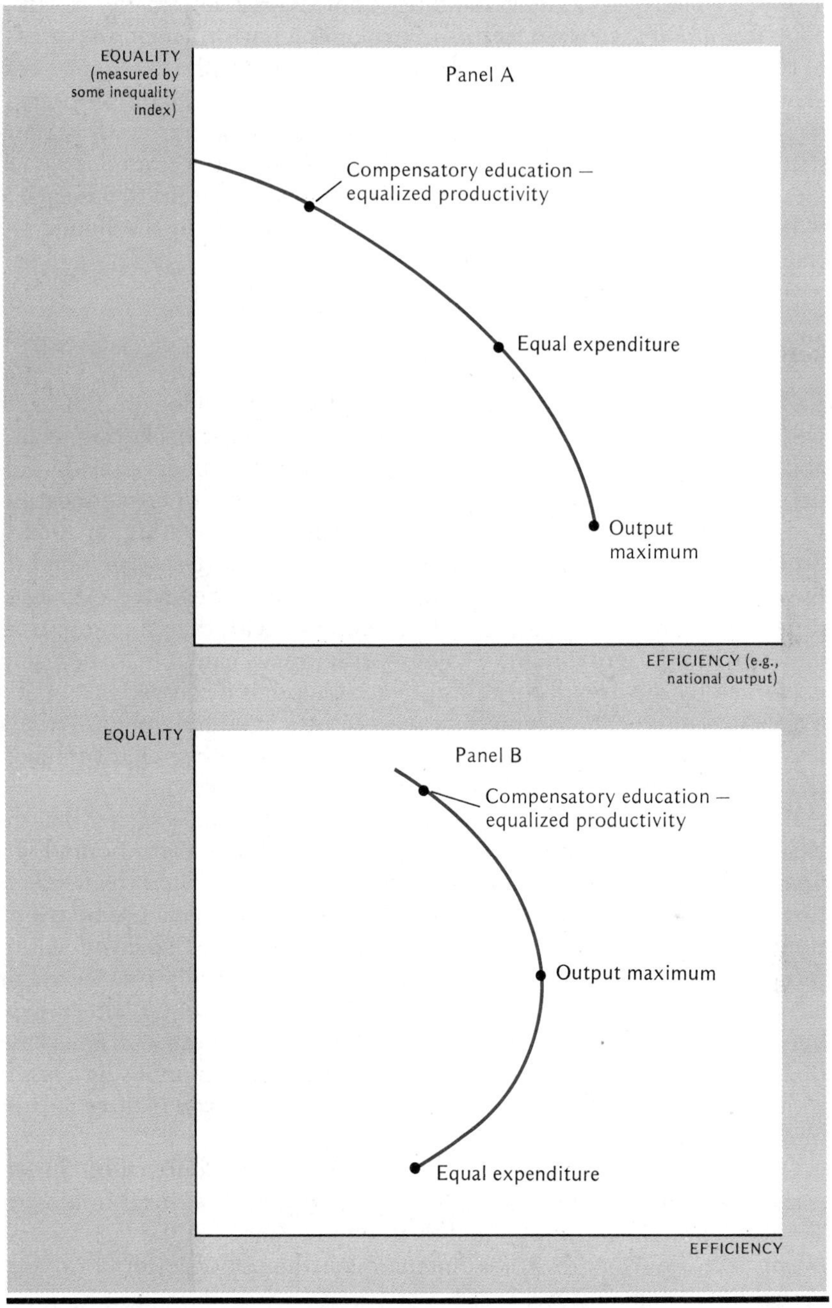

15.2 EQUITY-EFFICIENCY TRADE-OFFS IN EDUCATION EXPENDITURES
(A) There may be important equity-efficiency trade-offs in the allocation of educational expenditures. (B) Under some circumstances, providing more expenditures for the less advantaged both increases efficiency (increases national output) and reduces inequality.

ground). There is a long-standing controversy about the relative contribution of these two factors in explaining performance. In the case of two individuals with the same innate ability but different home backgrounds, the nature of the education-productivity relationships may depend on whether education in the home (home background) is a **substitute** for or a **complement** to schooling. If home background is a complement to schooling, it means that it increases the return to education. If it is a substitute, the more education that occurs in the home, the smaller the return to formal education.

Reforming the Financing of Education

The discussion so far has been concerned with the allocation of funds within a school district among students of different backgrounds and abilities. During the past two decades, there has been considerable debate concerning another aspect of resource allocation to education: expenditures per pupil in some communities are much higher than in others. Different communities have different resources with which to finance education. In addition, different communities have expressed different "tastes" for education. Communities with the same resources may spend different amounts. (These differences can at least be partly explained by the use of the kinds of voting models discussed in Chapter 6. We might expect a community with mostly aged individuals to have less commitment to education than a community with similar resources per student where most voters have school-aged children.)

In 1971, California's Supreme Court ruled in *Serrano* v. *Priest* that the existing manner in which that state's public schools were funded was unconstitutional. The California court held that the "right to an education in public schools is a fundamental interest which cannot be conditioned on wealth." Relying on local property taxes to finance education did just that. The ruling required that the State of California devise an alternative method of financing education. Subsequently, there have been similar decisions in a number of other states. These decisions have interpreted provisions of the states' constitutions as imposing certain requirements upon the states to ensure that all children receive an adequate education.

On the other hand, in 1972 the U.S. Supreme Court ruled, in *San Antonio Independent School District* v. *Rodriquez,* that local funding in Texas did not violate the "Equal Protection Clause" of the U.S. Constitution (the Fourteenth Amendment) even though it resulted in large variability in expenditures.

These decisions have focused attention on several important questions: Should spending be the same in every community within a state? Or should it only be required that a minimal level of education be provided in every community? If equality is mandated, that would seem to preclude communities from spending more on their children. Several states have, in fact, put caps on the levels of expenditures: equality is attained not only by raising the minimum level but by lowering the maximum level. If only a minimum standard is required, how is that to be determined? Obviously, if the standard is set at a low enough level, it will have no effect at all. If equality is insisted upon, what adjustments should be made for differences in the costs of education in different communities, or the nature of the student bodies? Is equality of spending enough? Some communities might use the funds to develop better athletic facilities, others to develop better programs for basic-skills development, others might allocate more funds to special educational programs. The result is differences of treatment of similar individuals who happen to reside in different communities. But to ensure equality would require eliminating community control and establishing a centralized educational system within each state.

What is at issue are not only the basic trade-offs of equity and efficiency; some individuals believe that every parent should have the right to make decisions concerning his or her child's education. With local control of education, parents at least feel that they can have some influence over the outcomes. Thus local autonomy of schools has become to many almost a principle in its own right; some individuals might still favor local control, even if it could be shown that central control was both more equitable and more efficient. To others, what is at issue is a trade-off between the rights of parents (to decide about their children's education) and the rights of children (to equality of opportunity, regardless of who their parents are).

The states have responded to these concerns by attempting to increase equality while retaining at least some degree of local autonomy. In New Jersey, for instance, the state has broadened its role in financing education (with poorer districts getting much more aid than better-off districts); it has set minimal educational standards that all districts must attain (when Trenton failed to meet these standards, and failed to take what the state thought was appropriate action to remedy the deficiencies, the state took over the school district); and it has placed ceilings on the amount that higher-spending school districts can spend.

LIMITATIONS ON EQUALITY IMPOSED BY PARENTAL CHOICE

Some of these attempts to attain greater equality, such as the ceilings on expenditures by richer school districts, have been criticized as self-defeating. What is of concern is not just the degree of inequality within public schools but the total extent of inequality in our society. So long as the government is not willing to prohibit individuals from going to private schools, any attempt to introduce too much equality into the public educational system will result in individuals transferring to private schools.

In England there have been periodic proposals for the government actively to discourage the private schools, on the grounds that private education leads to social stratification (only the upper and upper-middle classes send their children to private schools). But in the United States, restrictions on private schools might well be unconstitutional; in any case, though there has been controversy about whether private schools should receive public support, which we discuss below, there have been no suggestions that the private schools be actively discouraged.

Those who can afford to send their children to private schools may be induced to do so if they believe that the public schools are not providing an adequate level of education for their children. In narrow economic terms, parents may ascertain that the return to investing in their children exceeds the return to investing in other assets.

EDUCATION AS A SCREENING DEVICE

The view of education that we have presented so far is referred to as the **human capital** view. Education is an investment in individuals, which yields a return, just like any other capital investment.[10]

An alternative view holds that one of the important functions of education is to identify the abilities of different individuals. Those who go to school longer get a higher wage and are observed to be more productive; but this is not because the schools have increased the productivity of these individuals. Rather, the schools have identified those who are the most productive individuals. The school system is viewed as a **screening device,** separating the very able from the less able.[11]

If this view is correct, or even if a part of the return to education represents the identification of those who are more productive, there may be much less of a trade-off between efficiency and equity than would be the case if the primary reason that those who receive more education receive a higher wage is that they are made, by the education, more productive. Reducing "screening" may reduce the extent of inequality without reducing net national output. On the other hand, if this screening view is correct, it may be more difficult to use public education as a way of promoting equality. First, the expenditures on education may have relatively little effect on productivity and hence on incomes, which reflect individuals' productivity; and second, if the public school systems fail to identify the very able, those who believe that their children are in this category will pursue other means to signal ability, such as sending them to private schools. Even were the government successful in reducing inequality among those graduating from public schools, there might remain inequality between graduates of public and private schools.

Note that both the screening and human capital views are consistent with the systematic correlation between the level of education and

[10] There is a huge literature on the human capital view of education. See, for instance, Gary Becker, *Human Capital: A Theoretical and Empirical Analysis with Special References to Education* (New York: National Bureau of Economic Research, Columbia University Press, 2nd ed., 1975).

[11] This view has been put forward by J. E. Stiglitz, "The Theory of Screening Education and the Distribution of Income, "*American Economic Review* 65 (1975): 283–300, A. Michael Spence, "Job Market Signaling," *Quarterly Journal of Economics* 87 (1973): 355–74, and K. J. Arrow, "Higher Education as a Filter," *Journal of Public Economics* 2 (1973): 193–216.

wages: the average wage of the better educated is higher than that of the less educated.

Public Support for Private Schools

In recent years there has been increasing political support for financial aid to private schools. Traditionally, most private schools in the United States have been affiliated with religious institutions, and thus the controversy over aid to private schools has been closely related to issues of state support for religion, which is explicitly barred by the Constitution. In the last few years, the issue has ceased to be viewed primarily in this light. Most of the proposals involve financial assistance directly to the students rather than to the institution and thus sidestep the issue of state support of religious education (though the consequences may be much the same).

TUITION TAX CREDITS

There have been two major proposals for aid to private schools. The first of these is a tuition tax credit. Parents who pay for tuition in private schools would receive a credit against their income tax of a certain percentage of their expenditures. Were such a proposal to be adopted, it would be another example of a tax expenditure. The government could just as well not give a tax credit but simply send a check of a certain amount to those who have children enrolled in private schools (with the amount depending on the amount spent on a private school, and perhaps on the income of the parent). The expenditures on private education would then be an explicit item in the federal budget. Giving aid in the form of a tax credit has two disadvantages over direct grants. First, it does not provide aid to the poor, who pay little or nothing in income taxes and who would not be able to afford a private school even if the tax credit were refundable. Second, it makes the implicit expenditure on private education less obvious, less open. (This may, in fact, be one of its desirable characteristics from the point of view of supporters of aid to private education.)

SCHOOL VOUCHERS

A second major proposal is called the **school voucher** system.[12] Each child would be given a voucher, a piece of paper, which he could use at any school he wished.[13] He would turn over the voucher to the school, and the government would then send the school a fixed dollar sum. The school might or might not charge a fee in addition to the voucher. Public schools would, under this proposal, have to compete directly with pri-

[12] For a survey of the issues, see G. R. LaNoye, *Educational Vouchers: Concepts and Controversies* (New York: Teachers College Press, 1972).

[13] Note that the GI bill, which provided educational benefits for veterans, was essentially a voucher program. They could use their vouchers at any qualified educational institution.

vate schools. Public schools would have to raise their revenue by persuading students to attend, just as private schools would. If parents valued the kinds of programs provided by the public schools, then the public schools would do well.

In the view of supporters of the school voucher scheme, this competition would force public schools to be more responsive, and the competition would lead to greater innovation in education. In the view of voucher critics, the scheme would lead to a more socially and economically stratified society, with the children of wealthy and well-educated parents going to one school and the children of poor and less well-educated parents going to other schools. Though regulations to prevent racial discrimination might be easily enforced, regulations to ensure the absence of socioeconomic stratification might be difficult to implement. Finally, questions are raised about discipline problems: Would schools be prohibited from turning down students? Would they be allowed to expel them? Would public schools become a repository for students not acceptable elsewhere? Could one devise a system of giving "bonuses" to schools that take children with discipline problems?

Though the plan has received extensive attention, no state has yet adopted it even in a modified form. There was a limited voucher experiment in one school district in San Jose, California. One study, after examining the results of that experiment, concluded that

> education vouchers stand little chance of succeeding in American elementary and secondary schools. [Parents eventually] learn about their alternatives and the rules governing choice. But there is still some question about the social consequences of parents' or students' program choices. Specifically, there is some concern that parents pick programs which reinforce their class-related social values, so that poor children have little opportunity to acquire the beliefs, attitudes, and social competencies necessary for social mobility to the middle class. . . .[14]

When the Reagan administration introduced a voucher scheme for federal compensatory expenditures in 1986 (The Equity and Choice Act, TEACH), bipartisan opposition, mainly reflecting a concern that it would hurt public education, was so strong that the proposal was withdrawn by the end of the year.[15]

Aid to Higher Education

There has been a long tradition of government aid to higher education. At the time many states were established, the state constitutions provided for the founding of a state university. Often a considerable amount of land was set aside and the proceeds from the sale of this land were to

[14] Gary Bridge, "Citizen Choice in Public Services; Voucher System," in *Alternatives for Delivering Public Services*, ed. E. S. Savas (Boulder, CO: Westview Press, 1977).

[15] Concerns about civil-rights protections of the administration's bill led to an alternative proposal, called CHOICE (Children's Options for Intensive Compensatory Education Act).

be devoted to the use of higher education. Then in 1864 Congress passed the Morrill Act, establishing what are called the land-grant colleges, for the study of agricultural and other technical subjects (such as mining). The extension services provided by the states' agricultural colleges have played an important role in the improvement of agriculture in the United States. The state universities, colleges, and junior colleges have enabled many students who would not otherwise have been able to afford a college education to get one. In the 1985–1986 academic year, tuition charges for students in public colleges and universities averaged $1,040, compared to $5,720 for students in private institutions.[16]

The present system of government aid has been criticized on both equity and efficiency grounds. A major justification of government support has been that it leads to a more egalitarian distribution of income. But critics claim just the opposite: the major beneficiaries of government support for higher education are the advantaged. Since the average income of those who go to college will be higher than those who do not, aiding them (by subsidizing higher education) in effect constitutes aid to the better off. The net effect of the aid on income distribution is ambiguous: since the wealthier tend to pay more taxes, they bear a larger share of the costs, but receive a larger share of the benefits.[17]

Moreover, the subsidy to education results in excessive "consumption" of higher education. In deciding on whether to stay in school longer, individuals compare the increment to their well-being and future income with the extra costs (including the *opportunity* costs—their foregone earnings—while they are in school) that they have to bear. Since those costs are less than society's cost (by the amount of the subsidy), some individuals will stay in school even though the extra returns fall short of marginal *social* costs.

Thus if individuals could borrow to finance their education but had to pay the full costs of their schooling, they would balance the benefits and costs and make efficient decisions. Poor individuals of high ability would be just as able to go to universities as the child of a rich parent.[18] If individuals could borrow, no one for whom higher education was a worthwhile investment would be denied access to it.

In this view, then, the problem is one of inability to borrow (a market failure), and the appropriate remedy is for the government to provide (or guarantee) loans. Advocates of student loan programs claim that they are more equitable than tuition grants and encourage economic effi-

[16] U.S. Department of Education, *Digest of Education Statistics*, 1985–1986, p. 156.

[17] One study by W. L. Hansen and B. Weisbrod of the University of Wisconsin suggested that the net impact was regressive. The average income of those with children at the University of California was more than 50 percent greater than those with no children in public higher education in California and a third greater than those with children in junior college. The subsidy for those with children in junior colleges represented 12 percent of their income, while the subsidy for those with children in the University of California represented 41 percent of their income. See W. L. Hansen and B. A. Weisbrod, *Benefits, Costs, and Finance of Public Higher Education* (Chicago: Markham Publishing Co., 1969).

[18] Universities may provide "consumption goods"—tennis courts, swimming pools, good conversation—in addition to yielding an investment return. Children of rich parents are likely to consume more of such "consumption goods" just as they consume more of other consumption goods.

ciency. Proponents of subsidies (tuition grants), at least for the children of the poor, believe that the inefficiencies associated with "excessive" purchase of education are minimal—the schools tend to weed out those who cannot benefit from the education, and the subsidy is small relative to the total costs (which include the earnings foregone while the individual is in school). They believe that unsubsidized loans will discourage the children of the poor from getting a higher education (particularly since there is always a risk that the investment will not pay off in terms of higher wages; if it does not, they are still saddled with a large loan to repay).[19] In this view, subsidies are critical in encouraging upward mobility among the poor. Advocates of subsidies for children of the poor believe that these effects on mobility are of central concern.

SUMMARY

1. The past thirty-five years have seen marked changes in the structure of education in the United States. There has been increased federal involvement (although support has declined in recent years), and an increase in the fraction of funds provided by the states.
2. Education is not a pure public good, nor do externalities provide a persuasive justification for the role of the government. The major justification for public support of elementary and secondary education is the belief that the quality of education obtained should not be solely dependent on the resources of the child's parents. Imperfections of capital markets provide the main justification for public support for higher education.
3. There may be important trade-offs between equity and efficiency in the provision of education. Attempts to provide compensatory education, in which the government attempts to offset the disadvantages that children from a poor background face, may reduce net national output. Whether compensatory education has this effect depends on a technological issue about which there is not agreement: whether the marginal product of education is greater or smaller for individuals with disadvantaged backgrounds.
4. So long as parents have the option of sending children to private schools, there is only a limited degree of equality that can be obtained through the public school systems.
5. Though education is not the only determinant of an individual's future wages, there is a systematic correlation between the level of education and wages; there is, however, controversy concerning the explanation of this correlation. Some claim that it is primarily due to the increased skills that children obtain at school (the human capital view), while others claim that it is due to the schools' identifying the very able and differentiating them from the less able (the screening view).
6. There has been increasing public support for government aid to private education, either through tax credits or through a voucher scheme.
7. The government has long played an active role in higher education, though

[19] If there were perfect risk markets, individuals might be able to divest themselves of this risk. The absence of good risk markets can be viewed as another market failure; this market failure, in turn, can be related to problems of imperfect information. To remedy the risk problem, some have proposed a "contingent repayment loan program" in which the amount repaid would depend on the future income of the individual. Yale University actually instituted such a plan.

its dominance is not as great as at the elementary- and secondary-school levels. Some believe that government aid to higher education is regressive in its effects, since those who benefit from college are likely to have higher incomes. They believe that direct subsidies should be replaced by loan programs.

KEY CONCEPTS

Tax expenditures
Compensatory education
Human capital
Education as a screening device
School vouchers

QUESTIONS AND PROBLEMS

1. Discuss the equity and efficiency arguments for raising tuition at state universities. To what extent do your answers depend on whether there is a good college loan program available?
2. Discuss the equity and efficiency arguments for providing college loans at subsidized interest rates.
3. List some characteristics of our educational institutions that seem to be more consistent with the signaling-screening view of education than with the human capital view.
4. What might you anticipate to be the consequences of eliminating the deductibility of state and local taxes from the federal income tax for: (a) the level of expenditures per pupil in public schools, and (b) the mix of public and private schools in the country? If the price elasticity of the demand for education is unity, what should be the effect on the demand for education in a community in which the median voter is in the 33 percent marginal tax bracket? in the 15 percent tax bracket?
5. It is important to remember that the property tax per student is often as high in industrial centers as it is in the suburbs. Why might you still expect that expenditure per pupil would be lower in the industrial centers than in the suburbs?
6. An important study headed by James Coleman found that private schools were both more effective educationally and more integrated racially.[20] Assuming the results are valid, can you suggest arguments for why this might be so? Discuss the difficulties in drawing policy conclusions from such a study.
7. In another important study headed by Coleman, it was found that the expenditures per pupil in a school district did not seem to have a significant effect upon educational achievement (when account is taken of the ability of the students and their home backgrounds). What could account for these results? What policy implications might they have?
8. Discuss the trade-offs involved in deciding upon the appropriate level and form of decentralization/centralization within education. (In your discussion, bear in mind that different aspects—finance, control of curriculum, control of hiring—can be decentralized to different extents; and that the

[20] J. S. Coleman, T. Haffer, and S. Kilgore, *Achievement in High School: Public and Private Schools Compared* (New York: Basic Books, 1981).

issues of centralization/decentralization relate not only to the division of responsibility between the federal government, the state, and the local community, but also to the division of responsibility within the school district, between central office administrators, school principals, and teachers).

9. Discuss the trade-offs between parental choice and equality of opportunity. Should the principle of consumer sovereignty extend to parental rights to choose the amount and form of education for their children?
10. Provide an economic analysis of the issue of tracking (of putting individuals of similar abilities in the same classes). What empirical evidence would you like to have to decide on whether tracking is desirable? What are the trade-offs?

PART FOUR

TAXATION: THEORY

Parts Four and Five are concerned with taxation. This part develops the general theory of taxation, and the next examines in some detail taxation in the United States.

While Chapter 16 sets out the general principles of taxation, Chapter 17 discusses who bears the burden of taxation. Chapters 18 and 19 analyze the effects of taxation on economic efficiency, while Chapter 20 shows how equity and efficiency considerations may be balanced off against each other.

16

Taxation: An Introduction

Taxation is unlike most transfers of money from one individual to another: while most other transfers are entered into voluntarily, taxation is compulsory. In Chapter 5 we saw some of the reasons why the contributions to support public services need to be compulsory: because of the free rider problem, unless support for public goods is made compulsory no one will have an incentive to contribute. We showed, in particular, that all individuals might be made better off by voluntarily agreeing to be compelled to contribute to the support of public goods. Yet the ability to compel individuals to contribute to the support of public goods may also provide the government with the ability to compel individuals to contribute to support some special-interest group: the government has the power to force one group to give up its resources to another group. This forced transfer has been likened to theft, with one major difference: while both are involuntary transfers, transfers through the government wear the mantle of legality and respectability conferred upon them by the political process. In some countries and at some times, the distinction becomes, at best, blurred. The political process becomes detached from the citizenry and is used to transfer resources to the groups in power.

The difficulty arises in distinguishing the legitimate from the illegitimate uses of the power of taxation. Concern about these issues was central to the founders of the Republic. The rebellion that became the

Revolutionary War is often dated to the Boston Tea Party, which was motivated by a concern that unjust taxes were being levied on the colonies. The slogan "Taxation without representation is tyranny" provided one of the central motifs of the revolution.

BACKGROUND

Taxes have existed virtually as long as there have been organized governments. The Bible said that a tithe (one-tenth) of the crops should be set aside for purposes of redistribution and for the support of the priesthood. It was not clear what the enforcement mechanism was, and the Bible does not report on the extent of tax evasion. In the Middle Ages, individuals provided services directly to their manor lords; these were effectively taxes but they were not monetized. The fact that they were forced to provide these services meant that they were, to some extent, slaves. Some have argued that the fact that modern taxes are **monetized**—individuals are not compelled to provide services (except in the special case of the draft) but to provide money—should not obscure the underlying relationships. An individual who must give the government, say, one-fourth of his earnings is, effectively, working one-fourth of the time for the government. One important advantage of this monetization ought to be apparent: the government would face an enormous managerial problem if each individual had to work three months a year for the government.

There are, however, two critical distinctions between feudal levies and modern taxes. In the former case, individuals were not allowed to leave their manor (without the permission of their lord). The fact that (outside the Soviet bloc countries) individuals are allowed to choose where they wish to live, and therefore the jurisdiction that will impose taxes upon them, is a critical distinction. Second, while under the manorial system individuals were compelled to work, in modern taxation individuals are compelled only to share what they receive from working (or what they receive from investing, or what they spend) with the government. They can choose to pay less if they are willing to work less and receive less for themselves. Still, taxes remain essentially compulsory.

In the United States, concern about the possibility that the power to tax might be abused led to certain constitutional restrictions on the kinds of taxes that could be imposed.[1] For instance, because an export tax was felt to be a selective levy against the producers of a particular commodity, such taxes were explicitly barred by the Constitution. Other provisions of the Constitution attempted to ensure that taxes would not be imposed in a discriminatory manner (the uniformity clause, which says that taxes must be imposed in a uniform way, and the apportionment clause, which says that direct taxes have to be apportioned among the states on the basis of population). These constitutional restrictions were interpreted to imply that the government could not impose an income

[1] See Chapter 2.

tax. It was not until a constitutional amendment was passed in 1913 that the federal government could impose such a tax.

The restrictions on taxation reflected the experiences the colonies had had with discriminatory taxes levied by the British government. The writers of the Constitution did not and probably could not have anticipated all of the forms of discriminatory taxation. Thus in spite of the safeguards that the founders of the Republic attempted to provide through the Constitution, issues of taxation have been among the most divisive issues facing the country. In the early nineteenth century there was, for instance, considerable controversy over tariffs.[2] Tariffs on industrial goods, though they raised revenues, also served to protect the industrial North; but while the North may have benefited from these tariffs, the South suffered by having to pay higher prices for the protected goods.

Changing Patterns of Taxation in the United States

The passage of the Sixteenth Amendment in 1913, establishing the income tax, marked a turning point in the structure of taxation in the United States. Prior to that, the principal sources of federal revenues were excise taxes and customs duties. In the past sixty years, these have dwindled in importance, and individual income taxes and social security payroll taxes have become the principal source of revenue to the federal government.

Table 16.1 RECEIPTS OF THE FEDERAL GOVERNMENT, 1988 (estimates in billions of dollars)

Individual income tax	$392.8
Corporate income tax	117.2
Excise taxes	33.4
Customs duties	15.3
Social security payroll taxes	333.2
Estate and gift taxes	5.8
Miscellaneous	18.8
Total	$916.6

Source: Economic Report of the President, 1987, p. 333.

Table 16.1 shows the estimated receipts of the federal government in 1988, while Table 16.2 shows the changes in the relative importance of various taxes during the past century. In particular, we see: (a) a marked increase in the relative importance of taxes imposed directly on individuals and corporations (called *direct* taxes) and a steep drop in the importance of taxes on commodities (called *indirect* taxes); and (b) within direct taxes, a sharp decrease since 1960 in the role of the corporate income tax and a marked increase in the role of payroll taxes.

[2] Tariffs are taxes imposed on imported goods. By raising the prices of the imported goods, they enable domestic producers of similar goods to raise their prices as well. In this way tariffs "protect" domestic producers.

Table 16.2 PERCENT OF FEDERAL RECEIPTS FROM VARIOUS SOURCES

	1902	*1940*	*1960*	*1980*	*1988*
Direct taxes					
Individual income tax	—	16.9	44.0	47.2	42.9
Corporate income tax	—	19.8	23.2	12.5	12.8
Social security payroll tax	—	14.2	15.9	30.5	36.4
Estate and gift taxes	1.0	6.3	1.7	1.0	1.7
Indirect taxes					
Excise taxes	47.6	31.6	12.6	4.7	3.6
Customs	47.4	5.8	1.2	1.4	.6

Sources: 1902–1940: U.S. Bureau of the Census: *Historical Statistics for the U.S., Colonial Times to 1957,* pp. 724, 727, 729.
1960–1980: J. Pechman, *Federal Tax Policy* (Washington, D.C.: Brookings Institution, 1983), p. 353, derived from Office of Management and Budget.
1988 (estimates): *Economic Report of the President,* 1987, p. 333.

These trends have not, however, been universal: in Europe, during the past two decades there has been increasing reliance on what is called the **value-added tax,** which is effectively a national sales tax. The value-added tax is imposed on the value added by an enterprise—that is, the value of its sales minus what is purchased from other firms. There has been some discussion in the United States concerning the introduction of such a tax. The United States relies more heavily than Japan and most European countries on the individual income tax; the U.S. federal government gets almost half its revenue from this source.

Designing an Income Tax System

The concept of "income" seems simple enough in theory, but in practice defining what is and is not income turns out to be a very difficult matter. The government has made matters worse for itself by taxing different kinds of income at different rates and by allowing a variety of deductions. Each distinction introduced by the tax law necessitates a set of careful legal definitions; and when the legal distinctions do not correspond well to sound economic distinctions, there are clear incentives to make sure that income is received in a form that is taxed at a low rate.

The motive for introducing many of the distinctions has been quite reasonable. For instance, the deduction for certain medical expenses was introduced because people believe that those who are sick and have to pay high medical bills should be treated differently from those who are not sick. But no matter how good the motive, the consequences in terms of the complexity of the tax code and increased opportunities for tax avoidance are subjects of widespread concern.

In addition, these special provisions have incentive effects. The deductibility of medical expenses may induce individuals to spend more on medical care than they otherwise would. The recognition of these incentive effects of taxation has had a further consequence. Between 1960 and 1986 the tax system was increasingly used to encourage activities that were thought to be socially desirable. Among the examples of this were the energy tax credit (to encourage energy conservation) and the investment tax credit (to encourage individuals and firms to invest more).[3]

The increase in income tax rates between 1913 and 1986,[4] combined with the extension of special treatment to a growing number of categories of income, led to a marked increase in tax avoidance activities. **Tax shelters**—investment schemes by which individuals can reduce their tax liabilities—grew enormously in popularity. (We discuss some of these in Chapter 24.) These schemes undoubtedly enabled some individuals to increase their after-tax income, but they also provided a good source of income for the tax accountants, tax lawyers, and brokers who have put together the tax shelter schemes.

Not all individuals have equal access to these tax shelters; they have provided greater relief from taxation on capital—that is, on interest, capital gains, etc.—than on wages. Salaried individuals—such as schoolteachers—may have little opportunity for tax avoidance, or perhaps more accurately, they may perceive themselves as having little opportunity for tax avoidance. But in fact, many of their fringe benefits, such as health insurance and pensions, are provided in a way that permits this form of compensation to escape tax.

A vicious cycle developed: because of the variety of deductions and special provisions, tax rates needed to be higher than they otherwise would have been to raise the requisite revenue. The high tax rates increased the incentive to find loopholes and to obtain special treatment, further reducing the tax base and necessitating further increases in tax rates.

In the mid-1980s, there was an increasing perception that the income tax system needed to be reformed. Some were concerned that the high tax rates led to serious economic inefficiencies and contributed to the low rate of savings and investment in the United States, and thus to the slowdown in the rate of increase of productivity. Others were concerned with what they perceived as the gross inequities associated with the present tax system. As President Reagan expressed it when arguing for his tax reform bill, there was not a level playing field.

But while there seemed to be a consensus that the tax system ought to be reformed, the consensus on how to reform it, which resulted in the Tax Reform Act of 1986, was fragile. Important compromises had to be made to get the legislation passed. Indeed, earlier attempts at reforms were far from successful; for example, the Tax Reform Act of 1976 is

[3] For a discussion of this use of policy, see Charles Schultze, *The Public Use of Private Interests* (Washington, D.C.: Brookings Institution, 1977). Charles Schultze, currently at the Brookings Institution, served on the Council of Economic Advisers and as director of the Office of Management and Budget.

[4] See Chapter 25 for a comparison of income tax rates over time.

widely referred to as "The Lawyers' and Accountants' Relief Act of 1976." The tax reform bill that Congress eventually passed in 1986 is viewed by some to be the most significant tax bill passed since the adoption of the income tax. Others believe it is seriously flawed and will give rise to further reform efforts. We discuss these issues in Chapter 25.

Why is it so difficult to design a fair and efficient tax system? Are there not some simple principles, some unambiguous criteria by which we can evaluate alternative tax systems? There are some basic principles, but because there are more than one, there are trade-offs. Reasonable people may differ concerning how much weight should be given to each consideration.

THE FIVE DESIRABLE CHARACTERISTICS OF ANY TAX SYSTEM

It is widely believed that there are five properties of a "good" tax system:

1. Economic efficiency: the tax system should not interfere with the efficient allocation of resources.
2. Administrative simplicity: the tax system ought to be easy and relatively inexpensive to administer.
3. Flexibility: the tax system ought to be able to respond easily (in some cases automatically) to changed economic circumstances.
4. Political responsibility: the tax system should be designed so that individuals can ascertain what they are paying so that the political system can more accurately reflect the preferences of individuals.
5. Fairness: the tax system ought to be fair in its relative treatment of different individuals.

Economic Efficiency

A persistent concern in recent debates over tax policy is whether the present tax system discourages savings and work and whether it has distorted economic behavior in other ways. For instance, the large increase in the number of Arabian horses in the United States over the past two decades has been attributed to a peculiar loophole in the tax structure. The special treatment of gas and oil may have led to excessive drilling. Railroad box cars were used for a while as a tax shelter, until a glut of these developed.

The history of taxation is dotted with other examples of distortionary effects. As we mentioned in Chapter 1, the result of the window tax imposed in Britain was that houses without windows were constructed. Modern England provides other examples: three-wheel vehicles, though perhaps slightly less safe, and not much less costly, than four-wheel vehicles, were taxed more lightly than the latter. Hence many individuals chose them in preference to the more conventional four-wheel vehicle. Vans (station wagons without windows) were taxed more lightly than station wagons with windows, and again, many individuals were motivated to purchase these vehicles, but not by a preference for darkness in the rear of their vehicle.

BEHAVIORAL EFFECTS OF TAXATION

Most of the efficiency effects of taxation are far more subtle and difficult to assess. Income taxation may affect the length of time an individual stays in school by affecting the after-tax return to education, the choice of jobs (because for some jobs, a larger fraction of the return comes in untaxed "fringe benefits"), whether an individual enters the labor force or stays at home to take care of children, the number of hours a taxpayer works (when he or she has discretion over that), whether he or she takes a second job and the effort put into the job, the amount that the individual saves and the form savings take (the choice between bank accounts and the stock market), the age at which an individual retires, and whether he works part-time beyond the age of sixty-five.

The effects of taxation are not limited to decisions concerning work, savings, education, and consumption. While there is some question of the extent to which the tax system affects whether individuals get married or divorced, there is little doubt that it affects the timing of these decisions. For instance, the United States tax code considers a couple married for the entire calendar year even if the wedding is held on December 31. So two working people who earn similar incomes, choosing between a December and January wedding date, are strongly encouraged by the income tax to choose January. The reverse is true for divorce. Taxation affects risk taking, the allocation of resources to R&D, and, in the long run, the rate of growth of the economy. It affects not only the level of investment in firms but the form of the investment (including the durability of machines.) It affects the fraction of national savings that is allocated to housing, to other structures, and to equipment. It affects the rate at which our natural resources are depleted. There is hardly an important resource allocation decision in our economy that is not affected in some way or another by taxation.

With tax rates at the levels they have been in recent years, tax considerations are often of primary concern; one may be better off by allocating one's effort to reducing one's taxes than to designing better projects or producing more.

FINANCIAL EFFECTS OF TAXATION

Sometimes, taxation affects the form that a transaction takes more than its substance. For instance, in real terms it may make little difference whether an employer gives an employee money to purchase a Blue Cross health insurance policy or whether the employer purchases it for him. In tax terms, it makes a great deal of difference. In the former case the individual receives "income" upon which he is taxed; in the latter case the "fringe benefit" is not taxed. Similarly, in real terms it makes little difference whether I save directly for my retirement or whether my employer takes some of my salary and invests it in a (fully funded) pension plan. But the tax implications are quite different, and as a result individuals are induced to save through the pension plan rather than directly. These financial effects may, of course, have in turn further real effects on the economy: pension plans, because of the restrictions imposed on them, may invest their funds differently than the way an individual saving for his retirement might invest them. The restriction of individual choice resulting from the provision of these fringe benefits may, itself, have economic consequences.

Similarly, since dividends, capital gains (increases in the price of a stock), and interest are all treated differently, the tax structure may have a significant effect on the *financial* structure of U.S. corporations; for instance, on firms' decisions whether to finance additional investments by borrowing or issuing new shares.

DISTORTIONARY AND NONDISTORTIONARY TAXATION

Any tax system influences behavior. After all, the government is taking money away from an individual, and we would expect him to respond, in some way, to this lower income. When we say that we want the tax system to be nondistortionary, we clearly do not mean that we want the individual not to react at all.

A tax is **nondistortionary** if, and only if, there is nothing an individual can do to alter his tax liability. Economists call taxes that are nondistortionary **lump-sum taxes**. Distortions are associated with the individual's attempt to lower his tax liability. Virtually all of the taxes imposed in the United States are, in this sense, distortionary. A head tax—a tax one has to pay regardless of income or wealth—is a lump-sum tax. A tax that depends on nonalterable characteristics (age, sex) is also a lump-sum tax.

Any tax on commodities is distortionary: an individual can change his tax liability simply by reducing his purchases of the commodity. Any tax on income is also distortionary: an individual can reduce his tax liability simply by working less or by saving less.

In Chapter 18 we shall show that distortionary taxes are inefficient in the sense that *if* the government could replace them with a lump-sum tax, it could raise more revenue, with the same effect on the welfare of individuals, or equivalently, the government could raise the same revenue and increase the welfare of individuals.

CORRECTIVE TAXATION

So far, our discussion has emphasized the negative aspects of taxation: that we should attempt to design a tax system not to interfere with economic efficiency. Taxation can sometimes be used in a positive way, to correct some market failure. Recall our discussion in Chapter 8, where we showed that taxation could sometimes be used to correct for externalities. **Corrective taxes** (as these taxes are called) both raise revenue and improve the efficiency of resource allocations. The United States has made limited use of corrective taxes. A recently imposed tax on the chemical industry, to pay for the costs of cleaning up and disposing of toxic wastes, can be thought of as a corrective tax. Those who view American energy consumption as excessive—an admittedly controversial position—have argued for an energy tax, which would both raise revenue and reduce (what in their view is) profligate energy consumption.

GENERAL EQUILIBRIUM EFFECTS

The imposition of a tax such as that on wages or on the return to capital alters the equilibrium of the economy. A tax on interest may reduce the supply of savings and, eventually, the stock of capital; this in turn may reduce the productivity of workers and their wages. We refer to these indirect repercussions of the tax as its **general equilibrium effects.**

General equilibrium effects have important distributional consequences, sometimes in a direction quite the opposite of the intent of the legislation. A tax on capital may reduce the supply of capital, thereby increasing the return to capital; in some instances, the degree of inequality may actually be increased by such a tax.

ANNOUNCEMENT EFFECTS

The economy does not instantaneously adjust to a new tax. Often, the long-run distortions are much greater than the short-run distortions, as the economy is able to respond more fully to the new situation.

But some of the effects of the tax may be felt even before the tax is imposed, simply upon the announcement of the tax. When an announcement is made concerning the future tax treatment of an asset, it has an immediate impact on the value of the asset. If it is believed, for instance, that a particular category of assets (say, housing) is about to be subjected to greater taxation (e.g., the interest deduction on mortgages is about to be eliminated), then the price of that category of assets may fall markedly. Owners of those assets at the time the announcement is made will (perhaps unfairly) bear the major burden of the tax.

It is these announcement effects (or impact effects), which may be quite significant, that have given rise to the saying that "an old tax is a good tax." Not only may the announcement effect present serious equity problems, but the anticipation of it can affect the supply of assets. Discussions about eliminating the deduction of interest for mortgage interest may lead individuals to anticipate significant capital loss, were they to invest in housing, and hence the demand for new housing may be seriously reduced.

Administrative Costs

There are significant costs associated with administering our tax system. There are direct costs—the cost of running the Internal Revenue Service—and indirect costs, which taxpayers must bear. These indirect costs take on a variety of forms: the costs of time spent filling out the tax forms, costs of record keeping, and the costs of accountants and tax lawyers. Joel Slemrod of the University of Michigan has estimated, for instance, that the indirect costs are at least five times greater than the direct costs.

The administrative costs of running a tax system depend on a number of factors. First, they depend on what records would be kept in the absence of taxation. Businesses need to keep records for their own internal management purposes; the advent of high-speed computers has greatly reduced the costs of record keeping for large corporations. Thus the tax system imposes a relatively small additional burden on large corporations for reporting wage income of their employees. At the other extreme, individuals hiring household help typically do not need to keep detailed records of the wages they pay to their employees. Although they are required to do so by law, most such individuals probably do not report wages of household help; those who do find it very burdensome; the same holds for many small businesses.

The record keeping required for capital gains taxation is particularly onerous because the records often have to be kept over a long period of time. An extreme case of this is the tax levied on capital gains on owner-occupied homes. Individuals who obtain a capital gain when they sell their home are allowed to postpone their taxes, so long as they purchase a more expensive house. Consider an individual who, at the age of twenty-five, in 1955, bought a house for $20,000, sold it when he was thirty-five for $40,000, and then purchased a new house for $50,000. He kept this house for another twenty years and then sold it for $80,000. Assume he spent $1,000 in 1956 for a new roof, $1,000 for a new furnace in 1957, $8,000 for a new bathroom in 1972, and $5,000 for a new electrical system in 1980. When he finally sold his house in 1985 to move into a rented apartment, he would have to pay a tax on $80,000 less his total previous expenditures ($45,000—his initial $20,000 plus the $10,000 extra he had to put in when he moved into a new house in 1965, plus $2,000 in improvements to his old house, plus $13,000 in improvements to his current house). That is, he has to pay tax on a capital gain of $35,000. But he has to substantiate all his earlier expenditures; he must keep records of all the improvements to all of his houses since the first house he purchased at the age of twenty-five.

A second factor that determines the administrative costs of a tax system is its complexity. Much of the cost of administering the income tax system comes from special provisions. For instance, the deductibility of certain categories of expenditures (medicine, charity, interest) requires that records be kept on these expenditures.

Third, differentiation of rates across individuals (with some individuals paying a much higher rate than others) and across categories of income gives rise to attempts to "shift" income to members of one's family with lower tax rates or to categories of income that are more lightly taxed. Doing this costs money; and stopping individuals from doing this —designing and enforcing provisions of the tax code that prohibit such shifting—costs money. Restrictions on loss deductibility have similar effects. Individuals can deduct, for instance, only $3,000 of *net* capital losses (capital gains minus capital losses) in a year. If an individual has experienced a large loss, it makes a great deal of difference to him if the return to some other investment is characterized as a capital gain or as interest or dividends.

Fourth, taxing some categories of income may be more expensive than taxing others. There is widespread belief that the administrative costs associated with imposing taxes on capital are much larger than those associated with taxing labor.

Flexibility

Changes in economic circumstances require changes in tax rates. For some tax structures these adjustments are easy; for some they require extensive political debate; for still others they are done automatically.

AUTOMATIC STABILIZATION

For instance, as the economy goes into a recession, a reduction in revenues may be extremely desirable, for it can provide needed stimulus for the economy. When prices are stable, a progressive tax structure will provide "automatic" stabilization. When incomes drop, as a result of a recession, the average tax rate is reduced—individuals face lower tax rates because their incomes are lower. On the other hand, when income increases, the average tax rate increases. However, before 1981, when tax brackets were indexed (that is, adjusted to take account of inflation) in periods of *stagflation*—where the economy was in a recession but there was still inflation—the average tax rate increased, even though a lower rate was needed to move the economy out of the recession. Indexing thus contributes to stabilization when prices rise during recessions. Indexing reduces the built-in stabilizing effects of the income tax, however, during periods of expansion and inflation.

POLITICAL DIFFICULTIES OF ADJUSTING RATES

When it is considered desirable to change the tax rates, attempts to adjust the U.S. income tax are often beset by intense political debate. Given the complexity of the tax code, which rates ought to be adjusted? Should all rates be increased proportionately, or are the rich or the poor already bearing a disproportionately large share of the burden of taxation, so that their taxes should be increased less than proportionately? Indeed, it is not even clear how to assess the fairness of a reform proposal. Is it fairer to reduce the taxes of individuals at different income levels by the same *dollar* amount, or by the same *percentage* amount? Should one focus on the average tax rate individuals pay or on their marginal tax rates? Is a tax reform fair if it lowers the average rate faced by a "typical" family with one earner, but increases the average rate on a two-earner family? Should the tax rate on capital be decreased, to encourage more savings, or increased, because capital owners are in a better position to bear the tax?

The political difficulty of adjusting the income tax rate should be contrasted, for instance, with that of the property tax. The property tax is beset by a number of administrative problems, not the least of which is the difficulty of assessing the value of various pieces of property. Still, it has one advantage: adjustments in the tax rates are made annually in a simple manner as the revenues required for the provision of local public services change.

SPEED OF ADJUSTMENTS

Finally, an important aspect of the "flexibility" of a tax system for purposes of stabilizing the economy is timing: the speed with which changes in the tax code (once enacted) can be implemented and the lags in the collection of funds. If fluctuations in the economy are rapid, the lags may limit the efficacy of, say, the income tax, in stabilizing the economy. In Panel A of Figure 16.1 we have shown how, in an idealized economy, income might fluctuate over time. (Actual economies never fluctuate this regularly.) Panel B shows what the movements of tax revenues over time might look like if there were no lags in tax collection. In this case, the fact that tax revenues are low in the depth of the recession means that consumers have more to spend, and this spending will provide an important stimulus to the economy.

Now see what happens if there is a lag in the collection of the tax revenues, as illustrated in Panel C. Government revenues reach a peak (say, at point E) when the economy is already on the downturn (national income is falling); the government should be providing a stimulus for the economy just at this point, to get it going again. Instead, the fact that tax revenues are at their maximum implies that taxes are having a dampening effect. The opposite occurs as the economy heads out of a recession, say, at point E' in the figure. The government might like to restrain the economy so that it will not go into an inflationary spiral. Instead, since tax revenues depend on income in the previous year, when income was very low, tax revenues will be low, and consumer spending will thus be abetted by the lower tax.

Political Responsibility

The government has passed several pieces of legislation aimed at making businesses more "responsible" to their customers, restricting their ability to take advantage of the uninformed consumer. The Truth-in Lending Act of 1968 requiring that a lender present the complete cost of borrowing in a form such that the borrower can easily compare proposals from other lenders, is perhaps the most noted example of this kind

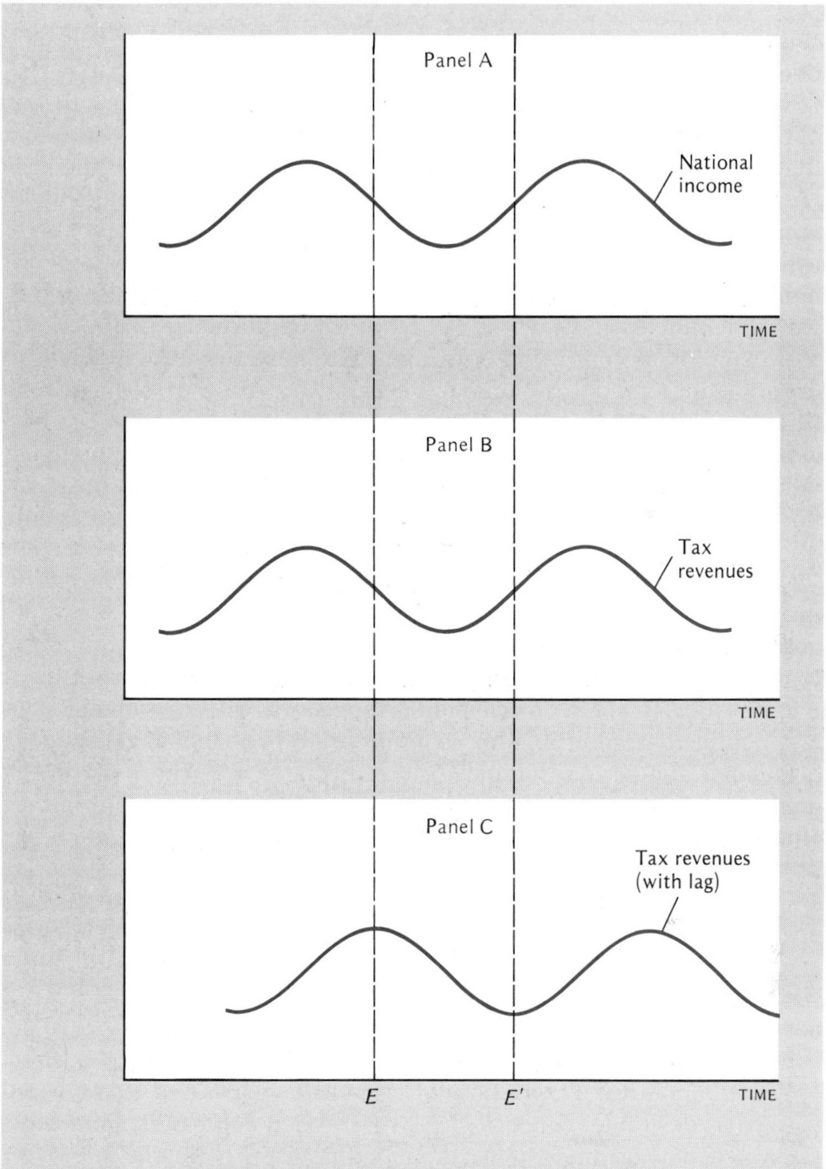

16.1 STABILIZING GNP WITH TAXES In an idealized economy, one might be able to match tax increases and decreases with fluctuations in GNP, as in panel B. Lags in the implementation of tax programs, however, can put well-intentioned tax policies out of sync, actually exacerbating the fluctuations.

of legislation. There is a feeling among many economists that it is equally desirable for the government not to try to take advantage of uninformed citizens.

In this view, those taxes where it is clear who pays are better than taxes where the burden is not so apparent. Thus the individual income tax is a good tax and the corporation tax is a bad tax. Not even economists can agree on who really pays the corporation tax, whether it is effectively a tax on stockholders, consumers, or all owners of capital.

Sometimes it seems as if the government misrepresents the true costs of the services it provides. For instance, there is widespread agreement that there is no meaningful distinction between the part of the social security tax that is paid by the employer and the part paid by the employee. (According to law, half is paid by each.) The employer is concerned only with the total costs of his employee, the employee only with his take-home pay. No one's economic behavior should be affected if it were announced that the entire tax was to be borne by the employee, were employers to give an equivalent pay raise to their employees to cover the increased tax. Would workers' attitudes toward social security be altered if they thought they had to bear the entire costs?

In some cases there is an almost deliberate attempt to persuade individuals that the cost of government is less than it is. Just as businesses find that they can sell cars more easily if they describe the cost as "only $340 a month for a short 40 months" than if they describe it as "$13,600 paid over 3½ years," so, too, governments sometimes show a preference for tax systems in which individuals never fully reckon the cost of government. One of the arguments put forward for sales taxes is that they are less noticed than other taxes, such as income taxes. Individuals never calculate the *total* amount they pay to the government.

A politically responsible tax structure is also one in which changes in taxes come about as a result of legislated changes, and where the government must repeatedly come back to the citizenry for an appraisal of whether the government is spending too much or too little. Steeply progressive tax rates (rates that rise as incomes rise) combined with a tax system that does not adjust for inflation, result in government's tax revenues in *real* terms (as a share of, say, national income) rising in inflationary times, as they did between 1975 and 1980. These increases in taxes were never directly legislated: indeed, many would argue that it would have been unlikely for Congress to have imposed directly, say, a 10 percent increase in taxes in 1980, although inflation had exactly this effect.

Though political responsibility, as we have defined it, is widely viewed as desirable, concerns have often been expressed about how a tax system may be misused in a democratic system to pursue interests of special minority groups, or even by a majority to pursue their interests to the disadvantage of the minority. Thus the Constitution imposed several constraints on the taxes Congress could impose, which we discussed in Chapter 2. Over the years, many of these constraints have been removed, either by constitutional amendment (one of which allowed the income tax) or by more liberal court interpretations. In 1984, for instance, the Supreme Court ruled that the windfall profits tax on oil companies, which exempted Alaskan oil from the North Slope, was not in violation of the provision of the Constitution requiring uniform taxation across the states (though lower courts had ruled that it was).

Fairness

Most criticisms of tax systems begin with their unfairness. It is, however, difficult to define precisely what is or is not fair, as we shall see. There are two distinct concepts of fairness: horizontal equity and vertical equity.

HORIZONTAL EQUITY

A tax system is said to be **horizontally equitable** if individuals who are the same in all relevant respects are treated equally. The principle of horizontal equity is so important that it is, in effect, enshrined in the Constitution as the Fourteenth Amendment (the Equal Protection Clause). Thus a tax system that discriminates on the basis of race, color, or creed would, in the United States, generally be viewed to be horizontally inequitable (and unconstitutional). Although the underlying idea is clear enough, there are two fuzzy notions in our definition: What does it mean for two individuals to be identical in all relevant respects? And what does it mean for two individuals to be treated the same?

Consider twins who are identical in every respect except that one likes chocolate ice cream and only chocolate ice cream, while the other likes vanilla ice cream, and only vanilla. For simplicity, we assume that chocolate and vanilla ice cream cost exactly the same amount. Is the tax system treating the two individuals in a horizontally equitable manner if it taxes vanilla and chocolate ice cream at different rates? One ends up paying more in taxes than the other, and in this sense the tax system appears to be unfair. But the twins faced the same "opportunity set." The chocolate lover could have bought vanilla ice cream if he had wanted (or vice versa). The tax system did not discriminate; it did not differentiate between individuals. This example is contrived so we could have two commodities that are "essentially" identical. In practice, there are many examples where the tax system treats differently individuals who differ in tastes—the higher taxes on hard liquor discriminate against those who prefer scotch relative to those who prefer wine or beer. Individuals who prefer to spend their vacations in their own vacation homes are treated preferentially, compared to those who prefer to travel during their vacation.

If we say that the differences in taste are an important economic difference, which the tax system may well take into account, then we can say that the principle of horizontal equity does not apply here. The twins are not identical in all relevant respects. Carried to this extreme, the principle quickly becomes vacuous: no two individuals are ever identical. What are to be acceptable distinctions? Unfortunately, the principle of horizontal equity gives us little guidance on how to answer this question.

One's first intuition might be that all distinctions are inadmissible: age, sex, and marital status should all be irrelevant. In fact, at present we make a distinction on the basis of age (those over sixty-five are allowed an extra exemption) and marital status (two individuals with the same income who marry pay more in taxes than they did before marriage). Congress has felt that those distinctions are relevant.

Perhaps age and marital status are relevant because they affect individuals' ability to pay. But if these are admissible bases for differentiation, are there other admissible bases? For instance, does variation in the economic costs associated with taxing different groups provide legitimate grounds for differentiation? In a later chapter we shall show that the inefficiencies arising out of a tax system depend on the magnitude of the responses to the tax. In households with two workers, the worker with the lower wage (usually the woman) displays much more sensitivity to the wage rate than the primary worker. While income taxes have almost no effect on the amount of labor supplied by the primary worker, they may have large effects on the secondary worker. Thus if the government were concerned with minimizing the inefficiencies arising out of the tax system, it would impose a lower tax on the secondary workers. Is this fair?

The following example illustrates the difficulty of even defining the meaning of equality of treatment. Assume we could agree that a man and a woman who had received the same income over their working lives should be treated equally for purposes of social security. Should the total expected benefits be the same for the man as for the woman, or should the annual benefit be the same? On average, women live significantly longer than men, so these two rules give different results. If the woman receives the same annual benefit as the man, the total expected value of her benefits will be much greater than the man's. Many would view this to be unfair.

VERTICAL EQUITY

While the principle of horizontal equity says that individuals who are essentially identical should be treated the same, the principle of **vertical equity** says that some individuals are in a position to pay higher taxes than others, and that these individuals should do so. There are three problems: determining who, in principle, should pay at the higher rate; implementing this principle—that is, writing tax rules corresponding to this principle; and deciding, if someone is in a position to pay the higher rate, how much more he should pay than others.

Three criteria are commonly proposed for judging whether one individual should pay more than another. Some individuals may be judged to have a greater ability to pay; some may be judged to have a higher level of economic well-being; and some may receive more benefits from general government spending.

Even if agreement were to be reached on which of these criteria should be employed, there would be controversies concerning how to measure ability to pay, economic well-being, or benefits received. In some cases the same measures—such as income or consumption—might be used to judge ability to pay *and* economic well-being.

ABILITY TO PAY VERSUS ECONOMIC WELFARE

The following examples may help illustrate why there is no agreement concerning what is the appropriate basis for taxation.

Consider first the view that those who are better off should contribute more. The critical question is how we are to tell whether one person is better off than another. Consider one individual who is an obsessive worker, who receives no enjoyment from his work. He is unhappy, his wife and three children have just been killed in an automobile accident, and he has been told that he will die of cancer in two years. Another individual is a happy beachcomber, young and attractive, with no source of income. There may be widespread agreement that the second individual is "better off" than the first, yet the tax system will tax the first at a higher rate than the second. It is apparent that a tax system must be based on a narrowly defined notion of welfare; it cannot attempt to measure overall well-being, and, as such, it must be inherently unfair.

This should be contrasted, for instance, with the allocation of tasks and goods within a family. There, it is possible for us to make overall assessments of both needs and capabilities. We may spend more on a child who has an unhappy experience, trying to compensate for it. There is more complete information than could ever possibly be available to the government.

Consider now the example of Joe Smith and his twin brother Jim, who have identical abilities and education. Joe decides to take a job as a high-school teacher of economics. He teaches six hours a day and the rest of the time he spends fishing, swimming, and sailing. He is very happy. Not surprisingly, his pay is very low. Jim becomes an economic consultant. He works seventy hours a week and has no time for fishing, swimming, or sailing. Their economic opportunity sets, what they could have done, are identical. (Jim and Joe have the same earning ability.) Yet they have made different choices. One has a high income, one a low income. Is it fair that Jim should pay far higher taxes than Joe? Joe believes that it is not economic opportunities that provide the fair basis of taxation but the extent to which individuals have seized advantage of whatever opportunities society has offered—in short, actual income provides the appropriate basis of taxation. Jim believes that it is not actual income that should be relevant but earning ability.

This example illustrates two points: first, while on philosophical grounds Jim and Joe differ on whether economic welfare or ability to pay would ideally be the appropriate basis of taxation, in practice, similar measures (e.g., income, potential income, consumption) will be employed. Secondly, even if they agreed that ability to pay provides the appropriate basis of taxation, controversy will remain concerning whether this is best measured by actual income or potential income. In practice, of course, it is virtually impossible to base a tax system on what individuals could have done. In the United States, we use income (with a variety of adjustments, to be discussed later) as the basis for measuring economic welfare. Some individuals believe that the wage rate provides a better indication of the individual's economic opportunity set than income, since the income tax makes those who choose to work longer hours pay more.

CONSUMPTION AS A BASIS OF TAXATION

But there is a widespread view that neither of these is a "fair" base of taxation. Both correspond to the individual's contribution to society, the value of his economic output. Is it not fairer to tax individuals on the basis of what they take out rather than what they contribute, which is to say, on the basis of consumption rather than income?

Income and consumption differ by savings.[5] That is, income (Y) is either consumed (C) or saved (S);

$$C + S = Y, \text{ or}$$
$$C = Y - S.$$

Thus a major issue is really whether savings ought to be exempt from taxation. It can be shown that this is equivalent to questioning whether the return to savings (interest, dividends, and capital gains) ought to be exempt from taxation. The following example illustrates again the conflicting views of equity.

Consider another pair of identical twins, whom we shall refer to as Prudence and Spendthrift. They both earn the same wages during their lifetimes. Prudence, however, saves 20 percent of her wages during her lifetime, accumulating a sizable nest egg for her retirement. Spendthrift, on the other hand, always spends what she receives and, when she reaches retirement, applies for welfare.[6] Under the present tax system, Prudence pays considerably higher taxes than Spendthrift (since Prudence must pay taxes on the interest that she earns on her savings), while she receives fewer government benefits.

Prudence views the present tax system as unfair, since their economic opportunity sets were, in fact, identical. She asks, "Should the government force me to be my sister's keeper, if my sister does not choose to help herself?" Is it unfair to punish Prudence with additional taxation and reward her high-living sister? Her sister replies that the past makes no difference: as they approach retirement their incomes differ. The fact is that Prudence's income is considerably in excess of Spendthrift's and Prudence is therefore better able to pay for the support of the government (and her sister).

[5] And bequests and inheritances. These involve a rather more complicated set of issues, discussion of which we postpone to a later chapter.

[6] Recall from Chapter 14 that the aged poor are eligible for Supplemental Security Income (SSI), in addition to the social security benefits that all elderly retirees receive.

Prudence's position is receiving more support today, partly on equity grounds but, more importantly, on the grounds that the current tax system may have contributed to the low U.S. savings rate. Under a view that is growing in support, the appropriate basis of taxation should be lifetime income, not income in one day or one hour, or even one year. Lifetime income is defined as the *present discounted value* of the individual's income.

Recall our discussion of Chapter 10, where we faced the problem of adding up the benefits (and costs) of a project that occurred at different dates. We argued there that \$1.00 in the next period was worth less than \$1.00 in this period. If we receive \$1.00 in this period, we could put it in the bank, and have $(1 + r)$ dollars in the next period, where r is the rate of interest. If r is 10 percent, we would have \$1.10 in the next period. Thus, we should be indifferent between receiving \$1.00 today or \$1.10 in the next period. We say that the present discounted value of \$1.10 in the next period is \$1.00. That is, we discount future receipts because they are less valuable. If an individual lives for two periods, and receives a wage of w_o in the first period and w_1 in the second, the present discounted value of his income, Y^* is

$$Y^* = w_o + \frac{w_1}{1 + r}.$$

Of course, the present discounted value of an individual's consumption over his lifetime must be equal to the present discounted value of his income (if we ignore bequests and inheritances). That is, if c_o is the individual's consumption in the first period of his life and c_1 is his consumption in the second,[7]

$$Y^* = c_o + \frac{c_1}{1 + r}.$$

It thus becomes clear that if we believe that the correct basis of taxation is the individual's lifetime income, this is equivalent to believing that the correct basis of taxation is the individual's lifetime consumption.

THE BENEFIT APPROACH

We noted earlier that one argument for the use of consumption as the appropriate basis for taxation is that it seems fairer to tax individuals on the basis of what they take out of the economic system. Some economists

[7] To confirm this, assume that the individual consumed an amount that is less than his wage income in the first period. His savings would then be $(w_o - c_o)$. Next period, he would have his wage income, plus his savings to consume, that is

$$c_1 = w_1 + (w_o - c_o)(1 + r).$$

We can rearrange terms to write

$$c_1 + c_o(1 + r) = w_1 + w_o(1 + r).$$

Divide by $(1 + r)$ to obtain the desired result.

have gone further, and have argued that individuals should contribute to the support of the government in proportion to the benefit they receive from public services. The principles of charging for public services should be analogous to those used for private services. And taxes can be viewed as simply the "charge" for the provision of public services.

In a few cases, the benefit approach is explicitly adopted: fees (taxes) are charged for the use of bridges and some toll roads. Using gasoline taxes to finance roads can be thought of as a simple mechanism for relating benefits (road usage, as measured by gasoline consumption) to taxes.

Economists have not, for the most part, been attracted to the benefit approach to taxation, largely because of the fact that it is impossible to identify the magnitude of the benefits received by different individuals. We all receive some benefit from defense expenditures, but how are we to apportion the relative benefits among different individuals? For many categories of expenditures, assessment of benefits is essentially impossible.[8] A second objection raised against benefit taxes when they are related to usage is that they are distortionary. Basing taxes on usage of a public facility (like a bridge) may discourage its use and thus lead to an inefficient allocation of resources.

There are often equity-efficiency trade-offs involved in levying benefit taxes (in those cases where it is possible to do so). In the absence of benefit taxes, it is impossible to ascertain who benefits from a public facility such as a bridge; if the bridge is financed out of general revenues, those who do not use the bridge are made worse off. It seems unfair to them that they should subsidize those who use the bridge.[9]

ALTERNATIVE BASES OF TAXATION

The principle of vertical equity says that those who are better off or have a greater ability to pay ought to contribute more than others to support the government. The principle of horizontal equity says that those who are equally well off (who have equal ability to pay) should all contribute the same amount. Our discussion of both principles has focused on the difficulties of determining whether an individual is better off than another, or of determining whether an individual has a greater ability to pay than another. How should we adjust for the myriad of differences in circumstances facing different individuals? We consider three examples. In all three cases, present tax laws make some adjustments for these differences in circumstances. There is, however, some controversy about whether the adjustments are appropriate.

The first example has to do with health. It is clear that an individual who is sick and has an income of $10,000 is different from an individual who is well and has the same income. Most of us would say that the indi-

[8] In Chapter 6 we showed how, under certain idealized circumstances, we could design mechanisms that induce individuals to reveal honestly their true marginal evaluations of public goods.

[9] The issue of government subsidies of public transportation systems, such as subways and trains, is currently a heated source of controversy in many metropolitan areas.

vidual who is sick is worse off (other things being equal) than the one who is well. Being sick or well is not readily observable. It is accordingly difficult for the tax code to make adjustments for health status. But there is a surrogate: medical expenditures. Those who spend more on hospital bills are, on average, worse off than those who have no hospital bills. The current tax law does allow for the deduction of medical expenses in excess of 7½ percent of the individual's income.

The second example has to do with marriage. Individuals who are married differ from those who are not. Surveys by sociologists indicate that married men, for instance, are happier. Whether much credence should be placed in such evidence or not, the fact is that married men do live longer and are, on average, in better health. This would suggest that a married man with a given income is better off than an unmarried man with the same income. Does the principle of vertical equity imply that the married man should pay higher taxes? The present tax structure does discriminate against married individuals where the husband and the wife have similar incomes (though probably not for the reasons just given), while marriage may reduce the taxes of a man and woman who have very different incomes.[10]

The third example has to do with the tax treatment of children. Consider two married couples with identical incomes. They both would like to have two children. One of the couples is infertile, the other is blessed with two children. Clearly, the couple with the two children is better off than the infertile couple. The principle that those who are better off should pay more taxes would suggest that this couple should pay more taxes; in fact, the tax law results in the couple with children paying lower taxes.

The analysis so far has shown that though the principles of vertical and horizontal equity seem, at first, to provide "reasonable" bases for designing a fair tax system, they are, in fact, of only limited help. The difficult questions—how do we tell which of two individuals is better off or which has a greater ability to pay, and what do we mean by equality of treatment?—are left unanswered. Furthermore, the principle of vertical equity does not tell us how much more someone who is better off should contribute to the support of the government; all it tells us is that he should pay more.

Because of these difficulties, economists have looked for other principles on which to base a "fair" tax.

Pareto-efficient taxation and social welfare functions

A somewhat different approach recasts the problem of the design of tax structures as a standard welfare economics problem (discussed in Chapter 4). First, it attempts to define (given the tools and information available to the government) what are the set of Pareto-efficient tax structures—i.e., tax structures such that no one can be made better off

[10] We will examine this more closely in Chapter 21.

without making someone else worse off. It then seeks to choose from among the many Pareto-efficient tax structures using a social welfare function, which summarizes society's attitudes towards the welfare of different individuals. The advantage of this approach is that it separates efficiency considerations from value judgments. Almost all would agree that if we could find a tax structure in which everyone was better off (or some better off and no one else worse off), it should be adopted. On the other hand, we often have to choose from among alternative tax systems, none of which Pareto-dominates the other; in one tax system the poor may be better off, the rich worse off. But are the gains to the poor sufficiently large to justify the losses to the rich? The answer depends on value judgments, over which reasonable people may differ.

Economists have made use of two special social welfare functions: the utilitarian (social welfare equals the sum of all individuals' utilities) and the Rawlsian (social welfare equals the utility of the worst-off individual). Using a social welfare function, one can say not only by how much taxes should increase with income but also, for instance, whether and under what circumstances a deduction for medical expenses should be allowed.[11] We now explore briefly what each of these two social welfare functions implies for tax design.

Utilitarianism. Traditionally, utilitarianism was thought to provide a rationale for progressive taxation, the taxation of rich individuals at higher rates than poor individuals. Under utilitarianism, taxes should be such that the marginal utility of income—the loss in utility from taking a dollar away from an individual—should be the same for all individuals.[12] If the marginal utility of income of Jim exceeds that of Joe, reducing Jim's tax by a dollar and increasing Joe's by a dollar increases total utility (social welfare), since the gain in utility to Jim exceeds the loss to Joe. Since taking a dollar away from a rich person causes him less loss of welfare than taking a dollar away from a poor person, utilitarianism seemed to provide a basis for progressive taxation.

But this argument fails to take into account that individuals' income depends on their work (effort), and raising taxes on those earning higher incomes may lead to a reduction in their work (effort). It is thus possible that raising the tax rate actually reduces the government's tax revenue, or that the marginal utility loss to the individual per dollar raised by the government may be very large. The earlier argument assumed, in other words, that income would not be affected by the imposition of taxes; it is now widely recognized that it generally will be. When it is, utilitarianism requires that we compare the loss in utility from an increase in a tax

[11] To make utilitarianism (or Rawlsianism) operational, one must make additional assumptions, as we noted in Chapter 4. It is conventionally assumed that all individuals have the same utility function (at each level of income all individuals benefit equally from an extra dollar), and that they exhibit diminishing returns (an extra dollar is worth less at progressively higher levels of income). The reader should also review the caveats noted in Chapter 4 about interpersonal utility comparisons. The difficulties of engaging in serious policy discussions without recourse to some comparisons should also be recalled.

[12] Thus under utilitarianism taxes are not *directly* related to the benefits one receives from a tax, or to the *level* of economic welfare. An individual who loses a limb may be less happy but also less able to enjoy a marginal increment in his income.

with the gain in revenue. We require that

$$\frac{\text{change in utility}}{\text{change in revenue}}$$

be the same for all individuals. If some group of individuals has a very elastic labor supply (that is, as tax rates are increased they greatly reduce their labor supply), an increase in the income tax rate on that group will yield relatively little revenue, so they should not be heavily taxed.

Utilitarianism was also once thought to provide a basis for the principle of horizontal equity. If everyone had the same utility function, individuals with the same income should be taxed the same. Assume that one individual faced a higher tax than another with the same income. Because of diminishing marginal utility, his marginal utility of income would be higher than the other's. Raising the tax on the individual with the *low* tax rate would cause him less loss in utility than the gain in utility from lowering the tax on the individual with the high tax rate. Again, this argument would be correct if income were unaffected. But it is, so the argument may no longer be valid.[13]

The argument that utilitarianism may imply horizontal *inequity* is perhaps best made by the story of the shipwrecked crew. The crew has enough food for all but one of its members to survive. Equality would thus imply that all individuals die, clearly a worse situation (from a utilitarian point of view) than one in which only one dies.

Rawlsian Social Welfare Function. Several economists and philosophers believe that the utilitarian approach is not sufficiently egalitarian, that it does not pay sufficient attention to inequality. In Chapter 4 we discussed the view of John Rawls that society should be concerned only with the welfare of the worst-off individual, that it ought to design the tax system (and other social policies) so as to maximize his welfare. This social welfare function, maximizing the welfare of the worst-off individual, has some simple and direct implications for tax policy: increase the tax rates on all individuals (other than the worst-off individual) to the point where the tax revenues one gleans from them are maximized. This does not necessarily imply that very rich individuals should be taxed at 80 percent or 90 percent of their income, or even that marginal tax rates should always increase with income. It may turn out that those with very high incomes have labor supplies that are more sensitive to tax rates than middle-income individuals.

There are those who argue that not even the Rawlsian criterion is sufficiently egalitarian. A change that makes one person better off but leaves everyone else unaffected, including the worst-off individual, might still be socially undesirable if the person who is made better off is, say, particularly rich. In this view, inequality itself is a social evil or gives

[13] It can be shown that, under plausible conditions, utilitarianism requires that with distortionary taxes individuals who appear to be essentially identical should be treated differently. A formal exposition of the argument is presented in J. E. Stiglitz, "Utilitarianism and Horizontal Equity: The Case for Random Taxation," *Journal of Public Economics* 21 (1982): 257–94.

rise to social evils. Differences in levels of wealth may give rise, for instance, to social tensions. Inequality of goods leads, in many political situations, to inequality in political power, and this may be used, eventually, to the advantage of the well off at the expense of the poor.

WHAT ECONOMISTS CAN CONTRIBUTE TO DISCUSSIONS OF FAIRNESS

Although economists (or philosophers) have not resolved the basic issues concerning the choice of the appropriate bases for judging fairness, there is still much that can be said. It is important, for instance, to be able to describe the full consequences of any tax, and these are seldom simply described by the amounts of tax each person pays directly. We can attempt to describe how various groups in the population are affected by different tax programs. In all tax systems there are certain groups that seem to pay less than their fair share—given any reasonable concept of fairness. We then need to ask, Why are they treated differentially? It may be (as we shall see in our later discussion) that to treat them fairly would necessitate introducing other, even worse inequities into the tax code. Tax systems must be based on certain *observable* variables, variables such as income or expenditures. As we noted earlier, many of the concepts involved in our more general philosophical discussions (e.g., welfare) are not directly measurable. Even income, as we shall see later, is not as well defined as might seem to be the case at first. Thus, many of the seeming inequities involved in our tax system are simply consequences of the inherent difficulties of translating what seem like well-defined concepts into the precise language required by any tax law.

In other cases, by considering carefully how different provisions of the tax code and changes in those provisions affect different groups, we can obtain some insights into why one group may claim that one set of provisions is unfair while another group claims that to change those provisions is unfair. We can attempt to distinguish those cases where fairness is used simply as a term to cover up a group's pursuit of self-interest from those cases where there is some reasonable ethical or philosophical position underlying individuals' claims.

SUMMARY

1. The five attributes that a good tax system should have are:
   economic efficiency,
   administrative simplicity,
   flexibility,
   political responsiveness, and
   fairness.
2. The two major aspects of fairness are horizontal equity and vertical equity.
3. While some argue that taxes should be related to the benefits received, others contend that taxes should be related to the individual's ability to pay. Still others believe they should be related to some measure of well-being. There is also disagreement about how best to measure ability to pay or eco-

nomic well-being. Any tax system must make use of easily observable variables, like income or consumption. Some contend that it is fairer to tax individuals on what they take out of the system (consumption) than on what they contribute (their income).

4. The utilitarian approach argues that the tax system should be chosen to maximize the sum of utilities. The Rawlsian approach argues that the tax system should be chosen to maximize the welfare of the worst-off individual.
5. Pareto-efficient tax structures are those that maximize the welfare of one (group of) individual(s), subject to the government attaining a given revenue, and subject to others' attaining prespecified levels of utility. No one can be made better off without someone else being made worse off.

KEY CONCEPTS

Monetized taxes	Pareto-efficient tax structures
Tax shelters	General equilibrium effects
Distortionary taxes	Horizontal equity
Nondistortionary taxes	Vertical equity
Lump-sum taxes	Benefit approach
Corrective taxation	Announcement effects

QUESTIONS AND PROBLEMS

1. Discuss how your views concerning the tax treatment of children might be affected by whether (a) you lived in a highly congested country or in an underpopulated country; (b) you viewed children as a consumption good (for their parents), like other consumption goods. Discuss both efficiency and equity considerations.
2. With a progressive tax structure, it makes a great deal of difference whether husbands' and wives' incomes are added together or whether each is taxed separately. Discuss some of the equity and efficiency considerations that bear on the tax treatment of the family.
3. Does utilitarianism necessarily imply that tax structures should be progressive?
4. Consider an individual who has lost a leg but, with a new artificial leg, has the same earning power he had before. How should his taxes differ from a similar individual who has not lost his leg (a) under utilitarianism; (b) under a Rawlsian social welfare function; (c) if you believed that ability to pay provided the appropriate basis for taxation?
5. The government has passed a number of pieces of legislation aimed at ensuring that firms do not take advantage of the limited information of consumers. What might be meant by a "truth in taxation" law? What might be the advantages of and the problems with such a law?
6. "Since the needs, other than medical, of the aged are typically not as great as those of younger individuals who have children to support, if the government provides free medical care to the aged, it should simultaneously subject the aged to higher income tax rates." Discuss the equity and efficiency consequences of doing this (consider alternative views of equity).
7. Suppose that the labor supply of married women is very sensitive to the after-tax wage (that is, it is very elastic), whereas the labor supply of men is not.

The government proposes to reduce the tax on income earned by married women by 5 percent, and to raise by 15 percent the tax on earnings of married men. How would this tax change affect total tax revenues? How would it affect the distribution of income?

8. To finance emergency road and bridge improvements, New York State considered several new taxes in 1987: increased fees on drivers' licenses, a personal property tax on motor vehicles, a tax on automobile parts (including tires), and higher taxes on cigarettes and liquor. Which of these taxes are benefit taxes, which are corrective taxes, which are both? Which of these taxes is least distortionary?

17

Who Really Pays the Tax: Tax Incidence

When Congress or a state legislature enacts a new tax, the debate usually includes some opinions about who should pay for running the government or for the particular program being supported by the tax. For example, when Congress adopted the social security tax to pay for the social security system, it levied half the tax on the employer and half on the employee. It thought that the employer and employee should share in the costs of the social security system. But economic reality, unfortunately, does not always follow the laws passed by legislators. Economists use the term **tax burden** to refer to those who, despite what the legislators say, bear the weight of a tax. **Tax incidence** is the study of tax burdens. In the case of social security, it turns out that the division of the tax burden does not depend at all on whether it is the employer or employee who is responsible for paying the tax.

In analyzing taxes, we say that a tax is *imposed* (or levied) on some person when he is made responsible for paying it. Thus, half of the social security tax is imposed on the employer, and half is imposed on the employee. But a tax may be *shifted* as it induces changes in relative prices. We say that the employer-paid portion of the social security tax is **shifted backward** if, as a result of the tax, the demand for labor declines and, hence, the wage declines. If the wage declines by less than the amount of the tax, we say that it is partially shifted backward; if the wage falls by exactly the amount of the tax, we say that the tax is fully shifted backward. Most economists believe that most of the social security tax (including the employer-paid portion) is borne by employees, who face lower wages as a result of the tax. Another result of a tax may be that employers raise the prices of their output. If so, the tax will be partially or wholly **shifted forward** onto customers. For example, consider the corporation income tax. This tax is popular because it is widely believed that the firm and its shareholders have to pay the tax. But if firms raise their prices as a result of the tax, the tax is borne by consumers. If, as a result of the tax, demand for labor falls and wages fall, the tax is partially borne by workers, not investors. If the tax makes investing in the corporate sector less attractive, capital will move out of the sector, driving down the return to capital elsewhere. Thus, part of the burden of the corporate tax is on capital as a whole, not just capital in the corporate sector.

incidence of corp. inc tax.

Let T be the burden of a tax on an individual (e.g., an owner of capital), and let I be that individual's total income. We call the ratio T/I the **effective tax rate** on that individual.[1] A tax for which the ratio T/I is higher for the rich than for the poor is called progressive; a tax for which the ratio is higher for the poor than for the rich is called **regressive**. If the ratio T/I is the same for individuals of all income levels, the tax is **proportional**. For instance, a cigarette tax is usually viewed as regressive, since the fraction of a poor individual's income that is spent on tobacco is higher than the fraction spent by a rich individual. On the other hand, a tax on perfume is progressive since the rich spend a larger fraction of their income on perfume.

rates

Clearly, whether the U.S. tax system as a whole is progressive or regressive depends on the incidence of the taxes imposed by the federal, state, and local governments. If the social security tax imposed on employers is borne by employees, the effective tax rate on workers is higher than it would be if that tax were not shifted. Similarly, if the corporation tax is shifted forward onto consumers or backward onto workers, the corporation tax is not as progressive as it would be if it were not shifted. Indeed, it is even possible that the corporation tax is regressive.

Thus to calculate how progressive our tax system is, one has to ascertain how individuals at different levels of income are affected by each of the taxes, as workers (through the wages they receive), consumers (through the prices they pay), or as investors.

The Tax Reform Act of 1986 reduced individual income taxes and increased corporation taxes. Thus, on average, individuals were led to believe that they had received a tax reduction, but this was only because they did not include in their calculations the effect of the higher corporation income tax on their real incomes as shareholders, consumers, and

[1] The term "*effective tax rate*" is, in other contexts, used to describe the rate of tax *liability* under a tax system, rather than to describe the tax *burden*. Throughout this chapter, we focus on tax burden. In Chapter 23, where we discuss the corporation income tax, we will use the term in the second sense. This should cause no confusion since corporations can't bear a tax burden, only people can (as workers, consumers, or owners of capital).

workers. To know whether the 1986 tax reform benefited you or hurt you, you would have to know the incidence of the corporation income tax—and this is a question about which there is no agreement.

This chapter first presents estimates of the incidence of the U.S. system of federal, state, and local taxes. Then it presents the theoretical tools that are used to predict the incidence of a tax.

INCIDENCE OF TAXES IN THE UNITED STATES

Joseph Pechman and Benjamin Okner of the Brookings Institution have attempted to estimate who bears the burden of taxes in the United States. They assumed that all taxes imposed directly on labor are not shifted and that sales taxes are borne only by consumers. They considered alternative sets of assumptions for the corporation tax and the social security (payroll) tax. In Case A, half the corporation tax is borne by stockholders, half by owners of property in general (as owners of corporations find that their after-tax return is lowered, they shift their investments in other directions, lowering the return to other forms of capital). Consistent with most economic theory, they assumed that the employers' share of the social security tax is borne by workers. In Case B, consumers (instead of stockholders) bear half of the corporation income tax; consumers also bear one-fourth of all social security taxes and a part of the property tax.

Even with these simplifications, the calculations are extremely difficult. One has to trace through how much individuals at different incomes spend on items subject to sales tax or produced by corporations, how much property that is subject to taxation is owned by individuals with different incomes, what dividends are received by individuals at different income levels, and how these dividend receipts are affected by the corporation tax.

There are a number of ways of reporting the results. One way is to ask how the effective tax rate varies as income varies, that is, what fraction of income is paid in taxes by individuals at different points in the income distribution. The results for 1985 are shown in Figure 17.1. In Case A (the black curve) there is a slight degree of progressivity to the tax system as a whole: those in the bottom tenth of the income distribution paid 17 percent of their income in taxes, those in the fifth tenth, 23 percent, and those in the top tenth, 26 percent. In Case B (the colored curve) the effective tax rate varied very little by income level. The poorest individuals effectively paid 24 percent of their income in taxes, and the richest people paid 25 percent.

Pechman's results for 1985 are similar to those he found for 1966 and various later years. How do we reconcile the apparent lack of progressivity with the widespread view that our tax structure is progressive?

The individual income tax is progressive. But the progressive effects of the income tax are offset by the regressive effects of sales taxes and, to a lesser extent, the payroll tax. The critical difference between Case A

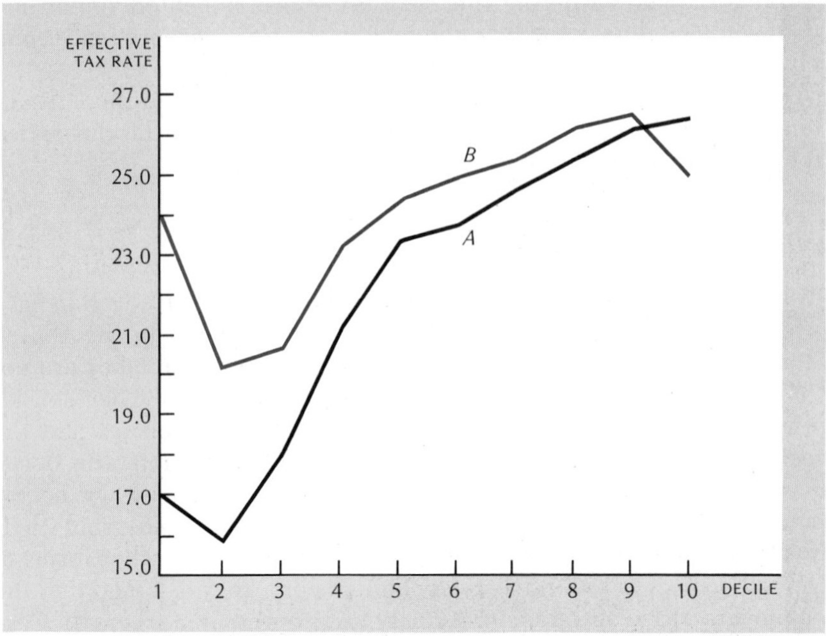

17.1 EFFECTIVE TAX RATES, 1985 Case A: Workers bear all of payroll tax; half of corporate tax borne by shareholders, half by property owners in general. Case B: Workers bear three-quarters of payroll tax; consumers bear one-fourth; half of corporate tax borne by consumers, half by property owners in general. SOURCE: A. Pechman, *Who Paid the Taxes, 1966–1985?, Revised Tables* (Washington, D.C.: Brookings Institution, 1987), Table 5.2.

and Case B arises from the corporation income tax. Under Case A, this tax is progressive (representing a tax on the poorest tenth of the population of 1.6 percent and a tax on the uppermost tenth of 3.6 percent); but under the second set of assumptions, where much of the tax is shifted forward to consumers, it is regressive, with the poorest tenth paying a 2.6 percent effective tax rate and higher-income groups paying rates varying from 1.8 percent to 2.2 percent.

The tax system obviously affects individuals differently, depending, as we have discussed, not only on income but on other important circumstances. Consumption patterns of aged and young, homeowners and renters, urban and rural, single and married individuals differ; hence their effective tax rates differ.

Pechman calculated the average effective tax rate on capital and labor (the sources of income) and on consumption (the uses of income) in various years between 1966 and 1985.[2] His results are shown in Table 17.1. Under both Assumptions A and B, the tax burden on capital exceeded that on labor in 1966. However, by 1985, the effective tax rate on capi-

[2] Joseph Pechman, *Who Paid the Taxes, 1966–1985?, Revised Tables* (Washington, D.C.: Brookings Institution, 1987), Table 5.5.

Table 17.1 EFFECTIVE RATES OF FEDERAL, STATE, AND LOCAL TAXES ON SOURCES AND USES OF INCOME, SELECTED YEARS, 1966–1985 (*percentages*)

	Case A			*Case B*		
Year	*Income from labor*[a]	*Income from capital*[b]	*Consumption*[c]	*Income from labor*[a]	*Income from capital*[b]	*Consumption*[c]
1966	17.6	33.0	8.3	16.0	21.0	17.6
1970	19.7	29.4	9.8	18.0	19.7	19.1
1975	23.9	22.3	10.6	21.9	13.9	21.9
1980	25.3	21.8	9.7	23.6	15.4	20.5
1985	25.9	18.1	7.7	23.8	11.9	17.0

[a] The sum of wages, salaries, wage supplements, and a portion of nonfarm and farm business income regarded as labor income.
[b] The sum of interest, corporation profits before tax, rents, royalties, capital gains, and a portion of nonfarm and farm business income regarded as capital income.
[c] The sum of total expenditures on consumption items generally subject to state sales and excise taxes.
Source: Joseph Pechman, *Who Paid the Taxes, 1966–1985?, Revised Tables* (Washington, D.C.: Brookings Institution, 1987), Table 5.5.

tal was only about half as high as that on labor in Case B. This change reflects the rise in the importance of payroll taxes and the decline in the relative importance of the corporation tax. The effective tax rate on consumption displays no time trend, but it is much higher under Case B than Case A. This is because Case B assumes that a major share of the corporation, property, and payroll taxes is shifted to consumers.

There are two important lessons to be learned from this kind of study. First, it is clear that the burden of taxes can be markedly different from that legislated; and second, it should be clear that the determination of the burden is a fairly complicated matter, and that there is likely to be considerable disagreement over it, even among experts. We have illustrated this by presenting two sets of results, under different assumptions. But even these do not fully span the controversy concerning the burden of taxation. Pechman's analysis assumed, for instance, that before-tax wages are unaffected by the income tax, and that before-tax consumer prices are unaffected by sales taxes. In other words, Pechman assumed that wage earners bear the burden of the income tax, and consumers bear the burden of sales taxes. How before-tax wages, prices, and interest rates are affected is one of the central concerns of the remainder of this chapter.

TAX INCIDENCE IN COMPETITIVE MARKETS

We begin our analysis by considering a competitive market. The basic principles may be illustrated by the demand-and-supply diagram for beer shown in Figure 17.2. The demand curve tells us how much of a commodity is demanded, at each price, while the supply curve tells us how much of the commodity is supplied at each price. The equilibrium

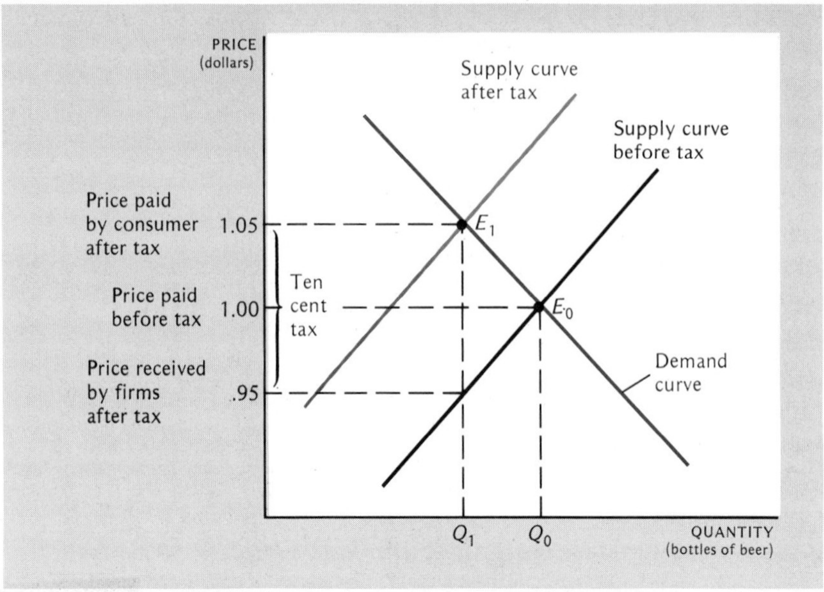

17.2 EFFECT OF TAX ON PRICES AND QUANTITIES The tax shifts the supply curve up by the amount of tax. This lowers the quantity consumed and raises the price paid by consumers.

before the imposition of taxes is depicted by point E_0. It occurs at the intersection of the demand and supply curves, where Q_0 bottles of beer are produced in equilibrium, at a price of $1 each.

Assume now that the government imposes a tax of 10 cents per bottle on producers. For each bottle of beer the producer manufactures, it must pay the government 10 cents. This means that for the producer to receive $1 a bottle after taxes, he must receive before taxes $1.10. What the manufacturer is concerned about is his net receipts (after paying taxes). Hence he will be willing to supply the same amount that he previously supplied at $1 at a price of $1.10 per bottle. The supply curve thus shifts up by the amount of the tax. The new equilibrium price is increased, but it does not increase by 10 cents. In our example, the price rises by 5 cents. The price received by the producer is thus 95 cents. In spite of the fact that the tax was nominally imposed on producers, consumers are forced to pay a part of the increased cost resulting from increased taxes, through higher prices.

The amount by which the price rises—the extent to which consumers bear the tax—depends on the shape of the demand and supply curves. In two limiting cases, the price rises by the full 10 cents, so the entire burden is borne by consumers. This occurs when the supply curve is perfectly horizontal, as in Figure 17.3, Panel A, or when the demand

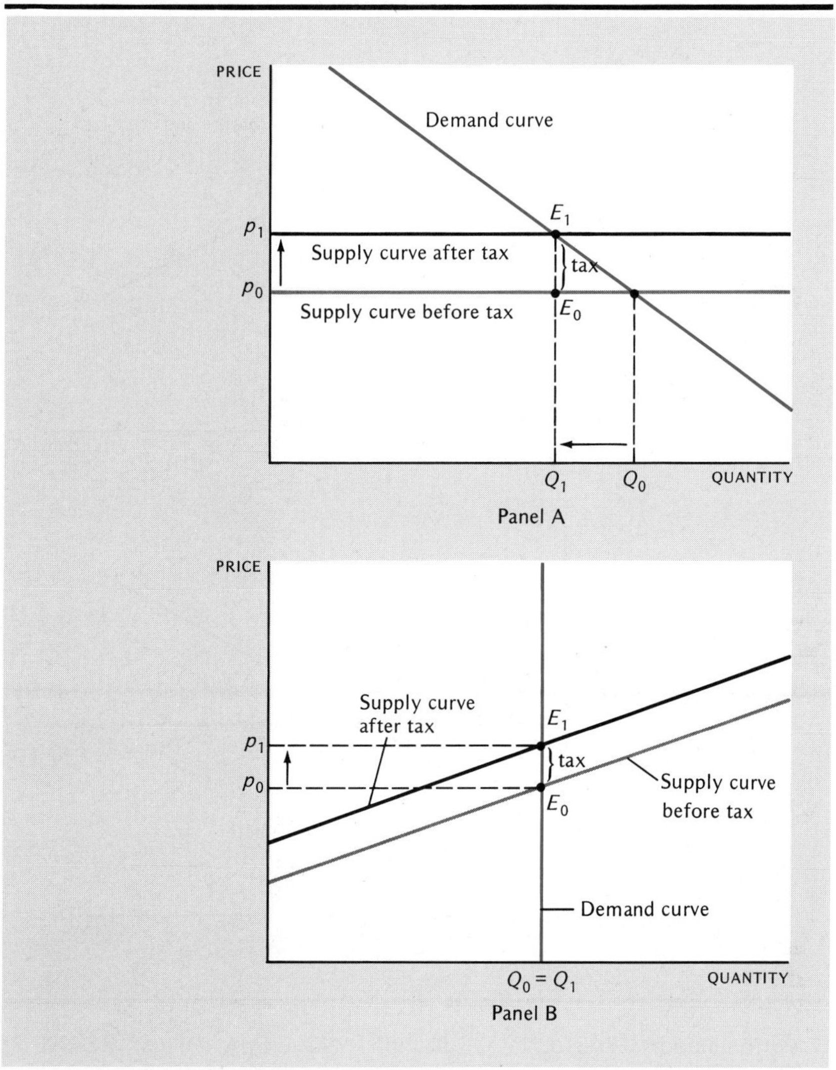

17.3 ELASTICITY OF SUPPLY AND DEMAND: TAX BORNE BY CONSUMERS
(A) Perfectly elastic supply curve; with a perfectly elastic supply curve (horizontal supply curve), the price rises by the full amount of the tax; the entire burden of the tax is on consumers. (B) Perfectly inelastic demand: with a perfectly inelastic demand curve, the price rises by the full amount of the tax; the entire burden of the tax is on the consumers.

curve is perfectly vertical (individuals insist on consuming a fixed amount of beer, regardless of price), as in Panel B.

There are also two cases in which the price paid by consumers does not rise at all; that is, in which the tax is borne entirely by producers, shown in panels C and D (p. 418). This occurs when the supply curve is perfectly vertical—the amount supplied does not depend at all on price—or when the demand curve is perfectly horizontal.

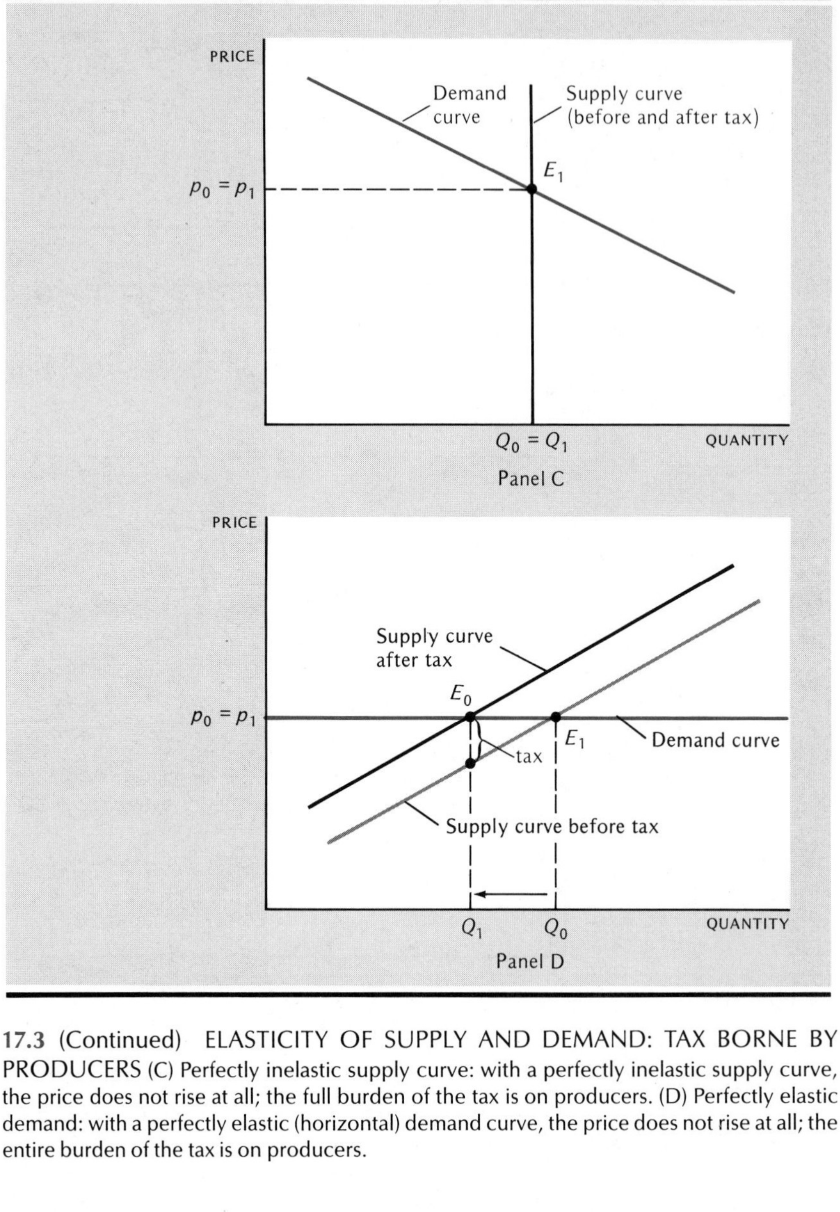

17.3 (Continued) ELASTICITY OF SUPPLY AND DEMAND: TAX BORNE BY PRODUCERS (C) Perfectly inelastic supply curve: with a perfectly inelastic supply curve, the price does not rise at all; the full burden of the tax is on producers. (D) Perfectly elastic demand: with a perfectly elastic (horizontal) demand curve, the price does not rise at all; the entire burden of the tax is on producers.

The Effect of Elasticity

The steeper the demand curve or the flatter the supply curve, the more the tax will be borne by consumers; the flatter the demand curve or the steeper the supply curve, the more the tax will be borne by producers. We measure the steepness of a demand curve by the **elasticity of demand;** the elasticity of demand gives the percentage change in the quantity of the good consumed due to a percentage change in its price. We thus say that the horizontal demand curve, where a small reduction in the price results in an enormous increase in demand, is infinitely elastic; and we say that the vertical demand curve, where demand does not change at all with a reduction in price, has zero elasticity.

Similarly, we measure the steepness of the supply curve by the **elasticity of supply;** the elasticity of supply gives the percentage change in the quantity of the good supplied due to a percentage change in its price. We thus say that a vertical supply curve, where the supply does not change at all with a change in price, has zero elasticity, while a horizontal supply curve has infinite elasticity.

The more elastic the demand curve and the less elastic the supply curve, the more the tax is borne by producers; the less elastic the demand curve and the more elastic the supply curve, the more of the tax will be borne by consumers.

Does It Matter Whether the Tax Is Levied on Consumers or Producers?

Consider now what would happen if Congress passed a beer tax but this time said that consumers would have to pay the tax. For each bottle of beer purchased, consumers would have to pay a 10-cent tax. What consumers care about, of course, is not who receives the money they pay. They simply care about the total cost of the beer.

The effect of this tax is displayed in Figure 17.4. If we now interpret

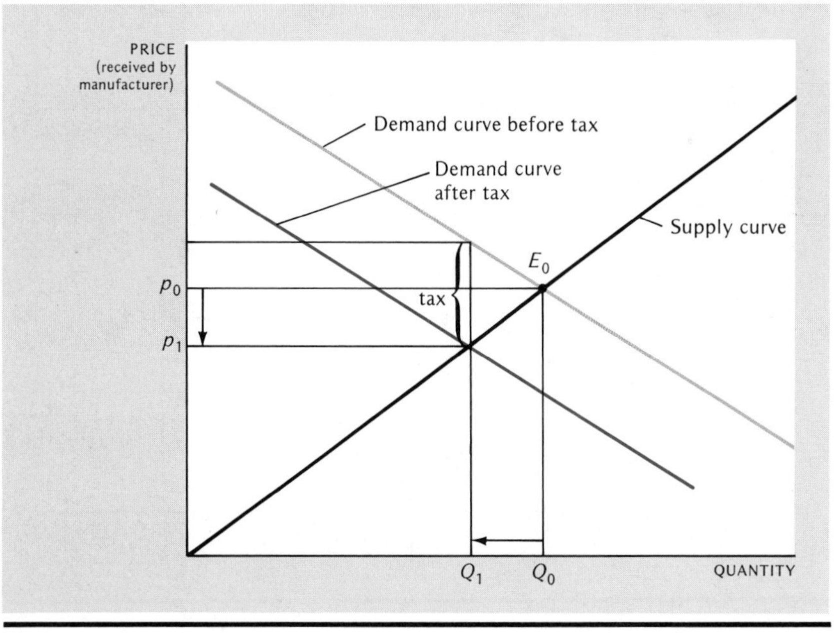

17.4 ALTERNATE VIEWS OF A TAX The effects of a tax can be viewed as either a downward shift in the demand curve or an upward shift in the supply curve (compare with Figure 17.2).

the price on the vertical axis of the diagram to be the price received by the manufacturer (rather than the price paid by the consumer), the tax on consumers can be represented by a downward shift in the demand curve, by the amount of the tax. That is, if the manufacturer receives p_1, the consumer must pay $p_1 + t$, and the level of demand is Q_1, just as it would be if, in the before-tax situation, manufacturers had charged $p_1 + t$. It should be apparent that it makes no difference whether Congress imposes the tax on the producers of beer or on the consumers of beer.

Analysis of the Effect of the Tax at the Level of the Firm

The analysis so far has focused on the impact of the tax on the industry equilibrium. It is useful to see how the tax affects the behavior of the individual firm. In Figure 17.5, before the imposition of the tax, the firm faced the price p_0 and had a rising marginal cost schedule, *MC*. It maximized its profits by setting its price (what it got from producing an extra unit of output) equal to marginal cost (the extra cost of producing an extra unit of output).

Now the government imposes a tax of t per unit of output on the firm.

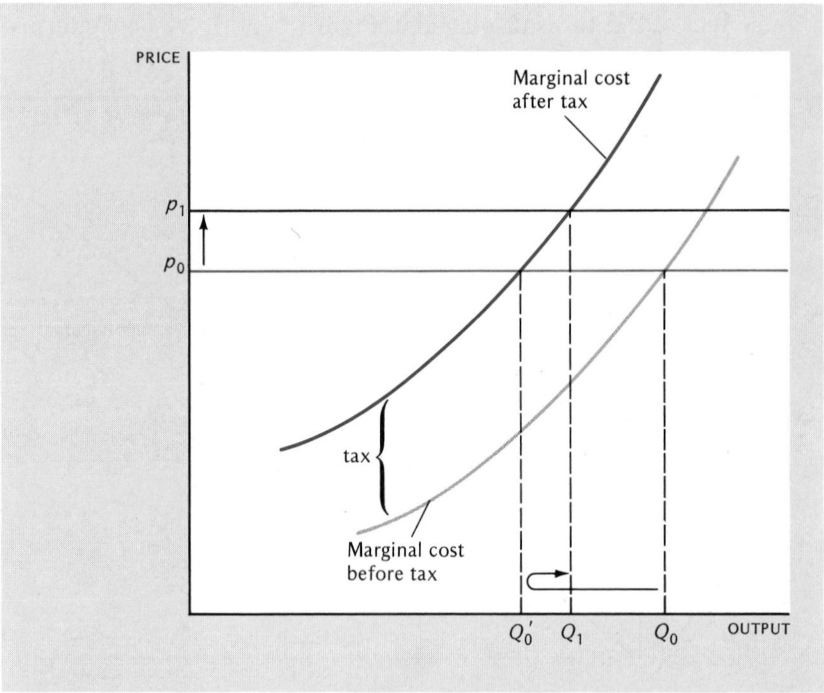

17.5 THE EFFECT OF A TAX ON MARGINAL COST Equilibrium for a competitive firm occurs at the point where price equals marginal cost. The tax shifts the effective marginal cost schedule up.

The cost to the firm of producing an extra unit is now $MC' = MC + t$, its marginal production cost plus the tax; it will thus reduce its output to Q_0'. But when all firms reduce their output, prices rise. The new equilibrium entails a price p_1 and output of Q_1, where the new price is equal to marginal production cost plus tax.

Tax Incidence and the Demand and Supply for Labor

The basic principles we have just derived apply to all taxes in competitive markets. In Figure 17.6A we have depicted the market demand and supply curves for labor. It makes no difference whether a tax on labor is imposed on the consumer (in this case, the firms who pay for the use of labor) or on producers (in this case, the individuals who are selling their labor services). The incidence of the tax is the same. The distinction made by Congress, that half of the social security tax should be paid by the employer and half by the employee, makes absolutely no difference for the effect of the tax. The consequences would have been the same had Congress said that firms must pay the entire tax or that individuals must pay the entire tax.[3]

Who effectively pays the tax depends on the elasticity of demand and supply for labor. If, as is frequently claimed, the supply of labor is relatively inelastic (i.e., almost vertical), most of the burden of the tax falls on workers, regardless of the legal imposition of the tax.

Some economists believe that the supply curve of labor actually is backward-bending, as illustrated in Figure 17.6B. As the wage rises above a certain level, the supply of labor actually decreases. Individuals decide that, at the higher standards of living that they can attain with the higher wages, they prefer to work less. Thus, higher wages reduce the supply of labor rather than increase it. In this case, a tax on labor may result in a reduction in the wage rate that is greater than the tax itself, as the decrease in wages induces a larger labor supply, which drives down the wage.

Taxation of Inelastic Factors and Commodities

As we have noted, if the supply elasticity of labor or of a commodity is zero, the tax is borne fully by the supplier. The classic example of a commodity with a zero supply elasticity is unimproved land. Thus, if a tax is imposed on unimproved land, the total burden of the tax will fall on the landowners.

[3] There may be a short-run difference. If Congress had imposed the entire tax on firms, it is unlikely that wages would have fallen immediately. In the short run, the labor market would not have been in equilibrium, and firms would have absorbed a large part of the social security tax.

There are also some differences arising out of the income tax. While the employee's contribution to social security is included in his income (upon which he must pay income tax), the employer's contribution to social security is not. Also, if the individual works for more than one employer and pays more than the maximum social security, he can claim a refund of the excess, but the employer is not entitled to any refund.

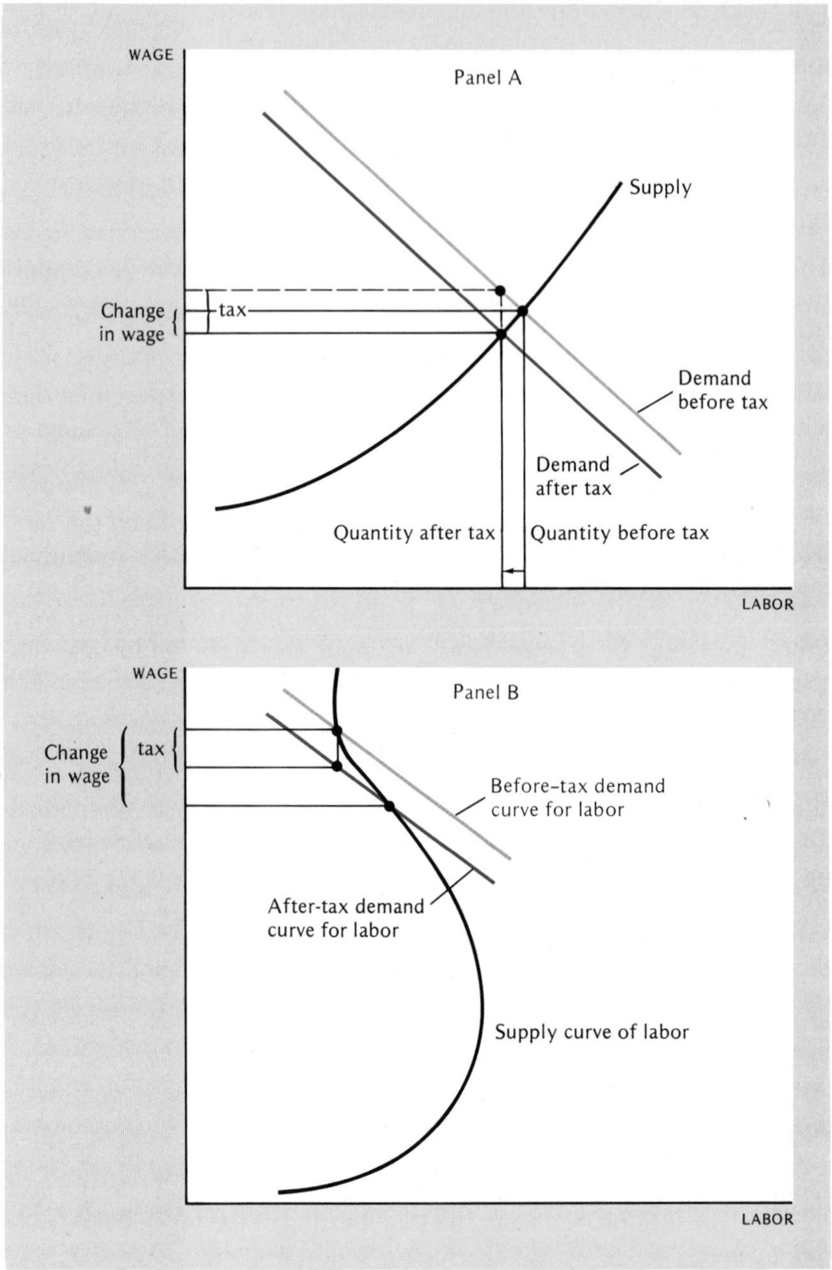

17.6 COMPARING THE EFFECTS OF A TAX ON THE DEMAND FOR LABOR
(A) The effect of a tax on labor is to shift the demand curve for labor down. A tax on labor will lead to a lower wage and a lower level of employment. (B) With a backward-bending supply schedule, the wage may fall by more than the amount of the tax.

Unfortunately, it is difficult to distinguish between the value of improved land and unimproved land. In many parts of the United States, for instance, land in the wilderness, with no access to roads, sewers, or water, is almost valueless. How much of the value of land in urban areas can be attributed to "improvements" (so we can attribute the residual to the value of the unimproved land) is difficult to ascertain. Because the supply elasticity of land improvements is large, a land tax may be largely shifted.

Another example of a factor in long-run inelastic supply is crude oil. Hence, a tax on oil is borne primarily by the owners of oil deposits. Since a disproportionate share of the world's oil is owned by those outside of the major consuming nations, the consuming nations have strong incentives to impose taxes on oil. Of course, owners of oil wells in the United States actively resist these taxes, and they are a sufficiently powerful lobby group to have done so quite successfully. In the United States, taxes on oil are far less than those in most Western European nations.

This analysis applies to taxes imposed on the users of oil as well as on the producers. As we have seen, it makes little difference what the legal imposition of the tax is. Thus, a tax on gasoline is likely to be borne largely by the owners of oil wells. This is equally true when there are several factors of production. To produce gasoline requires inputs of labor and capital, in addition to the inputs of crude oil. But the gasoline industry, while large, is only one of the many users of labor and capital, and thus the imposition of a gasoline tax is not likely to have a significant effect on the price the gasoline industry has to pay for its labor or capital. If the (before-tax) price of gasoline falls, the full burden of the decline lies on the owners of the crude oil. (In the short run, there may be some excess capacity of refineries, and a small portion of the burden may fall on the owners of capital in the oil industry. In the long run, however, refinery capacity will adjust to the lower level of demand.)

TAX INCIDENCE IN MONOPOLISTIC VERSUS COMPETITIVE ENVIRONMENTS

The effect of the imposition of a tax depends critically on the nature of the market. The analysis in the preceding sections assumed that markets were competitive. But if the industry is a monopoly (or acts collusively, so that its behavior is similar to that of a monopoly), the effect of a tax could be markedly different.

In the absence of a tax, a monopolist will choose that level of output such that the cost of producing any additional output (the **marginal cost**) is just equal to the additional sales revenue he would receive (his **marginal revenue**). To maximize profits, the monopolist thus sets his marginal cost equal to his marginal revenue.

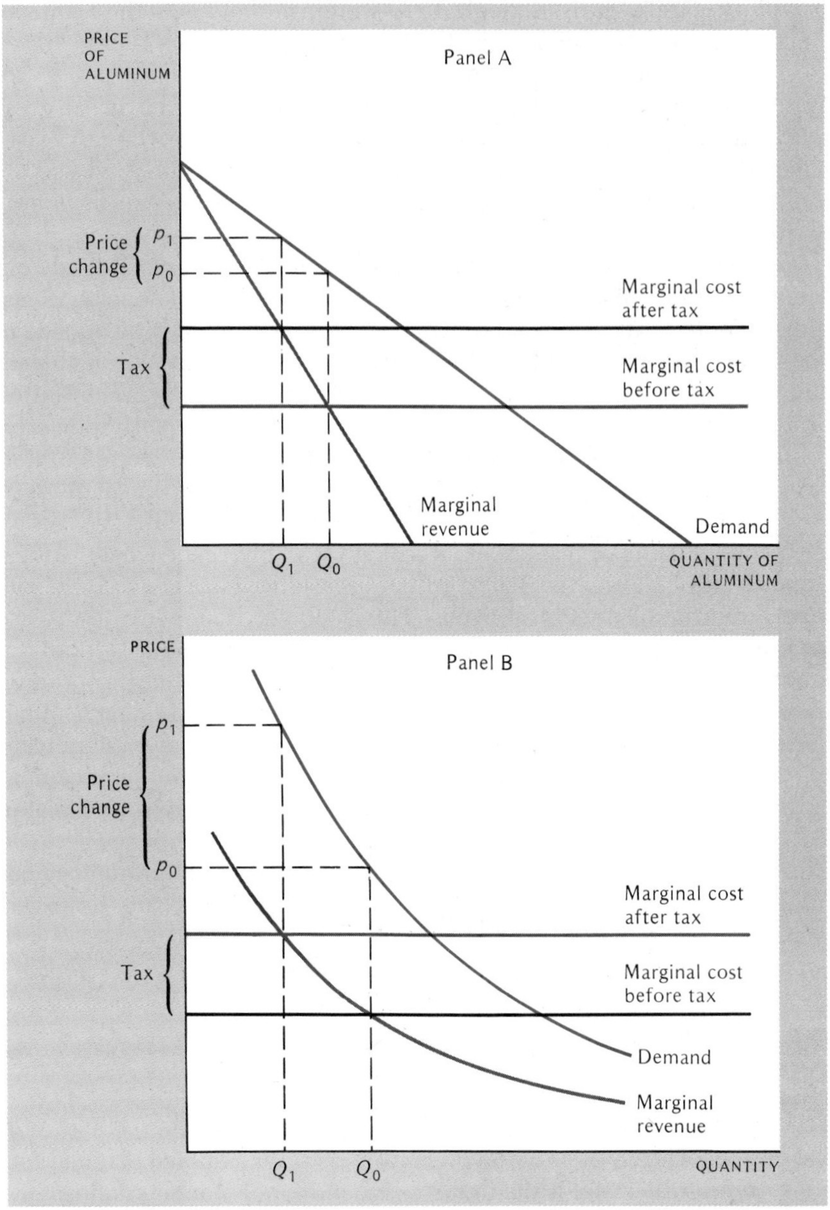

17.7 TAXING A MONOPOLY (A) With linear demand and supply curves, the price paid by consumers rises by exactly half the tax; consumers and producers share the burden of the tax. (B) With constant elasticity demand curves, the price rises by more than the tax.

Figure 17.7 depicts the demand curve for aluminum, the marginal revenue curve, and the marginal cost of production. The marginal revenue curve lies below the demand curve. It represents the extra revenue the firm receives from selling an extra unit of output. The marginal revenue is the price the firm receives for that extra unit, minus the loss it sustains on the other units it sells, because as it attempts to sell more, it must lower the price. The monopolist chooses Q_0 as his level of output, the quantity where the marginal cost and marginal revenue curves intersect. To find the price charged by the monopolist, we go up to the demand curve and locate price p_o.

A tax on aluminum can be viewed simply as an increase in the cost of production, which is to say a shift upward in the marginal cost curve. This will reduce output to Q_1 and increase the price to p_1.

Relationship between the Change in the Price and the Tax

In the case of a competitive industry, we showed that the consumer price increased by an amount that normally was less than the tax, and that the magnitude of the price increase depended on the demand and supply elasticities. The results for a monopolist are more complicated.

First, the steeper the marginal cost curve, the smaller the change in output and hence the smaller the increase in price. With a perfectly vertical marginal cost schedule, there is no change in output and no change in price; the tax is borne by producers. A supply (or marginal cost) curve is perfectly vertical if no increase in price calls forth an increase in supply. Standard examples are the supply of unimproved land or the supply of Van Gogh paintings. This result parallels that for competitive markets.

On the other hand, with a horizontal marginal cost schedule, as in Figure 17.7, the extent to which producers or consumers bear the tax depends on the *shape* of the demand curve. (Contrast this to competitive markets, where the consumer would bear the entire tax.) Panels A and B of Figure 17.7 illustrate two possibilities. With a linear demand curve, as in Panel A, the price rises by exactly half the tax. With a constant elasticity demand curve (where a 1 percent increase in the price results in, say, a 2 percent reduction in the demand, regardless of the price level), as in Panel B, price is always a constant multiple of marginal revenue. Hence if marginal revenue increases by t, price must increase by even more: the increase in price always exceeds the magnitude of the tax. There is more than 100 percent shifting onto consumers.[4]

Ad Valorem versus Specific Taxes

There is another important difference between the taxation of competitive and monopolistic industries. In the case of competitive industries, the form in which we levy the tax makes no difference. We can choose

[4] The marginal revenue *(MR)* is related to the price by the formula $MR = p\,(1 - 1/\eta^d)$ where η^d is the price elasticity of demand, and it is defined to be positive. (For a monopolist, it would be more than one.) Since $MR = MC + t$,

$$p = \frac{MC + t}{1 - 1/\eta^d}.$$

An increase in the tax by 10 cents increases price by $(\frac{1}{1 - 1/\eta^d}) \times 10¢$. If $\eta^d = 2$, the increase in the price is 20 cents.

between a **specific tax,** which is specified as a fixed amount per unit of output, and an **ad valorem tax,** which is specified as a percentage of the value of the output. All that matters for determining the effect of the tax is the magnitude of the difference (in equilibrium) between the price received by producers and the price paid by consumers, what we refer to as the wedge between the two.

In the case of monopolistic industries, however, the effects of an ad valorem and a specific tax are quite different. We show in the Appendix that for any given revenue raised by the government, the monopolist's output will be higher with an ad valorem tax than with a specific tax. On this ground, an ad valorem tax is superior to a specific tax.

Both in competitive and monopolistic industries, the administration of the two taxes may raise different problems. In general, the same tax must be applied across a wide variety of commodities of differing qualities. If the tax is on a per unit of output basis, then it represents a higher percentage tax on lower-quality units and thus serves effectively to discourage the production of these lower-quality (lower-priced) items.

On the other hand, it is often easier to monitor the quantity of a good sold than its price, particularly when firms sell more than one commodity. If these commodities are taxed at different ad valorem rates, there is an incentive to strike deals in which the higher-taxed commodity is "underpriced" on invoices, and the tax administrator may not be able to detect this. These administrative problems have perhaps played a more important role in determining the form of taxation than the economists' analysis of their comparative distortionary effects.

TAX INCIDENCE IN OLIGOPOLIES

Between the extremes of perfect competition and monopoly is the oligopoly market structure. In oligopolies, such as the airline market and the rental car market, each producer interacts strategically with every other producer. If one producer changes its price or output, the other producers may also change their prices or outputs, but these responses may be hard to predict. The oligopolist, unlike the perfect competitor or monopolist, faces a demand curve that he can only guess at.

There is no widely accepted theory of firm behavior in oligopoly, and so it is impossible to make any definite predictions about the incidence of taxation in this case. Some economists believe that oligopolists are not likely to raise the prices they charge consumers when taxes change. Each oligopolist may believe that if he raises his price, other firms will steal his market share. An opposite conclusion follows if each oligopolist expects that his competitors will match his price increase after a tax is imposed. In this case, all will raise their prices and thereby shift the burden of the tax to consumers.

Until economists gain a better understanding of oligopolistic behavior, there can be no general theory of the incidence of a tax in an oligopolistic market.

EQUIVALENT TAXES

Up to now, we have pointed out several instances where taxes that appear to be different—a tax on employers to finance social security and a tax on employees, a tax on the producers of beer or a tax on consumers of beer—are really equivalent. There are many other examples of what appear to be very different taxes (and from an administrative point of view *are* different taxes) that are, from an economic point of view, equivalent.

Income Tax and Value-Added Tax

An obvious example follows from the basic identity between national income (what all the individuals in our society receive) and national output (what they all produce). Since the value of income and the value of output must be the same, a uniform tax on income (that is, a tax that taxes all sources of income at the same rate) and a uniform tax on output (that is, a tax that taxes all outputs at the same rate) must be equivalent. A comprehensive uniform sales tax is a uniform tax on output and is thus equivalent to a uniform income tax.

The production of any commodity entails a large number of steps. The value of the final product represents the sum of the *value added* at each stage of production. We could impose the tax at the end of the production process or at each stage along the way. A tax at the end of the production process is called a sales tax. A tax imposed at each stage of the production process is called a value-added tax. Thus, a uniform value-added tax and a comprehensive uniform sales tax are equivalent; and both are equivalent to a uniform income tax.

The value-added tax is used in most European countries, and there has been some discussion about introducing such a tax into the United States. Since a uniform value-added tax is equivalent to a uniform (proportional) income tax, replacing our current income tax system with a value-added tax would be equivalent to replacing it with a proportional income tax system.

Equivalence of Consumption and Wage Taxes

Suppose that individuals receive no inheritances and leave no bequests. Then a uniform tax on wages and a uniform tax on consumption are equivalent. To put it another way, a consumption tax is equivalent to an income tax in which interest and other returns to capital have been exempted. (Our present tax system, in which part of the return to capital is tax exempt, can be viewed as somewhere between a consumption tax and an income tax.)

The equivalence may be seen most clearly by looking at the lifetime budget constraint of an individual (with no inheritances or bequests). For simplicity, we divide the life of the individual into two periods. His wage income is w_1 in the first period and w_2 in the second. The individ-

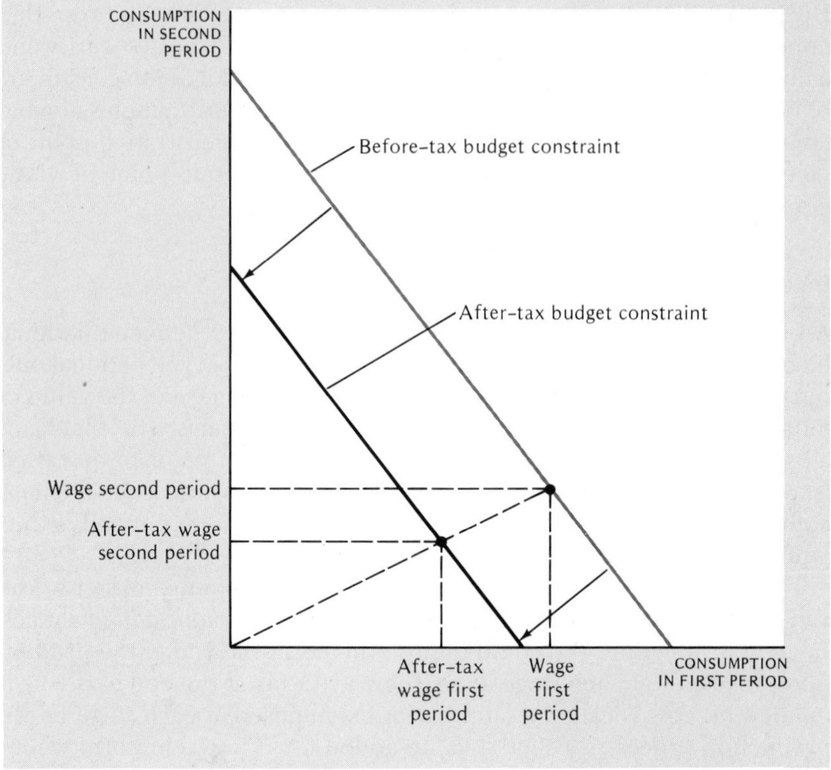

17.8 COMPARING THE EFFECTS OF A CONSUMPTION TAX AND WAGE TAX
A consumption tax and a wage tax have exactly the same effect on the individual's budget constraint.

ual has to decide how much to consume the first period of his life, while he is young, and how much while he is old. If he reduces his consumption today by a dollar and invests it, next period he will have $\$1 + r$ dollars, where r is the rate of interest. With a 10 percent interest rate, he will have \$1.10. The budget constraint is a straight line, depicted in Figure 17.8.

Consider what happens to his budget constraint when a wage tax of 20 percent is imposed. The amount that he can consume shifts down. The *slope* of the budget constraint remains unchanged: it is still the case that by giving up \$1 of consumption in the first period, he can get \$1.10 next period.

Now consider what happens to his budget constraint when a 20 percent consumption tax is imposed. Just as before, the amount that he can consume shifts down, and the slope of the budget constraint remains unchanged. If the individual spends \$1 today, he gets 20 percent fewer goods because of the tax; but when he spends \$1 tomorrow, he also gets

20 percent fewer goods because of the tax. The trade-off between spending today and spending tomorrow remains unchanged. A wage tax and a consumption tax are equivalent.[5] Only the timing of the revenues to the government differs between the two taxes; this may be important if capital markets are imperfect.

There are, again, several ways that we can impose these equivalent taxes. We can impose a tax on wage income in each period, exempting all interest, dividends, and other returns on capital. Or we can tax consumption in each period, which can be calculated by having the individual report his total income minus total savings.

Equivalence of Lifetime Consumption and Lifetime Income Taxes

This analysis has one other important interpretation. Continuing with our example in which the life of an individual is divided into two periods, we can write the budget constraint[6] as:

$$C_1 + C_2/1 + r = w_1 + w_2/1 + r.$$

The left-hand side is the present discounted value of the individual's consumption, and the right-hand side is the present discounted value of wage income. In the absence of bequests and inheritances, the present discounted value of consumption must equal the present discounted value of (wage) income. Thus, a lifetime consumption tax and a tax based on lifetime income are equivalent, as we saw in Chapter 16.

FACTORS AFFECTING TAX INCIDENCE ANALYSIS

So far, we have shown that what is important in determining who bears the burden of any tax is not who Congress says should bear the burden of the tax but: (a) certain properties of demand and supply, and (b) the nature of the market, whether it is competitive or monopolistic or oligopolistic.

[5] If there are bequests and inheritances, a wage-plus-inheritance tax is equivalent to a consumption-plus-bequest tax. These equivalency relations require a perfect capital market but are true even if there is risk. See A. B. Atkinson and J. E. Stiglitz, *Lectures on Public Economics* (New York: McGraw-Hill, 1980), Lecture 3.

[6] This can be seen in a slightly different way. An individual's savings (borrowings) are the difference between wages and consumption in the first period:

$$w_1 - C_1.$$

Consumption in the second period is thus second-period wage income plus the savings with its interest (minus borrowings, with interest):

$$C_2 = w_2 + (1 + r)(w_1 - C_1).$$

Rearranging terms, we have

$$C_1(1 + r) + C_2 = (1 + r)w_1 + w_2.$$

Dividing by $(1 + r)$ we obtain the budget constraint in the form presented in the text.

There are several other important factors that need to be taken into account in any complete incidence analysis. First, there is an important distinction between a tax in a single industry and a tax affecting many industries. We considered above a tax on a small industry (beer). The presumption is that such a tax will not, for instance, have any significant effect on the wage rate. Though the reduction in the demand for beer will reduce the demand for labor in the beer industry, the assumption is that this industry is so small that workers released from their jobs can find employment elsewhere without any significant effect on the wage rate. We refer to this kind of analysis, where we assume that all prices and wages (other than those on which attention is explicitly focused) remain constant, as **partial equilibrium analysis.**

Unfortunately, many taxes affect many industries simultaneously. The corporate income tax affects all incorporated businesses. If, as a result of the tax, incorporated businesses reduce their demand for capital, the capital released cannot be absorbed by the rest of the economy (the unincorporated sector) without reducing the return to capital there. Thus, we cannot assume that what the corporate sector must pay to obtain capital is independent of the tax imposed on that sector. To analyze the impact of the corporation tax requires an analysis of the equilibrium of the entire economy, not just the businesses on which the tax is imposed. We call such an analysis a **general equilibrium analysis.** There are many instances where the general equilibrium impact of a tax may be markedly different from the partial equilibrium effect. For instance, if capital can be shifted relatively easily from the incorporated to the unincorporated sectors of the economy, the tax on corporate capital must be borne equally by capital in *both* sectors of the economy; they both must have the same after-tax return.

Short-run versus Long-run Effects

A distinction must also be made between the incidence of the tax in the long run and in the short run. In the short run, many things are fixed that, in the long run, can vary. While capital presently being used in some industry (like steel) cannot easily be shifted for use into another, in the long run new investment can be shifted to other industries. Thus a tax on the return to capital in the steel industry may have markedly different effects in the long run than in the short run.

If savings are taxed, the short-run effect may be minimal. But in the long run, the tax may discourage savings, and this may reduce the capital stock. The reduction in the capital stock will reduce the demand for (and productivity of) labor, and this, in turn, will lead to a lowering of wages. As a result, the *long-run incidence* of a tax on savings (or capital) may be on workers, even if the *short-run incidence* is not.

Open versus Closed Economy

The distinction between short-run and long-run effects is important, because governments and politicians are often shortsighted. They observe the immediate effect without realizing that the full consequences of the tax may not be those that they intended. The nature of the general equilibrium effects depends on whether the economy is closed (does not trade with other countries) or open. If a small, open country like Switzerland imposed a tax on capital, the before-tax rate of return would have to adjust fully to offset the tax (or else investors would withdraw their funds from Switzerland and invest elsewhere); the tax would be borne by other factors. Effectively, the supply schedule for capital is infinitely elastic. The same analysis applies, of course, to any state within the United States.

Associated Policy Changes

The final aspect of incidence analysis that we need to discuss is this: it is almost never possible for the government to change only one policy at a time. There is a basic government budget constraint, which says that tax revenues plus the increase in the size of the deficit (increased borrowing) must equal government expenditures. If the government raises some tax rate, it must either lower another, reduce its borrowing, or increase its expenditure. Different combinations of policies will have different effects. We cannot simply ask the question, What would happen if the government increased income taxes? We need to specify whether the income tax is to be accompanied by a reduction in some other tax, an increase in government expenditure, or a reduction in government borrowing. (Often the accompanying change is taken to be understood but not made explicit; e.g., if taxes are raised, there will be a smaller deficit.)

We call the analysis of a tax increase accompanied by a decrease in some other tax **differential tax incidence analysis;** we call the analysis of a tax increase accompanied by an increase in government expenditure a **balanced budget tax incidence** analysis.

Sometimes we are interested in analyzing combinations of policies that leave some important economic variable unchanged. Thus, a tax increase may lead to a reduction in the level of aggregate demand and to a lowering of national income (when income is demand-determined). We may want to distinguish the effects of a tax program on the level of national income (and the effects that this may have, say, on its distribution) from the direct effects of the tax itself; we thus may look at combinations of policies that leave the level of national income unaffected.

Similarly, many taxes have an effect on the level of capital accumulation. The fall in the capital stock in turn may lower wages. Again, one may want to distinguish the direct from the indirect effects of a tax resulting from its impact on capital accumulation. This is particularly the case if one believes that other instruments can be used to offset these indirect effects. If an inheritance tax reduces capital accumulation, it may be possible to undo the effects by providing an investment tax credit. We may examine a set of policies the effect of which is to leave capital accumulation unaffected; we call incidence analysis of this sort **balanced growth incidence analysis.**

More generally, government expenditures may affect wages and prices just as taxes do, and those who ultimately benefit may differ from those for whom the government program was intended. If the government raises tax rates and uses the proceeds to buy consumption goods, and if those consumption goods it supplies are at least partial substitutes for private consumption goods, the tax will discourage current private consumption (encourage saving); this will be true whether the individual is a lender or a borrower. If the government uses the tax proceeds to buy a capital good, which will increase future consumption, and if this government-provided future consumption is at least a partial substitute for future private consumption, then the tax will discourage savings and encourage private (current) consumption. Again, this will be true for both borrowers and lenders.

This chapter has focused solely on the distribution of the tax burden, not on the distributive consequences of government expenditure programs and not on the effect of taxation on economic efficiency. In the next two chapters, we turn to the efficiency cost of taxation. In Chapter 20, we show how distributional and efficiency considerations may be balanced off against each other in the design of a tax.

SUMMARY

1. It makes no difference whether a tax is imposed on the suppliers of a factor or commodity rather than on the consumers. Who bears the burden of the tax depends instead on the demand and supply elasticities, and on whether the market is competitive or noncompetitive. Taxes induce changes in relative prices, and it is this market response that determines who bears the tax.
2. In a competitive market, if the supply is completely inelastic or demand completely elastic, the tax is borne by producers. If the supply is completely elastic or demand completely inelastic, the tax is entirely borne by consumers.
3. A tax on a monopolist may be shifted more than 100 percent—that is, the price paid by consumers may rise by more than the tax.
4. A tax on output (a uniform sales tax), a proportional income tax, and a uniform value-added tax are all equivalent. A uniform tax on wages and a uniform tax on consumption are equivalent.
5. Empirical studies of who bears the burden of the set of taxes imposed in the United States show that the degree of progressivity of the tax structure depends critically on assumptions concerning the incidence of taxes on capital and on payrolls. While under one set of assumptions, the current United States tax structure has some progressivity, under another set, there is very little progressivity.

6. The general equilibrium incidence of a tax, taking into account repercussions in all industries, may differ from the partial equilibrium incidence. The incidence of a tax may be different in the long run than in the short run.
7. It is almost never possible for the government to change one policy at a time. Differential tax incidence focuses on how substituting one tax for another will affect the distribution of the tax burden.

KEY CONCEPTS

Burden	Specific tax
Incidence	Marginal revenue
Shifting forward	Marginal cost
Shifting backward	Oligopoly
Effective tax rate	Partial equilibrium analysis
Progressive	General equilibrium analysis
Regressive	Differential tax incidence analysis
Elasticity of demand	Balanced budget tax incidence
Elasticity of supply	Balanced growth incidence analysis
Ad valorem tax	

QUESTIONS AND PROBLEMS

1. Consider a mineral that is in fixed supply, $Q^s = 4$. The demand for the mineral is given by $Q^D = 10 - 2p$, where p is the price per pound, and Q^D is the quantity demanded. The government imposes a tax of \$2 per pound on the consumer,
   a) What is the price paid by the consumer before the tax is imposed, and in the post-tax equilibrium?
   b) What is the price received by producers?
   c) How much revenue is raised?
2. Consider a small town in which workers are highly mobile (i.e., can be induced to leave the town if opportunities elsewhere improve slightly). What do you think the incidence of a tax on wages in that town would be, compared to the incidence in a town in which workers are immobile?
3. Consider a small country, in a world in which capital is highly mobile (i.e., capital will flow into the country quickly if the return offered is greater than elsewhere and will flow out if the return offered is less than elsewhere). What do you think the incidence of a tax on the return to capital would be in such a country?
4. It is frequently asserted that taxes on cigarettes and beer are regressive, because poor individuals spend a large fraction of their income on such items. How would your estimate of the degree of regressivity be affected if you thought these commodities were produced (a) by competitive industries with inelastic supply schedules; (b) by a monopoly with a linear demand schedule; (c) by a monopoly facing a constant elasticity demand schedule?
5. It is often asserted that gasoline taxes used to finance highway construction and maintenance are "fair" because they make those who use the roads pay for them. Who do you think bears the burden of such taxes?
6. If you believed that a proportional consumption tax was the "best tax," what are various ways in which you could levy it? Might there be differences in administrative costs associated with levying such a tax in different ways?

7. In what ways may the actual incidence of a government expenditure program differ from the "legislated intent"? Why might the effects be different in the short run and in the long run? Illustrate with examples drawn from Part III of the book, or with a discussion of the effects of government farm programs. Similarly, discuss how the short-run and long-run effects of a regulatory program, such as rent control, may differ from one another.
8. The demand for a product is described by the linear demand curve,

$$p = a - bQ,$$

where p = price, Q = output, $a = 100$, $b = 1$. Draw the demand curve. Revenue, $R = pQ$. How does revenue depend on output? Draw the relationship between revenue and output. Show that the marginal revenue, $MR = a - 2bQ$. Show that in equilibrium, the monopolist sets

$$p = \frac{MC + t + a}{2}$$

where MC is the marginal cost of production, and t is a specific tax on the output of the commodity. What does this imply about shifting of the tax?

APPENDIX: COMPARISON OF THE EFFECTS OF AN AD VALOREM AND SPECIFIC COMMODITY TAX ON A MONOPOLIST

Suppose the government imposes a tax on the output of a monopolist. We asserted in the text that an ad valorem tax (a tax based on a fixed percentage of the value of sales) would reduce output less than a specific tax (a fixed tax on each unit sold) for any given revenue raised by the government.

The reason for this is that the ad valorem tax reduces marginal revenues by less than the tax, while the specific tax reduces marginal revenues by exactly the amount of the tax. Since a monopolist sets marginal revenue equal to marginal cost, if marginal revenue is reduced by less, output is reduced by less.

We can see this diagrammatically in Figure 17.9. Panel A illustrates the effect of a specific commodity tax. Earlier, we represented the effects of such a tax by an increase in the marginal cost. We can alternatively represent the effects of this tax as a *decrease* in the price received by the firm at any given quantity sold, that is, as a downward shift in the demand schedule. Both the demand and marginal revenue schedules shift down by the magnitude of the tax, t.[7]

With an ad valorem tax, if an individual pays a price p for a commodity, the amount received by the producer is $p(1 - \hat{t})$ where $\hat{t}$ represents the ad valorem tax rate. Thus the tax paid is a function of the market price. If the price were

[7] Marginal revenue before tax is

$$p + Q(dp/dQ).$$

The firm receives p for the extra unit sold, but because price falls as it attempts to sell more (by dp/dQ) it loses revenues on all other units it sells. The total loss on these units is $Q(dp/dQ)$. With the tax, marginal revenue is

$$p - t + Q(dp/dQ),$$

that is, it is lowered by exactly the amount of the tax.

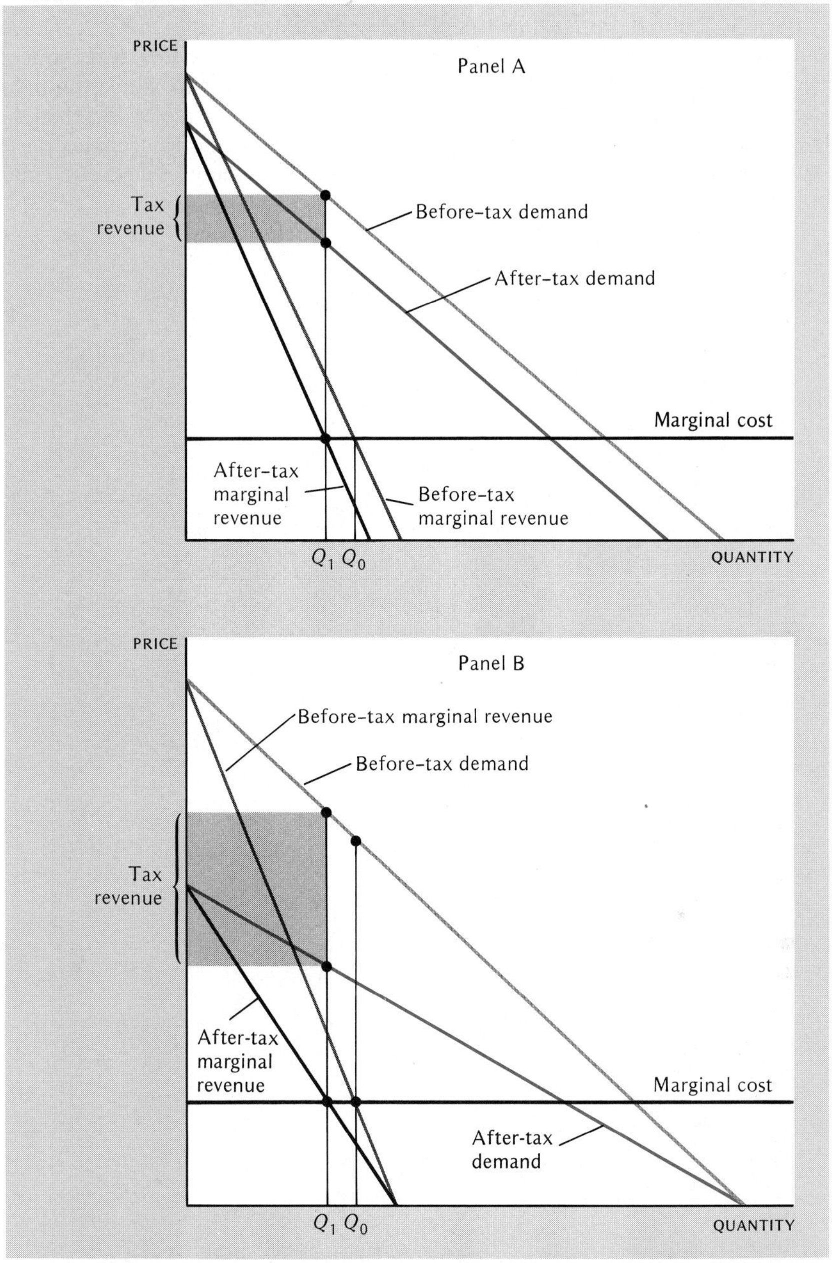

17.9 COMPARING THE EFFECTS OF A SPECIFIC TAX AND AN AD VALOREM TAX ON A MONOPOLIST (A) The effects of a specific commodity tax on a monopolist can be viewed either as a shift upward in the marginal cost schedule (as in the earlier diagrams) or, as here, a shift downward in the demand and marginal revenue schedules. (B) Analysis of the effects of an ad valorem tax on a monopolist. For any given level of output, Q_1, tax revenue is higher with an ad valorem tax than with a specific tax.

zero, there would be no tax paid. The effect of the tax is to rotate the demand curve as in Panel B, rather than to shift it down uniformly, as in Panel A. The ad valorem tax reduces the marginal revenue to $(1 - \hat{t})MR$—that is, it is reduced by $\hat{t}MR$, while the revenue received by the government is $\hat{t}p$. Since the price exceeds the marginal revenue, the marginal revenue is reduced by less than the tax. Hence for any given level of equilibrium output, the ad valorem tax raises more revenue, as shown in the figure; or equivalently, for any given tax revenue, output will be higher with an ad valorem tax.

18

Taxation and Economic Efficiency: Consumption

All taxes affect economic behavior. They transfer resources from the individual to the government. As a result, individuals must alter their behavior in some way. If they do not adjust the amount of work they do, they must reduce their consumption. They may work more, enjoying less leisure; by working more, they need reduce their consumption less.

No matter how individuals adjust, an increase in taxes must make them worse off.[1] But some taxes reduce individuals' welfare less, for each dollar of revenue raised, than do other taxes. This is because some taxes induce greater economic inefficiencies than others. The only tax that does not induce any economic inefficiencies is a lump-sum tax. In Chapter 16 we defined a lump-sum tax as a tax whose yield was independent of the behavior of any individual. The classic examples of a lump-sum tax are a tax on unimproved land or a head tax on an individual. We said such taxes were nondistortionary. Lump-sum taxes do affect behavior: they might reduce the demands for some commodities or induce individuals to work harder. But these effects are associated

[1] This ignores, of course, the benefits that may accrue from the increased government expenditures that result from the increased taxes. Throughout this chapter we also ignore general equilibrium effects: before-tax wages and prices will be assumed to be unaffected by the imposition of a tax.

only with the fact that individuals have less income to spend. They are thus called **income effects.** Because lump-sum taxes are nondistortionary, they raise the most revenue for any given loss to individual welfare.

This chapter addresses several questions: What determines how individuals adjust to the taxes imposed upon them? What determines the magnitude of the welfare losses arising from the use of distortionary taxation? Finally, how can we *measure* the inefficiency associated with the use of distortionary taxation? This inefficiency is called the **excess burden** of a tax. We also refer to the excess burden as the **deadweight loss** of the tax. As we will show, it can be measured in dollars.

We consider first the simplest case of a tax borne fully by consumers. Then we will consider the case of taxes borne at least partly by producers. In the next chapter, we discuss the effect of taxes on labor.

EFFECT OF TAXES BORNE BY CONSUMERS

Assume that each individual's income is fixed, and he can choose between purchasing two commodities, soda and beer. His budget constraint is the line *SB* in Figure 18.1. This gives the various combinations of soda and beer that the individual can purchase. If he spent all his income on soda, he could purchase the amount *S;* if he spent all his income on beer, he could purchase the amount *B*.

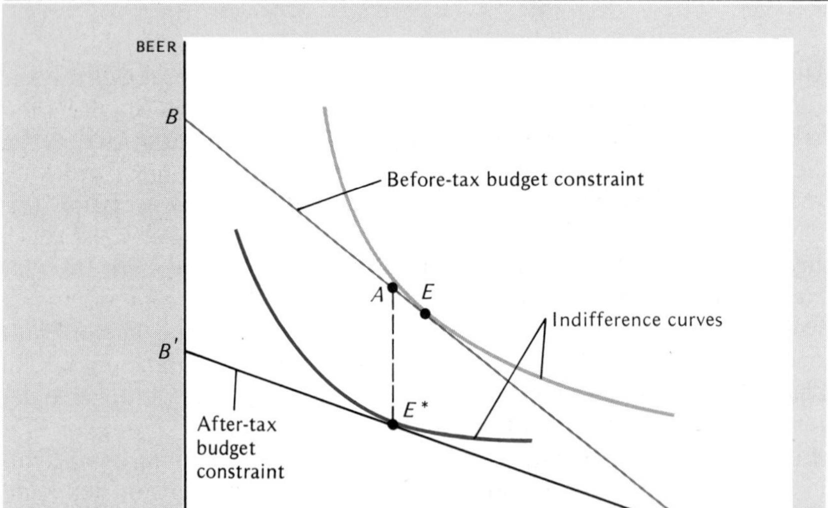

18.1 EQUILIBRIUM AFTER THE IMPOSITION OF A TAX ON BEER The effect of the tax is to shift the budget constraint down and, thus, the equilibrium changes from *E* to *E**.

Suppose that the government imposes a tax on beer. What will be the effect? (Throughout this section, we will assume that the consumer price rises by the full amount of the tax; that is, consumers bear the full burden of the tax. This will happen if the supply curves for beer and soda are infinitely elastic, as we showed in Chapter 17.) The tax on beer shifts the budget constraint in to *SB′*. The individual can still, if he wishes, spend all his income on soda, in which case he obtains *S* units of soda. But beer is now more expensive, so he can purchase less of it with his income.

Initially, the individual allocated his income by choosing point *E* on this budget constraint. This is the point of tangency between the budget constraint and the indifference curve. After the imposition of the tax, there is a new equilibrium, at point E^*.

The individual is clearly worse off at E^* than at *E*. Any tax would make him worse off to the extent that it reduces his income. The revenue raised by the tax, measured in terms of beer, is AE^*,[2] the vertical distance between *SB* and *SB′* at the individual's new consumption level, E^*.

Could a lump-sum tax provide even more revenues than AE^* to the government without making the individual worse off than he is at E^*? (The beer tax is not a lump-sum tax because the revenue yield depends upon the individual's beer consumption, which is sensitive to the price of beer.)

Suppose, then, that the government repeals the beer tax and instead imposes a lump-sum tax of *AF*—as we see in Figure 18.2A. The new budget line is parallel to *SB;* it is generated simply by subtracting a distance *AF* from each point along the initial budget line *SB*. With the lump-sum tax, the individual allocates his income by choosing point $\hat{E}$ on his budget constraint.

Now notice a remarkable result. Even though the lump-sum tax revenue is more than the revenue from the beer tax[3]—*AF* is more than AE^*—the individual is no worse off: $\hat{E}$ and E^* are on the same indifference curve. The distance between the lump-sum tax revenue and the beer tax revenue, E^*F, is the excess burden or deadweight loss of the beer tax.[4]

It is useful to decompose the individual's response to the beer tax (the movement from *E* to E^*) into two parts. The movement from *E* to $\hat{E}$ shows the effect of a change in income (a parallel shift down of the budget constraint). It is called the **income effect of the tax.** The movement from $\hat{E}$ to E^* is due to the change in the slope of the budget constraint, with the individual remaining on the same indifference curve. It is the **substitution effect** of the beer tax. The individual substitutes soda for the now higher-priced beer. The substitution effect of a tax is sometimes called the *distortion* caused by the tax.

[2] In money terms, the tax revenue is AE^* multiplied by the before-tax price of beer.

[3] The government revenue is measured by the vertical distance $\hat{A}\hat{E}$ between the before-tax and after-tax budget constraints, at the new point of consumption, $\hat{E}$. But because with a lump-sum tax, the after-tax budget constraint is parallel to the before-tax budget constraint, $\hat{A}\hat{E} = AE^*$.

[4] In money terms, the excess burden is E^*F multiplied by the before-tax price of beer.

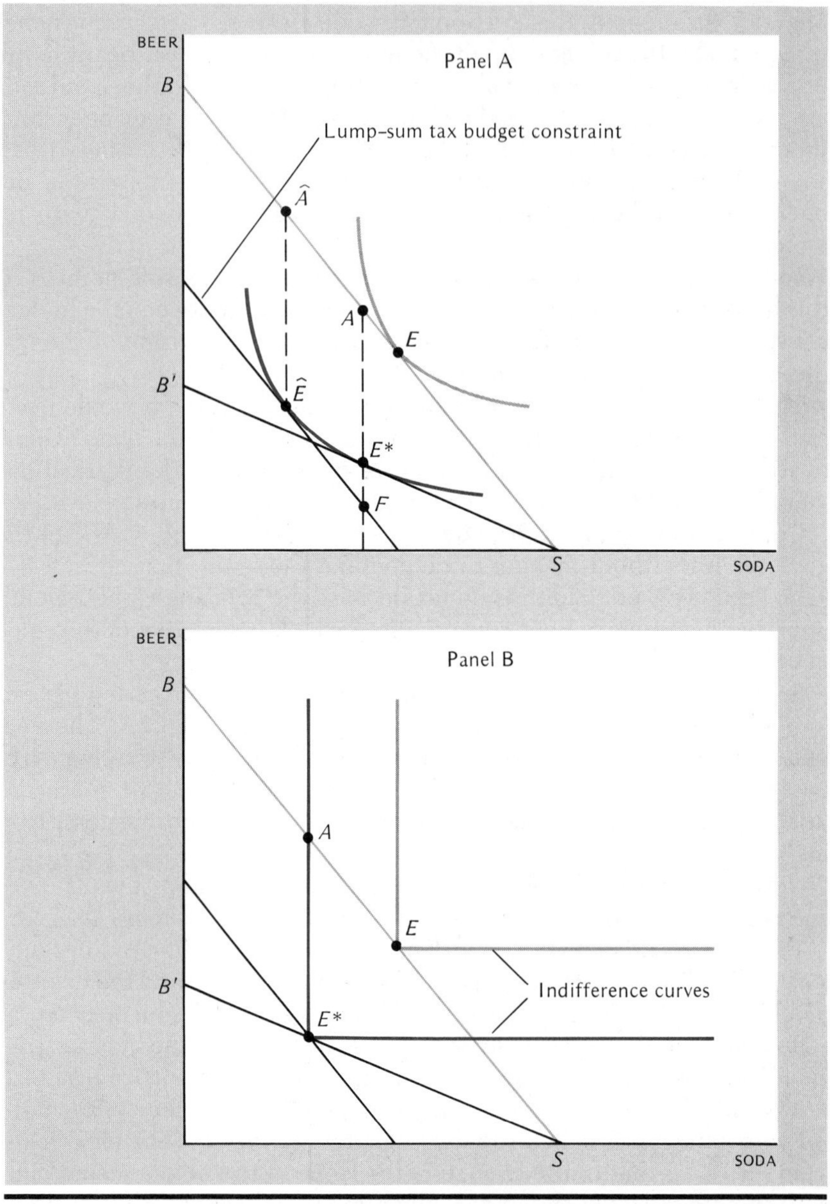

18.2 THE SHAPE OF THE INDIFFERENCE CURVE AND THE DEADWEIGHT LOSS (A) A lump-sum tax generating the same (after-tax) utility as a proportional beer tax raises more revenue and leads to higher consumption of beer (but less than in the before-tax equilibrium). The difference in revenues is the deadweight loss associated with the tax. (B) With L-shaped indifference curves, there is no substitution effect, and hence no deadweight loss.

Income and substitution effects work in the same direction in the case of a beer tax: beer consumption drops continually as we move from E to $\hat{E}$ to E^*, since each point is lower than the one before. However, the extent to which the drop in beer consumption is a result of the income effect or the substitution effect makes a critical difference in the analysis of taxes. If there is no substitution effect, then the tax gives rise to no deadweight loss.

To see this, consider Panel B of Figure 18.2. Panel B shows the special case where the individual has L-shaped indifference curves. There is then no substitution effect: at a fixed level of utility, a change in the price has no effect on the level of consumption of beer and soda. Consumption with a lump-sum tax and with a beer tax (which leaves individuals on the same indifference curve) is identical: in both cases, the individual chooses point E^*. Thus, the government gains no extra revenue by replacing the beer tax with a lump-sum tax that leaves the individual on the same indifference curve. This proves that there is no deadweight loss associated with the beer tax if beer consumption (along an indifference curve) is not sensitive to price.

If it is very difficult to substitute soda for beer—i.e., if the indifference curves, though not L-shaped, are very curved—the distortion associated with the tax is very small. The magnitude of the distortion can vary from individual to individual, and from commodity to commodity. Some individuals believe that for those addicted to alcohol the indifference curves between food and alcohol are also close to L-shaped, so that the substitution effect is small. Therefore, the deadweight loss is small. For most commodities, a reasonable degree of substitution is possible, and hence taxes imposed on these commodities will give rise to excess burdens.

Present and Future Consumption

The individual's allocation of his income between consumption this period and consumption in the future is very much like his decision about allocating his income between two different commodities.

Consumption today can be viewed as one commodity; consumption in the future can be viewed as another commodity. By giving up one dollar of consumption today, the individual can obtain $(1 + r)$ of extra consumption dollars next period, where r is the interest rate. That is, if the individual saves the dollar and deposits it in a bank, he gets back at the end of the period his dollar plus the interest it has earned. Thus, $1 / 1 + r$ is the price of consumption tomorrow, relative to consumption today.[5]

If the individual neither borrowed nor lent money, he would consume whatever his wages were in the two periods. We denote the wages in the initial period by w_0 and wages in the next by w_1. Suppose that w_0 and w_1 correspond to point W in Figure 18.3. By borrowing, the individual can consume more today, but at the expense of less next period. By saving,

[5] Recall our discussion of present discounted value from Chapter 10. The individual's budget constraint can be interpreted as requiring that the present discounted value of his consumption equals the present discounted value of his wages (ignoring bequests and inheritances).

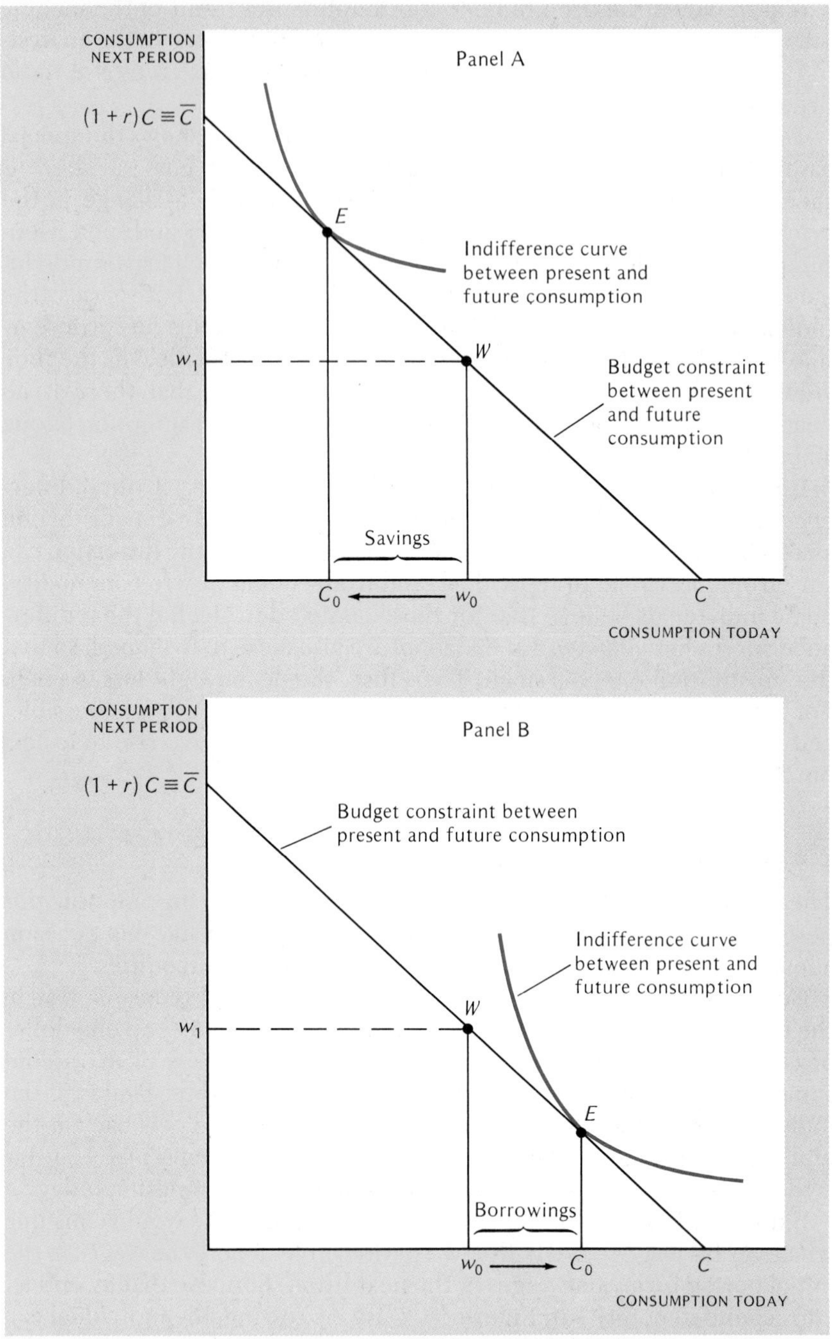

18.3 CONSUMPTION, SAVINGS, AND BORROWINGS The individual allocates his income between consumption this period and next period. In Panel A the individual saves, while in Panel B he borrows.

the individual can consume more next period, but at the expense of less consumption this period.

The individual thus faces a budget constraint. He can either have C units of consumption today, or $(1 + r)C \equiv \overline{C}$ units of consumption tomorrow, or any point on the straight line joining the two points, as depicted in Figure 18.3. The individual has a set of indifference curves between present consumption and future consumption, just as he has between beer and soda; each indifference curve gives those combinations of current and future consumption that leave the individual at the same level of utility. The individual is willing to consume less today in return for more future consumption. As his present consumption gets smaller and smaller, he becomes less willing to give up more; and as his future consumption gets larger and larger, the extra benefit he gets from each additional unit of future consumption gets smaller and smaller. Thus, the amount of increased consumption next period required to compensate the individual for a reduction by one unit in current consumption becomes larger and larger. That is why the indifference curve has the shape depicted. The individual chooses that point, denoted by E, on his budget constraint which is tangent to his indifference curve.

In Panel A of Figure 18.3 we illustrate a situation where the individual wishes to consume less than his wage income the first period and so saves the rest, while in Panel B the individual wishes to consume more than his wage income the first period and so borrows the difference.

Consider now the effect of a proportional tax, at the rate t, on total income, including interest income, but assume that interest payments are tax deductible, as is the practice in the United States. Assume further, that if net income, after interest payments are deducted, is negative, the individual *receives* money from the government; if his net income is $-Y$, he receives tY from the government, just as if his net income had been Y, he would have paid tY to the government.[6] Figure 18.4 shows how the income tax can be decomposed into two parts. The taxes on wages reduce his after-tax wage income each period proportionately, and thus his budget constraint is moved down in a parallel fashion. If he neither borrowed nor lent, his before-tax consumption would be represented by the point W, his after-tax consumption by the point W'. On the other hand, the interest income tax would rotate the budget constraint around the point W'.

Let us now focus our attention on a saver, someone whose first-period consumption is less than his (after-tax) first-period wage income. The tax has both an income effect and a substitution effect. Because the individual is worse off, he normally will reduce his consumption in both periods. Thus the income effect leads to lower current consumption. (Remember that savings is just the difference between after-tax wage income the first period and first-period consumption.) But because the

[6] There are, in fact, limitations on the deductibility of interest under U.S. tax law, which we discuss in later chapters; if net income, including interest payments, is ever negative, the individual does not get a check from the government.

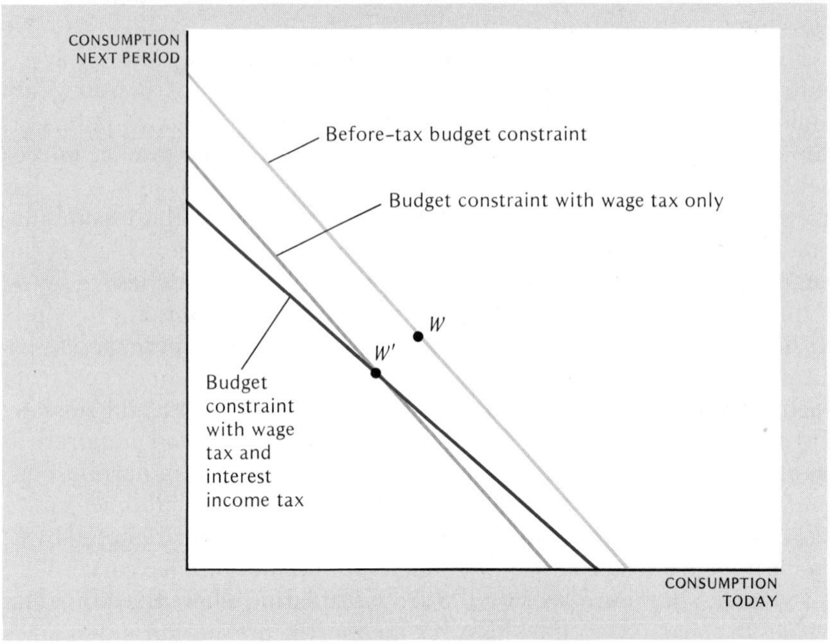

18.4 THE EFFECT OF AN INCOME TAX The effect of an income tax can be decomposed into two parts, a wage tax plus a tax on interest income. A wage tax shifts the budget constraint down in parallel. An interest income tax (with deductibility of interest payments) rotates the budget constraint.

individual receives a lower return from postponing consumption, the substitution effect discourages future consumption and encourages current consumption; it leads individuals to reduce their savings. The net effect on current consumption—and hence on savings—is ambiguous. If the substitution effect is large enough, savings are reduced.

If the substitution effect and the income effect were exactly to cancel each other, leaving savings unchanged, would this imply that the tax is nondistortionary? No, for the tax is distortionary so long as it causes the individual to substitute between current and future consumption along his indifference curve. To see this, let us consider a pure interest tax. We focus on the effect of such a tax on a saver.

Figure 18.5 depicts the case where the income effect of the interest tax (the movement from E to $\hat{E}$) is just offset by the substitution effect (the movement from $\hat{E}$ to E^*). Therefore savings $w_0 - C_0$, are the same before and after the tax. Nonetheless, there is a substantial distortion in second-period consumption. The change in the consumption bundle between $\hat{E}$ and E^* causes a deadweight loss of E^*F.

We could contrast the effect of the interest income tax with a lump-sum tax, a tax that affected consumption at both dates equally. Again, it is straightforward to show that such a tax will, for any given effect on the

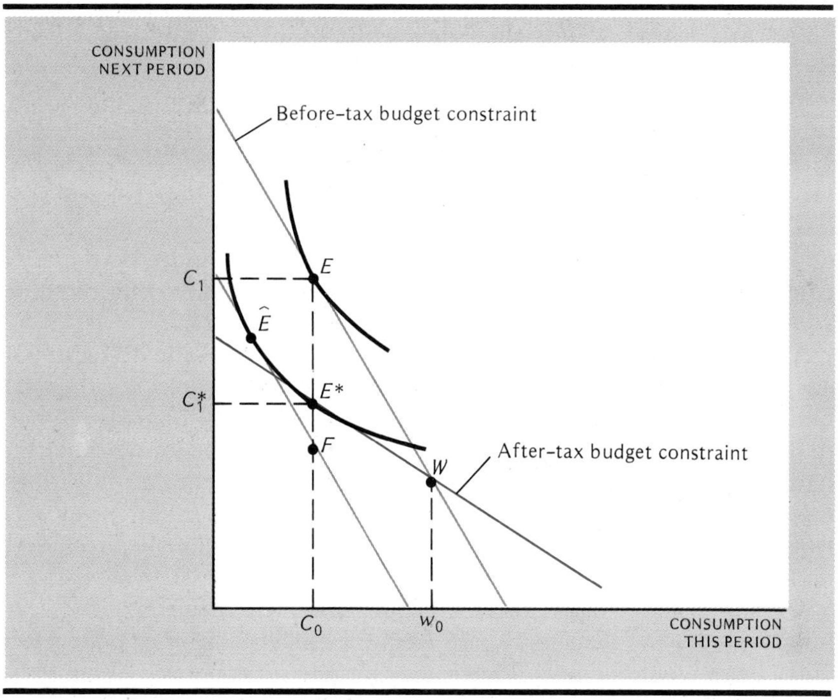

18.5 EFFECT OF INTEREST INCOME TAX The income effect of the interest tax is just offset by the substitution effect in the first period. But there is still a deadweight loss of E^*F.

individual's utility, raise more revenue; or that for any given level of revenue, individuals will be better off with the lump-sum tax than with the interest income tax. The magnitude of the distortion depends on the magnitude of the substitution effect, which in turn depends on how substitutable current and future consumption are.

The Consumer Surplus Approach to Deadweight Loss

In the preceding section we measured the inefficiency (the deadweight loss) from the imposition of a distortionary tax as the additional revenue that government could have raised, with exactly the same effect on consumer utility, had government imposed a lump-sum tax.

The concept of consumer surplus, which we discussed in Chapter 10, is often employed for calculating the loss associated with a distortionary tax.

Assume we have imposed a tax of 30 cents per bottle of beer, and, with the tax, the individual consumes ten bottles a week. We ask the individual how much he would be willing to give to the government if the tax were eliminated. In other words, what lump-sum tax would leave him at the same utility level he reached when he was subject to the 30-cent tax on beer? Clearly, he would be willing to pay at least 30 cents × 10 per week. Any extra revenue that such a tax would generate is the deadweight loss associated with the use of a distortionary tax system.

We now show how to calculate the deadweight loss using a consumer's **compensated demand curve.** The compensated demand curve gives the individual's demand for beer, assuming that as the price is lowered, income is being taken away from the individual in such a way as to leave him on the same indifference curve. We use the compensated demand curve because we wish to know how much more revenue we could have achieved with a nondistortionary tax, still leaving the individual just as well off as he was with the distortionary tax.

Assume initially the price of a bottle of beer is $1.50, including the 30 cent tax, and the individual consumes ten bottles a week. We then ask him how much extra he would be willing to pay to consume eleven bottles a week. He is willing to pay only $1.40. The total amount that the individual would thus be willing to pay us as a lump-sum tax if we lowered the tax from 30 cents to 20 cents (and lowered the price of beer from $1.50 to $1.40) is 10 cents × 10 bottles he previously purchased, or $1.00 (the area *FGCD* in Figure 18.6A).

We now ask him to assume he is in a situation where we levied a $1.00 lump-sum tax and charged $1.40 each for eleven bottles of beer. How much *extra* would he be willing to pay for one extra bottle? Assume the individual said $1.30. We can now calculate the total lump-sum tax that an individual would be willing to pay if the price were reduced from $1.50 to $1.30. He would be willing to pay 20 cents a bottle for the first ten bottles (the area *JKCD*) and 10 cents for the next (the area *GKLH*), for a total of $2.10.

Finally, we ask him to assume he is in a situation where we levied a $2.10 lump-sum tax and charged $1.30 each for twelve bottles. How much extra would he be willing to pay for one extra bottle? Assume the individual said $1.20. We could now calculate the total lump sum tax that an individual would be willing to pay for the elimination of the 30 cents tax. He would be willing to pay 30 cents on the first ten bottles (the area *ABCD*), 20 cents on the next bottle (the area *BNHG*), 10 cents on the twelfth bottle (the area *NRML*) for a total of $3.30. The tax revenue from the tax was $3.00 (the area *ABCD*). The deadweight loss is 30 cents (the shaded area.)

Measuring the Deadweight Loss

More generally, the amount that an individual would be willing to pay to have the price reduced by 1 cent is just 1 cent times the quantity consumed. As we lower the price, the quantity consumed increases. In Figure 18.6B the total an individual would be willing to pay to have the price reduced from *D* to *A* is the area *AECD*, which takes account of the change in the after-tax quantity consumed as the price is reduced. But of that, *ABCD* is the tax revenue (the tax *AD*, times the quantity consumed,

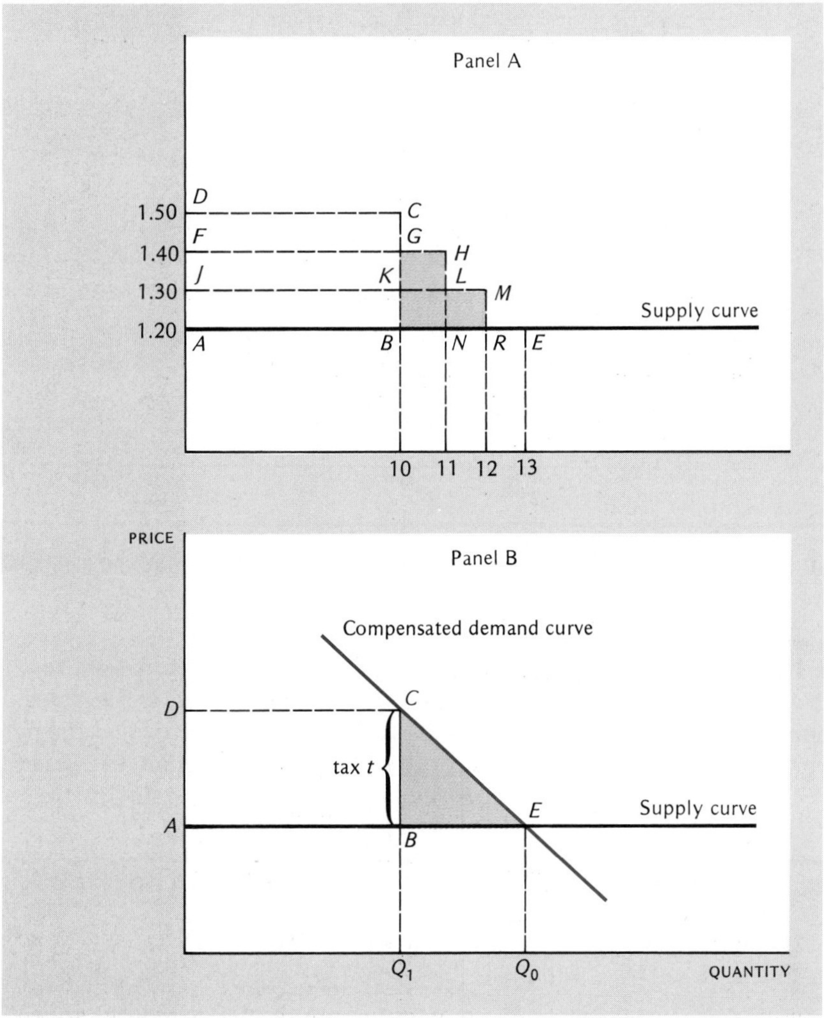

18.6 USING COMPENSATED DEMAND CURVES TO MEASURE DEADWEIGHT LOSS Government revenue is area *ABCD*. In Panel A, we show how much the individual would be willing to pay to have the price of beer reduced from $1.50 to $1.20 (keeping him at the same level of utility). The difference between this and the tax revenue raised (the area *ABCD*) is the deadweight loss (the shaded area). Panel B illustrates the case where the level of consumption can be varied in very small increments.

AB). Hence the deadweight loss, the difference between the two, is just the triangle *BCE*.

Figure 18.7 shows that as we double the tax rate, we more than double the deadweight loss. In fact, the triangle *C′B′E* is four times the size of the triangle *CBE*. The deadweight loss increases with the *square* of the tax rate.

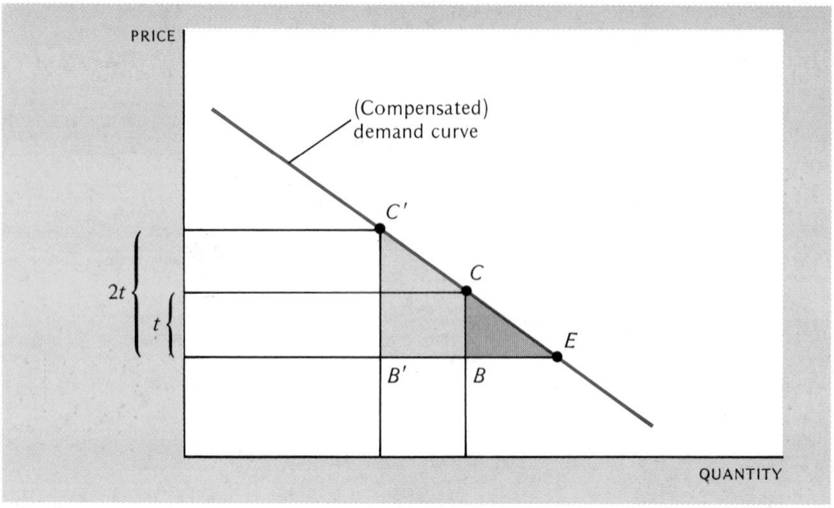

18.7 EFFECT OF AN INCREASE IN TAX RATE ON THE DEADWEIGHT LOSS
A doubling of the tax rate more than doubles the deadweight loss.

Figure 18.8 shows that, for a given tax rate, the deadweight loss is greater the flatter (or more precisely, the more elastic) is the demand curve. (Remember that the elasticity of the demand curve gives the percentage change in demand as a result of a one percent change in price.)

There is, in fact, a simple formula relating deadweight loss to tax

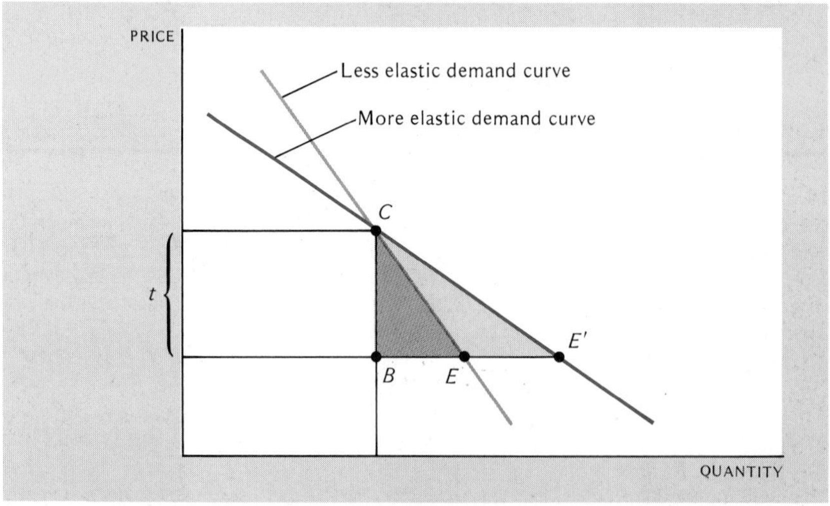

18.8 EFFECT OF AN INCREASE IN THE (COMPENSATED) ELASTICITY OF DEMAND ON DEADWEIGHT LOSS An increase in the elasticity of the (compensated) demand curve increases the deadweight loss. (*BEC* is deadweight loss from the less elastic demand curve, *BE'C* from the more elastic demand curve.)

revenue:

$$\frac{\text{Deadweight loss}}{\text{tax revenue}} = \frac{1}{2}\frac{t}{p} \times \text{the elasticity of the compensated demand curve}$$

This formula shows that the ratio of the deadweight loss to the revenue raised increases proportionally with the tax rate and with the elasticity of the compensated demand schedule (t/p is the ratio of the tax to the price).

As we noted in Chapter 10, consumer surplus calculations are widely employed to evaluate government programs, as well as to measure the inefficiencies associated with various taxes.[7] In chapter 3 (Figure 3.5), we used the same method to measure the welfare loss resulting from monopoly; we can think of the difference between the monopolist's price and his marginal cost as a "tax" imposed and collected by the monopolist.

But consumer surplus has been widely criticized. These criticisms have as much to do with how the calculations are done in practice as with the theory. Note in particular that our formula made use of the *compensated* demand elasticity. Moreover, our calculation of the area assumed either that the demand curve was linear or that the tax was small enough that a linear approximation was reasonably accurate. If we are calculating the deadweight loss associated with 30 percent marginal tax rates, the approximation must be used with considerable caution.

A second limitation of our analysis is that it has focused only on how a tax affects the sector in which it is levied. But any tax may also have repercussions on other sectors. Whenever the tax rates in these other sectors are not zero (or whenever there is imperfect competition in these other sectors), we have to pay attention to these repercussions. Assume, for instance, that the government has a tax on both beer and cigarettes. Assume that individuals drink more beer when they are smoking. If the government increases its tax on cigarettes, it will reduce beer consumption, and this will reduce the revenue raised by the beer tax.[8] In Chapter 20, we discuss briefly how these interactions may be taken into account in designing the optimal tax structure.

EFFECT OF TAXES BORNE BY PRODUCERS

Up to now, this chapter has focused on the distortionary effects of a tax on a consumption good. We assumed that supply curves were horizontal, so the entire burden of the tax was on consumers.

[7] In measuring the deadweight loss in an economy from a tax, we use the elasticity of the compensated market demand curve. The number can be estimated through statistical techniques. For a recent discussion of these techniques, see J. Hausman, "Exact Consumer Surplus and Deadweight Loss," *American Economic Review* 11 (1981); 662–76.

[8] In this example, the loss in beer tax revenues can be related to the increase in the beer tax's deadweight loss. Both changes arise because the cigarette tax distorts individuals' consumption of beer. For a proof, see A. Harberger, "Taxation, Resource Allocation, and Welfare," in *Taxation and Welfare*, ed. A. Harberger (Boston: Little, Brown, 1974) pp. 32–35.

But, at least in the short run, most supply curves are upward-sloping. This means that part of the burden of any tax on a consumption good will fall on producers. Will this cause an excess burden on producers, above and beyond the direct burden of the tax revenue? The answer is yes, except in the special case where the supply curve is vertical (that is, the elasticity of supply is zero).

Recall how a supply schedule is constructed. At each price, firms produce up to the point where price equals marginal cost. If the supply schedule is upward-sloping, the marginal cost rises as production rises. The area between the supply curve and price measures the **producer surplus,** which is just the difference between revenues and total variable costs. Changes in this area thus measure changes in profits.[9]

Consider the example illustrated in Figure 18.9A. What happens to profits as price increases from 1 to 4 and output increases from 1 to 4? The first unit of output costs $1; the next, $2; the third, $3; and the fourth, $4. If we pay the firm $4, so it produces 4 units, the firm gets $3 more than marginal costs for producing the first unit, $2 more than marginal costs for producing the second unit, and $1 more than marginal costs for producing the third unit. The total profits are $3 + 2 + 1 = $6.

This can be seen more generally in Figure 18.9B. Assume initially the producer is receiving the price p. Then a tax is imposed that lowers the amount he receives to $p - t$. In the initial situation, his total profits are given by the area *DBC*.[10] Now, his profits are reduced to *DGE*. The change in his profits area is *EGBC*. But of this change, part accrues to the government as tax revenue—the rectangle *EGHC*. The tax on producers has resulted in producers' profits being reduced by more than government revenue has increased. The difference between the two is the deadweight loss associated with the tax. It is simply the shaded area *BGH*. To put it another way, the government could have imposed a lump-sum tax on the firm, which left price at p and which left the firm at the same level of profits as it had with a price of $p - t$. That lump-sum tax would have generated higher revenues, by the amount *BGH*, than the tax on the output of the firm.

It is clear that the steeper—the more inelastic—the supply schedule, the smaller the deadweight loss. In particular, we can, as before, show that for small taxes the deadweight loss increases with the square of the tax rate and with the supply elasticity.

A similar analysis applies to taxes on goods that are used in production. Assume, for instance, we had a tax on some input, such as steel, into an industry (automobiles). We can ask what lump-sum tax we could impose on the industry that would have the same effect on profits as the

[9] This is because profits = revenues − variable costs − fixed costs = producer surplus − fixed costs. (Fixed costs are costs that are incurred as long as the firm operates; they do not depend on the scale of production.)

[10] More accurately, the shaded area measures the difference between revenues and total variable costs. To calculate profits, we need to subtract fixed costs.

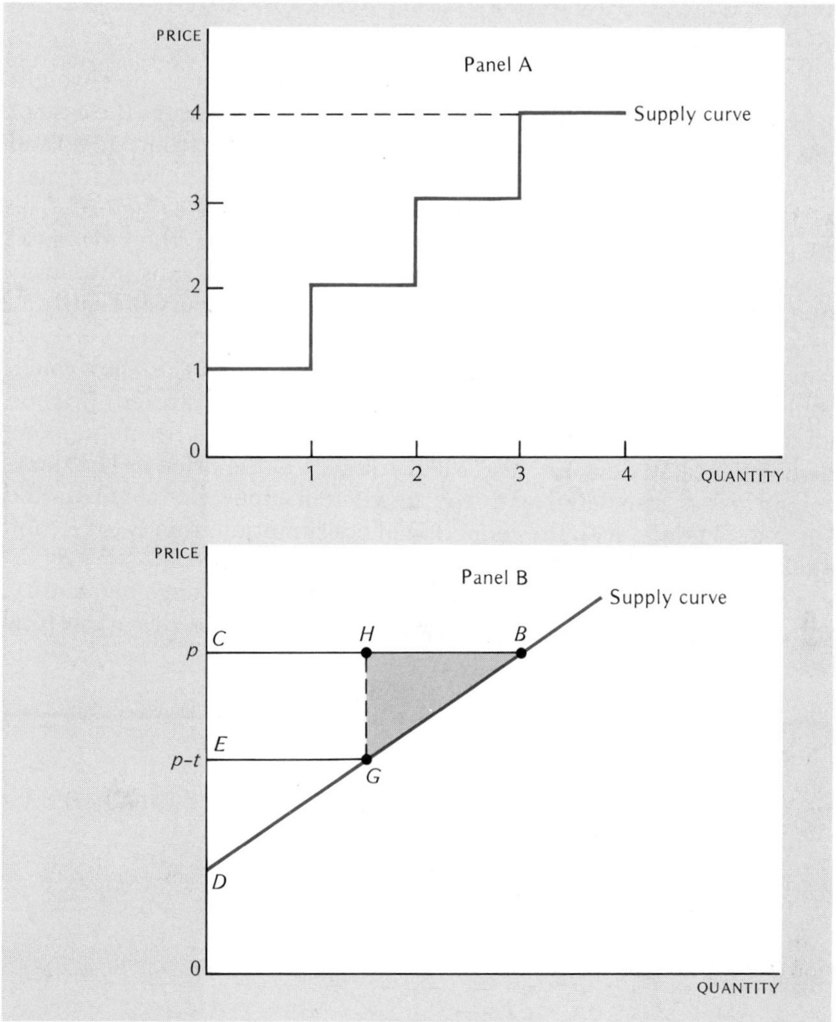

18.9 THE DEADWEIGHT LOSS OF A TAX ON PRODUCTION *BGH* measures the deadweight loss of a tax on production.

tax on steel.[11] The difference in revenues raised by the lump-sum tax and the tax on steel is the deadweight loss from the tax. The magnitude of the deadweight loss will depend on the possibilities of substitution. If the firm cannot substitute any other input for steel (even partially), the tax on steel is no different from a tax on output. There is no distortionary effect on the input mix and, hence, no deadweight loss associated with a change in the input mix.

[11] This is not, of course, the only deadweight loss arising from the input tax. Since it increases the marginal cost of production, it will result in an increase in the price consumers pay, and there will be a deadweight loss to consumers.

EFFECTS OF TAXES BORNE PARTLY BY CONSUMERS, PARTLY BY PRODUCERS

It is straightforward to combine our analysis of producer deadweight loss with consumer deadweight loss. Figure 18.10 illustrates the case of a tax that is borne partly by producers (whose price falls from p to p_s) and partly by consumers (whose price rises from p to p_c). The change in market demand can be decomposed into two parts, just as before. The movement from Q to $\hat{Q}$ is the income effect of the tax; the movement from $\hat{Q}$ to Q^* is the substitution effect, as consumers substitute away from the taxed good along the compensated demand curve. That is, in the new equilibrium, at the price p_c, consumers are clearly worse off than they were at the original equilibrium price, p. If we ask how much would they have consumed, at the original (non-tax-distorted) price p, but at the new lower level of welfare, the answer is $\hat{Q}$, the point along the compensated demand schedule through A at the price p. The deadweight loss is associated with the movement along the compensated demand schedule, with the reduction of consumption from $\hat{Q}$ to Q^*, and is given by the triangle ABD.

What matters, however, for producers is the total change in quantity, from Q to Q^*, so their deadweight loss is the triangle BCE. The total

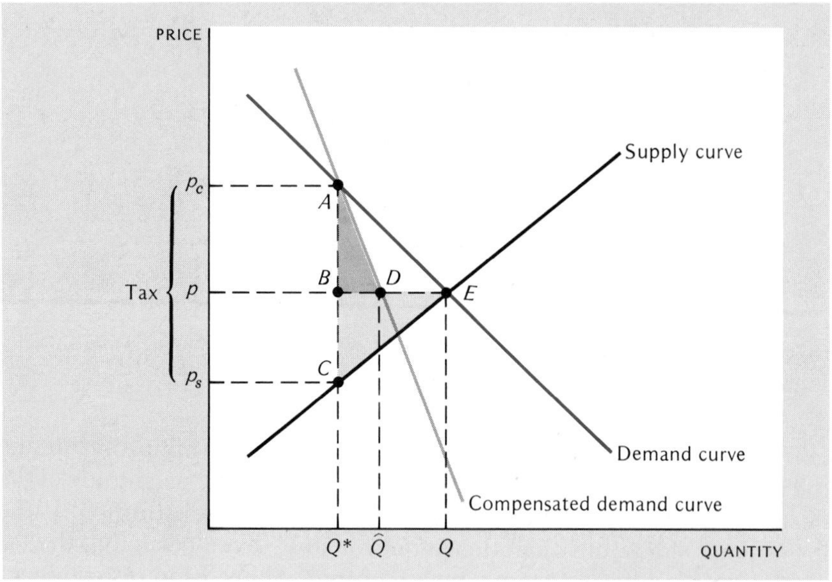

18.10 DEADWEIGHT LOSS FROM A TAX THAT IS BORNE PARTLY BY CONSUMERS AND PARTLY BY PRODUCERS The consumers' deadweight loss is the triangle *ABD;* the producers' is the triangle *BCE.* If the compensated and uncompensated demand schedules coincide, as they will if the demand curve is not sensitive to small changes in income, then the total deadweight loss is the big triangle *ABCE.*

deadweight loss is the sum of these two triangles, and depends, as before, on the elasticities of demand and supply.

SUMMARY

1. The imposition of a tax that is not a lump-sum tax introduces inefficiencies. The magnitude of the inefficiencies is measured by the deadweight loss, the difference in revenues that could be obtained from a lump-sum tax as compared to a distortionary tax, with the same effect on the level of welfare of consumers.
2. The effect of any tax can be decomposed into an income effect and a substitution effect.
3. There is an income effect associated with a lump-sum tax but no substitution effect. Thus the magnitude of the distortion associated with any tax is related to the magnitude of the substitution effect. The greater the substitution effect, the greater the deadweight loss.
4. For a tax on a commodity, both the income effect and the substitution effect usually lead to a reduction in the level of consumption of that commodity.
5. For an interest income tax as viewed by a saver, the income effect typically leads to an increase in savings and the substitution effect leads to a decrease in savings: the net effect is ambiguous. But even if the net effect is to leave savings unchanged, there is still a distortion associated with the interest income tax. For borrowers, the income effect and the substitution effect both lead to an increase in borrowing (assuming that interest payments are tax-deductible). Now the effect is unambiguous.
6. The deadweight loss from a tax-induced increase in a consumer price may be measured by the area under the compensated demand schedule, as the change in the level of consumer surplus associated with the tax minus the tax revenue.
7. There is also a deadweight loss associated with the reduction in the price received by producers. The reduction in their profits exceeds the tax revenues they effectively pay to the government.
8. The deadweight loss increases more than proportionately with increases in the tax. It also increases with the (compensated) elasticity of demand and with the elasticity of supply.

KEY CONCEPTS

Deadweight loss
Excess burden
Income effects
Substitution effects
Compensated demand curve
Consumer surplus
Producer surplus

QUESTIONS AND PROBLEMS

1. If savings do not respond to changes in the interest rate, does it mean that there is no deadweight loss associated with the taxation of interest?
2. What is the deadweight loss from the mineral tax in Problem 1, Chapter 17? What does this imply about the relationship between deadweight loss and supply curves? Relate this to our discussion of lump-sum taxes.

3. Under what circumstances will a government tax or subsidy have income and substitution effects that: (a) strengthen each other? (b) offset each other?
4. Compare the effects of a tax on beer and of a lump-sum tax raising the same revenue. In particular, show that the individual's utility is higher with the lump-sum tax than with the tax on beer.
5. Show that for linear compensated demand schedules,

$$Q = a - bp$$

and that with constant marginal cost of production, the deadweight loss is

$$.5\, b\, t^2.$$

Show that the elasticity of the compensated demand schedule is

$$\frac{bp}{Q}.$$

What is the revenue raised?
Show that the ratio of the deadweight loss to the revenue raised is

$$\frac{.5\, bt}{Q} = .5 \times \text{elasticity of the compensated demand schedule} \times \text{percentage tax rate } (t/p).$$

APPENDIX: MEASURING DEADWEIGHT LOSS

Earlier, we showed how the deadweight loss from a tax can be measured as the area of the triangle *BCE* in Figure 18.6. The height of the triangle, *BC*, is equal to the tax, *t*. *BE* is the change in quantity as a result of the tax. Recall that the *elasticity of demand* gives the percentage change in quantity as a result of a one percent change in price, that is

$$\eta = \frac{\Delta Q/Q}{\Delta p/p}$$

where the symbol ΔQ represents the change in quantity and the symbol Δp represents the change in price. The symbol Δ is the (capital) Greek letter "Delta" and is conventionally used to represent a change. The symbol η is the Greek letter "eta" and is conventionally used to represent the elasticity of demand. Rearranging, we can write the change in quantity as

$$\Delta Q = \frac{\Delta p}{p}\, Q\, \eta.$$

This equation has the natural interpretation that the change in quantity will be larger, the larger the change in price and the larger the elasticity of demand. But the change in price is just the per-unit tax, *t*. Thus, substituting, we obtain

$$BE = \frac{t}{p}\, Q\eta.$$

Now the area of the triangle *BCE* is just

$$\frac{t \cdot BE}{2} = \frac{1}{2}\frac{t^2}{p}Q\eta$$
$$= \frac{1}{2}\left[\frac{t}{p}\right]\left[\frac{t}{p}\right]pQ\eta$$
$$= \frac{1}{2}\hat{t}^2 pQ\eta$$

where $\hat{t} \equiv \dfrac{t}{p}$ is the tax *rate*. That is, $t = \hat{t}p$ is the tax per unit output, while $\hat{t}$ is the *ad valorem* tax rate.[12]

[12] Any per unit tax can be expressed as an equivalent ad valorem tax using this formula.

19

Taxation and Economic Efficiency: Labor Supply

In 1986, over 100 million Americans worked an average of thirty-five hours per week and earned total wages and benefits of $2.5 trillion. On average, Americans faced a marginal tax rate on their wages of close to 40 percent.[1] How did these taxes affect the supply and productivity of labor? What was the deadweight loss from U.S. labor taxes?

The economic theory we described in the last chapter tells us how to analyze these questions, but substantial controversies about their precise answers remain. Many economists believe that our tax system has had a negative effect on both the quantity and quality of labor supplied, and that it has caused a significant deadweight loss.

EFFECTS OF TAXATION ON THE QUANTITY OF LABOR SUPPLIED

Has the tax system led individuals to work more or fewer hours than they otherwise would have worked?

Many students' (and a few economists') first reaction to this question is that taxes have little to do with the number of hours worked; most jobs specify the number of hours to work; the individual has little discretion. The number of hours specified by the job, in turn, is a consequence of technological or institutional considerations, and union and government

[1] *Economic Report of the President*, p. 91, and Statistical Tables. The marginal tax rate takes account of the social security and Medicare payroll taxes, and federal, state, and local income taxes. It does not take into account the implicit taxes on earnings of individuals who receive public assistance.

regulations. These institutional considerations do mean that, in the short run, individuals may have less choice about the number of hours that they work than they otherwise would. But institutions do change. The standard work week has been drastically shortened over the past century; in manufacturing, for instance, it declined from fifty-five hours in 1900 to fewer than forty today.

Most economists would argue that this marked change in hours worked is at least partly a response to economic forces. Though each individual may not have full discretion over the number of hours he works, the contracts firms offer and the bargains unions make reflect the preferences of the workers. A rise in wages has two effects. The income effect leads individuals to work less, taking some of their gains in the form of increased leisure; the substitution effect leads individuals to work more. The fact that as wages have risen hours have declined implies that the income effect has dominated the substitution effect. This implies that the labor supply schedule is backward-bending, as shown in Figure 19.1[2]

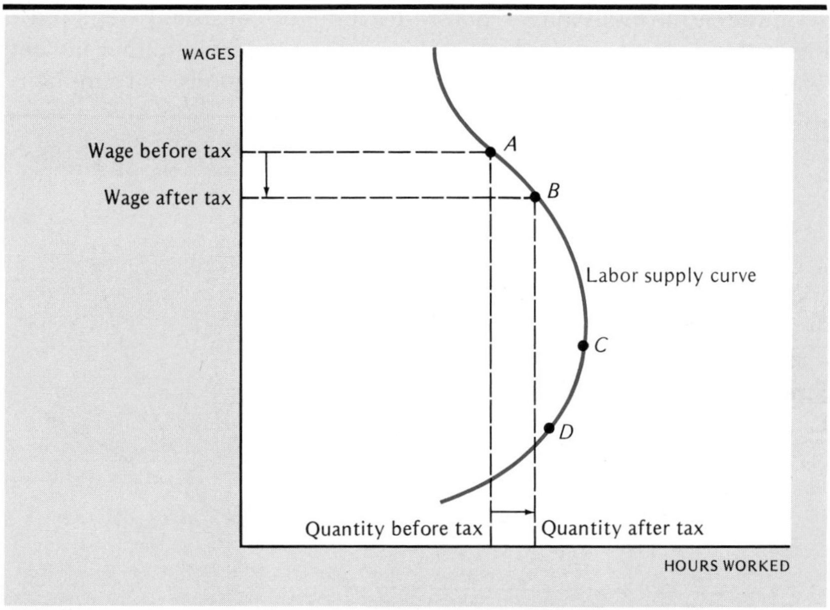

19.1 LABOR SUPPLY CURVE With a backward-bending supply curve, at some wage levels an increase in a tax on wages—equivalent to a decrease in wages—increases labor supply. Below point *C*, a tax on wages reduces labor supply.

[2] One has to be careful in using time-series data to predict what would happen were the wage today to be (permanently) decreased. There have been many changes other than wage increases that have affected labor supply (such as the evolution of social insurance programs and changes in the relative prices of different goods, including those that might affect the demand for leisure). But the "suggestion" from time-series data that the labor supply curve is backward bending is consistent with other data discussed in footnote 4.

The imposition of a *proportional* income tax is equivalent to a reduction in wages received, assuming that the before-tax wage does not change. With a backward-bending labor supply schedule, a proportional income tax leads to an increase in total work (from what it otherwise would have been), moving from point *A* to point *B* in Figure 19.1. (Of course, the change in the supply of labor will affect the before-tax wage, but for purposes of this chapter we will, for the most part, ignore these effects.)

Relationship between Labor and Consumption

The supply curve for labor is the relationship between the price of labor and the quantity of labor supplied by one (or all) individuals. Another way to depict the relationship between an individual's labor supply and the wage is shown in Figure 19.2. This figure shows how the individual chooses between consumption and leisure. (The more leisure he gives up, the greater his hours of work, and hence the greater his consumption or income.) It is analogous to Figure 18.1, which shows how the individual chooses between beer and soda.

Consider the individual's before-tax budget constraint depicted in Figure 19.2. As the individual works more, he obtains a higher income, which enables him to purchase more consumption goods. For simplicity,

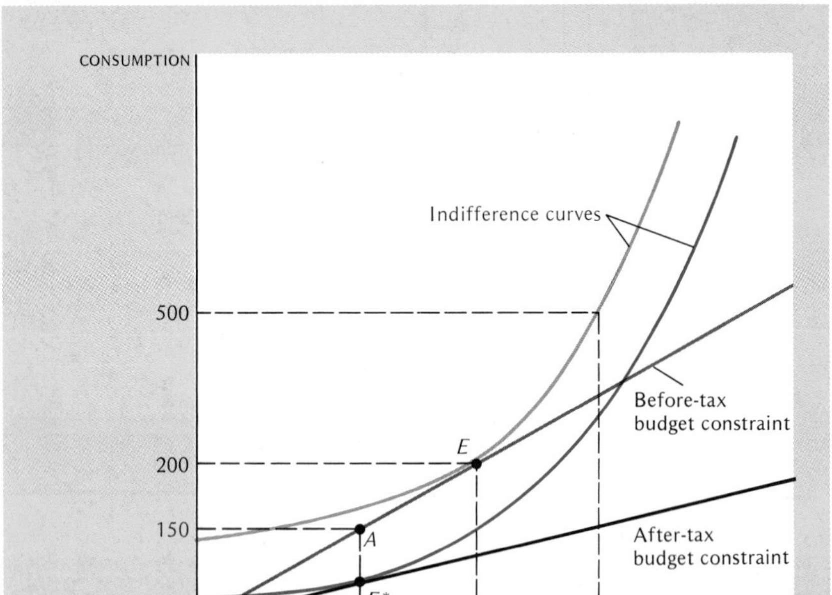

19.2 EQUILIBRIUM BEFORE AND AFTER TAXES The effect of the tax is to shift the budget constraint down, and thus the equilibrium changes from *E* to *E**.

we assume there is a single consumption good and the individual cannot save.

The budget constraint shows the alternative levels of consumption and labor that are possible. In this example, the individual gets paid $5 an hour. If he works thirty hours a week he gets $150. If he works forty hours a week he receives $200, and if he works fifty hours a week he receives $250.

The figure also shows the individual's indifference curves for work and consumption, giving the combinations of work and consumption goods among which the individual is indifferent. The individual is indifferent, for instance, when choosing among working thirty hours a week and receiving $175, working forty hours a week and receiving $200, and working fifty hours a week and receiving $500. Note that the individual requires a much larger increase in his weekly income to compensate him for increasing his work from forty to fifty hours than for compensating him for increasing his work from thirty to forty hours. As he works more and more, his leisure becomes more valuable relative to consumption goods. That is why he requires larger and larger increases in consumption to compensate him for successive increases in his labor supply.

In the absence of taxation, the individual would choose that point on his budget constraint where his indifference curve is tangent to his budget constraint, point E in Figure 19.2.

At E, the individual requires precisely $5 extra compensation for working an additional hour, and he receives $5 extra for working an extra hour. In other words, the slope of the individual's indifference curve (his *marginal rate of substitution*) is just equal to the slope of his budget constraint, his wage. (The slope of the budget constraint specifies how much his consumption increases in response to an increase in his labor supply. In our example, for each extra hour the individual works, he gets an extra $5.)

Income and Substitution Effects of Taxation

We now examine how taxes alter this. Assume that there is a proportional income tax. That is, a given fraction of the income the individual earns must be turned over to the government. This shifts his budget constraint down, as depicted by the after-tax budget constraint in Figure 19.2. There is now a new equilibrium, denoted by E^*. The tax revenue is the vertical distance, at E^*, between the after-tax and the before-tax budget constraints, E^*A. The before-tax budget constraint gives the individual's income—before tax—at the labor supply corresponding to E^*. The after-tax budget constraint gives his level of consumption. The difference is just what he pays in taxes.

In our example, we have imposed a 50 percent tax, and the individual, as a result of the tax, has reduced his labor supply from forty hours a week to thirty hours a week. Thus, the government's tax revenue is $30 \times \$2.50 = \$75$.

As we just saw, the effect of a rise in wages can be broken down into two parts: the income effect and the substitution effect. First, the wage tax makes the individual worse off. As a result of being worse off, the individual will consume less and work more hours. This is the **income effect** of the tax. The second effect is that the return for working is reduced; for each hour the individual works, he used to receive a wage of w; now he receives a wage of $w(1 - t)$, where t is the tax rate; that is, his return for working is reduced by the amount of the tax. Since the individual's return for his labor is reduced, he has less incentive to work. We refer to this as the **substitution effect** of the tax; he substitutes leisure for consumption goods.

In Figure 19.3 we illustrate the two effects. We first observe that if we shift the individual's budget constraint down in a parallel way (from *OA* to *CD*), keeping the slope—representing the increased consumption for working an extra hour, the wage—fixed, we increase labor supply. This movement from point E to $\hat{E}$ is the income effect. Because the individual is poorer, he consumes fewer goods and less leisure.[3] Next, we observe that if we rotate the budget constraint (from *CD* to *OB*)—keeping the individual on the same indifference curve—labor supply decreases. This movement from $\hat{E}$ to E^* is the substitution effect. Because the wage is lower, at any given level of utility individuals substitute leisure for consumption goods: they work less.

In the case of a proportional income tax, the substitution effect and the income effect work in opposite directions. While the income effect leads the individual to work more, the substitution effect leads the individual to work less. It is impossible to say, on theoretical grounds, which effect will dominate. In Panel A of Figure 19.3 the substitution effect dominates the income effect, so that the individual reduces his labor supply; E^* is left of E. In Panel B we have depicted a case where the two effects exactly cancel each other, and the labor supply is unaffected; E^* is directly below E.

We showed earlier that the question of whether a proportional tax decreases or increases labor supply is equivalent to asking whether the labor supply curve is upward sloping or backward bending. Thus, in Figure 19.1, as the wage is reduced from A to B, labor supply rises. As the wage is reduced further, say, from C to D, labor supply falls.

A measure of how labor supply changes when the wage changes is the elasticity of labor supply. This gives the percentage change in the labor supply resulting from a percent change in the wage:

$$\text{Elasticity of labor supply} = \frac{\%\text{ change in labor supply}}{\%\text{ change in wage}}.$$

[3] We say that a good is "normal" when, as the budget constraint shifts down at fixed wages and prices, consumption of the good decreases. Similarly, we say that leisure is a normal good when leisure decreases as the budget constraint shifts down in a parallel fashion. Throughout most of the remaining analysis, we shall assume that leisure and consumption goods are "normal."

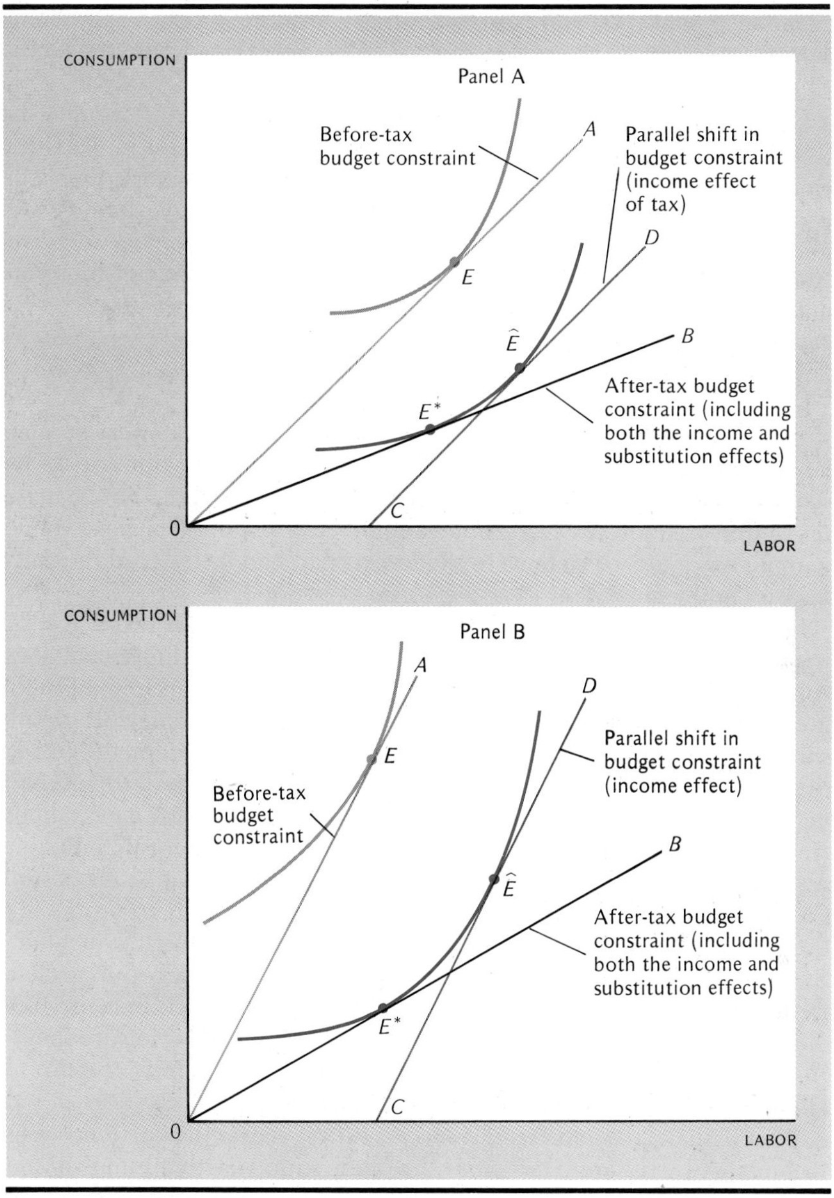

19.3 THE INCOME AND SUBSTITUTION EFFECTS (A) The income effect normally leads to increased labor supply. The substitution effect always leads to decreased labor supply. The net effect is ambiguous. (B) In this example, income and substitution effects exactly cancel; the tax has no effect on labor supply.

If a 1 percent increase in the wage increases the labor supply by .25 percent, we say that the elasticity of labor supply is .25. If a 1 percent increase in the wage decreases the labor supply by 0.5 percent, we say that the elasticity of labor supply is −0.5. There is a consensus among economists that the labor supply elasticity for men is very small.[4] Some economists' empirical work suggests that it is negative in sign, so that the labor supply curve is slightly backward bending.

On the other hand, there is a consensus that for married women the labor supply response is positive, and much larger than for men.[5] If the married female labor supply elasticity is taken to be around 1, then a 25 percent tax would reduce the amount of labor supplied by women by 25 percent. As changes in the role of women in the workplace occur, corresponding changes in labor supply elasticities may occur, but these are not yet well reflected in the data.

Distortionary Effects of Wage Taxation

We have seen that a tax on wages may have only a slight effect on male labor supply. Does this mean that such a tax is nondistortionary? As we shall now show, the answer is no. Even if an individual has not changed his supply of labor, the government could have obtained more revenue, with no extra loss of welfare to the individual, had it replaced the wage tax by a lump-sum tax.

Recall from Chapter 18 the definition of a lump-sum tax: it is a tax whose magnitude does not depend on anything that the individual does. A lump-sum tax would require each citizen to pay a given amount to the government—say, $100 per week—regardless of income. It simply shifts the individual's budget constraint downward, as depicted in Figure 19.4. The slope of the budget constraint is unchanged; the individual still receives the same extra consumption for working an extra hour. (In our example, with a $5 wage rate, for each extra hour the individual works, he still receives $5.) If he works forty hours a week, his before-tax income is $200. But his after-tax income is $100. If he works fifty hours a week, his before-tax income is $250, but his after-tax income is $150. At each level of labor supply, his income is reduced by exactly $100.[6] Notice that a lump-sum tax has an income effect: because individuals are worse off, they consume fewer goods and less leisure (hence they work more). Indeed, the effect of the tax is precisely the *income effect* we described earlier.

We compare the effects of a lump-sum tax and a proportional wage income tax by asking: How does the labor supply with a lump-sum tax compare with that under a proportional income tax, assuming that we choose the tax rate so as to leave the individual at precisely the same

[4] The results of the major empirical studies are summarized in J. Pencavel, "Labor Supply of Men," *Handbook of Labor Economics,* Vol. 1, O. Ashenfelter and R. Layard, eds. (Amsterdam: North Holland, 1986). The wage elasticities in representative studies range from −0.29 to 0.06. A simple average of all these is −0.12. Technically, these elasticities are called *uncompensated* elasticities, because they include both the income effect and the substitution effect of the wage change.

[5] See M. Killingsworth and J. Heckman, "Female Labor Supply," *Handbook of Labor Economics.* The estimates of married women's labor supply elasticity are quite varied, but a majority ranges from about 0.5 to 2.5.

[6] In this simple exposition, we ignore what happens if the individual's income is less than the amount of lump-sum tax that has been imposed.

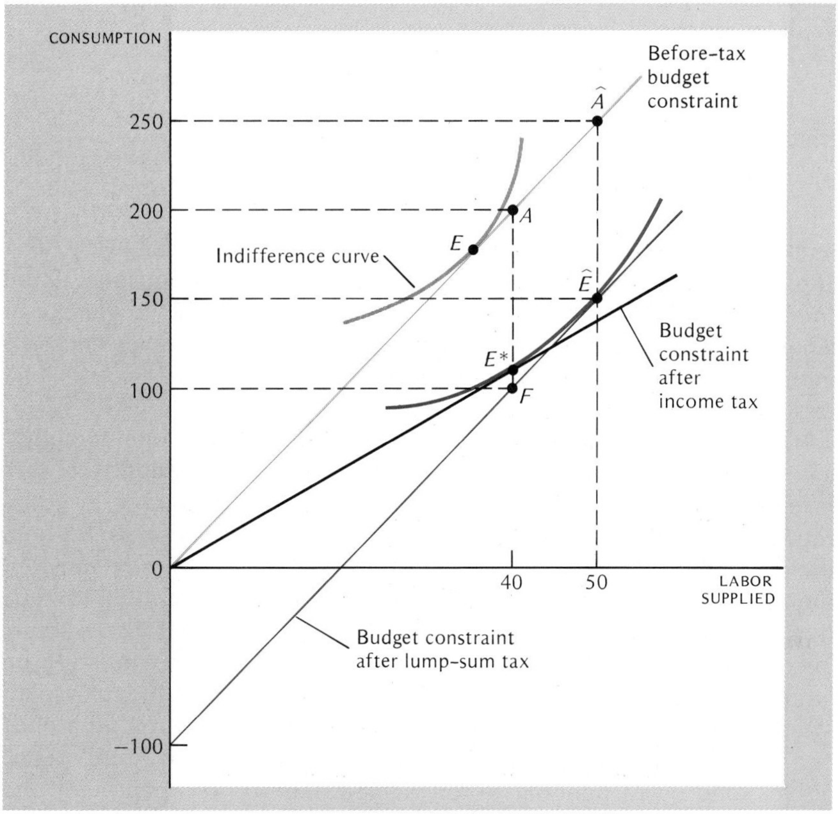

19.4 COMPARING THE EFFECTS OF A LUMP-SUM TAX AND A PROPORTIONAL TAX ON WAGE INCOME With the income tax, the individual chooses E^* and pays tax of AE^*. With a lump-sum tax of $AF = \hat{A}\hat{E}$ the individual chooses $\hat{E}$. The excess burden is the difference, E^*F.

level of utility (on the same indifference curve) that he had with the lump-sum tax? This comparison is also depicted in Figure 19.4. With the lump-sum tax the individual chooses point $\hat{E}$; with the income tax the individual chooses point E^*. It is clear that with the income tax there is less labor supplied; this is precisely the substitution effect we identified earlier.

We now wish to compare the amount of revenue raised by the government. The amount of revenue raised is measured by the difference between the before-tax and after-tax budget constraints at the level of labor actually supplied. The revenue raised by the income tax is the distance AE^*.

For the lump-sum tax, the distance between the before- and after-tax budget constraints is the lump-sum tax and is the same no matter what the amount of labor supplied. Thus the distance $\hat{A}\hat{E}$ is equal to the distance AF, and both equal the revenue raised by the lump-sum tax. It is apparent from the figure that with a lump-sum tax, the government raises more revenue than with an income tax. The extra revenue is depicted by the distance E^*F in Figure 19.4.

Distortion with Inelastic Labor Supply

We now return to our original question: Is there a distortion associated with an income tax, if the labor supply elasticity is zero, so that the number of hours worked remains the same after the tax as before? The answer is yes, and the magnitude of the distortion is proportional to the *compensated labor supply elasticity.* This is the percentage change in labor supply in response to the combination of (a) a percentage decrease in the wage rate, and (b) sufficient compensation to keep the individual at the original (pre-wage change) level of utility.

If, as individuals move along an indifference curve, obtaining higher levels of income (but lower levels of leisure or, equivalently higher levels of work), their willingness to give up additional hours of leisure in return for additional consumption remains relatively undiminished, their compensated labor supply elasticity will be large; equivalently, their indifference curve between consumption and leisure will be relatively flat. If, as they work harder and have higher incomes, they rapidly become increasingly unwilling to give up more leisure, insisting on larger and larger increments to income as compensation, their compensated elasticity of labor supply will be small, and their indifference curves will be very curved. In Figure 19.5 we have drawn indifference curves, one corresponding to low substitutability between labor and goods (a low compensated elasticity of labor supply), the other to high substitutability (high compensated elasticity of labor supply).

It is apparent that the magnitude of the deadweight loss with high substitutability (large compensated elasticity) is much higher than it is with low substitutability.

The magnitude of the deadweight loss also increases rapidly with the magnitude of the tax, as we saw in the previous chapter. In fact, for small taxes, it increases with the *square* of the tax rate; that is, doubling the tax rate multiplies the deadweight loss by a factor of four. This becomes particularly important when we remember that what is relevant is the total marginal tax rate faced by the individual. For instance, consider a lower-middle-income individual facing a 15 percent marginal tax rate under the federal income tax. The distortion is not just that associated with a 15 percent income tax. If we view the individual as paying the entire social security tax, the total marginal tax rate he faces from federal taxes alone is approximately 30 percent, so the deadweight loss will be approximately four times that at a 15 percent rate. (If the individual spends all that he earns, and lives in a state with a 8 percent sales tax, the effective marginal tax rate and the deadweight loss are even higher).

In the previous chapter, we pointed out that for small commodity taxes, the ratio of the deadweight loss to the revenue raised was propor-

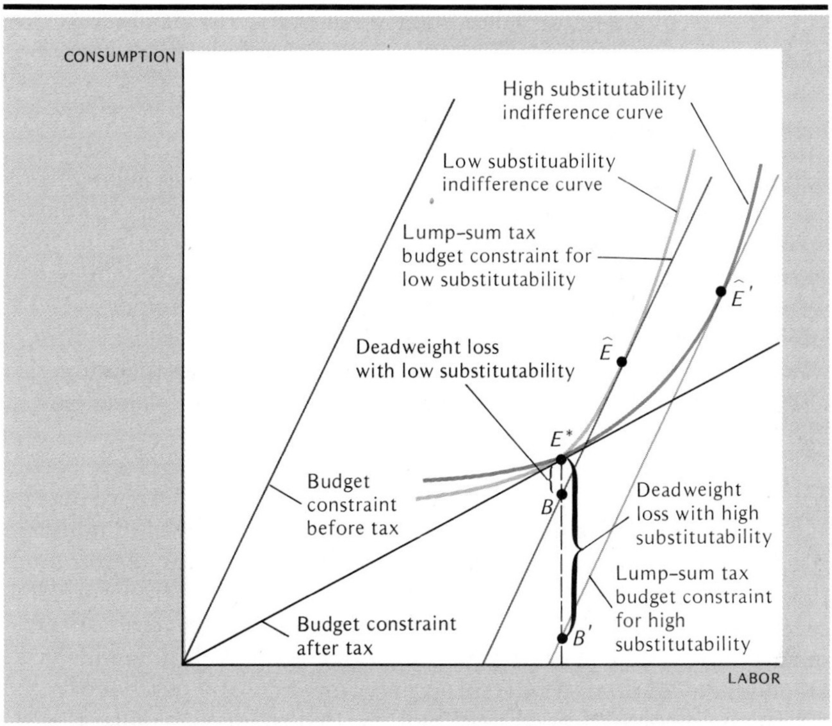

19.5 THE SUBSTITUTION EFFECT AND THE DEADWEIGHT LOSS FROM A TAX The greater the substitution effect, the greater the deadweight loss from a tax.

tional to the percentage tax rate and to the compensated elasticity of demand. With a tax on wage income, the ratio of the deadweight loss to the revenue raised is proportional to the percentage tax rate and to the compensated elasticity of labor supply:

$$\frac{\text{Deadweight loss}}{\text{Revenue raised}} = .5t\left\{\begin{matrix}\text{compensated elasticity of} \\ \text{labor supply}\end{matrix}\right\}$$

Unfortunately, different approaches to estimating the responsiveness of labor supply to changes in wages have led to quite different estimates of the compensated labor supply elasticity. Of fourteen major studies surveyed recently by John Pencavel of Stanford University, five actually yielded a negative estimate of the compensated elasticity, which is inconsistent with theory. Of the positive estimates, the largest is .84 and the smallest is .04. If labor economists had to vote on the best elasticity, the average might be .11.[7] With a 28 percent tax on wage income, and using the .11 estimate, the deadweight loss of the wage tax is less than 2 percent (= 1/2 × .28 × .11) of revenue raised, while under the largest

[7] J. Pencavel, "Labor Supply of Men," Chapter 1.

estimate of compensated labor supply elasticity, the deadweight loss from the tax is almost 12 percent of revenue raised (= $1/2 \times .28 \times .84$).

Taxes and Female Labor Force Participation

In the past eighty years there have been dramatic changes in **labor force participation** of different groups. The percentage of women working has more than doubled, from 20.4 percent in 1900 to 55.3 percent in 1986.[8] There are many factors affecting decisions to work, but economic considerations—and hence taxes—are among the more important. The labor force participation of women might have increased even more were it not for the discouragement provided by the tax structure. The effect may be particularly significant for both very low-income families and high-income families.

To see how the tax-welfare system may discourage labor force participation for a low-income woman, turn to Figure 19.6, where we depict a case where the government has accompanied a high level of minimum guaranteed income with a high (here 100 percent) marginal tax rate. In this situation, there will be no increase in consumption from foregoing leisure up to point H. This is precisely the case with several aspects of our welfare system. For instance, since 1981 the Aid to Families with Dependent Children (AFDC) program provided a 100 percent effective tax rate on income earned by the mother; that is, for each dollar that she earned (or that she reported earning) she lost one dollar of benefits. Figure 19.6 depicts her budget constraint. If her preferences correspond to indifference curves u and u', it is clear that her optimal decision will be not to work. When she does not work, she collects the full AFDC grant, and she reaches the indifference curve marked u. It is also clear that letting her keep 50 cents on the dollar will lead her to work, will reduce government outlays, and will make her better off. (The new equilibrium is marked E' and is on the higher indifference curve marked u'.)

On the other hand, some women who previously found it unattractive to apply for AFDC might do so after the welfare reform, and these women might be induced to work less. Thus, the woman with the dark indifference curves v and v' worked h hours before welfare reform, and she reduced her work to h' hours after welfare reform.

The reason that women in high-income families are discouraged from working is rather different. There are theoretical reasons to expect that taxation may have different effects on the head of the household (usually men) than on secondary workers (usually married women). Because most families file joint returns, the marginal tax rate on the secondary worker's first dollar earned is likely to be high. Thus the substitution effect is large, and the reduction in labor supply and the deadweight loss are likely to be much higher than for the primary worker. The empirical findings that we describe later in this chapter are consistent with this view.

[8] *Economic Report of the President*, 1987, Table B-34.

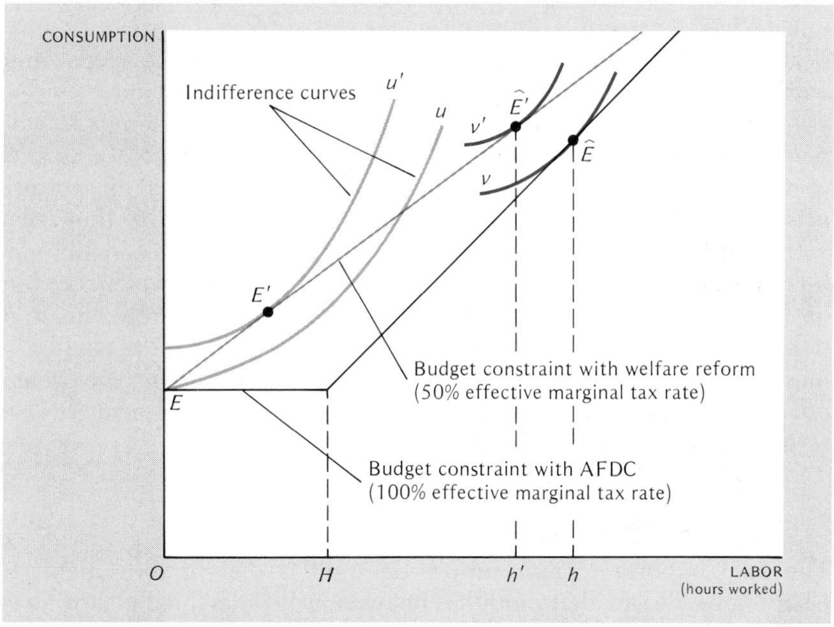

19.6 EFFECT OF *AFDC* ON BUDGET CONSTRAINTS AND LABOR SUPPLY
With *AFDC* there is a 100 percent tax rate. This discourages labor force participation of those who participate in the program. A reduction of the effective marginal tax rate to 50 percent would increase their labor supply from zero to *E'*. However, a reduction in the *AFDC* tax rate would also induce more women to participate in *AFDC*, and these women might reduce hours worked, from *h* to *h'*.

(Of course, the total effect of wage taxes on female labor supply are, on theoretical grounds, ambiguous. While the income effect—including the reduction in the husband's after-tax income—leads to an increase in labor supply, the substitution effect leads to a reduction.)

There are, moreover, some grounds for expecting females to be quite sensitive to changes in after-tax wage. When the married woman does not work outside of the home, she is still being productive; it is only that her services are not monetized, and therefore not taxed. Frequently, when she goes to work, the family will have to replace those services in one way or another. It may hire someone to do the cleaning or cooking; it may rely more on frozen dinners or eat out more often (effectively purchasing the cooking services that the wife previously supplied). Thus the net gain to the family is much less than the gross income of the wife. Assume, for instance, that the wife earns \$10,000 a year, but the family spends an extra \$7,000 to purchase services to replace those she had previously performed. The net gain to the family is only \$3,000. From the point of view of economic efficiency, the woman should choose to work. Her productivity in the workplace exceeds her productivity at home. But consider what happens if, as a result of her husband's income, she is in the 33 percent tax bracket. Her after-tax income is only $6,700, but she has to pay out $7,000 to replace the services she previously had performed. The family's after-tax income is reduced by her decision to work. To the extent her decision to work is based on economic considerations, she will be discouraged from working. The tax, though only 33 percent of her income, represents more than 100 percent of the surplus of her income over the costs of replacing her services. It is thus not surprising to find that women are very sensitive to the wage rate they face.

Institutional factors which limit the availability of part-time jobs may further exacerbate the negative effect of the income tax/welfare system on labor force participation. Individuals may face a discrete choice of either working, say, forty hours, or not working at all.[9] If she could, she might prefer to work twenty hours, but of the two extremes, she prefers not to work than to work full time, given the marked reduction in returns from working resulting from the income tax.

Retirement Decision

The final important labor supply decision is that of retirement. In Chapter 13 we saw that there has been a marked decline in labor force participation by those over sixty-five; we also saw how the retirement decision was affected by the social security program. But it is also affected by a variety of other measures taken by the government. Thus the tax treatment of savings affects individuals' incentives for saving, and this has a strong interaction with individuals' retirement decisions. The public provision of high-quality education reduces the demands on savings imposed on those with children; and this implies that these individuals are likely to have more savings available for retirement.

MEASURING THE EFFECTS OF TAXES ON LABOR SUPPLIED

The fact that theoretically the effect of an income tax on labor supply is indeterminate makes it all the more important to attempt to determine empirically what has, in fact, been its effects. Research in this area has been extensive and has yielded important (but not uncontroversial) results. Three methods have been employed to study these questions: surveys, cross-section econometric models, and experiments.

Surveys

The first involves surveying individuals, asking them whether they were led to work more or less than they otherwise would as a result of taxation. Not surprisingly, the responses obtained were mixed; some claimed, in effect, that they worked harder because they needed to

[9] Although it is often "feasible" to work part time, pay for part-time work is often much lower than pay for the equivalent full-time work.

make up for what the government had taken away (for them, evidently, the income effect exceeded the substitution effect), while others claimed just the opposite (implicitly, the substitution effect dominated the income effect).[10] Although the studies do confirm the theorists' belief that the effects of taxation on labor supply are indeterminate, they are of limited use: they do not provide a very accurate quantitative indication of the magnitude of the effects.[11]

Statistical Techniques Using Market Data

The second method entails using statistical techniques to analyze how individuals in the past have responded to changes in their after-tax wages. In general, we do not have data on how particular individuals responded to changes in wages. Rather, we have data on how many hours individuals who have different wages work. Those who have higher wages seem to work more hours. We can calculate from this the "average" effect of wages on hours worked.

To this point, we have simply described a *correlation*, an observed relationship between two economic variables. We now wish to use this to make an *inference*, a prediction or a statement about the effect of lowering take-home wages resulting from, say, the imposition of a tax. To make such an inference, we must make an assumption: that the reason individuals who receive higher wages are observed to work more is that they choose to work more because of the higher wage; in other words, an individual who receives a higher wage is essentially like the one who receives a lower wage; the only important difference is the difference in pay, and it is this difference that leads to a difference in the number of hours worked. There are, of course, other important differences, and more sophisticated statistical analyses attempt to take as many of these differences (say, age or occupation or sex) into account; they attempt to see, of individuals of the same age, occupation, or sex (or who have other characteristics in common), whether those who receive higher wages work more.

There are two consistent findings across these studies of the effect of wage changes on labor supply. The total effect on labor supply of men is small, but the effect on female labor supply may be substantial. Recall that the deadweight loss associated with a tax is related to the substitution effect. Though the total effect of a tax may be negligible, with the income effect offsetting the substitution effect, it is possible that there is a substantial substitution effect and, hence, a substantial deadweight

[10] Among the most famous of these studies are those by Dan Holland of M.I.T. (D. M. Holland, "The Effect of Taxation on Effort: Some Results for Business Executives," *National Tax Association Proceedings of the Sixty-Second Annual Conference,* September 29–October 3, 1969), and George Break, of the University of California (G. Break, "Income Taxes and Incentives to Work: An Empirical Study," *American Economic Review* 47 [1957]: 529–49).

[11] Moreover, surveys have, in other contexts, proven an unreliable indicator of how individuals behave: they reflect how individuals perceive their behavior to be affected, but there are often marked discrepancies between individuals' perception of their behavior and the behavior itself.

loss. There is not a consensus concerning whether the deadweight loss is large or small.

A recent study of labor supply by Jerry Hausman of M.I.T. attempted to take into account both the fact that individuals differed in their tastes for goods versus leisure and relevant details of our tax structure and welfare program. His major findings include the following:[12]

a. Federal taxes (at 1988 rates) reduce labor supply of the average married man by approximately 6.5 percent. Labor supply was little changed by the 1986 Tax Reform Act; the overall increase was only .9 percent. Because it lowered the marginal tax rate of upper-income individuals more, the tax reform stimulated labor supply of upper-income individuals somewhat more, by approximately 1.5 percent.

b. As a percentage of revenue raised, the deadweight loss from all taxes on labor (including social security taxes and average state income and sales taxes) remains substantial, even after tax reform: for the average married man, 13.5 percent (as compared to 16.5 percent before 1986). For upper-income married men (an income of $45,000 in 1985 dollars), the deadweight loss is 25.6 percent of revenue now, compared to 32.6 percent under the old law, and 54.2 percent before 1981. These high estimates of deadweight loss are a result of Hausman's high estimate of the magnitude of the substitution effect. As our earlier discussion noted, there is no consensus on the magnitude of the substitution effect. Most studies suggest, however, that it might be considerably smaller, with commensurately smaller deadweight losses.

c. While male labor supply is relatively unresponsive to wage changes, female labor supply is relatively elastic. Hausman's estimate of the female labor supply elasticity was .9 (most of the supply response is accounted for by an increase in the number of women working rather than by an increase in the average hours of the female work force). It is estimated that in 1988 the average married woman working full time faces a marginal federal income tax rate of 28 percent, reducing female labor supply by $.9 \times 28 = 25.2\%$.[13] The marginal tax rate is only slightly lower than with the old law when it was just under 30 percent. On the other hand, lower income (part-time) workers had a substantial reduction in the tax rates they faced. The net effect was that the 1986 Tax Reform Act is estimated to have increased the labor supply of wives by 2.64 percent. Again, the ratio of the deadweight loss to revenue raised remains high, at 25 percent, but it is still substantially below the estimate of 58 percent based on the pre-1981 code.

The magnitude of the labor responses for female-headed households lies between that of men and married women.

[12] From J. Hausman, "Labor Supply," in *How Taxes Affect Economic Behavior*, H. J. Aaron and J. Pechman, eds. (Washington, D.C.: Brookings Institution, 1981), pp. 27–72; and J. A. Hausman and J. M. Poterba, "Household Behavior and the Tax Reform Act of 1986," *Journal of Economic Perspectives*, Summer 1987.

[13] This calculation would be correct if the income tax were approximately proportional. With a progressive income tax, the effect on labor supply is greater.

Experiments

The third approach to obtaining a quantitative estimate of the magnitude of the labor supply responses to tax changes is an experimental approach. The question we are interested in is: What would happen to the labor supply if we raised or lowered tax rates (or changed the tax structure in some other way)? One approach is to say, "Let's change the tax structure and see what happens." This could be an expensive approach: the change might have a very negative effect on labor supply, but before the effects were recognized and the tax structure changed again, considerable damage (welfare loss) could have occurred.

But we can learn something by changing the tax structure for just a small portion of the population. Just as opinion polls can give fairly accurate estimates of how voters will vote in an election, simply by asking a small sample of the population (often fewer than 1,000 individuals), so too the response of a small sample may give a fairly reliable indication of how other, similar individuals would respond were they to face the alternative tax structure. Opinion polls are careful to obtain a representative sample of views; that is, they make sure that views of young and old, of the rich and poor, of skilled and unskilled workers, of married and unmarried individuals, etc., are all represented, and in forming their estimate of how the population as a whole will vote, they assign weights corresponding to the relative importance of the various groups in the population (when they are attempting to predict the outcome of elections, they assign weights corresponding to the known likelihood that members of different groups vote).

In the late 1960s and early 1970s there was a series of such experiments, attempting to ascertain in particular the effects of changes in the tax structure and welfare system on the labor supplied by poorer individuals. Different individuals were confronted with different tax structures, making it possible, in principle, not only to estimate the overall effect of tax changes but to separate out the income effects from the substitution effects.

For instance, while our current welfare system has a fairly high effective marginal tax rate, with a negative income tax the government might reduce an individual's benefits by less as his income rose. Since the negative income tax experiments focused on lower-income individuals, they were mainly concerned with the effect of alternative subsidy systems on labor supply. The government attempted to assess the effects of different levels of guaranteed income and different tax rates. Similar individuals were confronted with different support levels but the same tax rate, or different tax rates with the same support levels. In principle, therefore, the experiments enable the identification of income and substitution effects.

The results were consistent with the view that the overall effect of taxes on labor supply is relatively small. The report on the first such experiment, conducted in New Jersey, described it as presenting "a picture of generally small absolute labor supply differentials between" those who were confronted with the alternative tax/welfare structures and those who faced the existing tax/welfare structure. "Only among wives, whose mean labor supply is quite small to begin with, are the differentials large in relative terms."[14]

The experiments yielded some further results concerning the possible effects of changes in the welfare/tax system. Providing more income to the poor resulted in their searching longer for a job when they became unemployed.

While the early experiments focused on the effect of alternative tax-subsidy schemes on labor supply (and related variables, like job search), later studies attempted to ascertain whether there were other effects as well. For instance, an experiment in Gary, Indiana, found a higher birth weight of babies—an indication of the health of the child—in families whose income had been increased. A large-scale experiment conducted in Seattle, Washington, and Denver, Colorado, found that providing women with a guaranteed income, as the negative income tax does, might contribute to the break-up of families. However, the most generous negative income tax programs in the Seattle-Denver experiment had the least effect on family dissolution rates. It has been argued that income guarantees have two opposing effects on dissolution rates: On the one hand, they stabilize marriages by improving the family's ability to buy essential goods and services. On the other hand, they destabilize them by improving the economic quality of alternatives to marriage. Under this theory, the experimental results suggest that for low guaranteed income levels, the second effect (the "independence effect") dominates the first effect.[15]

The experiments represent an important advance in the tools that are available to social scientists. At the same time, there are some important limitations to the experimental approach in general—and to the above-mentioned experiments in particular—that have to be borne in mind in evaluating the results.

First, there is a well-known phenomenon called the **Hawthorne effect,** which plagues all experimental work with individuals: when an individual is included in an experiment, and he knows his behavior is being examined, his behavior is often altered.

Second, there are problems associated with ensuring that one obtains a representative sample. Since participation in the experiment is voluntary, there may be systematic biases associated with the kinds of individuals who refuse to participate.

[14] U.S. Department of Health, Education and Welfare, *Summary Report: New Jersey Graduated Work Incentive Experiments* (Washington, D.C.: Government Printing Office, 1973).

[15] The Seattle-Denver experiment had guaranteed levels of support ranging from 50 percent to 100 percent of the poverty line, and tax rates varying from .5 to .8. A total of 4,800 families, including a control group, participated in the experiment over the period 1970–1978. See SRI International, *Final Report of the Seattle-Denver Income Maintenance Experiment*, Vol. 1 (Washington, D.C.: U.S. Government Printing Office, May 1983), pp. 1–18, 345, 358.

Third, the response of individuals to short-run changes may be different from their responses to long-run changes. On the one hand, a temporary change in the tax structure that leads them to be better off has a smaller effect on lifetime income than a permanent change in the tax structure; hence the income effect may be understated. On the other hand, since the experiment often involved individuals facing a higher or lower marginal tax rate during the course of the experiment, the after-tax wage was temporarily reduced or increased; a temporary reduction in the wage may have different effects than a permanent reduction. In the absence of costs of adjustment there is a presumption that individuals will reduce their work (increase their leisure) more than they would with a permanent wage reduction. Thus an individual who was planning to take some time off from work (a woman who was thinking of having children at some time in the not too distant future) might have taken advantage of the temporary availability of the subsidy. If this is true, the experiments overstated the substitution effect. On the other hand, costs of adjustment may be very high; an individual might be reluctant to quit his current job, knowing that he will want it back in three years' time (when the experiment is over), because he believes it will be difficult to get it back then. If these effects are important, the experiment may have understated not only the income effects but the substitution effects. Some of the more recent experiments have attempted to ascertain the magnitude of the biases in the estimates resulting from the fact that the change in tax structure/welfare payments was only temporary by guaranteeing to the individual the same tax structure/welfare structure over a more extended period (up to twenty years).

A final important qualification on interpreting whether the experiments provide an accurate statement of the extent to which labor supply would be affected by changes in tax laws or welfare programs relates to the role of institutions in determining the length of the work week. We commented earlier that, in the short run, institutional practices play an important role in restricting individuals' choices over the number of hours worked. But in the long run, these institutional practices themselves change, partly in response to changes in the economic environment. Thus many of the individuals in the experiment may have had only limited discretion over the number of hours they worked; but if everyone in society were confronted with the new tax/welfare payments structure, pressures might develop to alter these institutional practices to bring them more into conformity with individuals' preferences.

OTHER DIMENSIONS TO LABOR SUPPLY

The preceding discussion focused on how the current tax rate may affect the individual's decision to participate in the labor force and, if so, how many hours to work. Such a discussion oversimplifies the analysis of the effect of taxation in several important respects.

Effort

First, it ignores the many important decisions of the individual that affect the quality of labor supplied in the market. Individuals have considerable discretion about the effort they put into a job; one of the important returns to putting in more effort is the financial return obtained from the higher pay one is likely to receive, either directly or indirectly, as a result of promotions. Pay, of course, is only one of the reasons that individuals work hard. They also work hard for status, recognition from their peers, etc. Without denying the importance of these factors—though they tend to be more important in more skilled, professional, and managerial occupations than in unskilled jobs—all that our analysis requires is that individuals are partly motivated by financial returns. For most individuals, working in most jobs, this is clearly true.

Job Choice

The tax structure affects the choice of jobs. Individuals of equal ability do not, in general, receive the same wage in all jobs. Some jobs are particularly unpleasant, and individuals have to be compensated to undertake them. Examples of this may include work as a sanitary engineer or a job with long or inconvenient hours.

Other jobs are viewed to be particularly pleasant; individuals are willing to take them even when they pay less than other jobs for individuals of comparable skills. Teachers, for instance, work fewer hours per year than others. Ski instructors get to spend part of every day skiing. Other jobs confer status or provide other "perks."

The wages at which individuals are willing to work at a job depend on these **nonpecuniary** attributes. When the job has very attractive features, wages can be lower. When the job has negative nonpecuniary attributes, wages must be higher to compensate. The tax system penalizes such occupations, since individuals in these occupations are taxed on all of their monetary compensation, part of which is intended to compensate them for these negative nonpecuniary attributes of the job. Assume, for instance, individuals are indifferent between being a ski instructor at $10,000 a year, or a sanitary engineer at $20,000 a year. Since the two individuals are just as well off (by assumption), one might argue that they should pay the same tax. Let us now impose a progressive income tax, which levies a 15 percent tax on incomes in excess of $5,000. The ski instructor will pay a tax of only $750, the sanitary engineer will pay $1,500 more, for a total tax of $2,250. Given their *after-tax* income, individuals prefer to work as ski instructors. More generally, the tax system induces a distortion in the pattern of allocation of labor.

We discussed earlier how a variety of government programs affect individuals' decisions concerning when to leave the labor force (that is, the date of retirement). Similarly, a variety of government programs affect the decision of when to enter the labor force (that is, how long to remain in school). Subsidized colleges and universities and subsidized loan programs encourage students to remain in school; not allowing tuition expenditures to be deductible discourages educational expenditures, since the returns to education, in the form of higher income, are taxed.

Labor Supply and Other Household Decisions

The decisions we have described concerning labor supply both affect and are affected by a variety of other decisions made within the household, decisions that themselves are affected by a variety of government policies. Both marriage and divorce are affected by tax policy (see Chapter 21 for a discussion of the marriage tax and the tax treatment of alimony). Social security rules penalize short marriages that end in divorce: the ex-wife is entitled to benefits only if the couple remain married for ten years. Current tax policy, to the extent that it discourages labor force participation by wives, simultaneously encourages children: a major part of the cost of a child is the opportunity cost of the mother's time, her lost wages. In some countries where there has been concern about a declining population, governments have enacted policies (such as child subsidies, more favorable income tax treatment for larger families, provision of child-care facilities) to encourage reproduction. Other countries, such as China, where there is a concern about the economic consequences of rapid population growth, have enacted policies designed to reduce dramatically the birth rate.

We have already noted the importance of savings for the retirement decision. Savings, in turn, are affected by tax policy (the special treatment of pensions, IRA accounts, etc.), and by government expenditure programs. The provision of medical insurance (encouraged by current tax policy) and Medicare make precautionary savings (savings for medical expenses) less important; student loan programs make savings for children's education less important.

The important point to remember is that though we study the effects of each policy (tax, expenditure) on each decision (savings, labor supply) alone, in fact all the decisions are interconnected, and virtually all government policies have some effects, direct or indirect, on each of the decisions.

Form of Compensation

Finally, the tax structure affects the form in which individuals receive their pay. It encourages firms to compensate their employees in forms that are not taxable. This provides one of the explanations of the rapid growth of fringe benefits (of, for instance, employer-sponsored health programs) during the past three decades. Expense accounts, training programs held in attractive resorts, and subsidized meals are all forms of nontaxable compensation. Perhaps the most important effect of the tax structure on the form of pay is the encouragement that it provides for "deferred compensation"—pensions and stock options.

SUMMARY

1. On theoretical grounds, the effect of taxation on labor supply is ambiguous. The income effect and substitution effect work in opposite directions. The income effect leads to an increase in the amount of labor; the substitution effect to a decrease.
2. Empirical evidence suggests that for males, the substitution and income effects virtually cancel, so that the total effect of the tax on the male labor supply is probably not large; while for females, there may be a marked effect on labor force participation. On the other hand, even though the total effect may be small for males, the substitution effect, and hence the deadweight loss associated with the tax, may be very large.
3. The tax system encourages jobs with large nonpecuniary benefits and encourages compensation in forms that are not taxed or receive preferential tax treatment.

KEY CONCEPTS

Labor force participation
Hawthorne effect
Nonpecuniary benefits
Compensated supply elasticity of labor
Negative income tax

QUESTIONS AND PROBLEMS

1. Prior to 1981, the government imposed only a 67 percent (instead of a 100 percent) marginal tax rate on income earned by a mother receiving AFDC. Draw the budget constraint before 1981 and after 1981. Draw the indifference curve of someone who prefers to remain out of the labor force under both regimes. Draw the indifference curve of someone who worked before 1981 but chose not to work after 1981. Show how, for this person, lowering the tax rate will increase utility, reduce costs, and increase labor supply. Finally, draw the indifference curve of someone who worked both before and after 1981. Show how, for this person, the lower tax rate affects AFDC costs and affects labor supply. What can you say about government policy if there are some individuals of the first type, some of the second type, and some of the third type?
2. What will be the effect of a switch to taxing individuals on the basis of their own income (rather than family income) on labor force participation of wives?

3. Taxes and government expenditure programs affect a variety of other aspects of household behavior. Some economists, for instance, argue that they affect birth rates. What provisions of the tax system might affect the decision to have a child? What government expenditure programs?
4. Instead of representing the individual's decisions as a choice between consumption and work, as in Figures 19.2 and 19.3, they could have been represented in terms of a choice between consumption and leisure. Draw the indifference curves, and identify the income and substitution effects resulting from a change in the tax rate on labor.
5. Compare the effects of an income tax and a lump-sum tax raising the same revenue. In particular, show that the individual's utility is higher with the lump-sum tax than with the income tax.
6. Compare the effects of a proportional income tax and a progressive flat rate income tax (i.e., one in which there is a lump-sum grant from the government of, say, $3,000, and then a constant marginal tax rate on all income). In particular, show that if the two taxes raise the same revenue, and all individuals have the same income, utility will be higher with the proportional tax.

20

Optimal Taxation

In the previous two chapters we observed that there may be a significant welfare loss (the *deadweight loss*) associated with any tax other than a lump-sum tax. Two questions immediately arise. Why, if this is the case, do we not just impose a lump-sum tax? And if we are to impose distortionary taxes, is there some way that they can be designed to minimize the deadweight loss? These questions have been at the center of much of the theoretical research in taxation during the past two decades. The research has produced some remarkably simple and insightful answers, answers that may help to design better tax systems in the future.

THE FALLACY OF COUNTING DISTORTIONS

Before turning to these questions, we need to dispose of an argument that has misled a number of distinguished economists. It makes no sense simply to count the number of distortions introduced by the tax system. For instance, some economists have argued that we should have a tax on income but no special taxes on goods (say, on cigarettes, alcohol, or luxuries), because one distortion is better than several distortions. This conclusion would be correct if there were no distortions associated with the income tax. But we showed in the previous chapters that an income tax usually distorts individuals' decisions to save and to work, and it is not necessarily the case that two large distortions are better than several smaller distortions. Chapter 18 showed that the deadweight loss from a tax was proportional to the square of the tax rate. This *suggests* that it may be better to have a number of small taxes than a single large tax.

The same fallacy was held to by those who argued that it is better not to tax interest income but rather to impose a tax just on wage income, because taxing interest income, by affecting the decision to save or borrow, introduces an additional distortion into the economy. Again, though the conclusion that we should not tax interest income may be correct, the argument is fallacious. One cannot simply count the number of distortions to arrive at the desirable tax structure.

THE SECOND-BEST FALLACY

On the other hand, it is important to guard against an equally dangerous fallacy. The example we gave where more distortions may be better than fewer, illustrates the general proposition that whenever there are inefficiencies (distortions) in several markets, removing one of them may not improve matters. In earlier chapters we characterized Pareto-efficient resource allocations. All of the required conditions are seldom satisfied. And it may be virtually impossible to remove all the distortions in all sectors. The theory of the second best is concerned with the design of government policy in situations where the economy is characterized by some important distortions that cannot be removed.[1] (This is in contrast to "first-best" economies, where all the conditions for Pareto efficiency can be satisfied.) Thus, second-best considerations say that it may not be desirable to remove distortions in those sectors where they can be removed. The theory of the second best is often interpreted fallaciously as saying that as long as there are some distortions, economic theory has nothing to say. This is incorrect, as we shall shortly show. Economic theory can tell us under what circumstances two small distortions are preferable to one large one, when it is better to have inefficiencies in both consumption and production, and when it is better not to have inefficiencies in production. Second-best theory tells us that we cannot blindly apply the lessons of first-best economics. Finding out what we should do when some distortions exist is often a difficult—but not impossible—task.

OPTIMAL REDISTRIBUTIVE INCOME TAXATION

In Chapter 16 we discussed two fundamental principles of taxation, economic efficiency and equity. We are concerned in this chapter with tax structures that raise a given revenue and obtain given distribution objectives, at least cost in loss in efficiency. As always in economics, there are trade-offs: if the government wishes more redistribution, it may be able to obtain it only at the cost of greater economic inefficiency

[1] Early formulations of the theory of the second best include those of James Meade, *Trade and Welfare: Mathematical Supplement* (Oxford: Oxford University Press, 1955), and R. G. Lipsey and K. Lancaster, "The General Theory of Second Best," *Review of Economic Studies* 24 (1956–1957): 11–32.

(greater deadweight loss). The **optimal tax** structure is the one that maximizes social welfare, in which the choice between equity and efficiency best reflects society's attitude toward these competing goals. In this section we describe why distortionary taxes are imposed, why there is a trade-off between redistribution and economic efficiency, and how we can analyze the choice among alternative tax structures.

Why Impose Distortionary Taxes?

If the government had perfect information about the characteristics of each individual in our society, there is a strong argument that it would not impose distortionary taxes. Individuals who can more easily pay taxes should, it is widely believed, pay more in taxes than those who cannot easily pay. If the government could ascertain who had greater abilities, and who therefore was in a better position to pay taxes, it would simply impose higher lump-sum taxes on those individuals.

But how can abilities be measured? Consider a family. Parents often believe that they have good information concerning the abilities of their children. A parent who has two children, one of whom has a great deal of ability but chooses to become a beachcomber, and the other of whom has limited ability that he uses to the fullest, is more likely to provide financial assistance to the latter than the former; the assistance is made not on the basis of income—the beachcomber may in fact have a lower income than a hard-working but low-ability brother.

The government, however, is not in the position of the parent who can observe the ability and drive of his children. The government can base its tax only on observable variables, such as income and expenditure (and even these, as we shall see, are not easily observable). The choice facing the government is either to have a *uniform lump-sum tax,* one that individuals pay regardless of what they do or their abilities, or to have a tax that depends on easily measured variables, such as expenditures or wages, and such a tax is inevitably distortionary. An income tax does not always succeed in taxing those we might think ought to be taxed—it treats equally the individual who has low ability but works extremely hard and the individual who is of high ability, and takes it easy, provided the two have the same income. Still, most people believe that those who have a higher income ought to pay a higher share of government costs because those with a higher income are, *on average,* more able or have had better than average luck. Moreover, society may reasonably value the loss of income by the rich (implying, say, one less yacht) less than it values the loss of income to lower-income individuals.

The Trade-off between Inequality and Inefficiency

If everyone were identical, there would be no reason to impose distortionary taxes. It would be far simpler administratively and more efficient (in terms of minimizing deadweight loss) simply to impose a uniform lump-sum tax. The use of distortionary taxes is an inevitable consequence of our desire to redistribute income, in a world in which the government can observe the characteristics of individuals only imperfectly.

There is thus a trade-off. We can impose a more progressive tax, one that redistributes more income by laying on the rich a larger fraction of the burden of government spending—but we do so at the expense of a loss in economic efficiency. The government can reduce the degree of inequality but only at the expense of a larger deadweight loss.

The optimal tax structure is defined as that tax structure that maximizes society's welfare, where the balance between deadweight loss and inequality reflects attitudes towards equality and efficiency. Different societies might choose different tax systems if they had different attitudes towards inequality. We can view much of the political debate concerning how progressive the tax structure should be—that is, how much more high-income individuals should pay in taxes than low-income individuals—as one involving differences in values, in how much deadweight loss one is willing to accept for a given decrease in inequality.

There may be disagreements not only about values but also about the empirical question of what the trade-offs are. Those who advocate the desirability of more progressive taxes tend also to argue that the cost, in terms of the deadweight loss, of reducing inequality is smaller than the cost perceived by those who argue that there should be less progressivity to the tax structure. In Chapters 18 and 19 we showed that the magnitude of the deadweight loss from a tax was related to the substitution effect. If leisure and consumption goods are very substitutable, then the compensated labor supply schedule will be very elastic, and there will be a large deadweight loss from a tax on consumption or labor income. If consumption this period and consumption next period are very substitutable, then the savings schedule will be very elastic, and the deadweight loss associated with an interest income tax will be large. Those who believe that the deadweight losses are small are often referred to as *elasticity optimists;* they believe, for instance, that the (compensated) labor supply elasticity and the savings elasticity are low, so that the distortions associated with high tax rates are low; while those who believe that the distortions are large are often referred to as *elasticity pessimists;* they believe that the labor supply and savings elasticities are large. The evidence supporting each view is ambiguous.

Why Does More Progressivity Imply More Deadweight Loss?

The preceding section argued that as we use our tax system to attain greater equality, the deadweight loss increases. Panels A and B of Figure 20.1 illustrate this general proposition by contrasting two tax schedules. The first (in color) is a proportional income tax, in which the tax liability is the same percentage of income for all individuals, no matter how large or small their income. The second is a simple progressive income tax that

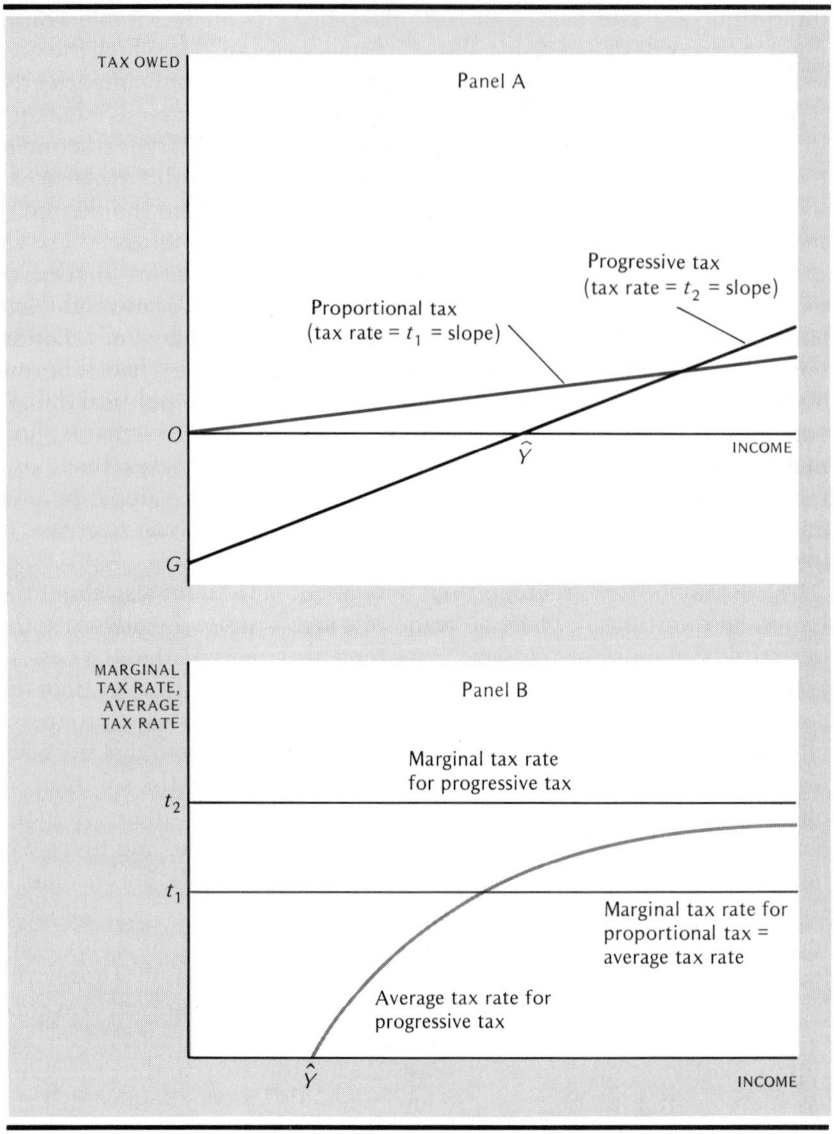

20.1 FLAT-RATE INCOME TAX SCHEDULES Panel A compares the tax schedule of a proportional flat-rate income tax with that of a progressive flat-rate income tax. Panel B compares average and marginal tax rates for these two taxes.

imposes a tax at a flat rate on the difference between the individual's income and some critical level of income, $\hat{Y}$. Individuals whose income falls below the critical level receive a grant from the government equal to the tax rate times the shortfall between their income and the critical level. Notice from Panel B that the marginal tax rate, the extra tax an individual pays or receives on an extra dollar of income, is constant for both tax systems. Therefore, both are popularly called **flat-rate taxes.**

But with the progressive tax, the *average* tax rate, the ratio of the total tax payments to the individual's income, increases with income. This is why we call the tax progressive.[2]

Because, as we have depicted it, the progressive flat tax provides for a payment to individuals whose income falls short of the critical level, we sometimes refer to that portion of the tax schedule below $\hat{Y}$ as a *negative income tax.*[3]

The progressive flat tax can be thought of as a combination of a uniform lump-sum grant to all individuals and a proportional income tax. Thus, in Figure 20.1A, a proportional tax at the rate t_2, combined with a grant of OG, is identical to an income tax on incomes in excess of $\hat{Y}$ ($\hat{Y}$ is the exemption level) at a rate of t_2, provided those with incomes less than $\hat{Y}$ receive a rebate (sometimes called a cashable tax credit) equal to t_2 times the difference between $\hat{Y}$ and their income. If the government is both to finance its public goods and other public expenditures *and* pay everyone a uniform lump-sum grant, the revenue raised must be higher, so the marginal tax rate must be higher than with just a proportional tax. But the deadweight loss is associated with the magnitude of the marginal tax rate. Hence the greater the lump-sum grant, the more progressive the tax structure, and the greater the deadweight loss.

A Diagrammatic Analysis of the Deadweight Loss of Progressive Taxation

To compare the effects of a proportional and a progressive tax, we employ the same kinds of diagrammatic techniques we employed in the previous chapter. Figure 20.2 shows an individual's before-tax budget constraint, showing how much income (consumption) he has for each level of work, and his indifference curve between consumption goods and work. It also depicts his after-tax budget constraint assuming that the government takes a given fraction of his income, which is to say it imposes a proportional tax. This part of the diagram is identical to Figure 19.4, which we used to analyze the deadweight loss of a proportional income tax. Finally, the figure shows the after-tax budget constraint for a progressive flat tax with implicit grant OG.

We now compare the revenue that the government can raise from a progressive income tax that leaves the given individual at the same level of utility with the revenue that can be raised with a proportional income tax. The revenue raised by the tax is the vertical distance between the before-tax budget constraint and the after-tax budget constraint at the

[2] Usage is not standardized. Some prefer to reserve the term *progressive* for tax structures where the *marginal* tax rate increases. Nothing important hinges on these semantic points. Notice that a flat-rate tax combined with a lump-sum tax is regressive, in the sense that the average tax rate decreases with income. For a more general discussion of the definition of progressive and regressive tax structures, see A. B. Atkinson and J. E. Stiglitz, *Lectures on Public Economics* (New York: McGraw-Hill, 1980), Chapter 2.

[3] In some tax systems, those with income above $\hat{Y}$ are taxed on the difference between their income and this exemption level, but those below the critical level neither pay taxes nor receive a rebate.

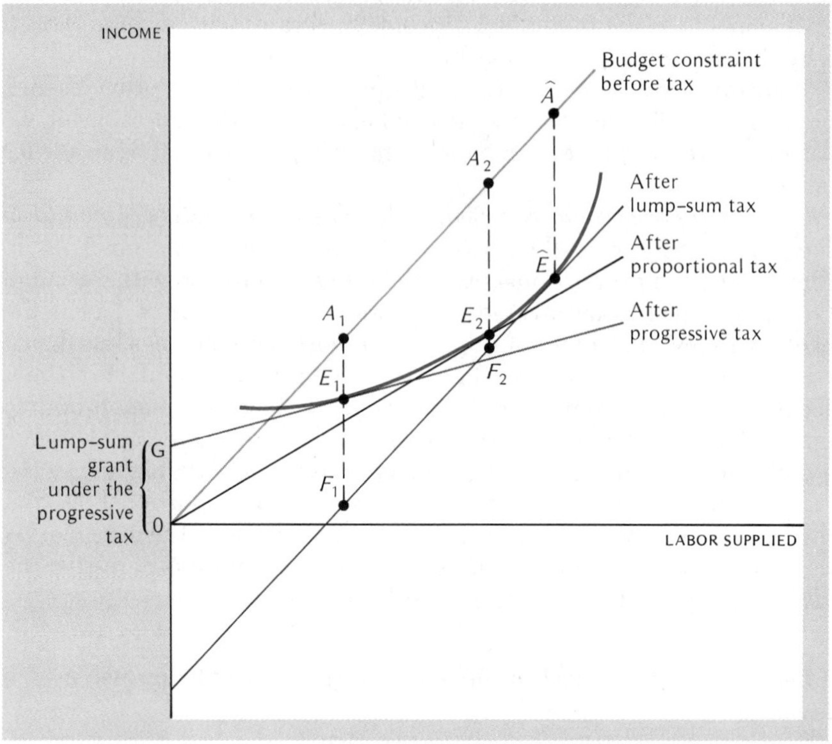

20.2 COMPARING A PROGRESSIVE, A PROPORTIONAL, AND A LUMP-SUM TAX WHICH HAVE THE SAME EFFECT ON THE INDIVIDUAL'S UTILITY With the progressive tax, the individual chooses E_1, and the tax revenue is A_1E_1. With the proportional tax, the individual chooses E_2 and the tax revenue is A_2E_2. With the lump-sum tax, the individual chooses $\hat{E}$ and the tax revenue is $\hat{A}\hat{E}(= A_2F_2 = A_1F_1)$.

level of work that the individual chooses to put forth. Thus, in Figure 20.2, the tax revenue from the proportional income tax is A_2E_2, while the tax revenue from the progressive tax is A_1E_1, much less. There is an additional deadweight loss resulting from the progressivity; E_1F_1 is much greater than E_2F_2. This is not surprising. We argued before that the deadweight loss is associated with the substitution effect, the change in the hours worked resulting from the lowering of the after-tax wage below the true productivity of labor. Because the marginal tax rate is higher, the substitution effect is larger with a progressive income tax than it is with a proportional income tax, and thus the deadweight loss is larger.[4]

[4] In Figure 20.2 it is clear that the marginal tax rate is higher (the slope of the budget constraint is smaller) for the progressive tax than for the proportional tax. This is always the case: if the tax rate were the same or lower, clearly the individual would be better off with the tax system with a lump-sum grant than with one without it. He could not be on the same indifference curve.

Relationship between Deadweight Loss and Redistribution

We now turn to see how, as we attempt to redistribute income further, we increase the deadweight loss. As we argued before, a progressive flat-rate tax can be viewed as a combination of a proportional tax and a lump-sum grant. As we increase the lump-sum grant from *OG* to *OG′* in Figure 20.3, we must raise the tax rate in order to keep net government revenues constant.

Assume we have two groups in the population, one with incomes below the exemption level and one with incomes above. As we increase the lump-sum grant, the group below the exemption level is better off, the group above the exemption level is worse off: inequality has been reduced. But *both* groups face higher marginal tax rates, and hence the deadweight loss associated with both groups has increased.

There may be a maximum of redistribution that is feasible. As we increase the marginal tax rate, the upper-income individuals eventually may start to reduce the labor supply; they may reduce it enough that the revenue raised by the tax on them is reduced. In that case, the lump-sum grant would have to be reduced.

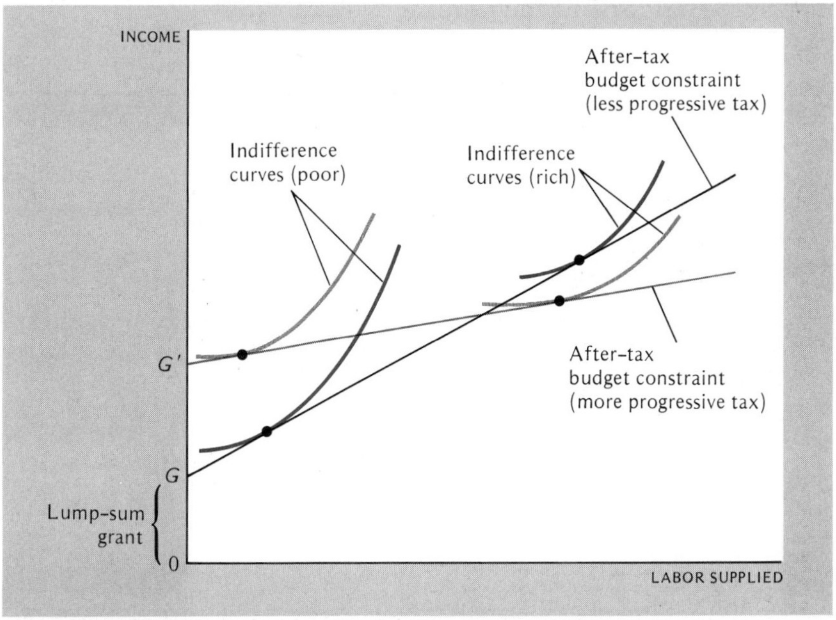

20.3 EFFECTS OF INCREASING THE DEGREE OF PROGRESSIVITY When the lump-sum grant is increased from *OG* to *OG′*, the marginal tax rate must be increased if the government is to obtain the requisite revenue. Thus the after-tax budget constraint will be flatter. Poor individuals, those below the exemption level, will be better off; rich individuals will be worse off. For poor individuals, income and substitution effects reinforce each other, and they work less. For rich individuals, the income and substitution effects are offsetting, and the net effect can't be predicted. In the case shown here, rich individuals also work less. But both groups face greater deadweight losses.

The Utility Possibilities Curve and Distortionary Taxation

We can depict the choices facing society in a slightly different way. In Chapter 4 we derived the utility possibilities frontier for a simple Robinson Crusoe economy, showing the maximum level of utility for Friday that can be obtained for each level of Crusoe's utility. We did that under the assumption that as the government attempts to redistribute more and more income (more and more oranges) from Crusoe to Friday, a larger fraction of the oranges taken away from Crusoe is lost before Friday receives them. The loss of oranges in this simple example was intended to suggest the excess burden (the deadweight loss) of the distortionary orange tax. The utilities possibilities schedule must take into account the distortions that arise out of our attempt to redistribute income.

Two utility possibilities schedules are shown in Figure 20.4. The gray one assumes the lump-sum tax option and the black one makes the more realistic assumption of distortionary taxation. The two curves coincide at the point along the original utility possibilities schedule that would emerge as the competitive equilibrium with no redistributive taxes—point *C*. If there are public goods to be financed by the taxation, then the two curves coincide at the competitive equilibrium corresponding to a *uniform* lump-sum tax on the two groups of individuals.

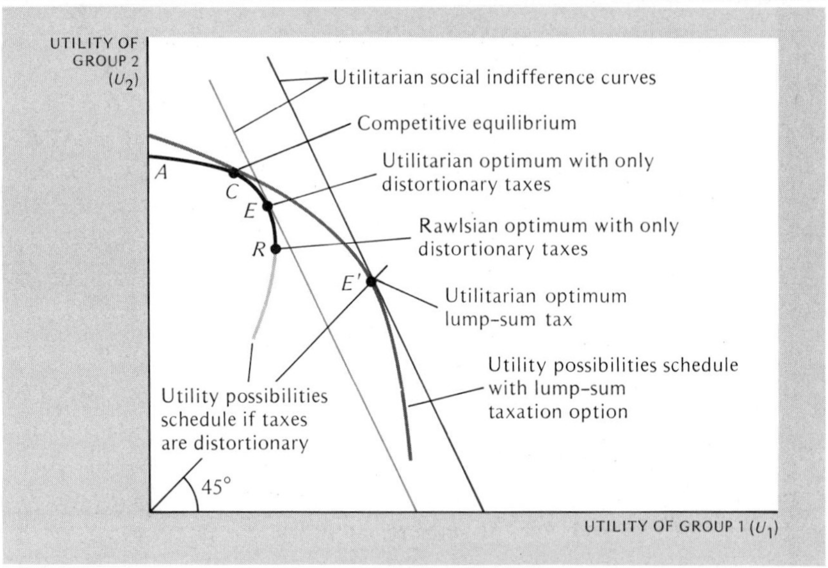

20.4 UTILITY POSSIBILITIES SCHEDULES WITH LUMP-SUM AND DISTORTIONARY TAXES Society finds the point on the utility possibilities schedule that maximizes social welfare. If society's welfare function is utilitarian (so the social indifference curves are linear), optimal distortionary taxes correspond to point *E*. If government can impose lump-sum taxes on Group 2, then the optimal tax corresponds to point *E'*.

As government uses distortionary taxes to move the equilibrium point away from C, we cannot avoid some deadweight loss. Hence, the distortionary tax utility possibilities schedule lies inside the lump-sum tax utility possibilities schedule. If the method of redistributing income that we have available is a progressive flat-rate income tax, we can easily derive the utility possibilities schedule. For each level of exemption, we find the level of tax rate that raises the required revenue. We then plot the levels of utility that the two groups attain. As we increase the level of exemption, the utility of the lower-income group increases and that of the higher-income group decreases.

It is clear that the utility possibilities curve is affected by what information is available and by the methods available for the redistribution of income.

Any tax structure that (given the available information and tax instruments) gets the economy to a point on the utility possibilities schedule is called a **Pareto-efficient tax structure.**[5] Under certain circumstances, for instance, it can be shown that if the government can impose taxes on wages and on the consumption of different commodities, it should in fact impose taxes only on wage income. This is true regardless of one's attitudes toward inequality; that is, a system that imposes taxes on different commodities at different rates is Pareto inefficient.[6]

Society's first problem (after determining the possible set of taxes) is thus to determine what are the Pareto-efficient tax structures. Having done this, the second problem is choosing among alternative Pareto-efficient tax structures. This is equivalent to deciding on a point along the utility possibilities schedule.

Earlier, we called the tax structure that maximizes society's social welfare the optimal tax structure. The optimal tax structure thus will depend on: (a) society's social welfare function and (b) the information available to the government and, correspondingly, the kinds of taxes that can be imposed. If the government could identify the abilities of each individual and could levy lump-sum taxes on each according to his ability, the income tax would not be part of a Pareto-efficient tax structure (and hence, it would not be part of an optimal tax structure).

The relationship between the optimal tax structure and the social welfare function is easy to see in Figure 20.4. A utilitarian would maximize the sum of the utilities of the two groups; that is, the social indifference curves, giving those combinations of U_1 and U_2 among which society is indifferent, are linear. Society is willing to give up some welfare of Group 1 for an equal increase in the welfare of Group 2. The utilitarian optimal tax structure, given that the government can only infer the dif-

[5] The term *constrained Pareto-efficient* is sometimes used to describe such tax structures to remind us of the limitations imposed by information inperfections. For a more detailed description of Pareto-efficient tax structures see J. E. Stiglitz, "Self-Selection and Pareto-Efficient Taxation," *Journal of Public Economics* 17 (1982): 213–40.

[6] The circumstances under which this is true are that (a) the sole source of differences among individuals is their differences in productivity, and (b) their marginal rates of substitution between different commodities do not depend on the amount of leisure they enjoy. See A. B. Atkinson and J. E. Stiglitz, "The Design of Tax Structures," *Journal of Public Economics* 6 (1976): 55–75.

ferences in ability from observations of income, is depicted as point E. (If government could distinguish between people of different ability, so that it could impose differential lump-sum taxes, then E' would correspond to the optimal tax structure.)

Rawlsian Taxation

Notice in Figure 20.4 that we have drawn the utility possibilities schedule with distortionary taxation as backward bending.[7] There is a maximum amount of revenue that we can extract from the higher-income individuals (without direct compulsion). Assume, for instance, that we imposed simply a proportional tax on those with high incomes. Although we observed earlier that the effect of increasing the tax (lowering the wage) was in general ambiguous, beyond some point the tax will lead the individual to work less. (More accurately, the individual will engage in fewer transactions through the market: he may be working just as hard, but not for cash. He will be induced to bake his own bread, paint his own house, etc.) There is thus a maximum revenue that can be raised. (If the government attempts to raise this revenue through a progressive flat-rate tax, the maximum that the government can raise from the rich is even lower.) This means that there is a maximum amount that the government can redistribute to the poor. This is the point at which the utility possibilities schedule turns back. Further increases in the tax rate mean that to finance the given level of public goods the exemption level must be decreased. We have marked this point on Figure 20.4 with R, after John Rawls,[8] who argued that society should choose the tax rate that maximizes the welfare of the worst-off individual.

Notice that there is a maximum tax rate consistent with the Rawlsian position. Society can have too high a tax rate. Such tax rates are Pareto inferior—i.e., by lowering the tax rate, everyone could be made better off. There are those who believe that many Western European countries have reached tax rates that, if not exceeding this point, are close to it. In the United States, this view was popularized through what has come to be called the **Laffer curve,** which, as we described in Chapter 5, is simply the curve relating revenues to the tax rates, showing that beyond some point further increases in the tax rate actually lead to a lowering of tax revenues. As part of President Reagan's economic program, it was argued that a lowering of the tax rate would lead to such a large increase in national output that tax revenues would actually increase. The administration's belief, in other words, was that we were beyond the point at which the maximum tax revenue was raised. There was scanty empirical evidence in support of this view, and considerable evidence against it.[9]

[7] Since the definition of the utility possibilities schedule is the maximum level of utility that Group 1 can obtain given the level of utility obtained by Group 2, formally the utility possibilities schedule is only the portion AR of the black curve depicted in Figure 20.4.

[8] John Rawls, *A Theory of Justice* (Cambridge, MA: Harvard University Press, 1971).

[9] See, for instance, Don Fullerton, "On the Possibility of An Inverse Relationship between Tax Rates and Government Revenues," *Journal of Public Economics* 19 (1982): 3–23.

As it turned out, the short-run supply responses were far less than the advocates of the tax cut had predicted; but these short-run responses may have been dominated by other factors, such as the high rates of interest, which occurred simultaneously. And the long-run responses may be much greater. Still, the consensus among most economists is that even before the tax acts of 1981 and 1986 reduced marginal tax rates, we were not near the point of maximum government revenue.

Relationship between Progressivity and Government Expenditures

Several points are, however, clear. First, if society values equality, then even if it does not have to raise any revenue at all to finance public expenditures, it would still want to redistribute income through a progressive tax structure. There is a negligible deadweight loss from a small tax, but a finite gain in redistribution. Those whose income fell below some critical level would receive some income from the government.

Second, if society wishes to raise a great deal of revenue for public expenditures, more than the maximum amount that can be attained through a proportional income tax, it may need to impose a lump-sum tax on all individuals *plus* a proportional rate on all income. More generally, the greater the government's expenditure on pure public goods (e.g., military expenditures), the lower, in general, will be the funds that are available for redistribution, and the less progressive will be the optimal tax structure.

A Numerical Calculation of the Optimal Flat-Rate Tax

Nick Stern, of the London School of Economics, calculated the optimal linear flat-rate tax using what he thought were reasonable estimates of the labor supply elasticity and the distribution of individuals' productivity in the economy.[10] He found, assuming that government expenditures on public goods amounted to 20 percent of national income, that while with a utilitarian social welfare function the optimal flat-rate tax was 19 percent, with a Rawlsian social welfare function—where the only concern is with the poorest individual—it was around 80 percent.

THE OPTIMAL STRUCTURE OF INCOME TAXES

The United States—and most other Western countries—does not employ a progressive flat-rate tax. Before the Tax Reform Act of 1986, marginal tax rates under the personal income tax increased steeply with income, from 11 percent to 50 percent. The issue of whether this was

[10] Nicholas H. Stern, "On the Specification of Models of Optimum Income Taxation," *Journal of Public Economics* 6 (1976): 123–62. The results of the calculations are very sensitive to all the assumptions made, and in particular to assumptions concerning the compensated elasticity of labor supply. Therefore they need to be considered with a great deal of caution. As we noted in Chapter 19, there is considerable controversy concerning the magnitude of the compensated elasticity of labor supply.

desirable was the subject of considerable debate in the United States. The Reagan tax reform proposals were based on the premise that marginal tax rates for the rich were too high; as of 1988 the maximum marginal tax rate on the wealthiest individuals is only 28 percent.[11] Here, we attempt to identify the trade-offs between deadweight loss and redistribution that result from having a tax structure with varying marginal tax rates.

The distortion (the deadweight loss) associated with a tax system is related to the magnitude of the marginal tax rate. By raising the marginal tax rate at one income level—say, between $15,000 and $20,000—the government can raise the *average* tax rate at higher income levels without altering the marginal tax rate at these higher income levels. Consider what happens to an individual making $25,000. His average tax has gone up, because he has to pay more on his income between $15,000 and $20,000. But his marginal rate—the tax on the 25,000th dollar—remains the same. The extra distortion introduced by the higher taxes is measured only through its effect on individuals making $15,000 to $20,000, those whose marginal rate has increased. There is a trade-off between a greater deadweight loss at the lower-income level and greater revenue for the same deadweight loss at upper-income levels.

Some elementary considerations determine whether increasing the rate on one income bracket is likely to be welfare-enhancing. If for instance, there are relatively few individuals in the group whose marginal tax rate has been increased, the welfare loss (from the deadweight loss) will be small.

The fact that by raising marginal tax rates on middle-income individuals one can obtain greater revenue from the rich, with the same deadweight loss, suggests that it may be desirable for middle-income individuals to have higher marginal tax rates than upper-income individuals. However, the fact that there are many middle-income individuals, so that the deadweight loss from increasing marginal tax rates on middle-income individuals is very large, suggests that they should face lower marginal tax rates. In the examples investigated in detail by James Mirrlees of Oxford University these two effects offset each other, and the optimal tax schedule was close to a progressive flat tax.[12]

Labor Supply Elasticities and Tax Rates

If the labor supply response of different groups (individuals with different incomes) differs systematically, the tax rates they should face should differ.

Assume that the government could impose, for instance, one tax rate on unskilled workers and another on skilled workers. It wishes to do so

[11] For a single individual, the 28 percent marginal tax rate applies to all income above $100,750. See Chapter 21.

[12] J. Mirrlees, "An Exploration in the Theory of Optimum Income Taxation," *Review of Economic Studies* 38 (1971): 175–208.

to maximize the sum of utilities (a utilitarian social welfare function). Assume it has to raise a fixed amount of revenue between the two groups. Clearly, it will set the tax rates so that the loss in utility from an increase in revenues by a dollar (resulting from an increase in tax rates) on one group is exactly equal to the loss in utility from an increase in revenues by a dollar on the other group.

Increasing the tax rate on some group is equivalent to reducing the wage paid that group. We plot utility as a function of tax rate in Panel A of Figure 20.5. As the tax rate increases, utility decreases. The loss in utility from an increase in the tax rate is proportional to the labor supply of the group and its marginal utility of income.[13]

The revenue obtained from an increase in the tax rate increases with the amount of labor supplied. But there is an indirect effect: the higher tax rate may reduce (or increase) the labor supplied. The tax revenue from tax rate $\hat{t}$ is $\hat{t}wL$, where w is the wage rate and L is the labor supplied. As $\hat{t}$ increases, tax revenue will not increase as much if L decreases as it would if L remained unchanged. In fact, if L decreases enough, total tax revenue could actually decline as $\hat{t}$ increases, as depicted in Panel B of Figure 20.5. The magnitude of the decrease in the labor supply is measured by the elasticity of labor supply. The greater the elasticity of labor supply, the smaller the increase in government revenue from an increase in the tax rate.[14]

The optimal tax rates must be such that the loss in utility from increasing the revenue raised by a dollar from each group is the same. The change in utility per unit change in revenue for two different groups is plotted in Panel C of the figure.

Thus a group with a lower income is likely to have a higher marginal utility of income, and this effect in itself suggests that it should have a lower tax rate. But if it reduces its labor supply less than some other group (other things being equal), its tax rate should be higher.

On the other hand, if the elasticity of labor supply among those in managerial, executive, and professional positions is lower than the labor supply elasticity of other workers, these high-income individuals should be taxed more heavily than others.

In Chapter 16 we showed how a utilitarian would impose much higher tax rates on high-income individuals than on low-income individuals; the taxes would be set so that the marginal utility of income would be equated. But that analysis assumed that labor supply was inelastic—the

[13] For those familiar with calculus, this result can be shown simply by using the indirect utility function $V(w,p,I)$, which gives the level of utility as a function of wages, prices, and other sources of income. It is possible to show that

$$\frac{dV}{dw} = L\frac{dV}{dI}.$$

dV/dI is just the marginal utility of income.

[14] $\frac{dR}{d\hat{t}} = wL + w\hat{t}\frac{dL}{d\hat{t}} = wL(1 - \hat{t}\frac{w}{L}\frac{\partial L}{\partial w})$, where $\frac{w}{L}\frac{\partial L}{\partial w}$ = elasticity of labor supply.

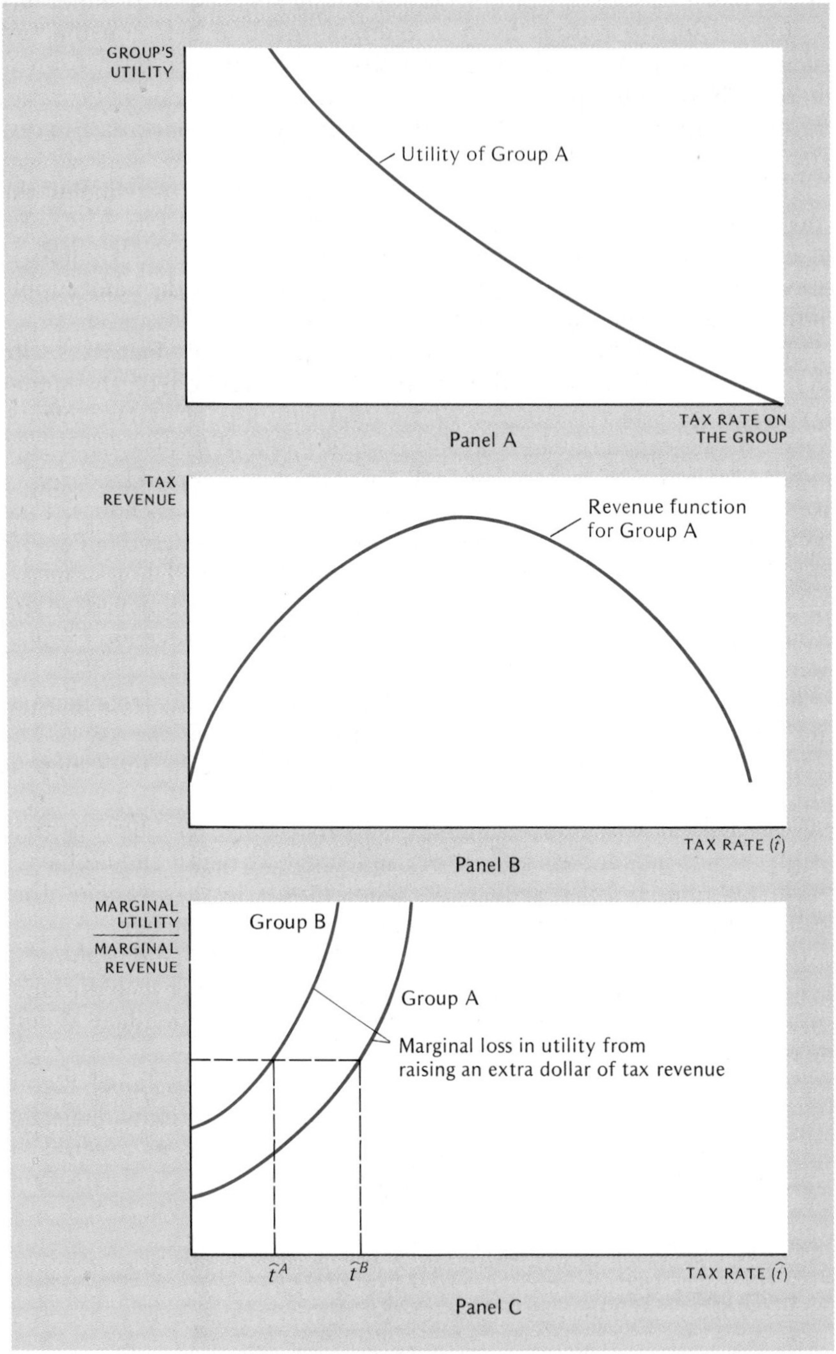

20.5 OPTIMAL TAXATION WITH DIFFERENT GROUPS If different tax rates can be imposed on different groups, maximizing the sum of utilities implies that the loss in utility per extra dollar raised should be the same for all groups. This ratio can be constructed as follows: in Panel A we plot the utility level as a function of the tax rate. In Panel B we plot the revenue raised as a function of the tax rate. At each level of $\hat{t}$, we calculate the loss in utility from a further increment in the tax rate and the increase in revenue; dividing one by the other, we obtain Panel C.

individual's before-tax income was not affected by the taxes imposed. The fact that individuals will respond to high tax rates by reducing labor supply limits the optimal degree of progressivity.

General Equilibrium Effects

So far we have assumed that the income tax has no effect on before-tax incomes, that there is, in other words, no *shifting* of the income tax. There are some economists, however, who believe that there may be considerable shifting.

There are several arguments that suggest, in particular, that the income tax system has increased the degree of before-tax inequality. First, there are some who believe that the wages and fees of managers and professionals adjust to the taxes, leaving their after-tax income relatively unchanged. Moreover, if as a result of the income tax, skilled workers supply less labor and investment is discouraged, unskilled laborers' productivity and, hence, their wage, will decline. At the present time, unfortunately, we do not know the quantitative significance of these effects. If they are important, it suggests that the benefits of progressivity are less than they seem when these effects are ignored.[15]

REDISTRIBUTION THROUGH COMMODITY TAXES

In the previous section we argued that the primary reason for resorting to distortionary taxation was to enable the government to redistribute income more effectively, to achieve a more egalitarian society than could be obtained with *uniform* lump-sum taxes.

Should government use commodity taxes in addition to income taxes to raise revenue and redistribute income? That is, if we supplement a well-designed income tax (as described in the previous paragraphs) with taxes on, say, perfume and luxury cars, can we raise the same revenue, achieve the same distribution goals, at less loss in efficiency? Is a tax system that uses both commodity taxes and income taxes more efficient than just an income tax?

The Inefficiency of Commodity Taxation

The question has been a subject of continuing debate among economists. In Chapter 17 we noted that taxing all output (consumption goods plus investment goods) at the same rate was equivalent to an income tax. Hence, we are concerned here only with the imposition of taxes on dif-

[15] The importance of these general equilibrium effects in the design of optimal taxes was noted by Martin Feldstein, "On the Optimal Progressivity of the Income Tax," *Journal of Public Economics* 2 (1973): 357–76, using a simulation model. His results were corroborated and extended in subsequent theoretical work by N. Stern, "Optimum Taxation with Errors in Administration," *Journal of Public Economics* 17 (1982): 181–211; F. Allen, "Optimal Linear Income Taxation with General Equilibrium Effects on Wages," *Journal of Public Economics* 17 (1982): 135–43; J. E. Stiglitz, "Self-Selection and Pareto-Efficient Taxation," *Journal of Public Economics* 17 (1982): 213–40.

ferent commodities at different rates, what are sometimes referred to as *differential commodity taxes.* One often-quoted argument, that taxing commodities at different rates introduces additional distortions, has already been shown to be fallacious: one simply cannot count the number of distortions.

It can be shown that if one has a well-designed income tax, adding differential commodity taxation is likely to add little, if anything, to the ability to redistribute income.[16] The caveat that there be a well-designed income tax is important: in many countries income tax evasion is sufficiently prevalent that virtually the only way effective redistribution can occur is through the taxation of commodities consumed by the rich.

Further Arguments against Differential Commodity Taxation

There are two further arguments against taxing different commodities at different rates. The first is that such differential taxation is administratively complex; there are always some commodities that might fall into either the high-tax or low-tax categories, and there are thus administrative problems (and inequities) associated with drawing these distinctions.

Second, differential taxation might well be used to serve other purposes; it opens up the possibility of some groups using the tax system to discriminate against others. For instance, in the United Kingdom, scotch is the prevalent drink in Scotland, while beer is more popular in England. It would not, of course, be acceptable to impose a tax on those citizens of the United Kingdom who happened to live in Scotland that would be different from that imposed on those who live in England. But much the same effect could be obtained by taxing beer and scotch at different rates.

In the United States prior to the passage of the Sixteenth Amendment, which made income taxes legal, the federal government had to rely on commodity taxes. Different patterns of taxation had important differential effects on different regions. A tariff on industrial products benefited the Northeast at the expense of the South. In many countries today, the crops grown and the products produced and consumed in different areas may differ markedly. Differential taxation opens up the way for those in one region to use the tax structure to exploit those in another.

Ramsey Taxes

More than fifty years ago the great Cambridge economist Frank Ramsey asked: What taxes should the government impose on different commodi-

[16] A. B. Atkinson and J. E. Stiglitz, *Lectures on Public Economics*, Lecture 14. One intuitive way of seeing their result is to observe that, to increase society's ability to redistribute, one must tax commodities that are income-elastic more heavily than those that are income-inelastic—e.g., perfume should be taxed more heavily than bread. But many of the income-elastic commodities are also price-elastic, and hence the distortions associated with taxing them are greater. The optimal tax balances off the two effects; and in the balance, there is little gain from taxing different commodities at different rates.

ties, assuming it could not levy lump-sum taxes?[17] He was not concerned with redistribution but simply with identifying what we today would call the Pareto-efficient set of taxes under the assumption that lump-sum taxes are infeasible. In other words, he asked what tax structure would minimize the deadweight loss associated with raising a given amount of government revenue. In his analysis, Ramsey assumed all individuals were identical.

The commodity taxes that minimize the deadweight loss are called **Ramsey taxes** and have a remarkably simple form. Under certain simplifying conditions, Ramsey taxes are proportional to the sum of the reciprocals of the elasticities of demand and supply:

$$\frac{t}{p} = k(1/\eta_u^d + 1/\eta^s),$$

where k is a proportionality factor that depends on the total amount of revenue the government is attempting to raise, t is the per unit tax rate, p is the (after-tax) price, η_u^d is the compensated elasticity of demand, and η^s is the elasticity of supply. If the elasticity of supply is infinite (a horizontal supply schedule), the tax should simply be inversely proportional to the compensated elasticity of demand. Ramsey's result should not come as a surprise. In Chapter 18 we showed that the deadweight loss from a tax increased with the compensated elasticity of demand and the elasticity of supply. (Recall Figure 18.8.)

Figure 20.6 shows the solution to the optimal commodity tax problem. Panel A depicts the deadweight loss as a function of the tax rate imposed on commodity *i*. Panel B shows the revenue raised as a function of the tax rate imposed on commodity *i*. From these two diagrams we can calculate, at each tax rate, the ratio of the increase in deadweight loss to the increase in tax revenues from raising the tax a little bit. A similar curve can be derived for commodity *j*, as shown in Panel C. The tax rates should be set so that the increase in deadweight loss per extra dollar raised is the same for each commodity. If the increase in excess burden per extra dollar raised were greater for one commodity than for another, by adjusting tax rates so that one less dollar was raised on the first commodity and one more dollar was raised on the second commodity, total excess burden would be reduced. Notice that we have drawn the curves not only so that excess burden increases as the revenue raised increases, but also so that each increment in revenue increases the excess burden more. This follows from the fact that the deadweight loss increases with the square of the tax rate.[18]

[17] F. Ramsey, "A Contribution to the Theory of Taxation," *Economic Journal* 37 (1927): 47–61. The question had been posed to him by his teacher, A. C. Pigou. See A. C. Pigou, *A Study in Public Finance* (London: Macmillan, 3rd ed., 1947).

[18] The proof is in the Appendix to Chapter 18.

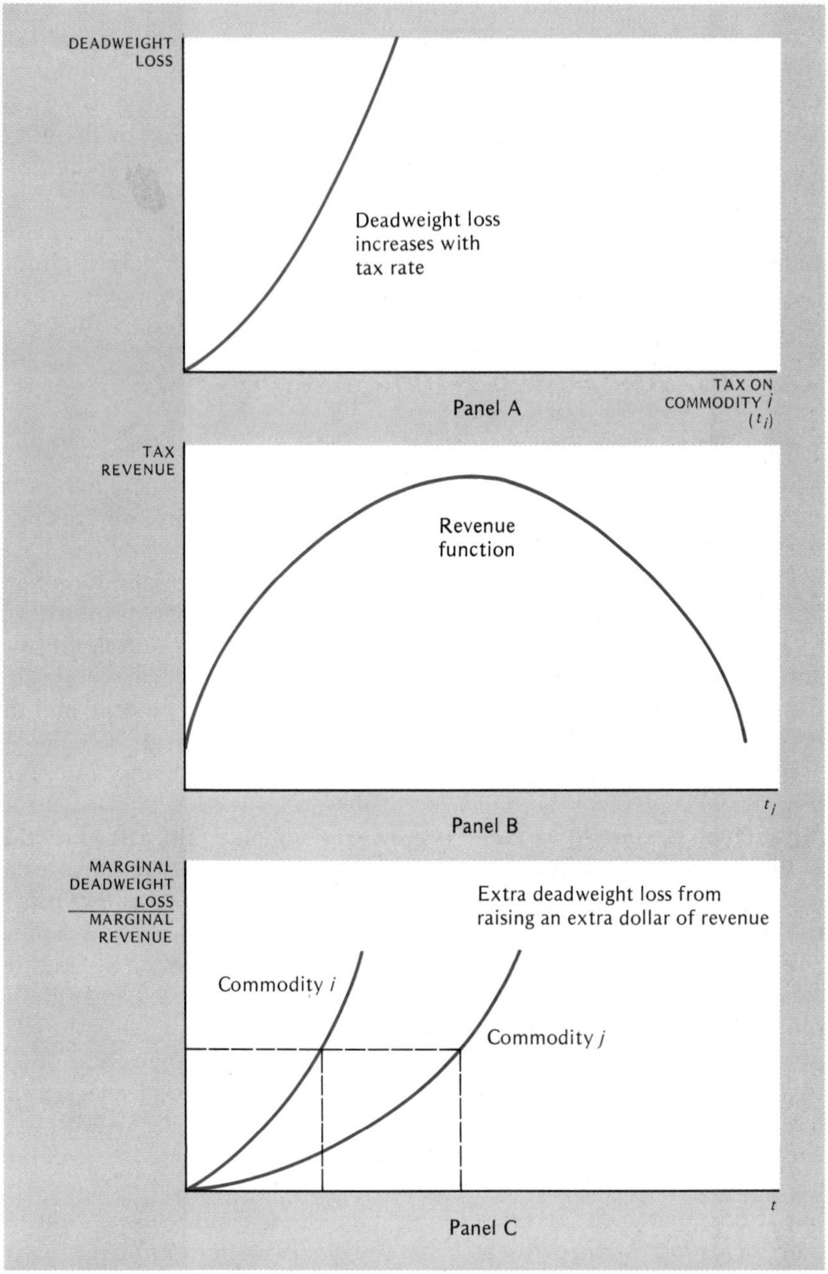

20.6 OPTIMAL COMMODITY TAXATION Optimal commodity taxes entail that marginal excess burden per marginal dollar raised be the same for all commodities.

OPTIMAL COMMODITY TAXATION WITH INTERDEPENDENT DEMANDS

The result we have just given requires that the compensated demand curves of each commodity are independent; that is, the demand for one commodity does not depend on the price of another. Another interpretation of Ramsey's result holds when supply curves are infinitely elastic, whether or not demand curves are interdependent; *the optimal tax structure is such that the percentage reduction in the compensated demand for each commodity is the same.*[19]

ALTERNATIVE INTERPRETATION: OPTIMAL COMMODITY TAX STRUCTURE WITH INTERDEPENDENT DEMANDS

We showed in Chapter 17 that a uniform tax on consumption is equivalent to a tax on labor (income). An income tax is distortionary because it induces individuals to make incorrect decisions concerning the amount of labor they wish to supply. Commodity taxation may help correct that distortion. If we tax commodities that are complements for leisure and subsidize commodities that are complements for work, we encourage individuals to work, and thus reduce the distortion caused by a uniform tax. For instance, by taxing ski equipment and subsidizing commuter costs we induce individuals to work more and consume less leisure.[20]

REDISTRIBUTION AND RAMSEY TAXES

There is one very disturbing feature of Ramsey's analysis. The major reason that governments use distortionary rather than uniform lump-sum taxes is that they have certain redistributive goals that they cannot achieve otherwise. Thus it is peculiar that the early discussions of optimal taxation assumed that all individuals were identical (in which case the natural assumption would be that the government would employ uniform lump-sum taxation).

This failure was particularly vexing since the results described earlier suggest that high tax rates should be imposed on commodities with low price elasticities, such as food. These commodities often have low income elasticities, so that if a high tax is imposed on them the poor will have to bear a larger burden than the rich. But the original reason for employing commodity taxation was to shift more of the burden onto the rich than they would face, say, with a uniform lump-sum or uniform commodity tax. Ramsey's analysis thus seemed to provide little guidance for any serious policy analysis and was, accordingly, largely dismissed.

Subsequent research has extended Ramsey's original analysis to include redistributive goals.[21] Not surprisingly, whether one wishes to tax income-elastic and price-elastic commodities, such as perfume, at a

[19] Note that if $\eta^s = \infty$, $t/p = k/\eta^d_u$; with horizontal supply curves, the percentage tax is inversely proportional to the compensated demand elasticity. The percentage change in output is equal to the percentage increase in price × percent change in demand from a percent change in price $= k/\eta^d_u \times \eta^d_u = k$—i.e., it is the same for all commodities.

[20] This interpretation was noted in W. J. Corlett and D. C. Hague, "Complementarity and the Excess Burden of Taxation," *Review of Economic Studies* 21 (1953): 21–30.

[21] See, in particular, P. Diamond and J. Mirrlees, "Optimal Taxation and Public Production, I: Production Efficiency and II: Tax Rules," *American Economic Review* 61 (1971): 8–27 and 261–78; P. Diamond, "A Many-Person Ramsey Tax Rule," *Journal of Public Economics* 4 (1975): 335–42; A. B. Atkinson and J. E. Stiglitz, "The Structure of Indirect Taxation and Economic Efficiency," *Journal of Public Economics* 1 (1972): 97–119; A. B. Atkinson and J. E. Stiglitz, "The Design of Tax Structure: Direct versus Indirect Taxation," *Journal of Public Economics* 6 (1976): 55–75.

higher or lower rate than income-inelastic and price-inelastic commodities like food depends, in part, on the strength of one's concern for income redistribution. But, as we noted earlier, regardless of one's attitudes toward income redistribution, with a well-designed income tax little appears to be gained by adding differential commodity taxation.

Interest Income Taxation and Commodity Taxation

In our earlier discussion we showed how a tax on interest income changes the slope of the budget constraint (between current and future consumption). It discourages future consumption. It changes the slope of the budget constraint in the same way that a tax on future consumption only would.

Thus an income tax that taxes interest can be viewed as a differential commodity tax in which future consumption is taxed more heavily than current consumption. The question of whether it is desirable to tax interest income is then equivalent to the question of whether it is desirable to tax future consumption at higher rates than current consumption.

Just as, with a well-designed income tax, there may be little to be gained by adding differential commodity taxation, so too there is little to be gained from taxing consumption at different dates at different rates. This means, in effect, that interest income should be exempt from taxation. An income tax that exempts interest income is, of course, equivalent to a wage tax, and we showed in Chapter 17 that a wage tax was equivalent to a consumption tax (in the absence of bequests). This suggests that it may be optimal to have a consumption tax. We discuss this further in Chapter 25.

OPTIMAL TAXATION AND PRODUCTION EFFICIENCY

Consumption taxes have the effect of putting a wedge between the individual's marginal rate of substitution and the marginal rate of transformation. Figure 20.7 depicts the loss in welfare from distortionary commodity taxation. The economy is still on its production possibilities schedule, but the representative individual's indifference curve is no longer tangent to the production possibilities schedule. As a result, the individual is worse off. (E_1 is on a lower indifference curve than E_2.) This is the cost associated with the distortion.

Many of our taxes also affect the production efficiency of the economy, which is to say that they result in the economy not being on its production possibilities schedule. Production efficiency requires that the marginal rate of technical substitution between any two inputs be the same in all firms, and the marginal rate of transformation between any two outputs (or between an input and an output) be the same in all firms. Productive efficiency is attained when all firms face the same prices for inputs and outputs. Thus, any tax on an input that is not uniform across all firms, or any tax on an output that is not uniform across all firms,

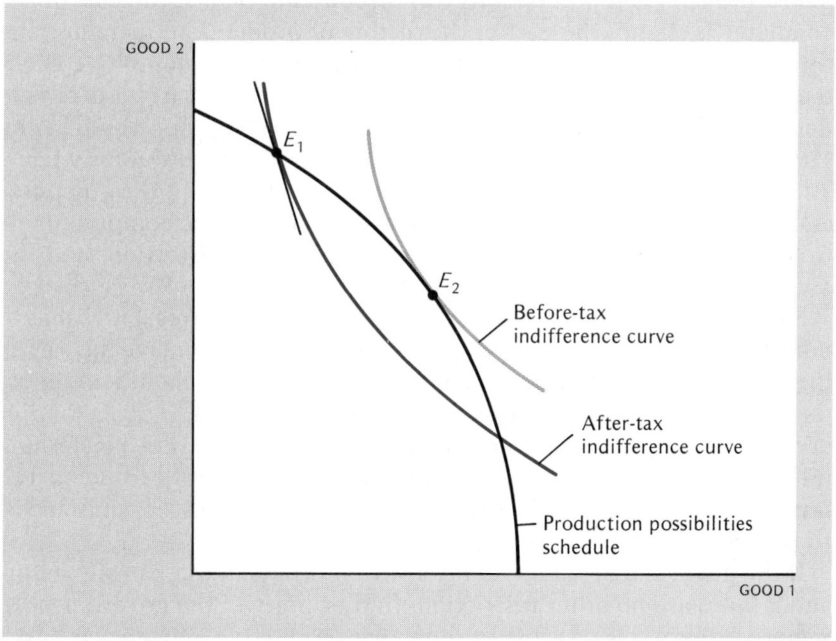

20.7 GENERAL EQUILIBRIUM EFFECTS OF COMMODITY TAXATION If the tax rate on Good 1 is different from that on Good 2, the economy will produce on its production possibilities schedule, but the marginal rate of substitution (the slope of the indifference curve) will not be equal to the marginal rate of transformation (the slope of the production possibilities schedule).

results in the economy not being productively efficient. For instance, the corporation income tax is widely viewed as a tax on capital inputs used in incorporated firms. Thus it raises the after-tax cost of capital in corporations above that in unincorporated businesses. Also, while gasoline that is used for most business purposes is taxed, gasoline used for farming is not. But these are only the most obvious examples.

Many production activities are performed both in the market and nonmarket sectors. Only those performed in the market sector are taxed. Thus an individual driving himself to work is performing the same service that a taxi cab driver who drives the individual to work performs. Yet, there is a tax on the latter and not on the former. A person who bakes a loaf of bread at home is performing a service similar to that of a baker but is not taxed in the same way that the baker is taxed. There is thus a distortion between the marketed and nonmarketed sectors, and the economy is not productively efficient.

Whenever a commodity is used both by businesses and consumers and the tax is imposed on both (businesses are not exempted), there is a loss in productive efficiency. Thus import duties and sales taxes create a production distortion. To see this most clearly, consider a firm that produces and uses computers in its own production plants; the cost of the computer is simply the cost of the factors of production (including the return to capital employed in the production). In a competitive economy this firm would be forced to sell the computers at its costs of production, so that the cost of any other firm using a computer would be the same as the cost of the manufacturing firm in using it. But now, when a sales tax is imposed, the cost to the firm manufacturing the computer and using it is less than the cost to another firm using the computer in its production processes. There is thus an important distortion, and the economy is no longer productively efficient.

Should the government impose such distortionary taxes if it wishes to minimize the deadweight loss of the tax system? One naïve answer to this question is to say, of course not. The government should not introduce any additional distortions that it does not need to. This kind of argument is similar to the arguments we discussed earlier concerning differential commodity taxes. It makes no sense simply to count the number of distortions. Yet it turns out that under some circumstances, the conclusion of the naïve argument is correct.

If the government is able to tax away all profits in the private sector, and if there are no other restrictions in the ability of the government to impose taxes,[22] it is possible to show that productive efficiency is desirable. Hence, the government should impose no distortionary taxes on businesses. Whatever the government could do with a distortionary tax on producers, it could do better with a direct tax on consumers that maintained the economy on the production possibilities schedule.[23]

This analysis has some very strong implications. It suggests, in particular, the undesirability of import duties and of taxes on corporations that differ from those on unincorporated businesses.

There are many instances, however, when the government cannot make distinctions it would like to make, and hence cannot impose taxes it would like to impose. For instance, it cannot distinguish between final consumer use of a commodity and the use of the commodity by a business. It cannot distinguish between capital and wage income in the unincorporated sector, and hence an unincorporated profits tax is not feasible. It cannot distinguish between pure profits and return to entrepreneurship. Whenever the government is not able to identify and tax away all pure profits in the private sector and whenever there are other restrictions on the ability of the government to impose taxes, it may be desirable to impose distortionary taxes on producers.[24]

The arguments in favor of the productive efficiency of the economy also have some important implications for the choice of projects in the public sector. The government, in its role as a producer, can be viewed as just like any other producer; thus if the economy is to be productively

[22] The sole restriction is that the government cannot impose lump-sum taxes.

[23] This result was originally established in the important paper by Diamond and Mirrlees, "Optimal Taxation and Public Production, I: Production Efficiency," *American Economic Review* 61 (1971): 8–27.

[24] This result was established in J. E. Stiglitz and P. Dasgupta, "Differential Taxation, Public Goods and Economic Efficiency," *Review of Economic Studies* 39 (1971): 151–74.

efficient, the marginal rates of substitution among inputs in the public sector must be the same as in the private sector, and marginal rates of transformation between any two outputs must be the same. If the government is considering the construction of an electric power plant, it should use in its project evaluation exactly the same prices as a private firm would use; for instance, in evaluating outputs in different dates, it should use the rate of interest facing private producers.

One must be careful, however, not to push this argument too far. As we argued in Chapter 5, many public projects are concerned explicitly with distributional objectives that cannot be obtained in other ways. The distributional implications of labor training programs should probably not be ignored, for instance, in evaluating such programs.[25]

THE DEPENDENCE OF OPTIMAL TAX STRUCTURE ON THE SET OF AVAILABLE TAXES

Throughout this chapter, we have noted the dependence of the optimal tax results on the assumptions made concerning the set of available taxes. This was particularly true for commodity taxation. Whether there should be differential commodity taxation, and, if so, how the difference in rates should be chosen, depends on whether there is an income tax and if there is, on its structure. Ramsey showed that *in the absence of any income tax* (and assuming no redistributional objectives) different commodities should be taxed at different rates depending only on the elasticities of demand and supply; with 100 percent taxes on profits, the optimal tax depends only on the demand elasticities, not on supply elasticities.[26] When there is an optimally chosen income tax, it may not be desirable to impose differential commodity taxes. When it is desirable to impose differential commodity taxes, they do not depend simply on the elasticities of demand.[27]

[25] J. E. Stiglitz, "The Rate of Discount for Benefit-Cost Analysis and the Theory of the Second Best," in *Discounting for Time and Risk in Energy Policy*, ed. R C. Lind (Baltimore, MD: Johns Hopkins University Press, 1982), pp. 151–204. The conclusion concerning the use of private sector prices in evaluating public projects needs to be further qualified if there are important distortions in the economy, e.g., associated with monopoly.

[26] More generally, Stiglitz and Dasgupta establish that, under Ramsey's assumptions, and if there is a tax on profits at the rate τ, the optimal tax structure is of the form

$$\frac{t}{p} = k\left(\frac{1}{\eta_u^d} + \frac{1-\tau}{\eta^s}\right).$$

If $\tau = 1$ (100% profits taxes), this reduces to the rule that commodity tax rates be inversely related to compensated demand elasticities.

[27] The central question is whether the additional redistribution that might be obtained from differential commodity taxation is worth the extra deadweight loss.

When there is a flat-rate income tax, with the tax rate chosen optimally, the optimal tax rate on a commodity is simply inversely proportional to the elasticity of demand and proportional to a parameter that measures the extent to which the good is consumed relatively more by the rich (so that a tax on that good is progressive). In some simple cases, that distributional parameter itself is proportional to the elasticity of demand; goods with low elasticities of demand (like food) have low deadweight losses but a tax on them is regressive. The two effects (efficiency, or deadweight loss, and distribution) are offsetting, and there should either be no differential taxation on different commodities, or it should depend on parameters other than the elasticity of demand.

(cont.)

It should be emphasized, however, that the set of taxes that is feasible should itself be a subject for analysis: it depends, in particular, on what variables are easily observable and verifiable. In developing countries in which there are many barter transactions (trade not for cash) and in which the level of record keeping is low, it is difficult to enforce an income tax; commodity taxes must be relied on to redistribute income and to ensure that the burden of taxation is equitably borne. But in the United States, the case for the use of redistributive commodity taxation is weak.

SUMMARY

1. Pareto-efficient tax structures are such that there is no alternative that can make any individual better off without making some other individual(s) worse off. The nature of the Pareto-efficient tax structure, in turn, depends on the information available to the government.
2. There are important trade-offs in the design of tax structures between distributional goals and efficiency. The optimal tax structure balances the gains from additional redistribution with the costs in terms of loss in efficiency.
3. The deadweight loss associated with the magnitude of the substitution effect suggests that it is desirable to have low marginal tax rates in those parts of the income distribution where there are a large number of individuals, which is to say in the middle-income ranges. On the other hand, high marginal rates in such ranges enable the government to collect the same or greater revenue with a lower marginal tax rate from upper-income individuals. This reduces the deadweight loss per dollar of revenue raised from upper-income individuals. The net consequence of the two effects together is that it may be desirable to have a flat-rate tax.
4. If the government can impose a redistributive income tax, there appears to be little scope for additional redistribution through commodity taxation.
5. Ramsey taxes minimize the deadweight loss associated with raising a given revenue through commodity taxes alone. In the simple case of independent demand and supply curves, the tax rate on a good is lower, the higher are its supply and compensated demand elasticities.
6. Whether different commodities should be taxed at different rates depends on the taxes that are available to the government. If the government has imposed an optimal income tax, then in one central case, no commodity taxes should be imposed and, by the same token, there should be no taxation of interest income. Even if the government is restricted to imposing a flat-rate income tax, there is some presumption against the imposition of differential commodity taxes.
7. If there are no pure profits in the private sector (the economy is perfectly competitive, or the government can impose a 100 percent profits tax) and there are no other restrictions on the ability of the government to impose taxes, then the government should not impose any taxes that interfere with

In the more general case where an optimal income tax can be imposed that is not necessarily flat (that is, marginal rates can vary with income) a critical determinant of the commodity tax structure is how the marginal rate of substitution between two commodities depends on leisure; in the case where marginal rates of substitution among commodities do not depend at all on leisure, there should be no differential commodity taxation.

the productive efficiency of the economy. When these stringent assumptions are removed, it may be desirable to introduce taxes that interfere with productive efficiency and to take into account distributional considerations in the evaluation of public projects.

KEY CONCEPTS

Second best	Negative income tax
Pareto-efficient taxes	Progressive tax
Optimal tax	Regressive tax
Flat-rate taxes	Ramsey tax

QUESTIONS AND PROBLEMS

1. "If there are groups in the population who differ in their labor supply elasticity, they should be taxed at different rates." Justify this in terms of the theory of optimal taxation, and discuss its implications for the taxation of working spouses.
2. Earlier, we noted that consumption at different dates could be interpreted just like consumption of different commodities (at the same date). What do the results on optimal taxation imply about the desirability of taxing interest income? (Hint: recall that the price of consumption tomorrow relative to the consumption today is just $1/1 + r$, where r is the rate of interest.)
3. Explain why it might be desirable to have a regressive tax structure, even if the social welfare function is utilitarian, when general equilibrium effects of taxes are taken into account. Would it ever be desirable to impose a negative marginal tax rate on very high-income individuals?
4. If you believed that those who were more productive in earning income also had a higher marginal utility of income (they were more efficient in consumption), what would that imply for the design of tax structures? Discuss the reasonableness of alternative assumptions.
5. Under what circumstances will an increase in the progressivity of the tax schedule increase the degree of before-tax inequality?
6. To what extent do you think that differences in views concerning how progressive our tax structure should be reflect differences in values, and to what extent do they reflect differences in judgments concerning the economic consequences of progressivity (deadweight loss, shifting)?
7. One argument sometimes made in favor of the use of commodity taxation rather than income taxation is that people do not accurately perceive the amount they pay in commodity taxes. They will object less to a 20 percent income tax supplemented by a 10 percent sales tax than to a 30 percent income tax. Do you think this is true? If it is, what do you think it implies about the design of tax policy?

APPENDIX: DERIVING RAMSEY TAXES ON COMMODITIES

The formula for Ramsey taxation, given horizontal supply schedules, may be derived using calculus and certain standard results from microeconomic theory. We represent the individual's utility by his *indirect utility function,* giving his level of utility as a function of prices (p_1, p_2, p_3, . . .) and of income (I):

$V = V(p_1, p_2, p_3, \ldots, I)$. A standard result[28] is that the change in utility from a change in price is just equal to the (negative of the) quantity consumed times the marginal utility of income $\frac{\partial V}{\partial I}$:

$$\frac{\partial V}{\partial p_i} = -Q_i \frac{\partial V}{\partial I}.$$

Let us now increase the per unit tax on, say the first commodity (t_1) and reduce the per unit tax on the second commodity (t_2) in such a way as to leave utility unchanged. Then $dp_1 = dt_1 > 0$, $dp_2 = dt_2 < 0$. Clearly, to keep utility unchanged, the required change in the tax on the second commodity must satisfy $dV = \frac{\partial V}{\partial p_i} dt_1 + \frac{\partial V}{\partial p_2} dt_2 = 0$. We can substitute in the values of $\partial V/\partial p_1$ to obtain

$$\frac{dt_2}{dt_1} = -\frac{Q_1}{Q_2}.$$

Thus, if the quantity consumed of the first commodity is large (so the loss in welfare from the tax increase is large), the reduction in taxes on the second commodity must be large.

If the demand for each commodity depends only on its own price, then the change in revenue induced by an increase in the tax on the first commodity is just

$$\frac{\partial (t_1 Q_1)}{\partial t_1} = Q_1 + t_1 dQ/dp_1 = Q_1\left(1 + \frac{t_1}{p_1}\frac{dQ_1}{dp_1}\frac{p_1}{Q_1}\right) = Q_1\left(1 - \frac{t_1}{p_1}\eta_u^1\right),$$

where η_u^1 is the compensated demand elasticity for Good 1. The term, $t_1 \frac{dQ_1}{dp_1}$, represents the *loss* in revenue resulting from reduced sales in response to the changed price. The reason that it is the compensated demand elasticities that are relevant is that we are considering variations in two tax rates that, together, *leave the individual at the same level of welfare.*

Similarly, for each change in the tax on the second commodity, the change in revenue is given by

$$Q_2\left(1 - \frac{t_2}{p_2}\eta_u^2\right).$$

The total change in revenue is thus

$$\frac{dR}{dt_1} = Q_1\left(1 - \frac{t_1}{p_1}\eta_u^1\right) + \frac{dt_2}{dt_1} Q_2\left(1 - \frac{t_2}{p_2}\eta_u^2\right)$$

$$= Q_1\left[\left(1 - \frac{t_1}{p_1}\eta_u^1\right) - \left(1 - \frac{t_2}{p_2}\eta_u^2\right)\right] = Q_1\left[\frac{t_2}{p_2}\eta_u^2 - \frac{t_1}{p_1}\eta_u^1\right].$$

[28] This result is known as Roy's Identity. For a proof, see H. Varian, *Microeconomic Analysis* (New York: Norton, 1984), pp. 126–27, or A. Deaton and J. Muellbauer, *Economics and Consumer Behavior* (London: Cambridge University Press, 1980), pp. 37–41.

With an optimal tax structure, this must be zero, i.e., given that we are keeping the level of utility of the individual constant, revenues must be maximized. But this requires that

$$\frac{t_2}{p_2}\,\eta_u^2 - \frac{t_1}{p_1}\,\eta_u^1 = 0.$$

Generalizing this condition to all commodity taxes, $t_1, t_2, \ldots t_i, \ldots$, we know that $\frac{t_i}{p_i}\,\eta_u^i$ must be the same for all values of i. Let k be that value, so that

$$\frac{t_i}{p_i} = \frac{k}{\eta_u^i}.$$

This means that tax rates must be inversely proportional to compensated demand elasticities. This is the Ramsey rule.

PART FIVE

TAXATION IN THE UNITED STATES

Here we apply the general principles of taxation developed in Part Four to the analysis of taxation in the United States. During the past decade, there was increasing dissatisfaction with the U.S. income tax system, culminating in the passage of the Tax Reform Act in October 1986. After explaining the major provisions of the U.S. personal and corporate income tax, and their implications for both capital and labor, we discuss tax avoidance, evaluate the extent to which the 1986 Tax Reform Act addressed the central deficiencies of the tax system, and present some current proposals for further reform.

21

The Personal Income Tax

The personal (or individual) income tax is the single most important source of revenue for the federal government. It is also the tax that impinges on our lives more than any other. So important is the personal income tax that President Reagan put tax reform at the center of his agenda for his second administration. Though he heralded it as the beginning of the Second American Revolution, the Tax Reform Act of 1986 did not fundamentally alter the structure of the tax system; there was no major change in the underlying principles. Before undertaking an evaluation of the 1986 tax revision, however, we must understand the basic structure of the U.S. income tax, the principles underlying it, and the major problems faced in administering it.

The new tax law called for a two-year transition period before the new system takes full effect in 1989. Moreover, the new tax law calls for certain adjustments to reflect inflation. Accordingly, the tax rates that will be imposed on different levels of income in 1990 and afterwards will depend on how rapidly prices rise. In the discussion below, we describe the tax system as it will look in 1989.

AN OUTLINE OF THE U.S. INCOME TAX

There are four steps in the calculation of an individual's tax liability. First, one calculates **gross income.** One adds up the total of wages and salaries, dividends and interest received, net income from one's business, net rent (after expenses) from rental properties, and the net gains from the sale of assets. Unemployment compensation is now taxed fully, and pensions are taxable to the extent that receipts exceed contributions upon which tax has already been paid. Alimony is also included in income. Gambling earnings, reduced by gambling losses, are included. Illegal earnings (such as from prostitution), from whatever source, are taxable, but not generally reported. But there are several sources of income that are not taxable at all—for example, interest on state and local bonds, most social security benefits, interest on life insurance, welfare and veterans' benefits, and certain employer-paid fringe benefits. None of these amounts is included in gross income.

To get from gross income to **adjusted gross income,** one subtracts moving expenses, job-related expenses (to the extent they exceed 2 percent of gross income), contributions to certain tax-exempt savings plans (discussed in the next chapter), and alimony paid.

To get from adjusted gross income to **taxable income,** there are two alternatives. One can itemize personal deductions—for large medical expenses and casualty losses; for mortgage interest; for state and local taxes other than sales taxes; and for charitable contributions—and then subtract the sum from adjusted gross income. Alternatively, one can take what is referred to as the **standard deduction,** a subtraction of $5,000 for a married couple or $3,000 for an individual. This standard deduction is built into the tax tables. It is intended to simplify tax reporting for the majority of taxpayers, who have only a limited amount of deductions (interest, state and local income and property taxes, etc.) Thus, an individual with only $2,432 of itemized deductions would use the standard deduction.

Both those who itemize their personal deductions and those who take the standard deduction are entitled also to deduct one or more personal exemptions. What is left over after deducting these amounts from adjusted gross income is called **taxable income** (see Table 21.1). The personal exemption in 1989 is $2,000 per individual. For most families there is a personal exemption for each member of the family, but problems arise when there are individuals who are supported in part by more than one family, or who earn part of their support themselves.

The exemptions do not, of course, represent the additional cost of support for an additional person: these typically are far greater than $2,000. Rather, the exemptions, combined with the standard deduction, are intended to ensure that no taxes are imposed on the very poor. Historically, changes in the minimum income below which no tax is imposed have roughly followed what is called the poverty level.

Having arrived at taxable income, one can then calculate one's basic tax liability. The tax will depend on whether the individual is single, married filing jointly with a spouse, married filing separately, or a head of a household. Under the Tax Reform Act of 1986, there are officially only two rates, 15 percent on taxable income up to $29,750 for married

Table 21.1 CALCULATING TAX LIABILITIES

	Wages and Salaries	
	Interest Income, Dividends	
	Net Business Income	
	Net Rental Income	
+	Other Income	
	GROSS INCOME	
−	Moving Expenses	
−	Employee Expenses (in excess of 2% of income)	
−	IRA Contributions (when eligible), and contributions by self-employed to pension plans	
	ADJUSTED GROSS INCOME	
	Alternative 1	Alternative 2: Itemized Deductions
	− Standard Deduction	− Mortgage interest
		− State and local income and property taxes
		− Medical expenses in excess of 7.5% of adjusted gross income
		− Charitable contributions
		− Casualty losses
	− Exemptions	− Exemptions
	TAXABLE INCOME	
×	Tax rate	
	Tax liability	
−	Taxes previously withheld	
−	Tax credits (child care, foreign taxes paid)	
	TAXES DUE	

couples ($17,850 for single individuals), and 28 percent on income in excess of that amount.

The extra tax that an individual must pay as a result of earning an extra dollar of income is called his **marginal tax rate.** Although there are only two official tax rates, 15 percent and 28 percent, the top marginal rate under the new tax law is actually 33 percent, because the advantages of the lower first-bracket rate (15 percent) and the personal exemptions are phased out for high-income taxpayers. To accomplish these two phase outs, the law requires that an additional 5 percent tax (resulting in an overall tax rate of 33 percent) be imposed on each dollar of taxable income at certain levels—depending on the individual's filing status. For instance, the tax rate schedule for a family of four is as shown in Table 21.2 for 1988. In future years, the income levels at which each marginal tax rate applies will be adjusted for inflation.

Table 21.2 TAX RATE SCHEDULE FOR FAMILY OF FOUR

If taxable income is:	*The marginal tax rate is:*
Not over $29,750	15%
Over $29,750 up to $71,900	28%
Over $71,900 up to $194,050*	33%
Over $194,050	28%

* Range within which the 13 percentage point reduction (from 28 to 15 percent) in the first bracket and four personal exemptions are phased out. The top limit of the range increases or decreases by $11,200 for each exemption.

Under the new tax law, there are effectively not two but four marginal tax rates. For a family of four, which takes the standard deduction, with adjusted gross income of up to $42,750 (= $13,000 + $29,750) the marginal tax rate is 15 percent;[1] from $42,750 until $84,900 it is 28 percent; from $84,900 to $207,050 it is 33 percent; and beyond that it is 28 percent. While the marginal tax rate rises and then falls, the *average* tax rate, the ratio of taxes to income, increases gradually, from 0 to 28 percent.

Having arrived at the "tax," there is one further step to arrive at "total tax due." One is allowed to subtract certain tax credits. The major tax credit remaining under the current law is for child-care expenses. In families in which both parents work, a credit of up to 30 percent of child-care expenditures—up to $2,400 (for one child) or $4,800 (for two or more children)—is allowed. A family with two or more children whose child-care expenses equal or exceed $4,800 would have its tax liability reduced by

$$.30 \times \$4,800 = \$1,440.$$[2]

PRINCIPLES BEHIND THE U.S. INCOME TAX

The basic principles underlying the U.S. tax system are worth reviewing, even though the long political process from which they evolved has produced results that sometimes may not be consistent with these "basic principles."

The Income-Based Principle and the Haig-Simons Definition

The current U.S. tax code rests on the premise that the appropriate basis for assessing tax liability is the individual's income (net of expenses personally incurred on the job).

[1] The $13,000 is the sum of the $5,000 standard deduction, plus four $2,000 personal exemptions. Each of the subsequent figures ($84,000 and $207,050) are similarly $13,000 higher than those given in Table 21.2.

[2] The credit can only be taken against the income of the spouse with the lower income. Thus, if Joe earns $2,000 while his wife Jane earns $6,000, the credit is only 30 percent of $2,000. Note, however, that for these purposes, the government imputes an income of $400 a month for full-time students with two or more children, or $200 for those with one child. Thus, if Joe is a full-time student for six months, and Joe and Jane have two children, they get a credit of 30 percent of $4,400, or $1,320. The credit rate decreases with income. High-income individuals receive a maximum credit of 20 percent, or $960.

For the most part, economists have argued that a *comprehensive* definition of income should be used that includes not only cash income but capital gains (whether the gain is realized or simply accrued). A number of other adjustments have to be made to convert "cash" income into the "comprehensive" income that, in principle, should form the basis of taxation. This comprehensive definition of income is referred to as the **Haig-Simons concept,** after two early twentieth-century economists who advocated its use. They believed that such a comprehensive income measure most accurately reflects "ability to pay."

There are three major differences between how our tax system measures income and the Haig-Simons concept of "comprehensive" income.

1. *Cash Basis Market Transactions.* For the most part, only **cash-basis** market transactions are taxed. The tax is thus levied on a notion of income that is narrower than that which most economists would ideally like to see employed. Certain nonmarket (noncash) economic activities are excluded, though activities that appear to be identical and are marketed are subject to taxation. For instance, a maid who cleans house has her compensation taxed, while a spouse who performs exactly the same services in his or her home (and whose support by the spouse working outside the home can be thought of, at least partially, as compensation for the services performed) is not taxed. If an individual owns a house and rents it out, the net rental income is subject to taxation; if the individual lives in the house himself, no tax is due. The primary reason for this is the difficulty of determining appropriate values in the absence of market transactions; when there is a market transaction, there is an observable variable, the transaction price, which we can (and do) use to value the service.[3]

Some noncash transactions are listed in the tax code but are difficult to enforce. **Barter arrangements** (Sally Housepainter paints Joe Carpenter's house in return for his building her a new garage) are subject to tax. Also, when employers provide **in-kind payments** to their employees (such as making an automobile available for personal use), then, in principle, the individual is required to assess the value of these payments and report them on his 1040 form. In fact, noncash payments are often not reported.

A major category of income that the tax system fails to trap is **unrealized capital gains.** Capital gains (the increase in the value of an asset) are taxed only when the asset is sold. Capital gains are taxed, in other words, only upon *realization*, rather than on an *accrual* basis (that is, as they actually occur from year to year).

To see why economists have argued that income should include capital gains, consider two individuals: one puts his $100 savings in a bank and earns 10 percent interest. His income is $10. The other buys $100 worth of gold. During the course of the year, the price of gold rises by 10 percent. At the end of the year, he could sell his gold for $110. The capi-

[3] Some countries (such as Sweden) have attempted to tax the imputed "rent" on owner-occupied houses, as if the individual rented the house to himself.

tal gain increases the wealth of the individual just as the interest payments do; from an economic point of view, the two individuals appear to have an identical ability to pay. But their tax liabilities will differ: the individual who purchases gold only has to pay a tax on his capital gain *when* he sells the asset.[4]

2. *Equity-Based Adjustments.* A second difference between our tax system's measure of income and true "comprehensive" income is that our tax system allows individuals who have large medical expenses or casualty losses to deduct a portion of those expenses from their income. The rationale here is fairness. These individuals are not in as good a position for paying taxes as someone with the same income without those expenses.

3. *Incentive-Based Adjustments.* Finally, the tax code is used to encourage certain activities, such as charitable contributions, by allowing tax credits or deductions for those expenditures. The tax code also allows the exclusion from income of most health insurance and life insurance premiums provided by employers to employees, presumably to encourage employers to provide these benefits.

The Progressivity Principle

Our tax structure is based on the premise that those with higher incomes not only should pay more but should pay a larger fraction of their income in taxes. The effect of the differences between comprehensive income and the tax definition of income is to reduce significantly the effective degree of progressivity. To limit the extent to which individuals can avail themselves of these loopholes, Congress has passed a **minimum tax,** the intent of which is to ensure that upper-income individuals pay a tax at least equal to 21 percent of their income (in excess of a basic exemption level).

The magnitude of the discrepancy between the legislated tax rates and the effective tax rates under the old and the new law is illustrated in Table 21.3.[5] Under the old law, the **effective tax rate,** the ratio of tax payments to a measure of full income, on those with incomes over $1 million was actually lower than those with income between $500,000 and $1 million. The new tax law eliminates the lower tax rates on capital gains, which was of special importance to the very rich, and it restricts

[4] For certain assets, the government could easily calculate the magnitude of capital gains. For instance, the market value of most securities is printed daily in the newspaper. Since 1981, in fact, individuals trading in futures markets have been taxed on the basis of the actual market value of their holdings at the end of the year, whether or not gains or losses are realized. For other assets, however, estimating capital gains would be extremely difficult.

[5] In the table, reported adjusted gross income is increased to take account of income in tax-exempt forms. There is some controversy about some of the adjustments; in particular, the inclusion of tax-exempt interest. The rates of return on these assets are somewhat lower than on taxable bonds; the difference can be thought of as a tax payment (made to state and local governments). Nonetheless, the basic picture presented by Table 21.3 appears to be accurate.

Table 21.3 EFFECTIVE TAX RATES UNDER PRESENT LAW, BY INCOME CLASS, BEFORE AND AFTER TAX REFORM (1986) (*income classes in thousands of dollars; rate in percent*)

Expanded Adjusted Gross Income Class	*Old Law*	*1986 Tax Reform Act*
0–5,000	−0.6	−1.6
5,000–10,000	1.7	0.4
10,000–15,000	4.9	3.8
15,000–20,000	6.8	6.9
20,000–25,000	8.7	8.5
25,000–35,000	9.9	9.9
35,000–50,000	11.8	11.6
50,000–100,000	15.7	15.5
100,000–500,000	24.2	22.3
500,000–1,000,000	28.6	26.5
1,000,000 and over	26.3	26.6
AVERAGE	13.1	13.0

Source: J. A. Pechman "Tax Reform: Theory and Practice," 1986 Distinguished Lecture on Economics in Government, Joint Session of the American Economics Association and the Society of Government Economists, December 29, 1986.

several tax avoidance schemes; at the same time, the deductions for mortgage interest and state and local income and property taxes remain. Thus, the new tax law substantially reduces, but does not eliminate, the discrepancy between effective and legislated tax rates.

The Family-Based Principle

The basic unit of taxation in the United States is not the individual but the family. Two individuals who decide to get married (and thus change their family status) will find that their tax liabilities are altered. The tax code attempts to make some limited adjustments for families in different circumstances. Families in which there is only one adult face a rate that is halfway between those of an individual and a two-adult family. Families with children are allowed exemptions for each child, as mentioned earlier. Families in which both parents work are allowed a credit for child care. Whether these are "fair" or "appropriate" is a question we shall discuss later.

Although the tax system is basically family-based, it is not completely so: while income of children under fourteen is taxed at the family's marginal tax rate (that is, it is effectively included within the tax unit), income of children over fourteen is not. The United States is now one of the few countries still employing a family-based tax system. Other countries, such as Canada, have an individual-based system, where each individual is taxed on his own income.

Divorce presents problems for a family-based tax system. Under present provisions, alimony (but not child support) is deductible by the party paying it and taxable to the party receiving it.[6]

The Annual Measure of Income Principle

The U.S. income tax is based on annual income, not lifetime income. The consequence of this is that two individuals with the same lifetime income may, over their lifetimes, pay quite different taxes. The individual who decides to postpone more of his consumption until retirement will, for instance, pay more in taxes than his less frugal brother. Or consider two individuals with the same (before-tax) present discounted value of income, one of whom is a late bloomer, earning most of his income in later life. The present discounted value of his tax payments will be lower.

Because of the progressivity of the tax structure, the use of an annual measure of income also affects differently those with stable incomes and those with fluctuating income. Middle-income families with variable income are adversely affected, while some upper-income individuals with variable income are better off. Consider a middle-income family of four whose average income is $43,000, but in half the years it has an income of $53,000, while in the other years it has an income of only $33,000. Under the new tax law, in a good year, the family will be taxed at a marginal rate of 28 percent; in a bad year, it will be taxed at a marginal rate of 15 percent. Its total tax liability will be considerably greater than that of a family with a stable income of $43,000 which always faces a 15 percent marginal tax rate; the *average* additional annual tax payment of the family with a fluctuating income is $650.[7]

By contrast, consider an upper-income family of four whose average income is $207,000, but in half the years has an income of $247,000, while in the other years has an income of only $167,000. Under the new tax law, in a good year the marginal rate will be 28 percent; in a bad year it will be 33 percent. Now the family with a fluctuating income is better off than the family with the same average (but stable) income. The *average* annual tax payment of the family with the fluctuating income is $1,000 less than the family with the stable income.[8]

Prior to the 1986 Tax Reform Act, taxpayers were allowed to average income over periods when their income varied widely. By eliminating the privilege of income averaging, the Tax Reform Act aggravated the distortions produced by the annual basis of taxation.[9]

[6] Thus with the progressive tax structure, if the husband and wife are in very different tax brackets, it pays to label payments that are really child support as alimony. Like everything else in modern life, it requires care and thought to get divorced in a manner that minimizes tax liabilities.

[7] We assume that the family has no adjustments to income and takes the standard deduction. Then in the good year, the extra tax payment is .28 × $10,000. In the bad year, the reduced tax payment is .15 × $10,000. The total extra tax payment over a two-year period is thus $1,300. Dividing by 2, we obtain the *average* annual extra payment.

[8] In the good year, the family pays .28 × $40,000 = $11,200 extra. In the bad year, tax liabilities are reduced by .33 × $40,000 = $13,200. The total reduction over the two years is $2,000. Dividing by 2, we obtain the average annual reduction.

[9] The annual basis of taxation has other effects: an individual who has the option of paying some deductible expense on December 31 or on January 1 has a strong incentive to do so on December 31.

PRACTICAL PROBLEMS IN IMPLEMENTING AN INCOME TAX SYSTEM

In translating the basic *principles* of the income tax into a workable tax system, the tax law faces four extremely difficult problems: it must determine what "income" is; it must determine when somebody has received some income; it must decide what deductions from income to allow; and it must decide on the appropriate unit of taxation.

Determining Income

For most wage earners, determining income for tax purposes is a simple matter. They simply add up their paychecks, interest, dividends, etc. But for those who run their own business it is not. There are two central problems. The first is concerned with determining depreciation (the loss in value of machines and buildings as they age) and adjusting the cost of inventories for inflation. These are sufficiently difficult and complex questions that we postpone them for the next two chapters. The second problem is differentiating between consumption expenditures and legitimate business expenses.

The tax code recognizes that legitimate expenses required in order to earn a living ought to be deducted from an individual's income. The principle seems clear. Surely, a store owner who sells candy should not be taxed on the total value of his sales; his expenses—the rent for his store, the purchase of candy from the candy manufacturer, the salaries he pays his employees—should all be deducted from sales to calculate his gross income. But what about the candy he consumes while he is working? He may claim that his consumption of candy is a form of advertising; when customers see him chewing candy, they increase their purchases. But what of the candy that he consumes when no one is around? He may claim he is "testing" various samples, to ensure the quality of the candy he sells. One might suspect that the real motive lying behind the candy store owner's eating his candy is neither of these expressed explanations: he simply likes candy.

Similarly, in many businesses there is very little difference between advertising and entertainment expenses. Taking clients to dinner is a method of persuading them to buy your product, just as putting an advertisement in the newspaper is an attempt to persuade customers to buy your product. On the other hand, there are other instances where "business" entertainment is purely a matter of having a good dinner partly at Uncle Sam's expense.

These examples illustrate the two central problems:

1. In many instances it is impossible to ascertain what are and are not legitimate business expenses.

2. Even when the distinctions between legitimate and illegitimate

---

An individual who has an option of being paid on December 31 or on January 1 has a strong incentive to ask for a postponement of his check until January 1. Both statements are made on the assumption that the individual is in the same marginal tax bracket both years.

business expenses are conceptually clear, it is often impossible to perform the required monitoring. It is difficult to imagine the kinds of records that would be required to isolate the owner's consumption of candy (if we decided that consumption is not a legitimate business expense).

CONSEQUENCES OF ALTERNATIVE BUSINESS-EXPENSE RULES

It is impossible to devise a system of distinguishing between legitimate and illegitimate expenditures in a way most of us would consider to be fair; someone always either is unfairly burdened or benefits unfairly, no matter what rule is devised.

The government can either allow a fairly generous treatment of expenses—for instance, for travel—in which case the individual who is really traveling for recreation purposes is unfairly receiving a tax benefit; or the government can be fairly restrictive—for instance, by not allowing first-class travel and not allowing meal deductions above a certain amount—in which case the individual who has no recreational motive may be unfairly burdened. There is no way the tax code can be fair to both of these individuals. Moreover, any rule induces economic distortions. If deductions for travel expenses are restricted, businesses requiring travel will be discouraged; if travel expenses are not restricted, businesses requiring travel may be encouraged. The deductions are a form of tax-exempt income. Furthermore, if deductions for travel expenses are restricted, businesses may substitute less efficient communications methods for travel. This is because the relative after-tax price of travel will rise if travel expenses are not deductible, but other communication expenses (telephone, telex, etc.) are still deductible (see Figure 21.1A).

In Figure 21.1B, we consider a self-employed individual who is able to claim business entertainment as a deduction. The deductibility of these expenses shifts his budget constraint, the alternative combinations of "entertainment" and "other consumption goods" the individual can purchase. His before-tax budget constraint is E_oC_o. With no deductibility, it is E_1C_1. When entertainment is deductible, it is E_0C_1. Entertainment becomes relatively less expensive; if the individual is in the 33 percent tax bracket, he has to give up only 67 cents' worth of other goods to get a dollar's worth of entertainment. His consumption decisions are clearly distorted.

In the 1986 Tax Reform Act, Congress took an intermediate position: tax deductions for luxury cars were reduced, and only 80 percent of entertainment expenses and meals were deductible.

WHAT CONSTITUTES A BUSINESS?

Not only is it difficult to determine what are legitimate business expenses, in some cases it is even difficult to determine what is a business. For instance, individuals who raise horses could be raising horses as a business. On the other hand, they could be keeping the horses sim-

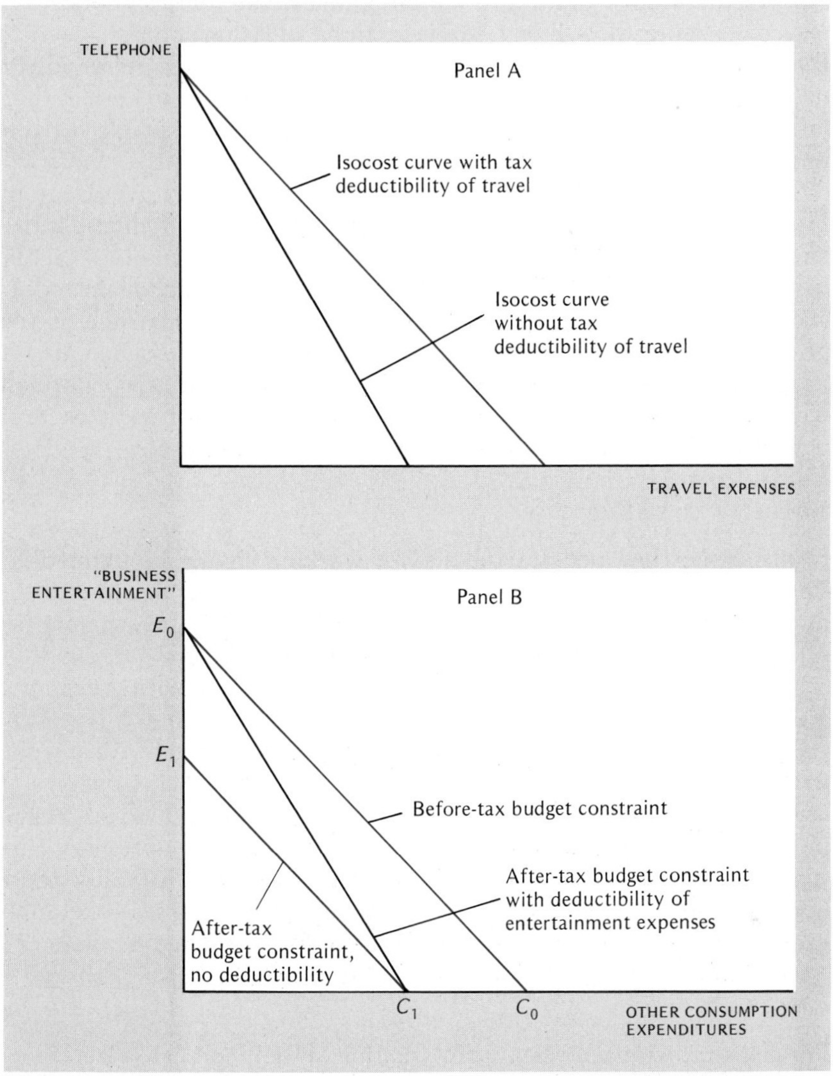

21.1 DILEMMAS OF TAX DEDUCTIBILITY OF TRAVEL, ENTERTAINMENT, AND RELATED EXPENDITURES (A) If firms were denied the right to deduct travel expenses for income as a legitimate business expense, travel would become a relatively more expensive way of communicating than other forms of communciation, such as telephone; thus production decisions would be distorted. (Isocost curves are similar to budget constraints. They give those combinations of inputs that together cost a given amount.) (B) For a self-employed individual who can claim a deduction for "business entertainment," the tax system reduces the cost of this form of consumption relative to other forms of consumption. There is a distortion (and hence a deadweight loss).

ply for their own pleasure. If they buy a horse, keep it for several years, sell it, and take a loss, the loss is really not on a business activity or on an asset but on an ordinary pleasurable activity. One could argue that there is no reason that their capital loss should be deducted from their income tax. On the other hand, there are individuals who do raise horses as a way of earning their living—buying them at a lower price, feeding them, and then selling them at a higher price. Not to allow these individuals who are in the business of raising horses for profit to deduct their losses would seem to be grossly unfair. The difficulty is that it is virtually impossible to distinguish between the two situations.

The government attempts to combat this kind of tax avoidance by insisting that serious businesses make a profit. The rule of thumb is that an individual must make a profit in at least three years out of five; in the case of horse breeding, this rule is relaxed so that an individual needs to show a profit in at least two years out of seven. Rules such as this obviously do succeed in reducing the amount of tax avoidance. At the same time, of course, there are individuals who are seriously in business who make losses year after year. Setting up a business often takes three or four years in order to establish a reputation—and a profit.

EMPLOYEE BUSINESS DEDUCTIONS

In principle, the "necessary costs" of working should be deductible. The difficulty is ascertaining what are necessary costs. Because of the impossibility of doing this on a case-by-case basis, the government has set up certain basic rules: some educational expenses are deductible, others are not. Moving expenses are deductible, commuting expenses are not.

Again, there are inequities and inefficiencies associated with any particular set of rules. In drafting the 1986 Tax Reform Act, Congress, in effect, decided that the old law resulted in too many individuals claiming employee business expenses for what were actually ordinary consumption expenditures. Accordingly, they decided that only those taxpayers with very large employee business expenses—expenses exceeding 2 percent of adjusted gross income—could deduct them.

FRINGE BENEFITS

For many individuals, a significant fraction of their compensation comes in forms other than direct cash payment. We have already discussed the problems arising from, for instance, travel. (Even those jobs not requiring extensive travel often pay for a trip to a convention at an attractive place, like Florida or Las Vegas.) Still other problems are posed by fringe benefits provided by the firm. The most important of these is medical insurance provided by the firm. Some workers are receiving thousands of dollars worth of medical and dental benefits that are exempt from taxation. Most economists believe that such benefits should be included within taxable income. There are again administrative problems in doing so: these benefits are clearly worth more to some individuals than to others. The tax reform proposed by the Treasury in 1985 called for taxing most of these benefits, but there was strong political opposition, and in the 1986 Tax Reform Act which was finally adopted these fringe benefits remain tax-exempt.

There are three lessons to be learned from this discussion of the problems of implementing the income tax. First, what may seem like minor details of a tax law can have important consequences. Second, many (but by no means all) of the provisions of the tax code that seem unfair and distortionary are not the result of politicians representing special-interest groups or of incompetent bureaucrats. There are real difficulties in determining what is income and what are legitimate business expenses. Thirdly, whatever rules that are chosen will entail both some inequities and some inefficiencies. In designing the tax code, one must weigh one inequity against another, one distortion against another. The objective of our discussion has been to clarify these trade-offs and to help explain the all-too-frequent situations where, in the process of correcting one inequity or distortion, the authorities discover that they have created a new one, as bad or worse than the first.

Timing

The second important practical problem of implementing an income tax is determining when somebody has received some income. Again, for most wage income, there is no problem. But consider an author writing a book. Authors are commonly paid a royalty, a certain fraction of the revenues generated by sales of the book. Usually, the publisher provides an advance payment, prior to the publication of the book in anticipation of future royalties. In principle, if the book fails to sell, the advance must be returned. Should the advance be treated as income to the author at the time he receives it? Or should the advance be more properly treated as a loan, which will be repaid with the proceeds of the book? In the latter case, the author would only have to pay the tax when the book has been sold.

There are, in fact, many transactions that are, or can be made, to take on this form. Consider a contractor building a building. The contract is not fulfilled unless, and until, the building is completed. But he receives payments as the building progresses. Are these payments to be treated as loans (in which case the builder only records the income when the building is completed)? Similar issues arise in any long-term project (such as defense contracts to develop a new airplane).

Or consider this example: Old Alfred A. agrees to sell his business to young Frank F., at a price considerably above what Alfred A. originally paid for it. Frank does not have all the necessary money. Alfred could sell it now, lending Frank the additional $100,000 required, which Frank will repay in four years. In this case, Alfred would have to pay a capital gains tax now. Alternatively, they could treat the transaction as an installment purchase, with title to the business not being transferred for four years, when Frank will have paid the full amount. Though there are some legal consequences (which might affect, for instance, what would happen in the case of a fire), for most purposes other than taxes the two arrangements are almost equivalent. But the tax consequences are markedly different. In the second case, Alfred can postpone paying the tax on his capital gains until he receives the actual payments for his business.

People care about timing because a dollar today is worth more than a dollar tomorrow. The **present discounted** value of tax liabilities is reduced by postponing the tax.

The importance of what may seem like minor technicalities should not be underrated: in the 1986 Tax Reform Act, almost half of the increased taxes raised from corporations ($60 billion over a five-year period) were the consequences of accounting changes, most of which were related to these issues of the timing of the "recognition" of income.

Personal Deductions

The third practical problem in implementing an income tax is deciding which deductions from income to allow. Thus, in going from adjusted gross income to taxable income, the government allows deductions that are designed to make a more equitable tax system and to encourage certain socially desirable activities. There are five important kinds of expenditures for which deductions are allowed: medical expenses, mortgage interest, state and local taxes except sales taxes, charitable contributions, and casualty losses.

MEDICAL EXPENSES

The motivation for allowing medical expenditures to be deducted from income seems perfectly obvious: health problems lead to costly medical bills and often reduce the individual's earnings as well. An individual who is spending all of his income on doctors' bills simply to stay alive has a lesser ability to pay than an individual with the same income but no medical expenses. Ability to pay is measured best not by total income but by discretionary income, the amount in excess of the amount required to survive.

This argument has been criticized on two grounds. First, there are other categories of expenditures (such as food) that, at least at some level, are equally necessary. But differences in the necessary amount of food are likely to be smaller than differences in the necessary amount of medical expenditures. Second, a significant fraction of medical expenses are discretionary (e.g., staying in a private room rather than a semiprivate room, having a television set in one's room, plastic surgery to stay young-looking, etc.), and the law makes no distinction between "necessary" and "discretionary" expenditures. Again, however, this is understandable, since the distinction, though clear in principle, is virtually impossible to make in practice. The tax rules now allow deductions for medical expenses only to the extent that they exceed 7.5 percent of adjusted gross income. This seems to reflect the judgment that significant inequities in ability to pay arise only with significant medical costs, and that these large medical costs are likely (but not always) to be nondiscretionary.

The provisions for deducting them effectively reduce the price of medical services. For someone in the 28 percent marginal tax bracket whose medical expenses exceed the 7.5 percent minimum, the private cost of an extra $100 of medical services is only $72. The distortions this introduces are obvious: to the extent that medical expenditures are discretionary, the individual has an incentive to spend too much on medical services (relative to other commodities).

Note that the amount by which the effective price of medical services is reduced depends on the marginal tax bracket of the individual. For an individual in the 15 percent bracket, an extra $100 of medical services costs $85. Whenever individuals face different prices for the same commodity, there is inefficiency.

Along with the inefficiencies introduced by the medical expense deduction, this deduction has also been objected to on grounds that it is unfair. The reduction in the tax liability as a result of say $1,000 of medical expenses for an individual at a higher income level is greater than that for an individual at a lower income level. Thus if an individual in the 28 percent bracket incurs a $1,000 medical expense (ignoring for the moment the provision limiting the amount that can be deducted), his tax liability is reduced by $280. On the other hand, an individual in the 15 percent bracket would have his tax liability reduced by only $150. The *value* of the provisions for deductibility of expenses is thus much greater for the individual in the higher bracket.

The efficiency and equity arguments against deducting medical expenses (which apply to other categories of deductions as well) have led many economists to conclude that credits are preferable to deductions. With a tax credit, an individual with a $1,000 medical expense would have his tax reduced by the same amount, regardless of his income. If there were a 20 percent tax credit, the government would, in effect be paying 20 percent of medical expenditures. Not only does this seem more fair to many individuals, it also seems more efficient. Recall that one of the requirements for the Pareto efficiency of the economy is that all individuals' marginal rates of substitution between different commodities be the same. (This was called the principle of exchange efficiency.) This is ensured if all individuals face the same price for every commodity. With tax credits, since the government is, in effect, paying part of medical costs, individuals do not pay net (after tax) the true marginal cost of the medical services they obtain; but all individuals face the same effective price. With deductions, as we have noted, upper-income individuals face a lower price than lower-income individuals.

The above arguments are not completely persuasive. Recall that the motivation for allowing the deduction was that we wished to base taxes on some measure of ability to pay. It was believed that medical expenses reduce the individual's ability to pay. If this is true, gross income by itself does not provide an appropriate basis for judging ability to pay. Gross income, net of "involuntary" medical expenses, provides a better measure. Though we know we cannot separate out "voluntary" from "involuntary" medical expenses, we may believe it is better to take account of medical expenses than to ignore them; that is, we may believe that gross income, net of all medical expenses, is a better measure (though admittedly imperfect) than gross income alone.

It is, of course, true that the deductibility of medical expenses produces distortions, particularly for individuals in the 28 percent or 33 percent marginal brackets. As we discussed earlier, there is an important equity/efficiency trade-off. The fraction of medical expenses that should be tax-deductible would presumably depend on the elasticity of demand for medical services. As we noted earlier, if the elasticity is low, the distortion is low, and there will be little gain in efficiency from making medical expenditures only partially deductible. On the other hand, if the elasticity of demand for medical expenditures is high, there are potentially great gains in efficiency, and then we may wish to have only a fraction of medical expenses deductible.

The 1986 Tax Reform Act, while raising the nondeductible portion of medical expenses, left intact the far more significant exemption of medical insurance provided by firms. Raising the threshold for medical deductions is anticipated to increase government tax revenues by approximately one billion dollars a year. Eliminating the exemption for employer-provided medical insurance and medical care would increase government revenue by twenty times as much.[10]

INTEREST

The motivation for the tax deductibility of interest is simple: income (as usually defined) includes wages plus net interest receipts—i.e., the difference between interest paid and interest received. If we believe that an individual who has positive net interest receipts has a higher ability to pay than someone with no interest receipts and that an individual with negative net interest receipts has a lower ability to pay, interest paid should be tax-deductible.

Those who believe that consumption is the appropriate basis of taxation argue that interest should not be taxed and that interest payments should not be tax-deductible. Even those who believe that income is the appropriate tax base have, however, been concerned with the inequities and inefficiencies to which interest deductibility gives rise. First, since some types of capital income receive favorable tax treatment, borrowing to finance favored types of investments provides one of the major classes of tax avoidance devices. (We discuss this later in Chapter 24.) Second, the present system encourages borrowing, and thus discourages saving.

The 1986 Tax Reform Act took a compromise position. It continued the tax deductibility of mortgage interest (for up to two homes). But it eliminated the deductibility of all consumer interest. Money, however, is fungible; money borrowed allegedly for one purpose can be used for

[10] *Special Analyses: Budget of the United States Government. Fiscal Year 1988,* Table G-2; *Tax Reform Act of 1986, Conference Report,* Table A.2.

another. An individual who is buying a house and a car, and who was planning to borrow money to pay, say, 80 percent of the cost of each, can obviously borrow a little more against the house, using the additional funds to pay cash for the car. In recent years banks have been making home equity loans, enabling an individual to borrow against the current market value of his house (which is often considerably more than the price at which it was purchased). These are treated as mortgages, and interest on these loans is tax deductible. The restriction on the deductibility of interest is thus likely to encourage this trend.

Congress was aware of this problem, and partially addressed it by limiting the size of the mortgage for which interest is deductible to the original purchase price plus borrowing for medical and educational purposes. Whether these provisions on the limitation of interest deductibility will be very effective remains to be seen.[11]

STATE AND LOCAL TAXES

State and local taxes (except sales taxes) are deductible. The primary motivation for this provision is the concern that without such a provision, the imposition of federal taxation would seriously impair the ability of the states to raise revenues. Indeed, without such a provision, during World War II, when federal marginal tax rates reached as high as 94 percent, some individuals would have faced total marginal tax rates (combining federal and state taxes) in excess of 100 percent. Some individuals also have expressed a concern that without such a provision, there would effectively be double taxation of the same income. Whether such double taxation is inequitable is, however, another question. If the taxes are thought of as being associated with the benefits of living in a particular locale, it is not obvious that these expenditures should be treated any differently from expenditures on other goods and services.

Indeed, the deductibility of local taxes may give rise to an important source of distortions and inequities. Many of the services provided by local communities—garbage collection, sewage disposal, education, tennis courts—differ little from similar commodities that can be purchased privately. Such services provided by local communities are known as "local publicly provided goods"—though all members of the community benefit from these goods, those outside it do not. Thus the deductibility of local taxes encourages the public provision of these goods and services (regardless of whether the services might be more efficiently provided privately) and encourages the consumption of those goods and services that can be provided through local communities.

To see this, consider a small community consisting of wealthy homeowners. They face a choice of having a token public school system and sending their children to private school, or having a first-rate public

[11] The provision limiting the size of the mortgage to the original purchase price plus borrowing for medical and educational purposes has an additional potential distortion: individuals whose houses have increased in value will have an incentive in effect to trade houses; the trade will allow both of them to borrow more.

school system. For simplicity, we ignore the costs of the token public school system (in fact, state laws may require a high level of expenditure on public schools, and the first option may not really be available; individuals in some rich communities where many of the children go to private school do, however, seem to spend less on their schools than do those in less well-to-do communities). With a private school system, the residents pay an average of, say, $\$E$ per family. If they now switch to the public school system, and again pay an average of $\$E$ per family, raised by means of taxes, the cost is only $\$(1 - t)\,E$, where t is the marginal federal income tax rate, since the taxes are deductible from income for those who itemize deductions on their federal tax return. All communities will have an incentive to spend an excessive amount on education, but the amount of the subsidy is greater the wealthier the community.

The same argument applies, of course, to garbage collection or any other publicly provided service. Note that communities that do not provide public sewage collection (individuals have to use septic tanks) are thus disadvantaged relative to communities with public sewage collection. And there will be instances where, on efficiency grounds, septic tanks would be preferable to public sewage collection, but given the subsidy for public sewage collection, the latter will be employed.

Not all economists are agreed upon the significance of these distortions or inequities. Although many goods provided by local communities are much like privately provided goods, many are basically public goods, little different from those associated with private charities (for which a deduction is allowed). The elderly, for instance, do not benefit directly from the expenditures on education (though in some instances they may benefit indirectly, from the increased value of their house). In the voting models discussed in Chapter 6, the outcome of the political process depends critically on the median voter, the one who is such that half want more public expenditures, and half less. In that case, what is critical is how the tax system affects the median voter. In most states and communities—but not all—the median voter does not itemize; that is, according to the median voter model, deductibility is essentially irrelevant. Still, many economists, and almost all politicians, were concerned that the elimination of the deductibility of state and local taxes would decrease the demand for state and local goods.

The 1986 Tax Reform Act represented a peculiar compromise. Sales taxes, which represent only 25 percent of all taxes collected at the state and local level, are no longer deductible; but all other taxes remain deductible. Moreover, states and localities may be induced, as a result of this provision, to switch from sales taxes to other sources of revenue. There is no convincing justification, other than political expediency, for this distinction in treatment between sales taxes and other taxes.

CHARITY

The deduction for gifts for charitable purposes—for education, religion, health, and welfare—is one of the more controversial provisions of the tax code. The motivation for allowing these expenditures to be deductible is clear. As we discussed at greater length in Chapter 5, there are insufficient private incentives for spending money on goods that generate benefits to others. Money spent to develop a polio vaccine may yield little direct benefit to the giver but may provide great benefits for mankind. Similarly, gifts to educational and other cultural institutions may contribute much to the welfare of society, but relatively few of the benefits accrue directly to the benefactors.

Opponents of the deduction for charity argue that:

1. Many of the expenditures are not really for public goods.

2. The public—i.e., the government—should determine directly how expenditures on public goods should be allocated.

3. The provision for deductibility of charitable gifts mainly benefits the rich and thus reduces the redistributive impact of our tax system.

4. Eliminating the provision of the deductibility of charitable gifts would have little effect on charitable giving.

It is difficult to assess the validity of these various claims. Many of the most important advances in medicine have been the outcome of research supported by private foundations. The Rockefeller Foundation's development of "miracle seeds" brought on a Green Revolution in developing countries that has greatly increased the availability of food in these countries.

There is also some evidence that elimination of the deductibility of charitable donations would have a substantial effect on gift giving.[12]

Whether the deductibility provisions result in the tax system being unfair is also not clear. To the extent that wealthy individuals create foundations that pay high salaries to their officers but spend little on true public goods, the provision for charitable donations may well be thought to be inequitable. But to the extent that the expenditures are really for public goods, the giver gets no more enjoyment out of the expenditure than do many other members of society. There is no more reason to include these expenditures in his income than in that of any other individual (who benefits equally by it).

If the appropriate basis of taxation is "income available for spending on private goods," the appropriate tax treatment is allowing a full deduction (just as we argued earlier that the appropriate tax treatment of medical expenses was a deduction, not a credit). But the consequence of this is that the marginal cost of charity is less for those in the 28 percent or 33 percent bracket than for those in the 15 percent bracket.

The charitable contribution has also sometimes been abused, with individuals giving away property (paintings), and assigning a value to the

[12] Martin Feldstein ("The Income Tax and Charitable Contributions, Part II: The Impact on Religious Education, and Other Organizations," *National Tax Journal*, June 1975, p. 217) estimated that eliminating tax deductibility for someone in the 50 percent tax bracket would reduce charitable contributions to educational institutions by three-quarters; the loss to the charities would be one and one-half times the gain to the federal government. (Someone who had been giving $1,000 would now give $250.) Hospitals would similarly be hard hit. The least sensitive were contributions to religious organizations. See also C. T. Clotfelter and E. Steuerle, "Charitable Contributions," in *How Taxes Affect Economic Behavior*, H. J. Aaron and J. A. Pechman, eds. (Washington, D.C.: Brookings Institution, 1981).

gift far in excess of the true value. Recent legislation has imposed severe penalties for those who get caught doing this.

The deductibility of charitable contributions raises a basic question concerning the manner in which decisions regarding the supply of public goods should be made. Critics claim that the tax deductibility of charitable contributions gives, in effect, undue power to the rich in deciding which public goods should be provided. On the other hand, political processes do not provide a very efficient mechanism for registering individuals' attitudes toward different public goods. Individuals vote for representatives and have little opportunity for expressing their views on the relative allocation, say, of educational and health expenditures.

The provision for charitable deductions has encouraged a system in which public goods are provided by a variety of institutions. Individuals can express their views about the importance of different categories of public goods in a variety of ways. If the government were the only source of funds for, say, health research, the views of that bureaucracy would exclusively determine the direction of health research; as it is, these decisions can be made independently in a variety of institutions. The arguments for the decentralization of decision making for public goods are closely parallel to those for the decentralization of decision making in other areas: having competing (or at least alternative) organizations providing similar services leads to greater efficiency, and it allows for diversification, so that the consequence of mistakes will be smaller.[13]

CASUALTY LOSSES

Individuals are allowed to deduct losses from thefts, fire, accident, and other casualties that exceed 10 percent of the individual's adjusted gross income. The motivation for these provisions is again clear. These losses reduce the individual's ability to pay; they represent "expenditures" that were not voluntary and from which the individual presumably got no enjoyment.

This provision has, however, some important consequences. In particular, it means that the government effectively provides a kind of insurance against these casualties. The magnitude of the insurance depends (as we noted in our discussion of the medical deduction) on the individual's marginal tax rate. Once they have suffered a loss, individuals are obviously much better off than if the government did not provide this kind of insurance. On the other hand, these provisions may seriously distort individuals' behavior. Insurance, in general, reduces individuals' incentives to avoid the losses in question. Thus, if the government pays

[13] The provision for the deductibility of expenditures on religious charities has another motivation: some argue that the constitutional prohibition against legislation interfering with the free exercise of religion prohibits taxation of religious organizations. Although this may provide a justification for exempting religious institutions directly from taxation, it does not seem to provide justification for deducting gifts to churches for purposes of the income tax.

33 percent of the loss, the individual may not make as much effort to avoid being robbed.

Unit of Taxation

The final practical problem in implementing an income tax involves determining the appropriate unit of taxation. The tax due to the government depends both on taxable income and on the filing status—i.e., whether single, married, or head of household. Our present tax system, as we noted earlier, is based on the family as the unit of taxation; because of some inequities that result, an allowance is made for child-care expenses. Our present tax structure penalizes marriages between partners with equal incomes and encourages marriages between partners with very unequal incomes. This is seen in Table 21.4, where we have calculated the cost of marriage for two couples. Abigail and Billy presently are living together but are not married; each earns \$25,000, and they pay a total of \$6,560 in income taxes. Were they to get married, their tax liability would increase by over \$1,000 to \$7,613. If they anticipate remaining married for, say, fifty years, and do not anticipate any change in their salaries (after adjusting for inflation) over that period, the total cost of getting married would exceed (with a 5 percent real interest rate) \$20,000. If Abigail and Billy have some doubts about whether to get married, this calculation might well resolve those doubts. The increased tax payment resulting from getting married is sometimes referred to as the marriage penalty.

By contrast, when Bradford marries his low-paid girlfriend, Amy, they find that their total tax liabilities are reduced by \$617. For this couple, the tax system acts to encourage marriage. Over the fifty years of their marriage, the value of the government's subsidy to this couple's tying the knot is nearly \$12,000. Rich girls used to worry that they were being married for their money. Now Amy worries that Bradford wishes to marry her because of the reduced tax liabilities.

Was it the intent of Congress, in enacting the tax code, to encourage marriages between individuals with very different incomes and discourage marriages such as that between Abigail and Billy? Probably not.

But consider now what happens if we change the tax code to have all individuals pay on the basis of their own income. Now, individuals nei-

Table 21.4 TAX EFFECT OF MARRIAGE

Filing status		*Earnings*	*Tax on individual*	*Total tax of A&B*
Single	Abigail	25,000	3,280	
	Billy	25,000	3,280	6,560
Single	Amy	10,000	750	
	Bradford	40,000	7,480	8,230
Married	A & B	50,000		7,613

ther benefit nor are penalized by marriage. This provision does eliminate the discrimination against those who choose to live together under the bonds of matrimony.

But consider Amy and Bradford. They have the same family income as Abigail and Billy. But now, their total tax liability is $8,230, as opposed to that of Abigail and Billy, whose tax bill is only $6,560. Not surprisingly, Bradford and Amy think this is unfair. Shouldn't the family's total tax burden depend simply on family income, not on how much each member of the family earns? There is no tax arrangement that appears to be "fair" in all circumstances.

Do the general theories of fairness we discussed in Chapter 16 provide any guidance? The ability-to-pay approach suggests that two families (with the same number of children and with both parents working) with the same income ought to pay the same taxes. Since the costs of two individuals living together are much lower than twice the costs of two individuals living singly, the ability-to-pay approach would suggest that whenever two individuals cohabit, they should be subjected to higher taxation than if they live singly. Unfortunately, the tax authorities cannot easily monitor cohabitation; so long as the vast majority of cohabitators are married, and so long as most married individuals live together, basing taxes on whether individuals are married (which is relatively easy to ascertain) rather than on whether they cohabit (which is not easy to ascertain) does not create too many inequities. Thus, provided the distortionary effects of the marriage tax are not too large (and there is little evidence to suggest that many individuals' decisions are strongly affected), the present tax structure may not be unreasonable.

The utilitarian view attempts to ascertain how the family circumstances in which individuals find themselves affect their marginal utility of income.

In both the utilitarian and ability-to-pay approaches, one might want to distinguish between the family with two workers and that with one worker. Assume the families have the same total income. The current tax system treats the two alike. Yet the family with both individuals working has to purchase many services that the nonworking spouse provides free. Both those who believe in ability to pay and in utilitarianism might well argue that the family with two working individuals should pay a lower tax than the family with one worker.

The Tax Reform Act of 1986 affected the size of the marriage penalty in two ways. First, the magnitude of the marriage penalty depends greatly on the degree of progressivity. The reduction of the maximum marginal tax rate to only 33 percent, and the fact that most working individuals are either at a marginal tax rate of 15 percent, 28 percent, or 33 percent has reduced the size of the marriage penalty.

On the other hand, the old tax law allowed the deduction of 10 percent of the income of the spouse with the lower income (with a maximum deduction of $3,000). This provision has now been eliminated. For most couples, the first effect is, however, more important, and the 1986 Tax Reform Act has reduced the marriage penalty.

CHILD-CARE PROBLEMS

The problem of designing a tax system that is fair to families under different circumstances is exacerbated by the presence of children. The tax credit for child-care that we discussed earlier is designed to reduce the inequities and inefficiencies that arise when both individuals work and someone must be hired to take care of the children.

Present tax law allows a credit on up to $2,400 of child-care expenses if there is one child, or $4,800 if there are two or more children, for households in which both parents work. If a woman with a child goes to work and has to pay someone to take care of her child, her *net* income, measuring her ability to pay, is just the difference between what she receives and what she must pay out. If she receives $15,000 and must pay out $5,000 in child-care expenses, her net income is only $10,000. Not allowing the deduction of these expenses creates strong distortions. Assume the woman is married, and as a result of her husband's income is in the 33 percent bracket. If she pays $5,000 for child care, her total increase in spending income (after taxes) is less than $5,000. Not only is she thereby discouraged from taking the job, it seems a grossly unfair reward for working. Allowing a credit of $480 (= .20 × $2,400) goes only a little way toward fully alleviating the distortions or correcting the inequities.

The problems—both the inequities and the distortions—arise from the inability to measure (and therefore to tax) the household services provided within the family. Here, the failure to tax the "imputed" value of household services discriminates against the purchase of those services in the market.

In designing the child-care tax credit, the government was apparently more concerned about equity considerations than about efficiency. A deduction for child-care expenses would have benefited upper-income individuals more than lower-income individuals. But the distortion—in deciding whether to enter the labor force or not—is higher among individuals who face higher marginal tax rates; the present tax system leaves a significant distortion for families who face tax rates of 28 or 33 percent.

Decisions concerning the tax treatment of child-care expenditures have not only economic consequences; these decisions reflect, and have consequences for, social values and family structure. Family life where both parents work is different from that where the woman remains at home. A tax system that penalizes women who enter the marketplace may be thought to reflect and perpetuate a particular set of attitudes concerning the role of women. A tax system that encourages women to enter the labor force may have adverse effects on family structure, and, in particular, on the educational attainments of children.[14]

[14] These effects have been a subject of increasing concern, both to academics and politicians. New York Senator Patrick Moynihan (formerly a professor at Harvard) has repeatedly articulated these concerns. The Senate subcommittee of which he is chairman has had its name altered from the Subcommittee on Social Security to that of "Social Security and Family Policy."

University of Chicago's James Coleman, one of the country's leading sociologists, addressed these

THE ADVANTAGES OF A FLAT-RATE TAX SCHEDULE

There is one—and only one—way of avoiding the inequities surrounding the choice of unit of taxation. That is to impose a **flat-rate tax schedule.** If all individuals pay a proportional tax on income in excess of a basic exemption level (and those with an income below this exemption level receive a cash payment from the government), there is no penalty and no reward for marriage, and no reward for divorce. We shall see later, in Chapter 25, that a flat-rate schedule also reduces the seriousness of many other problems we have noted in this chapter.

AVERAGE AND MARGINAL TAX RATES: A CLOSER LOOK

The net impact of the variety of special provisions we have discussed in this chapter is that effective average tax rates (the ratio of tax payments to a measure of full income) are less than those legislated, and the degree of progressivity is also less. Under the old tax law, the differences between the legislated rates and the effective rates were large as a result of various special deductions and credits and the partial exemption of capital gains. As we suggested earlier, the 1986 Tax Reform Act has reduced, but not eliminated, the discrepancies.

It is important to realize, however, that though the effective average tax rate may be much lower than the nominal rate, the effective marginal tax rate may not be that much different from (and in some cases it may be higher than) the nominal rate. To see how this could happen, consider a divorced individual who earns \$26,000, has two children, and pays \$4,800 in child-care expenses, \$2,000 in interest payments, \$500 in drug expenses, and \$4,000 in other medical expenses. When his income rises by \$2,001, the amount he is allowed to deduct for medical expenses is reduced and his child-care credit is also reduced. The net effect is that while at his income level, he should be paying a marginal tax rate of 15 percent, his actual marginal tax rate is more than 21 percent (see Table 21.5). (This excludes state taxes and social security, which will make his marginal tax rate even higher.) As we have repeatedly emphasized, the distortions in any tax system are associated with the marginal tax rates.

SUMMARY

1. The U.S. income tax system is based on the principle that taxes should be related progressively to the family's cash (marketed) annual income. The tax code discriminates in favor of nonmarket transactions and against those with fluctuating income.
2. There are problems in implementing an income tax system, both in defining income and determining the time at which the tax should be imposed. A principal difficulty encountered in defining income is distinguishing activities

concerns in his invited lecture before the American Educational Research Association, "Families and Schools," Washington, D.C., April 1987.

Table 21.5 TAX LAWS MAKE AVERAGE TAX RATES LOW, WHILE MARGINAL TAX RATES ARE HIGH

Calculation of Taxes		*Initially*			*After $2,001 Pay Raise*	
Adjusted gross income			26,000			28,001
Drugs	500			500		
less 1% of adjusted gross income	260			280		
Equals deduction for drugs		240			220	
Other medical expenses	4,000			4,000		
less 7.5% adjusted gross income	1,950			2,100		
Equals deduction for medical expenses		2,050			1,900	
Interest		2,000			2,000	
Total deductions			4,290			4,120
Personal exemptions			6,000			6,000
Taxable income			15,710			17,881
Tax			2,356			2,682
Child-care tax credit						
22 percent of $4,800			1,056			
20 percent of $4,800						960
Net tax liability			1,300			1,722
Average tax rate			5.0%			6.1%
Change in tax liability						$422
Ratio of change in tax liability to change in income						21.1%
Legislated Marginal Tax Rate						15.0%

that are motivated by business considerations from ordinary consumption activities.

3. Many of the problems associated with designing a workable income tax system arise from the unobservability (or costs of observing) the essential variables, e.g., of knowing whether some medical procedure was really "necessary."
4. The tax code allows a number of adjustments to income and personal deductions, motivated both by equity and by incentive considerations. But regardless of their motivations, the deductions have both incentive and equity effects that need to be taken into account. For instance, the medical deduction effectively lowers the price of medical care; and it lowers it more for high-income individuals.
5. The basic unit of taxation in the United States (unlike most other countries) is the family. The tax system has a number of provisions that are intended to ensure that those in different family situations face equitable taxes. There is a limited tax credit for child-care expenses and different rate schedules for married couples and single individuals. Still, the current system imposes a marriage penalty on individuals with similar incomes and a marriage subsidy on individuals with very dissimilar incomes.
6. The 1986 Tax Reform Act reduced the degree of progressivity, but it did not eliminate many of the special provisions. Because of these special provisions,

such as the nontaxability of certain fringe benefits and the deduction for medical expenses, effective rates on a full measure of income are likely to remain below legislated rates; and effective marginal rates for some individuals may be considerably greater than the legislated rates.

KEY CONCEPTS

Adjusted gross income	Capital gains
Standard deduction	Realization versus accrual
Tax credits	Marriage tax
Haig-Simons income	Child-care tax credit
Cash basis	Marginal tax rate
Effective tax rate	Minimum tax

QUESTIONS AND PROBLEMS

1. For each of the provisions of the tax code listed below, which provides the best explanation: incentives; horizontal equity; vertical equity; administrative reasons; or special-interest groups?
   a) deductibility of mortgage interest
   b) deductibility of casualty losses
   c) deductibility of medical expenses
   d) deductibility of charitable contributions
   e) child-care tax credit
   f) credit on taxes paid to foreign governments
2. Discuss the arguments for and against using a tax credit rather than a deduction for: medical expenses; charitable contributions; and child-care expenses.
3. If you were asked to write the regulations concerning the deductibility of business expenses, how would you treat the following items, and why? Discuss the inequities and inefficiencies associated with alternative possible rules:
   a) educational expenses required to maintain one's current job
   b) educational expenses incurred to obtain a better job
   c) moving expenses arising from a reassignment by one's present employer
   d) moving expenses incurred in obtaining a new job
   e) business suit worn by an individual who does not wear suits except for business
   f) business lunches costing more than $25
   g) expensive cars
   h) commuting costs
   i) car expenses of a traveling salesman
   j) subsidized cafeteria lunches
4. Under the old tax law money that scientists received from winning the Nobel Prize (or similar prizes) was not taxable. Now it is. Which treatment do you think is appropriate? Under both the old and the new tax law, money received by lottery winners (as well as gambling receipts) is taxable, while the losses are not deductible. Is this fair? What distortions does this introduce?

5. Do you think that the current tax treatment of children is fair? (There is a $2,000 exemption for each child beginning in 1989. Thus individuals in higher tax brackets have their taxes reduced more by having an additional child than do individuals in lower tax brackets.) Should the exemptions be related to the cost of rearing a child, which will depend on the income of the parent? Does your answer depend on whether you think the appropriate basis of taxation is ability to pay? On whether you think that the current population of the United States is too small? Too large?
6. Discuss the efficiency and equity consequences of:
   a) not allowing the deduction of expenses on summer vacation homes for the ten months a year when the owner puts the house up for rent. Is this a "legitimate" business?
   b) not allowing the deduction of commuting expenses
   c) not allowing the deduction of educational expenses incurred to change one's profession (e.g., from accountant to tax lawyer)

   In each case, consider what would happen if the current rules were modified. Can you suggest modifications that would make the rules seem "fairer" or more efficient?

22

The Taxation of Capital

The United States, like most other countries, imposes a wide variety of taxes on the return to savings; that is, on the interest individuals receive on their bank accounts, the dividends they receive on their stocks, and the capital gains they receive from the sale of their assets. States and communities often impose taxes on property. When rich individuals die, what they leave to their descendants is taxed. The income of corporations, partly a return on the capital that is invested in the corporate sector, is taxed. We refer to all of these taxes as taxes on capital.

Some have attributed the slowdown of growth in the United States over the past decade to the oppressive effects of the taxation of capital. It is alleged that such taxes have discouraged savings, investment, and risk taking. Furthermore, these taxes have a number of elaborate provisions that enable those who can afford good tax lawyers and accountants to avoid, not only most of their taxes on capital income, but also some of the taxes they otherwise would have faced on their wage income. Many economists believe that the inequities and inefficiencies that we associate with capital income taxation are for the most part the consequence of these special provisions. Others believe that the inequities and inefficiencies arise from the inherent difficulties in measuring capital income. Some of these economists argue for the abolition of taxation of capital.

The two most important taxes on the return to capital are the individual income tax and the corporation income tax.[1] This chapter focuses on

[1] As we shall see in the next chapter, the extent to which the corporation tax should be viewed as a tax on capital is debatable.

the individual income tax, though many of the central issues, such as those relating to **depreciation** (as capital goods get older, they may wear out or become obsolete; they depreciate in value; the allowances made by the tax law for this are called **depreciation allowances**) are equally applicable to the corporation income tax, which we examine in the next chapter.

DEFINITION OF INCOME FROM CAPITAL

In our study of the U.S. income tax in the last chapter, we noted the problems of defining income. Indeed, the most difficult problem in taxing income from capital is defining income from capital, and, in particular, ascertaining "when" the income was created. In Chapter 21, we stressed the importance of timing: individuals and firms are always interested in postponing taxes; a dollar of taxes paid tomorrow is less costly than a dollar of taxes paid today.

Assume an individual has his tax liability reduced by $100 this year and increased by $100 next year. He could have taken the $100 in tax savings, invested it, and earned, say, an extra $5 (after he pays any tax on the interest). After he pays his tax next year, he will still have the $5 extra to keep. The present discounted value of $100 next period is only $100 divided by 1.05 (one plus the interest rate); that is, the individual is indifferent between receiving $100/1.05 today or $100 tomorrow. The reason he is indifferent is that he can take the $100/1.05, invest it at 5 percent, and end up with precisely $100. We thus say that the present discounted value of the tax payment is smaller if the individual can postpone the tax.

Important issues of definition of income and timing arise in determining depreciation allowances and in taxing capital gains and pensions.

Depreciation

Consider a machine that lasts for three years, costs $1,000, and yields $400 each year. Surely, one would not want to impose a tax on $400 each year; indeed, the total *net* income of the individual over the three-year period is only $200 ($1,200 minus the original $1,000 investment). In defining **net income** for purposes of income taxation, one needs to take into account the fact that the machine wears out in the process of producing output. In our example, we know that the machine will be totally worn out after three years. We say that the machine will have fully depreciated in value. Thus, over the three-year life of the machine, we need to provide $1,000 in depreciation allowances. The question is one of timing.

The *correct* way of doing so would be to attempt to ascertain the value of the machine at the end of the first year, and at the end of the second year. We know the value at the end of the third year is zero. The decrease in the value of the machine from the time it is purchased until the end of the first year should be the first year's depreciation allowance; the decrease in value during the second year should be the second year's depreciation allowance, and the decrease in value during the third year should be the third year's depreciation allowance. This is referred to as **true economic depreciation.**

In fact, however, there are often no markets for used machines in which we can value a one-year-old or two-year-old machine. We cannot easily observe the true decrease in the value of the machine. Accordingly, the government must *impute* how the machine's value decreases over its lifetime.

The simplest rule for the government to use would be to assume that a three-year-old machine loses one-third of its value in each year, or a machine that lives for N years loses $1/N$ of its value. This is referred to as **straight-line depreciation.**

For many capital goods, straight-line depreciation represents a faster depreciation of the asset than true economic depreciation; that is, more of the depreciation allowances are allowed in the early years of the investment than would be allowed under true economic depreciation, so that the present discounted value of tax liabilities is smaller than it would be under true economic depreciation.

ACCELERATED DEPRECIATION

Since 1954, the government has allowed firms to depreciate capital goods at a still faster rate. It has done this by allowing individual firms to depreciate their assets over a shorter period than their actual lives, and by allowing them to take still more of the depreciation allowances in the early years. There is, in other words, **accelerated depreciation.**

Under the post-1986 accelerated depreciation rules, machines are placed into several categories, depending on their expected life;[2] as Table 22.1 shows, in all cases, the period over which the asset is depreciated is considerably shorter than the life of the asset.

In addition, under the 1986 Tax Reform Act, firms have been allowed to depreciate their machines at a much faster rate than straight-line depreciation (and indeed, at a faster rate than they had been allowed to depreciate assets under the old law).[3] For three- and five-year assets, the depreciation allowances are given in Table 22.2.

While the 1981 law, the last major revision of the tax code prior to 1986, said that buildings should be depreciated over fifteen years, it was subsequently felt that this was far too generous; now real estate is depreciated over approximately thirty years.

[2] Certain categories of assets are assigned to depreciation categories that enable them to be depreciated at rates faster than other assets of comparable lifetimes. Thus railroad tracks are placed in the seven-year category, waste-water treatment plants in the fifteen-year category, and municipal sewers in the twenty-year category.

[3] The depreciation system is called Modified Accelerated Cost Recovery System (MACRS) and uses a rule called "200 percent declining balance." If n is the asset life, then the depreciation allowance is $2/n$ multiplied by the *book value* of the asset. In the first year, the book value is just the asset's original cost, but in later years it is original cost less all previous years' depreciation allowances. The book value declines each year, and that is why the annual depreciation allowance also declines. In the last few years of the life of the asset, depreciation allowances switch to straight line.

Table 22.1 DEPRECIATION PERIODS FOR ASSETS WITH DIFFERENT LIFETIMES

Expected lifetime	*Period over which the asset is to be depreciated*
Less than five years	*3*
5–9	*5*
10–15	*7*
16–19	*10*
20–24	*15*
25 or more	*20*

Table 22.2 DEPRECIATION ALLOWANCES FOR THREE-, FIVE-, AND SEVEN-YEAR ASSETS*

	3-Year Asset	*5-Year Asset*	*7-Year Asset*
1.	*33%*	*20%*	*14.3%*
2.	*45*	*32*	*24.5*
3.	*15*	*19.2*	*17.5*
4.	*7*	*11.5*	*12.5*
5.		*11.5*	*8.9*
6.		*5.8*	*8.9*
7.			*8.9*
8.			*4.5*

* The reason that the first year's depreciation allowance is less than subsequent years' is that the tax authorities assume that the machine was bought halfway through the year (regardless of when it was actually bought). Thus, under straight-line depreciation, a three-year asset would have a depreciation allowance of 16 2/3 percent, in contrast with the accelerated depreciation allowance of 33 percent.

The impact of these accelerated depreciation allowances can be seen in Table 22.3. There, we consider an asset that has a five-year lifetime and costs $100 but that the government allows to be depreciated in three years. The asset is assumed to yield a constant amount each year ($24) and to have no salvage value after five years. The interest rate is assumed to be 10 percent. In the first column of Table 22.3 we show the true economic depreciation, in the second the present discounted value of these depreciation allowances (as viewed at the time of purchase). The third and fourth columns show straight-line depreciation, and the fifth and sixth columns show depreciation under the current system. It is clear that there is a very large subsidy.

Table 22.3 COMPARISON OF TRUE ECONOMIC DEPRECIATION, STRAIGHT-LINE DEPRECIATION, AND DEPRECIATION UNDER THE CURRENT TAX LAW

Year	*Discount Factor (10% interest rate)*	*1 True Economic Depreciation*	*2 Present Value*	*3 Straight Line*	*4 Present Value*	*5 Current System*	*6 Present Value*
1	1	16	16	20	20	33	33
2	$1/(1.10) = .909$	18	16.36	20	18.18	45	40.9
3	$1/(1.10)^2 = .826$	20	16.52	20	16.52	15	12.4
4	$1/(1.10)^3 = .751$	22	16.52	20	15.02	7	5.3
5	$1/(1.10)^4 = .683$	24	16.39	20	13.65		
			81.79		83.37		91.6

Far more disturbing, however, is the fact that the magnitude of the subsidy varies greatly from one asset to another. For some assets the current system is only slightly favorable; but for long-lived assets it provides a major subsidy.

As a result, not only are some assets favored over others, but industries that use the favored assets gain at the expense of those that use the less-favored assets.

To those who advocated the introduction of these accelerated depreciation allowances, this difference is not a fault but a virtue. The depreciation allowances were designed to benefit "smokestack America," the industrial heart of America—including its automobile and steel industries—which, in the perception of many, had been lagging during the past decade.

Critics of accelerated depreciation provisions claim that they represent an inefficient (and politically irresponsible, because it is so hidden) subsidy; they claim that the subsidies have been ineffective in rekindling older American industries. They argue, moreover, that America should build on its current strengths, and if these are not in the steel and automobile industries, so much the worse for these industries. The government should, perhaps, assist in the transitional movement of workers from declining industries to the growing ones (as the Swedish government does, for instance); but it should not attempt to shore up these declining industries.

The Tax Reform Act of 1986 was intended, in part, to reduce tax-induced distortions in the allocation of investment. It eliminated, for instance, the **investment tax credit,** which allowed firms to take a credit of 10 percent of the value of long-lived machines or 6 percent of short-lived machines. The investment tax credit meant the government was, in effect, paying for 10 percent of the cost of any long-lived machine. So powerful was this provision when combined with the accelerated depreciation allowances that the effective tax rate on many capital goods was zero or negative. The provisions for accelerated depreciation were, however, retained, and hence there remain important tax-induced distortions in the allocation of investment.[4]

NEUTRAL TAXATION

To achieve neutrality in the choice of investment projects, the government has two options. One we have already described: it would allow true economic depreciation allowances (or at least attempt to devise rules that more closely approximate true economic depreciation).

The second method entails the government allowing a 100 percent deduction for the cost of the investment. Then the government is reducing the costs of the project by exactly the same amount (for most individual investors, 28 percent) that it is reducing the benefits (the returns

[4] In addition, there remain a variety of other distortions, to be discussed below, such as between owner-occupied housing and other investment opportunities.

that the investor receives). The government is, in effect, entering as a silent partner into the enterprise. A project for which the present discounted value of returns exceeds the cost—which therefore would have been undertaken in the absence of the tax—will still be undertaken.

While the first method corresponds to a neutral capital income tax (i.e., one that does not distort the choice of investment projects), the second method corresponds to a neutral pure profits tax: the difference between the present discounted value of the returns to an investment project and its costs can be thought of as pure profits.[5]

Capital Gains

Capital gains present the second important problem in the definition of income from capital. While depreciation allowances are intended to reflect decreases in the value of an asset as it is used, here we are concerned with increases in the market value of assets. The treatment of capital gains raises problems that are not so much conceptual as operational: for many assets, we cannot measure the capital gain until the asset is actually sold. Though for stocks and bonds listed on the New York Exchange market, one could impose a tax on capital gains as they occur, there is concern that doing so would disadvantage those assets relative to others. Thus, capital gains are taxed only upon *realization*. Again, the issue is one of timing: by postponing the tax, the present discounted value of the tax is reduced.

THE LOCKED-IN EFFECT

The fact that capital gains are taxed only upon realization gives rise to an important distortion, referred to as the **locked-in effect.** Because capital gains are taxed only upon realization, an individual who owns a security that has increased in value may be reluctant to sell it. He knows that if he sells it he will have to pay a tax. If he continues to hold the asset, he can postpone the tax until some later date. The present discounted value of his tax liabilities is reduced by the postponement of the tax. The individual is thus induced to hold on to his securities rather than to sell them. This is referred to as the locked-in effect.

The consequences of this may easily be seen. Assume that an individual had bought a security at $1, and that it suddenly rose to $101. He now expects that it will earn a return lower than the return he could obtain elsewhere. Assume, for instance, that he believes that there is another investment opportunity that could earn a return of 10 percent. In the absence of taxation, he would simply sell his security and buy the new investment.

Consider now what happens if he sells his stock. He must immediately

[5] Some of the return may be attributed to managerial efforts, in which case the difference between the present discounted value of the returns and the *direct* costs (excluding those associated with management) are a mixture of pure profits and return to management and entrepreneurship.

pay a capital gains tax. Assume he is in the 33 percent tax bracket. He must pay a tax of \$33. He would thus have only \$68 to reinvest.

Assume he believes he will need money in one year's time. His after-tax yield in the new investment is $(1 - .33) \times 10\% = 6.7\%$. In one year's time he will thus have $\$68 \times 1.067 = \$72.56$. On the other hand, if he keeps his \$101 in the old investment for one more year, and it increases in value at only 8 percent, he will have $\$101 \times 1.08 = \$109.08$. He must pay a capital gains tax of 33 percent on his gain (that is, his tax is $.33 \times \$108.08 = \$35.67$). Thus, after tax he has \$73.41. He is better off with his money yielding a return of only 8 percent in his current asset than he would be if he sold his asset and purchased an asset yielding a much higher return of 10 percent.

CONSEQUENCES AND IMPORTANCE OF THE LOCKED-IN EFFECT

There is considerable debate about the consequences and importance of this locked-in effect. Martin Feldstein, former Chairman of the Council of Economic Advisers, has claimed that the effect is so large that reducing the capital gains tax would lead individuals to sell securities that they previously had refused to sell, to such an extent that government revenues would actually increase.[6]

Critics of this view, while questioning the statistical studies upon which Feldstein reached his conclusions, point out that this is only a short-run revenue gain; the taxes that individuals pay now will not be paid later. There may be a short-run gain, but little or no change in government revenues in the long run. Moreover, because the reduction in the tax makes individuals better off, the tax may lead to an increase in current consumption and a decrease in aggregate savings at the same time that current government revenues are increased.

There are further debates about the welfare consequences of the locked-in effect. Much of the discussion has focused on individuals' purchases of securities. Economic efficiency requires that each security be held by the individual who values it the most, who thinks that it will yield the highest return.[7] The locked-in effect means that an individual may retain a security, even though there is someone else who values it more. This results in what is referred to as **exchange inefficiency.** There are some economists, however, who believe that the economic consequences of this should not be taken too seriously. They argue that the stock market is essentially a rich man's gambling casino and that though the locked-in effect may impair the efficiency of this gambling casino, it has few further repercussions for the economy. There is not, in this view, a very direct or strong relationship between the effect of the capital gains tax on the performance of the stock market and the decisions

[6] M. S. Feldstein, J. Slemrod, and S. Yitzhaki, "The Effects of Taxing on Selling and Switching of Common Stock and the Realization of Capital Gains," *Quarterly Journal of Economics* 94 (1980): 777–91.

[7] We define economic efficiency in the usual sense of Pareto efficiency. In the presence of risk, however, there is some question about the appropriate way of measuring the welfare of each individual. The sense in which we use the term here is in terms of the individual's own expectations concerning the outcome, regardless of the objective reality of those expectations.

made by the managers and owners of firms concerning, for instance, their investment and production.

The one area in which the capital gains tax may have a significant effect on the production efficiency of the economy is in smaller, owner-managed firms. There comes a point in the life cycle of such firms where the original owner-manager's skills and talents become less appropriate for the development of the firm. In the absence of capital gains taxation, the original owner-manager might like to sell his firm to some other entrepreneurs, but he is discouraged from doing so because of the high cost imposed by the capital gains tax.

Pensions and Retirement Income

Today, most employers have pension programs providing income to their employees upon retirement. Here, the central problem in defining income from capital is once again one of timing. Consider an individual who uses $1,000 of his before-tax income to save for his retirement. If his marginal tax rate is 28 percent, then he saves $720 after taxes and puts it in the bank for his retirement in twenty years. If the interest rate is 10 percent, his after-tax return will be 7.2 percent. When he retires he will receive with compound interest—that is, taking into account the interest he will earn on his interest—$2,892 ($720 \times 1.072^{20}$).

Consider now what would have happened if his employers, instead of paying the $1,000 directly, had put it into a bank account under the employee's name, but with the restriction that he could not take it out until he retired. This is the way pension plans work. Under current law, a tax is imposed only when the money is taken out. Thus, by the time the employee has retired, his account will have grown, again as a result of compound interest, to $\$1,000 \times 1.1^{20} = \$6,728$; and after he pays a 28 percent tax on that amount, he will still have $4,844, considerably more than in the case where he undertook the savings directly. There seems no good reason for the difference in treatment. In the second case, the individual actually *earned* $1,000 in 1987, although he would not receive the money until twenty years later. If we wish to have an income tax, the money should be taxed in the year in which it is earned.

But matters are never quite so simple as they seem. First, the employee might claim that $1,000 tied up in an account that he cannot use until he retires is not worth as much as $1,000 cash in the hand, which he can do with as he pleases. Surely then, he claims, he should not be taxed as if the two were the same.

Secondly, the employee's retirement program may have a proviso that if he quits before working for an additional five years, he loses all (or a portion) of his retirement benefit. Now, the $1,000 that is put into an account for his benefit is not really his at all. Should he be taxed when he has earned it (i.e., when it is put into his account) or five years later, when he is sure that he will get it?

Thirdly, most pension plans are still more complicated. They do not set aside a certain amount for the individual, but rather provide for a pension that is related, by a complicated formula, to the length of service and the pay of the individual, with particular emphasis on the pay in the last few years. Working for the firm this year, he may clearly have a higher pension than he otherwise would; but it is a difficult matter to determine—today—how much of his future pension should be attributed to this year's work, and thus, how much in total he has earned this year. These complexities are so great that the tax authorities do not even attempt to allocate to an employee's current income a portion of employer contributions to the firm's pension plan. Instead, they impose a tax on pensions only when they are received.

This raises both equity and efficiency issues. First, this tax treatment encourages savings through pension plans. Secondly, it creates an inequity between the individual who has saved on his own account, and the individual who has an employer who saves on his behalf. The significance of this kind of inequity is of some dispute: in the long run, firms will respond to the incentives provided by the tax system. Still, there is an inequity associated with the self-employed. And employer pension plans often do not have the flexibility of allowing those who wish to save more for their retirement to do so. Congress responded to these concerns by adopting three programs. First, it allowed the self-employed to put money into retirement plans of their own design (called **Keogh plans**), with the contributions being tax-deductible, and taxes on the return being imposed only when the money is withdrawn from the account. Second, it allowed firms to establish a kind of flexible account, into which individuals could make discretionary contributions (up to some relatively high maximum), with again the contributions being tax-deductible and a tax being imposed only at the time of the withdrawal of funds.

Thirdly, it established **Independent Retirement Accounts** (IRAs), into which an employee or self-employed individual could contribute a maximum of $2,000 per year, or $2,250 if he had a nonworking spouse. Eligibility standards for IRAs have varied over time. In 1981, eligibility was extended to virtually all working individuals, but the 1986 Tax Reform Act severely restricted it: higher-income individuals covered by employer-provided pension plans are no longer eligible for the IRA deduction.[8]

The way IRAs work is simple. The individual just subtracts the amount he contributes to this account from his gross income tax. So long as the money remains in the IRA account, the individual does not have to pay any tax on the interest that accumulates. The individual is allowed to take money out of the IRA when he turns fifty-nine (or at any time before that, provided he pays a 10 percent penalty). He is then taxed on the money he takes out.

[8] Money previously contributed to these accounts will still be taxed only upon withdrawal; in other words, the tax on the return on this capital is still deferred. Moreover, the higher-income individuals covered by employer-provided pension schemes can continue to make contributions as before; although those contributions will not be tax deductible, taxes on the return to this capital will be deferred until the funds are withdrawn.

The tax benefits provided for pensions, Keogh plans, and IRAs are equivalent to a tax exemption for the interest earned on these accounts. To see this, consider the tax liabilities of an individual who saves \$100 in one of these programs and then retires in two years. For simplicity, we assume his marginal tax rate both now and at retirement is 33 percent. His savings earn, say, 10 percent per year, so that at the end of the first year he has \$110, and at the end of the second year \$121. He then pays 33 percent tax. His total after-tax income is \$81.07.

Now consider what would have happened if the government had simply exempted interest income. The \$100 would have been taxed at the time he received it at 33 percent, leaving \$67, which he would have invested. At the end of the first year he would have had \$73.70. Since interest income would be exempt, he would be able to reinvest the entire amount, yielding, at the end of the second year, \$81.07. In general, if r is the before-tax interest rate and t is the marginal tax rate, then \$100 deposited in a tax-deferred saving plan yields \$100 $(1 + r)^2$ in two years. Upon withdrawal, a tax is due, and we are left with \$100 $(1 + r)^2 (1 - t)$. If, alternatively, the savings deduction *and* the tax on interest are both abolished, \$100 of before-tax income becomes \$100 $(1 - t)$ of savings, which in two years yields \$100 $(1 - t)(1 + r)^2$, just the same as in the first case.

On the other hand, many individuals have a lower income when they retire than when they worked and thus are subject to lower tax rates at retirement. The current system allows income that is used in retirement to be taxed at the lower marginal rates prevalent then.

Our present tax structure allows, in most cases, preferential treatment on savings only for retirement. Other savings are not tax-deferred. However, because the penalties are sufficiently low (at interest rates of 10 percent or more) it pays most individuals to save through these tax-deferred methods even if they plan to hold their savings only for several years.

Inflation

Inflation presents several difficult problems in the definition of income from capital. One wants to tax *real* returns to capital, not nominal returns. If an individual owns an asset, and it increases in value by 10 percent, but prices in general have gone up by 10 percent, the individual is no better off. His **real capital gain** is zero, even though his **nominal capital gain** is positive. Similarly, consider an individual who puts \$1,000 in a savings account and receives \$100 in interest. If the rate of inflation is 10 percent, the *real return* is zero. The \$100 in interest is just enough to compensate him for the decrease in the real value of his savings account.

By the same token, inflation reduces the *real value* of the depreciation allowances, which are tied to the nominal price that the individual or the firm paid for the asset and it does so much more for long-lived assets than for short-lived assets. In the late 1970s and early 1980s, the United

States went through a period of high inflation, with annual rates of price increases exceeding 10 percent. (This was low by standards in other countries, where in extraordinary cases inflation rates have exceeded 100 percent per month.) It became clear that when inflation rates were high, our tax system did not treat returns to capital in a fair or efficient manner.

The tax system taxes nominal returns, not real returns. Thus, the first consequence of the presence of inflation is that individuals who have a small positive before-tax real return on capital find that they have a large negative after-tax real return.

Consider an individual in the 33 percent tax bracket, receiving a 12 percent return (say, in the form of interest) with an inflation rate of 10 percent. Most of the return in periods of high inflation is just an adjustment for the decreased purchasing power of money. His real return is only 2 percent. (The real rate of return on an asset is the nominal return minus the rate of inflation.) But the present tax laws do not take account of this. This individual would have to pay 33 percent of the nominal return to the government (ignoring state and local income taxes), leaving him a net after-tax return of 8 percent. With inflation, his real return is 8 percent −10 percent = −2 percent. He loses 2 percent of his ability to consume simply by postponing consumption by one year. One would expect that this would serve as a strong discouragement to savings.

Between 1974 and 1982 the price of stock was doing little more than keeping up with inflation (and in many cases not even doing that). But since the price level doubled, individuals found themselves paying a large capital gains tax if they sold their shares. Again, this seemed unfair. The attempt to correct for this by excluding 60 percent of capital gains —as was done prior to the 1986 Tax Reform Act—seemed a particularly rough adjustment. It would be no more difficult to have only real capital gains taxed: only increases in price in excess of the rate of inflation would be taxed. If inflation rates once again return to the high levels of the late 1970s, the present system under which nominal capital gains are taxed at full rates will be viewed to be excessively inequitable and distortionary; some change in the tax structure will be almost inevitable.

There has been strong support for indexing tax brackets, and the 1986 tax law provides for indexing of tax brackets, as well as for indexing the standard deduction and personal exemptions. As a result, the income levels at which taxpayers become subject to higher tax rates will increase with the price level. Far more complicated than indexing the tax brackets, however, is designing the tax system so that only real returns to capital are taxed. Not only must capital gains be indexed, but so must interest payments, as well as interest receipts and depreciation. Thus, investors who have borrowed money would be able to deduct only their real interest payments, not their nominal interest payments. If capital gains were indexed, but interest payments were not indexed, individuals would find it profitable in inflationary times to borrow to purchase capital assets that were increasing in value at the same rate as the rate of inflation.

Indeed, there has been some controversy over whether the tax system encouraged or discouraged investment in the inflationary period of the late 1970s. On the one hand, the fact that nominal interest payments were fully tax-deductible while 60 percent of capital gains was tax-exempt created, in some cases, effective subsidies to capital. On the other hand, the fact that depreciation allowances were not indexed served to discourage investment.

It is apparent that our current tax system is not inflation-neutral; that as a result of inflation, in some circumstances, assets with a positive before-tax return have a negative after-tax return, discouraging investment, while in other cases, the tax system encourages investment.

What is required to obtain an inflation-neutral tax system is full indexation. Partial indexation of capital income (such as indexing capital gains but not debt) would exacerbate some of the distortions and would leave other distortions unchanged.

SPECIAL TREATMENT OF CAPITAL INCOME

In the preceding section, we saw how problems of defining and measuring income from capital give rise to a number of difficulties. The tax law has to specify how assets are to be depreciated, when to tax capital gains, and how to tax pensions. In each case, the resolution of these problems has been to give the taxpayer at least some "benefit of the doubt": depreciation is accelerated, capital gains are taxed only upon realization, and pensions are taxed only when the income is received.

The tax code contains still more provisions for treating income from capital favorably.

Housing

The most important investment for the majority of individuals is a home. The return to this asset—the housing service it provides—is not taxed in the United States.

In spite of the fact that the returns to housing—the housing services or imputed rent—are not taxed, money that individuals borrow to purchase houses (the interest on their mortgages) is tax deductible; indeed, under the new tax law, this is the only form of consumer interest that is tax deductible.

Housing is favored in still one more way: the tax on capital gains on owner-occupied dwellings is deferred if the individual repurchases a house at least equal in value (called a rollover provision); and if the individual is over fifty-five, he is only taxed on the capital gain in excess of $125,000.[9]

As a result of these provisions, a capital gains liability is incurred on only a small fraction of house sales.

[9] He can only take advantage of this provision once.

The reason that the imputed rent on owner-occupied housing is not taxed has already been discussed: the difficulties of imputing what the return is. But this is probably not the only reason. The tax laws reflect the values of our society, and there is a strong belief that it is good for individuals to own their own home (perhaps an extension of the Jeffersonian ideal that America should be a country of small landholders). Individuals who own their own home may be more likely to feel a member of the community and to participate as constructive citizens. It was considerations such as these—as well as the lobbying of the new home construction industry—that were dominant in retaining the favorable treatment of housing under the 1986 Tax Reform Act.

Interest on State and Municipal Bonds

Interest on state and municipal bonds is tax-exempt. These may include bonds used by municipalities to finance schools and by states to finance roads; industrial revenue bonds, which raise funds that are re-lent to businesses located in the town; and community-issued bonds which raise funds to be re-lent for mortgages for lower- and middle-income individuals. Some states have set up special agencies to borrow funds to finance dormitories at private as well as state universities, to build sports complexes, and to construct hospitals.

The original motivation for the interest exemption was a concern about the constitutionality of taxing interest on state and local bonds. But the expansion of this provision to include bonds issued by municipalities for money to re-lend to private individuals was clearly viewed as a form of federal subsidy to the localities. Many municipalities took up this federal subsidy with such enthusiasm that in recent years severe curbs have been imposed on the issuance of tax-exempt bonds.

Other Special Provisions

There are a host of other provisions related to particular sources of capital income. Over the years, the oil and gas industry has benefited from a number of special provisions.

We noted earlier that prior to the 1986 Tax Reform Act, capital gains were only partially taxable. Not surprisingly, many industries attempted to have their income treated as if it were capital gains. Cattle and timber succeeded. The value to the timber industry of this special treatment was estimated in 1986, the last year before the new tax law took effect, to exceed $400 million.[10]

Even under the new tax law, favorable treatment is granted to certain types of low-income housing investments.

[10] Source: *Special Analyses of the United States Budget, Fiscal Year 1987*, Table G–2.

SOME EXPLANATIONS FOR THE COMPLEXITY OF CAPITAL TAXATION

Why is the taxation of capital so complicated? Part of the complexity stems from attempts to design an equitable and efficient tax structure, and part of it arises from the political processes by which the tax structure is determined.

Administrative Costs

Much of the return to capital is not taxed or is taxed in a favorable way because of the costs of ascertaining what the returns are or to whom they accrue.

We have emphasized the importance of these difficulties in the taxation of capital gains, in the determination of depreciation allowances, in the taxation of the imputed return to owner-occupied housing, and in the taxation of pensions.

Horizontal Equity and Efficiency

In several of these instances, there were closely related categories of assets for which the returns were observable, where the problems of the definition of income would not arise, and where taxes could be imposed with relatively low administrative costs. But to do so would introduce horizontal inequities and distortions.

Thus, it would be possible to tax pension plans where a contribution is made into an account under the individual's name (so-called defined contribution plans). But to tax these pension schemes and not others seems inequitable and would be distortionary; firms simply would not employ defined contribution plans were they the only kinds of pensions that were taxed.

But then equitable treatment of those who are self-employed, in comparison with those who are employed by firms with pensions, requires that the self-employed be able to provide tax-deferred pensions for themselves. Keogh plans allow for this. But what, then, of the individual who works for a firm that does not have a pension plan? And what of the individual's spouse who stays at home? She or he could be thought of as being employed by the individual, and was it not equally important for her or him to put aside money for old age?[11] Thus, the IRA was born.

Similarly, though it is virtually impossible to tax the gains on many assets as they accrue, there are some assets for which it is possible to do so (marketable securities). But to tax these assets and not nonmarketed assets would introduce an inequity and a distortion.

[11] This inequity in not allowing homemakers to set aside money for their retirement in tax-free accounts is perhaps more apparent than real: homemakers are also not taxed on their imputed income (the income that they would receive were they performing similar services in the marketplace).

Incentive Effects

Congress has been persuaded, from time to time, to attempt to encourage savings (by exempting interest income in certain instances); to encourage investment in general (by the investment tax credit and accelerated depreciation allowances); to encourage risk taking (one of the objectives of the special treatment of capital gains prior to 1986); and to encourage particular types of investments (in research and development, low-income housing, and oil and gas exploration, for instance).

In some cases, the incentives do not seem to have been very effective. Accelerated depreciation, which was supposed to revitalize the smokestack industries such as steel, had at best limited effects. In other cases, the incentives were too effective. The real estate boom, partly resulting from the favorable treatment under the 1981 Tax Act, led by the mid-1980s to vacancy rates in excess of 20 percent in commercial real estate in many areas.

In some cases, the incentives were badly designed. We have repeatedly seen the importance of **marginal incentives.** In the case of IRA accounts, the limit on the amount that could be deducted eliminates the intended marginal incentives for savings for many individuals.

By the mid-1980s, there was a consensus among economists that whatever the merits of one or another of the special provisions, the hodgepodge of provisions had resulted in a tax system riddled with inequities and inefficiencies.

EFFECTS OF UNIFORM TAXES

Before turning in later chapters to how the Tax Reform Act of 1986 attempted to remedy the problems of the tax system, we first need to understand the consequences of a uniform tax on capital. The difficulties of taxing capital income that we have discussed mean that no economy has ever imposed a uniform tax on capital income. Yet it is necessary to understand what would be the consequences of such a tax, were it feasible, before we can understand the consequences of the kind of tax system we actually have.

The two most important sets of effects of a uniform tax on capital income are on savings and investment and on risk taking.

Effect of Capital Income Taxation on Savings and Investment

From Chapter 18 we know that we can decompose the effects of a tax on interest income from savings into an income effect and a substitution effect. The substitution effect always leads to increased current-period consumption (reduced savings). Whether the income effect is positive or negative depends on whether the individual is a borrower or a lender. The tax deductibility of interest implies that borrowers are better off; their income effect is positive; they increase their current-period consumption. Hence for borrowers, income and substitution effects both work to increase current consumption and to decrease savings. Lenders (net suppliers of capital) are worse off: they decrease current consumption. Hence substitution and income effects work in opposite directions.

Most of the empirical evidence on whether aggregate savings increase or decrease with a raising of the after-tax return to savings indicates that taxes reduce savings slightly.[12]

CORPORATE AND HOUSEHOLD SAVINGS: THE CORPORATE VEIL

Most of savings is done not directly by households but by corporations, through their retained earnings (what the firm keeps from sales after paying costs, interest, and dividends). As we will see in Chapter 23, the provisions of the corporate tax greatly affect the incentives for savings to be done in this form. There is considerable controversy about the implications of this for household savings. There are those who believe that individuals see through the *corporate veil*—that is, they can see accurately what is going on inside the firm—that they treat $1,000 saved by the corporation in which they own a 1 percent interest as if they had saved $10.[13]

It is important to realize that not all investors need to be well informed about firms' savings and investment to see through the corporate veil. All that is required is that enough investors realize that a firm that has saved and invested $1 million should have a market value $1 million larger than it was before for the stock price to rise by the requisite amount. Uninformed shareholders may not know why the firm's shares have increased in value. All they know is that they have. And the increase in wealth leads to increased current consumption (decreased savings).

In this view, then, the division of savings between household savings and corporate savings is purely an artifact of our current tax laws. It is *as if* the corporation distributed all of its profits to its shareholders, and then they decided how much to save.

Many economists believe, however, that individuals do not have enough information or are not so rational as to fully integrate corporate savings into their household accounts. Individuals cannot, in this view, fully see through the corporate veil. Exponents of this view point out, for instance, that individual shareholders seldom read the annual accounts of the firm, and that even were they to do so, they would find it difficult to ascertain the magnitude of savings that had been done on

[12] Michael Boskin of Stanford University has obtained perhaps the strongest negative response, arguing that an increase in the return to savings by one percentage point, say, from 4 percent to 5 percent, reduces savings by one percentage point. Howrey and Hymans of the University of Michigan claim that they have been unable to isolate a significant interest rate effect. See M. Boskin, "Taxation, Savings, and the Rate of Interest," *Journal of Political Economy* 86 (1978): S3–S27, and E. Philip Howrey and Saul H. Hymans, in *What Should Be Taxed: Income or Expenditures*, J. A. Pechman, ed. (Washington, D.C.: Brookings Institution, 1980).

[13] In this view, then, in the absence of taxation, whether firms paid dividends or retained earnings would make no difference. This view has been put forward by F. Modigliani and M. H. Miller, "The Cost of Capital, Corporation Finance, and the Theory of Investment," *American Economic Review* 48 (1958): 261–97, and by J. E. Stiglitz, "On the Irrelevance of Corporation Financial Policy," *American Economic Review* 64 (1974): 851–66.

their behalf by the firm. If one believed that the stock market values accurately reflected the true capital value of the firm, then households could infer how much had been saved. But economists who believe in the corporate veil tend also to believe that the stock market reflects true capital values only imperfectly and that households do not pay much attention to the day-to-day variations in the market value of their securities. In this view, then, one can (at least for short-term purposes) analyze separately the effect of capital taxation on corporation savings and on household savings.

Both sides agree that in the long run any policy that led systematically to increased corporate savings would *eventually* have an impact on household savings, if only because such a policy would have a systematic effect on the value of corporations and, through this, on the shareholders' views of their net worth.

THE CONSEQUENCES OF A REDUCTION IN SAVINGS

While there is some controversy about the magnitude, and possibly even the sign, of the change in savings resulting from an interest income tax, the general view is that there is probably a slight negative effect. The next question is: What are the consequences of this? Should it be a matter of concern? The reduction in savings will normally lead to a reduction in capital accumulation and, in the long run, to a reduction in output per capita.

These effects may, however, be offset in four different ways. First, the government can attempt to encourage savings in some other way: if, for instance, it reduces social security benefits, individuals may be induced to save more for their retirement. Second, it can attempt to reduce the fraction of savings that go into government bonds, thus increasing the fraction of savings that can go into real private investment. (It can do this by reducing the government's indebtedness.) Third, a decrease in the amount of capital affects the market value of other assets and, in particular, land. If land and capital are complementary, the decrease in capital reduces the return to land and hence reduces the market value of land. The decrease in capital is thus smaller than the decrease in savings.[14] (That is, some of the decreased savings takes the form of a decrease in the value of land holdings.)

Fourth, it can encourage investment by providing an investment tax credit or accelerated depreciation. The effect of this is seen in Figure 22.1, where, for simplicity, we assume all savings are invested in capital (we ignore, in other words, savings in government bonds or land). The interest income tax decreases the supply of savings at each interest rate,

[14] The market value of land before taxes (in long-run equilibrium) is just the present discounted value of rentals, or R/r, where R is the rental flow and r is the rate of interest. In the short run, with a fixed supply of capital, a tax on the return to land and capital leaves the value of land unchanged at $(1 - t)\,R/\,(1 - t)\,r = R/r$. But as capital decreases, the real rate of interest increases and (if capital and land are complements) R decreases. Both effects lead to a decrease in the value of land. (Note that it is possible that, if land and capital are substitutes, the decrease in capital will actually increase the market value of land, thus exacerbating the decline in capital stock.)

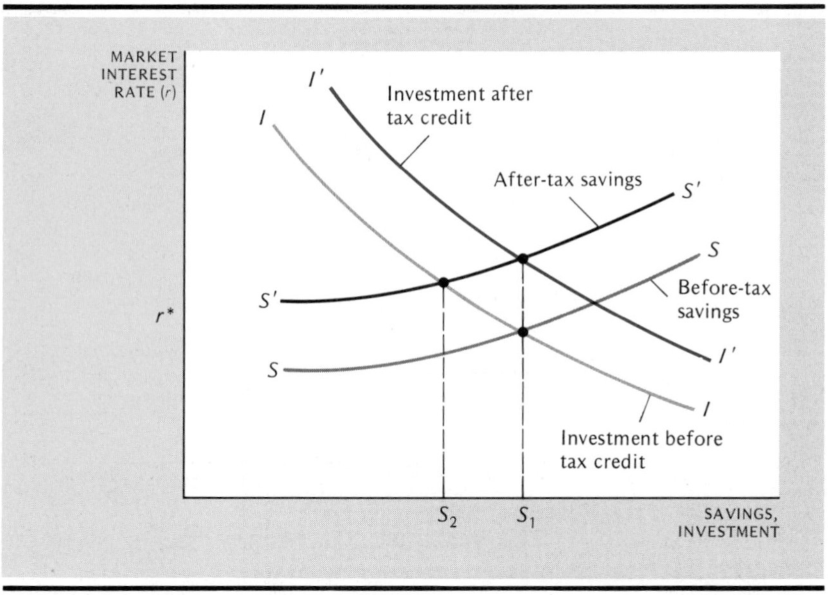

22.1 ENCOURAGING INVESTMENT THROUGH THE INVESTMENT TAX CREDIT The effects of the reduction in savings can be offset by an investment tax credit.

so the market equilibrium level of savings (investment) decreases from S_1 to S_2. An investment tax credit shifts the investment schedule so that at each *r*, the demand for investment is increased. This is the movement from *II* to *I′I′*. A sufficiently large investment credit shifts it enough to restore investment to its original level, S_1. At the new equilibrium, the after-tax return has also been restored to its original level. The question arises: would it not have been simpler and probably less distortionary to exempt interest income from taxation and not to have provided the investment tax credit?[15]

EFFECTS OF CAPITAL INCOME TAXATION IN AN OPEN ECONOMY

During the past quarter century, an international capital market, allowing funds to flow from one country to another, has developed. In recent years, the United States has been borrowing hundreds of billions of dollars from Europe and Japan.[16] Slight increases in the U.S. rate of interest can draw into America large amounts of money. Many economists believe that as a result, the supply curve for funds to the United States is close to horizontal (see Figure 22.2).

[15] The investment tax credit affects only new investment, while a reduction in the tax on the return to capital affects old investments as well. Thus there may be large redistributive consequences of a change from one policy to the other.

[16] Between 1982 and 1986, the United States borrowed so heavily from abroad that it went from being the world's largest creditor nation to the largest debtor. The U.S. net international investment position—the excess of foreign assets owned by U.S. banks, multinational corporations, and individuals over and above the value of U.S. assets held by foreigners—stood at $147 billion in 1982 and at approximately *negative* $250 billion in 1986. (The main reasons for this change were the large federal deficits, discussed in Chapter 2, and the strong U.S. economic growth relative to the rest of the world.)

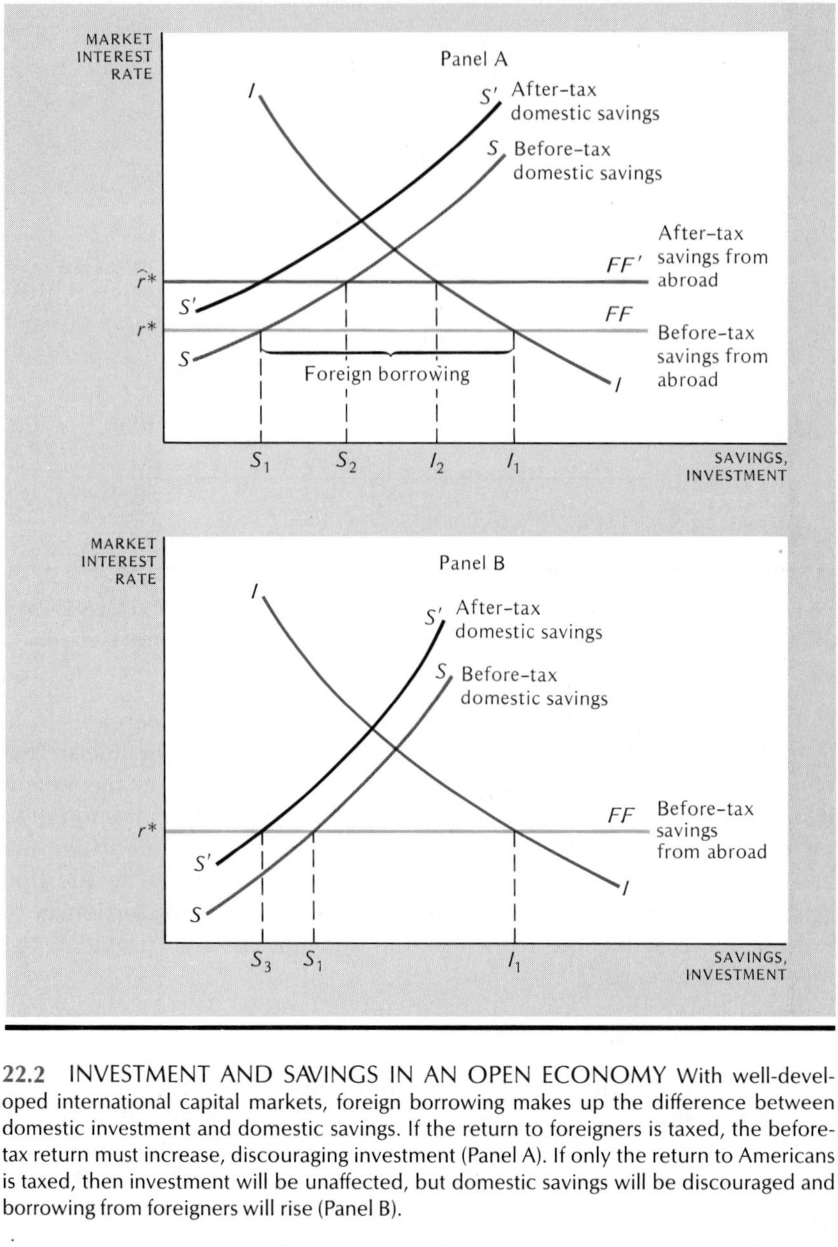

22.2 INVESTMENT AND SAVINGS IN AN OPEN ECONOMY With well-developed international capital markets, foreign borrowing makes up the difference between domestic investment and domestic savings. If the return to foreigners is taxed, the before-tax return must increase, discouraging investment (Panel A). If only the return to Americans is taxed, then investment will be unaffected, but domestic savings will be discouraged and borrowing from foreigners will rise (Panel B).

Suppose that there are no taxes, and consider the limiting case where foreigners are willing to supply funds at an interest rate of r^*. That is, the supply of funds is infinitely elastic. The equilibrium interest rate would then be r^*, with S_1 being domestic savings, I_1 domestic investment, and the difference, $I_1 - S_1$, being financed by foreign borrowing.

Now, a tax at the rate t on the return to capital that foreigners must pay will discourage investment in the United States. The before-tax return rises by the full amount of the tax, so that the *after-tax return* remains at r^* (at least in the long run). If Americans must also pay the tax, then *SS* shifts to $S'S'$, as we saw before. But since after-tax returns will remain the same, domestic savings will remain unchanged at S_1. The tax reduces investment to I_2, and foreign borrowing will fall to $I_2 - S_1$ (see Figure 22.2A), and borrowing will be discouraged.

Now assume that there are some special provisions (say IRA accounts) that allow for the return to capital for American savers to escape taxation. Then the domestic savings schedule will remain at *SS*. But, as in the preceding case, the market interest rate will be $\hat{r}^*$. Thus, the equilibrium will be characterized by the same level of investment as in the preceding case (I_2), a higher level of savings (S_2) and, hence, a lower level of borrowing ($I_2 - S_2$).

The important point to realize is that encouraging savings is not the same as encouraging investment in an open economy. The effect of encouraging savings is to reduce the amount that the United States borrows abroad, but in the limiting case of a perfectly elastic supply of foreign funds, there is no effect on investment. In particular, a provision that exempted foreigners from paying tax on interest earned in the United States would mean that the before-tax return would therefore remain at r^*. The taxation of interest earned by Americans would discourage savings, shifting *SS* to $S'S'$ in Figure 22.2B, lead to more foreign borrowing ($I_1 - S_3$), but leave investment at the same level as it would have been in the absence of any taxation of capital income.

Effect of Capital Income Taxes on Risk Taking

There has long been a concern that the taxation of capital income leads to a reduction in risk taking. We shall see that it is possible for an appropriately designed tax on capital income actually to lead to an increase in risk taking, but some of the features of our tax system do serve to discourage risk taking.

Although some individuals enjoy taking risks on a regular basis, and almost all individuals enjoy taking small risks occasionally (as evidenced by the popularity of state lotteries and the gambling casinos of Atlantic City and Las Vegas), most individuals take a more conservative position when it comes to managing their wealth. They are willing to take risks, but only if they receive, as compensation, a sufficiently high expected return over what they could have obtained in a safe investment. There is widespread concern that by taxing the return to capital, one is effectively taxing the return to risk bearing, the risk premium that individuals receive for bearing additional risks. As a result, there will be less risk taking.

The reason that this is of such concern is the belief that entrepreneurship is central to the vitality of capitalism, and entrepreneurship involves risk taking in an essential way. If entrepreneurs are discouraged from undertaking new risky ventures, the effect on the growth of the American economy would be extremely deleterious.

WHY CAPITAL TAXATION MAY INCREASE RISK TAKING

There is some controversy over the extent to which current taxes reduce risk taking. It is possible that they may actually increase it.

That the income tax might increase risk taking can be seen most easily by considering an extreme example. Assume that the individual has to decide between two assets: a safe asset yielding no return, and a risky asset that has a 50 percent chance of yielding a very large return and a 50 percent chance of yielding a negative return. The average return is positive, to compensate the individual for risk taking. The individual is conservative and so allocates a fraction of his wealth to the safe asset and the remainder to the risky asset.

We now impose a tax on the return to capital, but we allow a full deduction against other income for losses. The safe asset is unaffected. The risky asset has its return reduced by half, but the losses are also reduced by half. How does the individual respond to this? If he doubles the amount he previously invested in the risky asset, his after-tax income when the return is positive is the same, and his after-tax income when the return is negative is also the same. The tax has left him completely unaffected. Effectively, the government is sharing in the risks of the individual. By its willingness to share the risks—the losses as well as the gains—it is acting as a silent partner. And because the government is willing to share the risk, the individual is willing to increase his risk taking.[17]

This situation has one other interesting property: the tax yields on average a return to the government, but it has no effect on the welfare of the individual. The individual is unaffected because his after-tax position is the same as it was in the before-tax situation (whether the risky asset turns out to have a positive or negative return). This tax seems to do what no other tax seems capable of doing: it raises revenue without lowering welfare.

WHY CAPITAL TAXATION MAY REDUCE RISK TAKING

Before becoming too excited about the prospect of raising revenue without lowering welfare, one must keep several caveats in mind. First, with a progressive tax structure, returns to a successful investment are taxed more heavily than losses from unsuccessful investments are subsidized. There is thus a bias against risk taking.

Second, there are limitations on the magnitudes of the losses that can be offset. Thus the government, while sharing in the gains, shares only in some of the losses. Again, there is a bias against risk taking.

The importance of having the government share in risk taking

[17] For an early discussion of the effect of taxation on risk taking, see E. D. Domar and R. A. Musgrave, "Proportional Income Taxation and Risk-Taking," *Quarterly Journal of Economics* 58 (1944): 388–422. The standard current view is presented in J. E. Stiglitz, "The Effects of Income, Wealth and Capital Gains Taxation on Risk Taking," *Quarterly Journal of Economics* 83 (1969): 262–83. See also A. B. Atkinson and J. E. Stiglitz, *Lectures on Public Economics* (New York: McGraw-Hill, 1980), Chapter 4 and A. Sandmo, "The Effects of Taxation on Savings and Risk-Taking," in A. Auerbach and M. Feldstein, eds., *Handbook of Public Economics*, vol. 1 (Amsterdam: North Holland, 1985), 293–309.

depends on how well the private market does. For securities that are actively traded on the stock market, the risks are widely spread throughout the economy, and there is no reason to believe that the government can significantly increase the degree of risk sharing. For smaller firms the government may, however, be able to provide risk-sharing opportunities that the market cannot provide.

A final difficulty is that we have assumed that the safe rate of return is zero. If there is a significant positive return on safe assets, and it is taxed, there will be a significant wealth effect associated with the capital income tax. This wealth effect may lead to the reduction in the demand for risky assets.

In short, a proportional tax on the return to capital would probably encourage risk taking, but this positive effect may well be more than offset by the negative effects we have just described. Probably the single provision that has the most deleterious effect on risk taking is the limitation on loss deductibility.[18] The 1986 Tax Reform Act increased the severity of this limitation by providing that individuals cannot subtract losses from certain investment activities from their wage income in computing their income for tax purposes.

Although the government in effect shares in the financial costs of investments, it does not share in the effort costs of entrepreneurs. The stories of the long hours put in by the innovators who contributed so much to the computer industry, such as Stephen Jobs, the founder of Apple Computers, are by now legendary. Most of the returns they obtained from this effort were in the form of capital gains on the sale of the companies that they started. There has been a real concern that high rates of taxation of capital gains will serve to discourage this kind of risk taking and entrepreneurship. Others contend, however, that these individuals are driven by other than monetary incentives, and raising the tax on capital gains (say, from the maximum 20 percent level prior to the 1986 Tax Reform Act,[19] to the current maximum level of 28 percent) will have only minimal effects.

CONSEQUENCES OF NON-UNIFORM TAXES

In the previous sections, we have described the effects of a uniform capital tax. But no government has imposed a uniform capital tax. Many of the most important consequences of our tax system are a result of this non-uniform treatment.

This non-uniform treatment results in both inefficiencies and inequities. The inefficiencies are obvious: investment gets pulled into less productive tax-favored uses. The inequities are often more subtle. There

[18] This limitation serves some important positive functions within our present tax structure in limiting, for instance, the extent to which individuals can use tax shelters to reduce their tax liabilities.

[19] Prior to the 1986 Tax Reform Act, only 40 percent of capital gains on the sale of an asset were subject to tax (provided that the taxpayer had owned the asset for at least six months). The maximum *effective* tax rate on such gain was therefore $0.4 \times 50\% = 20\%$, since 50 percent was the maximum statutory tax rate before 1986.

are two reasons for this. First, because resources get pulled into tax-favored areas, the after-tax return in those areas may get driven down; individuals in those industries in the long run obtain the same after-tax return that individuals in other industries do. Those in the industry at the time the special treatment is introduced receive some extra income during the transition period until others have entered the industry. By the same token, those in the industry at the time the special treatment is removed are hurt, but only temporarily, until others have left the industry.

In some cases, however, entry may be limited. Special treatment of some natural resources (say, uranium) may not have a significant effect in increasing its supply. Those who own the mines at the time the special treatment is introduced receive a capital gain. Their assets are worth more. We say that the preferential tax treatment is **capitalized** in the value of the asset. Once the price has risen, the owners receive a normal return on the value of their asset. Thus in the long run, once again, owners of assets with preferential tax treatment do not receive a higher than normal after-tax return on the value of their assets.

Just as it is the owners of the assets at the time the special provisions are introduced (or when it is believed that they will be introduced) that receive a benefit, so too if a tax preference is removed, those who are hurt are those who are the owners at that time. That individual may well not be the individual who originally benefited when the tax preference was introduced.

Housing: An Example of Non-Uniform Treatment

Housing provides perhaps the best and most important example of the consequences of non-uniform treatment. Housing is extremely important, accounting for approximately one-third of capital stock. As we have noted, owner-occupied housing receives favorable treatment.

Owner-occupied housing provides a good illustration of both the complexity of the tax law and the difficulty of ascertaining the nature and magnitude of the bias. There is concern not only that owner-occupied housing is favored over other forms of investment, but that it is also favored over rental housing (which has distributional as well as efficiency consequences).

The tax advantages of owner-occupied housing are: (a) the return is not taxed (in contrast to rental housing, where the landlord pays a tax on his income, and the renter cannot deduct his rent); (b) interest payments and property taxes are deductible; and (c) capital gains enjoy particularly favorable treatment. On the other hand, the owner of a rental property can depreciate his property and can deduct maintenance expenses (and may even be able to deduct some capital expenditures under the guise of maintenance expenditures). (He too can deduct both interest payments and property taxes.)[20] In recent years, the allowances for

[20] There are further problems associated with ascertaining who bears the property tax. In the work described below, it is assumed that the tax is borne by the person paying the tax. But in fact, insofar as

depreciation have far exceeded true economic depreciation. In a competitive market, the tax savings of the marginal investor (the investor who is just indifferent when choosing between investing in real estate and investing somewhere else) are passed along to the renter.

Whether renters or owners are favored by the tax code, and whether owner-occupied housing is favored relative to other forms of investment, is greatly dependent on tax rates, interest rates, inflation rates, and depreciation allowances.

During the period 1981–1986, the favorable treatment accorded rental housing was sufficiently generous that it appears that renters were actually favored.[21] Since the 1986 Tax Reform Act, the much lower depreciation allowances and the increase in the tax on capital gains will almost surely imply that the longstanding presumption that those who own their own home are favored will once again be valid.

Again, during the period 1981–1986, the generous depreciation allowances for many forms of capital, combined with the investment tax credit, temporarily increased the tax advantages of investing in equipment and machines relative to investing in owner-occupied housing. However, since 1986, the increase in the tax rate on capital gains, together with the fact that the special tax treatment for capital gains on housing was retained and that mortgage interest is the only tax deductible form of consumer interest, may actually serve to increase the incentives to invest in owner-occupied housing. For many Americans, their own homes look increasingly like the best available tax shelter.

The retention of the special treatment of housing under the 1986 Tax Reform Act means that the net effect of the law on the efficiency with which investment gets allocated is ambiguous. So long as one important distortion remains, reducing other distortions need not increase the overall efficiency of the economy. The tax law may have reduced the distortions within different classes of assets within manufacturing, but increased the distortion between manufacturing and owner-occupied housing.

ESTATE AND GIFT TAXES

Estate and gift taxes tax the transfer of wealth from one individual to another.[22] The objective of the tax is partly to limit accumulations of wealth (though if that were its sole objective, the appropriate basis of taxation would be the individual receiving the bequest rather than the individual giving it. Under current law, the estate of the deceased pays the tax. The recipient of a bequest pays no tax. He does not include the bequest in his income, even though the inheritance clearly increases his "ability to pay").

---

the tax is a tax on land, it may simply change property values; it affects owners of property at the time the tax is imposed, but not current owners.

[21] See M. King and D. Fullerton, *The Taxation of Income from Capital* (Chicago: University of Chicago Press, 1984).

[22] We shall limit ourselves to the federal estate and gift tax. These two are now integrated.

The minimum size estate that is subject to taxation is $600,000. The maximum rate has been reduced in recent years from 77 percent to 50 percent. There are special provisions for the transfer of assets from an individual to his or her spouse.

The tax can be thought of as a tax imposed on a particular category of expenditures: on bequests and gifts. Like any tax, it has an income effect and a substitution effect. Because bequests are "more expensive"—the individual has to give up more of his current consumption to give a unit of consumption to his heirs—he increases his current consumption; because his wealth will ultimately be reduced by the tax, he decreases his current consumption. Thus the net effect on consumption is ambiguous. On the other hand, there is a strong presumption that at the confiscatory tax rates imposed by some foreign governments (exceeding 90 percent of the estate), the substitution effect probably outweighs the income effect, and savings are reduced.

The significance of this is controversial. There are at least two primary motivations for savings: to provide for retirement (this is called life-cycle savings) and to provide for one's heirs. It used to be thought that most savings were motivated by life-cycle considerations, so that even if the estate tax discouraged inheritances, it would have an insignificant effect on total savings. More recent studies have suggested that inheritance may play a more important role: not only is it difficult to account for the aggregate level of savings with a life-cycle model, but the distribution of wealth ownership (which is very skewed—that is, a small percentage of the population has a fairly large percentage of the wealth, a much larger percentage of wealth than of income) implies that inheritances play an important role in motivating savings.[23]

One aspect of the 1986 Tax Reform Act has served to encourage inheritances. The partial tax exemption for realized capital gains was repealed, so that the effective tax rate on capital gains has actually been increased. At the same time, the special treatment of capital gains at death has been retained. When an individual leaves an asset to her heirs, there is a *step-up in basis* to market value; that is, if she buys stock at $30 that is selling for $60 ten years later when she dies, her heir can hold the stock and use $60 as the basis for the capital gains tax when he sells it. The gain accrued from the time the asset was first acquired until death completely escapes income taxation. This obviously provides an incentive for individuals to leave appreciated assets to their children.

Avoiding or reducing the estate and gift tax is probably an even more important activity for the wealthy than avoiding the income tax. The complexities of the tax code and the opportunities for tax avoidance are sufficiently great that one expert referred to the tax as a "voluntary tax,"

[23] A recent study by Laurence Kotlikoff of Boston University and Lawrence Summers of Harvard suggests that as much as two-thirds of capital accumulation is due to inheritances. See L. Kotlikoff and L. Summers, "The Role of Intergenerational Transfers in Aggregate Capital Accumulation," *Journal of Political Economy* 89 (1981): 706–32. See also J. S. Fleming, "The Effects of Earnings Inequality, Imperfect Capital Markets, and Dynastic Altruism on the Distribution of Wealth in Life Cycle Models," *Economica* 46 (1979): 363–80.

paid only by those who were foolish enough not to plan for their death in an appropriate manner.[24]

One of the easiest ways to avoid paying the tax is transferring assets to one's children before death (a married couple can transfer $20,000 to each child per year). Since children are usually at a lower income tax bracket than their parents, such transfers also reduce the government's tax collections from the individual income tax. Stanford economist Douglas Bernheim has concluded that the loss in revenue to the income tax may actually be as large as the total income collected by the estate tax: the *net* revenue of the estate tax may be negligible.[25]

OUR HYBRID TAX SYSTEM

The tax system in the United States has evolved so that it is far from a pure income tax system; but neither is it a pure *consumption* tax system, in which the return from capital would be exempt from taxation. Our system is sometimes referred to as a *hybrid*, a cross between a consumption tax and an income tax. A large fraction of the return to capital is exempt from tax; for example, most savings for retirement (through pensions), as well as owner-occupied housing. Other returns to capital receive preferential treatment. Capital gains, though no longer partially tax-exempt, are taxed only upon realization.

SUMMARY

1. There are a number of important problems in defining and measuring "income from capital," in particular, problems in timing, i.e., in ascertaining when the income has occurred. Problems of defining real income accurately become particularly acute in inflationary periods. Our tax system is not inflation-neutral.
2. Depreciation allowances are adjustments to income to reflect the fact that the value of plant and equipment decreases with use and age. Under current law, there is accelerated depreciation. Thus depreciation allowances in the early years of an asset may substantially exceed the true decrease in its value. Current law benefits some categories of assets more than others.
3. Capital gains are taxed only upon realization. As a result, there is a locked-in effect. There is some controversy over the magnitude and economic significance of the locked-in effect.
4. The complexities in the provisions governing the taxation of capital arise partly out of concern for equity, partly for administrative reasons, and partly because the government is using the tax system to encourage certain kinds of economic activities.
5. In the analysis of the effects of capital taxation, we differentiated between the effects of a general (uniform) tax on the return to capital and *selective* taxes. Many of the distortions associated with capital taxation are attributed

[24] G. Cooper, *A Voluntary Tax? New Perspectives on Sophisticated Estate Tax Avoidance* (Washington, D.C.: Brookings Institution, 1979).
[25] D. Bernheim, "Does the Estate Tax Raise Revenue?" in L. Summers, ed., *Tax Policy and the Economy* (Cambridge, MA: MIT Press, 1987).

to its selective nature, and to the fact that depreciation allowances do not correspond closely to true economic depreciation.

6. On theoretical grounds it is possible for a general tax on the return to savings either to increase or to decrease savings. Some empirical evidence suggests that lowering the after-tax return may reduce savings slightly. In an open economy, a tax only on interest income accruing to Americans, while it may reduce savings, will leave investment unaffected. The gap will be made up by lending and investment by foreigners. Taxes on all returns to capital (including those accruing to foreigners) will reduce the equilibrium level of investment.
7. Though a proportional tax on the return to capital might induce an increase in risk taking, a progressive tax, with limited loss offsets (such as in the United States), may discourage risk taking. An evaluation of the effect depends partly on one's views concerning the market's abilities to share risks.
8. Many tax benefits become capitalized in the value of the asset. The true beneficiary of the special treatment is thus the owner of the asset at the time the special provision is introduced.
9. Our tax system is a hybrid tax system, a cross between a pure income tax and a pure consumption tax.

KEY CONCEPTS

Depreciation allowances	Locked-in effect
Straight-line depreciation	Individual retirement accounts (IRAs)
True economic depreciation	Keogh plans
Accelerated depreciation	Real versus nominal capital gains
Investment tax credit	Capitalized

QUESTIONS AND PROBLEMS

1. It is difficult to ascertain precisely the decline in the value of most assets as they grow older. An exception is automobiles. Assume a new car costs \$5,000, that its value at the end of one year is \$4,000, at the end of two years \$3,000, at the end of three years \$2,000, and that it loses \$250 in value for each of the following eight years. What is the true economic depreciation? What is the present discounted value of this, assuming a 5 percent after-tax interest rate? What will be the depreciation allowances under the current system? What is the present discounted value of these depreciation allowances? (Cars are treated as five-year assets.)
2. Supporters of accelerated depreciation and investment tax credits acknowledge that they favor heavy industry ("smokestack America") but argue that this is desirable. Why do economists tend to look askance at such arguments? Can you identify any major market failures? If it were decided to subsidize these industries, in what other ways might it be done?
3. What does economic theory suggest should have been the effect of IRAs on savings, under the old (pre-1986) law? Draw the individual's budget constraint (between consumption today and consumption at retirement) with and without the IRA. Describe the income and substitution effects for an individual who was planning to save a little. Describe them for an individual who was planning to save a great deal. What difference might it make if the individual has other assets, such as a savings account?

Discuss the equity and efficiency consequences of changing the rules so that only amounts in excess of $2,000 per year are afforded special tax treatment.

4. Do policies that encourage savings automatically lead to more investment? If you wanted to encourage investment in manufacturing, what policies might you advocate? How do current policies encourage, or discourage, investment in manufacturing? To what extent do your answers depend on alternative theories concerning the economy—e.g., how savings and investment are determined?
5. Who benefits from the provisions allowing for the tax exemption of interest income on municipal bonds? What do you think might happen to the interest rates these bonds pay if individuals were allowed to borrow to buy these bonds, deducting the interest on their loans?

23

The Corporation Income Tax

Early in 1983, in an offhand remark, President Reagan suggested that we should abolish our corporation income tax. The remark caused quite a stir: it was widely interpreted to reflect his pro-business orientation. What was not widely recognized at the time was that, two years earlier, the tax had, in effect, been almost abolished: the generous depreciation rules written into the 1981 Tax Act meant that the revenue derived from the federal corporate tax was rapidly dwindling. While in 1955, 27 percent of federal revenue came from the corporation income tax, and in 1980 12 percent, by 1983 it was down to just over 6 percent.

Surprisingly, one of the main features of the Tax Reform Act of 1986 was to increase corporate income tax revenues, while reducing revenues from the personal income tax. The revenue shift is approximately $120 billion over a five-year period. This shift was motivated more by political considerations than by a change in President Reagan's position concerning the undesirability of the corporation tax. To win acceptance for the reforms in the personal income tax that he thought were so important, personal tax revenues had to come down. To make up the lost revenues, other taxes had to be increased. The corporation tax was the obvious target, particularly since the 1981 and 1982 Tax Acts had created very uneven tax rates on income from alternative capital investments. The

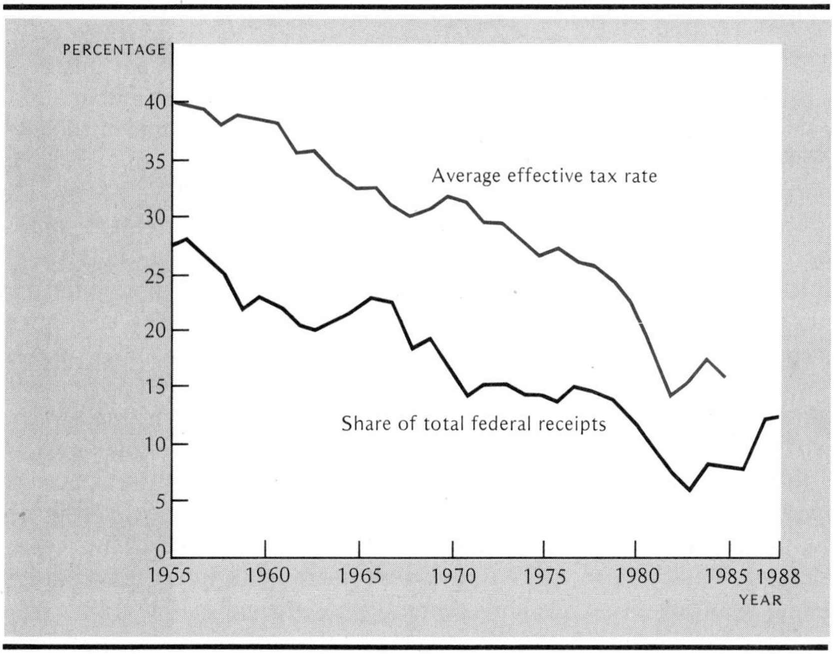

23.1 FEDERAL CORPORATE INCOME TAX: EFFECTIVE RATE AND SHARE OF TOTAL FEDERAL RECEIPTS Between 1955 and 1981, the effective tax on the domestic profits of U.S. corporations declined from 40.2 percent to 14.6 percent (shown in color). The decline of the effective tax rate, together with a fall in real corporate profits after 1978, meant that the share of corporate tax revenues in total federal receipts dwindled (shown in black). The 1986 Tax Reform Act is expected to reverse these trends. SOURCE: J.A. Pechman, *Federal Tax Policy,* 5th ed., (Washington, D.C.: Brookings Institution, 1987, Table D–15); *U.S. Budget in Brief, 1988,* Table 3.

elimination of some of these distortions would enable the government to lower legislated corporation tax rates, while increasing the revenues raised. As shown in Figure 23.1, when the changes of the 1986 Tax Act are fully implemented, the corporation income tax is expected to account for 12.8 percent of federal tax revenues.

Changes in aggregate revenues may not, however, convey much information about changes in the economic impact of the corporate tax. Economists believe that the corporate tax causes important distortions in the allocation of investment and in its overall level. This chapter addresses several questions:

1. What is the corporation tax a tax on, and who bears the burden—stockholders, workers, or consumers?
2. How does the corporation tax affect economic efficiency?
3. How does the corporation tax affect financial decisions—debt, dividends, and mergers?
4. Should there be a tax on corporations?

THE BASIC FEATURES OF THE CORPORATION INCOME TAX

The corporation income tax applies only to an *incorporated* business. The essential difference between an incorporated business and an unincorporated business is the liability of investors for the debts of the corporation. Corporations have limited liability; that is, investors in corporations can lose only the amount of money they have invested in the firm. In contrast, if an unincorporated business has debts it cannot pay, the creditors can attempt to recover their losses from the owners. Because of the protection provided to investors by the corporate form of organization, almost all large firms in the United States are incorporated.

The corporate tax is essentially a flat-rate tax, currently at 34 percent. As a concession to small business, the average tax rates for corporations with taxable incomes below $335,000 are somewhat lower, as shown in Table 23.1. The **tax base** is corporate taxable income. In general, taxable income is defined in the tax law to be gross revenues less wages, materials, interest paid, and legislated depreciation allowances. Thus, when Congress legislates more generous depreciation allowances, as it did in 1981, a corporation's taxable income is reduced and so is its tax.

Table 23.1 MARGINAL AND AVERAGE TAX RATES ON CORPORATE TAXABLE INCOME

Taxable Income	*Marginal Rate*	*Average Rate*
0–$50,000	15%	15%
$50,000–$75,000	25%	15–18%
$75,000–$100,000	34%	18–22%
$100,000–$335,000	39%	22–34%
Over $335,000	34%	34%

As with the individual income tax, after the tax liability is calculated, firms' taxes are reduced by *tax credits*. Before its repeal in 1986, the most important tax credit was for new investment. Firms still obtain a credit for a portion of their research and development expenditures and for most taxes paid to foreign governments.

THE INCIDENCE OF THE CORPORATION INCOME TAX AND ITS EFFECT ON EFFICIENCY

There is no agreement among economists about the incidence of the corporation tax—what it is a tax on and who bears it—or about the nature of the distortions it introduces. In the discussion below, we present the major views.

The Corporation Tax as a Tax on Income From Capital in the Corporate Sector

One of the earliest views of the corporation income tax on a producer was that it was a tax on the return to capital in the corporate sector. In the previous chapter, we analyzed the effect of a uniform personal tax on all capital incomes. Here, our concern is with the effects of a tax on the return to capital in one part of the economy, the corporate sector.

In discussing tax incidence, we pointed out that a tax could be shifted forward (onto consumers) or backward (onto workers). Even if the tax on corporate capital is not shifted onto consumers or workers, it will not be borne solely by owners of firms in the corporate sector. If the return to capital in one sector is taxed, investors will find it less attractive to invest in that sector. They will invest less in that sector and more in other sectors until the *after-tax returns* are equalized in both. Thus, in the long run, all capital, whether in the corporate or the unincorporated sector, will yield the same return after taxes.

Chapter 17 identified three critical determinants of the incidence of any tax: (a) the elasticity of demand, (b) the elasticity of supply, and (c) whether the market is competitive or not. Because long-run elasticities of supply might be much larger than short-run elasticities, the incidence of a tax in the long run might be markedly different from the short-run incidence.

THE SHORT RUN

In the short run, the supply of capital to the corporate sector is relatively fixed. Thus, a tax on income from capital in the corporate sector will be borne in the very short run by owners of corporate capital.[1] In Figure 23.2, the equilibrium falls along the vertical supply curve from point E to $\hat{E}$, and the return to owners of capital falls to $r^*(1-t)$.

But the capital of the corporate sector is not fixed for long: every year a significant fraction of it wears out and has to be replaced. If the return to this capital is below the return yielded elsewhere, individuals will not invest in the corporate sector. Capital will flow into the noncorporate sector at home or to industries abroad.

INFINITELY ELASTIC LONG-RUN SUPPLY RESPONSES

One hypothesis is that, at least at present, the long-run supply schedule of capital to the U.S. corporate sector is close to horizontal, as shown in Figure 23.2. There are two reasons for this. The first is that today there is a well-functioning international capital market; rates of return in the United States are closely linked to those in Europe, Japan, and other countries. A small country like Switzerland faces a horizontal supply schedule for capital. The amount that it borrows or lends has virtually no effect on the rate of interest prevailing in the international market. Investment in the corporate sector in the United States is obviously larger than that of Switzerland; but corporate bonds and equity still rep-

[1] This would be true both in perfectly competitive markets and in markets with a single monopolist. In oligopolies (markets in which there is more than one firm but not a large number of firms) the increase in taxes may serve as the basis of a coordinated price increase, shifting the burden onto consumers. Even in fairly competitive markets, however, the short-run response may entail some price increase; firms frequently set prices by certain rules of thumb, which entail a given markup over variable costs. The long-run equilibrium in these industries has the markup adjust to the competitive level. In the short run, the market may be out of equilibrium.

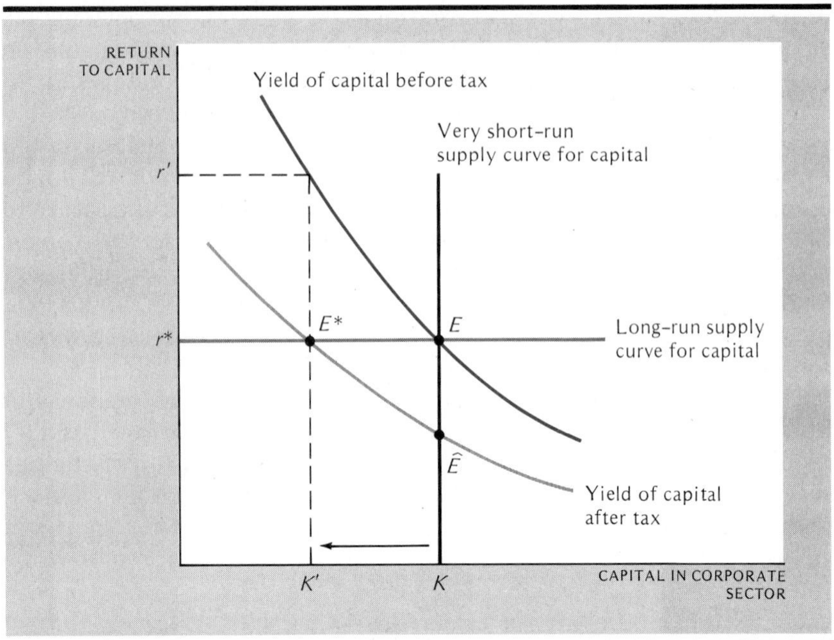

23.2 COMPARISON OF THE SHORT-RUN AND LONG-RUN EFFECTS OF A TAX ON CORPORATE CAPITAL In the short run, capital is fixed. A tax on capital income shifts the equilibrium from E to $\hat{E}$ and reduces the return to shareholders. If the long-run supply curve of capital to the corporate sector is perfectly elastic, then in the long run the equilibrium will shift to E^*, the quantity of capital in the corporate sector will fall from K to K', and the tax will not be borne by capital owners.

resent only a fraction of the assets of individuals in the United States. Thus the hypothesis that the interest rate is not changed significantly by a change in investment in the corporate sector is not implausible for the United States.

Alternatively, some economists have suggested that even in a closed economy (an economy in which there are no flows of capital, either into it from abroad or out of it), the long-run supply curve is close to horizontal, because the long-run response of savings to the return to capital is very elastic.[2]

If there is a horizontal long-run supply schedule of capital, the effect of the tax is to cause capital to flow out of the sector until the marginal product of capital (its before-tax yield) increases enough to leave the after-tax return unchanged (see Figure 23.2). Thus, if before the tax the rate of return on capital was r^*, the tax raises the rate of return to r', where $r'(1 - t) = r^*$, or $r' = r^*/(1 - t)$.

[2] This is implicit in many of the formal models economists have employed, where, for instance, savings are determined by individuals maximizing the discounted sum of their utility (over an indefinite future) with a constant discount rate. For a discussion of the use of these models, see R. Hall, "Consumption Taxes versus Income Taxes: Implications for Economic Growth," 1968 Proceedings of the 61st Annual Conference on Taxation, (Columbus, OH: National Tax Association, 1969), pp. 125–45; and R. Barro, "Are Government Bonds Net Wealth?," *Journal of Political Economy* 82 (1974): 1095–1117.

If a tax on capital income were imposed uniformly over the entire economy, the consequences of this would be simple: the amount of capital employed in the economy would decrease from K to K'. Since the amount of capital would be reduced, the income per capita would be smaller.

We are discussing here, however, a tax that is imposed on only part of the economy, on capital income in the incorporated sector. This tax has two effects: it discourages the use of capital (relative to labor) in the corporate sector; and because it increases the cost of capital in the corporate sector relative to the unincorporated sector, it discourages production in the corporate sector relative to the unincorporated sector.

In the long run, with an elastic supply of capital, the outflow of capital from the corporate sector will prevent the net return to capital from falling, and capital will not bear any of the tax. Instead, the burden will be shared by labor and by consumers of the goods produced by the corporate sector.[3]

THE "INTERMEDIATE RUN": THE HARBERGER MODEL

There is a peculiar case between the short run and the long run upon which economists have focused considerable attention. This is a situation in which the aggregate supply of capital is fixed, but capital can shift between sectors.[4] In that case, the supply schedule of capital to the corporate sector is neither vertical nor horizontal. Then, the magnitude of shifting depends on the elasticities of demand and supply for corporate capital. These are both *derived* functions—that is, the demand for capital in the corporate sector is equal to the demand for capital per unit output times the demand for the output of the corporate sector, and the supply of corporate capital depends on the demand for capital per unit output times the demand for the output of the *unincorporated* sector.

Now think of the entire set of goods produced in an economy as consisting of just two products—one product is made in the corporate sector, and the other is made in the noncorporate sector.[5] As a result of the tax on corporate capital, less capital (and more labor) is used to manufac-

[3] Workers are worse off because the amount of capital in the economy falls. Workers and owners of capital are both worse off to the extent that they consume the products of the corporate sector, whose relative price will increase.

[4] We call this case peculiar because the time involved for shifting capital between sectors is, with a few exceptions, the same as the time involved for the investment decision—i.e., the time for a change in the aggregate supply of capital. Some kinds of machines (cars) and some structures are readily shiftable, but most shifting of capital occurs through the diversion of new investment from corporate ventures into noncorporate ventures.

This model was first investigated in detail by Chicago economist Arnold Harberger and is often referred to as the Harberger model. See A. C. Harberger, "The Incidence of the Corporation Income Tax," *Journal of Political Economy,* 70 (1962): 215–40, reprinted in *Taxation and Welfare,* A. C. Harberger, ed. (Chicago: University of Chicago Press, 1974), pp. 135–70.

[5] Harberger based this distinction on his empirical work on the returns to capital between 1953 and 1955. He found that in those years, all industries other than real estate, agriculture, and miscellaneous repair services paid more than 20 percent of their capital income in corporate taxes, while those three industries paid less than 4 percent of their capital income in corporate taxes. See A. C. Harberger, "The Corporation Income Tax: An Empirical Appraisal," in U.S. House of Representatives, Ways and Means Committee, *Tax Revision Compendium,* Vol. 1 (Washington, D.C.: U.S. Government Printing Office, 1959), pp. 231–50.

ture each unit of the corporate good. Moreover, since the marginal cost of production increases when the cost of any input increases, the price of the corporate product increases, and this reduces the demand for the product. Thus an increase in the cost of capital to the corporate sector reduces the demand for capital in that sector on two accounts: The demand for capital will be elastic if the elasticity of demand for the corporate output is large (so that the demand decreases a great deal in response to a small increase in price) and if a slight increase in the cost of capital relative to the wage induces firms to substitute a lot of labor for capital (so we say that the elasticity of substitution is large).

Now consider the determinants of the *supply* of capital to the corporate sector. Since in the "intermediate run" the aggregate capital supply is fixed, the supply of capital to the corporate sector is just the total available capital less that used in the unincorporated sector. The elasticity of this supply curve thus depends on the elasticity of substitution of labor for capital in the unincorporated sector and the elasticity of demand for the output of that sector. The tax on capital in the corporate sector, by raising the relative price of output in the corporate sector, shifts demand towards the output of the unincorporated sector. At any interest rate, this will increase the demand for capital in the unincorporated sector, and, hence, reduce the supply of capital to the corporate sector.

In Figure 23.3 we divide the effect of a tax on capital in the corporate sector into two stages. First, at fixed relative prices of corporate and noncorporate goods, the tax shifts the demand curve for corporate capital down, from DD to $D'D'$. (The market rate of interest is r. To pay investors an after-tax return of r, the investment must yield a before-tax return greater than r; there will thus be less demand for capital.)

Secondly, as prices of outputs adjust to reflect the changed costs of production, there is a shift of demand toward the unincorporated sector; thus the demand curve for corporate capital shifts from $D'D'$ to $D''D''$ and the supply curve shifts from SS to $S'S'$. If the corporate sector is relatively capital-intensive (that is, the ratio of capital to labor exceeds that in the unincorporated sector), the net effect of this is to decrease the demand for, and hence the return to, capital. It is even possible for the after-tax return to decrease by more than the tax, as in Panel B. This may happen with reasonable values of the parameters (plausible values for the capital-labor ratios in both sectors, demand elasticities, and elasticities of substitution).

EMPIRICAL ESTIMATES

We have identified two distortions associated with a tax on corporate capital. First, there is a production distortion: the price of capital to the corporate sector is higher than the price of capital to the noncorporate sector, while production efficiency requires that all firms face the same input prices.

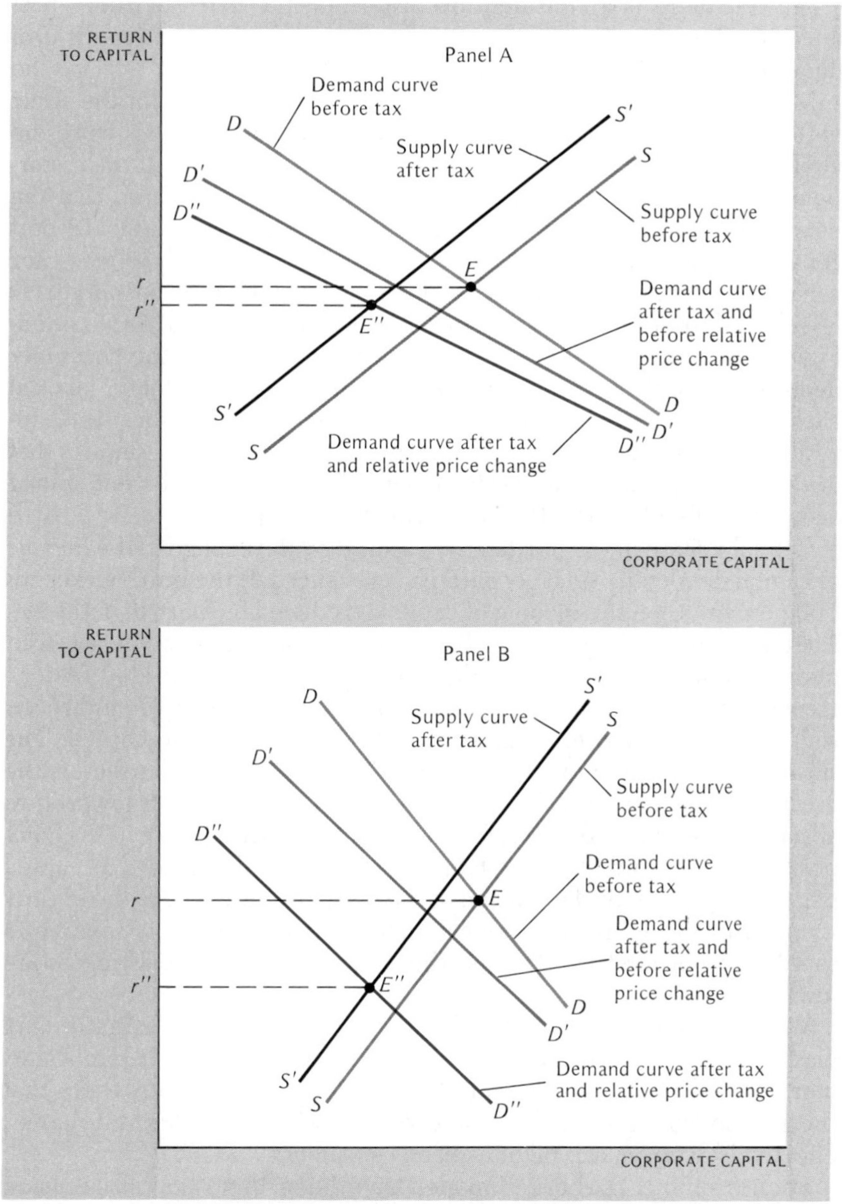

23.3 EFFECT OF A TAX ON CORPORATE CAPITAL IN THE "INTERMEDIATE RUN." In the intermediate run, the aggregate supply of capital is fixed, but capital can shift between the corporate and noncorporate sectors. A tax on capital income causes a leftward shift in the demand and supply schedules of corporate capital. In Panel A, the change in the after-tax return of capital owners is slight. In Panel B, the after-tax return to capital falls by more than the tax.

Second, there is a consumption distortion: the price of goods produced in the corporate sector rises relative to the price of goods produced by the non-corporate sector.

John Shoven of Stanford University has solved explicitly for the effect of the corporation tax in the "intermediate run," comparing the present equilibrium with what it would have been in the absence of the distortionary corporate tax on the return to capital. He estimated that the deadweight loss from the corporation income tax was roughly 12 percent of the tax revenue it generated.

He also estimated the extent to which the burden of the corporate tax was shifted from capital owners to consumers and workers. As we saw in Figure 23.3, the extent of shifting depends critically on the consumer demand elasticities and on how easy it is to substitute capital for labor in each of the two sectors. The elasticity of substitution measures the ease with which capital can be substituted for labor; a high value implies that it is easy to substitute capital for labor. There is no agreement among economists about what is the best estimate of this parameter.

Capital's share of the burden is measured by the change in the income of capital divided by total corporate tax revenues. If the burden exceeds 100 percent, then the income of capital is reduced by *more than* the tax. The corporate sector is relatively capital-intensive (that is, there is a lot more capital used for each worker than in the unincorporated sector). Hence a shift in demand toward the unincorporated sector indirectly reduces the demand for capital and, thus, the returns to capital. The smaller the elasticity of substitution in the unincorporated sector, the greater the extent to which the return to capital must be lowered to absorb all the capital that is released as a result of the change in the composition of demand. This explains why Shoven calculated that capital bears 162 percent of the burden of the tax in the case where the elasticity of substitution in the unincorporated sector is very low relative to that in the corporate sector and the consumer demand elasticities are low.

Without knowing precisely the value of the demand elasticities and elasticities of substitution, we cannot even tell whether capital bears more or less than 100 percent of the burden. No wonder, then, that there is no agreement about the extent to which the corporate tax is, effectively, a tax on capital or a tax on consumers!

Studies of the Harberger model have been important in focusing attention on the *general equilibrium* effects of taxes, in emphasizing that a tax imposed on capital in one sector has ramifications throughout the economy and that who ultimately bears the burden of the tax is uncertain. Still, these studies have limited use in assessing the effects of our corporation tax, largely because they have ignored the myriad of special provisions of the tax code. These provisions are critical in determining its ultimate effect. Moreover, these studies fail to take into account the *combined* effects of *all* taxes—the corporation income tax, the individual income tax, as well as other taxes on capital (the estate and gift tax, and state and local income and property taxes). They ignore international capital movements, which have become so important in recent years. Finally, they ignore the fact that the total tax payments associated with an investment depend on how that investment is financed, whether by debt or equity.[6]

The Corporation Tax as a Tax on Entrepreneurship

Up to now, we have treated the corporation income tax as if it were a uniform tax on the return to capital in the corporate sector. This would be true if the depreciation allowances were correct (which they are not), and if there were no deduction for interest paid (but there is). These provisions have an enormous effect on the impact of the tax; they are not just minor wrinkles in the tax code. To isolate the implications of the deductibility of interest payments, we will continue in this section to assume that depreciation allowances correctly reflect the decrease in the value of aging plant and equipment. What happens if (as in our tax code) interest payments are tax-deductible?

In deciding how much to invest, the firm wishes to know what the extra—i.e., marginal—return to the firm *after taxes* will be. It takes into account the extra taxes it pays as a result of its extra revenue; but it also takes into account the reduction in its tax liabilities, as a result of the additional depreciation allowances or the tax-deductibility of interest payments.

The net return to the firm from investing an extra dollar depends on how it finances that additional dollar of investment. Firms obtain capital in two forms, as debt in which the supplier of capital is guaranteed a given return provided that the firm does not go bankrupt (in which case the supplier of capital gets whatever is left), or in the form of equity (issuing new shares). Those who invest in equity (buy shares) do not get any guaranteed return, but if the firm does well, they share in the profits and capital gains.

If the firm borrows funds, in the absence of tax, the marginal cost of capital is simply the interest rate it has to pay on an additional loan to finance the additional investment. If the interest is tax-deductible, the after-tax marginal cost is $r(1 - t)$, where r is the rate of interest and t is the tax rate. If the interest rate is 10 percent and the tax rate is 34 percent, the after-tax cost is only 6.6 percent.

The firm's returns are reduced by 34 percent, but so is the cost of borrowing capital: hence if the net return to an investment financed by borrowing was positive before the imposition of the tax, it still is; if the net return was negative, it still is. Investment decisions are unaffected by the corporate tax.

This assumes that the firm had the option of financing its *marginal* investment project by borrowing; in other words, the firm, at the mar-

[6] Harberger and Shoven assumed that the marginal investment was financed in the same way as the average one, so that the relevant tax rate was the average tax rate currently being paid by the corporation. The theories we describe below argue that this may not be correct.

gin, asks itself: Is it worth borrowing a little bit more to invest a little bit more?[7]

Newly established firms sell shares to raise capital; it is often the only source of capital they can obtain—banks find long-term loans too risky, and these firms are too small to issue long-term bonds. The original entrepreneur usually takes his return largely in the form of stock ownership (rather than wage payments). Thus *the corporation income tax, which exempts interest payments, can be viewed effectively as a tax on entrepreneurship; it has an effect on the investment of new firms that cannot raise funds by borrowing additional amounts.*

If this view is correct, the long-run effects of the tax are not so much those associated with the reallocation of resources between the corporate and noncorporate sectors. Rather, they have to do with the degree of innovativeness of the corporate sector and the rate of technical progress. The magnitude of these effects depends on the elasticity of supply of entrepreneurship and risk taking, something about which economists have little knowledge.

The Effect of the Corporation Tax on Credit-Constrained Firms

The view that the corporation tax is nondistortionary for established firms is, however, somewhat controversial. Critics of this view argue that it ignores the fact that firms, at the margin, do finance a significant fraction of their investment by means other than borrowing. As we have noted, the argument presented above does not actually require that the firm borrow; it only requires that the firm can change its level of indebtedness in response to an increase in investment. If the firm would otherwise have used some of its funds to reduce its debt but chooses instead to increase its level of investment, the effects are precisely the same as those we have just described.

For a variety of reasons, however, firms may not be able to borrow (or they may have to pay much higher interest rates to borrow additional funds). Then the cost of inside funds (funds that have been retained inside the firm from past earnings) and outside funds (funds raised by issuing new equities or bonds or borrowing from a bank) may be markedly different.[8] There may be many projects worth undertaking at the marginal cost of inside funds but not at the marginal cost of outside funds. By reducing after-tax profits, the corporation income tax reduces the supply of inside funds and thus has a direct effect in reducing invest-

[7] Equivalently, a firm with outstanding debt that is not currently borrowing from the market but that is doing some investment can ask itself: Is it worth investing a little bit less, and using the extra funds to repay some of our outstanding debt obligations?

This view of the corporation income tax was put forward in J. E. Stiglitz, "Taxation, Corporate Financial Policy and the Cost of Capital," *Journal of Public Economics,* February 1973, pp. 1–34; and J. E. Stiglitz, "The Corporation Income Tax," *Journal of Public Economics,* April–May 1976, pp. 303–11.

[8] Recent theoretical work has emphasized the importance of imperfect information; those inside the firm (managers, large shareholders with controlling interests) know more about the firm's prospects than outsiders. The insiders will be particularly anxious, for instance, to sell shares of the firm when they observe that the market is overvaluing their company. See, for instance, B. Greenwald, J. E. Stiglitz, and A. Weiss, "Informational Imperfections and Macroeconomic Fluctuations," *American Economic Review,* May 1984, 194–99.

ment. To the extent this is true, the relevant factor in assessing the impact of the corporation tax is the average tax rate, not the marginal rate.

Many empirical studies of the effects of the corporation income tax simply assume that it increases the marginal cost of capital to the firm—the amount it would cost the firm to invest an additional dollar—by an amount equal to the average tax payments per unit of capital. That is, they assume that the marginal and average costs of capital are the same. We have seen that if firms can finance their marginal investment by borrowing (and if depreciation allowances are equal to true economic depreciation), there may be no marginal distortion caused by the tax system, and the marginal cost of capital may differ markedly from the average. Regardless of whether one holds the view that the marginal cost of capital is equal to (or less than) the marginal cost of funds raised by borrowing, there is no justification for the hypothesis that marginal and average costs of capital are the same.

The Corporation Tax as a Tax on Monopoly Profits

When there are monopolies, there are monopoly profits. A corporate income tax can then be viewed, in part, as a tax on pure (monopoly) profits. Pure profits, sometimes called excess profits, are total revenues less total costs, including a normal return on capital. (In long-run equilibrium, with competition, and with constant returns to scale, there are no pure profits.) That part of the tax corresponding to a tax on monopoly profits is, in effect, a lump-sum tax on monopolists.[9]

Whether the distortionary effects of the corporation income tax would be greater (per dollar raised) with monopoly or competition is uncertain. On the one hand, to the extent that the tax is partly a pure profits tax, it is nondistortionary; on the other hand, to the extent that it acts as an excise tax and, because of monopoly, production of the sector is already lower than the socially optimal level, the tax causes a greater distortion.[10]

Note that if the corporate sector can be viewed as consisting of a large number of monopolies (in different industries), the price may rise by more than the tax payments per unit output. As we saw in Chapter 17, under monopoly, with a demand curve of constant elasticity (that is, a 1 percent change in price has the same percentage effect on demand, regardless of the level of output), price is just a fixed markup over the marginal costs of production—including taxes. If the markup is, say, 20

[9] This assumes that the monopolist cannot avoid the tax by locating in a different country or by choosing not to be incorporated.

[10] We noted in Chapter 18 that the deadweight loss of a tax increases with the square of the tax. The effect of monopoly is similar to that of a tax. Indeed, if the demand curve has a constant elasticity of, say, 2, monopoly has the same effect on output and consumer prices as a 50 percent tax on the output of a competitive industry. Imposing a 10 percent tax on the output of the monopoly thus has the incremental deadweight loss associated with increasing the tax on a competitive industry from 50 percent to 70 percent (taking into account the fact that the monopoly price rises by twice the magnitude of the tax when there is a constant elasticity demand curve with elasticity of 2). This is substantially larger than the incremental deadweight loss from increasing the tax from 0 percent to 10 percent on the output of competitive industry.

percent, then if marginal costs increase by $1 from the imposition of the corporation tax, price will increase by $1.20.

Managerial Firms: An Alternative Perspective

The analysis so far has been predicated on firms' maximizing their after-tax returns. There are a number of aspects of firm behavior that seem hard to reconcile with this view. For instance, later we shall show that firms should not pay dividends; there are better (from a tax perspective) ways of distributing funds from the corporate to the household sector. The fact that firms have continued to distribute as much of their earnings as they have is called the "dividend paradox." Firms' dividend policy is not the only inexplicable aspect of corporate behavior.

Accelerated depreciation provides another "tax paradox." At times, the government has given firms and individuals the right to depreciate their assets at an accelerated rate. Again, the total nominal depreciation allowances are unaffected (they equal the cost of the machine, minus its salvage value, if any). But more rapid acceleration reduces reported income and, hence, taxes in the early years of the asset. All firms should want to take advantage of this opportunity. Yet firms were very slow to take advantage of this opportunity. This is true even though firms can make it clear to their shareholders that *reported* earnings are lower than they otherwise would be because the firm has made use of accelerated depreciation; indeed, one might have thought that shareholders would take such a report as a positive signal of good management, and the absence of such a report as a negative signal.

Firms have a choice of how to treat their inventories. Assume a firm that is selling steel beams bought some steel at $40 a ton and some at $100 a ton, a few months later, as a result of rapid inflation in the industry. Both kinds of steel beams are in its inventory. When it sells some steel beams for, say, $110 a ton, does it say its cost of purchase was $40 or $100? The Internal Revenue Service allows the firm to choose what to say, so long as it does so in a consistent manner. It can either say that it is always selling the item most recently acquired (this is called the last in, first out system, or LIFO) or that it is selling the first item acquired (first in, first out, or FIFO). In inflationary periods LIFO has a decided advantage over FIFO. Current tax liabilities are lower (though future tax liabilities are increased by the same amount). But the general principle that a dollar today is worth more than a dollar tomorrow implies that firms are better off with lower current tax liabilities. Yet, amazingly, firms were very slow to switch to LIFO, and even today, many firms continue to use FIFO.

EXPLANATIONS FOR TAX PARADOXES

Two explanations are offered for such seeming irrationalities. One is that managers of the firms are not profit maximizing and that the discipline afforded by a competitive marketplace, which is supposed to ensure efficiency, works only weakly. The second is that firms are rational but that shareholders are irrational. Shareholders do not understand how the tax system (or corporations) work. It is unlikely that they would notice a firm switch to the LIFO system, but they would see the firm's current reported profits decline, and they would believe that the firm is not doing as well as it was. As a result, the price of the firm's shares would decline. Consider what might happen if a firm failed to pay a dividend but instead distributed the same amount it previously had distributed as dividends in the form of capital gains (buying back shares). Consumers might get confused and value the firm less than they otherwise would. Managers, whose compensation often depends partly on the market value of the firm, thus prefer to keep shareholders "happy" by engaging in policies that do not minimize the firms' tax liabilities. Both explanations are probably partially correct.

THE CORPORATE VEIL

More generally, our analysis of firm behavior is predicated on the assumption that individuals can understand what is going on inside the firm: that they are indifferent, for instance, when choosing between owning 10 shares in a firm with 1,000 shares or 9 shares out of 900 shares in the same firm; that if the firm reduces its debt obligations by $1,000, the market will see that the net worth of the firm is now $1,000 greater, and its share prices will correspondingly increase; that if the firm invested $1 million of retained earnings, and a shareholder owns 1 percent, it is as if the shareholder himself had invested $10,000 directly. We assume, in other words, that individuals can see through the *corporate veil* to what is really going on; but as we have noted, there are several puzzling aspects of corporate behavior that seem inconsistent with the hypothesis that individuals do see through the corporate veil.

MANAGEMENT INTERESTS

Some economists believe that the managers of firms have considerable discretion in managing their firms, sometimes pursuing their own interests at the expense of that of the shareholders. For instance, in recent years there have been many instances of take-over bids, where one firm proposes to buy another at a price often considerably in excess of current market value. The management of the target firm often resists the bid, and in several cases has paid the firm attempting the take-over to withdraw its offer, even though doing so greatly reduces the value of the firm. (These payments are called **greenmail.**)

The divergence of interests between management and shareholders became evident in the discussions prior to the enactment of the 1986 Tax Reform Act. An earlier version of that act called for partial tax deductibility of dividend distributions. In spite of the advantages that such a provision would have had for shareholders, the provision was not greeted with enthusiasm by corporate managers, perhaps because it would have increased pressure on them to distribute earnings. With less retained earnings, they would have less discretionary power.

Though these theories call into question the assumptions we have made about "profit maximizing" firm behavior, their implications for the consequences of the corporate tax—its incidence and distortionary effects—remain unclear.

The Corporation Tax as a Tool of Economic Policy

Under the system of depreciation allowances adopted in 1981 there was frequently not a close connection between "true" economic depreciation—the decrease in the value of plant and equipment—and the deduction allowed under the law. As a result, some categories of investment faced effective tax rates that were much lower than others. Similarly, other special provisions affected a variety of industries, particularly oil and gas and timber.

Most economists viewed these as "distortionary," the result of special interest groups. On the other hand, some of those in government argued that these provisions were deliberately enacted to encourage certain industries, for which, for one reason or the other, there would otherwise be (so they contended) less investment than was socially optimal. The corporate tax should, in this view, be thought of as a tool of economic policy. As the Congressional Budget Office put it, "the corporate tax is used not only to raise revenue but to influence economic activities . . . the tax code allocates investment where it might not otherwise be undertaken."

The importance of the special provisions of the tax code was highlighted by a recent study by Eugene Steuerle of the Treasury Department and the Brookings Institution. He showed that of the total income from capital in the United States, 80 percent received some kind of preferential treatment.[11]

THE CORPORATION TAX AND ECONOMIC EFFICIENCY

We have presented several alternative views of the corporation tax. The nature of the distortions associated with the tax depends on which view one takes. When viewed as a tax on capital in the corporate sector, it discourages the use of capital in the corporate sector because the cost of capital is raised relative to the cost of labor. And because costs of production in the corporate sector are raised relative to costs of production in the noncorporate sector, it discourages production of goods by the corporate sector.

But we have emphasized that the effects of our corporate income tax are different from those of a uniform tax on capital in the corporate sector. In the section on credit constraints, we showed that the deductibility of interest meant that the tax discriminated between firms that

[11] E. Steuerle, "Is Income from Capital Subject to Individual Income Taxation?" *Public Finance Quarterly*, July 1982, pp. 283–303.

financed their marginal investment, in effect, through borrowing, and those which were credit constrained.

We have also noted the view that while the corporate system may alter the allocation of investment, it should *not* necessarily be viewed as distorting that allocation. Rather, the corporation tax is an economic policy instrument by which the government tries to divert investment in ways which it thinks particularly desirable.

Marginal Effective Tax Rates

To measure the magnitude of the allocative effects (whether viewed as desirable or not) of the tax code, economists have calculated the tax rate that firms face when considering new investments; this is the firm's marginal effective tax rate. Calculating it is not an easy matter.[12]

Consider a $100,000 investment yielding a return over ten years. The return stream is lowered by the corporate taxes associated with the marginal investment, though for some years the investment may lower the taxes the firm would otherwise have paid. In effect the tax payments may be negative because of depreciation allowances, deductions for interest payments on any loans to finance the investment, and (before 1986) the investment tax credit. Included in the tax payments are any property taxes that the firm must pay on its investment.

Figure 23.4 shows the marginal effective tax rates for equity-financed investments. The differences in the treatment of different assets increased enormously after 1979.

Alan Auerbach of the University of Pennsylvania has estimated that the welfare losses arising from the differential tax treatment of different categories of assets were five times as large (under the 1981 tax law) as the distortions between industries. (He estimates the total deadweight loss in 1981 to be approximately 10 percent of the revenue collected.)[13]

Distortions Arising Because Some Firms Do Not Have Taxable Income

Debt financing or economic losses on past investments may lower taxable income to the point where companies cannot use all their depreciation deductions and credits.[14]

Consider a firm with large depreciation allowances, say, because of accelerated depreciation on some new assets, which at the same time is making losses in a variety of other lines. If its taxable income is negative, the depreciation allowances have no value; when the tax is already zero, it cannot be reduced further.

[12] The firm's effective marginal tax rate takes into account the present value of all the taxes that a firm would expect to pay on the income from an asset, as well as the tax credits and deductions that accompany it.

[13] A. J. Auerbach, "Corporation Taxation in the United States," *Brookings Papers on Economic Activity*, 2 (Washington D.C.: Brookings Institution, 1983) pp. 451–513.

[14] Firms are allowed to carry over certain tax benefits to future years, but without interest or inflation adjustments to keep their present value unchanged.

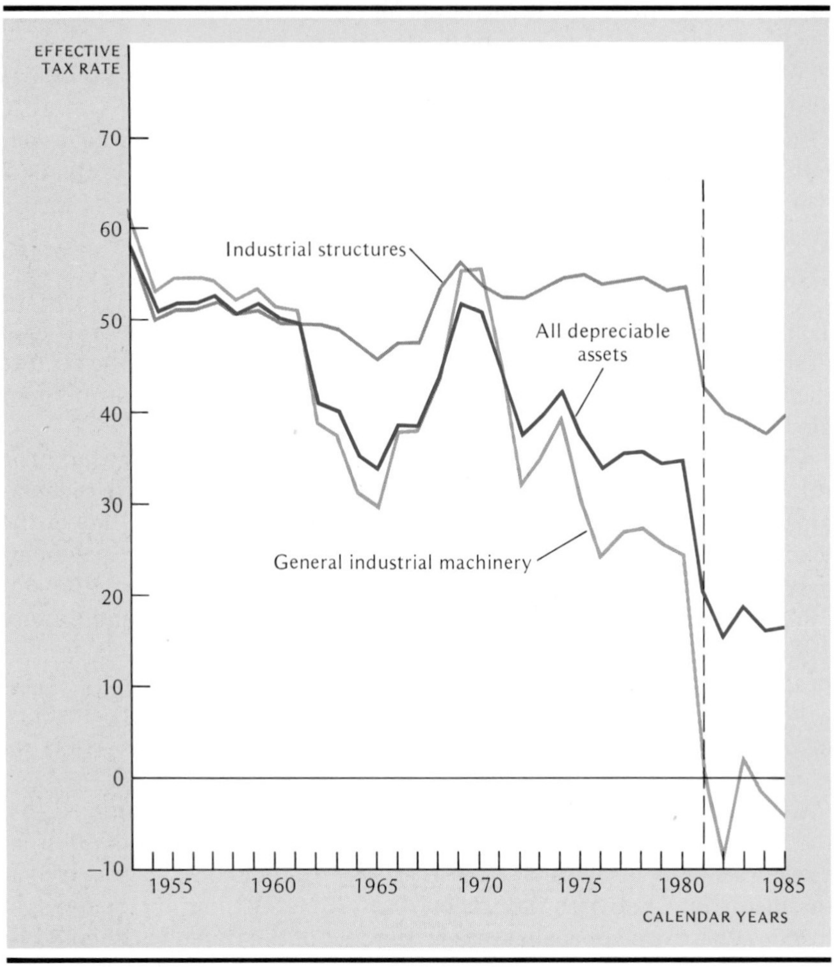

23.4 CORPORATE MARGINAL EFFECTIVE TAX RATES FOR EQUITY-FINANCED INVESTMENTS Disparities in marginal effective tax rates faced by different assets have increased enormously since 1979. SOURCE: Congressional Budget Office, *Revising the Corporate Income Tax* (Washington, D.C.: U.S. Congress, May 1985), p. 39.

Assume that the firm still will be doing poorly when the returns to the investment occur. Then, since the returns will not be taxed—there will be losses in other parts of the firm to offset the returns on this productive investment—the tax system may cause no distortion. But most firms that are doing badly and are investing anticipate doing better in the future; this implies that while the firm is not able to take advantage today of the depreciation allowances, it will have to pay taxes in the future on the returns to that investment just like any other firm. Thus the tax system causes a strong distortion *against* investment in firms that are currently not doing well and helps to perpetuate their weak position.

TAX-INDUCED MERGERS

The market always attempts to find ways of dealing with inefficiencies created by the tax system. One way is for the firm with losses to merge with a firm with profits. These are referred to as **tax-induced mergers.** There are many economists who are concerned about the long-run consequences of these mergers. Such mergers may limit competition in the economy. Moreover, it is believed that the vitality of a capitalist economy depends on having a large variety of firms; each firm has its own strengths and is thus in a position to take advantage of different situations. Some have made the analogy between firms and species of animals. Just as it may be advantageous to preserve a rich genetic pool, to be drawn upon in a variety of circumstances, so too may it be desirable to have a diversity of firms in the economy. The provisions of the tax code that encourage mergers (mergers that, apart from taxes, would not be undertaken) should, in this view, be altered.

LEASING

A second method of counteracting inefficiencies in the tax system is called **leasing.** Assume that a firm such as Chrysler has large losses and so cannot take full advantage of the depreciation allowances. To modernize its plants it would like to invest $1 billion. (Were General Motors to invest $1 billion, the government would, effectively, finance a fraction of that investment.) Chrysler approaches a firm that has large profits (Exxon) against which it can take the depreciation allowance. This firm buys the machines, and Chrysler rents the machines from it. Apart from the transactions costs, it is as if the government gave the tax benefits of the depreciation allowances directly to Chrysler.[15] In other words, it is as if Exxon had paid its full taxes, and the government had paid the investment subsidy to Chrysler. Instead, Exxon pays the subsidy to Chrysler.[16]

These leasing arrangements had been employed for years, but there were a number of restrictions that made them unattractive for many firms. The intent of the restrictions was to ensure that the lease was not done *simply* for tax reasons. Thus the nominal owner of the asset had to bear certain risks, much as it would if it were buying the asset for its own use.

[15] One way of doing this, for instance, would be *negative* taxes on negative income, i.e., when a firm has a loss, the government would share in part of that loss, that generated by depreciation allowances. Another alternative is to allow a *carry-forward* of losses with interest; under current law, firms are allowed to carry forward losses, but without interest. A dollar of reduced taxes in the future, however, is not worth a dollar of reduced taxes today. If, however, the firm lost $1 million today, but was allowed to deduct $1.1 million next year (assuming a 10 percent interest rate), then the *present value* of the tax reduction would be the same.

[16] Competition among firms with large profits ensures that most of the tax savings to firms like Exxon actually accrue to the firms like Chrysler.

The Tax Act of 1981 changed all that. It created what were called **safe-harbor leases,** the effect of which was to allow leases, the sole purpose of which was to permit corporations without taxable income to take advantage of the investment tax credit and depreciation allowances. Effectively, it allowed one firm to buy another firm's tax credits and tax deductions.

Though the Treasury Department had forecast fairly accurately the extent to which firms would take advantage of this provision, Congress and the public seem to have been taken by surprise: more than $20 billion of tax benefits were taken in the first year alone. This gave rise to a clamor against this giveaway to firms, and the Tax Act of 1982 reduced the benefits considerably. But in the clamor the basic issue became lost. The issue was simply whether firms that were doing poorly should receive the same subsidies to their investment that firms doing well received. The government may or may not wish to subsidize investment; there are good arguments that could be made either way. But it seems unlikely that as a matter of public policy, those subsidies should be restricted to old firms that are doing well.

COMBINING THE EFFECTS OF INDIVIDUAL AND CORPORATION INCOME TAXES

To assess fully the effects of the corporation income tax, we must see how it interacts with the individual income tax. The best way to see this is to imagine an individual who owns his own corporation. The more general case, with corporations owned by many individuals, is more complicated, but the results are similar.

Distributing Funds: The Basic Principles

In Figure 23.5 we have drawn a schematic picture of the relationship between the corporate and the household sector. Funds flow from the corporate sector to the household sector in the form of dividends, interest, and share repurchases. Funds flow from the household sector to the corporate sector in the form of new bonds and new equities. Funds flow within the household sector as individuals purchase shares and bonds from each other. And funds flow within the corporate sector as corporations purchase one another and are merged.

The tax authorities treat interest, dividends, and capital gains differently. Interest and dividends are taxed identically at the individual level, but payments from the corporation to the individual that are labeled "interest" are deductible from corporate income, while those labeled "dividends" are not. If the firm buys back shares, the individual is only taxed on the difference between the price at which the individual pur-

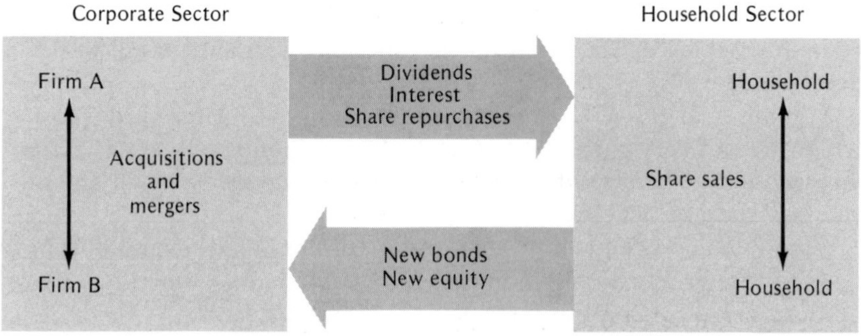

23.5 FLOW OF FUNDS BETWEEN AND WITHIN HOUSEHOLD AND CORPORATE SECTORS Funds flow from the corporate sector to the household sector, from the household sector to the corporate sector, and within each of the two sectors.

chased the share and the price at which the firm buys it back; in effect, the distribution of funds from the corporation to the household by share repurchases is only partially taxed. While there are legal constraints that prohibit a firm from regularly buying back a pro rata share of its stock from each of its stockholders in lieu of paying dividends, firms can simply buy back shares on the open market.[17]

The fact that our tax code does not tax all transactions at the same rate, and taxes transfers—whether in the form of interest, capital gain, or dividends—from the corporate sector to the household sector, has two basic implications:

1. Avoid transferring income from the corporate to the household sector whenever possible.

2. When income must be transferred, do it in a form so that it is eligible for capital gains treatment.

The Dividend Paradox

Corporations often seem to engage in financial transactions that are not consistent with the above principles. Dividends provide one important example. The puzzle of why firms pay dividends, when funds could be

[17] Note that if the firm bought back 5 percent of each individual's shares, the fraction of the firm that each owned would remain the same. This transaction is substantively the same as an equivalent cash dividend.

Note too that if the firm buys back the shares on the open market, the advantages of the share repurchase are even greater. Each individual could have sold back 5 percent of his shares; the fact that an individual chooses to buy back a different amount means that he is better off than if he were "forced" to buy back 5 percent of his shares. Individuals who bought the shares at a higher price may be more willing to sell their shares, since in doing so they encounter a smaller tax liability than those who bought the shares at a lower price. Thus, the transfer of funds from the corporate to the household sector will entail an even smaller tax liability than if the firm repurchased 5 percent of each shareholder's shares.

distributed from the corporate to the household sector in ways that encountered lower tax liabilities, is called, as we have noted, the **dividend paradox.**[18]

A number of possible explanations have been put forward, most of which are not very convincing. One is that dividends serve as a "signal" concerning the firm's net worth. Though this may be true, buying back shares should be an equally effective signal.

Though many owners of stock are tax-exempt (and thus indifferent to whether the firm issues dividends or buys back shares), individual shareholders who pay taxes should prefer share buy-backs.[19]

Mergers, Acquisitions, and Share Repurchases

The tax advantages of distributing funds from the corporate to the household sector through share repurchases (as opposed to dividends) can be obtained in other ways. When one firm buys another for cash, the receipts by the owners of the acquired firm are subject to capital gains taxation.

Though many firms have persisted in policies that appear not to minimize total tax liabilities, there is some evidence in recent years of increasing sensitivity to tax concerns.

During the ten years preceding the Tax Reform Act of 1986, mergers, acquisitions, and share repurchases increased enormously. While in the early 1970s, payments for mergers, acquisitions, and share repurchases amounted to approximately 15 percent of dividends, by 1984 they exceeded dividends, and in 1985 they amounted to almost 50 percent more than total dividends. The cost to the Treasury in foregone tax revenues exceeded $25 billion in 1985.[20] Many economists believe that these activities were tax-induced, that corporations had gradually come to recognize the advantages of distributing funds to the household sector in ways that subjected them to capital gains taxation.[21]

The 1986 Tax Reform Act not only reduced the tax advantages of capital gains by taxing them at full rates, but also repealed several provisions that resulted in capital gains taxes being avoided when a firm was liqui-

[18] The dividend paradox was discussed in J. E. Stiglitz, "Taxation, Corporate Financial Policy, and the Cost of Capital," *Journal of Public Economics,* 12 (1973): 1–34. Subsequent studies include J. Poterba and L. H. Summers, "Dividend Taxes, Corporate Investment, and 'Q'," *Journal of Public Economics,* 1983, pp. 135–67; A. Auerbach, "Wealth Maximization and the Cost of Capital," *Quarterly Journal of Economics,* August 1979, pp. 433–66; D. Bradford, "The Incidence and Allocation Effect of a Tax on Corporate Distributions," *Journal of Public Economics,* 15 (1981): 1–22; and M. King, *Public Policy and the Corporation* (London: Chapman and Hall, 1977).

[19] There are financial transactions that are even more puzzling than just paying dividends. For instance, when a firm simultaneously pays dividends and issues new shares, it unnecessarily increases tax payments. If the funds had been left in the corporate sector, the tax on the dividends could have been avoided. Even if some shareholders wanted the cash that the dividend provided, they would have been better off by selling an equivalent amount of their shares (to the individuals who would have bought the new share issues).

[20] From J. Shoven, "New Developments in Corporate Finance and Tax Avoidance: Some Evidence," in L. Summers, ed., *Tax Policy and the Economy,* National Bureau of Economic Research, 1987.

[21] But many economists argue that, though there may have been tax benefits, these mergers and acquisitions had other motivations. See M. Jensen, "The Take-over Controversy," *Journal of Economic Perspectives,* Winter 1988.

dated (either when it was sold to another firm, or when its assets were sold, with the proceeds distributed to the shareholders).[22]

Financial Restructuring

The principles entailed in financial restructuring are similar to those encountered in our discussion of how firms should distribute income to the household sector. A financial restructuring entails the firm borrowing to buy back shares, thus increasing its debt-equity ratio. In assessing the impact of financial restructuring, we need to include the changes in taxes paid by the corporation, by equity owners, and by bondholders. There is a cost: the taxes that must be paid on the capital gains on the repurchased shares (taxes that could have been postponed, or possibly even avoided, in the absence of a restructuring). There is a benefit: interest payments are deductible from the corporation income tax, dividends are not; on the other hand, if the firm had had a policy of share repurchases, the distributions to the shareholders would have received favorable tax treatment, relative to the distributions labeled "interest." One can show that so long as the corporation tax rate exceeds the effective individual income tax rate on the capital gains, if the firm had always paid out returns to shareholders in the form of dividends, the financial restructuring is desirable.[23] We suggested earlier that there were strong incentives for firms to distribute funds to the household sector in a form that was subjected to capital gains treatment, and that by 1985, a substantial portion of funds were in fact distributed in this form. In that case, a financial restructuring becomes much less desirable.[24]

Under the 1986 Tax Reform Act, the difference in the corporate and (marginal) individual tax rates is sufficiently small for high-income individuals that the tax savings from restructuring are relatively small, and, if a substantial part of the returns to shareholders is distributed in

[22] Indeed, some tax lawyers argue that the repeal of the "General Utilities Doctrine"—which permitted a liquidating corporation to avoid paying capital gains on distributions—to be one of the most important provisions of the new tax act. Consider a firm that has assets (accumulated, say, through retained earnings) that have increased enormously in value. Under the old law, if the firm liquidated, the (maximum) *total* tax rate was 20 percent. Under the new law, the corporation must pay a 34 percent tax; the remainder, when distributed, will be taxed at full rates. Thus, the effective rate is 52.5 percent ($.34 + .28 \times .66$).

[23] If r is the rate of interest, t_g the *effective* tax on any distribution (the effective capital gains tax rate will always be less than the legislated rate, because the effective rate takes into account that capital gains taxes are only paid upon realization, and some capital gains manage even to escape taxation), t_c the corporate tax, and t the individual income tax rate, then the tax savings to the corporation each year per dollar increase in its debt are rt_c. If these additional savings are distributed to the individual, the after-tax receipts of the individual are increased by $rt_c(1-t)$. The *present discounted value* of a perpetual stream of this amount (discounting at the after-tax interest rate of $r(1-t)$) can be shown to be just t_c. The extra tax the first period from the financial restructuring is t_g.

[24] If the firm borrows to buy back one dollar in shares, the flow of return to shareholders will be reduced by $r(1-t_c)$. The after-tax present discounted value of this (discounting at rate $r(1-t)$) is $\frac{(1-t_g)(1-t_c)}{1-t}$, under the assumption that the returns are distributed in a form subject to capital gains taxation. The increase in the present discounted value of after-tax receipts by bondholders is $1. At the time of the restructuring, a tax of t_g is paid. It can be shown that the present discounted value of household after-tax receipts increases if the corporate rate exceeds the personal rate.

Note that even though it does not pay the firm to borrow to buy back shares, it also does not pay the firm to issue equities to reduce its debt. When it buys back shares, a tax liability (t_g) is encountered; when it issues new shares, there is no corresponding current change in tax liabilities.

forms subjected to capital gains treatment,[25] a financial restructuring may actually increase tax liabilities.

New Investment

Most firms finance most of their investment out of retained earnings, what they have left over from their after-tax profits, after paying any interest to bondholders and after paying out dividends. If investment exceeds retained earnings, they obtain the additional required financing by borrowing.

While debt has the advantage that interest payments are deductible from the corporation income tax, equity has several advantages: only part of what is received from share repurchases (the "capital gain") is taxed; and even though under the 1986 Tax Reform Act capital gains are taxed at full rates, capital gains are only levied upon realization and are not levied upon death.[26] Under current tax law, these advantages are largely offsetting. While some individuals (those at the 33 percent bracket) might prefer the firm not to engage in any financial restructuring and to finance new investments first out of retained earnings, and then by borrowing, others such as tax-exempt institutions would prefer firms to pursue a high-debt policy. Thus, it is argued that different firms should cater to different *clientele.* It is not apparent to what extent they in fact do so, perhaps because these tax effects are not as important as other considerations.

COST OF CAPITAL

In the absence of taxation, firms would invest to the point where the return to capital was equal to its cost. If a firm borrowed all the funds to buy a machine, the total cost of owning the machine for a year would be the interest on the loan plus the decrease in the value of the machine (from use and/or obsolescence) over the year. This cost is sometimes referred to as the **user cost of capital.**

Taxes affect both the return to a machine and its costs. Firms will invest to the point where the after-tax marginal return to capital equals the after-tax cost of capital. If the tax rate is t, and the before-tax marginal return is denoted by MR, then the after-tax marginal return is $(1 - t)MR$. If $\hat{c}$ is what the firm must pay (after taxes) to get one more dollar of capital, the firm sets $(1 - t)MR = \hat{c}$ or $MR = \frac{\hat{c}}{1 - t}$. We call $\hat{c}/1 - t$ the **effective after-tax cost of capital.** The marginal return is set equal to the effective after-tax cost of capital. It is a useful concept,

[25] Even though capital gains are taxed at the same rate, recall that with share repurchases (mergers, etc.) only the difference between the price the individual receives and the price he paid is subject to tax.

[26] The importance of the latter advantage is particularly transparent in the case of a firm owned by an individual who plans to leave his entire wealth as a bequest to his children. By postponing distributing the profits of his firm until his death, he eventually escapes all taxes.

because if the effective after-tax cost of capital increases, investment will be reduced; if it decreases, it will be increased.

The exact formula for the effective after-tax cost of capital depends, as we have seen, on how the marginal investment is financed, as well as on the rules for depreciation. If there is accelerated depreciation, the effective after-tax cost of capital will be lowered. If there is true economic depreciation (see Chapter 22), and the marginal investment is financed by debt, then the after-tax cost of borrowing is just $r(1 - t)$ and the effective after-tax cost of capital is just r. As we have already noted, in these circumstances taxes leave unaffected the level of investment; the marginal return is reduced by the same amount that the marginal cost is.

CALCULATING EFFECTIVE MARGINAL TAX RATES ON NEW INVESTMENT

There have been several attempts at a full calculation of the effective marginal tax rate, taking into account all of the marginal taxes—corporate, property, and personal—that are paid as a result of a new investment.

Perhaps the most thorough recent study of overall effective marginal tax rates on investment is that of Don Fullerton and Yolanda Henderson. They asked: If an individual invests a dollar more in an asset that yields a before-tax return of, say, 10 percent, what will his after-tax return be, after paying property taxes, capital gains taxes, corporation taxes, taxes on dividends, interest, etc? Alternatively, what before-tax rate of return is required if the individual is to obtain, say, an after-tax return of 10 percent? Table 23.2 shows their calculation for a *debt-financed* investment under 1982 law. Effective marginal tax rates in the corporate sector (for equipment, structures, public utilities, inventories, and land) were negative. A negative tax rate means that the government is effectively subsidizing the investment; a tax rate of −208.2 percent (corporate equipment) means that if the after-tax return is 10 percent, the before-tax return is less than −10 percent. Thus, investments that yield

Table 23.2 EFFECTIVE MARGINAL TAX RATES: DEBT-FINANCED INVESTMENTS, 1982

	Corporate	*Noncorporate*
Equipment	−2.082	−.528
Structures	−.464	.082
Public Utilities	−.561	.026
Inventories	−.890	.088
Land	−.665	.144
	Owner-occupied	*Noncorporate*
Residential structures	.203	.155

Source: D. Fullerton and Y. K. Henderson, "Incentive Effects of Taxes on Income from Capital: Alternative Policies in the 1980s," in C. R. Hulten and I. V. Sawhill, eds., *The Legacy of Reaganomics: Prospects for Long-Term Growth* (Washington, D.C.: The Urban Institute Press, 1984).

a negative return are still profitable, so long as the return is not too negative.[27]

These calculations assume that the marginal investment is financed by debt. If the marginal investment was financed in the same way that the average investment was financed (the same ratio of debt to equity),[28] the effective marginal tax rates would be higher; but there would still be many categories of investment with negative effective marginal tax rates, and the differences in effective marginal tax rates among categories of assets would remain large. The overall effective marginal tax rate in the noncorporate sector of 11.6 percent was low—lower than on most wage income. Note too that residential structures faced *higher* effective marginal tax rates than other categories of investment, and that owner-occupied housing was taxed even more than residential structures.

The 1986 Tax Reform Act substantially increased effective marginal tax rates in the corporate sector and on non–owner-occupied residential structures. It was far from successful, however, in creating a level playing field.

SHOULD THERE BE A CORPORATION INCOME TAX?

The rationale for the corporation income tax has never been completely clear. Some believe that corporations, like individuals, ought to pay taxes. But most economists find this argument unpersuasive; it is not the corporation that pays the tax, but people: those who work for the corporation, those who supply capital to it, and those who buy the goods produced by it. The tax can be viewed as a tax on the corporate form of organization (on limited liability). Is there any reason that the government should wish to discourage this form of organization, or to penalize those who derive income from this form of organization? Most economists cannot see any strong argument for differential treatment. Many economists also question the value of imposing any tax on capital. While politicians often justify the corporate taxes in terms of their progressive effects, it is possible that they have no significant redistributive effect. This is hard to determine because of the difficulties of ascertaining who really bears the corporate tax burden.

There are two main arguments in favor of the corporate income tax. In the first, the corporation tax is viewed as a withholding tax on those who receive capital income from the corporation (like the withholding tax that is imposed on wage earners). Without such a tax, it is feared that many wealthy individuals might escape taxation. But there are two criticisms of this view. First, if it were viewed as a withholding tax, the eventual beneficiaries of corporate income should be credited with having paid taxes on this income. Although there have been proposals to do

[27] From M. King and D. Fullerton, *The Taxation of Income from Capital* (Chicago: University of Chicago Press, 1984), p. 256. They also provide comparisons of effective marginal tax rates between the United States and several other countries.

[28] But there is no reason to expect the marginal debt-equity ratio to be the same as the average.

that, at present it is not being done. Secondly, there is no persuasive reason that interest payments should be exempt from the withholding tax but dividend payments should not be exempt.

The second argument in favor of the tax is political: politicians like it precisely because it is not clear who pays the tax. Most taxpayers never know how much their income is reduced by the corporate income tax. But most economists would argue that the difficulty in ascertaining who bears the burden of the tax is actually an argument against the tax.[29] The corporation income tax does not do well on the criterion of "political responsiveness" that we presented in Chapter 16.

Thus, many economists argue that the corporation income tax should be **integrated** with the individual income tax (combining the two systems into one). The distortions associated with discouraging the flow of funds from the corporate to the household sector, in the decisions firms make in how to finance their investments and the encouragement of mergers and acquisitions, seem not to be justified by any compensating arguments, for instance, in terms of equity. Several countries have in fact integrated the two. There are a variety of ways in which such integration might work. One simple way is the following: There would be some reckoning of the taxes the corporation has paid on behalf of its shareholders, and some reckoning of the income of the corporation that can be attributed to each shareholder; the income would be added to the individual's tax base, the tax to what has been withheld on his wage income. Such an integration, its advocates claim, would not only be fair but would eliminate some of the important distortions we discussed in the preceding sections.

In this scheme, dividends would not be included in income separately. To do so would be double counting, since earnings—which include retained earnings and dividends—would already be included in income. Retained earnings cause a slight problem: in the absence of taxation, we could have imagined the firm paying out all of the earnings to the shareholders, and then the shareholders investing a part of what they receive back to the firm. Retained earnings are equivalent to a reinvestment by the individual in his firm. If there is a capital gains tax, account of this must be taken in determining what tax is due. Effectively, an individual's "share" of the retained earnings ought to be included in his "cost" of acquiring the shares. Assume an individual bought a share for $1,000. The next year the firm had a profit of $1,000 *per share,* of which it (invested) retained $300. The next year the individual sold his share for $1,400. What is his capital gain? His total investment in the share is his original expenditure of $1,000, *plus* the $300 of retained earnings, for a total of $1,300. Thus his capital gain is only $100.[30]

[29] A third argument is that one might like to tax capital income more heavily than wage income. One cannot easily differentiate wage and capital income in the unincorporated sector. One can in the corporate sector. But this view is not consistent with the deductibility of interest payments from the corporate tax base. (Besides, for reasons discussed in Chapters 20 and 25, it is not clear that the return to capital should be taxed at all, let alone more heavily than wage income.)

[30] Some economists, such as Joseph Pechman of the Brookings Institution, believe that the administrative problems associated with full integration make this infeasible. These problems are particularly

The tax treatment we have described for corporations is essentially the treatment that partnerships presently receive. At the end of a year, the income of the partnership is allocated to each of the partners. The only difference is that there is no "withholding tax" on partnerships.

The system just described represents a partial withholding tax on income to capital earned in the corporate sector. One could either extend the degree of withholding (making interest payments also subject to withholding) or decrease the degree of withholding (putting all the responsibility for payment on the individual). Prior to computerization, a strong argument could be made for withholding, since there was a fairly low degree of tax compliance among those who receive dividends and interest. Now all firms report dividend and interest payments to the Internal Revenue Service (IRS), which is in charge of administering federal taxes; because these reports are matched by computers with individuals' tax returns, compliance is not as significant a problem. In 1983 Congress passed a law extending withholding to interest, but after powerful lobbying by banks and other institutions who claimed that it would impose high administrative costs on them, the bill was rescinded. How significant these administrative costs are (given the computerization almost universally employed) is a moot question. The major disadvantage of making the corporations withhold the tax is that it may reduce the amount of funds available for reinvestment, and firms would have to raise more funds from the outside. The costs of raising funds may be significant. On the other hand, forcing firms to justify their additional capital requirements to suppliers of capital may have certain advantages.[31]

In the discussions leading up to the Tax Reform Act of 1986, a proposal that 10 percent of dividends be deductible from a corporation's income (for determining its tax liability) was given serious consideration. It was viewed by some as a first step toward the full integration of the personal and corporation income taxes, while to others, it represented but a minor redressing of the imbalance between the treatment of interest and dividends. The lack of enthusiasm by managers of corporations, who were perhaps concerned that it would increase pressure for them to distribute earnings, combined with the high cost to the Treasury in foregone revenues, led to the eventual elimination of this provision.

SUMMARY

1. If the supply of capital is perfectly elastic in the long run and the economy is competitive, a tax on the return to corporate capital is borne by consumers and workers. The after-tax return to capital is unchanged. The tax causes two

---

severe, as we have noted, if capital gains are taxed; individuals would have to keep a running account of the funds invested on their behalf by the firm through retained earnings. With modern computer technology, this problem is not as formidable as it would previously have seemed.

[31] This becomes particularly important when many shareholders are less informed than the firm's managers about the firm's prospects; under these conditions of imperfect information, there is an important distinction between inside funds and outside funds, and shareholders may not see perfectly through the corporate veil.

distortions, in the production efficiency of the economy (the economy no longer operates along its production possibilities schedule) and in the output mix (production is shifted toward the noncorporate sector).

2. If the supply of capital in the economy is fixed and the economy is competitive, the effect of the tax is to shift capital out of the corporate sector into the noncorporate sector, because after-tax returns in both must be the same. The after-tax equilibrium return will normally be lower than prior to the imposition of the tax, so that some of the burden of the tax lies on owners of capital. After-tax returns to capital may be lowered by even more than the tax.
3. If the corporate sector is noncompetitive, the tax is partially a tax on monopoly profits, and to that extent it is nondistortive. But the tax may also be a tax on the return to corporate capital and to that extent it may increase consumer prices by more than the increase in the costs of production resulting from the tax. There may appear to be more than 100 percent shifting.
4. Under our present tax system, interest payments are tax-deductible. This means that if marginal investment can be thought of as being financed through debt, a uniform corporation tax causes no distortion in the investment of the firm. The tax is best viewed as a tax on credit-constrained firms, which include many new firms, and hence it can be viewed as a tax on entrepreneurship.
5. In assessing the impact of the corporation income tax, one needs to consider the effect of the corporation tax simultaneously with the effect of the individual income tax.
6. The total (corporate plus individual) tax liability associated with a marginal investment depends on how that investment is financed, whether through debt or equity. The tax structure may affect how firms raise capital. There is no reason to believe that they finance new investments in the same way as they financed their previous investments, so that taxes may affect the marginal cost of capital differently from how they affect the average cost of capital.
7. The fact that firms pay dividends when there are other ways of distributing income to shareholders which result in lower total tax payments is called the dividend paradox. It is only one example of paradoxical behavior by firms, where they do not seem to minimize their tax liabilities.
8. The corporation tax falls unevenly on different forms of corporate investment, thereby biasing investment decisions toward certain favored assets or industries and against others that are not so favored. The economic cost of these uneven effective marginal tax rates is a misallocation of capital and a loss of output.
9. Many economists believe that the corporation and individual income taxes should be integrated.

KEY CONCEPTS

Tax base	Integration of corporate and individual income tax
Debt	Pure profits
Equity	Corporate veil
Retained earnings	Elasticity of substitution
Leasing	Tax-induced mergers
Dividend paradox	

QUESTIONS AND PROBLEMS

1. Discuss some of the controversies concerning who bears the burden of the corporation income tax. To what extent are differences in views accounted for by:
   a) differences in assumptions concerning the nature of the tax;
   b) differences in assumptions concerning the nature of the economy; and
   c) differences in interpretation of the data?
2. Is it possible for: (a) the price of output of the corporate sector to rise by more than the tax revenues collected (per unit of output); (b) the after-tax rate of return in the corporate sector to increase, after the imposition of the corporate income tax? Give conditions under which either of these may occur.
3. As a result of the provisions of leasing, several firms that had high profits paid no taxes. Discuss the equity and efficiency implications of this.
4. In the process of drawing up the Tax Reform Act of 1986, some congressmen wanted to increase the corporation tax rate further. Discuss the problems that arise when the corporation tax rate exceeds the highest personal income tax rates by a substantial amount.
5. Many firms pay their top executives with stock options, which give them the right to purchase shares in the company at a fixed price. When the firm does well, the value of the stocks increases, and hence the value of the option increases. Moreover, the income they obtain this way receives capital gains treatment, which prior to 1986, was taxed at much lower rates than ordinary income. Some critics of stock options claim that similar incentive effects can be obtained by tying executives' pay to the performance of the stock, but that paying executives directly has overall favorable tax consequences, once all taxes—including corporate taxes, the taxes paid by executives, and the taxes of shareholders—are taken into account. Discuss. (When the company pays executives directly, the wages are deductible from the firms' income subject to the corporate income tax; the "costs" of stock options are not deductible.)
6. There have been proposals to allow firms interest on the losses they carry forward on their tax returns from one year to the next. That is, if a firm has a loss this year of \$100,000, and the interest rate is 10 percent, it can deduct \$110,000 from its income next year (assuming that it is positive). Why might such a proposal be desirable? Would it completely resolve the problems that it is intended to address?
7. Why do economists make a great deal out of the difference between average taxes and marginal tax rates? Under what circumstances might these two differ significantly? Are there any circumstances in which you might be particularly concerned about what the average tax rate is?
8. Assume that at the end of the year, a machine costing \$1,000 is worth a fraction $1 - \delta$ of its value at the beginning of the year. $\delta \times 1{,}000$ is the true economic depreciation. In the absence of taxation, the firm will set the marginal return to investing, *MR*, as

$$MR = \delta + r.$$

Assume that the tax law allows the firm to take a deduction of δ^*. Assume that interest is tax deductible. Describe the new equilibrium condition for investment for the firm. What is the effective after-tax cost of capital? What would be the consequence of (a) using true economic depreciation? (b) eliminating the provision for interest deductibility?

24

A Student's Guide to Tax Avoidance

There is a widespread belief that the rich are able to avoid much of the taxes that they otherwise would pay by taking advantage of loopholes within the tax law. Most of these loopholes arise from the special provisions that govern the rates at which different kinds of capital income are taxed. Though closing these loopholes was one of the major motivations of the 1986 Tax Reform Act, which we discuss in the next chapter, the extent to which it was successful in this objective remains to be seen.

Although tax laws change, there is a constant duel between the tax authorities and the tax lawyers, with the tax lawyers developing new loopholes almost as fast as the tax authorities close old ones. If you understand the basic principles of tax avoidance, you will be able to adapt to these changes in the tax law.

From the public policy point of view, it is imperative to understand the nature of tax loopholes for two reasons. The total impact of the tax law depends as much on these special provisions as it does on the overall design. It may make little difference that we have enacted a progressive tax structure if the loopholes provide a method by which the rich can avoid paying high tax rates. Secondly, distortions in the patterns of investment and savings caused by these special provisions may be more significant than the distortions in the level of savings and investment caused by uniform capital taxation.

It is important to emphasize that we are concerned here with **tax avoidance,** as opposed to **tax evasion.** Tax evasion is illegal; tax avoid-

"Now, this over here, this is why you're going to have to go to jail."

Drawing by Mankoff; © 1982 *The New Yorker Magazine, Inc.*

ance entails taking full advantage of the provisions of the tax code to reduce one's tax obligations.

It is also worth noting that there may be disagreements about what is or is not a **loophole.** A loophole is a provision in the tax code that allows an individual to "escape" paying taxes. Consider, for example, a provision that has been introduced, say to encourage expansion of the oil industry. Should it be viewed as a loophole—because it reduces taxes in that industry—or as a *tax expenditure?* Those who think that the special provision is unwarranted will call it a loophole, those who think the special provision is an important incentive device will call it a tax expenditure. Like beauty, loopholes are often in the eyes of the beholder![1]

PRINCIPLES OF TAX AVOIDANCE

There are three basic principles involved in tax avoidance: income shifting, postponement of taxes, and arbitrage among the different rates at which the returns to capital are taxed. The next three sections discuss each of these in turn.

Income Shifting

The first principle is quite simple. Under a tax structure with increasing marginal rates, a taxpayer at a high marginal rate will always want to

[1] There are some loopholes that are put inadvertently into the tax law. Some of these are corrected in the "technical corrections acts," which are passed a year or so after the passage of every major tax act.

"shift" income to one with a low marginal rate. In particular, it pays parents to shift income to their children, for instance, by giving them some assets. The 1986 Tax Reform Act tried to limit this by taxing those under fourteen at the marginal tax rate of the parent.

There are several important points to note about income shifting. First, it requires the transfer of an asset such as stocks, bonds, real estate, or a share in the parents' business. Working parents cannot simply ask their employer to make out their paychecks in their children's names.

Secondly, income shifting works simply because of the fact that marginal tax rates increase with income. With a flat-rate tax structure, in which the marginal rate is constant (the individual is taxed, at a fixed rate, on the excess of his income over some exemption level), there is no incentive for income shifting, provided that the exemption level for a family is proportional to the number of individuals in the family.

Thirdly, there is a limit to the tax savings an individual can achieve through income shifting. Consider an individual with a wife and two children and total family income of $200,000. By shifting $48,150 to his fifteen-year-old son, the father can reduce total family taxes by $6,128,[2] a substantial amount, but still a relatively small percentage of his total tax liability.[3]

Fourthly, the government has attempted to limit income shifting, with only partial success. Consider the problems posed by divorce: How should the income from the ex-husband to the ex-wife and their children be treated? Under current law, alimony is tax deductible (taxable to the recipient), while child-support payments are not. Characterizing payments from an ex-husband as alimony (rather than a property settlement or child support) may have significant tax advantages. We noted in Chapter 21 how taxes intrude into the marriage decision; here we see how they also intrude into divorce.

Postponement of Taxes

A dollar today is worth more than a dollar next year. Accordingly, if one has a choice, it is always better to postpone one's taxes. There are several major methods of postponing taxes.

ACCOUNTING TRICKS

There are a variety of ways of using accounting devices to postpone the recognition of income. For instance, one way to postpone the capital gains tax on the sale of an asset is to postpone the date at which the transfer of the asset finally occurs. When an individual buys a house (or any other large asset), the seller often lends the buyer part of the pur-

[2] $5,000 escapes taxation completely (hence saving $1,650). $17,850 is taxed at 15 percent rather than 33 percent (for a saving of $3,213), and $25,300 is taxed at 28 percent, rather than 33 percent (for a saving of $1,265).

[3] With income of $200,000, his tax would be $54,248, and hence the reduction in his taxes would be just 11 percent.

chase price, which the buyer repays over several years. When does the sale of the asset actually occur and, hence, when must the seller pay capital gains tax? Is it when "control" of the asset is transferred, or when the buyer pays off the loan? The answer depends at least in part in how you "design" the sale. If title is not transferred until all funds are received, the later payments may be deemed payment of part of the purchase price rather than debt repayment. In this case, the seller will be able to postpone the capital gains tax. (These transactions are called **installment purchases.**)

In Chapters 21 and 22 we noted other problems in defining the *timing* of income. For instance, in construction projects and defense contracts, payments made prior to the completion of the contract are sometimes viewed as "loans" to the contractor, rather than payment for the project. Almost half of the projected increase in corporate tax revenues under the 1986 Reform Act is due to changes in accounting rules, including those related to construction and defense contracts.

CAPITAL GAINS AND THE POSTPONEMENT OF TAXES

Capital gains on an asset, as we have observed, are taxed only upon realization, that is, when the asset is sold. If one buys a capital asset and it goes up in value, one can postpone paying the tax simply by not selling the asset. If one would like to sell part of the asset in order to buy, say, some consumer goods, it may be better to borrow, using the asset as collateral. This method has a further advantage: if one postpones the sale until death, no capital gains tax is due (even by your heirs).

Tax Arbitrage

Arbitrage involves taking advantage of price differences for the same commodity, that is, when the asset is sold. If gold is selling for $350 an ounce in New York, and $375 in Zurich, and the cost of shipping gold between the two is $20, someone can buy gold in New York and ship it to Zurich for a sure profit. **Tax arbitrage** entails taking advantage of the different rates at which different kinds of income or different individuals are taxed.

Strictly speaking, the term "arbitrage" refers to situations where there is a sure gain—i.e., there is no risk assumed. Though in theory the tax code provides many opportunities for riskless tax arbitrage, in practice most tax avoidance activities involve the assumption of some risk. This is partly because of the general provision in the tax code that asserts that a set of transactions undertaken solely to avoid taxes will not be granted the favorable tax treatment. There are many situations where individuals must show that they are "at risk" to obtain the favorable tax treatment. But the risks that have to be borne are minimal.

The term is also applied to situations where different individuals face different tax rates, and a set of riskless transactions can be so designed so that both are better off as a result of the reduction in their joint tax liabilities.

We encountered one example of this in the preceding chapter in our discussion of leasing. A firm, which we shall refer to as NTB, Inc. ("near to bankruptcy"), which had insufficient income against which it could write off the accelerated depreciation allowances, sells its machines to a firm with a large income, CC, Inc. (for Cash Cow). NTB then leases the machines back. The bank that would have lent money to NTB for the machine now lends it to CC. Nothing *real* has occurred. The transaction is desirable because of the fact that NTB and CC face markedly different tax rates. The transaction reduces the total taxes paid by the two firms together, and there is a way in which the contract can be written so that they can split this gain (which is at the expense of the government).

STATE AND LOCAL (TAX-EXEMPT) BONDS

State and local bonds also provide an arbitrage possibility. Assume that state and local bonds yield 10 percent, and the individual can borrow money from the bank at 12 percent. If the individual is in the 33 percent marginal tax bracket, it pays for him to borrow, say, $10,000 to buy a tax-exempt bond. Every year he will have to pay the bank $1,200 in interest, but the after-tax cost of this is only $800. On the other hand, his tax-exempt bond yields him $1,000. He makes a clear profit (after taxes) of $200. The government, not surprisingly, does not allow this: it does not allow you to deduct interest on funds borrowed to buy tax-exempt bonds. But money is fungible: it may be impossible for the government to know whether you borrowed more than was needed when you constructed your house, so that you had money left over to buy tax-exempt bonds. This problem is sufficiently prevalent that there are precise rules specifying the conditions under which a loan will be treated as if it were made for the purpose of buying a tax-exempt bond.

IRAS AND KEOGH PLANS

Retirement plans, such as IRAs, provide limited opportunities for tax arbitrage. Again, the principle is the same as with state and local tax-exempt bonds. The individual can borrow money to deposit in these accounts. The interest payments may be tax deductible (if he borrows using his house as collateral), while the interest received will not be taxed until the individual withdraws funds from his account.

The individual may, of course, not consciously perceive himself as borrowing for these purposes; he may say to himself in April that it would be a good idea to put money into an IRA account; and then in June, he may decide that he would like to buy a new car; given his available cash, he finds that he needs to borrow more than he otherwise would have. He is smart enough to know, however, that if he borrows to buy the car, interest is not tax deductible. He has opened up a home equity loan account, which uses his house as collateral on the loan, and so long as the total amount he has borrowed (including his original mortgage) is less than the original purchase price of the house, his interest is deductible.

INSURANCE

Insurance provides further opportunities for tax arbitrage. Many life insurance policies can be thought of as both insurance and an investment. This is seen most clearly with what are called *single-payment* policies, where the individual purchases the policy with a single payment. The interest on this payment effectively is tax deferred until the individual cashes in the policy, or receives the proceeds as an annuity (a fixed annual payment) upon retirement. Again, if the individual borrows to buy his insurance (by using, for instance, a home equity loan), there is a possibility for tax arbitrage; the interest payments are tax deductible, while the interest earned largely escapes taxation.

TAX SHELTERS

Investment schemes devised primarily to reduce one's tax liabilities are called **tax shelters.** A tax shelter exists when deductions from one income source (e.g., oil and gas or real estate) can be offset against income from another source (e.g., salaries and wages). As we have noted before, for a tax shelter to be valid, there has to be an economic motive involved other than the avoidance of taxation.

There are a wide variety of tax shelters, but exploration of gas and oil represents perhaps the most notorious one. This tax shelter is based on a number of special, favorable tax provisions for the gas and oil industries. In Chapter 22, we discussed depreciation allowances. These are provided to take account of the fact that as a machine is used, it becomes less valuable (it wears out and becomes obsolete). Similarly, as oil is extracted from a well, the well becomes less valuable. To compensate for this, the government provides **depletion allowances.** These are related not directly to the change in the value of the asset but to the value of the oil extracted. Their level has varied over time, at one time reaching 27 ½ percent of the value of the oil sold. The correspondence between the depletion allowance and the change in the value of the well is even weaker than that between the depreciation allowance for a machine and "true economic depreciation." Over the life of the well, the depletion allowance may, for instance, exceed the purchase price of the asset. Moreover, when an oil well (or lease) is sold, a capital loss can be taken against the original purchase price without accounting for the depletion allowances taken in the interim. It is as if the government is allowing two tax deductions for the decrease in the value of the asset.

The taxpayer can use these deductions to shelter other income from taxation.

But we need to ask who gains by these tax loopholes. Industry experts claim that the return to capital in the oil industry, after tax, is no higher than elsewhere. But this is exactly what theory would predict: the benefits of the tax loopholes accrue to the owners of the inelastic factors, the land under which there is oil, not to "mobile" factors, like capital and labor. Thus if there were only inelastic factors involved, this tax loophole would have equity consequences but no distortionary consequences.

The 1986 Tax Reform Act and Tax Shelters

One of the major objectives of the 1986 Tax Reform Act was to design a tax system that was, and appeared to be, more fair. This meant that something had to be done about tax shelters. There were three approaches that were considered by the Treasury Department. The first was the elimination of the provisions, such as the favorable treatment of capital gains and the special treatment of the gas and oil industry, that gave rise to tax shelters. The second was limiting the extent to which losses on one category of income could be used to offset income in other categories. The third was the imposition of a more effective minimum tax. After careful consideration, the Treasury in formulating its original proposals decided on the first approach, to go after the basic source of the problem, and clearly rejected the second. Unfortunately, when Congress took up the matter, members found it politically difficult to attack many of the shelters directly, though one change, the full taxation of capital gains, reduced the value of many tax shelters. Because Congress left many of the loopholes in place, it had to turn to the second and third methods of attacking tax shelters.

The most important way it did this was to divide income into three categories, ordinary (earned) income, investment income, and passive income. Income generated by tax shelters (in which the individual did not take an active role) was categorized as passive income. So was most real estate income. Losses in one category could not be used to offset income in another. Thus interest expenses on one investment could be used to offset income from another investment, but net losses on investments as a whole could not be used to offset ordinary income. Nor could losses on real estate be used to offset ordinary income.

The Treasury had rejected this approach to controlling tax shelters for two reasons. First, one of the original objectives of tax reform had been to *simplify* the tax code. Distinguishing among passive, investment, and ordinary income will require a host of definitions, regulations, and court cases that will inevitably make the tax code even more complicated. Secondly, there is concern that these provisions will be of only limited effectiveness. Though they limit the extent to which tax loopholes can be used to avoid taxation of wage income, they do not effectively limit the extent to which (particularly rich) individuals can avoid taxation of capital income. They increase the transaction costs of tax avoidance. Real estate projects that generate taxable income will be bundled together with real estate projects that generate taxable losses. Taxes on real estate can thus continue to be avoided.

MINIMUM TAX ON INDIVIDUALS

The new tax act also attempted to reduce tax avoidance activities by imposing a somewhat stiffer minimum tax. The minimum tax on individuals is levied on a much broader definition of income; for instance, state and local income and property taxes are not deductible, and depreciation allowances are far less generous. The rules allowing individuals to take tax shelter losses are even more stringent than under the ordinary income tax.

The most important change provided by the new law was the increase in the minimum tax rate relative to the ordinary income tax rate. Most upper-income individuals will face a minimum tax rate of 21%, which is 75% of the regular rate they face, though because of some special features, some individuals will face a rate of 26.25 percent under the minimum tax.

By narrowing the gap between regular rates and the minimum tax rates, by lowering the top marginal tax rates, and by taxing capital gains at full rates the new tax act may have substantially reduced the demand for tax shelters and the opportunities for tax avoidance.

MINIMUM TAX ON CORPORATIONS

A minimum tax, at a 20 percent rate, has also been imposed on corporations. The toughening of the corporate minimum tax was partly a reaction of Congress to the widespread newspaper reports of major, apparently highly profitable, corporations not paying taxes. These corporations reported income to their shareholders, but income as defined for tax purposes may differ markedly from the income reported to shareholders (the *book* income of the firm). Thus Congress introduced a provision which required that, when book income exceeded taxable income for purposes of the minimum tax, as defined by the Internal Revenue Code, one-half the difference was to be added to the amount subject to the minimum tax. This is one of the most controversial aspects of the tax reform; the definition of income is taken at least partly out of the hands of the IRS and put into the hands of accountants. Since different firms use different accounting rules, firms in similar situations may pay very different taxes. Moreover, there will be incentives to change the accounting rules; in many cases, these rules were designed to convey critical information to the shareholders on how well the firm is doing. Though the provision is only temporary, economists have been concerned with the myriad of distortions and inequities that will inevitably arise (including the transition into and out of this "book income" minimum tax).

The Remaining Tax Shelters

Even at 28 percent or 33 percent, individuals have an incentive to avoid taxes if they can. The tax authorities have made it more difficult to avoid taxes, but not impossible (particularly on capital income). Among the available tax "shelters" we have already discussed are tax-exempt bonds and insurance. Individuals with moderate incomes can still defer taxes by using IRAs (although in recent years tax-exempt bonds have yielded higher returns with fewer restrictions).

One tax shelter that is particularly attractive for individuals with limited capital wishing to save for their children's education is provided by

U.S. government savings bonds. Interest on these bonds is taxable only when the bond is cashed in. Thus, if you purchase the bond in the name of your child, and postpone cashing it in until the child is at least fourteen, the income will be taxed at the child's rate (for most people, this means that the income will be tax-exempt; income has been shifted, and the restrictions applying to children under fourteen have been avoided).

GENERAL EQUILIBRIUM ANALYSIS OF TAX AVOIDANCE

To ascertain who benefits from a tax avoidance device is often difficult. It is often *not* the seeming beneficiary (or at least, he is not the only one who benefits). Consider, for instance, tax-exempt bonds. If ordinary bonds are yielding, say, 12 percent, and tax-exempt bonds of comparable risk are yielding 8 percent, then someone in the 33 percent bracket gets no benefit at all. All the benefit accrues to the community issuing the bonds (which has its cost of borrowing reduced by a third). If the tax-exempt bond yields 9 percent, individuals at the 28 percent and 33 percent brackets gain a little, but still, most of the benefit accrues to the community.

Under the leasing arrangements we discussed in Chapter 23, corporations with high incomes have their taxes reduced. But most of the benefits accrue to corporations with tax losses. If there are enough firms with high income looking for leasing arrangements, they will bid for the right to lease machines to the firms without income, that can offset their accelerated depreciation allowances.

By the same token, changes in the tax law which make tax avoidance more difficult may have unintended consequences. Thus, the firms that are hurt by provisions making leasing arrangements more difficult are not the high-income firms that appear to be avoiding taxes; they may actually be helped. Such provisions may reduce the number of firms that are willing to take up the leases; as a result of the less intense bidding, the low-income firms may find that they cannot find firms willing to lease machines to them, or that they may have to offer the high-income firms more attractive terms to induce them to undertake arrangements similar to those that they had undertaken before.

EQUITY AND EFFICIENCY CONSEQUENCES

We have not attempted in this chapter to provide an exhaustive list of loopholes, tax avoidance devices, and tax shelters. These change rapidly; at a given moment, some of the loopholes will have been closed and others opened up. The principles involved, however, remain the same.

Different industries have very strong incentives to attempt to garner for themselves special treatment. There is often some small justification for the special treatment. This special treatment opens up a loophole, which can usually be put into one of the categories that we have described in this chapter. It is important to note, however, to whom the benefits of these tax shelters accrue. They usually do not accrue to the investor attempting to take advantage of them. The competitive market takes care of that: different investors compete sufficiently vigorously to take advantage of the special tax advantages that the after-tax return—which, after all, is what the individual is really concerned with—is driven down to the after-tax return on other, less advantaged investments.

The consequences of the special treatment, then, are twofold. First, it diverts resources into the industry that is receiving the special treatment. This may be the intention of the legislation, but it usually is not. The return to perfectly mobile factors—such as capital—will be unaffected by such a subsidy. All the benefits will accrue to the owners of factors that are specific to the industry, such as land that cannot be used for other purposes. If all factors are "mobile," most of the benefits will accrue to customers.

Secondly, the major beneficiaries are the owners of the assets in the industry at the time that the loophole is opened up. It usually takes some time before real resources get diverted into the industry. In the meanwhile the original owners enjoy a windfall capital gain. The tax advantages are capitalized in the value of their assets; that is, if they sell their assets, they will receive a higher price for them; the individual buying the asset will pay a sufficiently high price that *his* after-tax return will be the same as it would be on any other asset.

Just as the imposition of such a tax benefit causes an inequity, a windfall capital gain for the current owners, the removal of the tax benefit causes an inequity, a windfall capital loss for the current owners. If the assets in the industry are owned by the same individuals when the benefit is granted as when it is withdrawn, the two cancel each other. But frequently, the removal of the special treatment occurs several years later, and it is often different individuals who will be affected by the removal of the special treatment. Closing the loophole is likely to be inequitable.

SUMMARY

1. There are three major principles underlying most of the devices by which individuals can legally attempt to reduce their tax liabilities: income shifting, tax deferral, and tax arbitrage.
2. Income shifting occurs under progressive taxes, where a family, by transferring assets to children, reduces its total family tax liability.
3. Tax deferral is based on the concept that a dollar today is worth more than a dollar tomorrow, so taxes paid in the future are less costly than those paid today.
4. Tax arbitrage takes advantage of the different tax treatment of various forms of capital income, and, in particular, of provisions that allow certain types of capital income to go untaxed until the individual withdraws funds from his account.
5. Tax loopholes have distortionary effects, and the benefits often do not accrue to those that they seem to be benefiting. The tax benefits of industry-specific loopholes (such as those relating to oil and gas) accrue to the owners of the inelastic factors in the industry (the land under which the hydrocarbon deposits lie), not to elastic factors (labor and capital).

6. The Tax Reform Act of 1986 attempts to restrict tax loopholes, not by eliminating them, but by imposing a more effective minimum tax and by dividing income into three categories (ordinary income, investment income, and passive income); losses attributable to one category cannot be used to offset income in another.

KEY CONCEPTS

Tax avoidance	Income shifting
Tax evasion	Tax arbitrage
Tax shelters	

QUESTIONS AND PROBLEMS

1. A common method of income shifting prior to 1984 was the granting of interest-free loans within a family. (These are referred to as Crown loans.) What would be the tax savings for an individual in the 28 percent marginal tax bracket from a $20,000 loan made to a child who had no other income, if the interest rate is 10 percent? Assume the child, as a dependent, cannot claim a personal exemption and can take only a $500 standard deduction.
2. A tax avoidance device that became popular in the late 1970s and early 1980s was the zero coupon bond. This was a bond that paid no interest. When the interest rate was 7 percent, a ten-year bond promising to pay $100 in 1990 would sell for $50 when issued. The government required the individual to *impute* the receipt of interest, to assume that one-tenth of the $50 gain that occurred between 1980 and 1990 occurred in each year. At the same time, the issuer of the bond could impute the payment of interest. If the two (the issuer of the bond and the purchaser) were in the same tax bracket, what would be the consequences of these imputed interest payments and receipts? If they were in different tax brackets?
3. Another popularly used tax avoidance device before 1981 was *straddles*, in which an individual would at the same time sign a contract to buy a commodity (like wheat) at some future time, and sign another contract to sell the same commodity at a date that was shortly earlier or later. Thus, when he had a gain on the first contract, he generally would have a loss on the second. What he gained on one, he lost on the other. Can you think how you could use straddles to postpone taxes? (Hint: Consider the consequences of selling one of the securities on December 31, the other on January 1.) Prior to 1986, long-term capital gains were taxed much more lightly than short-term capital gains. Can you think how you could use straddles to take advantage of this difference?
4. Describe the tax savings for someone in the 28 percent marginal tax bracket who owns a business with $10,000 in "profits" if he incorporates, giving his child (over fourteen) a 50 percent interest in the business. Assume his child has no other income and, as a dependent, cannot claim a personal exemption and can take only a $500 standard deduction.
5. Use a demand and supply curve diagram to contrast the effects of special treatment to cattle (assuming a horizontal supply schedule) and to oil (assuming a vertical supply schedule).

25

Reform of the Tax System

On May 29, 1985, President Reagan transmitted to Congress a proposal for a major tax reform. In his message to Congress, he wrote:

> We face an historic challenge: to change our present tax system into a model of fairness, simplicity, efficiency, and compassion, to remove the obstacle to growth and unlock the door to a future of unparalleled innovation and achievement.
>
> For too long our tax code has been a source of ridicule and resentment, violating our Nation's most fundamental principles of justice and fair play. While most Americans labor under excessively high tax rates that discourage work and cut drastically into savings, many are able to exploit the tangled mess of loopholes that has grown up around our tax code to avoid paying their fair share—and sometimes paying any taxes at all . . . .

His sentiments reflected the feelings of the majority of Americans. One poll, in early 1985, for instance, reported that 69 percent of those asked said that they believed that people who have more money than they did paid too little in taxes.[1]

After a tumultuous history, in which it appeared on several occasions that the tax reform bill would be defeated, it was finally passed by Congress and signed into law on October 22, 1986. This chapter describes

[1] The New York Times/CBS News Poll, reported in *The New York Times*, January 24, 1985, p. D1.

the impetus for reform, the major successes and failures of the act, some key aspects of the tax reform process, and the prospects for the future.

THE IMPETUS FOR REFORM

The impetus for a major reform in our tax system came from the widespread belief that its administrative costs were excessive, that even with these high administrative costs compliance was decreasing, that the tax system was riddled with inequities, and that the high marginal tax rates and the myriad special provisions gave rise to significant inefficiencies and contributed to the marked slowdown in productivity growth in recent years.

Administrative Costs

The brunt of the administrative costs of the U.S. income tax system is borne by the taxpayers, and the costs are not only the direct costs of filling out the tax returns but the indirect costs of record keeping required to comply with the tax laws.

The tax laws are so complex that nearly half of all taxpayers use tax preparers. Joel Slemrod of the University of Michigan estimated that in recent years taxpayers spent from 5 percent to 7 percent of the revenue raised by the federal and state income tax systems on compliance costs (the value of their time plus what they paid to tax preparers).[2]

In one recent year alone taxpayers spent around 2 billion hours filling out tax returns, and between $3.0 and $3.4 billion on professional assistance.

Complexity

The complexity of the tax code contributes to the high administrative costs, to the low level of compliance, and to the widespread sense of inequity. There are many indicators of this complexity. We have already noted that almost half of all taxpayers resort to professional assistance to complete their tax returns. There are more than 250 different forms. Of the 180 volumes comprising the Code of Federal Regulations (describing all general and permanent laws in force in the U.S.), the Internal Revenue Code is responsible for 14. Of these, 8 volumes, filling 5,105 pages, are devoted to the income tax.[3]

The complexity is reflected in the difficulties that even the Internal Revenue Service has in accurately assessing tax liabilities. Ralph Nader's Tax Reform Research Group created a tax schedule for a fictional couple that they sent to twenty-two IRS offices. The tax liabilities assessed by the different offices differed markedly, from a high refund of $811.96 to

[2] Slemrod's estimates were based on a 1982 survey of Minnesota taxpayers. See J. Slemrod and N. Sorum, "The Compliance Cost of the U.S. Individual Income Tax System," February 1984, University of Minnesota (mimeographed).

[3] R. Hall and A. Rabushka, *Low Tax, Simple Tax, Flat Rate* (New York: McGraw-Hill, 1983).

a tax underpayment of $52.14. IRS studies have shown that commercial firms which fill out tax returns for individuals with low incomes make errors on 82% of the returns. And people trained and employed by the IRS computed the wrong tax 72 percent of the time when handling relatively simple tax problems.[4]

Another indication of the complexity of the code—the difficulty that individuals have of knowing whether they are or are not complying with the law—is provided by the fact that, when individuals go to court to challenge the IRS, they generally win: the IRS recovers only about one-third of what it claims.[5] Instances where one court has ruled one way and another a different way on the same issue make the plight of the taxpayer even more difficult. For example, as we noted in Chapter 21, commuting costs are not, in general, deductible. A Federal Appeals Court in New York ruled, however, that airplane pilots could deduct the costs of using their automobiles to transport their heavy paraphernalia (and themselves) between their homes and the airport. But a tax court in Florida, not bound by a decision in New York, ruled the other way.[6]

Compliance

To collect its taxes, the federal government relies on a combination of voluntary compliance coupled with the threat of stiff fines and prosecution for outright fraud. To assist individuals whose sense of moral responsibility might be too weak to induce them to report all of their income, the government requires employers to report what wages they pay to their workers and firms to report what dividends and interest they pay to shareholders and bondholders. The government has only limited facilities, however, for checking on cash transactions, and the ability to avoid taxes by using cash has encouraged the growth of unreported transactions, referred to as the **underground economy.** Though precise estimates of the size of the underground economy are hard to come by, some observers believe that it may involve up to one-quarter of the work force and 15 percent of GNP. It includes unreported income not only of drug dealers, babysitters, and domestic help but of carpenters, gardeners, and those who sell merchandise on the street.[7] By 1986, the IRS estimated the income tax owed on unreported cash transactions, or resulting from overstated deductions or unjustified tax credits, had grown to $103 billion, an amount equal to about half the massive deficit of that year.

Though no comprehensive study of noncompliance has been done since passage of the 1986 Tax Reform Act, the sources of noncompliance

[4] *Consumer Reports,* March 1976.
[5] *Business Week,* April 16, 1984.
[6] Ibid.
[7] By its nature, it is difficult to obtain accurate measures of the underground economy. One survey of studies provided a range (as a percentage of GNP) from 3.5 percent to 33 percent for the United States. See Bruno S. Frey and Werner W. Pommerehne, "Measuring the Hidden Economy: Though This Be Madness, There Is Method in It," in V. Tanzi, *The Underground Economy in the United States and Abroad* (Lexington, MA: Lexington Books, 1982).

Table 25.1 INDIVIDUAL INCOME THAT ESCAPES THE TAX NET (1981 ESTIMATES)

	Shown on Tax Returns	*Should Have Been Shown*	*Percent Unreported on Tax Returns*
	(in billions of dollars)		
Wages and salaries	$1,455.2	$1,549.7	6.1%
Pensions and annuities	58.5	67.3	13.1
Interest	129.1	149.6	13.7
Dividends	44.9	53.7	16.4
Estate and trust income	3.9	5.2	25.8
State income tax refunds and alimony	11.7	18.9	38.0
Royalties	4.4	7.1	38.8
Capital gains	25.9	43.7	40.7
Nonfarm proprietor income	53.5	106.5	49.7
Partnership and small busines income	14.9	31.6	52.9
Rents	2.5	6.9	62.8
Off-the-book services	4.5	21.5	79.1
Farm proprietor income	−2.0	11.1	NA
Total Income	$1,807.0	$2,072.8	12.8%

NA = not applicable (total farm income reported was negative).

Source: Business Week, April 16, 1984, p. 9. Internal Revenue Service, *Income Tax Compliance Research, Estimates for 1973–1981,* July 1983, pp. 22, 37.

shown in Table 25.1, based on the old tax law, are likely to remain important under the new law. A major source of noncompliance is farm income: in the year in which the government did its comprehensive study, aggregate farm income was reported as a *negative* $2 billion, while estimated farm income that should have been reported was in excess of $11 billion.[8]

Some believe that compliance has decreased in recent years, partly as a result of the increasing complexity of the tax code and the sense that it is inequitable; partly because the increased marginal tax rates make compliance more expensive; and partly because of the decreased likelihood of being caught. While the government audited 2.25 percent of the tax returns in 1976, the percentage has been less than 1.5 percent in the years 1983–1987.[9]

The relative importance of these three explanations will become clearer as compliance with the new law is observed. Marginal tax rates have been reduced, complexity has been increased, and auditing has remained essentially unchanged. On the other hand, there is concern that the habits of thought and attitudes towards compliance, developed under the old tax law, will persist despite the change in the law.

[8] Unreported illegal income, though not so important as some of the sources of tax evasion given in Table 25.1, is still an important source of tax evasion. (Al Capone, the 1920s mobster, was convicted for failing to report his illegal income when other charges would not stick.) The government estimated that in 1981 it lost $6.1 billion from unreported income from heroin, cocaine, and marijuana, $1.9 billion from unreported female prostitution (it did not estimate the corresponding figure for male prostitution), and $900 million from unreported gambling earnings.

[9] On the other hand, the IRS may have grown more efficient in spotting tax evaders. Three out of four taxpayers audited in 1986 were assessed extra tax and penalties, up from 62 percent in 1980 (*U.S. News & World Report,* March 2, 1987, p. 63).

Tax Avoidance

Tax avoidance—taking advantage of all the loopholes in the tax structure—results in a significant erosion of the tax base and has increased rapidly in recent years. In the previous chapter we discussed the principles of tax avoidance as well as some of the more important tax shelters.

The line between tax avoidance and evasion, as we have noted, is not always easily defined. Thus in 1983 IRS agents audited 96,000 returns with tax shelters, obtaining an additional $1.8 billion in tax.

Whether as a result of tax avoidance or tax evasion, the net effect is that certain industries—such as real estate—were almost effectively exempt from taxation before 1986.

Most tax shelters take the form of partnerships. By the early 1980s tax avoidance had become so rampant that *all of the partnerships in the country, in aggregate, showed a large aggregate loss.*

There is indeed a market for tax avoidance activities, just as there are markets for conventional commodities. The demand for tax avoidance activities depends on how much one can save. This, in turn, depends on several factors, the most important of which is probably the marginal tax rate. Since the boundary between tax avoidance and tax evasion is often blurred, IRS auditing policy (and the penalties imposed on those who use shelters that are disallowed) is another important determinant of the demand for tax shelters. The supply of tax shelters, on the other hand, depends on the loopholes that are built into the tax law.

It might have been thought that the Economic Recovery Tax Act of 1981, which reduced the maximum tax bracket from 70 percent to 50 percent, would have decreased the demand for tax shelters. But at the same time its generous provisions for depreciation, leasing, and research and development expenditures increased the benefits of certain categories of tax shelters, and this "supply effect" more than offset the effect of the reduction in the marginal tax rates. The consequences were predictable: a large growth in shelters involving research and development, equipment leasing, and, in particular, real estate. One tax shelter expert, Robert Stanger, suggested that the Economic Recovery Tax Act of 1981 might more aptly have been called "the Real Estate Benefit Act."[10]

The widespread publicity given to tax avoidance activities undoubtedly contributed to the general public impression that the tax system was not working. While it was clear that some, perhaps many, individuals were avoiding taxes, there was disagreement among economists about how important this was.

Brookings Institution economist Joseph Pechman has argued that the popular discussions magnified the problem out of proportion. He pointed out that the ratio of income reported on tax returns to personal income (as calculated by the Department of Commerce) had actually increased from less than 40 percent in 1950 to almost 50 percent in 1981 (see Figure 25.1).

[10] Quoted in *Newsweek,* April 16, 1984, p. 58.

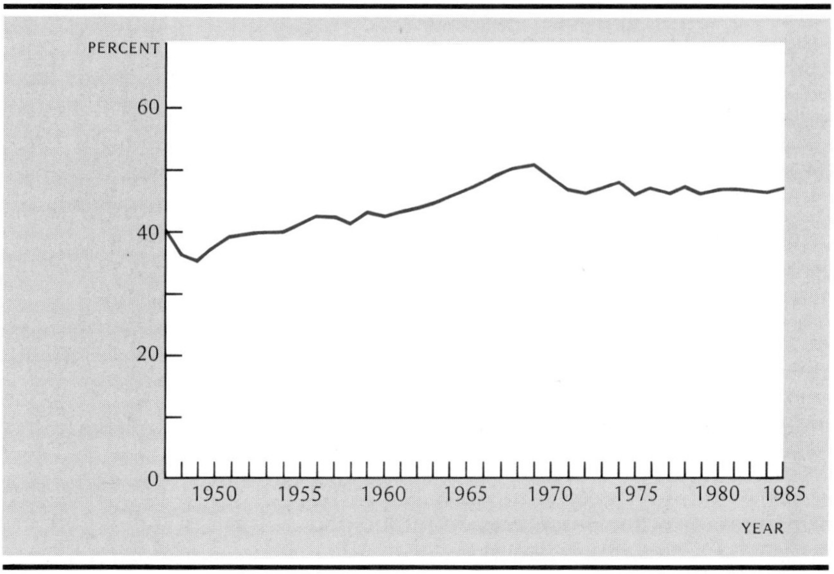

25.1 RATIO OF TAXABLE INDIVIDUAL INCOME TO PERSONAL INCOME, 1947–1985. The ratio of income reported on tax returns to personal income as calculated by the Department of Commerce has not changed radically in recent years. SOURCE: J. A. Pechman, *Federal Tax Policy* (Washington, D.C.: Brookings Institution, 1987), p. 67.

Pechman and other economists agreed that loopholes should be closed, but they were concerned that in the process of tax reform some of the desirable characteristics of the tax law, in particular its progressivity, would be adversely affected.

PRINCIPLES OF TAX REFORM

Our discussion provides several guidelines for the reform of the tax system.

First, the magnitude of the distortions is associated with the magnitude of the marginal tax rate. Thus one should attempt to design tax systems with low marginal rates.

Second, tax avoidance schemes are associated primarily with the progressivity of the tax schedule and with the taxation of capital—in particular, the taxation of different kinds of capital income at different rates. Reducing the level of marginal tax rates would reduce incentives to engage in tax evasion and tax avoidance. Reducing (or eliminating) the differential treatment of income would reduce the incentive, and ability, to engage in tax arbitrage.

Third, the complexity of the tax code arises from many of the same sources that give rise to tax avoidance. For instance, whenever different categories of income are taxed differently, individuals will attempt to ensure that their income receives the favored treatment. It seems a general rule that defining clear distinctions in tax law is much harder in practice than in theory.

Tax avoidance and tax evasion, besides making the tax system less progressive (and less equitable, since some individuals are in a better position to take advantage of these tax avoidance schemes and to evade taxes than others) than it otherwise would be, introduce important inefficiencies. Not only should the costs of designing and implementing these schemes (the accountants' and tax lawyers' fees) be treated as a deadweight loss, but there are further deadweight losses resulting from the resource allocation distortions to which these tax avoidance schemes give rise. For instance, the tax shelter provided to the oil and gas industry may have led to excessive investment in that industry.

A quite different argument in favor of simple, direct taxes is that a "good tax" has the property that one should know upon whom it falls, who bears the tax. Because its burden is passed along either to consumers or to stockholders, the corporate income tax is, as we have noted, a particularly bad tax in this respect.

The general principles we have outlined often run counter to other principles, or other objectives, of public policy. For instance, there are those who believe that a good tax is one that is not painful. As a finance minister to Louis XIV wrote: "The art of taxation consists in so plucking the goose as to obtain the largest amount of feathers with the least possible amount of hissing."[11] The corporate income tax may be a good tax in this respect.

Similarly, we noted in our earlier discussions that many of the distinctions that make the tax code complex, possibly unfair, and undoubtedly distortionary were introduced at least partly to make the tax system reflect more accurately society's view of equity (for instance, the sick should not pay so much as the healthy), and partly to improve the efficiency with which resources are allocated (the energy conservation credits, for example, were introduced because it was believed that private incentives to conserve energy were insufficient).

What had emerged clearly by the mid–1980s was that the tax system could not do everything. If we ask it to do too much, it may not do well in any of its objectives. The basic questions facing tax reform were thus:

1. Are there ways of simplifying the tax system that, while not sacrificing "too much" of the distributive objectives, gain significantly in economic efficiency?

2. Though society as a whole may be better off as a result of tax reforms, the reforms are seldom "Pareto improvements." Are there ways of designing the transition from the old system to the new system in which relatively few individuals are significantly disadvantaged? This is important, in part to make the reforms politically acceptable.

3. The tax system has been viewed as a relatively efficient means to pursue certain nonrevenue objectives. For example, to design a direct grant system for encouraging energy conservation would have been extremely difficult. Encouraging energy conservation through the tax system seemed a particularly effective (and administratively inexpen-

[11] Quoted in *Newsweek*, April 16, 1984, p. 69.

sive) way by which this national objective could be pursued. Indeed, there has been a long tradition in economics of advocating the use of "corrective taxes" to alleviate the inefficiencies arising from externalities. If a simplification of the tax system entails an abandonment of the use of corrective taxes, are there other ways by which these objectives could be attained, with at least the same degree of effectiveness that they are achieved at present?

THE 1986 TAX REFORM ACT

To what extent was the 1986 Tax Reform Act consistent with these basic principles of tax reform? Did it succeed in achieving the objectives that it had set for itself?

The Successes

There were three major achievements of the 1986 Tax Reform Act. First, it lowered the highest marginal rate from 50 percent to 33 percent, effective in 1988. Only eight years earlier, the highest rate had been 70 percent. As we have emphasized, many of the distortions, as well as much of the incentive for tax avoidance, are directly related to the high marginal rates.

Concern about the distortionary effects of high marginal rates has not been limited to the United States. In recent years, Sweden cut its top marginal rate from 87 percent to 80 percent, Portugal from 80 percent to 69 percent, Ireland from 77 percent to 65 percent, Italy from 72 percent to 62 percent, and Britain from 83 percent to 60 percent. Marginal tax rates in the United States remain much lower than in other countries.

The second major achievement was raising the personal exemption and standard deduction, thereby removing 6 million individuals from the tax rolls. The goal that those whose income was below the poverty level should not be taxed was at last achieved (see Figure 25.2).

The third achievement was that tax avoidance activities have been made both more difficult and less attractive. This is partly because some of the provisions that gave rise to tax avoidance activities—in particular, the favorable treatment of long-term capital gains and the rapid acceleration of real estate depreciation—were repealed. But the most important new obstacles to tax avoidance are the stiffer minimum tax and the restrictions on the use of losses on one category of income (such as real estate) to offset income in other categories (such as wage income), both of which we discussed in Chapter 24.

The 1986 Tax Reform Act divides income into three categories, *ordinary (earned) income, investment income,* and *passive income.* Income generated by tax shelters (in which the individual does not take an active role) is categorized as passive income. So is most real estate income. Losses in one category cannot be used to offset income in another. These provisions limit the extent to which tax loopholes can be used to avoid taxation of wage income. However, the extent to which they will effec-

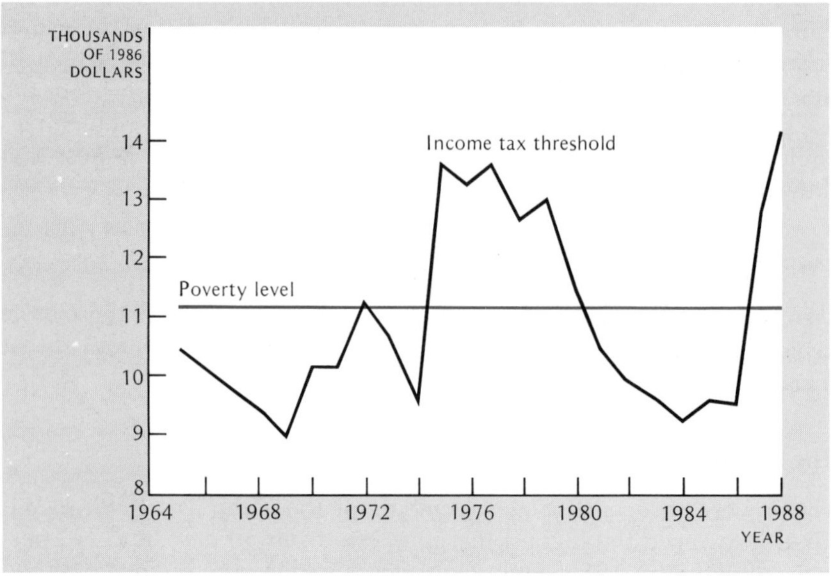

25.2 RELATIONSHIP BETWEEN THE POVERTY LEVEL AND INCOME TAX THRESHOLD FOR A FAMILY OF FOUR (in 1986 dollars) The figure compares the level of income below which a family is considered to live in poverty (shown in color) with the level of income at which a family begins to pay federal income tax (shown in black). The tax threshold (below which the family pays no taxes) dipped below the poverty level after 1980, but was dramatically increased by the 1986 Tax Reform Act. The tax threshold depends on the level of the personal exemption, standard deduction, and earned income tax credit. SOURCE: Joint Committee on Taxation, *Federal Tax Treatment of Individuals Below the Poverty Level,* June 14, 1985, p. 4; and estimates for 1987 and 1988 by the author.

tively limit the ability of (particularly rich) individuals to avoid taxation of capital income is questionable. (Real estate and other passive income projects that generate taxable losses will be bundled together with those that generate taxable income, so that taxes on, say, income-generating properties can be avoided.)

Though there had been a minimum tax prior to 1986, the new tax law was more inclusive in its definition of income (the minimum tax is imposed on the basis of a definition of income which allows fewer deductions and tax preferences). In addition, not only was the minimum tax rate increased, but the rate is now much closer to the ordinary income tax rate, thus greatly limiting the advantages to be had by tax avoidance activities.

Putting the Successes in Perspective

Some perspective must be put on these successes, as important as they are. First, marginal tax rate changes are large for only a few Americans. While 4 percent experience a marginal tax rate increase of more than 10

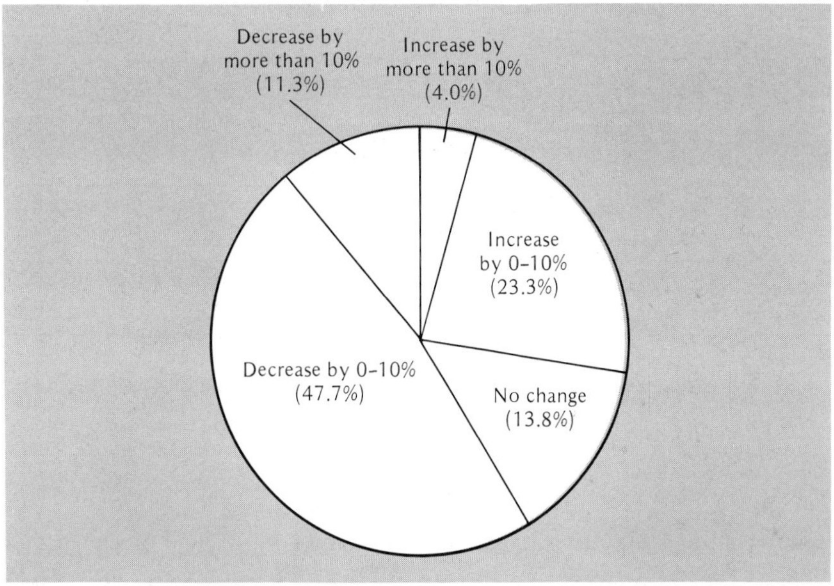

25.3 MARGINAL TAX RATE CHANGES Only a quarter of the population had a marginal tax rate change of more than 10 percent. SOURCE: J. Hausman and J. Poterba, "Household Behavior and the Tax Reform Act of 1986," *Journal of Economic Perspectives,* Summer 1987, pp. 101–20.

percent, 11.3 percent experience a marginal tax rate decrease of more than 10 percent (see Figure 25.3). Secondly, much of the reduction in marginal tax rates has simply reversed the bracket creep resulting from inflation that had occurred during the 1970s. Indeed, for a married couple with two children with an income in 1985 real dollars of $40,000, the marginal tax rate in 1988 of 28 percent was the same as in 1985, and still considerably above that in 1970 and 1960. For such a family, the big reduction in marginal rates occurred under the 1981 act (see Table 25.2).

Because the change in the marginal rate for so many individuals is so small, it is not surprising that it is estimated that the new tax law will have negligible effects on labor supply and savings.[12]

Some of the changes in the new tax law serve actually to increase marginal tax rates. For example, the provision under the old law by which 10 percent of earnings of working spouses was deductible (up to $3,000) has been eliminated.

For families with two earners who have similar incomes, the reduction in progressivity reduced the "marriage tax" in spite of the elimination of the proviso for deducting 10 percent of the spouse's earnings. For families with one earner, the marriage subsidy was reduced. Still, it is esti-

[12] See Jerry A. Hausman and James M. Poterba, "Household Behavior and the Tax Reform Act of 1986," *Journal of Economic Perspectives,* Summer 1987: 101–19.

Table 25.2 MARGINAL TAX RATES OVER THREE DECADES

Filing Status	*Income*	*Marginal Tax Rate*				
	($1985)	**1960**	**1970**	**1980**	**1985**	**1988**
Single	$14,000	22	22.6	21	18	15
Married Filing Jointly (2 Children)	25,000	20	19.5	21	18	15
Married Filing Jointly (2 Children)	$40,000	22	22.6	32	28	28
Married Filing Jointly (2 Children)	$200,000	62	56.4	64	50	28

Source: Jerry A. Hausman and James M. Poterba, "Household Behavior and the Tax Reform Act of 1986," *Journal of Economic Perspectives,* Summer 1987, pp. 101–20. Based on simulations using the National Bureau of Economic Research's TAXSIM Model.

mated that in 1988, 40 percent of all married couples will pay an annual average marriage tax of $1,100, and 53 percent will receive an average marriage subsidy of about $600.[13]

We saw before that ascertaining the effective marginal tax rate requires taking into account *all* of the provisions of the tax code, as well as social security and welfare programs. The new tax law raises the earned income credit for low-income workers with children from 11 percent to 14 percent (that is, the government in effect supplements whatever they earn by 14 percent), and the maximum earned income credit a family can now receive is $800. There is a phase out of the earned income credit, at a 10 percent rate, as the individual's income increases. As a result of this phase out, a family with children faces an effective marginal tax rate of 25 percent between $900 and $17,000.

The Failures

The 1986 Tax Reform Act falls far short of achieving some of the major goals that it had set out for itself (let alone the hopes of tax reforming economists).

First, it does not achieve the objective of *simplification.* The major simplification that the supporters of the reform point to, the reduction in the number of tax brackets, is a superficial one. Looking up in the tax table the tax that is due, once one's taxable income has been calculated, is an easy task, regardless of the number of brackets.

The new distinctions introduced in the tax law between various categories of income have, in fact, made the tax law more complicated. As we said in Chapter 24, distinguishing among passive, investment, and ordinary income will require a host of definitions, regulations, and court

[13] From H. Rosen, "The Marriage Tax Is Down but Not Out," National Bureau of Economic Research Working Paper No. 2231, May 1987.

MacNelly Chicago Tribune
1986 Tax Reform Quiz
1. Which is the old tax code, and which is the new, revised, simplified version?
2. Why are these guys still smiling?
TAX
TAX
OUR FIRST FIN
CPA
TAX ATTY.

Reprinted by permission: Tribune Media Services

cases. Indeed, the new tax law did not result in any simplification of tax forms; some forms became more complicated, and several new forms were introduced.

Secondly, the 1986 Tax Reform Act is far from successful in achieving its original objective of a fair tax system based on a "level playing field." Many loopholes have been retained, such as the favorable tax treatment of the gas and oil industry. While depreciation for real estate now more closely approximates "true economic depreciation," the highly accelerated depreciation allowances for other capital goods is retained. The elimination of the investment tax credit, however, means that most capital goods at least face a *positive* effective marginal tax rate. (Under the old tax law, some kinds of assets actually faced a negative effective marginal tax rate.)

The preferential treatment of owner-occupied housing has been retained, and indeed, the closing of other loopholes and the elimination of interest deductibility for borrowing other than for mortgages has meant that housing has become, relative to other investments, even more attractive.

Many view the elimination of the exclusion of 60 percent of capital gains as a major achievement. However, the tax act goes too far: Nominal capital gains, not just real capital gains, are taxed. Some or all of the nominal gains on any asset reflects inflation and not a real increase in value. While the original tax reform proposal made by the Treasury Department attempted to devise a system of indexing, so that the tax system would be inflation-neutral and only real income would be taxed, the administrative and revenue cost of indexing appeared to be too great. Political expediency resulted in a tax act with nominal capital gains subject to tax at full rates. In Chapter 22 we discussed the significant distortionary consequences this may have, particularly in periods of high inflation.

Some economists believe that overall—taking into account all of its provisions—the net effect of the new tax law will be to increase the distortions in the economy.

BASE BROADENING

Perhaps the greatest failure of the 1986 Tax Reform Act is that it has broadened the tax base only to a very limited extent. The myriad of special provisions that we have discussed in previous chapters removed slightly more than half of all income received by individuals from the pre-1986 tax base. There were several major "leakages" in going from personal income to adjusted gross income. The largest arose from the exemption of most government transfer payments (e.g., social security), imputed income from the return on owner-occupied houses, and investment income in life insurance companies, pension funds, and other tax-exempt forms. Still further "leakages" arose in going from adjusted gross income to taxable income, for example, from the deduction for charity and state and local taxes.

With the shrunken tax base, the tax rates necessary to raise the required revenue must be high, particularly if some degree of progressivity is to be maintained. Thus, a major goal of tax reform has been to broaden the tax base and to lower tax rates. The early Treasury proposals contained a number of base-broadening provisions, but most of the important ones were eliminated by the time Congress passed the act.

Thus, while the deductibility of consumer interest was eliminated, the quantitatively far more important provision for the deductibility of home mortgage interest was retained. Since money is fungible (funds borrowed for one purpose can be used for another, or in any case, can result in the release of funds that can be used for another purpose), individuals are likely to borrow more against their home (where interest is deductible) rather than to borrow to purchase a car or go on a vacation. This will accelerate the process, already begun, of individuals' using **home equity loans** (loans where their house is used as collateral). Though Congress attempted to impose restrictions, limiting loans against which interest was deductible to the original purchase price of the house, plus loans for medical and educational purposes, it is questionable how effective this provision will be. The restrictions on the interest deduction will be particularly ineffective for persons owning and operating small businesses, since they can often characterize all of their borrowing as for business purposes.

One of the most controversial base-broadening proposals was to eliminate the deductibility of state and local taxes. The states and localities were outraged. The politicians, particularly in those states with high tax rates, were concerned that there would be pressure to reduce state and local taxes and expenditures. (Note that in almost all states, the *median*

Table 25.3 COMPARISON OF TAX EXPENDITURES RETAINED AND DROPPED BY THE 1986 TAX REFORM ACT

State and local tax deductions	
Sales tax (dropped)	$ 5.5 billion
Income and property tax (kept)	27.8
Interest deduction	
For consumer credit (dropped)	$17.6 billion
For mortgage interest on owner-occupied homes (kept)	26.9
Health care provisions	
Medical expense deduction (modified)	$ 3.8 billion
Exclusion of employer contributions for medical insurance premiums and medical care (kept)	23.5

voter[14] does not itemize, and thus would be unaffected by this provision; if the median voter model is relevant, eliminating the deductibility should not significantly affect state and local expenditures; the magnitude of the opposition suggests that politicians at least do not believe the median voter model.) They managed to retain the deductibility for all state taxes except sales taxes, which are relatively insignificant (see Table 25.3). It is likely that there will be political pressure for states and localities with sales taxes to adopt income and property taxes, which are still deductible. Thus, the total revenue to be raised by repealing the deduction for state sales taxes may not be significant.

Although under the 1986 act only medical expenditures in excess of 7.5 percent of income are tax deductible, a far more important provision, the exclusion of employer-financed medical insurance, is retained. Table 25.3 compares some of the tax expenditures dropped by the Tax Act with the tax expenditures that were retained.

The most controversial change in the taxation of capital income is the substantial curtailment of Independent Retirement Accounts (IRAs). Though the amount of money at stake was relatively small, this was viewed to be one of the few tax shelters (besides housing) available to middle-income individuals.

OTHER FAILURES

To the more ardent advocates of tax reform, the 1986 act represents a failure in two other ways. First, it fails even to address the problem of the *integration* of the corporate and individual income tax. Although the earlier Treasury proposals had made some efforts at partial integration (by allowing a deduction for a fraction of dividends paid out of after-tax corporate income), these were thought to be too expensive.

The 1986 Tax Reform Act did not attempt to change the *basis* on which taxes are levied. Our tax system remains a hybrid, a cross between an income tax (in which interest income and other capital income is fully

[14] See Chapter 6.

taxable) and a consumption tax (in which income from capital is excluded from the tax base). The taxation of capital gains at full rates has moved us slightly closer to an income tax, but a large fraction of capital income still retains favorable treatment.

Finally, many economists believe that the increase in the corporation tax, at the expense of the individual income tax, should be viewed as a swindle. By lowering the money raised by the individual income tax, individuals might consider themselves winners, not losers, as a result of tax reform. This is possible only because no one knows precisely who pays the corporation income tax. The fact that the tax changes were designed to be revenue-neutral in fact means that, *on average*, there are no winners and no losers (except through the important indirect effects, resulting from the change in distortions).

PROBLEMS IN CHANGING THE TAX LAW

When President Reagan sent to Congress his original proposal for tax reform, he made it clear that his objective was to change the *structure* of the income tax, not the level of taxation. Thus he insisted that it be **revenue-neutral** (that is, that it raise the same amount of revenue as was being raised under the existing laws). Indeed, he even insisted that the overall degree of progressivity (the percentage of taxes paid by those in different income categories) not be substantially changed. The concern was that nothing would come out of an open-ended discussion, in which all of the structural issues were up for debate. He wished the discussion to focus on particular inefficiencies and inadequacies of the tax code itself.

The notion of revenue neutrality is not, however, unambiguous. When tax expenditures (say for state and local governments) are eliminated, should we assume that there will be an offsetting increase in direct federal grants to state and local governments? In the congressional debate, no consideration was given to the possibility of such offsetting increases. If there are such increases, the tax change will *not* be revenue-neutral.

Accounting for how the economy is likely to respond to the changes in the tax law is also difficult. Some economists believe the government has underestimated the stimulus that will be provided by the lower marginal tax rates, while other economists are concerned that it has underestimated the ability of the economy to substitute one tax shelter for another. The government may, for instance, have underestimated the extent to which individuals will be able to borrow against their houses, and so the increase in revenue attributed to the elimination of the interest deductibility for consumer loans may have been greatly overestimated.

Finally, the tax law entails many changes in accounting practices. Indeed, almost half of the increases in corporate tax revenue were the result of changes in accounting rules. Many of these changes were changes in timing, such that the level of taxes may be increased in the first five years of the act, but it may be decreased in subsequent years.

Budget Constraints and Political Trade-Offs

Most economists believe that tax reform is desirable, because the reduction in the distortions associated with the tax system would enable the economy to function more efficiently. But most tax reforms are not Pareto improvements. Even if there are many more gainers than losers, and the gainers gain more than the losers lose, inevitably some individuals will be worse off after the tax change. This is what makes tax reform so difficult. Special interest groups spend a great deal of time and money to maintain their special treatment. Congress attempted to cope with this pressure by requiring that any congressman who proposed an amendment granting tax relief had to specify how the offsetting extra revenue would be raised, e.g., which taxes would be increased, or which loopholes would be eliminated. This procedure was critical. Whether it will provide a model for future tax (and budgetary) reform remains to be seen.

Transitions

Changes in tax laws always entail problems. (Indeed, there is an old maxim that "old taxes are good taxes.") We noted earlier that changes in taxes on capital assets often result in significant changes in the value of those assets. Some economists attributed at least a part of the boom in the stock market in late 1986 and early 1987 to the 1986 Tax Reform Act.

There is particular concern about how the new tax law will affect real estate. It may seem unfair that real estate projects that were started under one tax law, which allowed the asset to be depreciated over eighteen or nineteen years, but completed under the new tax law, will be taxed much more heavily than the investors had anticipated.

At the same time, it may seem unfair that those who were lucky (smart) enough to have invested under the old tax law get the further additional benefit of lower tax rates. Old capital thus receives a windfall gain. Economists who were concerned with stimulating investment in the economy were particularly critical of these provisions, which rewarded old capital at the expense of new investment.

Those who are hurt by a new tax law obviously get much more concerned about the inequities than those who benefit; they lobby Congress for special transition rules. In the final days of the passage of the 1986 Tax Reform Act, a host of special provisions were adopted, worth billions of dollars, benefiting particular companies, particularly in the congressional districts of those who had helped to get the bill through Congress. To some, this was just a reflection of the politics of taxation; to others, it symbolized the defeat of the principles of tax reform.

THE FUTURE OF TAX REFORM

There is an ongoing debate about the likely future of the U.S. tax structure. Some believe that the 1986 act is just the beginning of a reform movement, and that future legislation will bring the tax system closer to the economists' ideal. Others believe that the absence of principle in the 1986 act means that special interest groups will be able to reintroduce special treatment for themselves in subsequent years.

Nobel Prize–winning economist James Buchanan presents what to many seems like a particularly cynical view. He argues that what gave rise to tax reform had little to do with what we discussed earlier as providing the impetus for tax reform. Rather, the inefficiency of the tax system meant that the marginal cost of raising revenues was so high that politicians were meeting increasing resistance to increasing expenditures. Moreover, the entitlements embodied in government tax and expenditure programs meant that politicians had little discretion to grant tax favors. He anticipates in coming years both an increase in direct expenditures (with a corresponding increase in tax rates) and an increase in special provisions for special interest groups.

Even less pessimistic economists, however, are concerned about the magnitude and persistence of the government's deficit. This, they are convinced, will inevitably put pressure on Congress to raise tax rates. If this is done, then what is perhaps the major achievement of the 1986 Tax Reform Act, the lowering of marginal tax rates, will be eliminated.

Whether or not tax reform is temporarily dormant or not, reform issues will eventually arise again. When they do, debate will likely focus on one of four proposals: a flat-rate tax, a consumption tax, a value-added tax, or a comprehensive income tax. We have already studied the major ways in which the current law fails to be a comprehensive income tax. Now we turn to the other three alternatives.

The Flat-Rate Tax

A flat-rate tax is a tax that applies the same marginal rate to all income above some threshold. The difference between an individual's income and a given exemption level would be subject to the flat-tax rate.

Advocates of the flat-rate tax believe that the elimination of the nominally high tax rates on the rich would eliminate the incentives of the rich to take advantage of the inevitable loopholes that creep into any tax system. The *uniformity* of the tax rate would also eliminate many of the tax-avoidance schemes; for example, tax shifting and tax arbitrage no longer would be relevant.[15]

Under the current law it would pay an individual at a high marginal tax

[15] It should also be noted that some inequities and inefficiencies associated with the tax exemption of interest on state and local bonds arise from the fact that marginal tax rates increase with income. Presumably, if all individuals had the same marginal tax rate, returns on these bonds would adjust so that all individuals would have the same after-tax return, whether on tax-exempt or taxable bonds. The distortion associated with excessive expenditures on local public goods (and in particular, on local capital goods) would, of course, remain.

rate to borrow money from an individual at a low marginal tax rate, since the tax savings in the interest deduction to the former exceed the tax liability on the latter. These noneconomic motives for lending would be eliminated if everyone were taxed at the same marginal tax rate.

ADMINISTRATIVE ADVANTAGES OF THE FLAT-RATE TAX

The uniformity of marginal tax rates—with its implication that it does not make any difference to whom one assigns a given income—has some administrative advantage as well. It means that income can be taxed at its source; taxing income at its source will reduce compliance costs and increase compliance rates. It would also be easy to impose a tax on fringe benefits (such as hospital insurance), since the tax paid would be the same, no matter who received the benefit; the government would not need to ascertain who benefited from a particular fringe-benefit program.

In fact, since all wages would be taxed at the same rate, the government could impose a (value-added) tax on net revenues of the firm. To make the tax system progressive, the government could then provide a fixed lump-sum grant to each individual. The result would be equivalent to a flat-rate income tax. Advocates of the flat-rate tax also point to the marked administrative advantages that could result from the integration of the corporation income tax and a flat-rate individual income tax.

REDISTRIBUTION AND THE FLAT-RATE TAX

Redistributive objectives could still be attained with a flat-rate tax. The higher the level of the exemption, the greater the proportion of the tax burden that will be borne by higher-income individuals. Jerry Hausman of M.I.T. claims that by introducing a flat-rate tax, it may be possible to lower the tax rate facing almost all income groups, because the reduction in the distortions would generate such a large increase in labor supply.[16]

These results are, however, controversial. Those who believe that the labor supply is relatively inelastic are concerned that to provide a reasonable level of exemption would require imposing a high marginal tax rate on those with incomes over the exemption level.

The Tax Reform Act of 1986 can be viewed as a modified flat-rate tax. But many of the advantages of a flat-rate tax come only from a pure flat-rate tax, not from its modified form. Thus, advocates of the flat-rate tax, such as Stanford economists Robert Hall and Alvin Rabushka, continue to advocate the adoption of the pure flat-rate income tax.

Consumption Tax

Many advocates of tax reform were disappointed that the reform act did not address the fundamental question of what should be the appropriate

[16] J. Hausman, "Labor Supply," in *How Taxes Affect Economic Behavior*, H. J. Aaron and J. Pechman, eds. (Washington, D.C.: Brookings Institution, 1981), pp. 27–72.

basis of taxation. We retained our hybrid system, in which much but not all of the income from capital escapes taxation. While advocates of a *comprehensive income tax*, who believe that all income should be subject to taxation, were pleased that the preferential treatment of capital gains was eliminated, they were disappointed that so many other tax preferences were retained.

But a large number of economists argue that *all* of the income from capital should be tax-exempt, or equivalently, that the appropriate basis of taxation is consumption. Sixty years ago Irving Fisher of Yale argued that it was more appropriate to tax individuals on the basis of what they take out of society (consumption) rather than what they contribute to society (measured by their income).

To tax consumption, one does not need actually to monitor an individual's purchases of goods. Rather, all one needs to observe is an individual's cash flow. Since

$$\text{Income} = \text{Consumption} + \text{Savings}$$

if one can measure income (total receipts) and savings, one can infer what the level of consumption is. The measurement of income involves problems of the kind we have encountered in our analysis of the income tax (distinguishing between legitimate business expenditure and consumption expenditure). The consumption tax does not solve these problems, but neither does it make them any worse. The problem of measuring an individual's savings is also not particularly difficult: one simple method calculates the total value of sales of securities during a year, less the total value of purchases during the same period. The difference plus the individual's wage income is his cash flow and is equal to his consumption.

EQUIVALENCE BETWEEN THE WAGE TAX AND THE CONSUMPTION TAX

In Chapter 17 we showed that a proportional consumption tax is equivalent to a proportional wage tax (ignoring for the moment bequests and inheritances). Taxing consumption alone is equivalent to giving a tax exemption for the income from capital. Those who believe that the major problems with our present tax system arise from the taxation of income from capital thus believe that a consumption tax will eliminate most of our current tax problems. Those who believe that exempting interest income is inequitable believe that a consumption tax is unfair. (A proposal for a tax on wages only would be politically much less popular than a proposal for a tax on consumption, though the two are in fact equivalent, in the absence of bequests and inheritances.)

The fact that a wage tax and a consumption tax are equivalent provides two alternative ways of levying the tax. We have described one way: the cash flow approach. The alternative way is simply to tax wage income. The cash flow approach has a major problem with the treatment of consumer durables, such as housing; the individual spends a large amount of money at one particular moment and would thus have a large tax liability. To avoid the problems to which this gives rise, the Treasury Department proposed in 1977 a mixture of the two approaches, which are described below.

Though a wage tax and a consumption tax give rise to the same tax (in present value terms) over an individual's lifetime, they differ in the pattern of cash flow to the government and in the problems that arise in the process of going from our present income tax system to the new tax basis. If individuals are on average saving, wage income on average exceeds consumption. Thus, though the present discounted value of tax revenues from a wage tax and a consumption tax would be the same, in the switch to a consumption tax, there would be a delay in the receipt of revenues; the government would have to finance its expenditures in the intervening period by an increase in debt.

Since, if bequests are included, consumption and income are equivalent (in present value terms), a consumption tax can also be viewed as lifetime income tax. Most economists would argue that lifetime income is a better basis for levying taxes than annual income. In this view, then, there is little disagreement between advocates of a consumption tax and advocates of an income tax.

ARGUMENTS FOR THE CONSUMPTION TAX

Recent arguments for the consumption tax are based on its advantages in terms of administrative simplicity; these arguments stand in marked contrast to the traditional arguments in favor of the consumption tax, which we have presented in previous chapters. The most important traditional arguments are: (a) consumption is a "fairer basis of taxation": it seems fairer to tax individuals on the basis of what they take out of society (consumption) than on what they contribute (income); and (b) consumption is a less distortionary basis of taxation.

The traditional form in which the efficiency argument was cast, that there were fewer distortions with a consumption tax than with an income tax, was shown to be incorrect. In the discussion of Chapter 20, we argued that we cannot compare taxes by counting the number of distortions. We showed there that if the only difference in individuals' incomes arise from differences in abilities, if relative wages are fixed, and if individuals' marginal rates of substitution between consumption early in life and later in life do not depend on how much they work, a consumption tax will be the optimal form of taxation: no tax should be imposed on interest income. If these assumptions are not satisfied, in some cases it was desirable to impose an interest income *subsidy*, not an interest income tax. There are two circumstances under which a persuasive case for an interest income tax (in addition to a consumption tax) can be made: First, an interest income tax may be desirable if such a tax changes the *before-tax* distribution in a desirable way; that is, if decreasing the after-tax return to capital discourages savings, and if unskilled labor and capital are substitutes, the lower capital supply will increase the relative wages of the unskilled; since there is a deadweight loss in redistributing income, it is always desirable to incur some deadweight loss to change the before-tax distribution of income. Secondly, an interest income tax may be desirable if individuals differ in their ability to invest, with some individuals obtaining a much higher return to their investments than others; then a wage tax alone (or, equivalently, a consumption tax) will not be able to redistribute income efficiently.

The recent resurgence of interest in the consumption tax has been motivated not so much by the traditional issues of equity (double taxation, whether consumption is a fairer basis of judging ability to pay than income, etc.) or efficiency (whether it is distortionary to tax interest income), which we have just discussed. Rather, it has been motivated by two concerns. First, as we noted in Chapter 22, many of the distortions in our tax system arise from the myriad of special provisions relating to the treatment of capital. Under the current tax system, a significant fraction of the return to capital is tax-exempt (owner-occupied housing, pensions, IRAs, etc.) or taxed at preferential rates. We thus have a system that is partly a consumption tax, partly an income tax. This hybrid may be less equitable, more distortionary, and more administratively complex than either a true income tax or a true consumption tax.

Concern with the administrative complexity of our tax laws, and the belief that much of this complexity arises from the taxation of capital, provides a second major motivation for interest in a consumption tax. In the previous chapter we noted too that most of the tax-avoidance schemes were related to the taxation of capital. For example, income shifting typically requires the transfer (or loan) of an asset. Most forms of tax deferral are attempts to avoid the taxation of interest.

The complexity and distortions that arise from the interaction of our individual income tax and corporate income tax systems could also be reduced with a switch to a consumption tax, particularly one based on the cash flow approach. Receipts from the corporate sector would be added to the cash flow (subject to tax), while payments to the corporate sector would be subtracted. All the complexity of the corporation tax, including the distortionary provisions for depreciation, could simply be eliminated, without fear that the corporations would be used as a vehicle for tax avoidance.

The consumption tax would not eliminate all administrative problems. As we have noted, there would remain a problem in identifying legitimate business expenses. But this problem would be no more severe—and no less severe—than under the current income tax system.

Critics of the consumption tax are not persuaded by the arguments for it based on its administrative advantages. First, they point out that the administrative problems with any tax can be eliminated simply by eliminating the tax. The fact that there are administrative problems with a tax on the income from capital is an argument for its abolition only if it can be shown that it is impossible to design a "reasonably" nondistortionary and "reasonably" equitable tax. Advocates of a broadly based *income* tax believe that such a tax can be designed. Though the imputed return to housing will escape taxation, and pension schemes will defer taxation of interest on savings for retirement until actual receipt, it is still possible (they believe) to tax a significant fraction of the return to capital; and they believe that the distortions arising from taxing some of the returns to capital and not others are worth the gains in revenue and equity from the tax.

Moreover, critics of the consumption tax fear that while we know the problems with our current system, we will only gradually find out those associated with running a consumption tax. These, they suspect, are no less severe than those of our current system.

THE DESIGN OF A CONSUMPTION TAX

During President Ford's administration, the Office of Tax Analysis of the Treasury Department, headed by economist David Bradford of Princeton, gave careful consideration to how one might design a consumption tax in practice. These economists were convinced that the administrative problems of a consumption tax were, overall, much less severe than those under the present system. In the following paragraphs we discuss three of the difficulties encountered.

1. *Housing under the Consumption Tax.* Housing presents a problem for the consumption tax, just as it does for the income tax. We argued in our discussion of the income tax that the theoretically appropriate way of dealing with housing was to *impute* to income an amount corresponding to the services yielded by the house—i.e., to impute a rental value. Similarly, with the cash flow approach to the consumption tax, the purchase of a house represents an investment, and the expenditures to purchase a house should be subtracted from income to determine the tax base. Later, however, the services yielded by the house should be included as "consumption" and added to the tax base. But given the difficulties of imputing the services yielded by the house, an alternative procedure (in which the expenditures on the purchase of a house are not subtracted from income, and the services yielded by the assets are not added back) has certain advantages.

The major disadvantage arises when the tax rates on consumption are progressive. Then, an individual who sells some of his securities to buy a house would appear to be dissaving (the reduction in his ownership of his securities is viewed as dissaving), and the value of this dissaving would be added to his income to form an estimate of his consumption. In fact, of course, the individual is simply changing the *form* in which he holds his assets; that is, he is substituting one set of assets (housing) for another (securities).[17] Thus any system of consumption taxation must make some special provisions for housing.

[17] With a flat-rate consumption tax, this makes no difference; his tax liability would be increased at one date and decreased at another. With a system of lifetime effective averaging described below, the increased tax this period (with a reduced tax liability at some date in the future) again would cause no problems provided the individual had the liquidity to pay the tax.

(cont'd.)

2. *Bequests.* The second problem has to do with bequests and inheritances. Should these be treated as consumption by the donor and as income by the receiver? One view treats the individual and his descendants as a single extended family. In this view, transfers between a parent and his child should not be taxed. Each consumption unit should be taxed only once. If a parent gives an asset to a child and the child sells the asset to buy consumption goods, a tax will be levied on the child. The other view says that giving money to a child is no different from spending money in any other way. The parent does it presumably because he receives pleasure from it. From this point of view, it is a "consumption" expenditure. Thus bequests ought to be taxed as if they were consumption expenditures. At the same time, bequests ought to be treated as income to the child; if the child sells the asset to purchase consumption goods, the child will be liable to pay the consumption tax.

The different approaches obviously may have different consequences for bequests. Some critics of the consumption tax are concerned that exempting bequests totally from taxation may lead to excessive concentration of wealth. Defenders of the consumption tax claim that if one is concerned about the concentration of wealth, one ought to attack that problem directly; for instance, by imposing a progressive wealth tax. Critics of the consumption tax claim that wealthy individuals will find ways of avoiding such a tax, and the way to increase the likelihood that they pay their fair share is to tax both capital income and bequests.

3. *Problems of Transition.* Some economists have been concerned with the transition from the income tax to the consumption tax. One problem we have already discussed: the cash flow to the government might be reduced in the interim, requiring further government borrowing.[18]

A second problem is the treatment of previously accumulated capital. Should individuals be taxed when they sell their previously purchased assets to buy consumption goods? Assume the individual had been saving out of his wage income; he has already paid an income tax. To tax him again when he consumes seems unfair. It seems to be an unjust tax on the thrifty. (Notice that what we are talking about here is a tax not only on interest income but on the whole value of the asset when he sells it.) Such a tax is called a **capital levy.** If it is not anticipated, and if individuals do not believe that it will be imposed again, it is not distortionary. But if individuals believe that it may be imposed again, it can have a very discouraging effect on savings.

On the other hand, much of current savings is from income that escaped income taxation. When an individual leaves an asset that has increased in value to his child, the capital gain effectively escapes taxation. Not to tax this saving also seems unfair. The problem is that we can-

---

Modern computer technology makes it feasible to design taxes based on lifetime consumption. A running account could be kept of each individual's consumption (appropriately discounted over time) and tax payments. Individuals would be allowed to prepay or to defer taxes under stipulated conditions.

[18] This increased deficit should not, however, have a significant deleterious effect on the economy; since individuals should anticipate their future tax liability, they would increase their savings by a corresponding amount.

not distinguish between these two types of savings. The transition rules from an income tax to a consumption tax that one thinks are appropriate are determined by how one thinks one should deal with previously accumulated savings.

If one thinks that previous savings should not be taxed, there is no problem: individuals would be allowed to consume by selling assets they currently own without paying any tax. If one thinks that previous savings should be taxed, all individuals would be required to register their current assets. When these assets were sold, the cash flow would be recorded and a tax imposed. There is some concern that individuals might underreport their present assets and that their true consumption would thus exceed their reported consumption. How serious this problem would be in the United States is not clear. It would not appear to be a problem at least for stocks and bonds.

IS A CONSUMPTION TAX INEGALITARIAN?

There is a widespread view that a consumption tax would be less egalitarian than an income tax, that it would hurt the poor relative to the rich. This view is based on several misconceptions. First, there is a confusion between a sales tax and a consumption tax. The two are clearly similar. But sales taxes, as imposed in most states, are levied only on certain commodities. Since vacations abroad, luxury homes, and diamonds purchased out of state typically escape such taxes, the fraction of a rich person's income spent on goods on which he has to pay a sales tax is typically smaller than the fraction of a poor person's income. Thus sales taxes are usually viewed to be regressive. In contrast, a consumption tax is levied on all consumption. Moreover, sales taxes are usually levied as a fixed percentage of the amount spent. But a consumption tax could be highly progressive; that is, one could design a consumption tax where, for instance, the first $4,000 of consumption is tax-exempt, the next $10,000 is taxed at 20 percent, the next $10,000 at 30 percent, and consumption beyond $24,000 is taxed at 40 percent.

How we collect the revenues for a consumption tax does depend on whether it is progressive or proportional. If it is proportional, we can collect it as a sales tax. If we wish to impose a progressive consumption tax, we need to know the individual's total consumption. To do this we infer what his consumption is, by ascertaining what his income was and what additional saving (or dissaving) he did in the course of the year. Doing this is only a little more difficult than ascertaining simply what the individual's income is (or so the advocates of the consumption tax claim).

Finally, there is some confusion about the appropriate way of measuring the degree of progressivity of the tax system. If one believes that consumption is a fairer tax base than income, the correct way of measuring progressivity relates tax payments to consumption; this is true even if the ratio of consumption to income declines with income, so that the ratio of tax payments to income does not increase as rapidly as the ratio of tax payments to consumption.

A Flat-Rate Consumption Tax

Though the consumption tax can thus be made highly progressive, with marginal tax rates increasing with the level of consumption, some economists have advocated a flat-rate consumption tax. The marginal rate on all consumption would be the same. The tax would still be progressive, because there would be an exemption level (only consumption over the exemption level would be taxed).

Earlier, we noted that there were significant administrative advantages in a flat-rate income tax. The advantages of a flat-rate consumption tax are similar. Taxes can be imposed completely at the source: there would be a flat percentage withholding of all expenditures on personnel (wages and fringe benefits). The individual's entire tax form could be put onto a postcard. A flat-rate consumption tax has been proposed by Stanford political economists Robert Hall and Alvin Rabushka. They believe that a 19 percent flat-rate consumption tax with a $6,800 exemption for a married couple with no children would generate essentially the same revenue as the current system. (Their tax includes a one-time 19 percent capital levy—i.e., all previous savings would be taxed at 19 percent as well.)

Critics of the tax are skeptical. Because the consumption tax base is smaller than the flat-rate income tax base, the tax rate would have to be higher than with the flat-rate income tax. The magnitude of the required tax rate depends to some extent on the magnitudes of the responses of labor and capital. If labor supply increases significantly in response to the lowering of the marginal tax rate, and if investors are so encouraged that the growth of the economy is significantly affected, it is possible that the 19 percent flat-rate consumption tax would raise the requisite revenue. If labor supply elasticities are low and savings elasticities are low, it is unlikely to raise the requisite revenue.

The Value-Added Tax

The **value-added tax** (V.A.T.) is a tax that is imposed at each stage of production on the difference between the sales of a firm and what it purchases from other firms; that is, on the value added by the firm. Though the V.A.T. has typically not replaced the income tax, it has become a major source of revenue in most European countries, with rates as high as 20 percent.

The tax is equivalent to a national sales tax. The only advantage of this tax over a sales tax is the manner in which it is collected. While there are a large number of retail outlets, the number of producing firms is much smaller. Thus a large portion of the revenues is collected from relatively few sources, and these may be more easily monitored than the myriad of small retail establishments. Whether this is a significant advantage in the United States, where the level of tax compliance is relatively high, is a moot question.

Once one recognizes that the tax is really a sales tax, one sees clearly the advantages and disadvantages of such a tax. A uniform tax on output is equivalent to a uniform tax on input (recall our discussion of Chapter 17), since output must equal input. Thus a value-added tax is equivalent to a comprehensive flat-rate income tax with no exemption. The value-added tax, therefore, is neither progressive nor regressive; it does not redistribute income. This is only considered an advantage by those who think the government should not redistribute income; most view this as a serious disadvantage.

On the other hand, we noted the serious inequities and inefficiencies that arise from the myriad of special provisions of the income tax. There is a belief that compliance with the V.A.T. is more uniform, and in this sense the tax is more equitable and less distortionary than the income tax.

Some degree of progressivity can be added by exempting certain industries. If food is exempted (or taxed at a lower rate), the effective rate on the poor may be lower than on the rich, since the poor spend a larger fraction of their income on food. Similarly, by imposing a surtax (a tax in addition to the normal tax) on luxuries such as large cars, those with high income will pay a higher than average proportion of their income in taxes. But there is a cost to attempts to increase the degree of progressivity of the tax: one of the virtues of the value-added tax is its uniformity, its simplicity. As soon as there are differential rates on different industries, there are difficult problems of determining the boundaries. How large should a car be to be considered a luxury car? Should the family circumstances of the purchaser be taken into account in determining whether it is a luxury? (For a family with many children, a large car may be a necessity rather than a luxury.) And the pressures of special-interest groups, each trying to make sure that the commodities they sell are classified in the low-tax category, would be enormous.[19]

Another commonly proposed modification in the value-added tax is to exempt investment. Since (ignoring government spending)

$$\text{Investment} + \text{Consumption} = \text{National Output},$$

a value-added tax that exempts investment goods is equivalent to a proportional consumption tax. The issues we discussed earlier in the context of the consumption tax are relevant here in determining whether total national income or consumption provides a better basis for the value-added tax.

Most proponents of the value-added tax do not advocate that it should replace the income tax. Rather, they believe that it can be used to reduce substantially the revenues to be collected from the income tax, and hence the high marginal tax rates; since much of the tax-avoidance

[19] In Chapter 20 we discussed whether different commodities should be taxed at different rates. The results were inconclusive. If there was an optimal consumption tax, if the source of inequality was differences in individuals' productivity, and if individuals' marginal rates of substitution between different commodities did not depend on the amount they worked, all commodities should be taxed at the same rate. In the absence of a consumption tax, while distribution considerations argue for higher rates on luxury goods, concern about deadweight loss argues for lower rates.

activities are related to the level of marginal rates, advocates believe that it will decrease the distortions and increase the equity of the tax system. Critics of this proposal point out that the total distortion of the tax system is related to the sum of the (marginal) tax on income and the value-added tax and that, unless this is reduced, the deadweight loss associated with the tax will not be reduced. Moreover, the gains in compliance costs from the reduction in the marginal tax rate will be more than offset by the additional administrative costs associated with collecting the value-added tax. Finally, there are those who are concerned that because the value-added tax is collected in a piecemeal way, individuals will not be conscious of the full scale of the taxes they pay, and this will lead politicians to increase the overall tax burden: for those who would like to see a larger public sector, this is an advantage; but for those who would like to see a smaller public sector, it is a disadvantage.

SUMMARY

1. High compliance costs and low levels of compliance, the complexity of the tax code, the perceived inequities of the tax structure, and the large distortions associated with high marginal tax rates all contributed to the impetus for the 1986 Tax Reform Act.
2. Many of the problems of the income tax system have arisen because too much has been asked of it. It was supposed both to provide economic incentives (e.g., to invest, to save, to buy health insurance, to support state and local governments), and to redistribute income.
3. The 1986 Tax Reform Act decreased the highest marginal tax rate, removed those in poverty from the tax rolls, and made tax avoidance more difficult. Most Americans did not, however, face greatly reduced marginal tax rates, and the reductions for the most part simply reversed the effects of inflation of the 1970s.
4. The tax law did not simplify the tax code. It left some important loopholes. It did not substantially broaden the tax base.
5. Future tax reforms will probably focus on one of four proposals: a comprehensive income tax, a consumption tax, a flat-rate tax, or a value-added tax. The different reforms are not mutually exclusive.

KEY CONCEPTS

Compliance costs	Value-added tax
Comprehensive income tax	Revenue-neutral
Flat-rate tax	Capital levy
Consumption tax	Base-broadening

QUESTIONS AND PROBLEMS

1. List some of the special provisions of the tax code that remain after the 1986 Reform Act and that would be eliminated by a comprehensive income tax. Which of these do you think are justified on grounds of equity? efficiency?
2. There is a widespread view that a consumption tax would hurt the poor. Is this necessarily the case?

3. The adoption of a *comprehensive income tax* might have a significant effect on the market value of certain assets. Which assets are likely to decrease in value? Which to increase in value? Should the government do anything to compensate the losers or to tax the gainers? The adoption of a *consumption tax* would also have a significant effect on the market value of certain assets. Which assets are likely to decrease in value? Which to increase in value?
4. There is a widespread view that the appropriate basis for taxation is an individual's lifetime consumption (or lifetime income). Discuss the inequities and inefficiencies that would arise from a consumption tax which had increasing marginal tax rates but no provisions for averaging years of low consumption with years of high consumption. Would these problems also arise under a flat-rate consumption tax?
5. In Chapter 21 we discussed the problems associated with choosing the appropriate unit for taxation (family versus individual). How would these problems be affected by the adoption of a consumption tax? a flat-rate income tax?
6. Consider a flat-rate income tax at a rate of 20 percent with an exemption level of $11,000 (the poverty level for a four-person family). What is the average tax rate on a four-person family with $15,000? with $30,000? with $100,000? Can it be argued that this tax is progressive?
7. Many economists and politicians have argued that moving from an income tax to a consumption tax would be unfair unless a wealth tax or an inheritance tax were enacted at the same time. Explain the arguments on both sides of this issue.
8. Explain why the repeal of the investment tax credit might have increased the value of existing capital goods.
9. Explain why if the marginal tax rate decreases as income increases, individuals whose income is variable may be better off than individuals with a stable income of the same average value.

PART SIX

FURTHER ISSUES

The United States has a federal system, with some activities being undertaken at the state and local level, others at the national level. Chapter 26 explains the rationale for a federal system and some of the important interactions between the federal government and the state and local governments. We also explore the role of competition among communities in ensuring that the correct levels and kinds of public goods get produced and that they get produced efficiently.

Chapter 27 briefly describes expenditures and taxes at the state and local level. We are particularly concerned with the incidence of taxes and expenditure programs in situations where capital and labor are highly mobile.

Chapter 28 is addressed to two major issues on which public attention has focused in the past decade: America's mounting budget deficits and its declining competitiveness in world markets, both of which are reflected in large trade deficits. We analyze the impact of taxation, government expenditures, and deficits on economic growth and stability.

26

Fiscal Federalism

In his State of the Union address in January 1982, President Reagan proposed to "alter" the relationship between the states and the federal government in an important way. Certain areas, including education and welfare, in which the federal government had taken an increasingly active role within the past decade or two, would once again be placed more solidly under the purview of the states. At the same time, the federal government would take over responsibility for Medicaid (which provides medical assistance to the indigent).[1] His proposals were dubbed "the New Federalism."

Though most of Reagan's proposals were not adopted, they focused attention once again on the longstanding issue of the appropriate division of responsibility and authority between states and the federal government. The Constitution stipulated that those powers not expressly delegated to the federal government—such as providing for the national defense, printing money, and running the post office—rested with the states. This seemed to create the presumption that responsibility for the provision of most public services (such as education, police and fire protection, roads and highways) was left with the states; and this was the view that was held for a long time. But the Constitution is a flexible document, and court interpretations of it have essentially freed the federal government to provide many other services.

[1] Currently, the states administer the Medicaid programs and determine eligibility standards within guidelines set by the federal government. Funding for Medicaid is shared between the federal government and the states.

THE DIVISION OF RESPONSIBILITIES

The state and local governments have primary responsibility for education (providing 92 percent of the funds), highways and roads (other than the interstate highway system), police and fire protection, and sewage and other sanitation. While the federal government has been responsible for the establishment of the major social welfare programs, public welfare is still the second-largest category of state and local expenditures, accounting for more than one-eighth of total expenditures. Other major portions of state and local budgets are transportation, civilian safety, and health and hospitals. Figure 26.1 gives a breakdown of state and local expenditures, and Figure 26.2 shows the fraction of public-sector spending financed by the federal government in six major areas.

Just as there is a division of responsibility between the federal government, on the one hand, and the state and local governments on the other, so there is a division of responsibility between the state governments on the one hand, and the local governments on the other. The division is a complicated one, involving financing, regulation, and administration. Thus elementary and secondary schools are almost all run by local communities, but half of the financing comes from the states, which also

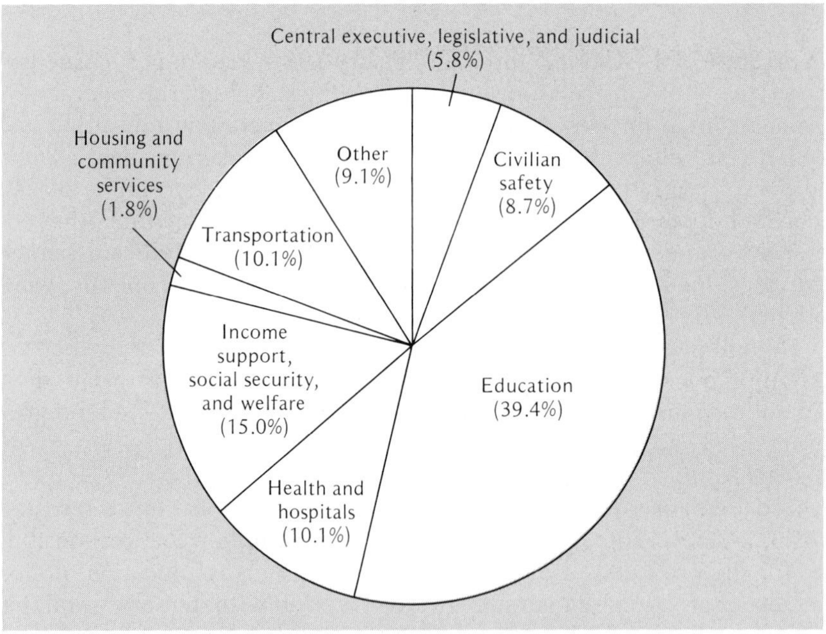

26.1 ALLOCATION OF STATE AND LOCAL EXPENDITURES IN 1985 (Total expenditures of $517 billion) Education is the largest state and local expenditure, followed by income-support programs, and health and hospitals. SOURCE: *Survey of Current Business,* July 1987, Table 3.16.

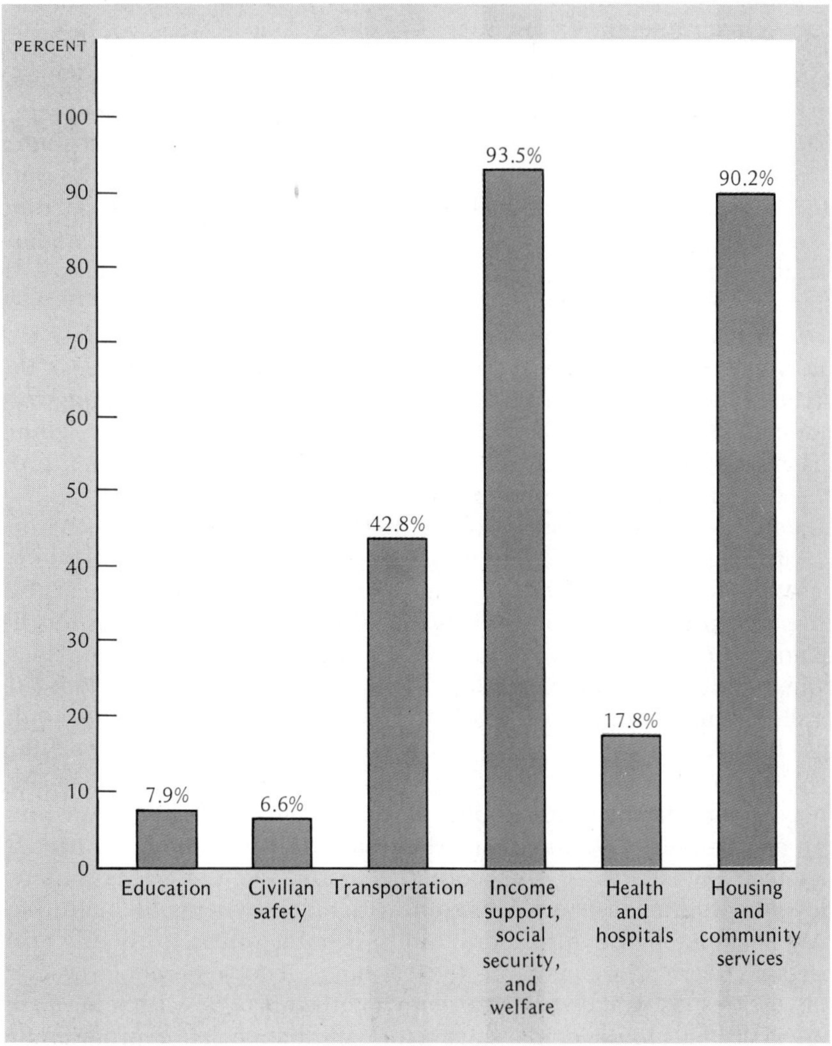

26.2 FRACTION OF GOVERNMENT EXPENDITURES FOR SELECTED CATEGORIES FINANCED AT THE FEDERAL LEVEL, 1985 The federal government finances most public-sector spending on social security, income support, and housing, but state and local governments finance most public-sector spending on education, police, and hospitals. Responsibility for transportation financing is almost evenly divided between the federal government and state and local governments. SOURCE: *Survey of Current Business,* July 1987, Tables 3.14 and 3.16.

impose a variety of regulations. While almost 60 percent of highway expenditures occur at the state level, almost all of sewage expenditures and expenditures on firefighting occur at the local level, along with 90 percent of police expenditures.

The Interaction between the Federal Government and the State and Local Governments

In earlier chapters, we saw the complexity of the interaction between the federal government and individuals and firms: the government regulates, subsidizes, taxes, provides goods and services, and redistributes income. The interaction between the federal government and the state and local governments is equally complex, including federal regulation of and incentives for state and local governments, state and local administration of federal programs, and the sharing of federal revenues with state and local governments.

1. *Regulation.* The Constitution restricts the laws that any state can pass. The states cannot enact legislation that deprives individuals of the right to a trial, no matter how heinous the crime they have committed, nor can states bar an individual from holding a job on racial or religious grounds. Many Supreme Court decisions in recent years have countered state actions that are in violation of the Constitution.

State agencies may also be subject to the same pollution and environmental regulations that apply to private firms and individuals. In some cases the federal government has mandated that the state and local governments provide certain services (for instance, access facilities for the handicapped) without providing the requisite funds. The states and local communities have, not surprisingly, complained, arguing that if the federal government attaches such importance to these services, it should also finance them.

2. *Incentives: Categorical Grants and Matching Grants.* Probably more important than direct controls are the efforts of the federal government to alter the actions of state and local governments through financial incentives. It uses both the carrot and the stick: if states develop programs that are consistent with federally set guidelines, they may become eligible for federal funds; if states refuse to comply with certain criteria, they may lose federal funds. Thus federal aid to state universities (as well as to private universities) may be withheld, if the university fails to develop a satisfactory affirmative action program for hiring women and minorities, or if it discriminates in any of its programs.[2] States become eligible to receive federal funds for Medicaid or for unemployment compensation provided that they develop appropriate programs. Federal grants to states and localities for specific purposes are called **categorical grants.** The most important categorical grant programs (outside of welfare programs) are for education and urban development. The magnitude of the grants may increase with state and local expenditures; that is, the government may match state expenditures (up to some maximum amount). These are called **matching grants.**

The federal government uses the threat of withholding federal funds

[2] There has been considerable controversy over whether failure to satisfy criteria in one program should entail cutoff of funds for other programs. New legislation resolved this controversy in 1988. Under the new law, federal anti-discrimination rules apply to an *entire* institution that accepts federal money.

as an inducement for states to act in accordance with its wishes. Thus highway speed limits are set by states, but the federal government threatened to withhold federal highway funds from any state that failed to enforce the fifty-five-mile-an-hour maximum speed limit.

3. *The Administration of Federal Funds.* In some cases, however, virtually all of the funds for some program come from the federal government. A state or local government agency is used to administer the program. For instance, Aid to Families with Dependent Children (AFDC) is a federal program, but it is administered by state and local government. The distinction between whether the state is essentially administering a federal program or whether the federal government is supporting a state program is not, of course, a clear one. The difference depends on the extent of discretion given to the state. In the case of the Medicaid program, eligibility standards and extent of coverage are both determined by the state, and there is a wide range of variation in practices among the states. Food stamp programs are also administered by the states, but they have far less discretion.

4. *General Revenue Sharing: Block Grants.* The federal government also transfers income back to the states and localities in **block grants,** grants that can be used for any purpose the states and localities desire. These programs are called **general revenue sharing,** as opposed to specific (or categorical) revenue sharing, which are grants designed for specific purposes. General revenue sharing has fallen in recent years: in 1986, it amounted to only $4 billion, compared to $103 billion in federal categorical grants to state and local governments.[3] There are two reasons for general revenue sharing programs. One is that the federal government may be a more efficient tax collector than the state and local governments; the extra administrative costs associated with adding a small increment to the federal tax rate to finance state and local activities is negligible. The second is that the wealth of different states, their potential tax bases, differs markedly, and thus the federal government engages in regional distribution of federal taxes, providing proportionately more to the poor states.

In recent years, the poorest states have had per capita incomes that were 20 percent to 30 percent less than the richest states; there were equally large disparities in per capita state and local taxes. The ratio of state and local taxes to per capita income varies from slightly more than 8 percent in Missouri to over 14 percent in New York.[4]

5. *Tax Expenditures.* This list of mechanisms by which the federal government affects states and localities is not meant to be exhaustive. One of the important ways that the federal government affects state and local expenditures is through the tax expenditures associated with the personal and corporate income taxes. These expenditures were estimated at $39 billion in 1987.[5]

[3] *Survey of Current Business,* July 1987, Table 3.15.

[4] In Alaska, tax revenues amounted to 43 percent of personal income, but this was largely because of taxes on oil.

[5] *Special Analyses, Budget of the U.S. Government, Fiscal Year 1988,* p. H–18.

The Size of Financial Transfers

In Chapter 2 we emphasized that the magnitude of governmental expenditures does not provide a complete picture of the role of the government in the economy. Similarly, the magnitude of federal transfers to states and localities does not tell us the extent to which state and local government expenditures are affected by federal activities. Still, it is worth noting several features of these transfers: (a) They have grown immensely in the last sixty years, from 1.6 percent of state and local revenues to 17 percent in 1986. This is down from the peak of 21.9 percent reached in 1977.[6] (b) Federal aid appears to be more important at the state level than at the local level, accounting for slightly more than one-quarter of state revenues and slightly less than 10 percent of local revenues.

But these figures are somewhat deceptive; much of the money to the states and localities simply passes through them to individuals. Thus 47 percent of the aid to state and local governments in 1986 went for AFDC and Medicaid. This proportion has been rising; for instance, in 1978 it was only 34 percent of state aid. Similarly, between one-fourth and one-third of federal aid received by state governments is then distributed by them to local governments.

THE PRINCIPLES OF FISCAL FEDERALISM

In Chapter 3 we discussed the rationale for government activities. The fundamental theorem of welfare economics—Adam Smith's "invisible hand" —implies that in the absence of a market failure, such as public goods, the economy will be Pareto efficient. Individuals, each acting in his own self-interest, will make decisions that lead to Pareto efficiency. Competition among producers leads them to supply the goods individuals want at the lowest possible cost.

An analogous argument can be made for the provision of public goods and services by state and local governments, as distinct from the federal government. Competition among communities, it is argued, will result in communities supplying the goods and services individuals want and producing these goods in an efficient manner. This is called the **Tiebout hypothesis,** after Charles Tiebout of the University of Washington, who first formalized the arguments in 1956.[7]

Tiebout was originally concerned with the problem of *preference revelation* discussed in Chapter 6: while individuals reveal their preferences for private goods simply by buying goods, how are they to reveal their preferences for public goods? When individuals vote, they choose candidates who reflect their overall values, but they cannot express in detail their views about particular categories of expenditures. Only limited use of referenda is made in most states. And even if individuals were

[6] Source: *Report of the Council of Economic Advisors,* 1984; *Survey of Current Business,* July 1987, Tables 3.3 and 3.15.

[7] See C. Tiebout, "A Pure Theory of Local Expenditure," *Journal of Political Economy* 64 (1956): 416–24.

asked to vote directly on expenditures for particular programs, the resulting equilibrium would not, in general, be Pareto efficient.

Tiebout argued that individuals could "vote with their feet," that their choice of communities revealed their preferences toward locally provided public goods in the same way the individuals' choices of products reveal their preferences for private goods. Moreover, just as there are incentives for firms to find out what commodities individuals prefer and to produce those commodities efficiently, so are there incentives for communities to find out what kinds of community-provided goods individuals prefer and to provide them efficiently. This is seen most strongly in the case of community developers. In recent years these developers have recognized that many individuals would like more security and more communal facilities (swimming pools, tennis courts) than are provided by the typical city. Hence they have formed large developments providing these services. Because these communities better meet the needs of the individuals than the alternatives that are available, individuals are willing to pay higher rents (or spend more to purchase homes in these communities); and it is this that provides the developer a return for his efforts to ascertain what it is that individuals want and to meet these desires.

More generally, communities that provide the services individuals like and provide them efficiently will find an influx of individuals; communities that fail to do so will find themselves with an outflux. This migration (with the consequent effect on property values) provides essentially the same kind of signal to the city manager that the market provides to the firm's manager (a firm that fails to provide a commodity individuals like will find its sales declining, a firm that succeeds will find its sales increasing). Politicians (sometimes under pressure from the electorate) respond to these signals in much the same way a firm's managers respond to market signals.

The analogy is an instructive one. Under certain assumptions, the separate decisions of each community concerning what public goods to provide and how to provide and finance them lead to a Pareto-efficient allocation, just as the separate decisions of firms and individuals concerning private goods lead to Pareto efficiency.

But these assumptions generally do not hold. And even were they to hold, the inequality in the distribution of welfare across communities might be unacceptably large.

The qualifications to the Tiebout hypothesis closely parallel those we discussed in Chapter 3, concerning the circumstances in which market allocations might not be Pareto efficient or, even if efficient, might not be desirable.[8] These qualifications were three-fold: the presence of

[8] Since Tiebout, an extensive literature has developed evaluating the conditions under which the result is valid. See, in particular, J. E. Stiglitz, "Public Goods in Open Economies with Heterogeneous Individuals," in *Locational Analysis of Public Facilities,* J. F. Thisse and H. G. Zoller, eds. (New York: Elsevier–North Holland, 1983); J. E. Stiglitz, "Theory of Local Public Goods," in *The Economics of Public Services,* M. Feldstein and R. Inman, eds. (New York: Macmillan, 1977), pp. 274–333; T. Bewley, "A Critique of Tiebout's Theory of Local Public Expenditures," *Econometrica* 49 (1981): 713–40; and G. R. Zodrow and P. Mieszkowski, "Pigou, Tiebout, Property Taxation, and the Underprovision of Local Public Goods," *Journal of Urban Economics* 19 (1986): 356–70.

some market failure; dissatisfaction with the distribution of income; and the belief that consumers might not take actions that were in their own self-interest (merit goods).

National Public Goods versus Local Public Goods

The benefits of some public goods accrue to those who live in a particular community. This is the case, for instance, with fire protection. The benefits of other public goods accrue to those who live anywhere. National defense is an example.

The same arguments that are used to show that if there is to be an efficient supply of public goods they must be provided publicly imply that if there is to be an efficient supply of national public goods they must be provided at the national level.

Pure public goods (that is, goods for which exclusion is impossible and undesirable) whose benefits are limited to a particular area are called **local pure public goods.** Traffic lights are an example. Just as most goods publicly provided at the national level are not pure public goods, so too most goods provided publicly at the local level are not local pure public goods. For some, such as public libraries, exclusion is easy but undesirable, since the cost of providing access to an additional individual is almost zero. Some goods which local governments provide—for example, education and public hospitals—are essentially private goods; exclusion is easy and the costs of providing services to additional individuals are significant. (See Chapter 5.)

In Chapter 7 we discussed the advantages and disadvantages of public versus private financing and production of goods, such as education, which are not pure public goods. If they are provided publicly, they may be provided nationally (education in France) or locally (education in the United States). The advantage of local provision is the greater adaptability to local needs and preferences; the disadvantage is the possibly higher transaction costs (as each community must spend resources choosing, for instance, its own curriculum). In addition, the inevitable inequality in the quality of the services provided in different communities when decisions are made locally may be viewed as a disadvantage, particularly in the case of education.

Externalities

The actions of one community may have marked effects on other communities. If a community constructs a smelly sewage plant or allows the development of an industrial area at its boundary, in a location such that the winds blow the bad odors over the neighboring communities, there is an important externality. We sometimes refer to these externalities as **spillovers.** Not all spillovers have negative consequences. Some economists believe that there are important public benefits from having an educated citizenry, and that this provides some justification for public support of education. To the extent that this is true, and to the extent that individuals move away from the community that provided them with a free education, there are spillovers from a local community's public education system.

Migration and location inefficiencies may be thought of as a particularly important class of externalities. Individuals, in deciding to move into a community, bring both benefits and costs; they may increase the tax base, but they also may lead to increased demands on public services, and increased congestion (for instance, of roads and parks). Since in many cases they neither pay for these costs nor are compensated for the benefits they confer, there are likely to be inefficiencies in location decisions. Many countries have become increasingly concerned about what they view as excessive concentration of population in the major cities (London, Paris, Mexico City) and have developed decentralization policies to attain what they view as a more efficient pattern of location.

Competition and Profit Maximization

A central assumption underlying the results concerning the efficiency of market economies is that there are many profit-maximizing firms. The Tiebout hypothesis similarly requires that there be many competing communities.[9] In most areas there are only a limited number of competing communities; there is, in effect, only limited competition. Moreover, communities do not make their decisions about which goods and services to provide on the basis of any simple profit maximization or land value maximization criterion, but by a political process along the lines discussed in Chapter 6. The kinds of inefficiencies to which this may give rise will be described in the next chapter. Here we simply note that limited competition provides an explanation for why we should be skeptical about the Tiebout hypothesis.

REDISTRIBUTION

Redistribution may be a more important explanation of the role of the federal government than are the market failures we have just described. There is concern about the distribution of income both among individuals and across communities.

Inequality among Individuals

Should the extent of redistribution—the level of welfare payments—be a local or national decision? Is "redistribution" a local public good? Assume individuals in some community believe strongly that no individual should live in a slum, and so they provide a good public housing pro-

[9] Indeed, there must be so many that all residents within each community who have the same skills also have the same tastes for public goods. Another implication is that (provided voters are rational) there would be complete unanimity in voting. Both of these implications are obviously not satisfied. See R. W. Eberts and T. J. Gronberg, "Jurisdictional Homogeneity and the Tiebout Hypothesis," *Journal of Urban Economics* 10 (1981): 227–39; and H. Pack and J. Pack, "Metropolitan Fragmentation and Local Public Expenditure," *National Tax Journal* 31 (1978): 349–62.

gram, while individuals in some other community have different ethical concerns. Is there any reason that individuals in the first community should attempt to impose their ethical beliefs on the second, by attempting to make minimal housing standards a national rather than a local issue?

The answer is yes. And the reason is that, with relatively free migration, the extent of redistribution that is feasible at the local level is very limited. Any community that decides to provide better housing for the poor or better medical care might find itself faced with an influx of the poor. Communities have an incentive to try to make their community unattractive to the poor, so that they will move on to the next community. Some communities, for instance, do this by passing zoning laws that require multi-acre lots.[10] Others do it by limiting the provision of certain public services that are particularly valued by the poor and for which the wealthier have good private substitutes, such as bus services.

Indeed, if there were perfect competition among communities, the efforts to provide local public services at least cost to the taxpayers would result in taxpayers paying taxes only commensurate with the benefits they themselves received. A community that had no welfare program and succeeded in excluding most of the poor would be able to provide public services (education, sewage treatment, libraries, etc.) at lower tax rates than a community that had an ambitious welfare program (public housing, good medical care, etc.) and educational programs aimed at disadvantaged children. The fact that competition is frequently limited and decisions concerning public services are made politically means that there often are local (and state) redistribution programs. But these remain limited.

Inequality across Communities

We have already noted the marked differences among the states in per capita income and tax rates. For a poor community to provide the same level of services as a rich one requires that it levy much higher tax rates.

But why should we be more concerned with the inequality associated with locally provided public goods (and tax rates) than we are with inequality in general? Is there any reason that there should be specific federal programs directed at reducing this particular kind of inequality? If we want more redistribution, why not simply impose a more progressive tax, letting individuals then choose how to spend their money? If they wish to live in communities that spend more or less on local public goods, why not let them? The issues are analogous to those that arose in earlier chapters concerning whether the government should have specific policies directed at decreasing the extent of inequality of access to specific goods, such an medicine, food, and housing. We introduced the concept of *specific egalitarianism*, the view that the consumption of certain commodities should not depend on one's (or one's parents') income

[10] Courts have recently restricted the use of zoning as an exclusionary device.

or wealth. Education, the most important locally and publicly provided good, is one of those for which the strongest argument for equality of access can be made.

There are, however, several arguments against programs aimed at reducing inequality in the provision of local public services.

CONSUMER SOVEREIGNTY

The first is the standard "consumer sovereignty" argument: individuals should be allowed to choose the goods they prefer. The federal government should not force its preferences—for food, housing, or education—on local communities. Programs aimed at reducing inequality in the provision of local public goods (to the extent that they are effective) distort consumption patterns; they may result in greater consumption of "local public goods" and less consumption of private goods than a redistributive program providing cash to individuals. Categorical grants (again, to the extent that they are effective) cause a distortion in the mix of locally provided goods; they may, for instance, result in more education and urban redevelopment and less frequent sewage collection. Whenever there are these distortions there is a deadweight loss.

This consumer sovereignty argument, though relevant, is somewhat less forceful for some locally provided goods than it is for others. For instance, decisions concerning elementary and secondary school education are made not by the individual but by his parents; and decisions concerning local public goods are made by a political process, which need not yield efficient outcomes, as we saw in Chapter 6.[11]

THE DIFFICULTY OF TARGETING COMMUNITIES FOR REDISTRIBUTION

A second argument against programs aimed at redistributing income across communities (localities, states) is that such programs are not well-targeted; that is, most communities contain a mix of poor and rich individuals. A program aimed at redistributing resources to a community whose average income is low may simply result in a lowering of the tax rate; the main beneficiaries of the program will thus be the rich individuals within the poor communities. On the other hand, certain specific programs, such as the school lunch program, may be more effective in redistributing income to *children* than programs aimed at redistributing income among families.

LOCATION INEFFICIENCIES

A third argument is that programs redistributing income across communities result in location inefficiencies. They distort the decisions of individuals about where to live and the decisions of businesses about where to locate.

[11] If the restrictive conditions under which the Tiebout hypothesis is valid hold, the supply of locally provided public goods will be efficient. By the same token, when these conditions are not satisfied, federal interventions in the local provision of public goods, the nature of which themselves is determined by a political process, need not enhance efficiency.

The United States is a very mobile society. We move often, and frequently quite far. There have been large migrations from the rural South to the urban North, and in more recent years, from the Snow Belt to the Sun Belt. A variety of reasons induce individuals to move, but economic considerations are among the more important. These include not only an individual's opportunities for employment and the wages he receives, but the taxes that are imposed and the public goods that are provided. As demands and technologies change, economic efficiency requires that individuals move to where they can be more productive. This will necessitate that some localities, and indeed even some regions, face declining populations, while others face rapidly rising populations. Federal aid aimed at redistributing income from one locality to another may interfere with the efficient allocation of labor and capital. The level of taxes and public services provided by one community will not correctly reflect the economic potential of that community. The inefficiencies to which this gives rise may be small in the short run but become large in the long run. Individuals will be encouraged to stay where they are rather than move to more productive localities. Indeed, it might be better to use the same funds to subsidize emigration out of the unproductive areas.

Similarly, with new highway systems, it may no longer be efficient to have the larger agglomerations of population associated with inner cities. Thus, aid to central cities may serve to perpetuate these inefficient patterns of location.[12]

Note that these inefficiencies arise from attempts to redistribute income among communities. If our basic concern is with inequality among individuals, redistribution should be aimed at individuals, not at regions or localities.

In addition, specific redistributive programs if they are not well designed, may give rise to large distortions. A program aimed at meeting measured housing shortages among the very poor, by providing federal subsidies, may encourage communities to undertake actions that exacerbate these housing shortages (such as rent control). A program to bail out cities that have borrowed excessively and appear to be in danger of defaulting on their bonds may encourage other communities to borrow more than they otherwise would, knowing that if they get into trouble the federal government is there to rescue them.

PRODUCTION VERSUS FINANCE

In our earlier discussions, we noted an important distinction between public production of some commodity and public financing of the provision of that commodity. A similar distinction needs to be made here: the federal government can deliver services directly or can use local governmental bodies for the delivery of those services (just as it could in princi-

[12] On the other hand, the aid may compensate for positive externalities produced by the inner cities.

ple use private contractors for the delivery of services). We noted earlier that the federal government frequently makes use of state and local governments for the administration of programs such as food stamps, job training, Medicaid, etc.

The arguments in favor of what we shall call local production, as opposed to federal production, are parallel to those we discussed in Chapter 7: (a) *Responsiveness to local preferences and needs.* Local communities have better information and incentives to provide the goods desired by local constituents. In cases where there are significant variations across communities (say, in education values), this may be an important advantage. (b) *Incentives for efficiency.* Just as competition among firms results in incentives to produce goods efficiently and in the form desired by consumers, so too does competition among communities result in incentives to produce publicly provided goods efficiently and in the form desired by consumers.

We have already noted one limitation to this argument; the limited number of communities may result in limited competition. There is, in addition, an important difference between privately provided goods and publicly provided goods: if a firm succeeds in building a better mousetrap or a mousetrap at less cost, the benefits accrue directly to the purchaser. It pays each individual to look for better and cheaper mousetraps. On the other hand, if voters spend resources to find out who is a better city manager, the benefits that result accrue to all taxpayers and all citizens.[13] Public management is, as we noted in Chapter 6, a public good. Whether these problems are more serious at the local level or the national level remains a matter of debate.

EFFECTIVENESS OF FEDERAL CATEGORICAL AID TO LOCAL COMMUNITIES

The intention of federal categorical aid to local communities is to encourage local spending on particular public services. Aid to bilingual education, aid to vocational education, and aid to school libraries is intended to result in an increase in expenditures in each of these categories. How effective is this aid? Do federal funds just substitute for local funds, or do they actually result in more expenditures for the intended purpose?

From a theoretical perspective, the issue is precisely the same as one that we discussed in Chapter 9. How effective is categorical aid to individuals in encouraging expenditures, say, on food or housing? The answer depends on whether there is a substitution effect or just an income effect.

We wish to compare three types of federal aid to local communities—a block grant (not tied to any specific use), nonmatching categorical aid, and matching categorical aid.

[13] Some have argued that there are incentives for politicians to provide public services more efficiently and to inform the electorate about their abilities.

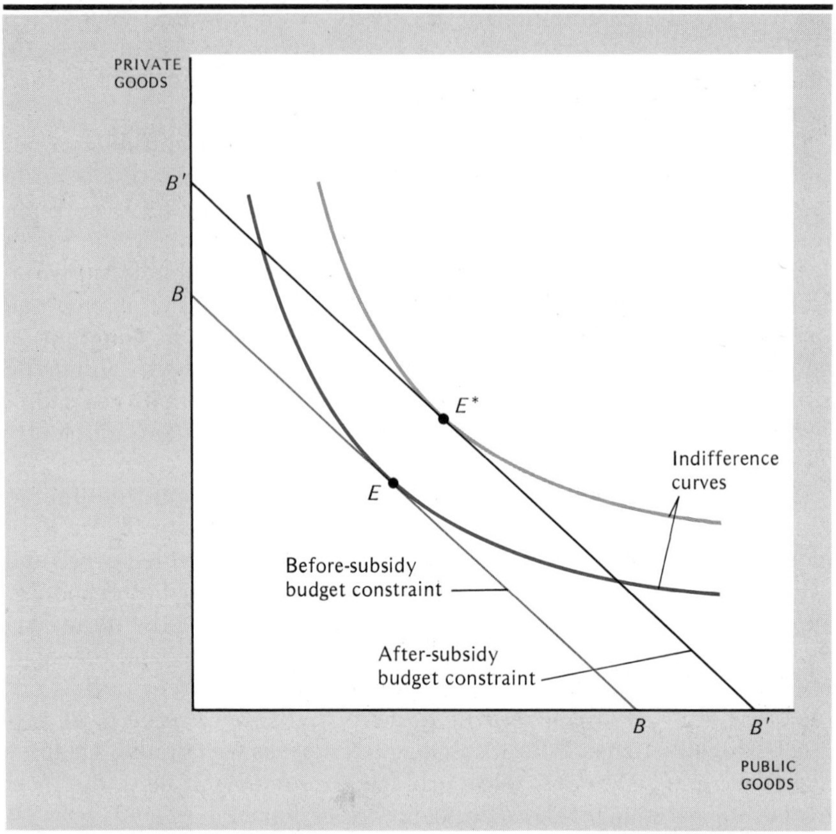

26.3 EFFECT OF BLOCK GRANTS A lump-sum transfer to a community will result in an increase in public expenditures, but by an amount less than the transfer; local taxes will go down.

In Figure 26.3 we have drawn the budget constraint of the community. (We simplify by assuming all individuals within the community are identical, so that we can ignore questions concerning differences in tastes.) The community would choose point E, the tangency between the budget constraint and the indifference curve of the representative individual. Now assume that the federal government provides a block grant to the community. This shifts out the budget constraint, to the line $B'B'$. There is now a new equilibrium, E^*. It entails a higher level of expenditure on local publicly provided goods and a higher level of per capita consumption of private goods. That is, the federal aid has in fact resulted in lowering the tax rate imposed on individuals. The federal money has *partially* substituted for local community money; the community, because it is better off, spends more on publicly provided goods as well as privately provided goods.

Assume now, however, that there are two different publicly provided goods, garbage collection and education, on which the community can spend funds. We represent the allocation decision of the community

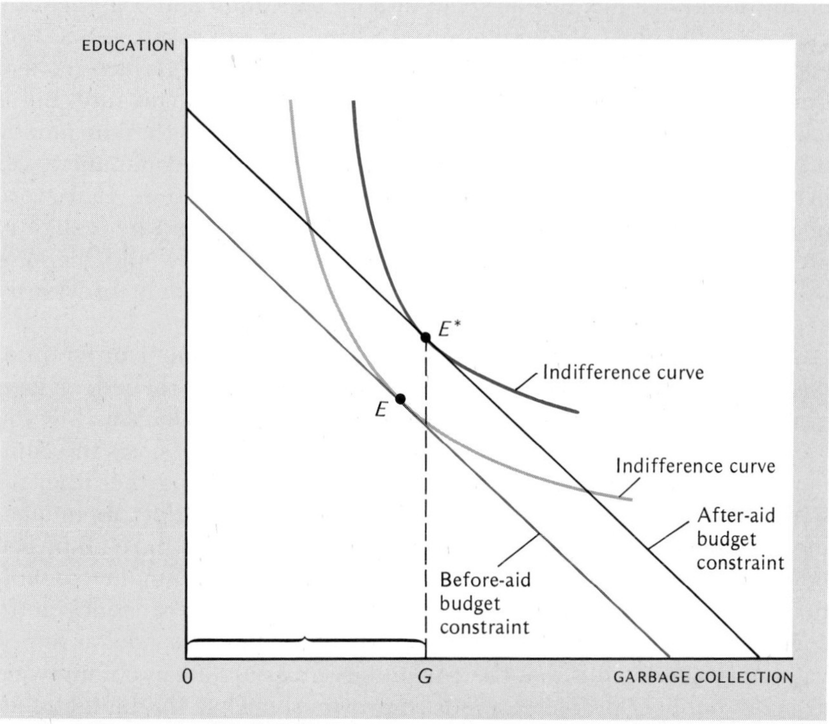

26.4 EFFECTS OF NONMATCHING CATEGORICAL AID It makes no difference whether the federal government stipulates that the funds be used for garbage collection or education, so long as the size of the federal government's grant is less than the total desired expenditure. (If the government stipulates that its funds be used for garbage collection, then, so long as the government gives less than the amount *OG*, the stipulation has no effect.)

between the two goods by the same kind of diagrammatic devices we have used to represent the allocation between private and publicly provided goods.[14] The community has a budget constraint; it needs to divide its total budget between the two goods, as represented by Figure 26.4. The community also has indifference curves between the two goods. The initial equilibrium is represented in Figure 26.4 by *E*. Now with the federal aid, the budget constraint has moved out, and the new equilibrium is *E**. Does it make any difference whether the government specifies that the funds be allocated to one public good or the other? Not usually. So long as the amount of federal aid that is tied to a good is less than the amount that the community wishes to spend on it, federal aid will substitute for local support for this particular good, on an almost dollar-for-dollar basis. That is, if the community spends, say, 5 percent

[14] This kind of analysis assumes that we can separate the allocation decision among publicly provided goods from the allocation decision between private and public goods. This kind of separation is possible only under a fairly stringent mathematical condition on preferences known as separability, where we assume that the marginal rate of substitution between public goods 1 and 2 does not depend on the level of consumption of other goods.

of any additional increase in its wealth on education and 5 percent on garbage collection, a federal grant of $1 million will result in $50,000 additional expenditure on education and $50,000 on garbage collection. The remaining $900,000 will be used to lower the tax rate. But it makes no difference whether the government stipulates that the money it gives be used for education or not, so long as the community was previously spending more than $1 million on education. If it were not spending this amount, then, of course, there would be a slightly greater effect on its education budget; expenditure would increase by the amount that the federal aid exceeded the amount previously expended.[15]

These results need to be contrasted with a government program of *matching* local expenditures (e.g., on libraries). Suppose the federal government matches local expenditures on a dollar-for-dollar basis. If the local community wishes to buy a book that costs $10, it costs the community only $5, with the federal government providing the other $5 with a matching grant. This obviously provides a considerable inducement to spend more on these services, as illustrated in Figure 26.5. The new budget constraint, with the subsidy for local government expenditures, is rotated around point *B*. If the community were to decide to spend nothing, it would not receive federal aid. For every dollar of privately provided goods that the community gives up, it can obtain twice as many publicly provided goods as previously. Thus the budget constraint is much flatter. This outward shift in the budget constraint has an income effect, as before; but now there is, in addition, a substitution effect. Since publicly provided goods are less expensive, the community will wish to spend more. The equilibrium will change from E to E^*.

In Figure 26.5 we have also drawn the community's budget constraint with a block grant that provides the community with the same welfare as the matching grant. (This budget constraint is clearly parallel to the before-subsidy budget constraint and the new equilibrium at E^{**} is on the same indifference curve as E^*.) Two things should be noted: the equilibrium level of public expenditure on the public good is lower than with the matching grant, and the cost to the federal government is lower. There is a deadweight loss associated with the matching grant (of DE^*, in terms of privately provided goods).

If the matching funds are provided for a particular good, the federal aid will have a marked effect on the composition of the community's budget; it will encourage those goods whose prices are lowered (perhaps partly at the expense of other publicly provided goods, whose relative prices can now be viewed as being higher).

By the same token, it should be clear that for any given level of federal grants, if the object of the federal government is to encourage the provision of particular goods, a system of matching grants is far more effective than block grants—i.e., a lump-sum subsidy—or than nonmatching categorical grants.

[15] A full analysis of this problem requires a three-dimensional diagram, with education, garbage collection, and private goods on the three axes.

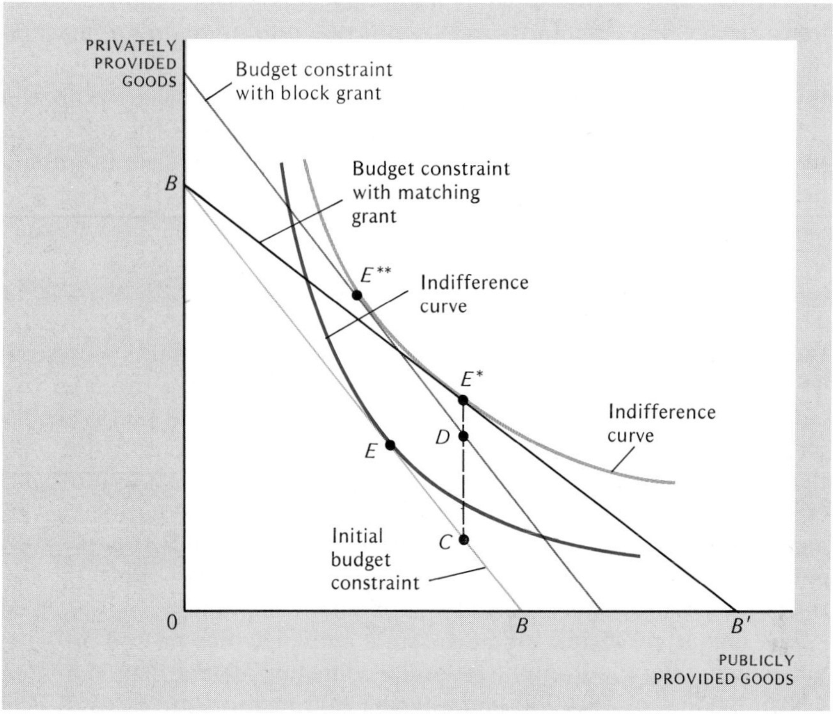

26.5 THE EFFECT OF MATCHING GRANTS Matching grants effectively lower the price of local public goods and result in an increase in the level of consumption of local public goods. With a 50 percent matching grant, to get $1 of public goods, the community need give up only 50 cents' worth of private goods. A block grant of *CD* gives the same level of utility as the matching grant of amount *CE**.

Theory and Practice

Evidence on actual government behavior supports our prediction that matching grants are more stimulative for local governmental spending than block grants, but does not support our prediction that nonmatching categorical grants have the same effects as a lump-sum increase in private income; the evidence suggests that categorical programs do have an effect on government budgets.[16] This has been referred to as the *flypaper effect:* money sticks where it hits.[17] Several explanations have been offered. One argument is that voters do not perceive the true marginal price of public expenditures when nonmatching grants are present; marginal costs exceed average costs, and voters are more aware of the latter than the former. Another explanation is that, at least in the short run, government bureaucrats have considerable discretion over

[16] See E. M. Gramlich, "Intergovernmental Grants: A Review of the Empirical Literature," in *The Political Economy of Fiscal Federalism*, ed. W. E. Oates (Lexington, MA: Lexington Books, 1977).

[17] P. N. Courant, E. M. Gramlich, and D. L. Rubinfeld, "The Stimulative Effect of Intergovernmental Grants: Or Why Money Sticks Where It Hits," in *Fiscal Federalism and Grants-in-Aid*, P. Mieszkowski and W. Oakland, eds. (Washington, D. C.: Urban Institute, 1979), pp. 5–21.

their budgets.[18] If they receive additional funds, the "voters" do not immediately know about it; and even if they did, they do not have the means by which to force the bureaucrats to pass the money back to them. A third argument has it that federal administrators can ensure that the money is spent in an incremental manner; they have enough discretion to withdraw funds if they believe that the federal funds are simply being used to substitute for state funds.

THE FEDERAL TAX SYSTEM AND LOCAL EXPENDITURES

The federal government affects local expenditures not only directly, through its aid programs, but indirectly, through the federal tax system. Two provisions of the income tax code have an important effect on local communities. The first is that interest on state and local bonds is completely exempt from taxation by the federal government. This means that if an individual faces a 33 percent marginal tax rate, a 6.7 return on a tax-exempt local government bond is equivalent to a 10 percent return on any other bond. After taxes, a 10 percent return yields $10\% (1 - .33) = 6.7\%$. This tax exemption for state and local bonds obviously lowers the cost to state and local authorities of borrowing funds.

The second provision is that the state and local income and property taxes are deductible from the federal income tax. That is, if an individual has an income of \$40,000 and pays \$1,000 in property taxes, he can deduct that amount from his income—i.e., he has to pay taxes on only \$39,000. This means that if the individual is in the 33 percent tax bracket, his net income (what he can spend to buy cars and other consumption goods) is reduced by only \$670. Of the \$1,000 in property taxes, the federal government is, effectively, paying one-third.

These tax benefits increase the level of expenditure on local public goods, encourage expenditures on capital projects, and induce some communities to finance their investments by debt.

Consider an idealized community in which all individuals are in the 33 percent tax bracket. If the community increases expenditures per family on education by \$1,000 and raises taxes to finance the increased expenditures, the after-federal income tax cost to the individual is only \$670. It is as if there is a federal matching grant for local public goods. The budget constraint facing the individual is identical to that depicted in Figure 26.5.

In most states, communities can only borrow to finance capital projects. If this restriction is binding (as it frequently is), the tax exemption of interest on local bonds implies that the effective cost of capital is lowered relative to that of current services (labor and materials); this results in a bias toward capital projects.

[18] For a discussion of this view see, for instance, J. Hannaway, "Administrative Structures: Why Do They Grow?" *Teachers College Record,* 79(1978): 413–36. The repeated attempts by taxpayers to restrict levels of taxation and expenditure through constitutional amendments suggest that there is a widespread perception that taxpayers have only limited control over the bureaucrats. For a discussion of these attempts, see A. Rabushka and P. Ryan, *The Tax Revolt* (Stanford, CA: Hoover Institution Press, 1982).

Inefficiency of Tax Benefits to Local Communities

There are four reasons why providing aid to local communities through the federal income tax system may be inefficient. The first we have just discussed: aid provides a large incentive for the public provision of goods, regardless of the efficiency with which the local communities are able to deliver these goods and services. It does not result in local communities concentrating their attention on areas in which they should.

The second is that a significant fraction of the benefits of interest exemption accrue not to the communities but to wealthy taxpayers. In the last few years, tax-exempt bonds have yielded higher after-tax returns than other bonds of comparable risk to individuals whose marginal tax rates were above 30 percent. With the lower marginal tax rates in effect beginning in 1988, the rich are likely to receive a much smaller fraction of the benefits of tax-exempt bonds, the lower yields just offsetting this tax-exempt advantage.

The third reason that tax exemption may not be an efficient way of subsidizing local communities is that because of competition among communities, some of the benefits may accrue to industries within the communities rather than to the communities themselves. Local communities can issue tax-exempt bonds to help finance some of the capital costs required to provide the infrastructure to attract firms to their communities. But if one community does this, other communities respond, either by trying to attract the firms to their community or by trying to prevent the firms from leaving. The net effect is that the level of public goods provided to businesses may be higher than it otherwise would be. If only one community provided the higher level of public goods, it would be reflected in the price firms are willing to pay for land in that community. But when all communities increase the level of public goods they provide, it may leave relatively unaffected the total demand for land and hence the level of rents.

The fourth consideration in an evaluation of federal tax and interest provisions are the inequities they create for individuals with different tastes and incomes. We have already noted that these provisions represent a considerable subsidy to the public provision of goods. Individuals who have a relatively strong preference for the goods that tend to be publicly provided at the local level benefit by such measures, at the expense of those who have a weak preference for these commodities.

Since the magnitude of the reduction in effective costs of publicly provided goods depends on the individuals' marginal tax rates, those who face a higher tax rate—usually the more wealthy individuals—receive a larger subsidy, and a larger reduction in their effective price of publicly provided goods. To some extent, the "taste" effect and the pure income effect offset each other; wealthier individuals are more likely to send their children to private school and, thus, though they may receive a larger subsidy for each dollar spent by their local government, communities with wealthy individuals may actually spend less on at least certain categories of goods.

It was partly because of the belief that using the tax system to aid local communities was a particularly inefficient and inequitable way of subsidizing them that President Reagan, in his proposal for tax reform, argued for the elimination of deductibility of state and local taxes. Not surprisingly, this proposal met with vehement opposition from those states and communities with high tax rates. There was particular concern because the federal government, at the same time, reduced direct grants. Local government officials were afraid that taxpayers would be unwilling to vote for expenditures as large as they had previously approved, and thus there would have to be major cutbacks in local services. Supporters of the president's proposal were less concerned. Since in all but a few states the median voter does not itemize his deductions, the elimination of tax deductibility would not have a significant effect on the level of expenditures approved by local communities (at least if the majority voting model discussed in Chapter 6 is approximately correct). Moreover, supporters of the president's proposal argued that if there were cutbacks, they would only result because voters had decided that, at the previous levels of expenditures, the marginal benefits were less than the marginal costs; and in that case there should be a cutback.

In the end, the opposition to the elimination of the tax deductibility of state and local income and property taxes prevailed. The 1986 Tax Reform Act made only minor changes in the rules for the deduction: sales taxes are no longer tax deductible. Also, new restrictions were imposed on the issue of tax-exempt bonds that are not used to finance public facilities. The lowering of the marginal tax rates reduced, however, the magnitude of the effective subsidy that the deduction and exemption provide.

SUMMARY

1. The federal government regulates and subsidizes states and localities. The direct subsidies consist of both categorical grants (grants for specific purposes) and block grants. In matching grants, the amount received by the states and localities depends on the amount they spend. Indirect aid is provided by the exemption from taxation of interest on state and local bonds, and the tax deductibility of state and local income and property taxes.
2. The Tiebout hypothesis postulates that competition among communities results in an efficient provision of local public goods. The reasons that federal intervention may be required include market failures (national public goods, externalities, particularly those associated with choice of location, and limited competition) and redistribution (the limited ability to redistribute income at the local level).
3. There are marked disparities in income per capita and in the provision of local public services across states and localities. Whether government policy should be directed at reducing inequalities across communities (rather than inequalities across individuals) is debatable.
4. The arguments favoring local production of public goods over federal production are that local governments will be more responsive to needs and preferences and have greater incentives to provide services efficiently.

5. Matching grants are more effective in encouraging expenditures in the direction desired, but if the purpose of the grant is to redistribute income, there may be a deadweight loss associated with their use. Though traditional theoretical arguments suggest that nonmatching categorical grants should have just income effects, and thus be equivalent to a block grant or an equal direct grant to the members of the community, the empirical evidence suggests the presence of a flypaper effect.
6. Tax subsidies lead to excessive expenditures on publicly provided goods and excessive capital investment by state and local governments.
7. Tax subsidies are an inefficient way of subsidizing state and local communities. Some of the benefit accrues to wealthy investors rather than to the communities; some of the benefit is passed along to businesses (and not to the residents of the communities); and the tax subsidies discriminate in favor of high-income individuals and individuals who have a strong preference for publicly provided goods.

KEY CONCEPTS

Matching grants	Spillovers
Categorical grants	Specific egalitarianism
Block grants	Flypaper effect
Local public goods	

QUESTIONS AND PROBLEMS

1. Discuss the advantages and disadvantages of state versus national determination of eligibility standards and benefits for: food stamps; Medicaid; unemployment insurance; Aid to Families with Dependent Children; and Old-Age and Survivors' insurance.
2. In President Reagan's State of the Union message in 1982, he proposed a trade with the states: in return for the states taking over responsibility for the full costs of food stamps and AFDC, the federal government would take over responsibility for Medicaid. In addition, he proposed phasing out most categorical grant programs (possibly substituting increases in block grants). Evaluate these proposals using the analysis of this chapter.
3. If the income elasticity of demand for education is 1, what will be the effect on expenditures on education of a small block grant of $100,000 if presently the community spends 5 percent of its total resources on education?
4. Many matching grant programs specify that the federal government matches on a dollar-for-dollar basis local expenditures up to some particular maximum. Draw the budget constraint between private goods and local public goods facing a community of identical individuals. Discuss the effect of such a matching program on communities that do not go to the maximum. Discuss the effect on communities that go beyond the maximum.
5. What would you expect to be the effects on spending on education if the federal income tax deduction for state and local taxes were eliminated? Show diagrammatically why you might expect such a change to increase the relative importance of private education.
6. Consider a community in which everyone is at the 33 percent marginal tax bracket. By how much would educational expenditures be reduced by the

elimination of the tax deductibility of state and local taxes, if the price elasticity of demand for education is 1?

7. On the basis of the discussion of Chapters 7, 8, and 9, discuss the relative merits of regulation versus matching grants as devices to elicit desired behavior on the part of state and local governments.

27

State and Local Taxes and Expenditures

In Chapter 2 we discussed the changing pattern of taxation at the state and local levels: the decreased importance of property taxes and the increased importance of sales and income taxes. Does this changing pattern of financing result in a change in who bears the burden of state and local taxes, or only a change in the manner in which they are collected? The first part of this chapter is concerned with answering the question: What is the incidence of state and local taxes? We also address the parallel question: Who benefits from the goods and services provided by local governments? What, in other words, is the incidence of these expenditures? It is necessary to answer these questions in order to answer our final question: What can we say about how the level and composition of public expenditures are determined locally?

INCIDENCE ANALYSIS APPLIED TO LOCAL PUBLIC FINANCE

In Chapter 17 we developed the basic principles of incidence analysis. There we showed that the incidence of a tax on a commodity or a factor depended on the elasticity of demand and supply for that commodity or factor.

The equilibrium return to a factor is determined by the intersection of the demand and supply schedules. Now assume that a tax is imposed on the use of a factor. That can be represented diagrammatically either as a shift upward in the supply curve (to elicit the given supply, the buyer must pay more, by an amount equal to the tax) or as a shift downward in the demand curve (the amount received by the seller, at each quantity, is smaller). The limiting case is where the supply schedule has an infinite elasticity—i.e., where the supply schedule is completely horizontal. Then the incidence of the tax lies entirely on the buyer. The price he pays goes up by the amount of the tax. The amount received by the seller is unaffected.

The implications of this for local taxes can easily be derived. In the long run most factors are mobile; that is, they can easily move from community to community. This is particularly the case for capital. Investors will invest in a community only if they can obtain the same return that they could obtain elsewhere.

Local Capital Taxes

A community that increases the taxes it imposes on capital will find that investors will invest less in their community; though it may not be possible for those with fixed capital equipment—such as steel mills—to remove their capital, new investments will be reduced until the before-tax return to capital is driven up. The process will continue until the after-tax return is equal to what it is elsewhere.

Thus the burden of the tax on capital is not felt, once capital can adjust, by the owners of capital. It is felt by land and labor. Because there is less capital, the productivity of land and labor (and hence their income) will be reduced.

If as a result of the tax on capital the productivity of workers is decreased, wages will be lowered. But then, in the long run, workers will emigrate; if labor is perfectly mobile, workers will continue to emigrate until their (after-tax) income is the same as it is elsewhere. This leaves land as the only factor that cannot emigrate. With less capital and less labor, the return to land is less: the full burden of the tax is borne by land owners in the long run.

This assumes that labor is perfectly mobile. Of course, in the short run, workers will not instantaneously migrate in response to a small change in the wage rate. Indeed, many individuals have strong preferences for living in the community in which they grew up. These laborers are only partially mobile. They will bear some part of the burden of the tax on capital. Their wages will be reduced as a result of the outflow of capital.

Ignoring these considerations may have dramatic consequences. Occasionally states have attempted to impose special taxes on particular industries. Some industries are especially "footloose." These industries will move out if higher taxes are imposed on them. They will "shop" for states and communities that offer the best deal.

Income, Wage, and Sales Taxes

Similar principles apply to the taxation of labor. If individuals had no particular attachment to their community, a small community would face a perfectly elastic long-run labor supply schedule. A tax on labor would simply increase the before-tax return to labor and leave the after-tax return unchanged. Again, the incidence of a wage tax is borne not by workers but by landlords. It is just an indirect—but inefficient—tax on land.

Uniform sales taxes on consumption and investment goods are, as we noted in Chapter 17, simply equivalent to proportional income taxes. They have effects that are analogous to wage taxes.[1] They are borne by land (and workers with limited labor mobility).

Distortions

The fact that all local taxes are borne by the same, immobile factors does not mean that the taxes all have the same consequences. While a direct tax on land is nondistortionary, all the other ways of raising revenue induce distortions. The property tax (which is partly a tax on land, partly a tax on capital) raises the cost of capital to the community and induces a bias against capital; a wage tax or a sales tax raises the cost of labor and thus induces a bias against the use of labor. In addition, it may induce individuals to do their shopping across state borders. For instance, the higher sales tax in New York City induces many individuals to do their shopping in New Jersey. When Washington, D.C., imposed a higher gasoline tax than neighboring Virginia and Maryland, drivers were induced to buy their gasoline outside the city. High state income taxes may induce individuals to live in one state and commute to another to avoid the high taxes that would be levied on their income.[2] New Hampshire imposes no income tax; many people find it advantageous to live there and commute to Massachusetts, which has an income tax. The tax is inefficient, both because it raises the cost of using labor in Massachusetts and because it induces unnecessary expenditures on commuting costs.

Limitations on the Ability to Redistribute Income

The fact that taxes are borne by immobile factors means that the extent of redistribution that is feasible at the local level is very limited. Assume, for instance, that some community decides doctors are too wealthy. The local government, accordingly, imposes a licensing tax on doctors in an attempt to redistribute income from this wealthy class of individuals to others. Doctors, in making their decision about where to set up practice,

[1] Income taxes are taxes on wages plus income from capital. These taxes have a particularly distortionary effect on location decisions of wealthy individuals: they may choose not to live and work in a location where their productivity is highest because the net return (taking into account the additional taxes they must pay on their capital income) is lower.

[2] In such situations, they typically must pay taxes on the wages they receive only to the state in which they reside.

will look at their prospects in different communities. When they discover that after-tax income is lower in this community than elsewhere, they will be discouraged from setting up practice in this community. If the tax is not too high, doctors who are already established will not leave; the costs of moving exceed the losses from the tax. The fact that its doctors do not leave may fool the community into thinking that it has been successful in extracting some additional tax out of doctors; in the short run, it may be right. But gradually, as fewer doctors move into the community, the scarcity of doctors will become felt, and their wages will be bid up. Wages will continue to be bid up until the after-tax wage of the doctor is equal to what he could have earned elsewhere. In the long run doctors do not bear the burden of the tax (although they do in the short run). In the long run, the community as a whole bears the burden of the tax, in the form of less medical services and higher prices for doctors.

The same principle holds for any factor that is mobile in the long run. A number of states have suffered under the false impression that they could in fact succeed in taxing capital within their state at higher rates than it is taxed elsewhere without either offering better public services or ultimately seeing an erosion of their capital base. Some states have attempted to include income of international enterprises operating outside the state (or country) in the tax base on which they levy a corporate profits tax. If the above analysis is correct, such attempts cannot, in the long run, be successful. These communities are often misled into believing that they can do this, because capital does not emigrate instantaneously.[3]

Rent Control

A number of communities have similarly been under the impression that they could reduce the return to landlords, who were viewed to be exploiting the poorer renters. They imposed rent control laws, the effect of which was to lower the rents paid by renters below what they otherwise would be. Again, in the short run, such measures may indeed be successful. In the long run, however, landlords will make decisions about the construction of additional apartments and the renovation and maintenance of existing apartments. If the return is lowered below the return they can obtain on capital invested in other sectors of the economy, there is no reason for them to continue to invest in housing. The consequence is that the rental market will "dry up." In the long run, renters will be worse off than they would be if the government had not imposed rent control; some renters cannot obtain a rental apartment at any price. (Not surprisingly, this then results in a demand for the public provision of housing for those dependent on rental markets, necessitat-

[3] It may not be the case that, in equilibrium, the after-tax return in all communities will be the same. Notions of loyalty may lead individuals to invest in their own country or community, even when they could obtain a higher return elsewhere.

Differences in information may also lead individuals to prefer investing in their own country and this reduces the mobility of capital.

ing that the community pay the subsidy to the renters through general revenues rather than having the owners of rental apartments bear the burden alone.)

CAPITALIZATION

Consider two communities that are identical in every aspect except that the taxes are higher in one than in the other (say, because of less efficiency in the provision of public services). Clearly, if the price of housing in the two communities were the same, everyone would prefer to live in the community with the lower tax rate. This cannot, of course, be an equilibrium. Individuals care only about the total cost of living in the community; they don't care whether the government or an individual receives the money that they pay. Thus in equilibrium the total cost of living in the two communities must be the same. This means that the community with the higher tax rates will find that the prices of its houses (land) are reduced proportionately (recalling our assumption that no extra services are provided with the taxes). We say that the taxes are **capitalized** in house prices.

The term *capitalized* is used here to refer to the fact that the price will reflect not only current taxes but all future taxes. To calculate the effect of a constant tax of, say, $1,000 per year on the house price, recall that a dollar next year is worth less than a dollar this year. If we got a dollar this year we could have invested it in a money market fund or bank and obtained a return of, say, 10 percent, so at the end of the year we could have $1.10. Thus getting a dollar today is worth (is equivalent to) $1.10 tomorrow. More generally, a dollar *today* is worth $1 + r$ next year, where r is the rate of interest (i.e., a dollar next year is worth $1/1 + r$ today).[4] Thus, the value of T taxes this year, next year, the year after, and so on is

$$T + \frac{T}{1+r} + \frac{T}{(1+r)^2} + \frac{T}{(1+r)^3} \cdots$$

This is the present discounted value of the tax liabilities. If the amount by which a house's price is reduced is given by the present discounted value of these tax liabilities, we say that the tax liabilities are fully capitalized in the value of the house. If two houses are identical except for their tax liabilities, and if the house prices differ by less than this amount, we say that the taxes are **partially capitalized** in the less expensive house.

Incentives for Pension Schemes

The fact that certain fiscal variables may not be fully capitalized has some important implications itself. There are incentives for communi-

[4] By the same reasoning, a dollar the year after next is equivalent to $\$1/1 + r = \$1/1.10$ next year; but this means that, since a dollar next year is worth $\$1/1 + r = \$1/1.10$ today, a dollar the year after next is worth $\$1/(1.10 \times 1.10)$ this year—i.e., $\$1(1 + r)^2$. See Chapter 10 for a more extensive discussion of present discounted value.

ties to take advantage of this. Someone living in a community who thinks there is a reasonable chance that he will move out in ten years or so might vote for a large, unfunded pension scheme for public employees, that is, a pension scheme which fails to set aside the funds that will be needed to pay the promised pensions, but relies instead on future taxes. A generous pension allows the community to attract workers while paying lower current wages. In effect, future house owners in the town will be forced to pay for current services. The future buyer of a house is being deceived in much the same way that the manufacturer of a product who does not disclose fully some important characteristics of his commodity may attempt to deceive a purchaser. An important characteristic of a house (or any piece of property) is the future tax liabilities that are associated with it, and to know these, one must know the debt and unfunded pension liabilities of the community. Whether the appropriate way to deal with this is through disclosure laws (each community might be required to notify all potential purchasers of a house of the debt obligations of the community prior to the completion of any sale) or through restrictions (not allowing unfunded pension schemes) is a debatable question.

Choice of Debt versus Tax Financing

The extent of capitalization has implications more generally for the decision about whether to finance local public expenditures by debt or taxes. With full capitalization, an increase in the local debt by a dollar would simply decrease the net market value of the community by a dollar. Since house buyers can choose to live in this community or in some other community, their assumption of the debt of the community is a voluntary action. Therefore they will have to be compensated for it, through a corresponding decrease in the price of a house. This is true no matter how far in the future the debt is to be repaid. It does not have to be repaid during the period in which the next owner owns the house.

Assume, for example, the debt is to be repaid in forty years, and each individual lives in the house for only ten years. The person who buys the house at the time that the debt is to be repaid clearly will pay less for the house, taking into account the increased tax liability associated with paying off the debt. But the preceding purchaser knows that the person to whom he will sell the house will be willing to pay less for it, and hence he will be willing to pay less for it (by the amount of the tax liability). Similarly, the previous purchaser knows that the price at which he can sell it will be lower by the amount of the increased debt, and so he too will be willing to pay less for it, and so on.

With full capitalization, current owners pay for current services, whether directly, through taxes, or indirectly through the expectation of a lower price on their house resulting from a higher debt used to finance the public services. Which of these two methods is then preferable turns out to depend on the treatment of local taxes and interest on local debt by the federal government, a question we discussed in the previous chapter.[5]

Short-run versus Long-run Capitalization

Assume that taxes are increased on apartment buildings. If the amenities the community provides are unchanged, the rents will remain unchanged: the rents individuals are willing to pay depend on the services provided by the community and the landlord, rather than on the costs to the landlord of those services. In the short run, the market value of the apartment will thus decrease. But this will make investing in apartments in the community less attractive; the supply of apartments will be reduced (as old apartments deteriorate) or in any case will not keep up with population growth. This will result in an increase in rents. Eventually, rents will increase to the point where the after-tax return on the apartment is the same as investors could obtain from investments in any other community. Thus, although the tax is imposed legally on buildings, in the long run it is land and immobile individuals (who must pay higher rents) who bear the tax.

Who Benefits from Local Public Goods? The Capitalization Hypothesis

The same reasoning that leads us to conclude that the incidence of any tax resides with the owners of land (or other partially immobile factors) implies that the incidence of any benefits resides with the owners of land (or partially immobile factors). Any public good that makes it more desirable to live in a community drives up the rents and hence increases the value of property in the community. In the short run, some of the benefits may be enjoyed by owners of buildings; but the increased rent on their buildings leads to increased investment in housing (new apartment buildings, replacing small, old apartment buildings with larger ones, etc.), and this drives down their return.[6] Ultimately the value of the public good is reflected in the price of land.

Similarly, some public goods make it more attractive to work in a given community. This will reduce the wage a firm must pay to recruit a worker. But again, the ultimate beneficiaries are the land owners.

To see the link between the wages that individuals receive and the level of public services provided, consider what happens if a city decides to spend more on its symphony orchestra, which provides free concerts in the parks in the summer. This makes the city a more attractive place in

[5] In the presence of credit rationing (limited availability of mortgages), the lower price of a house may increase its salability. The fact that communities may borrow more easily than individuals provides an argument for communities to borrow as much as they can.

[6] Current owners of buildings have an incentive to maintain their higher return by restricting further investments, by zoning. The higher returns they enjoy should be viewed not as a return to capital but as a return to the property rights the zoning board has created.

which to live and work. A worker who enjoys the symphony, contemplating a job offer in this city, will accept the job at a slightly lower wage than he would accept in a community that is identical in every respect except its level of exependiture on its symphony orchestra. Thus, to the extent that workers in the city (regardless of where they choose to live) value the amenities it provides, wages in the city will be lower; firms will find it attractive to locate there. As they move into this city, the price of land will be bid up. Equilibrium is attained when the price of land is bid up just enough to compensate for the lower wages, so that investors receive the same return to their capital that they receive from investing it elsewhere. The ultimate beneficiaries of the provision of better public goods are not the residents in the city but the land owners.

This analysis assumes, of course, that labor is highly mobile, so that when the city provides a more attractive public good, there is sufficient migration to decrease wages and increase rents. If labor is not very mobile (and in the short run it may well not be), wages will not fall to reflect fully the increased amenities, and some of the benefits of the increased provision of local public goods will accrue to the current residents. Note that some current residents may be hurt by the provision of the symphony. Those who do not enjoy music may find that, nonetheless, their rents are increased or wages reduced.

The provision of the symphony orchestra does have important spillovers to other communities. In particular, firms located in the suburbs will find that they too can hire workers at a lower wage than they previously could. This increases the value of their land as well. Bedroom suburbs will also find that the demand for their housing has increased.

Absolute versus Relative Capitalization

We have discussed how, if one community increases its level of expenditure on a public good, the differential expenditure will be reflected in the prices of the land in the community. There is, however, an important difference between the effects of a single community's increasing its expenditure on a public good and all communities' increasing their expenditures on that public good. If all communities increase their expenditures on a public good, the relative attractiveness of living in one community versus another is, of course, unchanged. Thus, in general, rentals will remain unchanged.[7]

This is an example of a phenomenon we noted in earlier chapters. The effects of a change in one community (a change in a tax on one commodity) may be quite different from the effects of a change in all communities (a change in the tax rate on all commodities).

[7] There are exceptions. If the communities provide a public good that makes land more desirable, all individuals will attempt to rent or purchase more land, and this will increase the value of land. The opposite will be true if communities provide a public good that makes owning land less desirable. Thus, since public parks are, in part at least, a substitute for back yards, it is conceivable that if all communities spend more on providing public parks, rents and land prices would actually decrease.

The Use of Changes in Land Rents to Measure Benefits

Changes in rents have often been used to measure the value of certain public services. In studies of the economic effects of American railroads in the nineteenth century, one commonly employed way of measuring the benefits is to measure the change in the land rents after the construction of the railroad. Again, one has to be careful to distinguish partial versus general equilibrium effects. Making one small plot of land more accessible will increase the demand for that plot of land; and the change in the rent will provide an accurate estimate of the reduction of the transportation costs of getting to that piece of land. However, changing the accessibility of a mass of land—as the railroad in fact did—has general equilibrium effects; the change in land rents will not correctly assess the value of such a change.[8]

Land values reflect the valuation of marginal individuals, those who are indifferent when choosing between living in this community and living somewhere else. When there are a sufficiently large number of communities, the valuation of these marginal individuals provides a good measure of the valuation of the entire community, but not otherwise.[9]

Testing the Capitalization Hypothesis

The question of the extent to which the benefits provided by public goods and taxes are reflected in property values has been extensively studied.

If some communities were more efficient in providing public goods than others, so that they could provide the same level of public goods with lower taxes, property values in the low-tax communities should be higher. If all communities were equally efficient and maximized their property values, differences in taxes would be matched with differences in benefits. In this case, there would be no systematic relationship between property values and expenditures. This is the result obtained by Jan Brueckner of the University of Illinois, in his study based on fifty-four Massachusetts communities.[10]

On the other hand, there is evidence that the value of amenities (such as clean air) for which there are not corresponding taxes is capitalized in property values.

[8] There is a second limitation on the use of land rents to measure the value of such changes: they provide a good measure only in the case where there are no inframarginal individuals, no individuals who are enjoying a consumer surplus from living in the community.

[9] R. Arnott and J. E. Stiglitz, "Aggregate Land Rents, Expenditure on Public Goods and Optimal City Size," *Quarterly Journal of Economics* 93 (1979): 472–500; R. Arnott and J. E. Stiglitz, "Aggregate Land Rents and Aggregate Transport Costs," *Economic Journal* 91 (1981): 331–47; D. Starrett, "Principles of Optimal Location in a Large Homogeneous Area," *Journal of Economic Theory* 9 (1974): 418–48.

[10] J. K. Brueckner, "A Test for the Allocative Efficiency in the Local Public Sector," *Journal of Public Economics* 19 (1982): 311–31.

In Chapter 6 we described how public choices are made; we showed that, with majority voting, the allocation to public goods reflects the preferences of the median voter.[11] This voter assesses the costs and benefits to him of the expenditure of an extra dollar on public goods. We then assessed the efficiency of the majority voting equilibrium.

The issues at the local level are identical; in both cases we need to focus our attention on the *incidence* of the benefits and costs associated with any increase in expenditure and taxation. We need to distinguish between the effects on renters and on land owners, under assumptions of perfect and imperfect mobility (with a large or small number of competing communities).

With perfect mobility and a large number of competing communities, any improvement in the amenities provided by a community will be fully reflected in rents; hence marginal renters will be indifferent with respect to the public services provided. Moreover, since their rents are affected only by the services that are provided, not by the tax rates, renters will be completely unconcerned about the efficiency with which public services are provided, that is, with their cost.

Under these same assumptions, land owners as a group will want public services to be increased so long as they lead to increases in rents exceeding the increases in taxes. Thus in a land owner-controlled community, in equilibrium an extra $1,000 spent on public goods should just increase aggregate rents by $1,000. But the increased rents represent renters' marginal evaluation of the services provided by the community. As a result, a land owner-controlled community will provide an efficient level of public services. Moreover, since if the community can provide the same services at less cost, the after-tax receipts of land owners will be increased, land owner-controlled communities have every incentive to ensure that public services are provided in an efficient manner. Thus, if the level of expenditures is chosen to maximize property values, and if there is effective competition among communities, the resulting allocation of resources will be Pareto efficient.

All of this changes if there are relatively few communities competing against each other. Consider a metropolitan region in which there are two towns, A and B. A has high taxes and a high level of local public goods; B has low taxes and a low level of public goods. Those who have a strong preference for public goods (relative to private goods) live in A; those who have a strong preference for private goods live in B. The individual who is indifferent with respect to living in the two communities we call the *marginal* individual; the extra public goods he receives in A just compensate him for the extra taxes he has to pay. All other individuals are called **inframarginal.** For those who live in A, for instance, the extra benefits more than offset the extra taxes they have to pay. Were A to increase its taxes slightly, without altering its benefits, they would still not wish to move to B.

[11] Assuming, of course, that a majority voting equilibrium exists.

Assume that there are houses for half the population in A, and half in B. All housing is rented. If B decides to provide fewer public goods, rents in B will have to adjust so that the *marginal* individual is still indifferent with respect to living in A or living in B. But of all the individuals who live in B, the marginal individual is the one with the *strongest* preference for public goods: the rents will fall in B to just compensate him for the lower level of public goods. If the rents decrease enough to make the marginal individual remain indifferent, the other individuals in B are actually better off. In particular, the median renter in B will have an incentive to vote for a very low level of expenditure on public goods, lower than is Pareto efficient. The same reasoning shows that the median renter in Community A will have an incentive to vote for a very high level of expenditure on public goods, higher than is Pareto efficient.

Land owners have exactly the opposite bias. They are concerned only with the effect of increased expenditure on land values (rents). If the increased rents exceed the increased expenditures, they are worth undertaking. In Community A, the increased rents from an increased expenditure reflect the *marginal* individual's evaluation; this is the individual who has the weakest preference for public goods. Thus the gain to others (the inframarginal renters) exceeds the gain to the marginal renter; but the land owners will pay no attention to this. As a result, they will vote for too little expenditure on public goods. By the same reasoning, in Community B, land owners will vote for too high an expenditure on public goods.

Thus, just as we saw in Chapter 6 that the majority voting equilibrium did not provide a Pareto-efficient level of expenditures on public goods, such is also the case even when there are only a small number of communities. When there is limited competition, there may be systematic biases in the patterns of allocation, and marked differences between communities in which renters dominate (in which case there may be excessive differences among communities) and those in which landlords dominate (in which case there may be insufficient diversification among communities). However, if there are a very large number of communities, and they all recognize that capital and labor (of different skills) are perfectly mobile, then they will compete effectively against each other, providing an efficient supply of public goods corresponding to the preferences of the different individuals in the different communities, and providing these public goods in an efficient manner. While, under these circumstances, renters will be indifferent to what the government does, land owners will not be.[12]

[12] There are, clearly, a number of communities within most metropolitan areas. But are there enough to ensure that the resulting equilibrium is "close" to Pareto efficient? There is no agreement among economists about the answer to this.

The case where there are a sufficiently large number of communities to ensure efficiency has some further peculiar implications. There would be unanimity among all voters about what the local government should do. All individuals of any skill type within the community would be identical. These implications are sufficiently counter to what is observed in most situations to suggest to many economists that models assuming limited competition are closer to the mark.

SUMMARY

1. If capital and labor are mobile, the incidence of any tax lies on land, the immobile factor. If labor is only partially mobile, some of the burden may lie upon it.
2. Local taxes that are imposed on mobile factors—sales taxes (which are equivalent to income taxes), wage taxes, corporation income taxes, property taxes —induce distortions.
3. Improved public services provided by the government get reflected in rents paid. In a perfectly competitive environment (with a large number of communities with similar individuals), the benefits of improved government services accrue solely to landlords.
4. Future benefits and taxes may be *capitalized* in current land values.
5. The effect of an increase in benefits on land rents (values) will depend on whether one community alone increases its benefits, or on whether all communities increase their benefits.
6. If the level of expenditures is chosen to maximize property values, and there is effective competition among communities, the resulting allocation of resources is Pareto efficient.
7. If there is limited competition, however, the resulting equilibrium is not Pareto efficient; there is a tendency for too little diversification in the services provided by the different owner-controlled communities.
8. In contrast, when renters control the community, there is a tendency (under the same circumstances) for excessive diversification. Communities that spend a great deal on public goods spend too much; communities that spend little spend too little.
9. Moreover, there is no incentive for renters to be concerned with the efficiency with which the government delivers its services.

KEY CONCEPTS

Rent control
Capitalization
Partial capitalization
Absolute versus relative capitalization
Inframarginal individual

QUESTIONS AND PROBLEMS

1. Explain why the property tax may lead to lower expenditures on capital (buildings) per unit of land.
2. Many firms have employees, plants, and sales in more than one state. In imposing state corporation income taxes, states use a rule for allocating a fraction of the firms' total profits to their state. Does it make a difference what rule is used? Discuss the consequences of alternative rules.
3. Many of the issues of state and local taxation are similar to issues that arise in international contexts. Many countries have, for instance, imposed taxes on capital owned by foreigners. Discuss the incidence of such taxes. Does it pay to subsidize capital owned by foreigners?
4. Discuss the incidence of a city wage tax.
5. Many cities have passed rent control legislation. Discuss carefully who benefits and loses, in the short run and in the long run, from such legislation. Discuss the political economy of such legislation. President Reagan has

proposed that no housing aid be given to communities with rent control legislation. Discuss the merits of this proposal.

6. Henry George, a famous nineteenth-century American economist, proposed that only land be taxed (not buildings). Would this be unfair to land owners? Would it distort resource allocations, making land more expensive relative to buildings?
7. Who is the main beneficiary of tax-exempt industrial development bonds (which enable communities to borrow funds to re-lend to firms constructing new plants within the city): (a) workers in the town; (b) land owners in the town; or (c) the industries that move into the town? Give your assumptions. Does it make a difference whether only one community provides these bonds or whether all communities provide them?
8. Who benefited from the construction of the subway system in Washington:
   a) owners of land near the subway line at the time the route was announced;
   b) owners of land near the subway line at the time the subway was completed;
   c) renters of apartments near the subway line at the time the route was announced;
   d) renters of apartments near the subway line after the subway was completed; or
   e) renters of apartments not near the subway line? In each case, give your assumptions.

28

DEFICITS, ECONOMIC STABILITY, AND GROWTH

In recent years, a subject of great concern to Americans has been the huge government deficits. The 1987 federal government deficit was estimated to be $186 billion. By then, the national debt, the accumulation of deficits over many years, had risen to $2.4 trillion dollars. These numbers are so large that it is hard to obtain a perspective on them. The accumulated deficit in the first six years of the Reagan administration was larger than the total national debt accumulated in the first 200 years of our country, including that required to finance both world wars. The deficit in 1987 amounted to 18 percent of federal government expenditure. Some of the increase in the deficit is, of course, illusionary; it is the consequence of inflation. But in Figure 28.1 we show that the real national debt, measured in constant dollars, has skyrocketed since 1980.

A second major concern of the past decade has been the decline in the competitiveness of American industries. **Labor productivity**—real output per employee hour—has been almost stagnant.[1] Many major American industries have lost much of their market to Japan and other countries. Our exports have not been growing as fast as our imports. We

[1] Labor productivity is also called just *productivity*. It is the total amount of GNP in inflation-corrected dollars, divided by the total number of hours spent on the job by the nation's workers.

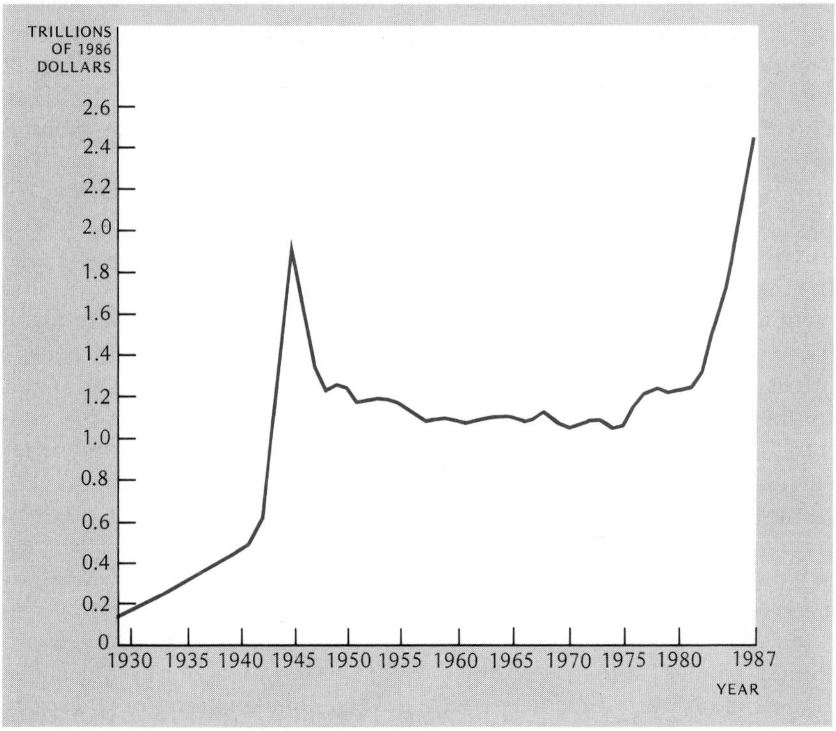

28.1 REAL FEDERAL DEBT (1986 prices) Real federal debt has increased enormously since 1980, exceeding the levels attained in World War II. SOURCE: *Economic Report of the President,* 1987, Tables B–3, B–74.

have been borrowing so much from abroad that in 1985, for the first time, we became a *debtor country:* the total value of what we owed foreigners exceeded what they owed us.

Many economists believe that these problems are related: that government policies, including the huge deficits, either have contributed to, or at least not been sufficiently active in preventing, the decline in productivity. Indeed, much of the debate over various tax, expenditure, and deficit policies centers on their implications for the growth and stability of the economy. For instance, it was widely thought in the early 1980s that lowering taxes would greatly stimulate the economy: individuals would work longer and harder and would invest more. The 1981 tax reductions were motivated more by these concerns than by a reduced need for revenue. The deep deficits that followed gave rise to concern; there was worry that they would lead to high interest rates, and thus to lower levels of output, investment, and growth. As a result, taxes were increased (with what were euphemistically called "revenue-enhancing measures" passed in 1982 and 1984).

These are not the only major problems that have confronted the economy in recent years. Unemployment rates, at least through 1987, remained persistently high. The average unemployment rate in the period 1974–1986 was 7.4 percent, much higher than the average rate of just 4.7 in the period 1962–1973. Professor Alan Blinder of Princeton University estimates that in the twelve years following 1974, the loss of output attributable to the rise in unemployment was close to $2 trillion. This staggering figure suggests that unemployment is the "biggest inefficiency of them all."[2]

DEFICITS AND ECONOMIC STABILITY

Before John Maynard Keynes, many economists thought that unemployment was largely due to too high wages relative to prices, which reduced the amount of labor that firms were willing to hire. The ratio of wages to prices is called the *real wage.* Lowering the real wage, it was thought, would increase the level of employment. Keynes argued, on the contrary, that the limitation on employment was the level of demand; firms would be willing to hire additional workers only if they could sell the goods that these workers produced.

Keynes not only provided a new diagnosis of the problem, he also provided a cure: if aggregate demand—either consumption, investment, or government spending—was increased, unemployment would be reduced. Keynes thought that, in deep recessions, it was difficult to stimulate investment, so that the most effective way of increasing aggregate demand was either to increase government spending or to reduce taxes, which would stimulate private consumption.

Critics of Keynesian economics have taken three positions: (a) Keynes's diagnosis of the problem was wrong, that at least in some important cases, unemployment is caused by too high wages, not insufficient aggregate demand. (b) Government policy is likely to be ineffective in increasing aggregate demand; for instance, public expenditures "crowd out" private expenditures—as public expenditures increase, private expenditures decrease on a dollar-for-dollar basis; in particular, public policies aimed at increasing either consumption or government spending reduce investment, and accordingly reduce the growth of the economy. (c) Even if government policy were effective, it is difficult for the government to time its interventions well, so it is likely that it will increase expenditures at precisely those times in which it should be decreasing them, and vice versa.

Most economists today believe that there are some important instances in which unemployment is caused by insufficient aggregate demand. But there is more controversy about how effective government policies have been, or can be, in countervailing unemployment.

In this chapter, we will focus on the role of tax, expenditure, and deficit policy in stimulating aggregate demand. There is another important instrument of government policy—monetary policy—which we will not discuss. In the ensuing discussion, the relationship between taxes,

[2] A. S. Blinder, *Hard Heads, Soft Hearts: Tough-Minded Economics for a Just Society,* (Reading, MA: Addison-Wesley, 1987), pp. 33–35. The $2 trillion figure is based on the rise in unemployment over a baseline level of 5.8 percent.

expenditures, and deficits needs to be kept in mind. If the government reduces taxes, keeping expenditures fixed, as it did in 1981, then the deficit increases.[3] Some of the effects of the change in policy may be attributed to the change in tax rates; and some may be attributed to the increased deficit. Sorting the two out may be difficult. Similarly, if the government increases its expenditures, and does not increase taxes, then again the deficit must increase. An increase in expenditure accompanied by a corresponding change in taxes is called a *balanced budget* increase in expenditures. We will discuss the determinants of consumption and investment spending, in turn.

Boosting Consumption

Earlier theories postulated that consumption depended on **disposable income.** Disposable income is an individual's income after paying taxes. In this view, reducing an individual's tax liabilities increases his disposable income and thereby increases aggregate demand.

In the last thirty years this view has been modified in several respects. Nobel laureates Milton Friedman and Franco Modigliani both argued that an individual's current consumption depended on more than his current disposable income. Friedman noted that there were large fluctuations in an individual's income from year to year. He said that consumption depended on what he called the individual's **permanent income,** the average value of his income over a number of years. In good years, an individual saved; in very bad years, he drew upon his savings; consumption was thus less variable than income.

Modigliani noted that the typical individual has an income stream that is low at the beginning and end of his life, and relatively high during the middle years of his life. An individual's consumption, however, tends to be more or less constant or increasing through life. Thus, it appears that individuals base their consumption decisions in each period on their lifetime income, rather than on the income they earn in that period. Modigliani's theory is called the **life-cycle theory of consumption.**

Under both theories, then, a *temporary* change in the level of taxes would have little effect on the level of consumption, for a temporary change in the level of taxes would have little effect on an individual's lifetime or permanent income. The individual would take this extra wealth and spread it over his life, rather than concentrate the increase in consumption in the year in which the tax reduction occurred. He would, in other words, save a large fraction of any temporary increase in his income.[4]

The effects of a temporary cut in an income tax may be contrasted with the effects of a temporary reduction in an excise tax on the pur-

[3] In fact, the government believed that the stimulating effect of the reduction in tax *rates* would be so great that tax revenues would actually increase, and hence the deficit would be reduced. This did not turn out to be the case.

[4] The income tax also taxes the return to savings. Traditional Keynesian analysis assumed that the interest elasticity of current consumption was small, and hence that this effect could be ignored, that income effects dominated any possible substitution effect.

chase of some durable. Such a tax would lead to an increased demand for that durable since individuals would prefer to purchase the good while it was temporarily less expensive.[5]

The distinction between the effects of a temporary cut in an income tax and a temporary cut in an excise tax corresponds to the distinction we saw in Chapter 18 between the income effect and substitution effect of a price change. A temporary cut in the income tax has primarily an income effect, shifting the budget constraint up as illustrated in Figure 28.2A, while a temporary reduction in an excise tax also has a substitution effect. The budget constraint "rotates" as in Figure 28.2B. Only by purchasing more today can the individual take advantage of the tax reduction.

One difficulty with temporary changes in excise taxes is that while they are effective in increasing the demand for consumption goods during recessionary periods, they also have effects in periods before and after the change in the tax rate. If the change in the tax rate is anticipated, then in periods before the tax is lowered, the demand for the goods that are about to have their tax reduced may be significantly lowered. Immediately prior to the return of the tax to its normal level, the demand for the good may go way up, and immediately after its return to its normal level, its demand may decrease significantly. Such shifts in the timing of purchases mean that temporary changes in the tax rate may have marked effects outside the period in which the intended effects are meant to occur.

LIQUIDITY EFFECTS

Some economists maintain, however, that there is a mechanism by which even temporary changes in the income tax may lead to significant changes in *current* consumption. Nobel laureate James Tobin of Yale University has emphasized that many individuals are **liquidity-constrained:** they would like to consume more than at present but they are constrained from doing so by limitations on their borrowing. To put it another way, they believe that their lifetime income warrants a higher level of consumption than their current level of consumption, but their bankers do not share that belief and hence are unwilling to give them loans. So long as the bankers remain unconvinced, the would-be higher spenders must limit their consumption to their current income. But when their current disposable income is increased—as it will be by a decrease in the income tax rate—opportunity knocks; they increase their expenditures on consumption goods.

The lack of liquidity is particularly important in constraining individ-

[5] A temporary reduction in an income tax should also have a short-run effect on labor supply. Because the return to working is higher while the income tax rate is low, individuals would prefer to work more, substituting future leisure for current leisure. This effect, however, is likely not to be significant in recessionary periods when individuals face limits on the amount of labor services that they can sell. Moreover, even in the best of times, many individuals have little discretion over the hours they work. For these reasons, most economists believe that the effect on labor supply of a temporary income tax change is slight.

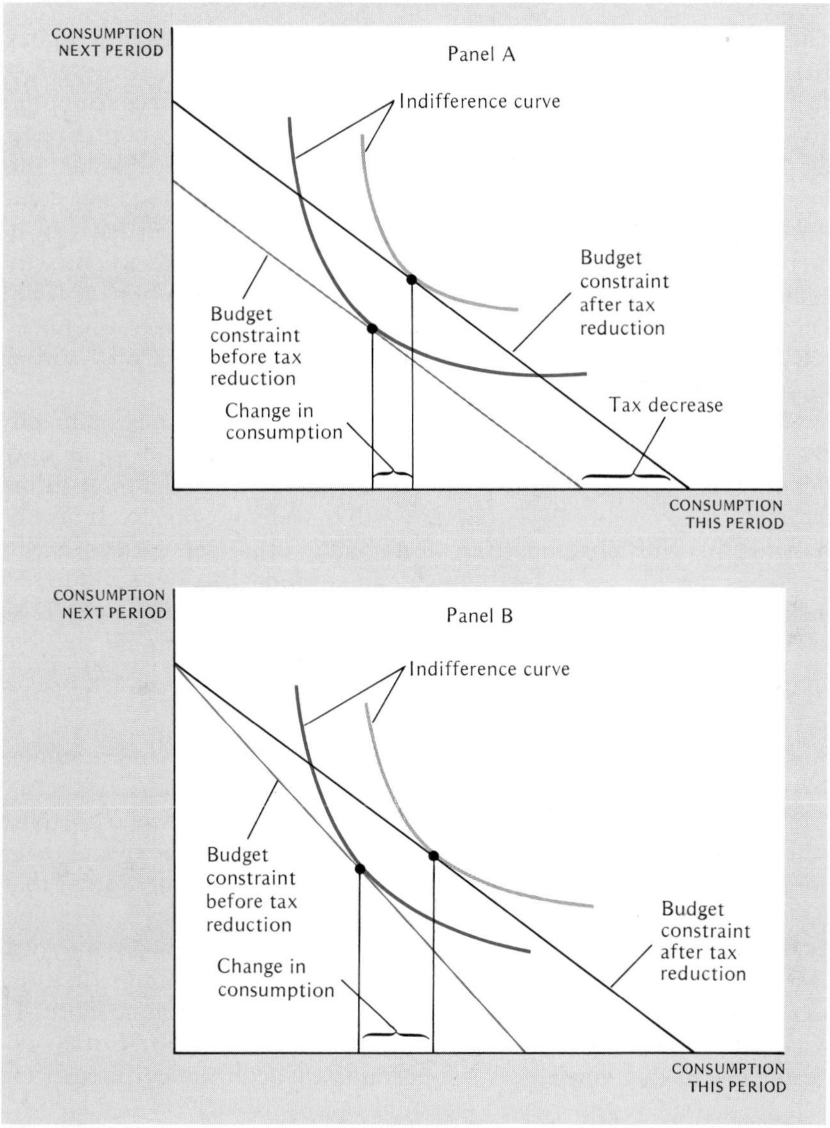

28.2 EFFECTS OF TEMPORARY REDUCTIONS IN INCOME TAX AND CONSUMPTION (EXCISE) TAX (A) A temporary cut in an income tax has a small effect on permanent income. The budget constraint is shifted up slightly, and current consumption is thus increased only slightly. (B) A temporary cut in an excise tax reduces the relative cost of current consumption, and thus may have a strong stimulating effect on current consumption.

uals' purchases of consumer durables, such as TVs, the benefits of which are received over a large number of years. When individuals find their disposable income reduced, and cannot borrow, the first thing they reduce is their purchases of durables. These exhibit much more cyclical variability than do nondurables such as food.

There are other economists, the most prominent of whom is Robert Barro of Harvard University, who believe that all of the views described so far exaggerate the likely increase in the demand for consumption goods resulting from a decrease in the tax rate. If the level of government expenditure remains unchanged, a decrease in the tax rate increases the government debt. Such an increase in the government debt implies that, at some time in the future, taxes will have to be increased. If individuals take the future tax increases into account, the reduction in their current taxes makes them feel no better off. They know it is simply a tax that has been postponed.[6] Accordingly, the lowering of the current tax rate leads to no income effect at all—and no increase in the level of consumption.[7]

The jury is still out on Barro's view. It supposes a degree of rationality for which there is little empirical evidence. Moreover, individuals must not only recognize that a tax cut today will increase taxes at some future date, but they must believe that they will have to pay the tax. It may be possible that a tax postponed is a tax not paid: future generations may be forced to pay the tax instead, in which case today's tax cut will in fact make the current generation feel better off and, hence, increase its level of consumption.[8]

CONSUMPTION EFFECTS OF REDUCTIONS IN THE CORPORATION TAX

Similar arguments concerning the degree of rationality of consumers arise in discussions of the effect of a corporate tax cut. To the extent that it leads to an increase in dividends and, thus, in disposable income, there will probably be some increase in consumption. But to the extent that a corporation tax cut leads to an increase in retained earnings rather than dividends, there will be an increase in consumption only if the stockholders of the firm see through its corporate veil. If they do, they will realize that as a result of the increased retained earnings they are wealthier, and because they feel wealthier they will consume more. To what extent do consumers see through the corporate veil? Most economists believe that consumers see *partially* through the corporate veil, that they treat the increased assets of the firm partly as if their own wealth were increased, and increase their consumption accordingly.[9]

Boosting Investment

There are three mechanisms by which government policy affects the level of investment: (1) it affects the investment function, the level of investment that firms desire at each interest rate; (2) it affects the sav-

[6] This view has, for instance, been put forward by R. Barro, "Are Government Bonds Net Wealth?" *Journal of Political Economy* 82 (1974): 1095–1117.

[7] Again, there may be a slight substitution effect—individuals would prefer to work during periods when the income tax rate is low.

[8] Barro maintains that even if future generations pay the tax, the current generation, concerned for their welfare, will increase their bequests by a corresponding amount.

[9] Recall the discussion of Chapter 23 on the effect of the corporate and public veils on savings.

ings function, the amount that individuals are willing to save at each interest rate; and (3) it affects the uses to which available savings are put.

CONSUMPTION MAY CROWD OUT INVESTMENT

In the previous section, we saw how government policies affect consumption. If what limits output is the level of aggregate demand, then an increase in aggregate demand will lead to an increase in output and employment.

But what happens if firms are unwilling to increase their output, say because wages, relative to prices, are too high? Then, instead of increasing output, the increase in consumption will be at the expense of savings; unless the country borrows from abroad, the scarcity of funds available for investment will lead to an increase in interest rates. Consumption will crowd out investment. Aggregate demand will not increase, nor will unemployment be reduced.

THE DEMAND FOR INVESTMENT

The major instrument that the government has employed to give a temporary boost to investment is the investment tax credit.[10] If there is a 10 percent investment tax credit, a \$100 machine costs a firm only \$90; the government effectively pays 10 percent of the cost. Thus, the effect of a temporary investment tax credit (or a temporary increase in the credit) is identical to the effect of a temporary sale of the investment good; firms will be tempted to purchase the investment good while the sale is on, rather than to wait to buy the machine until after the sale is over.

Like a temporary reduction in the excise tax on a durable consumption good, a temporary investment tax credit has effects on both earlier and later periods. If the increase is anticipated, those contemplating investment will postpone the investment decision until the investment tax credit is in effect; and at the end of the period, those who would have invested somewhat later will push their investments forward. The decrease in investment both before the investment tax credit is in effect, and after its removal, may have disruptive effects on the economy.

A temporary reduction in the tax rate on corporate profits may be much less effective in stimulating investment. In deciding whether to make a given investment, firms calculate the present discounted value of the after-tax returns from the investment, and compare it with the costs. A temporary lowering of the corporate tax rate has only a slight effect on the present discounted value of the returns to a long-term investment (even an announced permanent lowering of the corporate tax rate may be ineffective if firms do not believe that the lowering of the tax rate is in fact permanent).

If firms finance their marginal investment by borrowing, a change in the corporate tax rate has no effect on the marginal cost of capital. The reason for this is that interest payments are tax deductible. Thus, a firm

[10] The investment tax credit was first enacted in 1962 as part of the Kennedy administration's program to stimulate investment. After 1962, the credit was successively suspended, repealed, reenacted, and (in 1986) repealed once again.

that borrows at the interest rate r faces an effective cost of capital of $r(1 - t)$. On the other hand, the corporate tax reduces the marginal return from investing, again by a factor of $1 - t$. Since the marginal cost and the marginal return are both reduced proportionately, the corporate tax rate has no effect, at the margin, on the level of investment. Under these circumstances, lowering the corporation tax rate will have no direct effect on the level of investment.[11]

If firms are constrained in the amount they can borrow or in their ability to raise additional capital on the stock market, there is another mechanism by which a reduction in the corporation profits tax increases the level of investment; this mechanism is analogous to Tobin's theory of a liquidity effect on consumers. Many firms would like to invest more, but are constrained from doing so because funds are not available to them. They cannot borrow more (or can only borrow more if they can provide additional equity, which is hard to raise directly during recessionary periods). The lowering of the corporation tax provides the firm with funds that it can invest and that it can augment by borrowing, using the equity as collateral.

DEFICITS AND INVESTMENT

There has been considerable concern that government expenditures and deficits have reduced, or crowded out, private investment.

Savings can be used for two purposes: to finance investment and to finance government deficits. In Figure 28.3 we have depicted private

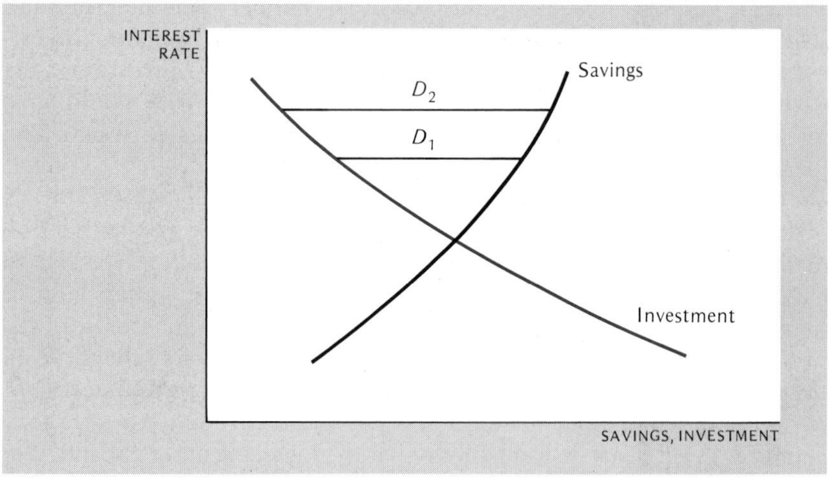

28.3 PRIVATE SAVINGS AND INVESTMENT AS A FUNCTION OF THE INTEREST RATE If the savings function is not shifted as a result of an increased deficit, an increase in the deficit from D_1 to D_2 results in reduced investment.

[11] There may be an indirect effect through a change in the interest rate. Also, this argument assumes that depreciation allowances equal economic depreciation.

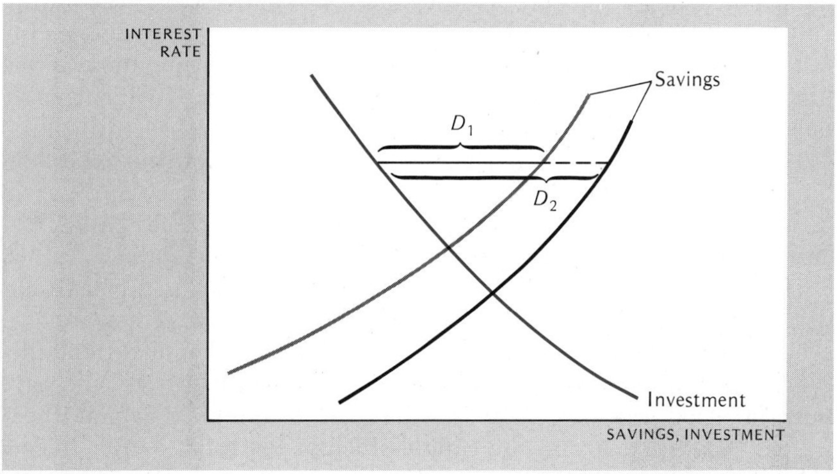

28.4 SPECIAL CASE WHERE DEFICITS LEAVE INVESTMENT UNCHANGED If an increase in the deficit from D_1 to D_2 shifts the savings function by the amount of the increase in the deficit, interest rates are unchanged, and investment unaltered.

savings and investment as a function of the rate of interest. The gap between private savings and investment is equal, in equilibrium, to the deficit. If the deficit increases, the government and private investors will compete for the supply of available funds, and interest rates must rise.[12] At the higher interest rates investment will be discouraged. Only if the increased deficit increases savings by an equal amount will interest rates not rise (see Figure 28.4). Even if one believes that higher deficits increase savings (as individuals set aside money for anticipated increases in taxes to pay off the increased deficit), savings are not likely to increase by a dollar for every dollar increase in the deficit.

The Burden of the Debt

The issue we have just been discussing is the central issue in the long-standing debate on the **burden of the debt.** If an individual were to bequeath a debt to his son (and if the courts forced his son to honor this debt, as they do in some countries), then his son would clearly be worse off. The larger the debt, the worse off he would be. Reasoning by analogy to the burden of private debt, many believe that the huge national debt in the United States imposes a burden on future generations. To increase the debt is to increase the burden we impose on future generations.

In the period after World War II, a view holding that the national debt did not represent a burden became fashionable. Since the national debt was simply money we owed to ourselves, how could we say it was a bur-

[12] This result will be modified once we take into account the possibility that domestic deficits can be financed by *foreign* savings. See the discussion below on deficits in open economies.

den? The analogy between private debt and public debt was, in this view, inappropriate. A private individual owes money to someone else. But in this view the cost of the war was borne at the time the war was fought: aggregate consumption was reduced at the time to finance military expenditures, and this was the true burden of the war.

Though there is a sense in which we do owe the debt to ourselves, different policies have different implications for the welfare of different generations. There are important trade-offs. Some policies benefit the current generation at the expense of future generations.

Thus, the generation that was alive at the time of World War II may not be the only generation that bears the cost of the war. When the government financed its expenditures by bonds rather than taxes, the lifetime consumption of the generations upon whom the taxes would have been imposed was increased. The bonds substituted for capital, there was less investment, and the capital stock in the future was reduced. Hence, the wages of future generations were reduced. The generation that fought the war may also vote themselves large veterans' benefits to be paid by the next generation. In both cases, the current generation has managed to impose some of the costs on future generations.

Deficits in Open Economies

The analysis so far has assumed that investment and the deficit must be financed out of domestic savings. The deficit may, however, be financed by borrowing abroad. Indeed, the deficit of a small open economy[13] has no significant effect on world interest rates. With interest rates unchanged, the level of investment remains unchanged, as does the level of savings (apart from the induced increase in savings resulting from anticipated future tax liabilities). The only effect of the deficit is to increase borrowing from abroad. Of course, from this perspective it makes no difference whether the government borrows abroad, or whether the government's borrowing induces private firms to borrow abroad. Since government deficits have no direct effect on investment (Figure 28.5), there is no effect on the growth of the gross national product of the country; but more of the output of the country must, in effect, be sent abroad to pay for the debts that have previously been incurred. The standard analogy between government debt and private debt appears, in this light, to be more reasonable: the increased deficit today does reduce what future generations can consume. This is true even though the actual government debt is held mostly by individuals within the country.[14]

The United States is not a small country; policies of the U.S. government do have an effect on international capital markets. Yet at the same

[13] An economy that has no economic relations with other economies is said to be *closed*. An economy that trades with other countries, or that can borrow from other countries, or that can obtain labor from other countries, is said to be *open*.

[14] There may be an indirect effect on investment: the lower level of domestic consumption that will eventually result from the lower level of income of the residents of the country eventually may have a negative effect on investment in the country.

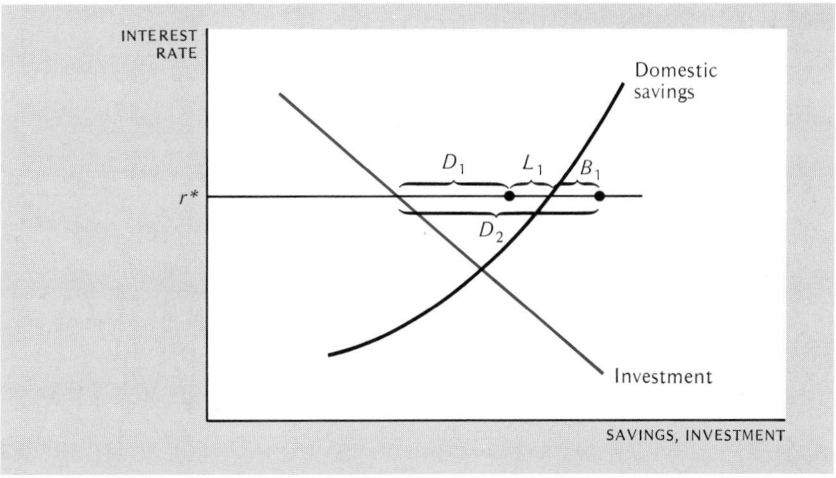

28.5 DEFICITS IN OPEN ECONOMIES For a small open economy, a change in the deficit leaves unchanged the market rate of interest (r^*) and the level of investment. With the deficit D_1, the country lends L_1 abroad, while with the deficit D_2, the country must borrow B_1 from abroad.

time it is important to remember that we are not a closed economy, and that even though the huge 1986 deficit represented more than a quarter of savings in the United States,[15] it represented a much smaller proportion of total world savings. Thus, while the deficit may have resulted in somewhat higher interest rates, it also resulted in an increase in the flow of capital from abroad (over what it otherwise would have been). The fact that the increased government deficits during the early 1980s closely corresponded to the increased borrowing from abroad was, in this perspective, no accident.[16] There is a burden on future generations from these deficits. Whether this is or is not desirable is a question of intertemporal distribution of income, whether one would like to distribute income towards or away from the current generation.

The History of Federal Deficits

Prior to 1930, there was a consensus that governments should not run a deficit. Following the Great Depression, the Keynesian view became popular, that the government should not run a deficit in normal years, but that a deficit may be desirable to stimulate the economy to get out of a recession or a depression. Thus economists calculate the **full employ-**

[15] In calendar year 1986, total savings by U.S. business, private individuals, and state and local governments amounted to $741 billion. Source: *Economic Report of the President,* 1987, Tables B–27 and B–78.

[16] Indeed, in this view, the government deficits were a central part of the explanation for why imports exceeded exports. Foreign borrowing increased to finance the deficit. Foreigners wishing to lend to the United States drove up the value of the dollar, which made our exports less attractive and imports more attractive. In this view, then, the trade deficit was a consequence of the foreign borrowing, which in turn was a consequence of the fiscal deficit.

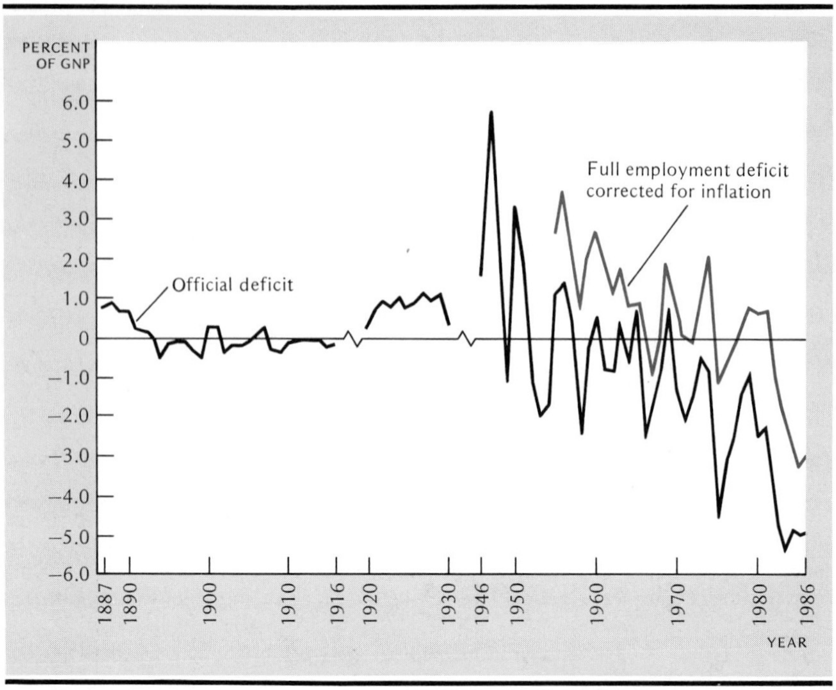

28.6 THE FEDERAL DEFICIT OF THE UNITED STATES OVER THE LAST CENTURY The official fiscal deficit is in black. The estimated full employment deficit corrected for inflation, 1955–1986, is in color. Deficits are not shown for the periods of the World Wars and the Great Depression. SOURCE: A. Modigliani and F. Modigliani, "The Growth of the Federal Deficit and the Role of Public Attitudes." *Public Opinion Quarterly* 51 (1987), pp. 459–80.

ment deficit, what the deficit in each year would have been had there been full employment. Keynesians become concerned only when the full employment deficit becomes large. In Figure 28.6 we show that until 1981, there were no major full employment federal deficits.

The large deficits of the 1980s arose in spite of the fact that President Reagan not only argued for a balanced budget, but went so far as to support a constitutional amendment for a balanced budget. While tax rates were drastically reduced in 1981, military expenditures were substantially increased. President Reagan called for reductions in other government programs, but exempted social security from these cuts. Given his positions on taxes, military expenditures, and social security, to attain a balanced budget was virtually impossible. Indeed, at its worst, the magnitude of the deficit was equal to the *total* of all federal nonmilitary, non–social security expenditures.

OTHER VIEWS OF THE EFFECTIVENESS OF GOVERNMENT POLICY

During the past two decades, there has been considerable controversy in macroeconomics. The standard Keynesian positions have been attacked on several grounds. In this text, we cannot present a comprehensive review of all of the competing theories. Here, we briefly note the implications of three competing schools of thought that have received considerable attention since the late 1970s and early 1980s.

Supply Side Economists

While Keynesian economists emphasize the role of aggregate demand, **supply side economists** such as Arthur Laffer of the University of Southern California emphasize the role of aggregate supply. This view was particularly popular in the early days of the Reagan administration. Supply side economists believed that if tax rates were cut, the spur to production (presumably through increased investment and an increase in effort and labor supply by workers and managers) would be so great that tax revenues would actually increase. Moreover, they believed that the increase in the supply of goods would dampen inflation.

The issue has not been whether it is *theoretically* possible for tax rates to be so high that a reduction in taxes actually increases output so much that government revenue increases. Rather, what has been at issue is whether current tax rates are so high that reductions in the tax rates would actually increase government revenue. Both econometric evidence[17] and the experience after the 1981 tax cut strongly suggest that they are not.[18]

Supply side economists seem to have made two errors. First, they overestimated the magnitude of the labor supply elasticity and the responsiveness of investment to changes in tax rates. Second, they underestimated the time it takes the economy to adjust to changes. Even if the long-run labor supply is very elastic, it might take several years before institutions adapt to the changed environment. Even if, in the long run, investment is very responsive to incentives, it might take firms several years to reexamine their investment strategies.

Supply side economics may have played a central role in the large deficits of the early 1980s. Reagan's willingness to push for large tax reductions was perhaps based on his belief that they would not produce the huge deficits they did, and indeed had the supply side theories been correct, the 1981 tax cut would not have resulted in huge deficits.

New Classical Economists

Supply side economists and Keynesian economists agree that government policies have a marked effect on the economy. Another important current school of thought, the **new classical** economists, such as Tom Sargent of Stanford and Robert Lucas of the University of Chicago, question the efficacy of government policies. These economists believe

[17] See Don Fullerton, "On the Possibility of an Inverse Relationship between Tax Rates and Government Revenues," *Journal of Public Economics* 19, No. 1 (October 1982), pp. 3–22.

[18] The supply siders may be correct in emphasizing the importance of supply side responses and the desirability of tax reductions. It is only their belief that the supply response is so great that a tax rate reduction will lead to an increase in tax revenues that is being questioned here.

that the private market responds to government actions in such a way as to offset the effect of those actions. We already discussed some examples of this viewpoint: we examined the conditions under which an increase in government expenditure leads to an offsetting decrease in private consumption. Of course, for private individuals to offset government actions, they have to observe these actions and understand their consequences. The new classical economists believe that individuals can do this. They believe that in making their decisions, individuals make full use of the information available to them to forecast, for instance, the consequences of each government action. When individuals form their expectations in this sophisticated way, they are said to have *rational expectations.* The new classical economists believe that individuals cannot be fooled by the government.

But the conclusions concerning the limited efficacy of government policy depend on more than the assumption of rational expectations. We saw earlier, for instance, that decreased government taxes might not be offset by increased private savings on a dollar-for-dollar basis if: (a) individuals faced liquidity constraints; or (b) there were intergenerational effects of the government policy.[19]

The new classical economists also share an assumption with the old classical economists. The old classical economists believed that markets worked well, that wages and prices were flexible and, in the absence of government intervention or possibly monopolistic unions, markets would quickly adjust to ensure that demand and supply were equal in all markets, including the market for labor. Unemployment, in this view, was either a short-run transitory phenomenon or the consequence of unions (or the government) keeping wages too high. Keynesian theory explicitly rejected these assumptions.

The new classical economists, however, have reinstated (often in a hidden form) the assumption of flexible wages and prices. With fully flexible wages and prices, with all markets (including that for labor) clearing so that demand equals supply, there is really little role for the government in determining the level of economic activity. It is the new classical economists' assumption of wage and price flexibility, more than their assumptions concerning rational expectations, which yield their conclusions concerning the inefficacy of government policy. Indeed, if there are wage and price rigidities, the "multiplier," the amount by which national income increases as a result of an increase in government expenditure by a dollar, is *greater* under the hypothesis of rational expectations than it is under the more standard Keynesian assumption that individuals' consumption simply depends on their disposable income.[20]

[19] That is, some individuals in the current generation did not have descendants in future generations, or did not care about them enough to increase their bequests on a dollar-for-dollar basis with the increase in their anticipated future tax liability.

[20] The reason for this is simple: individuals save largely for future consumption. When income today is increased, part of the increased income goes into savings. This increased savings today becomes increased consumption at some future date; this increased future consumption will increase aggregate demand and output at that future date. Individuals, anticipating this, will realize that their future

Monetarists

Monetarists such as Nobel laureate Milton Friedman believe that government policy affects the private sector mainly through the control the government has of the money supply. Most monetarists agree with the new classical economists that the government has, in the long run, little effect on the level of economic activity; in the short run, however, monetarists argue that it may have some significant effect. Most monetarists believe the best the government can attempt to do is to stabilize the price level, and this it can do by controlling the money supply, so that it increases roughly in proportion to real national income.

Monetarism reached its heyday during the late 1970s and early 1980s, when governments all over the world were concerned with the problem of inflation. It seemed to provide a simple policy for alleviating what was viewed to be the central problem of the times. It has subsequently fallen into some discredit, partly because of its lack of theoretical foundations; partly because the countries such as England that followed its dictates most closely enjoyed limited success in controlling inflation but suffered extremely high unemployment rates; and partly because the relationship between money and the value of output, which is central to the monetarist doctrine, has not been stable during the last few years.

TIMING OF POLICY CHANGES: DISCRETION VERSUS RULES

For the government to be able to stabilize the economy effectively through tax changes requires not only that its actions not be offset by countervailing actions on the part of consumers and producers, but also that the government be able to implement its policies in a timely way.

If the government attempts to reduce the level of demand to reduce inflation but acts too slowly, by the time the reduction in demand becomes effective the economy may already be in a downturn; the decrease in aggregate demand will then simply aggravate the ensuing recession. Similarly, if a government action to increase demand becomes effective when the economy is already on its way out of the recession and into a boom, government action may aggravate inflation.

The problems associated with timing of tax changes can be grouped in three categories: *lags in recognition* of a need for a change in policy, *lags in implementation* of policy, and *lags in effectiveness* of policies undertaken. Figure 28.7 traces out a business cycle. The economy begins to turn down at *A*, but the recession is not recognized until *B*. Once it is recognized that the economy is in a recession, political consensus must be formed on what to do about it; whether to cut personal taxes, increase government expenditure, or attempt to increase investment by using tax credits or monetary policy (lowering interest rates). Proposed changes

income will be higher than it otherwise would have been. And this higher future income makes them more willing to consume today, which increases aggregate demand today. See P. Neary and J. E. Stiglitz, "Towards a Reconstruction of Keynesian Economics: Constraints and Expectations," *Quarterly Journal of Economics*, 1983, Supplement, pp. 199–228.

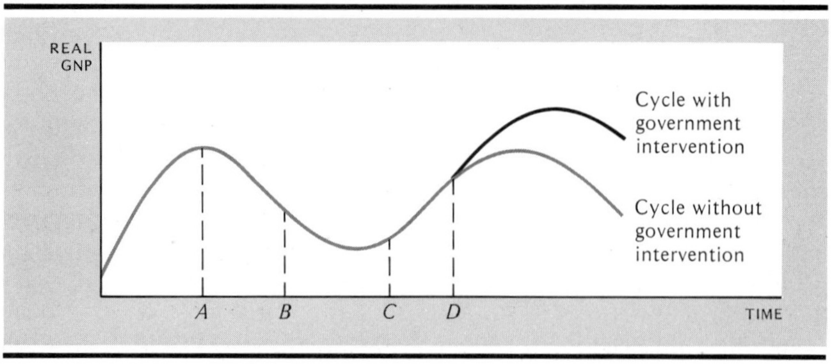

28.7 LAGS IN ANTI-RECESSIONARY POLICIES As a result of lags in recognition, implementation, and effectiveness, government policies may exacerbate cyclical fluctuations rather than dampen them. *A* - The economy begins to turn down. *B* - The government recognizes the downturn: *AB* = recognition lag. *C* - Government antirecessionary policy is implemented: *BC* = implementation lag. *D* - The government policy becomes effective: *CD* = effectiveness lag.

must make their way through the political process. This may take months; hence the lag denoted by *BC* in Figure 28.7.

Even after the legislative changes have been made, there are further lags before the changes take effect. Taxes are, for the most part, collected on a calendar-year basis. Thus, a tax cut passed by Congress in October will become effective, at the earliest, in the following January, resulting in another lag shown as *CD* in the figure.

And even after being enacted, there may be long lags before the full effects of the tax changes are felt. If an investment tax credit is unanticipated, firms will have to make new decisions concerning the timing of investments, and these decisions may take months. To draw up new investment projects (as opposed to simply moving forward projects that had previously been planned) may require years.

These lags are sufficiently long that unless the government is able to anticipate the recession, it finds itself implementing a policy change when the economy is well on its way to recovery. (The average period between recessions during the postwar period has been approximately five years.)

If the government could anticipate well in advance the peaks and troughs of the business cycle, then it could attempt to implement the policy changes in time for them to be effective. The government has not been very effective in anticipating these changes (or at least the evidence concerning forthcoming changes in the level of economic activity has been sufficiently ambiguous that no political consensus concerning what should be done has been reached until after the recession has actually arrived).

As a result, many economists (such as Milton Friedman) believe that the attempts by the government to stabilize the economy have actually increased its fluctuations. When they have not actually increased cyclical fluctuations, government policies have added to the uncertainty facing businesses and consumers. These economists argue that the government should not use *discretionary* instruments; rather, it should devise a set of rules, predicated on the performance of the economy, for the adjustment of tax rates, government expenditures, and other fiscal variables. The adoption of such rules would have the further advantage of avoiding the lags associated with the political process. The "rules" would represent a natural extension of the *built-in flexibility* already incorporated into our fiscal system. Under our present fiscal system, when the economy goes into a recession, there is some decrease in the average tax rate resulting from the progressivity of our tax structure, and there is some increase in government expenditure associated with higher unemployment benefits, higher welfare payments, and the increased social security payments resulting from individuals retiring early.

An example of a simple rule would be one that calls for a 5 percent reduction in income tax rates when the level of unemployment exceeds 10 percent, and another reduction in tax rates when the level of unemployment exceeds 12 percent.

Advocates of rules instead of discretion argue that individuals and firms will be able to plan much better if they can accurately predict what the government is going to do. One of the major uncertainties facing business is "policy uncertainty"—the uncertainty associated with knowing what actions the government will undertake.

Those who favor discretionary policy for stabilization argue that relying on rules is tantamount to tying one's hands: economic circumstances change sufficiently from one business cycle to another to make a simple rule inadequate. In contrast, supporters of rules claim that there are distinct advantages to "tying one's hands": reduction of policy uncertainty is of value in its own right.[21]

GROWTH

During the past decade, there has been increasing concern about the rate of growth of the American economy. Our overall growth rate (the average percentage increase in our output) and the rate of increase in our output per worker have lagged behind that of the Japanese and Germans, and in certain industries, such as automobiles, our share of the world market has declined significantly. There has also been a marked decease in the rate of growth of productivity in the United States, from 2.6 percent in the period 1962–1973 to 0.9 percent in the period 1973–1986.[22]

There is no consensus on the explanation for this; every economist has his favorite theory. What most economists do agree upon is that govern-

[21] "Tying one's hands" is sometimes referred to as *pre-commitment.* There are a variety of circumstances in which such commitments may be of value.

[22] A. S. Blinder, *Hard Heads, Soft Hearts,* (Reading, MA: Addison-Wesley, 1987), p. 40.

ment policies have had, and continue to have, an important effect on the rate of growth of our economy.

The growth of the economy depends on three critical factors: the growth in the capital stock (investment), technical progress (research and development), and the development and utilization of our natural resources.[23] The debate over growth inevitably involves equity questions as well, as we will see below.

Investment and Growth

Though there have been some controversies about the precise importance of investment to overall growth—with some economists, such as Harvard University's Dale Jorgenson, claiming that almost all of the increased output per worker over the past century is due to increases in our capital stock while other economists, such as Robert Solow of M.I.T., attribute a much larger role to technical progress[24]—there is little doubt that if investment is depressed in the economy, growth rates will quickly suffer.

At times, the prevailing view has been that the government should take an active role in encouraging investment. The previous sections described some of the ways in which government policies can do this. Today, the prevailing view is that the government should be careful not to dampen investment, but that it should not intervene directly to encourage it, because in doing so, it is at the same time likely to distort the patterns of investment, resulting in a misallocation of investment resources. The government should keep tax rates low, and deficits (which may crowd out investment) low; but its policy of on again–off again investment tax credits and accelerated depreciation do as much to distort the allocation of investment as they do to stimulate the level of investment.

R&D and Growth

The government plays an important role in research and development (R&D). Our discussion in Chapter 5 provides some explanation of this role. Recall from this discussion that there are two critical properties of public goods: the undesirability of exclusion (the zero marginal cost of providing the good to an additional individual) and the impossibility of exclusion. R&D (or more accurately, knowledge, the product of research) has the first property, and often has the second as well. Giving some piece of knowledge to additional individuals does not detract from what those who previously knew it know.[25] But if knowledge were pro-

[23] A fourth important factor is population growth and improvements in the quality of the labor force (human capital).

[24] Solow estimated that 87 percent of the growth in per capita income in the period 1909–1949 was due to technological change. Robert Solow, "Technical Change and the Aggregate Production Function," *Review of Economics and Statistics* 39 (1957), pp. 312–20.

[25] This fact should not be confused with the fact that the *return* that an individual can obtain from a particular piece of knowledge may depend on how many other people know that piece of information.

vided freely, it would not pay anyone to produce knowledge. Thus either the government must provide for the production of knowledge, through direct support of R&D, or it must ensure that individuals or firms that produce knowledge get compensated for doing so in some other way.

PATENTS

The government ensures compensation by providing "property rights" in knowledge; that is, it grants a **patent,** which allows the discoverer of the knowledge to have exclusive use of the knowledge (including the right to license others to use the knowledge) for a limited period of time. Not all ideas and discoveries are patentable, and even when a particular discovery is patentable, it is often possible to invent around the patent. Thus, while it is possible to patent a drug, it is often easy to devise a slight modification of the given drug, with the same medicinal properties. For this reason, and because to obtain a patent, a firm must disclose a considerable amount of information, many firms prefer not to patent their discoveries. Instead, they rely on secrecy to maintain their market advantage. For instance, the formula for Coca-Cola is not patented: its discoverers chose instead to keep the formula in a bank vault.

Notice that in those areas in which the product of research is patentable, R&D satisfies only one of the two properties of a public good (because the patent ensures that you can exclude others from the use of the R&D). In those areas in which the product of research cannot be protected either by secrecy or by patents, where others can easily imitate the discovery, R&D satisfies both of the critical properties of a pure public good.

In determining the life of a patent, the government faces a trade-off. By extending the life of the patent, it provides greater incentives for private firms to engage in R&D; but on the other hand, the knowledge that is produced will not be used efficiently for a longer period of time. Assume, for instance, that a firm has discovered a new, less expensive way of making a product. It is so much less expensive that the firm can undercut all its rivals. By patenting the discovery, the firm will be in a monopoly position. Less of the product will be produced than if the knowledge were freely disseminated.

The loss resulting from the patent can be seen in Figure 28.8, where we have drawn the market demand curve for the medicine. The cost of production prior to the invention was C_0, and the competitive equilibrium was thus (P_0, Q_0) at point D. The firm that makes the small invention has a lower cost of production C_1. It charges a price just below P_0, getting the entire market; its profits are thus *ABDE,* and its sales are Q_0.[26] If the information about the new innovation were made freely

A monopolist of a piece of information may be able to obtain a return, which he could not if the information were made freely available.

[26] The firm is not, of course, free to offer any price and quantity, since at any price at or above C_0 the firm *loses* its monopoly position. In other words, the firm maximizes its profits subject to the constraint that $P_1 < C_0$.

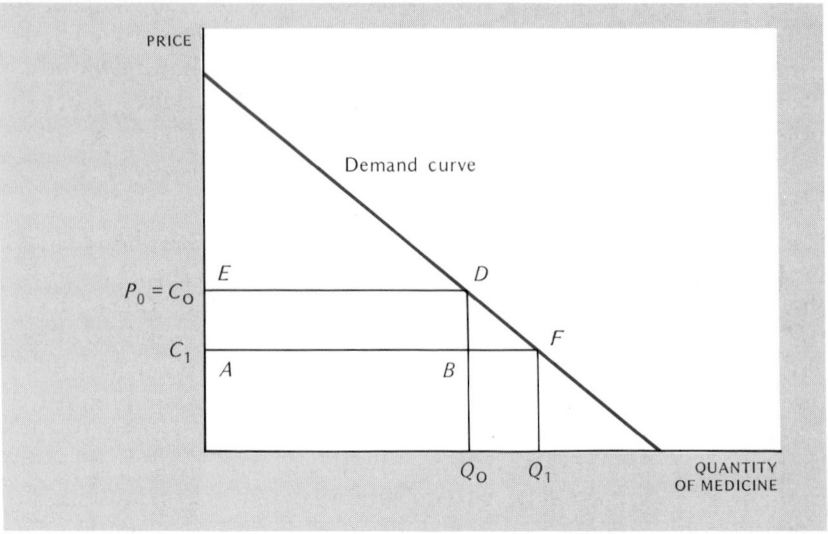

28.8 EFFECTS OF PATENTS A patent system results in a lower output than with free dissemination of knowledge. The deadweight loss is given by the triangle *BDF*.

available, the price would fall to C_1 and the quantity would rise to Q_1. Giving the firm with the patent a monopoly on its knowledge has resulted in output being smaller than it otherwise would be, and a deadweight loss of *BDF*. When the patent expires the price will fall to C_1, but the return to the innovator will drop to zero. Thus, the longer the life of the patent, the greater the deadweight loss associated with the inefficiency of giving the firm a monopoly over the use of the information; but the greater the return to the innovators and hence the greater the incentives for innovation.

Given the inefficiency associated with the patent system, why does the government not simply support research by direct grants? The patent system has two distinct advantages over a system of direct grants.

First, a system of direct grants requires some way of selecting among researchers, of making judgments about who are likely to be good researchers and which research projects are likely to have the highest payoffs. The patent system is a way of rewarding individuals for their research efforts on the basis of performance. Those who discover something that others value receive a reward. And those who believe that they have a good research project can enter the race, provided they have sufficient capital, or can persuade someone with sufficient capital to underwrite them.

Second, the patent system makes those who benefit from the innovation pay for it; it is a form of benefit taxation. When a better product is invented, the profit that accrues to the inventor, the compensation for his successful R&D program, is effectively paid by the consumer.

At the same time, it is important to realize that a patent system is still an imperfect way of rewarding research. The payments received by the inventor may not correspond well to his actual marginal contribution. If some invention would have been discovered anyway, the marginal contribution of someone who discovers it one day earlier is only the extra value arising from making the invention a day earlier. But the patent grants far more than that to that individual. Moreover, in making a discovery, the inventor draws upon a large pool of knowledge, and part of the value of the patentable invention may be attributed to this common pool of knowledge, rather than to the direct contribution of the inventor. But there is no practical way of distinguishing the two.

On the other hand, only a fraction of the value of any innovation is usually appropriated by the inventor. When DuPont produced rayon, it was able to patent that invention. But another product of its research was the knowledge that synthetic fibers could be developed. In addition, there may have been considerable benefits from the knowledge of how rayon was made, benefits that also could not be fully appropriated within the patent.

These nonappropriable benefits of research are particularly important for basic research, and that is the reason that some form of direct support for basic research is required if there is to be an efficient allocation of resources to it. Two recent "basic research" discoveries that have had a profound effect in many areas are transistors and lasers.

INCREMENTAL R&D TAX CREDIT

The government has also attempted to encourage R&D by providing an **incremental R&D tax credit;** that is, it provides firms with a 20 percent tax credit on increases in their R&D expenditures. This provision of the tax code has been criticized because it is difficult to identify what is and is not a research expenditure. Overhead expenditures and marketing research often get passed off as R&D expenditures.

Natural Resources and Economic Growth

During the past two decades, there has been concern that our limited supply of natural resources—of land, oil, coal, clean air and water, and a variety of minerals—will put a limit on the growth of the economy.[27] The steep rise in the price of oil in 1973–1974 and in 1979–1980 focused attention on our dependency on this exhaustible natural resource. There has been considerable debate over whether we have been too profligate with our resources, whether we are using them up too quickly. There is a widespread, popular feeling—not shared, however, by most economists—that markets will not do enough to ensure that there is an adequate supply of resources for future generations and that some form of government intervention is required.

In this section, we ask two questions: Are there market failures that

[27] The most famous study arguing this was published in 1972 by an M.I.T. project team. See D. Meadows et al., *The Limits to Growth* (New York: Universe Books), 1972.

necessitate government intervention regarding natural resources? What have been government policies aimed at improving the efficiency with which our natural resources have been used, and have they alleviated these market failures?

MARKET FAILURES AND NATURAL RESOURCES

In Chapter 3, we noted that one of the conditions required to ensure that the market provides an efficient allocation of resources is that there be a complete set of risk and futures markets; that is, for instance, firms could today sell oil for delivery in 2,000 years; and they could insure against even the wildest contingencies, such as the possibility that nuclear fusion turns out to be a feasible alternative source of energy, depressing the price of oil. When there is a complete set of futures markets, owners can decide whether to sell their oil today or next year or the year after. The prices of oil at each date give the scarcity value of oil at those dates. The prices will ensure that oil is allocated so that its marginal value at each date (in each use) is the same. The principles by which prices guide the allocation of resources over time are identical to the principles by which prices guide the allocation of resources at any moment of time among competing uses.

But when there is not a complete set of futures markets, owners of resources must make a *guess* about what the future prices will be. If their guesses are correct, then the allocation of resources will be the same as it would have been had there actually been the futures markets on which individuals could buy or sell oil for future delivery. The answer to the question of whether the market is excessively profligate depends then on whether the market has been excessively pessimistic about future prices of oil.[28]

How is it possible for the market, with selfish individuals living only seventy or eighty years, to make provision for generations yet to be born, one hundred or two hundred years from now? To do this, isn't some form of government intervention called for? The market can and does take into account consequences beyond the lives of those making the investment decision. This is seen most clearly in the case of forests. Men plant forests that will not mature for, say, thirty or forty years, well beyond the date at which they wish to harvest the trees. They do this knowing that in, say twenty years, a forest with half-mature trees will be highly valued; they can find some younger individuals to sell the asset to. Even if it took one hundred years for the trees to mature, the forest could be a profitable investment: the investor knows that he can sell it to some younger person, who knows that he can sell it to some still younger person, and so on.

[28] In the case of oil, there may be other market failures. In Chapter 8 we discussed the "common pool" problem. Not only will there be an excessive number of wells drilled, but in each person's attempt to get the oil before the others do, the total amount of oil that can be extracted may be reduced (because of effects of the excessive drilling on pressure). In countries where foreign oil companies are concerned about expropriation, oil may also be extracted too rapidly; the oil companies attempt to get as much oil out as they can before expropriation occurs.

The same principle applies to oil or other natural resources. If I know that the demand for oil is going to be high in forty years, it pays me to buy reserves, selling them in, say, twenty years, when the future need for the reserves becomes evident. This example illustrates, however, one difficulty with the argument that the market makes adequate provision for the future. If entrepreneurs believe that the market will not recognize its need for reserves for thirty-five years, but know that they will need to sell their assets in twenty years, oil may be a bad investment.

The question of whether the government ought to intervene is much more complicated. Is there any reason to believe that government forecasters will do a better job than private forecasters? If the information about future needs is widely recognized, the market price will reflect that information. And there are incentives for private firms to make long-range forecasts of energy needs.

GOVERNMENT POLICIES TOWARDS NATURAL RESOURCES

Government policies have focused on our limited resources of energy (though some economists believe that in the long run the limited supplies of other minerals may have more serious consequences). So concerned was the government with our limited energy supplies and our dependency on foreigners, that in 1977 it created a separate Cabinet-level Department of Energy.

The federal government has used a variety of instruments to influence the supply and demand for energy. In Chapter 24, we described some of the special provisions of the tax code that affect the oil and gas industry (depletion allowances and immediate expensing of certain drilling expenses).[29] In the period 1959–1973, the government imposed quotas on the importation of oil. These provisions probably did stimulate the development of our domestic oil and gas industry, but critics argue that they led to higher levels of consumption of domestic resources in periods when we could have obtained oil more cheaply abroad, making us more dependent now on foreign oil than we otherwise would have been.

The government has also regulated the oil and natural gas industries. Prices of natural gas were, for a long time, kept at below-market levels, leading again to inefficient use of gas. Only in recent years have these regulations been eliminated.

In the aftermath of the oil crisis of 1979, the government tried to regulate the allocation of oil. Many observers believe that the long queues at gas stations that occurred in 1979 were more a consequence of inept regulatory policy than of natural market shortages. To avoid the disruptive effects of an interruption in foreign supplies, the government has

[29] These are not the only special tax provisions relating to the oil industry. There was a concern that the large increase in oil prices in 1973 and 1979 created windfall profits for the oil companies, and that these gains should be shared with the rest of the nation. A windfall profits tax was imposed. The tax, however, was really a (temporary) excise tax on oil, and may have had, as a result, some distortionary effects. For a fuller discussion of the effect of a tax on the utilization of oil, see P. Dasgupta, G. Heal, and J. E. Stiglitz, "The Taxation of Exhaustible Resources," in *Public Policy and the Tax System*, G. A. Hughes and G. M. Heal, eds. (London: George Allen and Unwin, 1980), pp. 150–72.

established large reservoirs of oil. Finally, the government embarked on a large research and development program to develop synthetic substitutes for oil. The program was widely criticized as inefficient and not cost effective, and was virtually eliminated under the Reagan administration.[30]

Growth and Equity

Public policy has many objectives. One of these objectives is to encourage the efficient utilization of our resources. Another is to encourage the growth of the economy. Still another is to ensure a fair distribution of welfare, both across generations and within a generation (or at least to provide a safety net below which poor individuals cannot fall). There are often trade-offs among these policies.

For instance, for an exhaustible natural resource such as oil, it is clear that there may be important intergenerational trade-offs: oil that is consumed today is not available for future consumption. But economists are not so much interested in the relationship between the current generation's consumption of oil and that of future generations as they are in the relationship between the overall welfare of the generations. The fact that future generations may have less oil does not necessarily mean that they will be worse off. There are substitutes to oil (such as coal). By saving more, the present generation increases the stock of capital available to future generations, and this makes the future generation better off. Finally, technological changes may make it possible for future generations to do more with less oil. The marked increases in the fuel efficiency of American automobiles bear testimony to this possibility.

In the previous section, we noted a trade-off between short-run efficiency and growth. Stronger (longer-lived) patent policies result in greater incentives for R&D,[31] but the temporary grants of monopoly power result in static inefficiencies.

Similarly, there may be trade-offs between growth and distribution. Some policies to redistribute wealth may reduce the growth rate. Policies that increase the growth rate, by increasing the productivity of labor, may indirectly have a significantly beneficial effect on workers, particularly in the future.

Any policy that discourages savings (as inheritance taxes may) or investment may reduce the level of capital accumulation; the decrease in capital will lower wages and make workers worse off. Unless the government undertakes countervailing actions, inequality may actually increase. Tax measures aimed at redistributing income always introduce distortions that shrink the size of the pie to be divided; thus, the poor, while receiving a larger slice of a smaller pie, may not be helped much by such redistributive policies. On the other hand, governmental poli-

[30] For a history and analysis of U.S. energy policies, see Richard Victor, *Energy Policy in America: A Study of Business-Government Relations* (New York: Cambridge University Press, 1984).

[31] In some cases, patent policies that are too strong may have a negative effect on R&D. The granting of a central patent in some areas may discourage others from engaging in R&D in that area.

cies aimed at increasing growth may give the poor a smaller proportion of the pie; but if the pie is increased in size enough, the poor will be unambiguously better off.[32] Advocates of growth point out that a policy that simply increases the growth rate by 1½ percent a year for two generations (say, seventy years) will increase national income by a factor of 2, while even the most ambitious redistributive policies could not raise the income of the poorest quarter of the population by a similar factor. Today's poor may not, however, be content with the knowledge that their descendants may be much better off. Advocates of the poor also point out that the benefits of growth are unevenly divided; the long-term unemployed and those without an education may be among those least likely to gain.

SUMMARY

1. Government tax and expenditure policies affect the level of unemployment and growth. There is widespread belief that the government should take an active role in stabilizing the economy—in reducing aggregate demand during inflationary periods, and in increasing it during recessionary periods. By historical standards, the federal deficits of the 1980s have been enormous. Many economists believe that deficits have kept interest rates high and thereby hurt U.S. investment and productivity.
2. Policies that have primarily income effects may have limited ability to stimulate consumption in a recessionary period, except if spending is constrained by liquidity. Policies that have strong substitution effects, such as the temporary removal of excise taxes, may be more effective in stimulating investment and consumption during recessions, but they also will have adverse effects outside the period in which the taxes are lowered.
3. Some economists believe that there is only limited scope for government action to smooth out business cycles. First, there is a tendency for the private sector to take actions that offset those of the public sector. A government deficit may, for instance, crowd out private investment. Second, to be effective, the government must time its changes in expenditures and taxes correctly. There are important lags in recognition, implementation, and effectiveness, and these may result in the government exacerbating cyclical variations in income and employment, rather than reducing them.
4. Some economists believe that the government has been a major source of fluctuations in the economy. Those who hold this view believe that government fiscal and monetary policy should follow certain simple rules.
5. The decision to finance government expenditures by debt rather than taxation is likely to increase the welfare of the current generation at the expense of future generations. The increased debt reduces capital accumulation, and thus reduces future productivity.
6. There is no persuasive reason to believe that, in the case of most exhaustible resources, the market makes inadequate provision for the future.
7. Government policies towards R&D are important in determining the long-run prospects of the economy. The role of the government is motivated by the public goods characteristics of R&D. The patent system provides a tem-

[32] This assumes, of course, that their sense of well-being is related to their levels of material consumption, not to their *relative* consumption levels.

porary monopoly over the knowledge created by some inventor; it results in an allocative inefficiency (as does any monopoly).

8. The choice of government policies frequently involves trade-offs between the welfare of the current generation and the welfare of future generations, between static inefficiency and growth, and between growth and inequality.

KEY CONCEPTS

Disposable income
Permanent income
Life-cycle theory of consumption
Liquidity-constrained
Crowding out
Burden of the debt
Full-employment deficit
Supply side economists
New classical economists
Monetarists
Patents

QUESTIONS AND PROBLEMS

1. Compare the effect of a government deficit on investment in the case of a small country that can borrow as much as it wishes abroad at a fixed interest rate, and in the case of a country that cannot borrow or lend anything abroad.
2. "The resources that were spent fighting World War II were spent during the period 1940–1945. Hence, the generations that were alive, and paying taxes, during that period are the generations that bore the burden of the cost of the war, regardless of how it was financed." Discuss.
3. Why might social security affect the level of savings? Compare the effect of instituting a major unfunded social security program in a small country that can borrow as much as it wishes abroad at a fixed interest rate, and in a country that cannot borrow or lend anything abroad. (Recall from Chapter 13 the definition of an unfunded, or pay-as-you-go, social security program, such as ours.)
4. In Chapter 26, we distinguished between local and national public goods. To what extent is R&D an *international* public good? What implications does this have for government policy in the United States? What implications does this have for government policy in a small country?
5. List some examples of government policies where there are *intergenerational* trade-offs, i.e., where there are actions that the government can take that can improve the welfare of future generations, but at the expense of the current generation.
6. In the text, we described how the level of government expenditures might affect either consumption or investment. Discuss how *particular* expenditures (such as a new ski resort or a new road) might affect either consumption or investment. List some types of government expenditures that might encourage private investment. What types might crowd out private investment? What types might encourage private consumption? What types might crowd out private consumption?
7. Discuss how the government might use credit regulations to discourage private consumption. Can you think of how the government could use credit markets in recessionary periods to encourage consumption? Be clear about how your answer depends on what theory you believe concerning the determinants of aggregate consumption.

Selected Readings

CHAPTER 1 THE PUBLIC SECTOR IN A MIXED ECONOMY

A. O. Hirschman, *Shifting Involvements: Private Interest and Public Action* (Princeton, NJ: Princeton University Press, 1982).

A. B. Atkinson and J. E. Stiglitz, *Lectures on Public Economics* (New York: McGraw-Hill, 1980), Chapters 1 and 8.

C. Wolf, Jr., *Markets or Governments: Choosing between Imperfect Alternatives* (Cambridge, MA: MIT Press, 1988).

CHAPTER 2 THE PUBLIC SECTOR IN THE UNITED STATES

The question of the sources and explanation of the growth in government has been a subject of continuing debate. See, for instance, D. C. North, "The Growth of Government in the United States: An Economic Historian's Perspective," *Journal of Public Economics* 28 (1985): 383–99; W. G. Nutter, *Growth of Government in the West* (Washington, D.C.: American Enterprise Institute, 1978) and, in the context of the U.K., R. W. Bacon and W. A. Eltis, *Britain's Economic Problem: Too Few Producers* (London: Macmillan, 1978).

For a survey and appraisal of the U.S. public sector in this century, see G. F. Break, G. P. Shultz, and P. A. Samuelson, "The Role of Government: Taxes, Transfers, and Spending," in M. S. Feldstein, ed., *The American Economy in Transition* (Chicago: University of Chicago Press, 1980), pp. 617–74.

Official data on public expenditures at the federal, state, and local level (on a calendar year basis) are published in the *National Income and Product Accounts* (U.S. Department of Commerce, Bureau of Economic Analysis). Data for the most recent year appear in the July issue of the *Survey of Current Business* (U.S. Department of Commerce, Bureau of Economic Analysis).

Other good sources of current data include the *Annual Report of the Council of Economic Advisors* (published as the *Economic Report of the President*) and the *Bud-*

get of the United States Government, in particular the "Special Analyses." Unfortunately, the budget provides better data on how the government plans (or would like) to spend its funds than it does retrospective data on how the funds were actually spent.

For a highly readable account of public-sector spending that is *not* carried out through the appropriations process, see H. B. Leonard, *Checks Unbalanced: The Quiet Side of Public Spending* (New York: Basic Books, 1986).

There is an extensive literature on government as regulator. For a set of case studies of government regulations and the determinants of regulatory policy, see R. A. Leone, *Who Profits? Winners, Losers, and Government Regulations* (New York: Basic Books, 1986). For a brief survey of the results of deregulation, see E. E. Bailey, "Deregulation: Causes and Consequences," *Science,* Dec. 5, 1986, pp. 1211–16.

CHAPTER 3 THE ECONOMIC RATIONALE FOR GOVERNMENT

The classic expositions of the market-failure rationale for government are F. Bator's "The Anatomy of Market Failure," *Quarterly Journal of Economics* 72 (1958), and his "The Simple Analytics of Welfare Maximization," *American Economic Review* 47 (1957).

A nontechnical treatment of the income distribution rationale for government is in P. A. Samuelson, "Aspects of Public Expenditure Theories," *Review of Economics and Statistics* 40 (1958): 332–38.

CHAPTER 4 WELFARE ECONOMICS: EFFICIENCY VERSUS EQUITY

A basic discussion of welfare economics is provided by E. J. Mishan, *Introduction to Normative Economics* (New York: Oxford University Press, 1981).

The concept of social indifference curves was first developed by A. Bergson in "A Reformulation of Certain Aspects of Welfare Economics," *Quarterly Journal of Economics* 52 (1938).

A general discussion of the issues of welfare economics is provided by W. J. Baumol, *Welfare Economics and the Theory of the State* (Cambridge, MA: Harvard University Press, 2nd ed., 1965); I. Little, *A Critique of Welfare Economics* (Oxford: Clarendon Press, 2nd ed., 1957); and J. deV. Graaff, *Theoretical Welfare Economics* (London: Cambridge University Press, 1957).

W. A. Baumol's *Superfairness: Applications and Theory* (Cambridge, MA: MIT Press, 1986) explores the trade-off between equity and efficiency in specific areas—welfare programs, taxation, wage negotiations, divorce settlements, arbitration, rationing, and cross-subsidy pricing (as in telephone and utility services).

The controversy over the use of the compensation criterion involves contributions by N. Kaldor, "Welfare Propositions in Economics and Interpersonal Comparisons of Utility," *Economic Journal* 9 (1941): 549–52 and T. Scitovsky, "A Note on Welfare Propositions in Economics," *Review of Economic Studies,* November 1941.

Two philosophers whose ideas have received considerable attention among economists are John Rawls, *A Theory of Justice* (Cambridge, MA: Harvard University Press, 1971) and Robert Nozick, *Anarchy, State and Utopia* (New York: Basic Books, 1974). A concise statement of Rawls's position can be found in J. Rawls, "Concepts of Distributional Equity: Some Reasons for the Maximin Criterion," *American Economic Review* 64 (1974): 141–46.

Problems of introducing interpersonal comparisons into social choices are discussed in A. K. Sen, *On Economic Inequality* (Oxford: Clarendon Press, 1973).

CHAPTER 5 PUBLIC GOODS AND PUBLICLY PROVIDED PRIVATE GOODS

The classic references for the theory of pure public goods are P. A. Samuelson, "The Pure Theory of Public Expenditure," *Review of Economics and Statistics* 36 (1954): 387–89 and "Diagrammatic Exposition of a Theory of Public Expenditure," *Review of Economics and Statistics* 37 (1955): 350–56.

See also J. Buchanan, *The Demand and Supply of Public Goods* (Chicago: Rand McNally, 1968).

The concept of publicly provided private goods is discussed in J. E. Stiglitz, "The Demand for Education in Public and Private School Systems," *Journal of Public Economics* 3 (1974):349–85.

For a more advanced treatment of the topics covered in this chapter, see A. Atkinson and J. E. Stiglitz, *Lectures in Public Economics* (New York: McGraw-Hill, 1980), pp. 482–505.

CHAPTER 6 PUBLIC CHOICE

An excellent exposition of many of the topics covered here can be found in D. C. Mueller, *Public Choice* (New York: Cambridge University Press, 1979). A more advanced survey can be found in G. Kramer, "Theories of Political Processes," in *Frontiers of Quantitative Economics III,* ed. M. D. Intrilligator (Amsterdam: North Holland, 1977).

The classic reference on the voting paradox is K. Arrow, *Social Choice and Individual Values* (New York: Wiley, 2nd ed., 1963). An advanced textbook treatment may be found in A. Sen, *Collective Choice and Social Welfare* (Oakland, CA: Holden Day, 1970).

Two important books exploring the application of economic principles to political behavior are A. Downs, *An Economic Theory of Democracy* (New York: Harper and Row, 1957) and W. Niskanen, Jr., *Bureaucracy and Representative Government* (Chicago: Aldine, 1971).

The problem of revelation of preferences is dealt with by J. Green and J. J. Laffont, *Individual Incentives in Public Decision-Making* (Amsterdam: North Holland, 1979).

The argument that public-spirited motivation is important for the analysis of political behavior is made in S. Kelman, " 'Public Choice' and the Public Spirit," *The Public Interest* (Spring 1987): 80–94.

CHAPTER 7 PUBLIC PRODUCTION AND BUREAUCRACY

A recent study of privatization in Great Britain is J. Vickers and G. Yarrow, *Privatization* (Cambridge, MA: MIT Press, 1988).

For two contrasting views of government production, see E. S. Savas, *Privatizing the Public Sector* (Chatham, NJ: Chatham House Publishers, 1982) and C. T. Goodsell, *The Case for Bureaucracy* (Chatham, NJ: Chatham House Publishers, 1983).

See also W. A. Niskanen, Jr., *Bureaucracy and Representative Government* (Chicago: Aldine, 1971).

An early explanation of bureaucratic growth is provided by C. Parkinson, "Parkinson's Law," *Economist,* November 1955, reprinted in E. Mansfield, ed., *Managerial Economics and Operations Research* (New York: W. W. Norton, 4th ed., 1980).

Some of the important consequences of the absence of choice are discussed in A. Hirschman, *Exit, Voice, and Loyalty* (Cambridge, MA: Harvard University Press, 1970).

A popular summary of the Grace Commission report is available in W. R. Kennedy, Jr. and R. W. Lee, *A Taxpayer Survey of the Grace Commission Report* (Ottawa, IL: Jameson Books, 1984).

CHAPTER 8 EXTERNALITIES

For a good general discussion of externalities, see E. J. Mishan, *Introduction to Normative Economics* (New York: Oxford Univeristy Press, 1981).

An excellent, nontechnical introduction to the issues of pollution control is R. M. Solow, "The Economist's Approach to Pollution and Its Control," *Science*, Aug. 6, 1971, pp. 498–503. For a more technical discussion, see W. J. Baumol and W. E. Oates, *The Theory of Environmental Policy* (Englewood Cliffs, NJ: Prentice Hall, 1975) or P. Dasgupta, *The Control of Resources* (Oxford: Basil Blackwell, 1982). A more detailed discussion of particular pollution control programs is in A. L. Nichols, *Targeting Economic Incentives for Environmental Protection* (Cambridge, MA: MIT Press, 1984).

The Coase theorem is presented in R. Coase, "The Problem of Social Cost," *Journal of Law and Economics* 3 (1960): 1–44. It is reprinted, together with more recent extensions, in R. H. Coase, *The Firm, the Market, and the Law* (Chicago, IL: University of Chicago Press, 1988).

For a more advanced discussion of the design of optimal-corrective (Pigovian) taxes, see A. Sandmo, "Optimal Taxation in the Presence of Externalities," *Swedish Journal of Economics* 77 (1975): 86–98 and "Direct versus Indirect Pigovian Taxation," *European Economic Review* 7 (1976): 337–49.

CHAPTER 9 THE ANALYSIS OF EXPENDITURE POLICY

A useful collection of papers on the design and evaluation of public programs is assembled in *Public Expenditure and Policy Analysis*, R. H. Haveman and J. Margolis, eds. (Boston, MA: Houghton Mifflin, 3rd ed., 1983).

For a discussion of alternative ways of providing public services, and the circumstances under which each may be more desirable, see *Alternatives for Delivering Public Services*, ed. E. S. Savas (Boulder, CO: Westview Press, 1977).

CHAPTER 10 COST-BENEFIT ANALYSIS

There is an extensive literature on the principles and the applications of cost-benefit analysis. A good starting point is the Introduction to *Cost-Benefit Analysis*, R. Layard, ed. (Harmondsworth, England: Penguin Books, 1972), pp. 9–71. For those who doubt the value of cost-benefit analysis, a persuasive, nontechnical treatment is in C. J. Hitch, *Decision-Making for Defense* (Berkeley, CA: University of California Press, 1966), pp. 44–58. An excellent general review is provided by E. M. Gramlich, *Benefit Cost Analysis of Government Programs* (Englewood Cliffs, NJ: Prentice-Hall, 1981). Cost-benefit analysis has been extensively applied to less developed countries. A short overview is T. N. Srinivasan, "General Equilibrium Theory, Project Evaluation, and Economic Development," in M. Gersovitz et al., eds., *The Theory and Experience of Economic Development* (London: Allen and Unwin, 1982). Classics in this field are I. M. D. Little and J. A. Mirrlees, *Project Appraisal and Planning for Developing Countries* (London: Heinemann, 1974) and P. Dasgupta, S. Marglin, and A. Sen, *Guidelines for Project Evaluation* (New York: United Nations, 1972).

For recent discussions of the problems of valuing life, see W. K. Viscusi, "The Valuation of Risks to Life and Health: Guidelines for Policy Analysis," in J. Bentkover et al., eds., *Benefit Assessment: The State of the Art* (Boston, MA: D. Reidel, 1986), and J. Broome, "Trying to Value a Life," *Journal of Public Economics,* February 1978, pp. 91–200. For other applications of cost-benefit analysis, see R. C. Lind, "A Primer on the Major Issues Relating to the Discount Rate for Evaluating National Energy Options," in R. C. Lind et al., *Discounting for Time and Risk, in Energy Policy,* (Washington D.C.: Resources for the Future, 1982). *Measuring Benefits of Government Investments,* R. Dorfman, ed. (Washington, D.C.: Brookings Institution, 1965); J. Hirschleifer, J. C. deHaven, and J. W. Milliman, *Water Supply: Economics, Technology, and Policy* (Chicago: University of Chicago Press, 1969); L. G. Hines, *Environment Issues* (New York: W. W. Norton, 1973); and L. J. White, *Reforming Regulation,* (Englewood Cliffs, NJ: Prentice Hall, 1981).

CHAPTER 11 HEALTH CARE

The questions we have discussed in this chapter are part of what has become an important and growing area of specialization in economics, medical economics. See, for instance, P. Feldstein, *Health Care Economics* (New York: Wiley, 2nd. ed., 1983). Excellent discussion of the issues are contained in V. Fuchs, *Who Shall Live? Health, Economics, and Social Choice* (New York: Basic Books, 1983); V. Fuchs, *The Health Economy* (Cambridge, MA: Harvard University Press, 1986); and *A New Approach to the Economics of Health Care,* Mancur Olson, ed. (Washington, D.C.: American Enterprise Institute, 1981).

For an excellent treatment of the effect of insurance and U.S. tax rules on the market for medical care, see M. Pauly, "Taxation, Health Insurance, and Market Failure in the Medical Economy," *Journal of Economic Literature,* June 1986, pp. 629–75.

A major, scholarly work applying economic principles to medical malpractice is P. M. Danzon, *Medical Malpractice: Theory, Evidence, and Public Policy* (Cambridge, MA: Harvard University Press, 1985).

Statistics and analysis of the problem of the uninsured are contained in "Americans at Risk: The Case of the Medically Uninsured," Hearing before the Special Committee on Aging, U.S. Senate, 99th Congress, 1st Session, June 27, 1985.

Current issues are usually discussed in the annual Brookings Institution volume *Setting National Priorities;* see, for instance, Louise B. Russell, "Medical Care," in *Setting National Priorities: The 1984 Budget,* ed. J. Pechman (Washington, D.C.: Brookings Institution, 1983).

CHAPTER 12 DEFENSE

L. D. Olvey, J. R. Golden, and R. C. Kelly, *The Economics of National Security,* (Wayne, NJ: Avery Publishing Group, 1984) is perhaps the best up-to-date textbook on defense economics, by members of the West Point department. A broad discussion of defense issues, including the economic issues, is contained in James Fallows, *National Defense* (New York: Random House, 1981.)

Defense economics received considerable attention in the early 1960s. Among the notable books written in that period were C. J. Hitch and R. N. McKean, *The Economics of Defense in the Nuclear Age* (Cambridge, MA: Harvard University Press, 1965) and E. S. Quade, ed., *Analysis for Military Decisions* (Chicago: Rand McNally, 1964). See also A. C. Enthoven and K. W. Smith, *How Much Is Enough: Shaping the Defense Program, 1961–1969* (New York: Harper and Row, 1971).

A recent study of the organization of defense by Georgetown University's Center for Strategic and International Affairs is summarized in *Toward a More Effective Defense* (Washington, D.C.: Georgetown University, 1985).

The Grace Commission (see reference under Chapter 7) not only uncovered a number of systematic sources of inefficiency, but also prescribed several remedies.

The problems (economic and other) posed by the all-volunteer army are discussed in *The All-Volunteer Force after a Decade*, W. R. Bowman, R. D. Little, and G. T. Sicilia, eds. (New York: Pergamon-Brassey, 1986). An example of the economic analysis of recruitment is provided by J. R. Hosek and C. E. Peterson, "Enlistment Decisions of Young Men" (Santa Monica: Rand Corp.) July 1986.

The role of the military-industrial complex is discussed in M. Halperin, J. Stockfisch, and M. Weidenbaum, *The Political Economy of the Military-Industrial Complex* (Berkeley-University of California Press, 1973).

The American Enterprise Institute and the Brookings Institution frequently publish essays on current issues of defense economics. See, for instance, W. W. Kaufmann, *Defense in the 1980s* (Washington, D.C.: Brookings Institution, 1981) and J. M. Epstein, *The 1987 Defense Budget* (Washington, D.C.: Brookings Institution, 1986).

For a general discussion of defense expenditures, including whether such expenditures should be considered investments or consumption, see P. N. Courant and E. M. Gramlich, *Federal Budget Deficits: America's Great Consumption Binge* (Englewood Cliffs, NJ: Prentice-Hall, 1986).

CHAPTER 13 SOCIAL INSURANCE

An introductory survey of the issues raised by social insurance is M. Feldstein's "Social Insurance," *Public Policy* 25, Winter 1977.

Useful discussions of recent research on the effects of social security are contained in *Handbook of Public Economics*, A. Auerbach and M. Feldstein, eds. (Amsterdam: North Holland, 1985), pp. 230–31, 258–60, 283–86. More detailed studies of the social security system include: H. J. Aaron and G. Burtless, eds., *Retirement and Economic Behavior* (Washington, D.C.: Brookings Institution, 1984); M. J. Boskin, *The Social Security System* (New York: Twentieth Century Fund, 1984); Congressional Budget Office, *Financial Social Security: Issues and Options in the Long Run* (Washington, D.C.: U.S. Government Printing Office, 1982); L. H. Thompson, "The Social Security Reform Debate," *Journal of Economic Literature*, December 1983, pp. 1425–67.

Recent studies of income redistribution brought about by social security are M. J. Boskin and D. J. Puffert, "The Financial Impact of Social Security by Cohort Under Alternative Financing Assumptions," NBER Working Paper No. 2225, April 1987; and M. D. Hurd and J. B. Shoven, "The Distributional Impact of Social Security," in *Pensions, Labor, and Individual Choice*, D. A. Wise, ed. (Chicago: University of Chicago Press, 1985), pp. 193–215.

Issues raised by unemployment insurance are examined in: D. Hamermesh, *Jobless Pay and the Economy* (Baltimore, MD: Johns Hopkins University Press, 1977); Martin S. Feldstein, "Unemployment Insurance: Time for Reform," *Harvard Business Review*, March/April 1975; Martin S. Feldstein, "Unemployment Compensation: Adverse Incentives and Distributional Anomalies," *National Tax Journal* 27 (1974): 231–44.

CHAPTER 14 WELFARE PROGRAMS AND THE REDISTRIBUTION OF INCOME

A useful reference for current U.S. welfare programs is S. A. Levitan, *Programs in Aid of the Poor* (Baltimore, MD: Johns Hopkins University Press, 5th ed., 1985). A brief over-all appraisal of U.S. welfare programs is D. Ellwood and L. Summers, "Is Welfare Really the Problem?" *The Public Interest*, Spring 1986, pp. 57–78.

Excellent studies of specific aspects of U.S. public assistance are contained in *Fighting Poverty: What Works and What Doesn't*, S. Danziger and D. Weinberg, eds. (Cambridge, MA: Harvard University Press, 1986). For an historical study of U.S. public assistance programs, see J. Patterson, *America's Struggle Against Poverty: 1900–1980* (Cambridge, MA: Harvard University Press, 1981).

Post-war trends in poverty and income inequality are presented in A. S. Blinder, "The Level and Distribution of Economic Well-Being," in *The American Economy in Transition*, M. Feldstein, ed. (Chicago, IL: University of Chicago Press, 1980), pp. 415–79; M. A. King, "How Effective Have Fiscal Policies Been in Changing the Distribution of Income and Wealth?" *American Economic Review, Papers and Proceedings* 70 (1980): 72–76, and L. C. Thurow, "A Surge in Inequality," *Scientific American*, May 1987: pp. 30–37.

For general discussions of the issues involved in designing welfare programs, see A. Okun, *Equality and Efficiency: The Big Trade-Off* (Washington, D.C.: Brookings Institution, 1975); and H. Aaron, *Why Is Welfare So Hard to Reform* (Washington, D.C.: Brookings Institution, 1975).

CHAPTER 15 EDUCATION

For a recent survey of the literature on why education is publicly provided, see John R. Lott, Jr., "Why Is Education Publicly Provided," Working-paper, Hoover Institution, Domestic Studies Program, July 1987.

For a discussion of school vouchers, see Henry M. Levin, "Educational Vouchers and Social Policy," in James Guthrie, ed., *School Finance Policies and Practices: The 1980's* (Cambridge, MA: Ballinger, 1980).

For two surveys of the range of economic issues involved in education, see E. Cohn, *The Economics of Education* (Cambridge, MA: Ballinger, 1979) and *Economic Dimensions of Education*, A Report of a Committee of the National Academy of Education (Washington, D.C.: The Academy, 1979).

For two critiques of the role of the government in supporting higher education, see M. Friedman, "The Higher Schooling in America," *Public Interest*, April 1968 and D. M. Windham, "Social Benefits and the Subsidization of Higher Education: A Critique," *Higher Education* 5 (1976): 237–52.

Interest in reforming the financial structure of public schools peaked in the early 1970s. A major contribution to the debate at that time was J. E. Coons, W. H. Clune, and S. D. Sugarman, *Private Wealth and Public Education* (Cambridge, MA: Harvard University Press, 1970). A later survey of the issues can be found in the 1974 Winter-Spring issue of *Law and Contemporary Problems*, entitled "Future Directions for School Finance Reform."

For an example of the controversy raised by the first Coleman report, on *Equality of Opportunity*, see S. Bowles and H. M. Levin, "The Determinants of Scholastic Achievement: An Appraisal of Some Recent Findings," *Journal of Human Resources* 3 (1968): 3–24.

For a general discussion of the relationship between education and inequality, see J. E. Stiglitz, "Education and Inequality," *Annals of the American Academy of Political and Social Sciences* 409 (1973): 135–45.

For a discussion of the implications of the screening hypothesis for educational expenditures, see J. E. Stiglitz, "The Theory of Screening, Education, and the Distribution of Income," *American Economic Review* 65 (1975): 283–300.

A topic we did not discuss in this chapter is the equilibrium level of expenditures on education that emerges from a majority voting political model (as described in Chapter 6). This is analyzed in J. E. Stiglitz, "Demand for Education in Public and Private School Systems," *Journal of Public Economics* 3 (1974): 349–86.

CHAPTER 16 TAXATION: AN INTRODUCTION

For an overview of some of the equity issues, see W. J. Blum and H. Kalven, Jr., *The Uneasy Case for Progressive Taxation* (Chicago: University of Chicago Press, 1953).

For an overview of the United States tax system, see J. A. Pechman, *Federal Tax Policy* (Washington, D.C.: Brookings Institution, 5th ed. 1987).

CHAPTER 17 WHO REALLY PAYS THE TAX: TAX INCIDENCE

A more extensive discussion of the incidence of taxation in the United States is available in J. A. Pechman, *Who Paid the Taxes, 1966–1985* (Washington, D.C.: Brookings Institution, 1985). Somewhat different numbers are presented in E. K. Browning and W. R. Johnson, *The Distribution of the Tax Burden* (Washington, D.C.: American Enterprise Institute, 1979 and D. F. Bradford and the U.S. Treasury Tax Policy Staff, *Blueprints for Basic Tax Reform* (Washington, D.C.: Tax Analysts, 2nd. ed., 1984). A discussion of both U.S. and Foreign tax systems is contained in J. A. Pechman, *The Rich, the Poor, and the Taxes They Pay* (Boulder, CO: Westview Press, 1986).

A useful review of the effects of taxation in competitive industries is contained in E. Mansfield, *Microeconomics* (New York: W. W. Norton, 6th ed., 1988); for a review of price and output under pure monopoly, see Chapter 9.

CHAPTER 18 TAXATION AND ECONOMIC EFFICIENCY: CONSUMPTION

The classic articles are A. C. Harberger, "Three Basic Postulates for Applied Welfare Economics: An Interpretative Essay," *Journal of Economic Literature* 9 (1971): 785–97 and "Taxation, Resource Allocation, and Welfare," in *Taxation and Welfare*, Harberger, ed. (Boston, MA: Little, Brown, 1974). A useful review of this material is in E. Mansfield, *Microeconomics* (New York: W. W. Norton, 6th ed., 1988), Chapter 4.

CHAPTER 19 TAXATION AND ECONOMIC EFFICIENCY: LABOR SUPPLY

An overview of the issues is presented in H. S. Rosen, "What Is Labor Supply and Do Taxes Affect It?" *American Economic Review, Papers and Proceedings,* May 1980, pp. 171–76. For a recent paper arguing that U.S. tax-transfer policies cause only small distortions in our labor market, see G. T. Burtless and R. H. Haveman, "Taxes and Transfers: How Much Economic Loss?" *Challenge,* March/Apr. 1987, pp. 45–51.

A well-known study that showed that a reduction in the implicit tax rates in welfare programs might not improve work incentives is F. Levy, "The Labor Supply of Female Household Heads, or AFDC Work Incentives Don't Work Too Well," *Journal of Human Resources* 14 (1979): 76–97. See also P. K. Robbins, "The Labor Supply Results from the Negative Income Tax Experiments," *Journal of Human Resources* 20 (1985): 567–82.

Advanced studies on the determinants of labor supply are contained in:

O. Ashenfelter and R. Layard, eds., *Handbook of Labor Economics* (Amsterdam: North Holland, 1985).

J. Hausman, "Labor Supply," in H. J. Aaron and J. A. Pechman, eds., *How Taxes Affect Economic Behavior* (Washington, D.C.: Brookings Institution, 1981).

M. R. Killingsworth, *Labor Supply* (New York: Cambridge University Press, 1983).

J. A. Hausman, "Taxes and Labor Supply," in *Handbook of Public Economics,* ed. A. J. Auerbach and M. Feldstein (Amsterdam: North Holland, 1985).

CHAPTER 20 OPTIMAL TAXATION

A gentle introduction to this technical area is provided in A. Sandmo, "Optimal Taxation—An Introduction to the Literature," *Journal of Public Economics* 6 (1976): 37–54.

For a more advanced treatment of these topics, see A. B. Atkinson and J. E. Stiglitz, *Lectures in Public Economics* (New York: McGraw-Hill, 1980), Chapters 12, 13, 14. For a discussion of the concept of Pareto-efficient taxation, see J. E. Stiglitz, "Self-Selection and Pareto Efficient Taxation," *Journal of Public Economics* 17 (1982): 213–40.

For more recent surveys of what has become a vast literature, see the article by J. E. Stiglitz, "Pareto Efficient and Optimal Taxation and the New New Welfare Economics," in *Handbook of Public Economics,* Vol. II, A. Auerbach and M. Feldstein, eds. (Amsterdam: North Holland, 1988).

See also J. Slemrod, "Do We Know How Progressive the Income Tax System Should Be?" *National Tax Journal* 36 (1983): 361–70, and E. K. Browning and W. R. Johnson, "The Trade-off between Equality and Efficiency," *Journal of Political Economy,* 92 (1984): 175–203.

The classic paper on optimal income taxation is that of J. Mirrlees, "An Exploration in the Theory of Optimum Income Taxation," *Review of Economic Studies* 38 (1971): 175–208.

The classic papers on optimal commodity taxation include those of F. Ramsey, "A Contribution to the Theory of Taxation," *Economic Journal* 37 (1927): 47–61 and P. Diamond and J. Mirrlees, "Optimal Taxation and Public Production, I: Production Efficiency and II: Tax Rules," *American Economic Review* 61 (1971): 8–27 and 261–78.

The synthesis of the theory of optimal income taxation with optimal redistributive commodity taxation is presented in A. B. Atkinson and J. E. Stiglitz, "The Design of Tax Structures: Direct versus Indirect Taxation," *Journal of Public Economics* 6 (1976): 55–75.

CHAPTER 21 THE PERSONAL INCOME TAX

The best comprehensive elementary discussion of the United States income tax system is provided by J. A. Pechman, *Federal Tax Policy* (Washington, D.C.: Brookings Institution, 5th ed., 1987).

A rich source of legal cases pointing up the difficulty of measuring income is M. J. Graetz, *Federal Income Taxation: Principles and Policies* (New York: The Foundation Press, 1985).

The Economics of Taxation, H. J. Aaron and M. J. Boskin, eds. (Washington, D.C.: Brookings Institution, 1980), is a collection of essays on equity, the tax treatment of the family, and other issues which remain relevant today.

An aspect of the income tax which has been studied extensively is the effect of the deduction for charitable contributions. For a survey, see C. T. Clotfelter and C. E. Steuerle, "Charitable Contributions," in *How Taxes Affect Economic Behavior,* H. J. Aaron and J. A. Pechman, eds. (Washington, D.C.: Brookings Institution, 1981) or C. T. Clotfelter, *Federal Tax Policy and Charitable Giving* (Chicago: University of Chicago Press, 1985).

CHAPTER 22 THE TAXATION OF CAPITAL

Until recently, most studies have analyzed one tax on capital in isolation from others. An important exception is C. E. Steuerle, *Taxes, Loans, and Inflation* (Washington, D.C.: Brookings Institution, 1985).

For a discussion of the tax on capital gains, see M. David, *Alternative Approaches to Capital Gains Taxation* (Washington, D.C.: Brookings Institution, 1968).

For a more technical discussion, see J. E. Stiglitz, "Some Aspects of the Taxation on Capital Gains," *Journal of Public Economics* 21 (1983): 257–94.

For a sampling of the more recent controversies over the effects of this tax, see J. A. Minarik, "Capital Gains," in *How Taxes Affect Economic Behavior,* H. J. Aaron and J. A. Pechman, eds. (Washington, D.C.: Brookings Institution, 1981); M. S. Feldstein and S. Yitzhaki, "The Effects of the Capital Gains Tax on the Selling and Switching of Common Stock," *Journal of Public Economics* 9 (1978): 17–36; and M. S. Feldstein, J. Slemrod, and S. Yitzhaki, "The Effects of Taxation on the Selling of Corporate Stock and the Realization of Capital Gains," *Quarterly Journal of Economics* 94 (1980): 777–91.

For an extended survey of the way tax policy affects savings, see L. J. Kotlikoff, "Taxation and Savings—A Neoclassical Perspective," *Journal of Economic Literature,* December 1984, pp. 1576–1629.

See also E. P. Howley and S. H. Hymans, "The Measurement and Determination of Loanable-Funds Savings," in *What Should Be Taxed: Income or Expenditure,* J. Pechman, ed. (Washington, D.C.: Brookings Institution, 1980).

For a discussion of the United States estate and gift tax, see G. Cooper, *A Voluntary Tax? New Perspectives on Sophisticated Estate Tax Avoidance,* (Washington, D.C.: Brookings Institution, 1979); and B. D. Bernheim, "Does the Estate Tax Raise Revenue?" in *Tax Policy and the Economy,* L. H. Summers, ed., (Cambridge, MA: NBER and M.I.T. Press, 1987), pp. 87–111.

For a discussion of the effects of inflation, see H. J. Aaron, ed., *Inflation and the Income Tax* (Washington, D.C.: Brookings Institution, 1976). For more recent studies, see M. S. Feldstein, *Inflation, Tax Rules, and Capital Formation* (Chicago: University of Chicago Press, 1983) or A. Auerbach, "Inflation and the Choice of Asset Life," *Journal of Political Economy* 87 (1979): 621–38.

For a discussion of the effects of taxation on risk-taking, see E. D. Domar and R. A. Musgrave, "Proportional Income Taxation and Risk-taking," *Quarterly Journal of Economics* 58 (1944): 388–422 and J. E. Stiglitz, "The Effects of Income, Wealth and Capital Gains Taxation on Risk-taking," *Quarterly Journal of Economics* 83 (1969): 262–83.

For a more advanced discussion of some of the topics considered in this chapter, see A. B. Atkinson and J. E. Stiglitz, *Lectures in Public Economics* (New York: McGraw-Hill, 1980), Lecture 5; and A. Sandmo, "The Effects of Taxation on Savings and Risk Taking" in A. J. Auerbach and M. Feldstein, eds., *Handbook of Public Economics* (Amsterdam: North Holland, 1985).

For a cross-country comparison of capital taxation, see M. King and D. Fullerton, *The Taxation of Income from Capital* (Chicago: University of Chicago Press, 1984).

CHAPTER 23 THE CORPORATION INCOME TAX

For an excellent general discussion of the corporation income tax, see J. A. Pechman, *Federal Tax Policy* (Washington, D.C.: Brookings Institution, 5th ed., 1987). For a critical appraisal of the corporation income tax, see Congressional Budget Office, *Revising the Corporate Income Tax* (Washington, D.C.: U.S. Government Printing Office, 1985); and G. J. Ballentine, *Equity, Efficiency, and the U.S. Corporation Income Tax* (Washington, D.C.: American Enterprise Institute, 1980).

The system of depreciation enacted in 1981 gave rise to a large (almost universally critical) literature. See, for instance, A. Auerbach, "The New Economics of Accelerated Depreciation," *Boston College Law Review*, September 1982, pp. 1327–55. The new tax rules for corporations are analyzed in A. Auerbach, "The Tax Reform Act of 1986 and the Cost of Capital," *Journal of Economic Perspectives* 1, Summer 1987, pp. 73–86.

The issues of leasing are discussed in *Joint Committee on Taxation,* Analysis of Safe Harbor Leasing, (Washington, D.C.: Government Printing Office, 1982).

For slightly more advanced surveys of the issues discussed in this chapter, see Alan J. Auerbach, "The Economic Effects of the Corporate Income Tax: Changing Revenues and Changing Views" in *Financing Corporate Capital Formation,* B. M. Friedman, ed. (Chicago: University of Chicago Press, 1986), pp. 107–21, A. B. Atkinson and J. E. Stiglitz, *Lectures in Public Economics* (New York: McGraw-Hill, 1980) Lectures 5–7.

For a discussion of the problems of integrating the corporation and individual income tax, see C. E. McLure, *Must Corporate Income Be Taxed Twice?* (Washington, D.C.: Brookings Institution, 1979).

C. E. McLure and W. R. Thirsk provide "A Simplified Exposition of the Harberger Model I: Tax Incidence," *National Tax Journal* 28 (1975): 1–27.

CHAPTER 24 A STUDENT'S GUIDE TO TAX AVOIDANCE

The principles of tax avoidance are set out in more detail in J. E. Stiglitz, "The General Theory of Tax Avoidance," *National Tax Journal* 38, Sept. 1985, pp. 325–38.

There is a plethora of books about the specifics of tax avoidance. A good standard, popular book about how to fill in your income tax forms (and avoid paying some unnecessary taxes) is J. K. Lasser, *Your Income Tax* (New York: Simon and Schuster, annual edition). See also A. Bernstein, *Tax Guide for College Teachers* (College Park, MD: Academic Information Service, annual edition) and R. A. Stanger, *Tax Shelters: The Bottom Line* (Fair Haven, NJ: Robert A. Stanger and Co., 1982). A representative book promising "over 150 ways to reduce your taxes—to nothing" is J. A. Schnepper, *How to Pay Zero Taxes* (Reading, MA: Addison-Wesley, 1986).

CHAPTER 25 REFORM OF THE TAX SYSTEM

A lively history of the enactment of the Tax Reform Act of 1986 is in A. S. Blinder, *Hard Heads, Soft Hearts* (Reading, MA: Addison-Wesley, 1987), pp. 160–90.

The results of the Tax Reform Act are analyzed in H. J. Aaron et al., "Symposium on Tax Reform," *Journal of Economic Perspectives* 1, Summer 1987, pp. 7–119; and *Tax Reform and the U.S. Economy,* J. A. Pechman, ed. (Washington, D.C.: Brookings Institution, 1987).

D. Bradford, *Untangling the Income Tax* (Cambridge, MA: Harvard University Press, 1986) argues that much of the complexity of our income tax arises because it is a hybrid between a pure consumption tax and a pure income tax. He provides an excellent discussion of the consumption tax and how it might be implemented.

A study of the British tax system by a special commission, headed by Nobel laureate James Meade, *The Structure and Reform of Direct Taxation* (London: Allen and Unwin, 1978) also argues in favor of a consumption tax. Another excellent exposition of the British tax system, with an analysis of the advantages of the consumption tax, is provided in J. A. Kay and M. A. King, *The British Tax System* (London: Oxford University Press, 1978).

For an excellent discussion of the flat-rate consumption tax proposal, see R. E. Hall and A. Rabushka, *Low Tax, Simple Tax, Flat Tax* (New York: McGraw-Hill, 1983).

The value-added tax is discussed in H. Aaron, *The Value-Added Tax: Lessons from Europe* (Washington, D.C.: Brookings Institution, 1981).

For a discussion of the comprehensive income tax, see Joint Committee on Taxation, "Broadening the Tax Base," in *A Citizen's Guide to the New Tax Reforms,* J. A. Pechman, ed. (Totowa, NJ: Rowman and Allanheld, 1985), 21–57.

Problems with the corporate income tax are discussed in R. S. McIntyre and R. Folen, *Corporate Income Taxes in the Reagan Years: A Study of Three Years of Legalized Corporate Tax Avoidance* (Washington, D.C.: Citizens for Tax Justice, 1984) and *Revising the Corporate Income Tax* (Washington, D.C.: Congressional Budget Office, 1985).

The difficulties raised by any tax change are explained in M. S. Feldstein, "On the Theory of Tax Reform," *Journal of Public Economics,* 1976, pp. 77–104.

The problem of tax evasion is analysed in J. Skinner and J. Slemrod, "An Economic Perspective on Tax Evasion," *National Tax Journal* 38 (1985): pp. 345–53.

CHAPTER 26 FISCAL FEDERALISM

A general discussion of the issues of fiscal federalism is contained in W. Oates, *Fiscal Federalism* (New York: Harcourt Brace Jovanovich, 1972).

For a detailed look at current and past federal aid to state and local government, see *Special Analyses: Budget of the U.S. Government, 1988* (Washington, D.C.: U.S. Government Printing Office, 1987), pp. H-1–H-40 and Advisory Commission on Intergovernmental Relations, *Significant Features of Fiscal Federalism* (Washington, D.C.: U.S. Government Printing Office, periodic issues). Recent empirical research is presented in *Fiscal Federalism: Quantitative Studies,* H. S. Rosen, ed. (Chicago, IL: NBER Project Series, University of Chicago Press, 1988).

The classic article on the theory of local public goods is C. Tiebout, "A Pure Theory of Local Expenditures," *Journal of Political Economy* 64 (1956): 416–24.

A review of the ensuing literature is contained in *Local Provision of Public Services: The Tiebout Model after Twenty-five Years,* G. R. Zodrow, ed. (New York: Academic Press, 1983); and W. Oates, "On Local Finance and the Tiebout Model, *American Economic Review,* Papers and Proceedings, 71:2 (May 1981), pp. 93–98.

Under many conditions, the Tiebout model will not hold, as discussed in J. E. Stiglitz, "Public Goods in Open Economies with Heterogeneous Individuals," in *Locational Analysis of Public Facilities,* J. F. Thisse and H. G. Zoller, eds. (New York: Elsevier-North Holland, 1983); and G. R. Zodrow and P. Mieszkowski, "Pigou, Tiebout, Property Taxation, and the Underprovision of Local Public Goods," *Journal of Urban Economics* 19 (1986): 356–70.

Attempts by the courts to ensure a more even distribution of locally provided goods are discussed in R. P. Inman and D. L. Rubinfeld, "The Judicial Pursuit of Local Fiscal Equity," *Harvard Law Review* 92 (1979): 1662–750. A proposal to achieve greater equity within states is presented in K. L. Bradbury et al., "State Aid to Offset Fiscal Disparities across Communities," *National Tax Journal* 37 (1984): 151–70.

CHAPTER 27 STATE AND LOCAL TAXES AND EXPENDITURES

A useful, nontechnical set of papers on the major issues is contained in *State and Local Finance: The Pressures of the 1980s*, G. F. Break, ed. (Madison, WI: University of Wisconsin Press, 1983).

The diversity in tax structures among the fifty states is documented in D. R. Feenberg and H. S. Rosen, "State Personal Income and Sales Taxes, 1977–1983," in *Studies in State and Local Public Finance*, H. S. Rosen, ed. (NBER Project Report Series: Chicago, IL: University of Chicago Press, 1986).

For an analysis and critique of the corporate income taxes levied by states, see C. E. McLure, "The State Corporate Income Tax: Lambs in Wolves' Clothing," in *The Economics of Taxation*, H. J. Aaron and M. J. Boskin, eds. (Washington, D.C.: Brookings Institution, 1980), pp. 327–46.

The incidence of the property tax is discussed in P. Mieszkowski, "The Property Tax: An Excise or a Profits Tax," *Journal of Public Economics* 1 (1972): 73–96; C. E. McLure, Jr., "The 'New View' of the Property Tax: A Caveat," *National Tax Journal*, 30 (1977): 69–75; and H. J. Aaron, *Who Pays the Property Tax?* (Washington, D.C.: Brookings Institution, 1975).

The role of property taxes in the location of firms is studied in M. J. White, "Property Taxes and Firm Location: Evidence from Proposition 13," in *Studies in State and Local Public Finance*, H. S. Rosen, ed., cited above.

In the 1980s, many state and local governments faced a taxpayer revolt. See, for instance, D. O. Sears and J. Citrin, *Tax Revolt: Something for Nothing in California* (Cambridge, MA: Harvard University Press, 1982).

Many state and local governments use lotteries to raise revenues, and these are discussed in C. T. Clotfelter and P. J. Cook, "Implicit Taxation in Lottery Finance," NBER Working Paper No. 2246, April 1987.

CHAPTER 28 DEFICITS, ECONOMIC STABILITY, AND GROWTH

Explanations for the decline in U.S. productivity growth since the early 1970s are summarized in M. N. Baily, "What Has Happened to Productivity Growth?" *Science*, Oct. 24, 1986, pp. 443–51. The consequences of that decline are examined in F. Levy's *Dollars and Dreams, The Changing American Income Distribution* (New York: Russell Sage Foundation/Basic Books, 1988).

Chapters 2 and 3 of A. S. Blinder, *Hard Heads, Soft Hearts* (cited above, Chapter 25) explain the major issues in stabilization policy, and provide a lively critique of monetarism, new classical economics, and supply-side economics.

Two very different approaches to the problems of stabilization and growth were taken by the Kennedy administration and the Reagan administration. Kennedy relied on traditional Keynesian theories, while Reagan relied on lower taxes and less regulation to solve the economy's problems. Their two approaches are presented and analyzed in *Two Revolutions in Economic Policy: The First Economic Reports of Presidents Kennedy and Reagan*, J. Tobin and M. Weidenbaum, eds. (Cambridge, MA: MIT Press, 1988).

For an overview of the literature on the supply-side effects of tax policy on investment, see B. P. Bosworth, *Tax Incentives and Economic Growth*, (Washington, D.C.: Brookings Institution, 1984).

The question, "Why Is U.S. National Saving So Low?," and its implications for U.S. competitiveness are discussed by L. Summers and C. Carroll in *Brookings Papers on Economic Activity 1987*, Volume 2 (Washington, D.C.: Brookings Institution, 1987), pp. 607–35.

A case study of government support for R&D is provided in G. Eads and R. R. Nelson, "Government Support of Advanced Civilian Technology: Power Reactors and the Supersonic Transport," *Public Policy*, Summer 1971, pp. 405–27. For an analysis of the R&D tax credit, see R. Eisner, S. Albert, and M. Sullivan, "The New Incremental Tax Credit for R&D: Incentive or Disincentive," *National Tax Journal* 37 (1984): 171–83.

INDEX